Annotated Instructor's Edition

MATHEMATICS IN ACTION

Algebraic, Graphical, and Trigonometric Problem Solving

The Consortium for Foundation Mathematics

Ralph Bertelle — *Columbia-Greene Community College*
Judith Bloch — *University of Rochester*
Roy Cameron — *SUNY Cobleskill*
Carolyn Curley — *Erie Community College—South Campus*
Ernie Danforth — *Corning Community College*
Brian Gray — *Howard Community College*
Arlene Kleinstein — *SUNY Farmingdale*
Kathleen Milligan — *Monroe Community College*
Patricia Pacitti — *SUNY Oswego*
Rick Patrick — *Adirondack Community College*
Renan Sezer — *LaGuardia Community College*
Patricia Shuart — *SUNY Oswego*
Sylvia Svitak — *Queensborough Community College*
Assad J. Thompson — *LaGuardia Community College*

An Imprint of Addison Wesley Longman, Inc.

Boston • San Francisco • New York • Harlow, England
Don Mills, Ontario • Sydney • Mexico City • Madrid • Amsterdam

Publisher: Jason A. Jordan
Acquisitions Editor: Jennifer Crum
Editorial Project Manager: Ruth Berry
Managing Editor: Ron Hampton
Text and Cover Design Supervision: Susan C. Raymond
Cover Designer: Leslie Haimes
Production Coordinator: Sheila Spinney
Composition: Scott Silva, Lynn Lowell
Editorial Assistant: Greg Erb
Media Producer: Lorie Reilly
Marketing Manager: Dona Kenly
Marketing Coordinator: Elan Hanson
Prepress Services Buyer: Caroline Fell
First Print Buyer: Evelyn May Beaton

ISBN: 0-201-66044-X

2 3 4 5 6 7 8 9 10 CRW 03 02 01 00

Contents

CHAPTER 1 FUNCTION SENSE

Cluster 1 Modeling with Functions

Cluster 2 Linear Functions

CHAPTER 5 RATIONAL AND RADICAL FUNCTIONS

Cluster 1 Rational Functions

Cluster 2 Radical Functions and Equations

CHAPTER 6 INTRODUCTION TO THE TRIGONOMETRIC FUNCTIONS

Cluster 1 Introducing the Sine, Cosine, and Tangent Functions

Preface

Our Vision

Mathematics in Action: Algebraic, Graphical, and Trigonometric Problem Solving is intended to empower college mathematics students for mathematical literacy in the real world and simultaneously help them build a solid foundation for future study in mathematics and other disciplines.

Our team of fourteen faculty, primarily from the State University of New York and the City University of New York systems, used the AMATYC *Crossroads* standards to develop this two-book series to serve a very large population of college students who, for whatever reason, have not yet succeeded in learning mathematics. It became apparent to us that teaching the same content in the same way to students who have not previously comprehended it is not effective, and this realization motivated us to develop a new approach.

Mathematics in Action is based on the principle that students learn mathematics best by doing mathematics within a meaningful context. In keeping with this premise, students solve problems in a series of realistic situations from which the crucial need for mathematics arises. *Mathematics in Action* guides students toward developing a sense of independence and taking responsibility for their own learning. Students are encouraged to construct, reflect on, apply, and describe their own mathematical models, which they use to solve meaningful problems. We see this as the key to bridging the gap between abstraction and application and as the basis for transfer learning. Appropriate technology is integrated throughout the books, allowing students to interpret real-life data verbally, numerically, symbolically, and graphically.

We expect that by using the *Mathematics in Action* series, all students will be able to achieve the following goals:

- Develop mathematical intuition and a relevant base of mathematical knowledge.
- Gain experiences that connect classroom learning with real-world applications.
- Prepare effectively for further college work in mathematics and related disciplines.
- Learn to work in groups as well as independently.
- Increase knowledge of mathematics through explorations with appropriate technology.
- Develop a positive attitude about learning and using mathematics.
- Build reasoning techniques for effective problem solving.

- Learn to apply and display knowledge through alternative means of assessment, such as mathematical portfolios and journal writing.

Pedagogical Features

The pedagogical core of *Mathematics in Action* is a series of guided discovery activities in which students work in groups to discover mathematical principles embedded in realistic situations. The key principles of each activity are highlighted and summarized at the activity's conclusion. Each activity is followed by exercises that reinforce the concepts and skills revealed in the activity.

The activities are clustered within each chapter. Each cluster contains regular activities along with project and lab activities that relate to particular topics. The lab activities require more than just paper, pencil, and calculator; they also require measurement and data collection and are ideal for in-class group work. The project activities are designed to allow students to explore specific topics in greater depth, either individually or in groups. These activities are usually self-contained and have no accompanying exercises. For specific suggestions on how to use the three types of activities, we strongly encourage instructors to refer to the *Instructor's Resource Guide* that accompanies this text.

Each cluster concludes with two sections: What Have I Learned? and How Can I Practice? The What Have I Learned? activities are designed to help students pull together the key concepts of the cluster. The How Can I Practice? activities are designed primarily to provide additional work with the numeric, graphical, and algebraic skills of the cluster. Taken as a whole, these activities give students the tools they need to bridge the gaps between abstraction, skills, and application.

Changes from the Preliminary Edition

Instructors who have used the preliminary edition of *Mathematics in Action* will immediately notice a reorganization of the table of contents. Chapter 5 from the preliminary edition, Exponential and Logarithmic Functions, has been moved forward to Chapter 3. This was done because the Consortium acknowledges the many contexts for which the exponential functions serve as models. We also wanted to make a strong association between linear functions, in which the output changes by the same amount for a unit change in input, and exponential functions, in which the output changes by the same percentage for a unit change in input. This also led to a slight reorganization of the material related to the rules of exponents.

Other sections have been revised as a result of further class testing to clarify and increase emphasis on some skill areas, such as fractional exponents. Specific revisions include the following:

- All exercises have been carefully reviewed to ensure an appropriate level of difficulty for the intermediate college algebra course.
- Summaries have been added to the end of each activity.
- The exposition within the development of several topics, including negative and fractional exponents, has been expanded.
- Throughout the text, an icon refers students to Appendix C for instruction on how to use the TI-83 graphing calculator.

- Appendix A, Concept Review, has been expanded to include fractional exponents and addition and subtraction of polynomials.
- We have included appendix icons throughout the text to highlight concepts and/or skill areas that could be enhanced by the use of Appendix A, Concept Review, or Appendix B, Trigonometry.

World Wide Web Supplement
www.mathinaction.com

A new Web site accompanies the *Mathematics in Action* series, providing valuable resources for both instructors and students. Students can use the site to access InterAct Math® tutorial exercises for each chapter of the books in the series. Instructors will find teaching tips, sample syllabi, information about alternative assessment, and links to math forum sites.

General information about the *Mathematics in Action* series can also be found at Addison Wesley Longman's Developmental Mathematics Reform Forum Web site: **www.mathreform.com**

Instructor Supplements

Annotated Instructor's Edition
ISBN 0-201-66044-X

This special version of the text for instructors provides answers to all exercises directly beneath each problem.

Instructor's Resource Guide
ISBN 0-201-66046-6

This valuable teaching resource includes the following materials:

- Sample syllabi suggesting ways to structure the course around core and supplemental activities.
- Teaching notes for each chapter.
- Extra practice worksheets for topics with which students typically have difficulty.
- Sample chapter tests and final exams for in-class and take-home use by individual students and groups.*
- Information about incorporating technology in the classroom, including sample graphing calculator assignments.
- Extensive information about group learning.
- Guidance for alternative means of assessment.
- Journal assignments.

* Electronic versions of these tests are available on disk in Microsoft Word. To receive a copy, please send your request via e-mail to math@awl.com, specifying which *Mathematics in Action* text you are using to teach your course and providing your school mailing address and phone number.

TestGen-EQ with QuizMaster-EQ
ISBN 0-201-70717-9

Available on a dual-platform, Windows/Macintosh CD-ROM, this fully networkable software enables instructors to create, edit, and administer tests using a computerized test bank of questions organized according to the chapter content. Six question formats are available, and a built-in question editor allows the user to create graphs, import graphics, and insert mathematical symbols and templates, variable numbers, or text. An Export to HTML feature lets instructors post practice tests to the Web, and using QuizMaster-EQ, instructors can post quizzes to a local computer network so that students can take them on-line. QuizMaster-EQ automatically grades the quizzes, stores results, and lets the instructor view or print a variety of reports for individual students or for an entire class or section.

InterAct Math® Plus
Windows ISBN 0-201-63555-0
Macintosh ISBN 0-201-64805-9

This networkable software provides course-management capabilities and on-line test administration for Addison Wesley Longman's InterAct Math® Tutorial Software (see Student Supplements). InterAct Math® Plus enables instructors to create and administer on-line tests, summarize students' results, and monitor students' progress in the tutorial software, creating a valuable teaching and tracking resource.

Instructor Training Video
ISBN 0-201-70959-7

This innovative video discusses effective ways to implement the teaching pedagogy of the *Mathematics in Action* series, focusing on how to make collaborative learning, discovery learning, and alternative means of assessment work in the classroom.

Student Supplements

InterAct Math® Tutorial Software
ISBN 0-201-70715-2

Available on a dual-platform, Windows/Macintosh CD-ROM, this interactive tutorial software provides algorithmically generated practice exercises that are correlated to the chapter content of the texts. Every exercise in the program is accompanied by an example and a guided solution designed to involve students in the solution process. The software tracks students' activity and scores and can generate printed summaries of students' progress. The software also recognizes common student errors and provides appropriate feedback. Instructors can use the InterAct Math® Plus course-management software (see Instructor Supplements) to create, administer, and track on-line tests and monitor student performance during their practice sessions in InterAct Math®.

InterAct MathXL
http://www.mathxl.com
InterAct MathXL subscription bundled with text: ISBN 0-201-71346-2
InterAct MathXL subscription purchased separately: ISBN 0-201-71630-5

InterAct MathXL is a Web-based tutorial system that helps students prepare for tests by allowing them to take practice tests and receive a personalized study plan based on their results. Practice tests are correlated directly to chapter content. Once a student has taken an on-line practice test, the software scores the test and generates a study plan that identifies strengths, pinpoints topics where more review is needed, and links directly to the appropriate section(s) of the InterAct Math® tutorial software for additional practice and review. Students gain access to the InterAct MathXL Web site through a password-protected subscription; subscriptions can either be bundled with new copies of the *Mathematics in Action* texts or purchased separately.

Acknowledgments

The Consortium would like to acknowledge and thank the following people for their invaluable assistance in reviewing and testing material for this text:

Russell L. Baker, *Howard Community College*

Linda Bastian, *Portland Community College*

Judy Cain, *Tompkins Cortland Community College*

Tamara Carter, *Montgomery College*

Oiyin Pauline Chow, *Harrisburg Area Community College*

Ellen Clay, *Richard Stockton College of New Jersey*

Ruth Collins, *Delaware Technical and Community College, Wilmington Campus*

Jennifer M. Dollar, *Grand Rapids Community College*

Irene Duranczyk, *Eastern Michigan University*

Lorraie Edson-Perone, *Cerritos College*

Maryann B. Faller, *Adirondack Community College*

Susan Forman, *Bronx Community College*

Miguel Garcia, *Gateway Community-Technical College*

Johanna G. Halsey, *Dutchess Community College*

Marilyn Jacobi, *Gateway Community-Technical College*

Kandace Kling, *Portland Community College, Sylvania*

Linda Laine, *University of Hawaii*

Anne F. Landry, *Dutchess Community College*

J. Robert Malena, *Community College of Allegheny County, South Campus*

Raquel Mesa, *Xavier University of Louisiana*

Paula J. Mikowicz, *Howard Community College*

Elaine A. Nye, *Alfred State College*

Mark Omodt, *Anoka-Ramsey Community College*

Helen Salzberg, *Rhode Island College*

Barbara Schewe, *Anoka-Ramsey Community College*

Sharon Testone, *Onondaga Community College*

Jill C. Zimmerman, *Manchester Community-Technical College*

We would also like to thank our accuracy checkers, Deana Richmond and Bonnie Gillespie. Finally, a special thank you to our families for their unwavering support and sacrifice, which enabled us to make this text a reality.

The Consortium for Foundation Mathematics

To the Student

The book in your hands is most likely very different from any algebra book you have seen before. In this book, you will take an active role in developing the important ideas of algebra. You will be expected to add your own words to the text. This will be part of your daily work, both in and out of class. It is the belief of the authors that students learn mathematics best when they are actively involved in solving problems that are meaningful to them.

The text is primarily a collection of situations drawn from real life. Each situation leads to one or more problems. By answering a series of questions and solving each part of the problem, you will be led to use one or more ideas of introductory college mathematics. Sometimes, these will be basic skills that build on your knowledge of arithmetic. Other times, they will be new concepts that are more general and far reaching. The important point is that you won't be asked to master a skill until you see a real need for that skill as part of solving a realistic application.

Another important aspect of this text, and the course you are taking, is the benefit gained by collaborating with your classmates. Much of your work in class will result from being a member of a team. Working in small groups, you will help each other work through a problem situation. While you may feel uncomfortable working this way at first, there are several reasons we believe it is appropriate in this course. First, it is part of the learning-by-doing philosophy. You will be talking about mathematics, needing to express your thoughts in words. This is a key to learning. Secondly, you will be developing skills that will be very valuable when you leave the classroom. Currently, many jobs and careers require the ability to collaborate within a team environment. Your instructor will provide you with more specific information about this collaboration.

One more fundamental part of this course is that you will have access to appropriate technology at all times. You will have access to calculators and some form of graphics tool—either a calculator or computer. Technology is a part of our modern world, and learning to use technology goes hand in hand with learning mathematics. Your work in this course will help prepare you for whatever you pursue in your working life.

This course will help you develop both the mathematical and general skills necessary in today's workplace, such as organization, problem solving, communication, and collaborative skills. By keeping up with your work and following the suggested organization of the text, you will gain a valuable resource that will serve you well in the future. With hard work and dedication you will be ready for the next step.

The Consortium for Foundation Mathematics

CHAPTER 1

Function Sense

CLUSTER 1

Modeling with Functions

ACTIVITY 1.1

Parking Problems

Topics: *Function Notation, Graphical and Numerical Representations of a Function*

Did you have trouble finding a parking space this morning? Was the time that you arrived on campus a factor? As part of a reconstruction project at a small community college, the number of cars in the parking lot was counted each hour from 7:00 A.M. to 10:00 P.M. on a particular day. The results are shown in the following graphic.

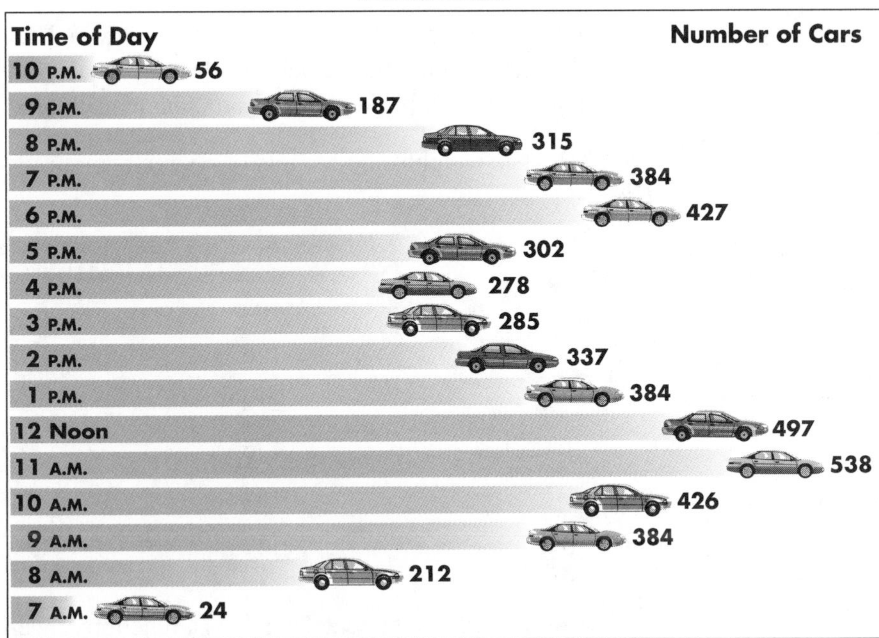

Notice that at each given time, there was a specific number of cars in the lot. For example, at 12:00 noon there were 497 cars. The set of data in this graphic is an example of a mathematical function.

A **function** is a correspondence between an input variable and an output variable that assigns a single, unique output value to each input value.

Such a relationship is stated as follows: "The output variable is a function of the input variable."

In our example, the number of cars in the lot is said to be a function of the time of day. The input for this function is the time of day, and the output is the number of cars in the lot at that time.

1. Explain how the data in the graphic fit the description of a function.

At each time of day (input) there is only one number of cars (output).

2. Interchange the input and the output. Let the number of cars in the lot be the input and the time of day be the output. Is the time of day a function of the number of cars in the lot? Write a sentence explaining why this switch does or does not fit the description of a function.

No, it is not a function, because for the input of 384, two output values correspond: 7 P.M. and 1 P.M. Therefore, it is not a function.

The notion of function is a key mathematical concept and the cornerstone of this course. Mathematicians and scientists may work with very complicated functions, but all of us use functions that describe the relationships between the objects we encounter on a daily basis.

For example, last year's daily high temperature where you live is a function of the date. The date is the input, and the high temperature is the output. For each date, there is exactly one high temperature.

If the input and output are switched, the daily high temperature becomes the input and the date becomes the output. The date is probably not a function of the high temperature, because it is likely that a particular temperature occurred on more than one date.

3. The weights and heights of six mathematics students are given in the following table.

WEIGHT (lb)	HEIGHT (cm)
165	172
123	157
212	183
175	178
165	163
147	167

a. In the statement "Height is a function of weight," which variable is the input and which is the output?

Weight is input. Height is output.

b. Is height a function of weight for the six students? Explain.

No, height is not a function of weight, because 2 students weigh 165 pounds.

4. a. In the statement "Weight is a function of height," which variable is the input and which is the output?

   Height is input. Weight is output.

   b. Is weight a function of height for the six students? Explain.

   Yes, no height has two different weights paired with it.

The function that described the number of cars in the parking lot as a function of the time of day was presented as a graphic. In such a situation, the function is defined **numerically.** Another way to define a function numerically is as a set of ordered pairs.

> An **ordered pair** of numbers consists of two numbers written in the form
>
> (input value, output value).
>
> The order in which they are listed is significant.

For example, the ordered pair (3, 4) is distinct from the ordered pair (4, 3). In the ordered pair (3, 4), 3 is the input and 4 is the output. In the ordered pair (4, 3), 4 is the input and 3 is the output.

A function may be expressed as a set of ordered pairs in which the first number of each pair represents the input value, and the second number represents the corresponding output value. For example, (9:00 A.M., 384) or (0900, 384) (using a 24-hour clock) is an ordered pair that is part of the parking lot function.

5. Using a 24-hour clock, write three other ordered pairs of this function.

   (1000, 426) (1300, 384) (1800, 427) Other pairs are acceptable.

You probably have seen an ordered pair before as the coordinates of a point in a rectangular coordinate system, typically (x, y). The first value, the horizontal coordinate, indicates the directed distance (right or left) from the vertical axis. The second value, the vertical coordinate, gives the directed distance (up or down) from the horizontal axis. In this book, the variables will not always be represented by x and y, but the horizontal axis will always be the input axis and the vertical axis will always be the output axis.

6. Using a 24-hour clock convert all the values in the graphic Park It to ordered pairs. Plot each ordered pair on the following grid. Set your axes and scales by noting the smallest and largest values for both input and output. Label each axis by both the variable name and its designation as input or output.

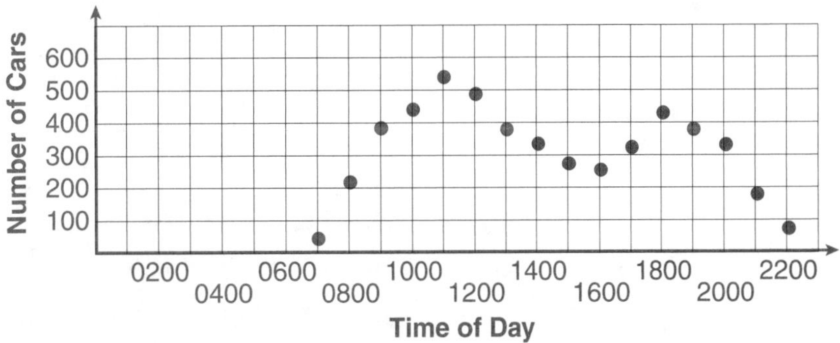

The graph, which consists of a set of labeled axes and 16 points, presents the same information that is in the graphic, Park It, but in a different way. It shows the information graphically and therefore defines the function **graphically.**

7. a. If you work for an hourly wage, your gross pay is a function of the number of hours that you work. The number of hours is the input, and the gross pay is the output. Using $7 per hour as the hourly wage, determine four ordered pairs for this function.

NUMBER OF HOURS (INPUT)	GROSS PAY (OUTPUT)
1	7.00
3	21.00
6	42.00
9	63.00

Answers will vary depending on the choice of input values.

b. Plot the ordered pairs determined in part a on an appropriately scaled and labeled set of axes.

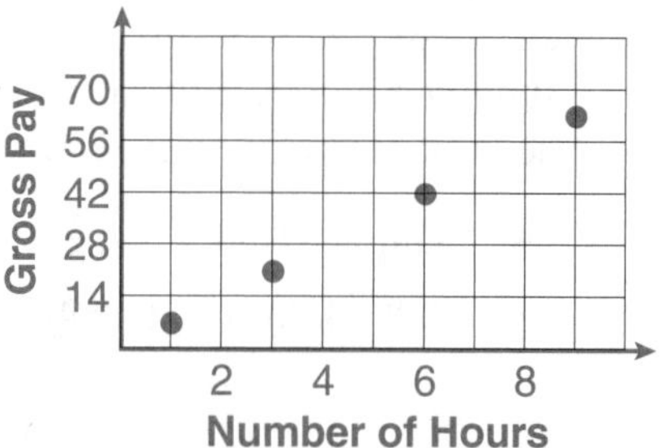

There is a special notation for functions in which the function itself is represented by a name or letter. For example, the function that relates the time of day to the number of cars can be represented by the letter f. Let t represent time, the input variable, and let c represent the number of cars, the output variable. The following simplification (really an abbreviation) is now possible.

The number of cars in the parking lot is a function of the time of day.

The number of cars in the parking lot is f (the time of day).

$$c = f(t).$$

The final symbolic notation is read "c equals f of t."

In general, function notation is written as follows:

Output variable = name of function(input variable).

The input variable, or input value, is also called the **argument** of the function.

8. a. Values from the table in Problem 6a for the parking function can be written using function notation, as follows:

$$212 = f(0800), \qquad 302 = f(1700), \qquad f(2100) = 187.$$

Rewrite the three examples just given as three ordered pairs. Pay attention to which is the input value and which is the output value.

(0800, 212) (1700, 302) (2100, 187)

b. Write a sentence explaining the meaning of $f(1600) = 278$.

There are 278 cars in the lot at 1600 (4:00 P.M.)

9. Represent the hourly wage function from Problem 7 by the letter g. Let n represent the number of hours worked, and let p represent the gross pay. Rewrite the statement "The gross pay is a function of the number of hours that you work" using function notation.

$p = g(n)$

SUMMARY

- A function is a relationship between an input variable (sometimes called the argument) and an output variable, where for every value of the input variable there is exactly one value of the output.
- Functions can be defined numerically using ordered pairs of numbers. The ordered pairs are always given in the form (input value, output value). These can be displayed as a table of values or on a graph.
- The function relationship is often expressed using function notation:

Output variable = name of the function (input variable).

$y = f(t)$ is read "y equals f of t."

EXERCISES

1. a. Give three examples of functions that you may encounter in your daily life or that describe something about the world around you. Identify the input and output variables. Write each function in the form "the output is a function of the input." Explain how each example fits the definition of a function.

For any given week, the number of loads of laundry is a function of the day of the week. There will be only one number of loads for each day.

The average amount of homework per night is a function of the class. There will be only one average for each class.

The grade on a true/false quiz is a function of the number of questions answered correctly. There will be one grade for each number of questions answered correctly.

Exercise numbers appearing in color are answered in the Selected Answers section of this book.

b. Switch the input and output of the three functions you presented in part a. Identify the input and the output. Explain how each example fits or does not fit the definition of a function.

The first may or may not be depending on whether or not the number of loads of laundry is repeated at least twice during a given week. Same is true for homework. Two classes could have the same average amount of homework.

If the grades are letter grades, then most likely the third is not either because different numbers of correct answers could result in the same letter grade.

c. Write each of the three functions you listed in part a in function notation. For each one, represent the input variable, the output variable, and the function itself by letters.

$l = f(d)$, $h = f(c)$, $g = f(n)$

For Exercises 2–6, determine whether or not each situation describes a function. Give a reason for your answer.

2. **a.** Your blood alcohol level is a function of the number of beers you drink in a 2-hour time period.

Yes, it is a function. For each number of beers you drink, you will have one blood-alcohol level.

b. The number of beers you drink in a 2-hour period is a function of your blood alcohol level.

This is probably not a function, because if you drank three beers early, your blood-alcohol level may be different than if you spread them out over two hours.

3. **a.** Your letter grade in this course is a function of your numerical grade.

Yes, each numerical grade will correspond with one letter grade.

b. Your numerical grade in this course is a function of your letter grade.

No, the letter grades may correspond to several different numerical grades.

4. a. The input is any number, and the output is the square of the number.

Yes, each input has one output.

b. The square of a number is the input, and the output is the number.

No, 4 can have 2 and −2 as outputs.

5. **a.** Snowfall is the input and elevation is the output, as indicated in the following table.

SNOWFALL (in.)	ELEVATION (ft)
4	2000
6	3000
9	4000
12	5000

Yes, each amount of snowfall is paired with one elevation in this table.

b. Elevation is the input and snowfall is the output; as indicated in the preceding table.

Yes, each elevation is paired with one quantity of snow in this table.

6. a. $(2, 5), (-3, 5), (10, 5), (\pi, 5)$

Yes, no first entry has two different second entries.

b. $(5, 2), (5, -3), (5, 10), (5, \pi)$

No, the one input 5 is paired with 4 different outputs.

7. Use the table in Exercise 5, with elevation as a function of snowfall and represent the function using function notation. Let f represent the function itself, s represent snowfall in inches; and h represent elevation in feet.

a. Write, in function notation, that a snowfall of 4 inches occurs at an elevation of 2000 feet.

$f(4) = 2000$

b. What is the practical meaning of $f(9) = 4000$?

At 4000 feet there is 9 inches of snow, or when there is 9 inches of snow, the elevation is 4000 ft.

c. Write the information in part b as an ordered pair.

(9, 4000)

d. When graphing this function, which variable will be represented on the vertical axis?

elevation

8. Identify the input, the output, and the name of each function. For each of the functions, write in words the equation as you would say it.

a. Sales tax $=$ T(price)

Sales tax is a function of price.

b. $h(a) = b$

h of *a* equals *b*.

c. $f(6) = 3.527$

f of 6 equals 3.527

d. $520 = g(t)$

520 equals *g* of *t*.

ACTIVITY 1.2

Fill 'er Up

Topics: *Function Notation, Symbolic Representation, Domain and Range*

You probably need to fill your car with gasoline more often than you would like, so you drive around looking for the best price per gallon.

1. There are two variables that determine the cost of a fill-up. What are they? Be specific.

The size of the gas tank and the price per gallon of the gasoline are the two variables.

2. Assume that the price of gas is $1.36\frac{9}{10}$. Now the cost of a fill-up is dependent on only one variable. Write a sentence that describes how the cost of a fill-up is determined.

To determine the cost of the fill-up, multiply the price per gallon by the number of gallons needed to fill the tank.

The result of Problem 2 is a **verbal** definition of a function. The cost function is defined using words.

3. Identify the input and output of the cost function.

The input is the number of gallons needed. The output is the cost of the fill-up.

The result of Problem 2 should be something like "The cost of a fill-up is determined by multiplying the number of gallons of gas needed by \$1.369 per gallon." Letting g represent the input variable and c the output variable, you can express this verbal definition in symbols as $c = 1.369g$. If f represents the function, then $c = f(g)$ and the symbolic rule $c = 1.369g$ can be written as $f(g) = 1.369g$.

$$c = f(g) = 1.369g$$

is the **symbolic** definition of the cost function using function notation. Now, suppose you want to determine the cost (output) of 5 gallons of gas (input). The notation $f(5)$ represents the cost of 5 gallons of gas, the output, when the input is 5 gallons. To evaluate $f(5)$, substitute 5 for g in $f(g) = 1.369g$, as follows:

$$f(5) = 1.369(5) = 6.845.$$

The results can be written as $f(5) = 6.845$ or as the ordered pair (5, 6.845). Therefore, 5 gallons of gas will cost \$6.85 (rounded to the nearest cent).

4. Write the cost of 8 gallons of gas using function notation and evaluate. Write the result as an ordered pair.

$f(8) = 1.369(8) = 10.95$; (8, 10.95)

5. Evaluate $f(12)$, and write a sentence describing its meaning. Write the result as an ordered pair.

$f(12) = 1.369(12) = 16.43$. The cost of 12 gallons of gas is \$16.43. (12, 16.43)

6. Can you replace the input variable in this function by any number? Describe the values of g that make sense and explain why they do.

   Negative numbers would not make sense as input values, nor real numbers much larger than 20, since most gas tanks are not much larger than 20 gal.

The collection of all meaningful replacement values of the input variable is called the **domain** of the function.

Since you were trying to identify the values of the input variable g that made sense, the answer in Problem 6 is called the practical domain. The practical domain is the set of real numbers 0 through 20, assuming that 20 is the maximum capacity of your gas tank. The value of g would be 0 if you do not need any gas and 20 if your gas tank is totally empty. The domain for the abstract function with no connection to the context of the problem is the set of all real numbers, since any real number can be substituted for g in $1.369g$.

The **practical domain** is so called because it is the domain that makes practical sense in the context of the problem.

When a value from the domain is substituted for the independent variable and the corresponding output is evaluated, the result is a value of the dependent variable.

In all functions, the output variable is called the **dependent variable.** The input variable is called the **independent variable.**

The collection of all values of the dependent variable is the **range** of the function. The practical range corresponds to the practical domain.

7. What is the range for this cost function?

   The range is all real numbers for the abstract function. The practical range of this function is $0 \leq y \leq 27.38$. 27.38 is the cost of a 20 gallon fill-up. Answers may vary depending on the assumed size of the tank.

8. Did you determine the practical range in Problem 7?

   Yes, it is labeled as such.

9. Use the symbolic form of the cost function, $f(g) = 1.369g$, to evaluate $f(0), f(5)$, $f(10), f(15)$, and $f(20)$, and complete the following table. Note that the input variable g increases by 5 units. In such a case, you say that the input increases by an **increment** of 5 units.

NUMBER OF GALLONS OF GAS NEEDED, g	COST OF FILL UP, $f(g)$
0	0
5	$6.85
10	$13.69
15	$20.54
20	$27.38

A *numerical* form for the cost function is a table or a collection of ordered pairs. When a function is defined in symbolic form, you can use technology to generate the table. The TI-83 is a function grapher. The variables $y1$, $y2$, and so on, represent function output (dependent) variables. The input, or independent variable, is x. The steps to build tables with the TI-83 can be found in Appendix C.

10. Use your grapher to generate a table of values for the function $f(g) = 1.369g$ to check your values in the table in Problem 9.

11. The directions for roasting a turkey say that the turkey should be cooked for 20 minutes per pound at 350°F.

a. Write a symbolic rule (equation) to determine the cooking time t (in minutes) of the turkey weighing w pounds.

$t = 20w$

b. Is the cooking time a function of the weight of the turkey? Explain.

Yes. The weight of the turkey is the input. The cooking time is the output.

c. Using h for the name of the function, rewrite the equation in part a using function notation.

$h(w) = 20w$

d. What is the independent variable? What is the dependent variable?

The weight of the turkey is the independent variable. The cooking time is the dependent variable.

e. What are the practical domain and the practical range of the function? Explain.

0 to 25 pounds. We either have no turkey or a big turkey; 0 to 500 minutes.

f. Evaluate $h(14)$, and write a sentence describing its meaning.

$h(14) = 280$ minutes or 4 hr and 40 minutes. A 14-lb turkey takes 4 hr 40 min to cook.

g. Use your grapher to generate a table, and fill in the output values in the following table.

WEIGHT OF TURKEY, w (lb)	COOKING TIME, t (min)
10	200
12	240
14	280
16	320
18	360

SUMMARY

- *Independent variable* is another name for the input variable of a function.
- *Dependent variable* is another name for the output variable of a function.
- The set of all values that can be used as meaningful input values is called the *domain of the function*. When a function describes a real situation or phenomenon, its domain is often called the practical domain.
- The set of all output values of a function is called the *range of the function.* When a function describes a real situation or phenomenon, its range is often called the practical range of the function.

EXERCISES

In Exercises 1 and 2, write the functions described in symbolic form. Be sure to indicate which letters represent the input and output variables, as well as the function itself.

1. Sales tax is a function of the price of an item. The amount of sales tax is 0.08 times the price of the item.

   $T(x) = 0.08x$, x is the input, $T(x)$ is the output, T is the function.

2. The Fahrenheit measure of temperature is a function of the Celsius measure. The Fahrenheit measure is 32 more than $\frac{9}{5}$ times the Celsius measure.

   $F(C) = \frac{9}{5}C + 32$, C is the input, $F(C)$ is the output, F is the function.

For each function in Exercises 3–5, evaluate $f(2)$, $f(-3.2)$, and $f(\pi)$.

3. $f(d) = 2d - 5$

   -1 $\quad$ -11.4 $\quad$ 1.2832

4. $f(t) = -16t^2 + 7.8t + 12$

   -36.4 $\quad$ -176.8 $\quad$ -121.4

5. $f(x) = 4$

   4 $\quad$ 4 $\quad$ 4

6. For the function in Exercise 3, write the sequence of operations on d indicated by the algebraic expression $2d - 5$.

   Multiply the input d by 2, then subtract 5.

Exercise numbers appearing in color are answered in the Selected Answers section of this book.

Use your calculator to generate a table in Exercises 7–9. Write 4 ordered pairs from the table.

7. $g(x) = x^2$. Start at 3 and increment by 2.

x	$g(x)$
3	9
5	25
7	49
9	81

8. $h(x) = \frac{1}{x}$. Start at 10 and increment by 10.

x	$h(x)$
10	0.1
20	0.05
30	0.03
40	0.025

9. $f(x) = \sqrt{100 - x}$. Start at 0 and increment by 5.

x	$f(x)$
0	10
5	9.75
10	9.49
15	9.22

10. a. The distance you travel while hiking is a function of how fast you hike and how long you hike at this rate. You usually maintain a speed of 3 miles per hour while hiking. Write a sentence that determines how the distance that you travel is determined.

The distance traveled is 3 times the number of hours I have hiked.

b. Identify the input and output variables of this function.

The input is hours. The output is distance.

c. Write the function in symbolic form using the letter g to represent the function itself.

$d = g(h) = 3h$

d. Which variable is the dependent variable? Explain.

d is the dependent variable.

e. Write the distance traveled in 4 hours using function notation and evaluate.

$g(4) = 3(4) = 12$ miles

f. Evaluate $g(7)$, and write a sentence describing its meaning. Write the result as an ordered pair.

$g(7) = 3(7) = 21$. If I hike for 7 hours, I expect to travel 21 miles.

g. Determine the domain and range of the function.

The domain is all real numbers. The range is all real numbers.

h. Determine the practical domain and the practical range of the function.

The domain depends on the individual probably real numbers from 0 to say 8. Using this domain the range is real numbers from 0 to 24.

i. Use your calculator to generate a table of values beginning at zero with an increment of 0.5.

x	$g(x)$
0	0
0.5	1.5
1	3
1.5	4.5
2	6
2.5	7.5
3	9

ACTIVITY 1.3

Skid Marks

Topic: *Modeling Data with Functions*

After an automobile accident, the investigating officers often estimate the speed of the vehicle by measuring the length of the skid marks. The following table gives the average skid distances for an automobile with good tires on dry pavement.

SKID MARK LENGTH (ft)	SPEED (mph)
28	25
54	35
89	45
132	55
184	65
244	75
313	85
390	95

1. Does the table data define speed as a function of the skid marks? Explain.

   Yes. For every skid mark there is one unique speed. Thus, it is a function.

2. Identify the independent variable and the dependent variable.

   The length of the skid marks is the independent variable. Speed is the dependent variable.

3. Plot the (input, output) ordered pairs on an appropriately scaled and labeled set of coordinate axes.

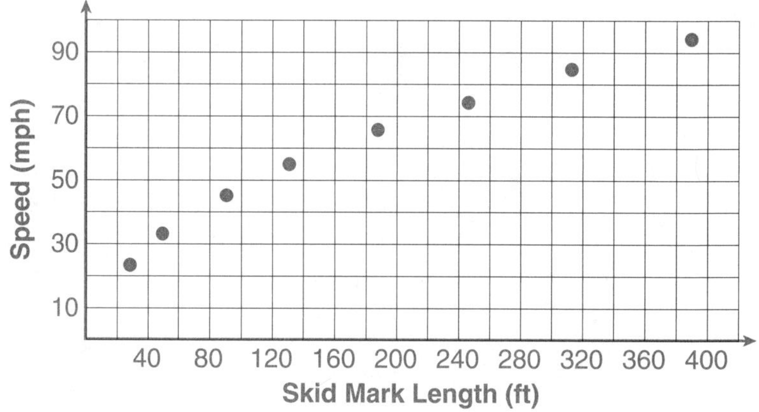

After a particular accident, the length of a skid mark is measured to be 200 feet. Using the table, the investigating officer knows that the speed of the vehicle was between 65 and 75 miles per hour. She would, however, like to be able to be more precise in reporting the speed. One way of getting values that are not listed in a table is to use a graph.

A **mathematical model** is a function that closely approximates the actual data and can be used to predict output values for input values not in the table.

Calculators can produce an equation that best models actual input/output data entered into tables. Using the data in the table on page 14, the TI-83 was used to generate the model

$$f(x) = -0.00029x^2 + 0.31x + 18.6 \quad \text{(coefficients are rounded)}$$

where x represents the length of skid marks and $f(x)$ represents the speed.

5. **a.** Enter the function $f(x)$ into your calculator. (For help with the TI-83, see Appendix C.)

   b. Use the table values to set appropriate window values to view the graph.

   c. Display your graph. A window defined by Xmin = 0, Xmax = 400, Ymin = 0, Ymax = 100 yields the following graph.

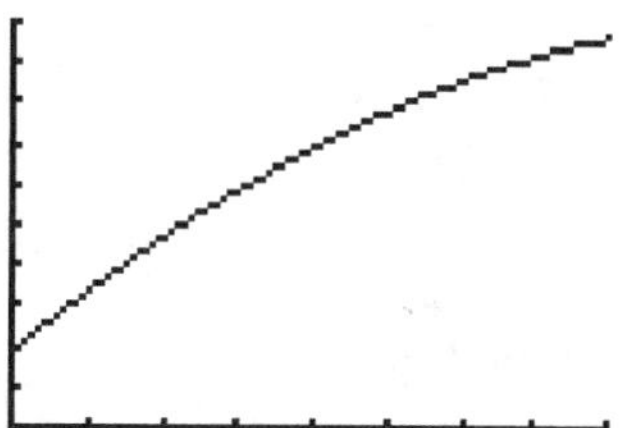

By pressing the trace key and the left and right arrow keys, you can display the input/output values of points on the graph on the bottom of the display.

5. Use the trace feature of your calculator to determine the speed of the car when the length of the skid marks is 200 feet.

   69 mph;

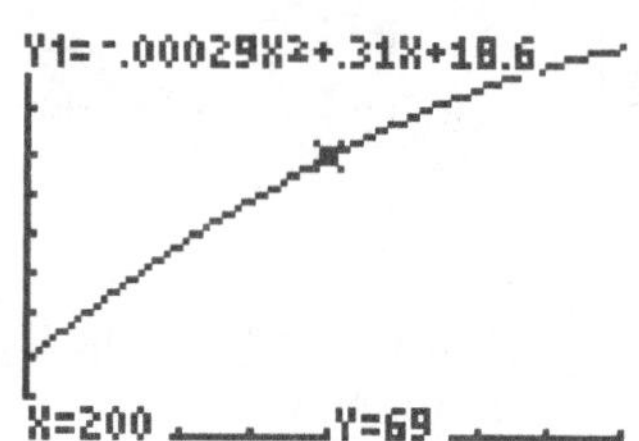

There are many other advantages to having the function in graphical form. For example, you are often interested in determining how the output values change as the input values increase.

A function is **increasing** if its graph goes up to the right, **decreasing** if its graph goes down to the right, and **constant** if its graph is horizontal.

6. a. Is the function $f(x) = -0.00029x^2 + 0.31x + 18.6$ increasing, decreasing, or constant over the domain displayed in the window?

The function is increasing.

b. Sketch the graph of a function that is everywhere decreasing.

(Answers will vary.)

c. What does the graph of a constant function look like?

The graph of a constant function is a horizontal line.

7. Plot the points (3, 1), (3, −2), and (3, 0), and then complete the following statement: If two or more plotted points have the same x-coordinate but different y-coordinates, then the points will all lie on ____a vertical line____.

Recall that when a set of ordered pairs represents a function, each input value is assigned a single unique output.

8. Can the three ordered pairs in Problem 7 represent a function? Explain.

No, because the input 3 has three different outputs.

A graph defines a function if every vertical line intersects the graph at most once. This is called the **vertical line test.**

9. Use the vertical line test to verify that the graph displayed in Problem 5c defines a function.

Yes, it represents a function.

10. Use the vertical line test to determine which graph (if any) represents a function.

a.

Yes

b.

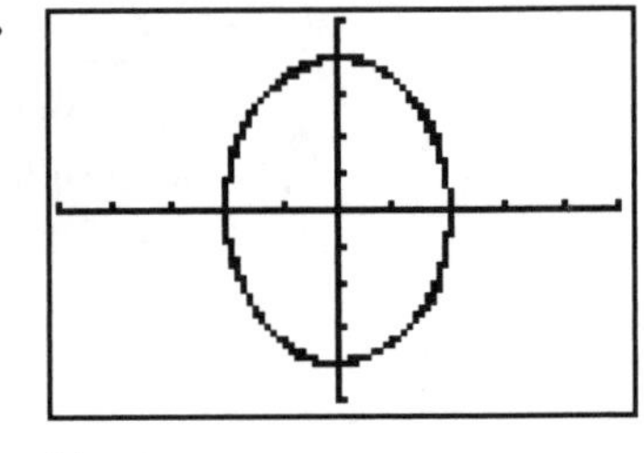

No

11. The following table defines snowfall as a function of elevation for a recent snowstorm in upstate New York.

ELEVATION (ft)	SNOWFALL (in.)
1000	4
2000	6
3000	9
4000	12

A function that closely models the data in the table is

$$f(x) = 0.0027x + 1.$$

Enter this function into a y variable on your calculator.

a. Using your calculator, complete the following table using the function f.

ELEVATION	1000	2000	3000	4000
$f(x)$	3.7	6.4	9.1	11.8

b. Write a sentence describing how the output values generated by the model compare with the data.

The model values rounded to the nearest whole number match the values in the table.

c. Determine $f(2500)$ and explain its practical meaning in this situation.

$f(2500) = 7.75$. At an elevation of 2500 feet there was 7.75 inches of snow.

d. Use the values in the table to set appropriate window values to view the graph. Graph the function on your calculator. Identify the window you used.

Xmin = 0, Xmax = 5000, Ymin = 0, Ymax = 15

e. Does the graph pass the vertical line test for a function? Explain.

Yes, any vertical line will intersect the graph at most once.

f. Does the graph indicate that the function is increasing, decreasing, or constant? Explain.

The graph indicates the function is increasing.

g. Use the trace feature of your calculator to determine $f(2500)$. Compare your answer with your result in part c.

It is the same, 7.75.

SUMMARY

- A mathematical model is a function that closely fits the actual data and can be used to predict output values for input values not given in the table.
- A function is increasing if its graph goes up to the right, decreasing if its graph goes down to the right, and constant if the graph is horizontal.
- A graph defines a function if every vertical line intersects the graph at most once. This is called the vertical line test.

EXERCISES

1. Use the vertical line test to determine which graph (if any) represents a function.

a.

A function.

b.

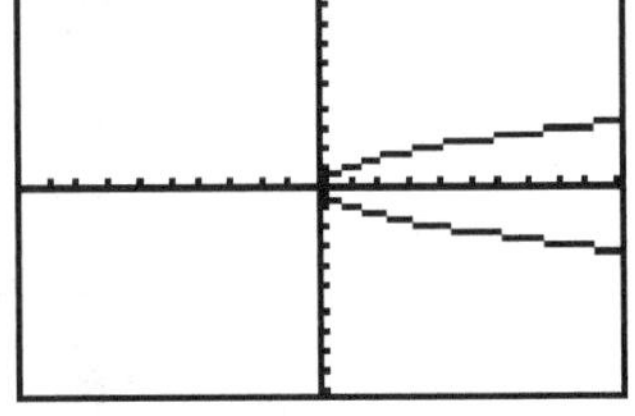

Not a function.

In Exercises 2 and 3, enter the given function into a y variable on your calculator. Match the graph given for the function by finding the appropriate window. (*Hint:* Use a table to help determine a window.) Give the Xmin, Xmax, Ymin, and Ymax window values determined.

2. $f(x) = 5400x + 3600$

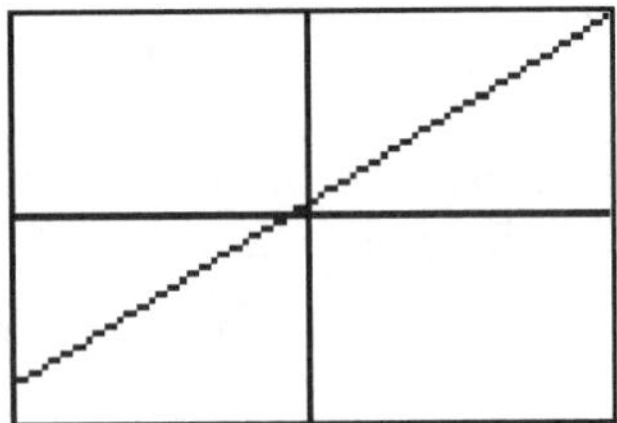

Xmin = −9, Xmax = 9, Ymin = −54,000, Ymax = 54,000

3. $g(x) = 2x^4 - 5x - 2$

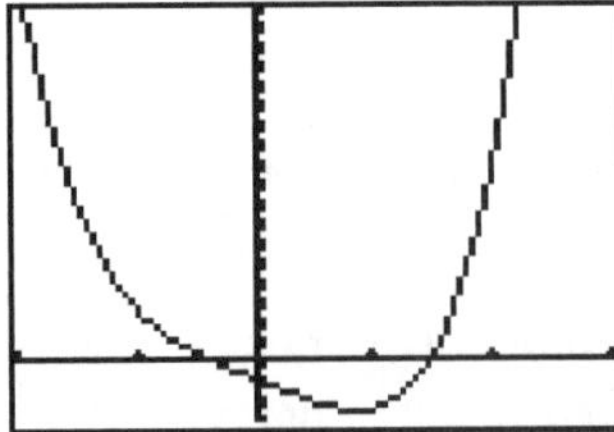

Xmin = −2, Xmax = 3, Ymin = −6, Ymax = 36

Exercise numbers appearing in color are answered in the Selected Answers section of this book.

4. You will need some string, a ruler, and some circular objects. Find as many circular objects in the room as you can: bottle caps, cans or bottles, perhaps a bracelet.

   a. Measure the circumferences and diameters of the objects. For each object, divide the circumference C by the diameter D, and call the result P. Make a table of these values.

C	D	$P = \frac{C}{D}$
25	8	3.125
3.15	1	3.15
7	2.25	3.11
12.6	4	3.15

   b. What do you notice about P?

   All values of P are close to 3.1

   c. A quantity that does not change is called a constant. P is a constant, usually represented by π, the Greek letter pi. Write C as a function of D, using the symbol π for pi.

   $C = f(D) = \pi D$

   d. Obtain π on your calculator and write its value to eight decimal places.

   3.14159265

5. You're having a party and you wish to fill balloons with helium gas. The volume of helium needed for one balloon is a function of the size of the balloon. You can write a symbolic rule to represent this function if you assume that the balloon is approximately the shape of a sphere. The volume V of a spherical balloon is given by the formula $V = \frac{4}{3}\pi r^3$, where r is the radius of the balloon.

   a. Complete the following table.

RADIUS OF THE BALLOON (cm)	12	14	16	18
HELIUM NEEDED (cm^3)	7238	11,494	17,157	24,429

   b. Identify the dependent (output) and independent (input) variables.

   The dependent variable is the helium. The independent variable is the radius of the balloon.

   c. Let the volume function be represented by the letter f. Fill in the blank: $V = f(\underline{\ r\ })$, where $\underline{\ r\ }$ is the argument of the volume function.

   d. What would be a practical domain and practical range for this function?

   Domain $0 \leq r \leq 25$. The corresponding range is $0 \leq h \leq 65{,}450$.

e. How much helium will you need to fill 100 balloons if each has a radius of 15 centimeters?

$100f(15) = 100(14{,}137) = 1{,}413{,}700 \text{ cm}^3$

f. How many balloons of radius 15 centimeters can you fill with 100,000 cubic centimeters of helium?

$\frac{100{,}000}{14{,}137} \approx 7$ balloons

g. You could say that the number of balloons of radius 15 centimeters that you can fill is a function of the amount of helium you have. For this function, what are the dependent and independent variables?

The helium is independent. The number of balloons is dependent.

h. How many balloons of radius 6 inches can you fill with 100,000 cubic centimeters of helium? (See the inside front cover for conversion facts.)

6 in. is approximately 15.4 cm. $f(15.4) = 15{,}299 \text{ cm}^3$ $\frac{100{,}000}{15{,}299} = 6$ balloons.

6. a. The Earth is roughly spherical. Approximate the volume of the Earth (always remember to include units), given that the radius of the Earth is approximately 4000 miles.

$V = \frac{4}{3}\pi r^3$

$\frac{4}{3}\pi(4000)^3 = 2.68 \cdot 10^{11}$ cu mi

b. What would the volume of the Earth be in cubic kilometers?

1 km = 0.62137 miles

6437.3884 km = 4000 miles

$\frac{4}{3}\pi(6437.3884)^3 = 1.1174 \cdot 10^{12} \text{ km}^3$

PROJECT ACTIVITY 1.4

Graphs Tell Stories

Topic: *Interpreting Graphs of Functions*

"A picture is worth a thousand words" is a cliché. It is used so often because it is true. Functions are often easier to understand when presented in visual form. To understand such pictures, you need to practice going back and forth between graphs and words.

The graphs in Problems 1–3 present a visual image of several functions. Each graph shows how the inputs and outputs change in relation to one another. As you read a graph from left to right, the input variable is increasing in value. The graph indicates the change in the output values (increasing, decreasing, or constant) as the input values increase.

For Problems 1–3, describe in words what the graph is telling you about the situation. Indicate what happens to the output as the input increases and if the function reaches either a minimum or maximum point.

1. Elevation of a hot-air balloon is a function of time.

The balloon rises rather rapidly at first, but then rises more slowly as it reaches its maximum. After it reaches a maximum, it starts to come down very rapidly, but later slows its descent. Later it levels off before it finally reaches the ground.

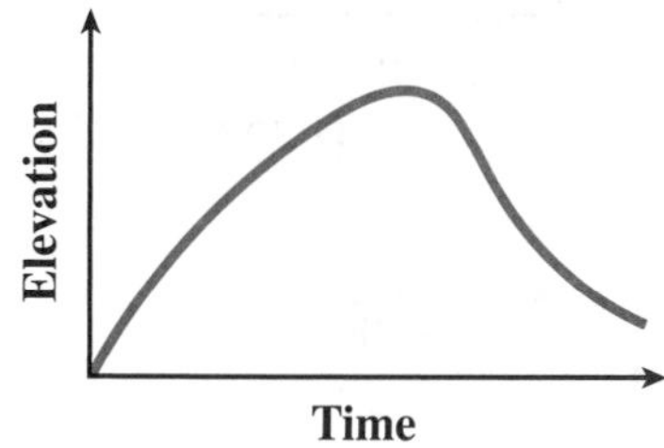

2. Profits at a juice-bar stand are a function of daily temperature.

The profits increase with temperature. First it is a medium increase, then it is a fast increase. It levels off briefly, but then continues a rather steady rise as the temperature rises.

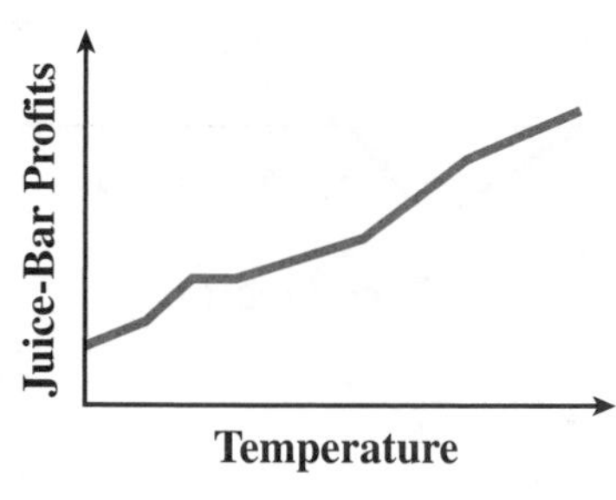

3. Average annual income is a function of years of education.

Annual income is low and rather constant for a low number of years of education. It increases steadily for a while as education increases, then it takes a dip, but as the number of years of education gets large, the annual income increases sharply.

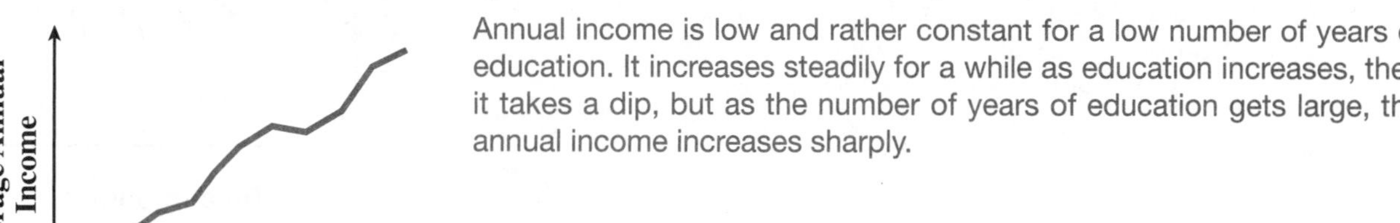

In Problems 4–11, sketch a graph that best represents the given situation. Notice that many times you won't know the actual values, so you will need to estimate what seems reasonable to you. Your graphs will be more qualitative than quantitative in these problems. Be sure to label your axes, with the input variable always on the horizontal axis. Provide numerical scales when appropriate.

Exercise numbers appearing in color are answered in the Selected Answers section of this book.

4. You leave home on Friday afternoon for your weekend getaway. Heavy traffic slows you down for the first half of your trip, but you make good time by the end. Express your distance from home as a function of time.

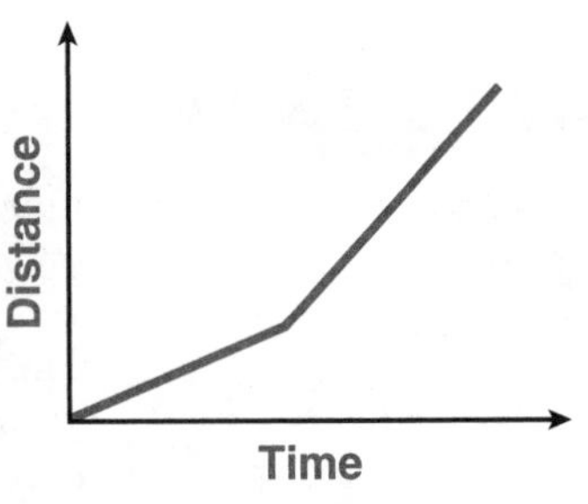

5. You started a job 5 years ago that paid \$8.00 per hour. You got a 50-cent raise after 6 months and another raise of \$1.00 3 years ago. You have been making your current wage of \$12.30 per hour for the past year. Express your hourly wage as the dependent variable and time as the independent variable.

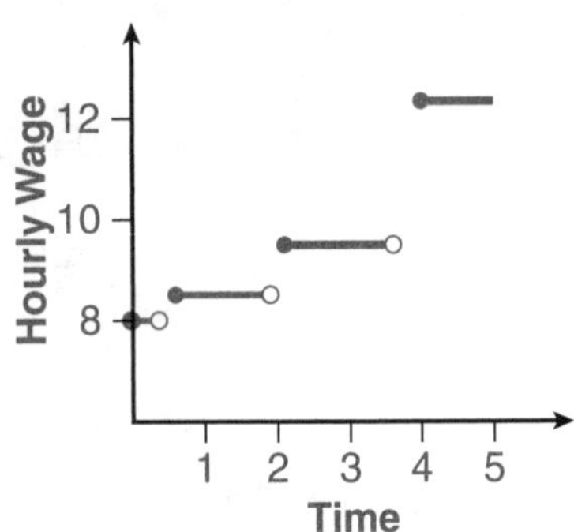

6. Your small business started slowly, losing money in its first 2 years, then breaking even in year 3. By the fourth year, you made as much as you lost in the first year, then doubled your profits each of the next 2 years. Graph your profit as the output and time as the input.

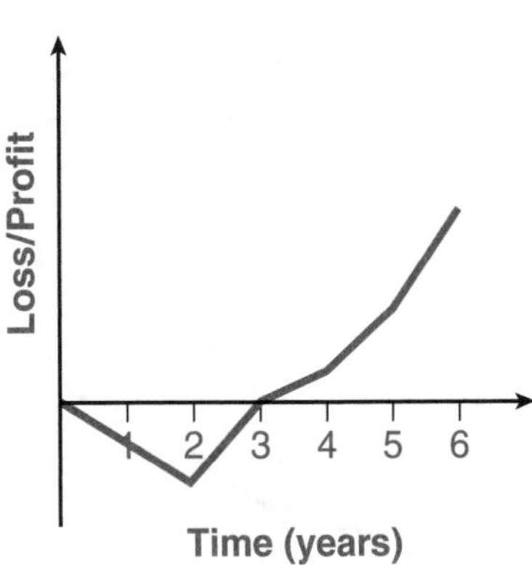

7. Hair grows at a steady rate. Suppose you get your hair cut every month. Measuring the longest hair on your head, graph your hair length over the course of one year.

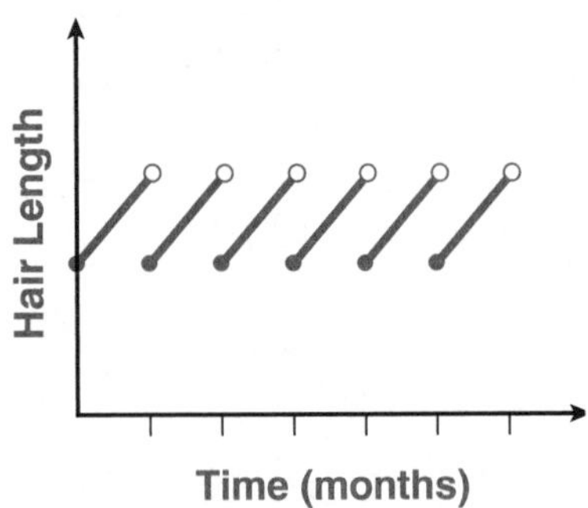

8. Hours of daylight depends on the day of the year.

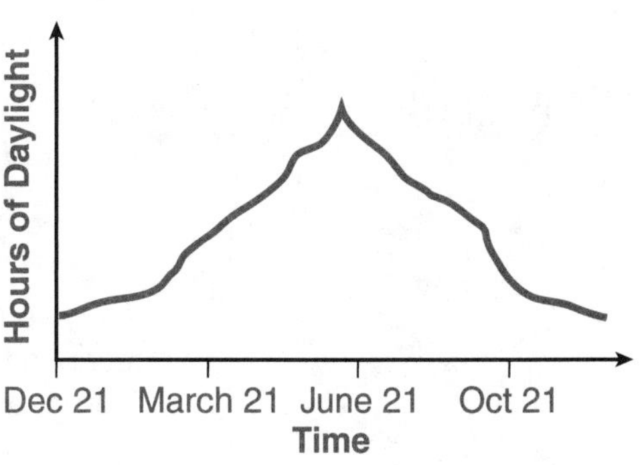

9. The distance traveled is a function of speed in a fixed time interval.

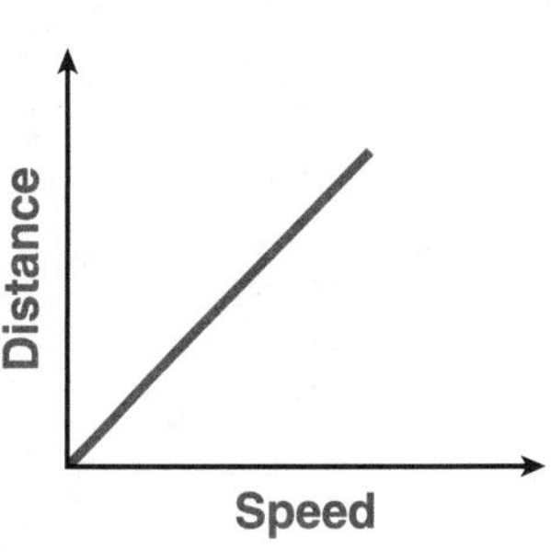

10. The sale price of a computer is a function of the percent of discount.

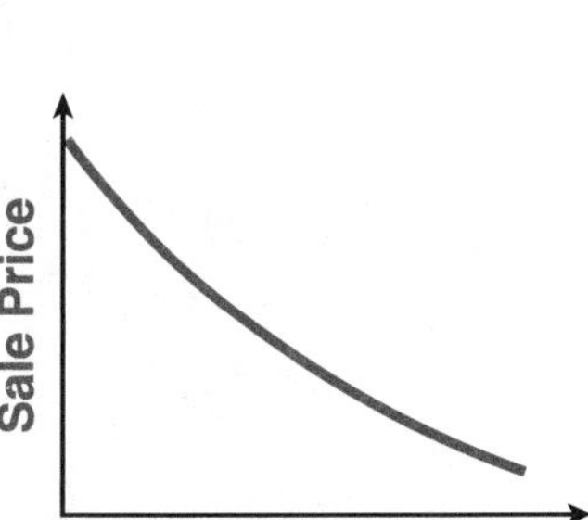

11. The area of a square is a function of the length of one side of the square.

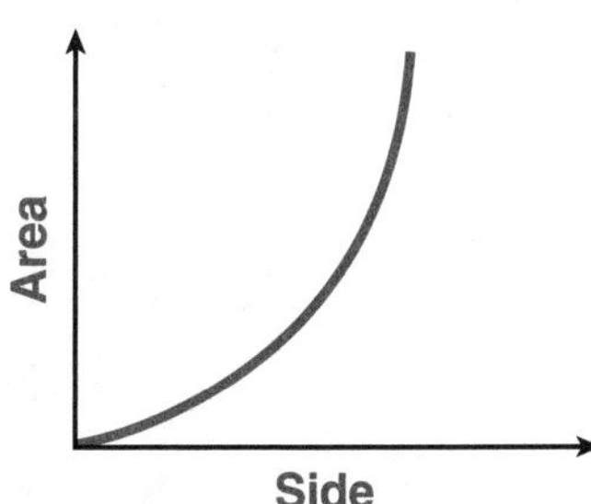

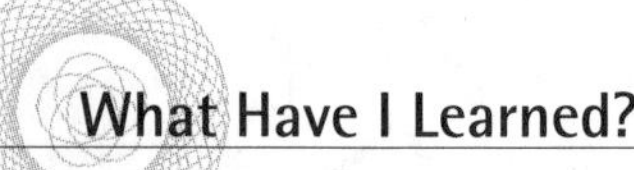

What Have I Learned?

1. Explain how to use a vertical line to determine if a graph represents a function, and explain why the vertical line test works.

If any vertical line crosses the graph more than once, the graph does not represent a function because the vertical line has located an input value that has more than one output paired with it.

2. You know that the point (1, 2) is on the graph of a function *f*. Give the coordinates of a point that you know cannot lie on the graph of *f*. Explain.

(1, 3) cannot be on the graph of the function because 1 is paired with 2 and cannot be paired with any other output.

3. Is it possible for an input/output relationship to represent a function if two different inputs produce the same output? Explain.

Yes, every input can be paired with the same output, but no input can be paired with more than one output.

4. Functions were defined four different ways in this cluster. List them.

Functions can be defined verbally, graphically, numerically, or symbolically.

5. Is there a difference between the domain of an abstract function and the practical domain of a contextually defined function if their symbolic representations are identical? Explain.

Yes, the domain contains all possible values of input. The practical domain contains only those values that make sense in the context of the problem situation.

6. What are two other words or phrases used in this cluster to represent the input variable and output variable?

The input variable is also called the independent variable or the argument. The output is also known as the dependent variable.

How Can I Practice?

1. The following table shows the total number of points accumulated by each student and the student's numerical grade in the course.

STUDENT	TOTAL POINTS	NUMERICAL GRADE
Tom	432	86.4
Jen	394	78.8
Kathy	495	99
Michael	330	66
Brady	213	42.6

a. Is the numerical grade a function of the total number of points? Explain.

Yes, because none of the total points values is repeated.

b. Is the total number of points a function of the numerical grade? Explain.

Yes. For each numerical grade in the table, there is one value of total points.

c. Using the total points as the input and the numerical grade as the output, write the ordered pairs that represent each student. Call this function *f*.

$f = \{(432, 86.4), (394, 78.8), (495, 99), (330, 66), (213, 42.6)\}$

d. Plot the ordered pairs determined in part c on an appropriately scaled and labeled set of axes.

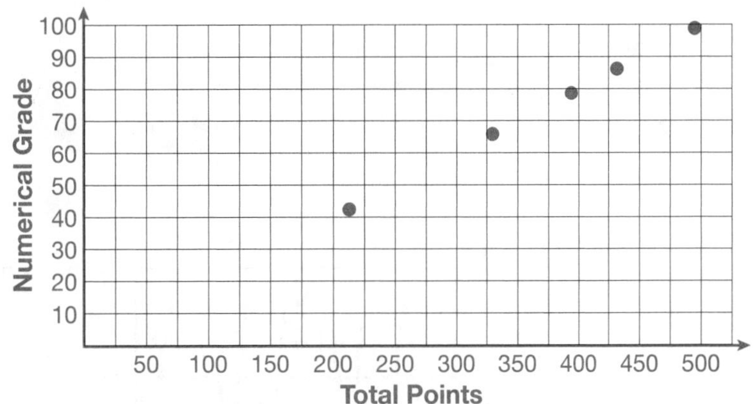

e. What is the value of $f(394)$?

$f(394) = 78.8$

f. What is the practical meaning of $f(394)$?

The numerical grade that corresponds to 394 points is 78.8.

g. What is the value of $f(213)$?

$f(213) = 42.6$

Exercise numbers appearing in color are answered in the Selected Answers section of this book.

h. What is the practical meaning of $f(213)$?

The numerical grade that corresponds to 213 points is 42.6.

i. Determine the numerical value n, given that $f(n) = 66$.

If $f(n) = 66$, then $n = 330$.

In Exercises 2–10, determine which of the given relationships represent functions.

2. The money you earn is a function of the number of hours you work.

This is a function.

3. Your heart rate is a function of your level of activity.

This could be a function, depending on how activity level is measured.

4. The cost of day care depends on the number of hours a child stays at the facility.

This is a function.

5. The number of children in a family is a function of the parents' last name.

This is not a function.

6. $\{(2, 3), (4, 3), (5, -5)\}$

This is a function.

7. $(-3, 4), (-3, 6), (2, 6)$

This is not a function.

8.

x	-3	5	7
$f(x)$	0	-5	9

This is a function.

9.

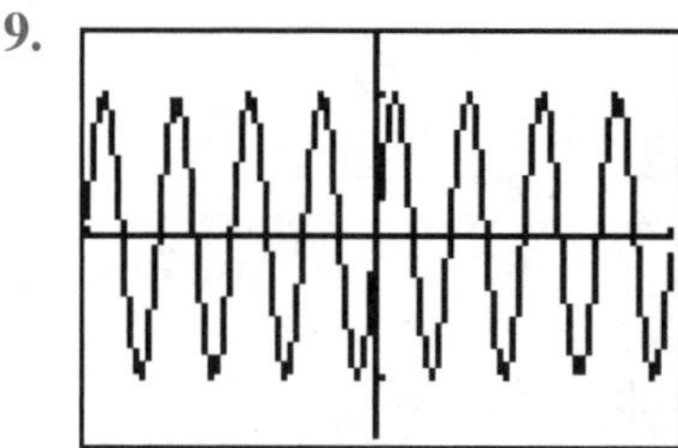

This is a function.

10.

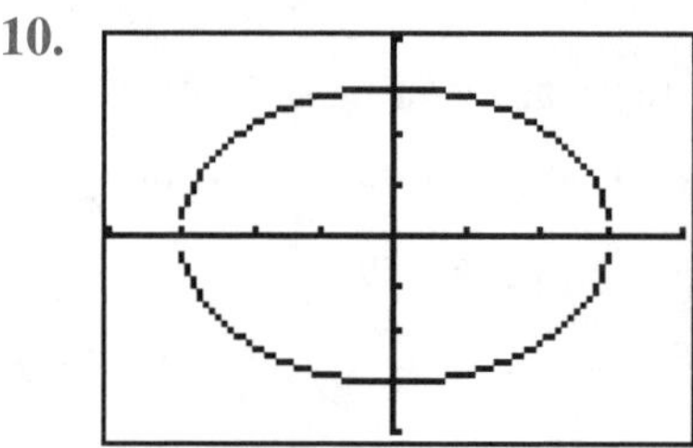

This is not a function.

11. a. For a part-time student, the cost of college tuition is a function of the number of hours the student is registered. If the cost per hour is $90, write the tuition cost c as a function of the number of hours h taken for the current semester.

$c = 90h$

b. Use $f(h)$ to represent the cost, and rewrite the rule in part a using function notation.

$f(h) = 90h$

c. Complete the table.

h	2	4	7	8	11
$f(h)$	180	360	630	720	990

d. Which variable is the output?

The output is cost.

e. Which is the independent variable?

The independent variable is hours.

f. Explain from the table how you know that it represents a function.

For each value of input, h, there is only one value of output.

g. What is the practical domain for this function? What is the practical range?

The practical domain is 0 to 20 depending on the school. The practical range is 0 to 1800.

h. Place the ordered pairs from part c on the graph. Which axis will represent the input data?

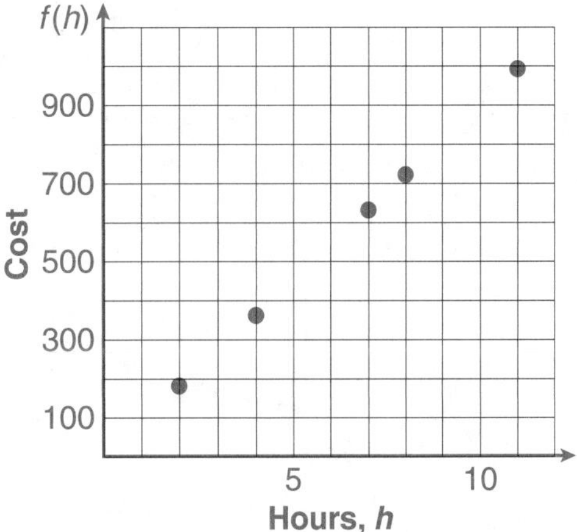

The horizontal axis represents the input.

i. Explain from the graph how you know that it represents a function.

$f(h)$ is a function because the graph passes the vertical line test.

j. Use your grapher to verify your answers to parts c and h.

k. Use the trace and table features to determine the cost of 9 hours.

The cost of 9 credit hours is $810.

12. Given $p(x) = 2x + 7$, determine each of the following.

a. $p(3)$

$p(3) = 13$

b. $p(-4)$

$p(-4) = -1$

c. $p\left(\frac{1}{2}\right)$

$p\left(\frac{1}{2}\right) = 8$

d. $p(0)$

$p(0) = 7$

13. Given $t(z) = 2z^2 - 3z - 5$, determine each of the following.

a. $t(2)$

$t(2) = -3$

b. $t(-3)$

$t(-3) = 18 + 9 - 5 = 22$

14. The following graphs present visual images of two functions. Each graph shows how the inputs and outputs change in relation to each other. Describe in words what the graph is telling you about the situation. Provide a reasonable explanation for the behavior you describe.

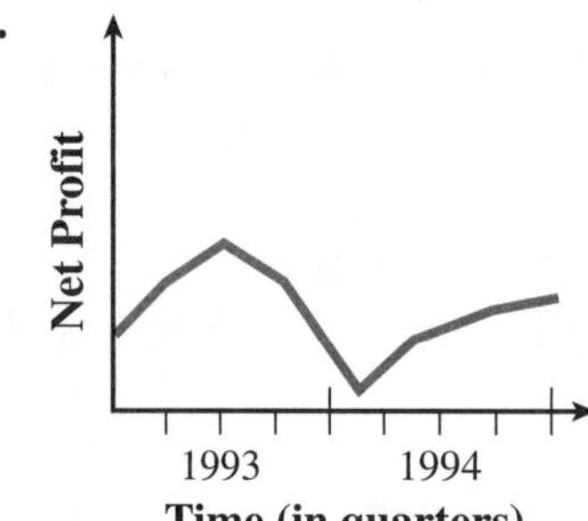

The net profit increases during the first 2 quarters of 1993. The net profit then decreases for about 2.5 quarters, and then increases through the final quarter of 1994.

b.

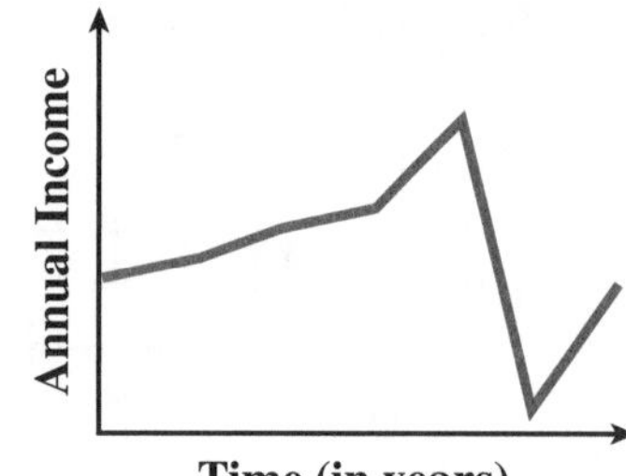

The annual income rises rather steadily for 3 years, in the 4th year, it rises sharply. Then it suffers a sharp decline during the next year. During the last year the income recovers to about the point it was originally.

CLUSTER 2

Linear Functions

ACTIVITY 1.5

Walking for Fitness

Topic: *Rate of Change*

Suppose you are a member of a health and fitness club. A special diet and exercise program has been developed for you by your personal trainer. At the beginning of the program and once a week thereafter, you are tested on the treadmill. The test consists of how many minutes it takes you to walk, jog, or run 3 miles on the treadmill. The following data give your time t over an 8-week period.

WEEKS, w	0	1	2	3	4	5	6	7	8
TIME, t, (MIN)	45	42	40	39	38	38	37	39	36

Note that $w = 0$ corresponds to the first time on the treadmill, $w = 1$ is the end of the first week, $w = 2$ is the end of the second week, and so on.

1. a. Is time t a function of weeks w? If so, what are the input and output variables?

Yes, t is a function of w. The input is weeks. The output is time.

b. Plot the data points using ordered pairs of the form (w, t).

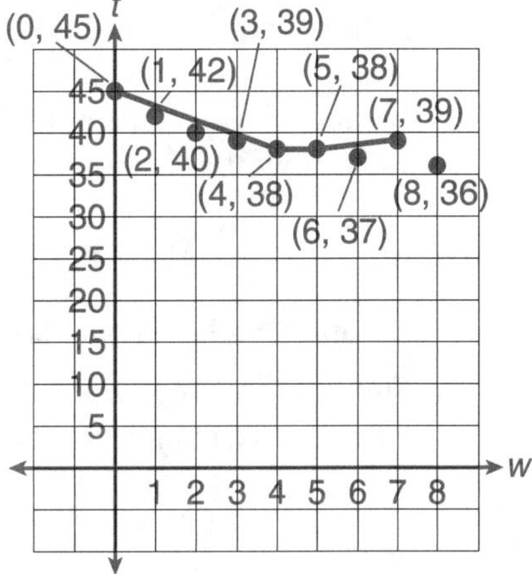

2. a. What was your treadmill time at the beginning of the program?

45 minutes

b. What was your treadmill time at the end of the first week?

42 minutes

An important question that can be asked about this situation is, how did your time change from one week to the next?

3. a. During which week(s) did your time increase?

Time increased in week 7.

b. During which week(s) did your time decrease?

Time decreased in weeks 1, 2, 3, 4, 6 and 8.

c. During which week(s) did your time remain unchanged?

Time was unchanged in week 5.

4. Your time decreased during each week of the first four weeks of the program.

a. Determine the total change in time t during the first four weeks of the program (i.e., from $t = 45$ to $t = 38$). Why should your answer contain a negative sign? Explain.

The time change is $38 - 45 = -7$. The negative makes sense because the time decreased.

b. Determine the change in weeks, w, during this period (that is, from $w = 0$ to $w = 4$).

$4 - 0 = 4$ weeks

NOTATION

The change in time t is represented by the symbol Δt. The symbol Δ (delta) is used to represent "change in." You generally calculate the change in time t from a first (initial) value to a second (final) value of t. The first time is represented by t_1 (read "t sub 1"), and the second time is represented by t_2 (read "t sub 2"). The change in t is then calculated by subtracting the first (initial) value from the second (final) value. This is symbolically represented by

$$\Delta t = t_2 - t_1 \text{ or } \Delta t = \text{final time} - \text{initial time}.$$

Because t is the output variable, Δt is the change in output.

Similarly, Δw represents the change in weeks w; w_1 represents the first (initial) value of w, and w_2 represents the second (final) value of w. Symbolically,

$$\Delta w = w_2 - w_1, \text{ or } \Delta w = \text{final week} - \text{initial week}.$$

Because w is the input variable, Δw is the change in input.

5. Use the Δ notation to express your results in Problems 4a and b.

$\Delta t = 38 - 45 = -7$

$\Delta w = 4 - 0 = 4$

Just knowing the change in treadmill time or the change in the number of weeks does not give a complete description of your progress during the first four weeks. The ratio of the change in t, Δt, to the change in w, Δw, written $\frac{\Delta t}{\Delta w}$, provides more relevant information about the effect of the exercise program over time. This ratio $\frac{\Delta t}{\Delta w}$ is simply how the time changed on average over the four-week period.

6. **a.** Use your results from Problem 5 to determine the ratio $\frac{\Delta t}{\Delta w}$ during the first four-week period. Interpret your answer.

$\frac{\Delta t}{\Delta w} = \frac{-7}{4} = -1.75$ min/wk

On average, your time decreased by 1.75 minutes every week.

b. What are the units of measurement of the ratio determined in part a?

Minutes per week.

c. On your graph from Problem 1, connect the points (0, 45) and (4, 38) with a line segment. Does the output increase, decrease, or remain unchanged on this interval?

The output decreases.

The ratio $\frac{\Delta t}{\Delta w}$ is called the **average rate of change** or simply the rate of change of time t with respect to weeks w. In general, the average rate of change is

$$\frac{\text{change in ouput}}{\text{change in input}}.$$

7. **a.** Determine the rate of change of t with respect to w during the sixth and seventh weeks (from the point where $w = 5$ to the point where $w = 7$).

$\frac{\Delta t}{\Delta w} = \frac{39 - 38}{7 - 5} = \frac{1}{2} = 0.5$ min/wk.

b. What is the significance of the positive sign of the rate of change in this situation?

The time increased over these two weeks.

c. Connect the data points (5, 38) and (7, 39) on your graph from Problem 1 using a line segment. Is the output increasing, decreasing, or constant on this interval?

Although it decreases in the middle, the output at 7 is greater than the output at 5 so over the interval there is an increase.

8. **a.** At what rate did your time change during the fifth week (from $w = 4$ to $w = 5$)?

$\frac{\Delta t}{\Delta w} = \frac{39 - 39}{1} = 0$

b. Interpret your answer in this situation.

The time was constant. The time did not change.

c. Connect the data points (4, 38) and (5, 38) on the graph from Problem 1 using a line segment. Is the output increasing, decreasing, or constant on this interval?

The graph is horizontal, so the output is constant.

9. **a.** At what rate is your time changing as w increases from $w = 3$ to $w = 7$?

$\frac{\Delta t}{\Delta w} = \frac{39 - 39}{7 - 3} = \frac{0}{4} = 0$

b. Does your answer in part a mean that your time did not change in this four-week period? Interpret your answer in part a in this situation.

No, it does not mean that there was no change at all. It means that we are in the same place after 7 weeks as we were after 3 weeks.

SUMMARY

- The average rate of change of a function over a specified input interval is the ratio $\frac{\text{change in output}}{\text{change in input}}$.
- The rate of change indicates how much, and in which direction, the output changes when the input increases by a single unit. It measures how the output changes on average.

EXERCISES

The baseball card industry has seen some great fluctuations in sales over the 1980s and 1990s. This is reflected in the following table, as reported by *Sports Collector's Digest* in their November 29, 1996, issue.

YEAR, t	78	79	81	86	88	89	90	91	92	93	94	95	96
s, SALES (IN MILLIONS OF CARDS)	9.2	10	30	90	25	45	80	120	110	85	85	70	65

Use the data in the table to answer Exercises 1–6.

1. **a.** Determine the rate of change in sales per year from 1981 to 1986.

$\frac{\Delta s}{\Delta t} = \frac{90 - 30}{86 - 81} = \frac{60}{5} = 12$ million/year.

b. Describe what the rate of change in part a represents in this situation.

Sales were increasing at a rate of 12 million cards per year.

2. Determine the rate of change in sales per year from 1991 to 1994.

$\frac{\Delta s}{\Delta t} = \frac{85 - 120}{94 - 91} = \frac{-35}{3} = -11.7$ million/year.

3. What was the rate of change over the 18-year period described in the table?

$\frac{\Delta s}{\Delta t} = \frac{65 - 9.2}{96 - 78} = \frac{55.8}{18} = 3.1$ million/year.

4. During what one-year period did card sales increase the most?

90–91.

5. **a.** What does it mean in this situation if a rate change is negative?

It means the sales decreased.

b. Determine at least one two-year period when the rate of change was negative.

Sales are decreasing. 86–88; 91–93; 94–96.

Exercise numbers appearing in color are answered in the Selected Answers section of this book.

c. What trend would you observe in the graph if the rate of change was negative? That is, would the graph go up, go down, or remain constant?

The graph would go down.

6. a. Was the average rate of change over any one-year period zero? If so, when?

93–94.

b. What does this mean in this situation?

This means sales stayed the same.

c. What trend would you observe in the graph during this period? That is, would the graph go up, go down, or remain constant?

The trend of the graph is horizontal.

d. Write a paragraph that describes what you have observed about the sales of baseball cards. You may refer to the graph or table in your narrative.

The sale of baseball cards has been anything but steady. In the early 80s, the sale of cards grew enormously reaching 90 million cards in 1986. However, by 1988 sales had plummeted to 25 million cards. Then sales grew again, reaching the 120 million card mark in 1991. Since 1991, the industry has shown a steady decline to 65 million cards in 1996, although sales were steady at 85 million cards in 1993 and 1994.

According to the *World Almanac*, the first year of sales for music videos was 1989, with 6.1 million videos sold for a net of $115,400,000. The following table lists the total number of music videos sold in each of the first seven years.

YEAR, t	89	90	91	92	93	94	95	96
SALES, s (IN MILLIONS)	6.1	9.2	6.1	7.6	11.0	11.2	12.6	16.9

Use the table of data to answer Exercises 7 and 8.

7. Plot the data points using ordered pairs of the form (t, s).

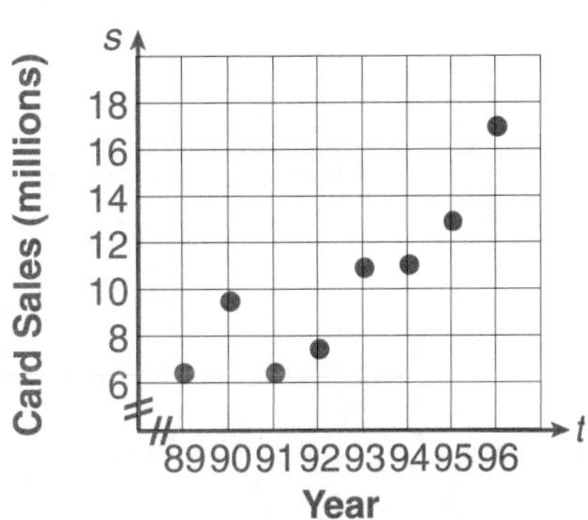

8. a. Determine the average rate of change of sales from 1989 to 1990.

$\frac{\Delta s}{\Delta t} = \frac{9.2 - 6.1}{90 - 89} = 3.1$ million per year.

b. Determine the average rate of change of sales from 1990 to 1991.

$\frac{\Delta s}{\Delta t} = \frac{6.1 - 9.2}{91 - 90} = -3.1$ million per year

c. Compare the rate of change in 1989–1990 with the rate of change in 1990–1991.

The rate of change of 89–90 is positive. The rate of change of 90–91 is negative.

d. When the rate of change is negative, what trend will you observe in the graph? What does this mean in this situation?

When the rate of change is negative, the graph falls to the right. This means that sales decrease.

e. Determine the average rate of change of sales from 1989 to 1991. Does this mean that the number of sales did not change during the period from 1989 to 1991? Explain.

$\frac{\Delta s}{\Delta t} = \frac{6.1 - 6.1}{91 - 89} = \frac{0}{2} = 0$ The average rate of change is 0. There may be changes in the middle but the final output is the same as the initial output.

f. From the graph, determine during what time period the rate of change was always positive.

The rate of change is always positive from 89–90 and 91–96.

Between 1989 and 1996 the net dollar value of music video sales more than doubled. Use the following table to answer Exercise 9.

YEAR, t	89	90	91	92	93	94	95	96
DOLLAR VALUE (IN MILLIONS)	115.4	172.3	118.1	157.4	213.3	231.1	220.3	236.1

9. **a.** Determine the rate of change, in millions of dollars per year, from 1989 to 1990.

$\frac{\Delta \$}{\Delta t} = \frac{172.3 - 115.4}{90 - 89} = 56.9$ million dollars per year.

b. Determine the rate of change, in millions of dollars per year, from 1990 to 1991.

$\frac{\Delta \$}{\Delta t} = \frac{118.1 - 172.3}{91 - 90} = -54.2$ million dollars per year.

c. Determine the rate of change, in millions of dollars per year, from 1989 to 1991.

$\frac{\Delta \$}{\Delta t} = \frac{118.1 - 115.4}{91 - 89} = \frac{2.7}{2} = 1.35$ million dollars per year.

d. Determine the rate of change, in millions of dollars per year, between 1989 and 1996.

$\frac{\Delta \$}{\Delta t} = \frac{236.1 - 115.4}{96 - 89} = \frac{120.7}{7} \approx 17.24$ million dollars per year.

ACTIVITY 1.6

Car Speed

Topics: *Linear Functions and Slope, Slope-Intercept Form*

Suppose you leave your home at noon and are driving down the interstate highway at 60 mph. The total distance traveled from your house is a function of the time you travel at 60 mph.

1. a. Complete the following table, in which t is the time (in hours) past noon and d is the total distance traveled (in miles).

TIME, t (hr)	DISTANCE, d (mi)
0	0
1	60
2	120
5	300
10	600

b. Consider ordered pairs of the form (t, d), and plot each on an appropriately scaled and labeled set of axes. Connect the points to see if there is a pattern.

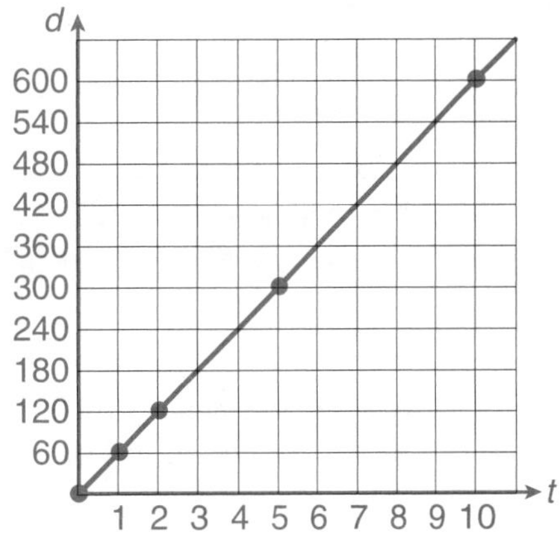

2. a. Use your results from Problem 1a to complete the following table.

TIME INTERVAL (hr)	Δt (hr)	Δd (mi)	RATE OF CHANGE $\frac{\Delta d}{\Delta t}$ (mph)
1 to 2	1	60	60 mph
2 to 5	3	180	60 mph
1 to 10	9	540	60 mph

b. Using the results in part a, what can you infer about the rate of change over any time interval?

The rate of change is constant. It does not change.

Any function for which the rate of change,

$$\frac{\text{Change in output}}{\text{Change in input}}$$

is constant is called a **linear function.** The graph of a linear function is a line. The constant rate of change is called the **slope** of the line and is denoted by the letter ***m.***

If x represents the input variable and y represents the output variable, then the slope m of the line between points (x_1, y_1) and (x_2, y_2) is

$$m = \frac{\Delta y}{\Delta x} = \frac{y_2 - y_1}{x_2 - x_1} \quad \text{where } x_1 \neq x_2$$

c. What is the slope of the line drawn in Problem 1b? What is the practical meaning of slope in this situation? (*Hint:* How does the output change when the input increases by 1 hour?)

The slope is $m = \frac{\Delta y}{\Delta x} = \frac{y_2 - y_1}{x_2 - x_1} = \frac{120 - 60}{2 - 1} = 60$. This is the average speed of 60 mph.

The **vertical intercept** is the point where the graph crosses, or intercepts, the vertical axis. The input value of the vertical intercept is always zero.

3. Using the graph in Problem 1b, determine the vertical intercept. What is the practical meaning of this point in this activity?

(0, 0) This represents the starting point, noon at home.

4. Suppose your friend also starts at noon, but she is already 30 miles down the highway from your home. Your friend travels at an average speed of 55 mph in the same direction as you.

a. Complete the following table, which gives the distance your friend is from your house.

TIME, t (hr)	DISTANCE, d (mi)
0	30
1	85
2	140
5	305
10	580

b. Use your results from part a to complete the following table.

TIME INTERVAL (hr)	Δt (hr)	Δd (mi)	RATE OF CHANGE $\frac{\Delta d}{\Delta t}$ (mph)
1 to 2	1	55	55 mph
2 to 5	3	165	55 mph
1 to 10	9	495	55 mph

c. Is the function defined by the table in part b linear? Explain.

Yes, the rate of change is constant.

d. Graph the data from part b. Use the same grid that you used in Problem 1b.

e. What is the slope of this line? What is its practical meaning in this situation?

$m = \frac{140 - 85}{2 - 1} = \frac{55}{1} = 55$ This is the car's constant speed.

f. What is the vertical intercept of this line? What is the practical meaning of the vertical intercept in this situation?

(0, 30) The friend started 30 miles from your home at noon.

5. Describe how you can determine which line represents the faster speed by examining the graphs in Problem 1b.

If the line is more vertical, the slope is steeper, and the speed is faster.

6. **a.** What would be the slope of the line if your friend were traveling 65 mph?

65

b. What would be the vertical intercept of the graph if your friend started 10 miles from your house?

(0, 10)

7. Let the slope of a line be represented by the letter *m*, and let the vertical intercept be represented by (0, *b*). Let (*x*, *y*) represent the coordinates of any other point on the line.

a. Determine an expression for the slope *m* of the line containing points (0, *b*) and (*x*, *y*).

$m = \frac{y - b}{x}$

b. Solve this equation for *y*.

$y = mx + b$

The coordinates of *all* points (x, y) on the line with slope m and vertical intercept $(0, b)$ satisfy the equation

$$y = mx + b \text{ or } y = b + mx.$$

This is called the **slope-intercept form** of the equation of a line.

Note that the coefficient of x, which is m, is the slope of the line. The constant term b is the y-coordinate of the vertical intercept. Replacing y with $f(x)$, the equation $y = mx + b$ can be written as

$$f(x) = mx + b.$$

Therefore, the slope-intercept form of the equation of the line with slope 3 and vertical intercept $(0, -6)$ is $y = 3x - 6$. Using function notation, this becomes $f(x) = 3x - 6$.

8. a. Write the slope-intercept form of the equation of the line whose graph you drew in Problem 1b.

$f(t) = 60t$

b. Write the slope-intercept form of the equation of the line whose graph you drew in Problem 4d.

$g(t) = 55t + 30$

9. Suppose your grandfather leaves his house, which is 10 miles west of your home, the same time as you. You both head west. You are both traveling at a speed of 50 mph.

a. Will you ever catch up with your grandfather? Explain.

No, because our rates are the same, I will always remain 10 miles behind.

b. Write a slope-intercept equation that represents the distance you are from your home as a function of time.

$f(t) = 50t$

c. Write a slope-intercept equation that represents the distance your grandfather is from your home as a function of time.

$g(t) = 50t + 10$

d. What did you notice about the slope of the two equations?

The slopes of the two equations are equal.

e. Use your grapher and the window; Xmin = 0, Xmax = 3, Ymin = 0, Ymax = 150 to graph both equations on the same axes. What do you notice about the steepness of each of the graphs? What do you conclude about the two lines?

The lines have the same steepness. The lines are parallel.

> The graphs of linear functions with the same slope are **parallel lines.**

10. The following table gives the distance d in miles from home as a function of time t in hours.

t (hr)	d (mi)
1	60
2	20

a. Assuming that the function is linear, determine the slope of the line.

$\frac{20-60}{2-1} = -40$

b. Sketch the graph of the function using the data from the table. Extend the graph through the horizontal and vertical axes.

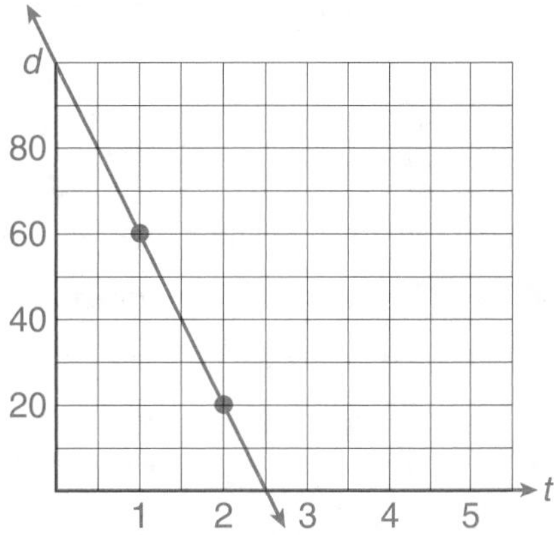

c. What is the graphical significance of the negative slope?

The line is decreasing. This means as time increases the distance is getting smaller.

d. Determine the vertical intercept from the graph.

(0, 100)

e. What is the practical significance of the slope and vertical intercept of the line?

I start 100 miles from home (0, 100) and I am getting closer to home every minute (negative slope).

f. Write the equation of the line in slope-intercept form.

$f(t) = -40t + 100$

g. Check that your equation is correct by graphing on your grapher. Be sure to set the window so that the given data points (1, 60) and (2, 20) are on the screen.

Yes, they are on my line.

A **horizontal intercept** of a graph is a point where the graph meets or crosses the horizontal axis.

h. What is the horizontal intercept of the graph in part b? Verify using the graph created in part g.

(2.5, 0).

i. What is the practical significance of the horizontal intercept in this situation?

This means that it takes 2.5 hours to reach home.

j. What is the *y*-coordinate of any point on the horizontal axis?

The *y*-coordinate of any point on the *x*-axis is 0.

k. Use the equation of the line you found in part f to obtain the horizontal intercept.

$-40t + 100 = 0 \quad \text{or} \quad t = \frac{-100}{-40} = 2.5$

11. Consider the equation $y = 2x - 10$.

a. Determine the vertical intercept.

(0, −10)

b. Determine the horizontal intercept.

(5, 0)

c. Sketch a graph of $y = 2x - 10$ by plotting the horizontal and vertical intercepts.

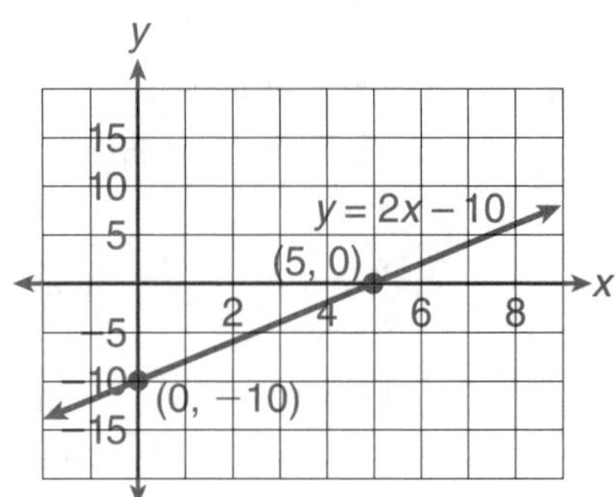

d. Verify your results in parts a, b, and c by graphing the equation $y = 2x - 10$ on your grapher.

SUMMARY

- A function for which the rate of change between any pair of points remains constant is called a *linear function.*
- The graph of linear function is a straight line. The constant rate of change is called the *slope* and is denoted by the letter m (from the French verb *monter,* "to climb or rise").
- The slope of a line segment joining two points (x_1, y_1) and (x_2, y_2) is denoted by m and defined by

$$m = \frac{y_2 - y_1}{x_2 - x_1} = \frac{\Delta y}{\Delta x} = \frac{\text{change in output}}{\text{change in input}}.$$

- The slope indicates how much the output changes when the input increases by a single unit.
- The vertical intercept $(0, b)$ of a graph is the point where the graph crosses the vertical axis. The horizontal intercept $(a, 0)$ of a graph is the point where the graph crosses the horizontal axis.
- The slope-intercept form of the equation of a line is $f(x) = mx + b$.
- To determine the b-value of the vertical intercept $(0, b)$ from $y = mx + b$, set $x = 0$ and solve for y.
- To determine the a-value of the horizontal intercept $(a, 0)$ from $y = mx + b$, set $y = 0$ and solve for x.
- If the slope of a linear function is positive, the graph of the function rises to the right.
- If the slope of a linear function is negative, the graph of the function falls to the right.
- The graphs of linear functions with the same slope are parallel lines.

EXERCISES

1. A function is linear if the rate of change between any two points is constant. Determine whether the following functions are linear. If they are, determine the constant rate of change, or slope of the line.

a.

x	y
0	−1
1	9
2	19

The function is linear. The slope is $\frac{19 - (-1)}{2 - 0} = 10$

b.

x	2	4	6
y	11	8	−1

This function is not linear. The slope between the first and second points is $\frac{8 - 11}{4 - 2} = -\frac{3}{2}$. The slope between the second and third points is $\frac{-1 - 8}{6 - 4} = -\frac{9}{2}$.

Exercise numbers appearing in color are answered in the Selected Answers section of this book.

c. $\{(-2, 18), (2, 9), (6, 0)\}$

This is a linear function. The constant slope is $\frac{9 - 18}{2 - (-2)} = -\frac{9}{4}$.

2. Determine whether the following tables contain input and output data that represent linear functions. Explain your reasoning.

a. You owe your grandmother $1000 because she paid for your first semester at your community college. The conditions of the loan are that you must pay her back the whole amount in one payment using a simple interest rate of 6%. She doesn't care in which year you pay her. The following table contains input and output values to represent how much money you will owe your grandmother one, two, three, and four years later.

YEAR	1	2	3	4
AMOUNT OWED ($)	1060	1120	1180	1240

This is linear. As the input increases by one, the output increases by 60.

b. You decide to invest $1000 of your 401(k) funds into an account that pays 5.5% compounded continuously. The table contains input and output values that represent the amount an initial investment of $1000 is worth at the end of each year.

YEAR	1	2	3	4	5
TOTAL INVESTMENT ($)	1057	1116	1179	1246	1317

Not linear because the input is increasing by one but the output increases by 59, 63, 67, and 71, not constant.

c. For a fee of $20 per month, you may have breakfast in the college snack bar each day (all you can eat). The following table contains input and output values that represent the total number of breakfasts consumed each month and the amount you pay each month.

NO. OF BREAKFASTS EACH MONTH	10	22	16	13
COST ($)	20	20	20	20

This is a constant linear function. The output does not change so the slope is zero.

3. You belong to a health and fitness center. You and your friends are enrolled in the center's weight loss program. The charts contain input and output values that represent the weight over a four-week period for you and your two friends. Determine which charts contain data that are linear and explain why.

a.

WEEK	1	2	3	4
WEIGHT (lb)	150	147	144	141

The data is linear because the input increases by 1 as the output decreases by 3.

b.

WEEK	1	2	3	4
WEIGHT (lb)	183	178	174	171

This data is not linear because as the input increases by 1, the output decreases by 5, then 4, then 3.

c.

WEEK	1	2	3	4
WEIGHT (lb)	160	160	160	160

This data is linear because the output is constant. The slope is zero.

4. Consider the equation $y = -2x + 5$.

a. What is the slope of the line represented by the equation?

$m = -2$

b. What is the vertical intercept?

(0, 5)

c. What is the horizontal intercept?

(2.5, 0)

d. Sketch a graph of the line.

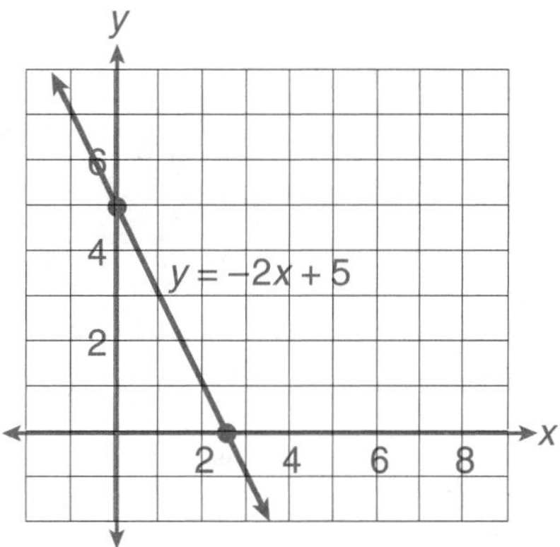

5. a. Determine the slope of the line through the points $(2, -7)$ and $(0, 5)$.

$m = \frac{5 - (-7)}{0 - 2} = -6$

b. Determine the vertical intercept of this line.

(0, 5)

c. What is the equation of the line through these points? Write the equation in function notation.

$f(x) = -6x + 5$

d. What is the horizontal intercept?

$\left(\frac{5}{6}, 0\right)$

6. A car is traveling on a highway. The distance (in miles) from its destination and the time (in hours) are given by the equation $d = 420 - 65t$.

a. What is the vertical intercept of the line represented by the equation?

(0, 420)

b. What is the practical meaning of the vertical intercept?

The car is starting 420 miles from its destination.

c. What is the slope of the line?

The slope is -65.

d. What is the speed at which the car is traveling?

The speed of the car is 65 mph.

e. Graph the equation, both by hand and with your grapher, to verify your answers.

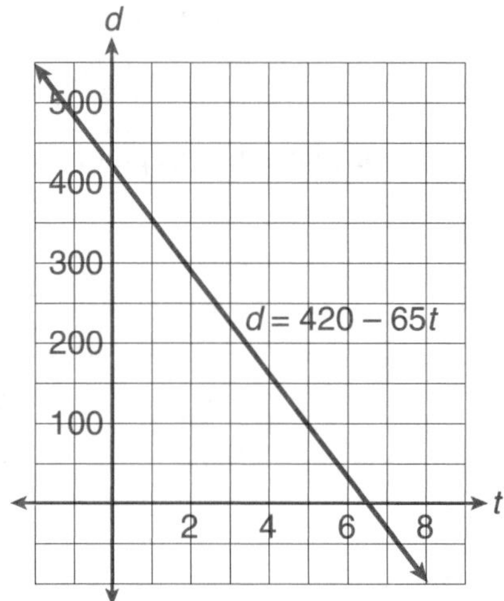

7. A jet is making its landing approach to the runway. Its height above the ground (in feet) as a function of time (in seconds) is given by the following table.

t (sec)	*h* (ft)
0	3500
5	3000
10	2500
15	2000
20	1500
25	1000

a. Is this function linear? Explain.

Yes, the table demonstrates a constant change in t, 5 sec, and a constant change in h, -500, so the rate of change is constant.

b. Calculate the slope $m = \frac{\Delta h}{\Delta t}$.

$m = -100$

c. What is the significance of the sign of the slope in part b?

The negative sign means the graph is decreasing and so is the jet's height above the ground.

d. Determine where the graph crosses the vertical axis.

(0, 3500)

e. Write the equation of the function in slope-intercept form.

$f(x) = -100x + 3500$

f. Determine the horizontal intercept. What is its significance in this situation?

(35, 0) This means it takes the jet 35 seconds to reach the ground from a height of 3500 feet.

8. Determine the horizontal intercept of the line whose equation is given.

a. $y = 4x + 2$

$(-0.5, 0)$

b. $y = \frac{x}{2} - 3$

(6, 0)

9. a. Use your grapher to graph the linear functions defined by the following equations: $y = 2x - 3$, $y = 2x$, $y = 2x + 2$, $y = 2x + 5$. Discuss the similarities and differences of the graphs.

The graphs are all parallel. They have the same slope, but different intercepts.

b. Use your grapher to graph the linear functions defined by the following equations: $y = x - 2$, $y = 2x - 2$, $y = -x - 2$, $y = -2$. Discuss the similarities and differences of the graphs.

Each graph has a different slope, but they all have the same vertical intercept.

ACTIVITY 1.7

A Visit to the Architect
Topic: *Determining Linear Models from Two Data Points*

You are traveling in your car to visit your architect to make final decisions on the plans for your new home. You stop at a convenience store near your home for a cup of coffee and then leave from there. The accompanying graph defines the distance d in miles from home as a function of time t measured in hours from the time you leave the convenience store. Each tick mark on the vertical axis represents 20 miles. Each tick mark on the horizontal axis represents 1 hour.

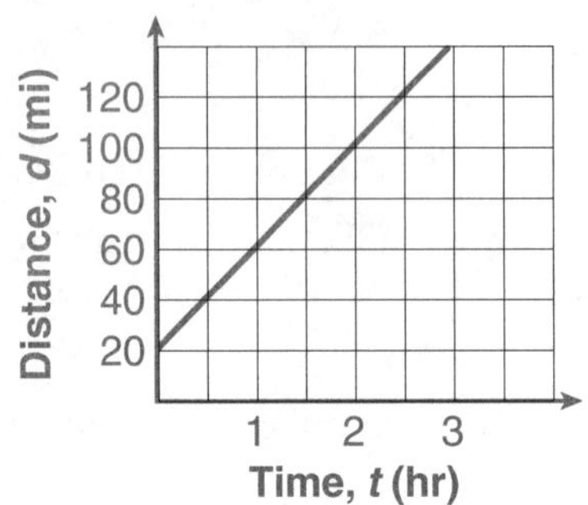

1. a. What is the vertical intercept? What is the practical significance of the vertical intercept?

   (0, 20) I start the trip 20 miles from home.

   b. Use the graph to determine the distance traveled after 1 hour. After 2 hours.

   After one hour, I have traveled 40 miles. After 2 hours, I have traveled 80 miles.

   c. Calculate the slope of the line using the values from part b using the formula $m = \frac{\Delta d}{\Delta t}$.

   $m = \frac{100 - 60}{2 - 1} = 40$

   d. How fast are you going? In which direction (toward or away from home)?

   I am traveling 40 mph away from home.

   e. Use the slope found in part c and the vertical intercept found in part a to write the equation of the line.

   $d = f(t) = 40t + 20$

   f. It took you 2.5 hours to reach the architect's office from the convenience store. How far did you travel?

   $d = f(2.5) = 40(2.5) + 20 = 100 + 20 = 120$ miles.

2. The architect shows you the plans for your roof. You must make a decision about the pitch. The pitch is the slope of the roof expressed as a ratio of the vertical (rise) to the horizontal (run). The following diagram shows this roof, with each tick mark representing 1 unit.

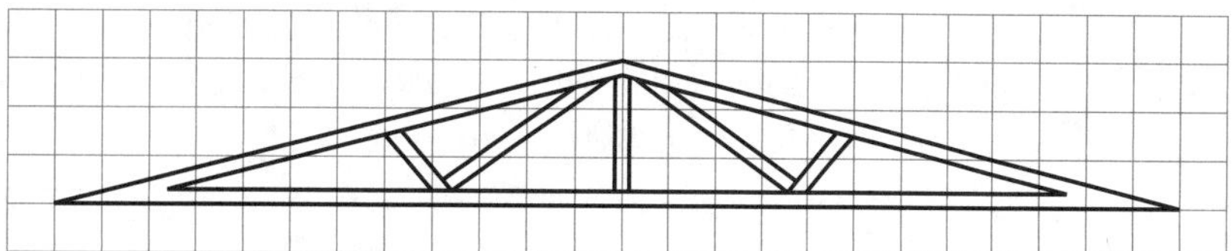

a. From the diagram, determine the slope (pitch) of the roof. Express this as a ratio.

$m = \frac{1}{4}$

b. If the rise of the actual roof must be 5 feet, then how long must the actual run be?

The run will be 20 feet.

c. You decide that you would prefer a pitch of 5 to 16. Draw a diagram of the roof on the following grid that shows this pitch.

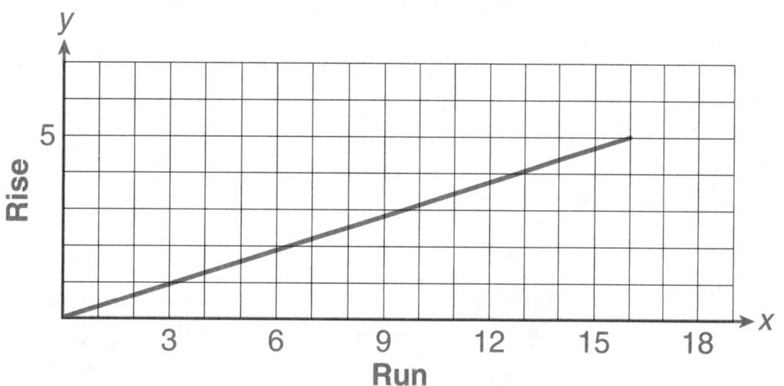

3. Your architect will charge you a flat fee of $2000 for the plans for your home. The cost of your home is estimated by the square footage. The following table gives the total estimated cost c of your home, including the architect's fees, as a function of the square footage h. Assume that the total cost is a linear function of square footage. You want to determine the equation of the line from the data you are given in the table.

TOTAL SQUARE FOOTAGE, h	TOTAL COST, c
0	2000
2500	152,000

a. What is the vertical intercept?

(0, 2000)

b. Using the data in the table and the formula $m = \frac{\Delta c}{\Delta h}$, calculate the slope. What is the practical meaning of the slope in this situation?

$m = \frac{152{,}000 - 2000}{2500 - 0} = \frac{150{,}000}{2500} = 60$ The cost is $60 per square foot.

c. Use the results from parts a and b to write the equation of the line in slope-intercept form.

$c = f(h) = 60h + 2000$

d. You decide that you cannot afford a house with 2500 square feet. Using the equation from part c what is the cost of your home if you decrease the size to 2000 square feet?

$f(2000) = 60(2000) + 2000 = 122,000$. The cost of the home is $122,000.

4. You leave the architect's office and travel further from your home to your favorite vacation spot. The following table gives the distance, *d*, in miles from your home as a function of time, *t*, the number of hours since you left the architect's office.

t (hr)	*d* (mi)
2	226
6	438

Assume that the distance *d* is a linear function of time *t*. You want to determine the equation of the line from the data in this table. Because *d* is the output variable and *t* is the input variable, the slope-intercept form of the line is $d = mt + b$.

a. Calculate the slope $m = \frac{\Delta d}{\Delta t}$ from the given data. What is the practical meaning of the slope in this situation?

$m = \frac{438 - 226}{6 - 2} = \frac{212}{4} = 53$ My average speed is 53 mph.

Notice that you do not know the vertical intercept *b*. From a graph, you can see the approximate vertical intercept, but not the exact value. You can determine the exact vertical intercept algebraically as follows.

b. Both ordered pairs (t, d) in the table must satisfy the equation of the line. Choose one ordered pair to replace *t* and *d* in the equation $d = mt + b$.

$226 = m(2) + b$

c. Now substitute the value for the slope *m* that you found in part a into the equation. With these substitutions, you now have only one unknown—the vertical intercept *b*.

$226 = 53(2) + b$

d. Solve the equation in part c for *b*, the vertical intercept. What is the practical meaning of the vertical intercept in this situation?

$226 = 106 + b$ $b = 120$ This means the architect is 120 miles from the house.

e. Write the equation of the line in slope-intercept form.

$d = f(t) = 53t + 120$

f. Check your equation by graphing on your grapher. Are the two data points on your line? If not, try to determine the source of your error.

The data points are on my line.

SUMMARY

To determine the equation of a line when two points on the line are known:

1. Determine the slope of the line, $m = \frac{\Delta y}{\Delta x} = \frac{\text{change in output}}{\text{change in input}}$.
2. Choose either of the given points (x, y).
3. Using the slope-intercept form, $y = mx + b$, replace m, x, and y with the values found from steps 1 and 2.
4. Solve the resulting equation for the only unknown, b.
5. Substitute the values for m and b into the slope-intercept form, $y = mx + b$.

EXERCISES

1. Write the equation of the line whose graph is given. Each tick mark is 1 unit.

   a.

   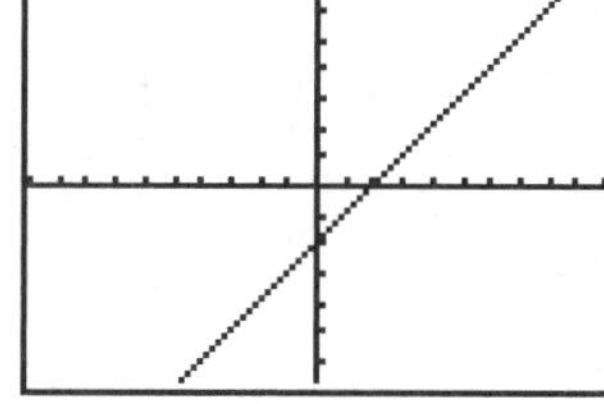

   $f(x) = x - 2$

   b.

   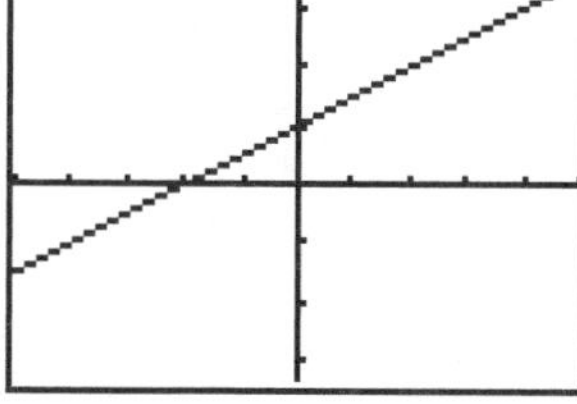

   $f(x) = \frac{1}{2}x + 1$

   c.

   $g(x) = -2x + 6$

   d.

   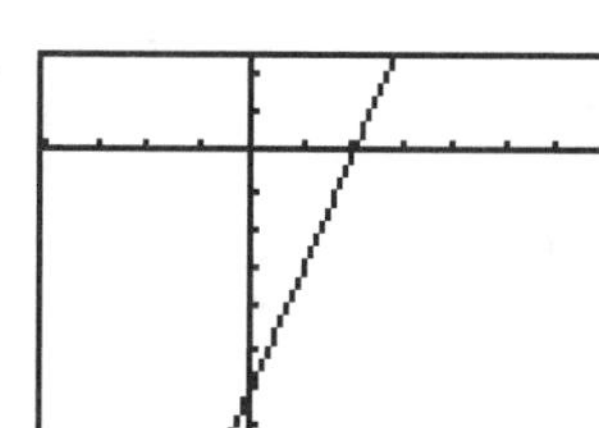

   $h(x) = 3x - 6$

2. The following graph represents the distance a car travels as a function of time (in hours). Each horizontal tick mark represents 1 hour. Each vertical tick mark represents 25 miles.

   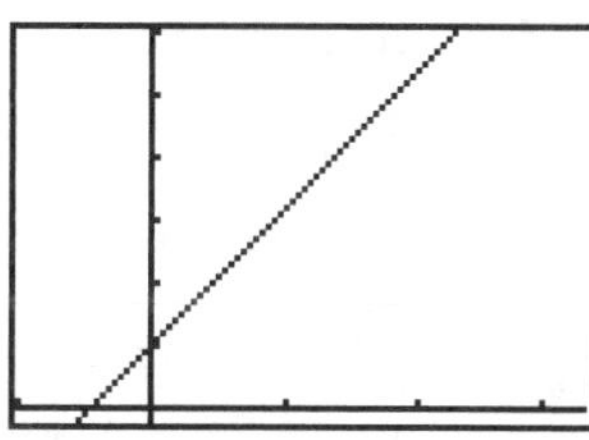

   a. How fast is the car traveling?

   50 mph

   b. Write the equation of the line in slope-intercept form.

   $d = 50t + 25$

Exercise numbers appearing in color are answered in the Selected Answers section of this book.

3. Instead of a graph, you are given the following table, which gives the cost c of a car rental as a function of miles driven, x.

x (mi)	c ($)
0	35
100	40

Assume that the function is linear and that you want to determine the equation of the line from the table.

a. What is the vertical intercept? How do you know this?

(0, 35) The vertical intercept occurs where $x = 0$.

b. Calculate the slope $m = \frac{\Delta c}{\Delta x}$ from the data in the table. What is the practical meaning of this slope?

$m = \frac{40 - 35}{100 - 0} = \frac{5}{100} = \frac{1}{20}$ The cost is $1 per 20 miles or $0.05 per mile.

c. Use your results from parts a and b to write the equation of the line in slope-intercept form.

$c = f(x) = \frac{1}{20}x + 35$

4. The following table gives the distance d in miles from the marina as a function of time t in hours.

t (hr)	d (mi)
2	75
4	145

a. Write the equation of the line in slope-intercept form.

The slope is $\frac{145 - 75}{4 - 2} = 35$ So, $d = 35t + b$ or $75 = 35(2) + b$
So, $b = 5$ Thus, the equation is $d = 35t + 5$.

b. What is the speed of your boat?

The speed of the boat is 35 mph.

5. Write the slope-intercept equation of the line satisfying the given conditions.

a. Slope $= \frac{1}{2}$, vertical intercept $= -1$

$y = \frac{1}{2}x - 1$

b. Contains the points $(-3, 5)$ and $(0, -1)$

$y = -2x - 1$

c. Contains the points $(-4, -3)$ and $(2, 6)$

$y = \frac{3}{2}x + 3$

d. Parallel to the line $y = 3x - 7$ and through the point $(2, -5)$

$y = 3x - 11$

6. a. Graph a line with a slope of 4 that goes through the point (1, 5). Write the equation of the line.

$y = 4x + 1$

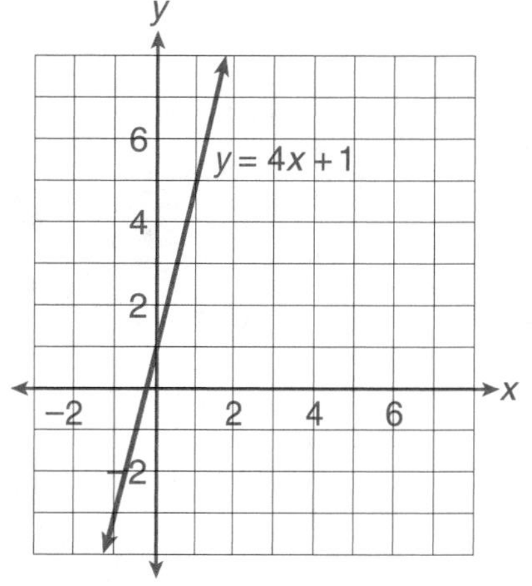

b. Graph a line with a slope of $-\frac{1}{2}$ that goes through the point (−2, 3). Write the equation of the line.

$y = -\frac{1}{2}x + 2$

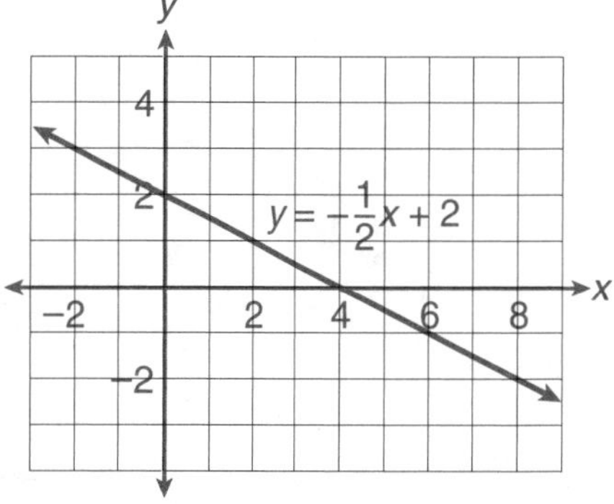

7. Determine five ordered pairs that satisfy each of the following equations, and then sketch the graph. Verify, if possible, using your grapher.

a. $y = 2x - 8$

b. $y = -\frac{1}{3}x + 6$

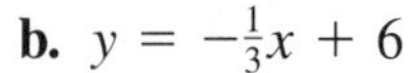

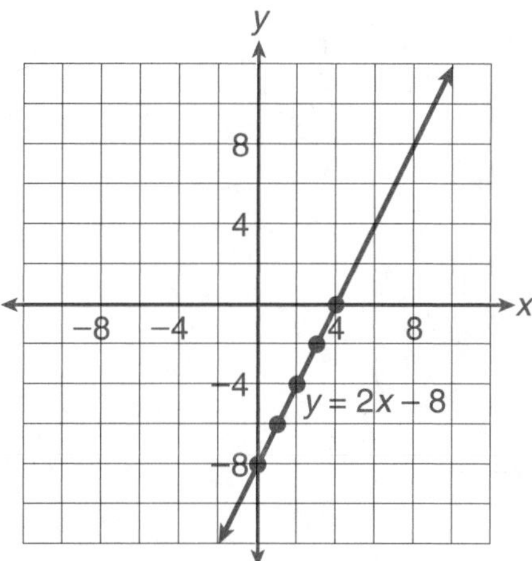

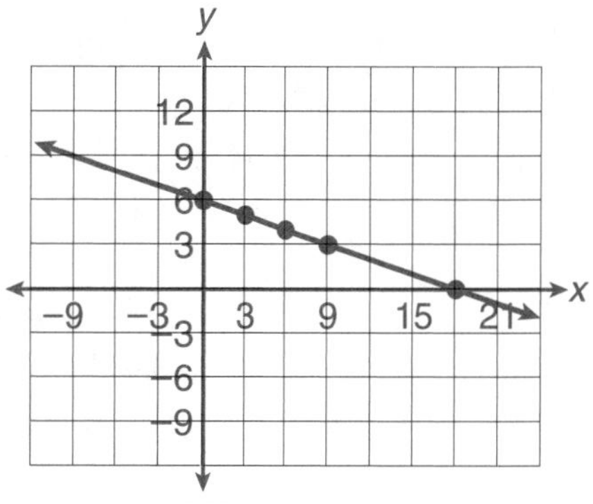

(0, −8), (1, −6), (3, −2), (4, 0), (2, −4)

(0, 6), (3, 5), (18, 0), (6, 4), (9, 3)

c. $4x - 2y = 1$

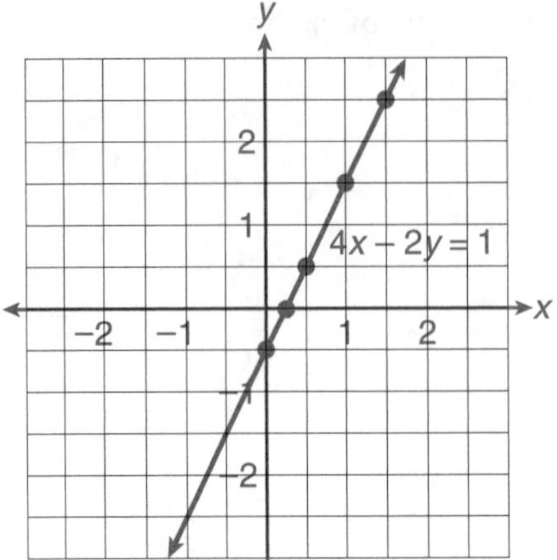

$(0, -\frac{1}{2})$, $(1, \frac{3}{2})$, $(\frac{1}{2}, \frac{1}{2})$, $(\frac{1}{4}, 0)$, $(\frac{3}{2}, \frac{5}{2})$

d. $y = 3x$

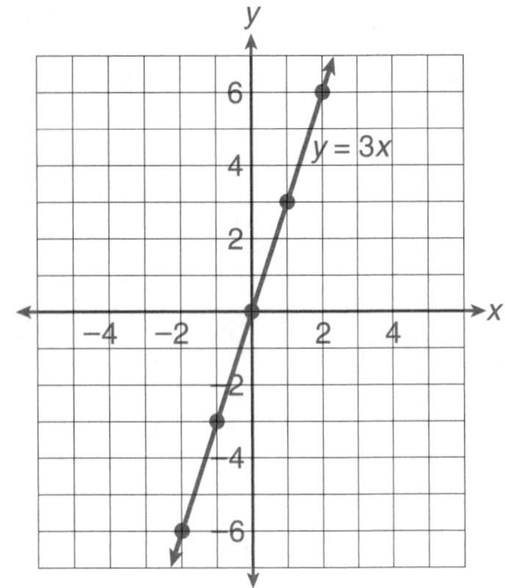

(0, 0), (1, 3), (2, 6), (−1, −3), (−2, −6)

e. $y = 5$

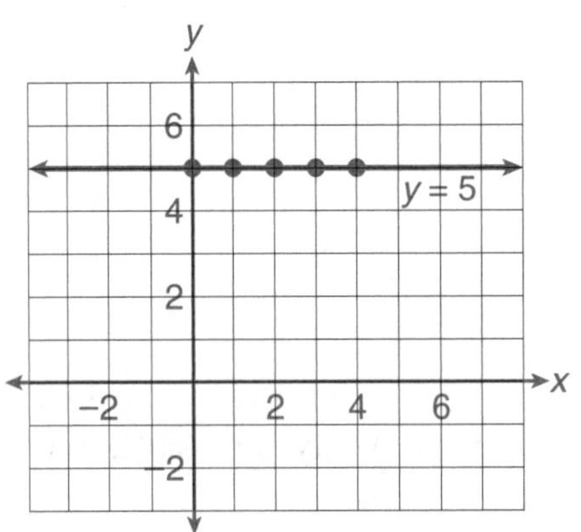

(0, 5), (1, 5), (2, 5), (3, 5), (4, 5)

f. $x = -3$

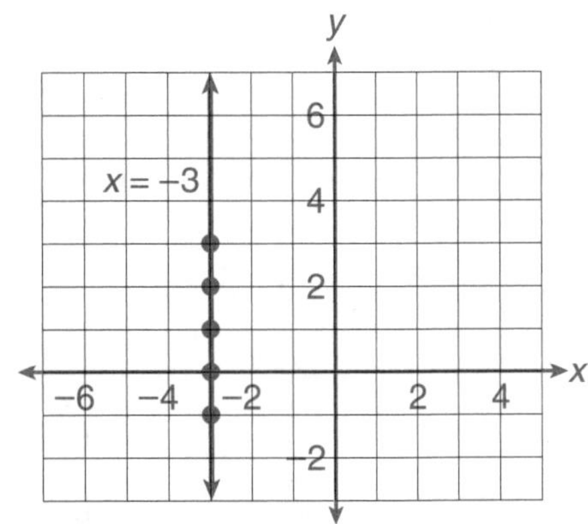

(−3, 0), (−3, 1), (−3, 2), (−3, 3), (−3, −1)

ACTIVITY 1.8

Skateboard Heaven
Topic: *General Form of Linear Equations*

Your town has just authorized funding to build a new ramp and pathways for skateboarding. The ramp and pathways must have a rectangular fence surrounding them for security. The monies allocated in the budget for fencing will be enough to purchase 350 feet of fence. The only stipulation is that the width must be between 35 and 60 feet to properly enclose the new ramp. The length will depend on the width you choose. Your task is to determine the length and width of the rectangular region so that you use all of the fencing.

1. a. What does the value of 350 represent with regard to the rectangular region?

350 represents the perimeter of the rectangle.

b. Using x to represent the width and y to represent the length, write an equation for the perimeter of this rectangular region.

$2x + 2y = 350$

c. The linear equation in part b should be in the form of $Ax + By = C$. Identify the values of the constants A, B, and C in the equation.

$A = 2, B = 2, C = 350$

2. Rewrite the equation from Problem 1b in slope-intercept form by isolating the dependent variable y. That is, solve the equation for y in terms of x.

$y = 175 - x$

3. Use function notation to write the length y as a function of the width, x. Let F represent the function.

$F(x) = 175 - x$

4. Complete the table to determine some possible lengths and widths for the rectangular region.

x	35	40	50	60
$F(x)$	140	135	125	115

5. What is the slope of the line represented by the equation that you wrote in Problem 2? What is the practical meaning of the slope in this situation?

The slope is -1. This means as the width increases by 1 foot, the length decreases by 1 foot.

6. What is the vertical intercept of the line represented by the equation you wrote in Problem 2? What is the practical meaning of the vertical intercept in this situation?

The vertical intercept is (0, 175). This means if the length is 175 the width is zero, so there is no rectangle.

7. What is the practical domain and range for this function?

$35 \le x \le 60$; $115 \le y \le 140$

When a linear equation is written in the form $Ax + By = C$, it is said to be in **general form.**

If either A, the coefficient of x, or B, the coefficient of y, equals zero, a special situation arises. You will explore this in the following problems.

8. a. When the ramp for skateboarding is complete, you will be able to pay a monthly fee of $12.50 to use the ramp as many hours as you wish. Complete the table of values, where x is the number of hours per month a person uses the ramp, and y is the cost per month.

x, TIME (hr)	5	10	15	20
y, COST ($)	12.50	12.50	12.50	12.50

b. Use the data points from the table to sketch the graph.

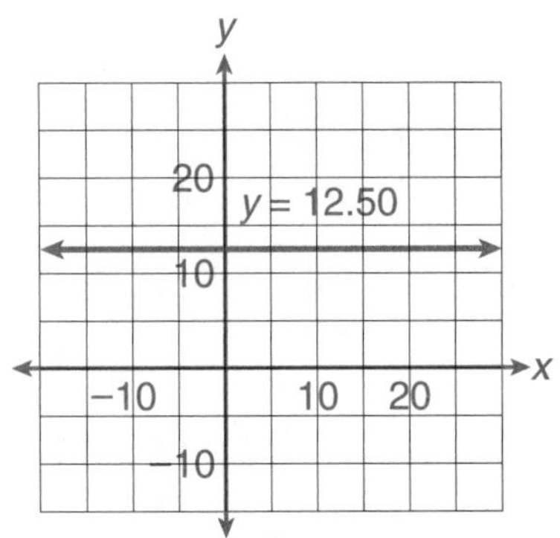

c. Describe the graph in words.

The graph is a horizontal line through (0, 12.50).

d. Choose two ordered pairs from part a and determine the slope m of the line. What is the practical meaning of the slope in this situation?

$m = 0$, this means that the cost does not change.

e. What are the intercepts (vertical and horizontal) of the line (if they exist)?

Vertical intercept: (0, 12.50); Horizontal intercept: none.

f. Write the equation of this line in slope-intercept form, $y = mx + b$.

$y = 0x + 12.50$

g. Compare your equation in part f with the general form $Ax + By = C$, and identify the values of A, B, and C. Note that when there is no input variable appearing in an equation, its coefficient is understood to be zero.

$A = 0, B = 1, C = 12.50$

9. Sketch the graphs of the following equations on the same coordinate axes. Verify using your grapher.

a. $y = -2$

b. $f(x) = 1$

c. $g(x) = \frac{5}{2}$

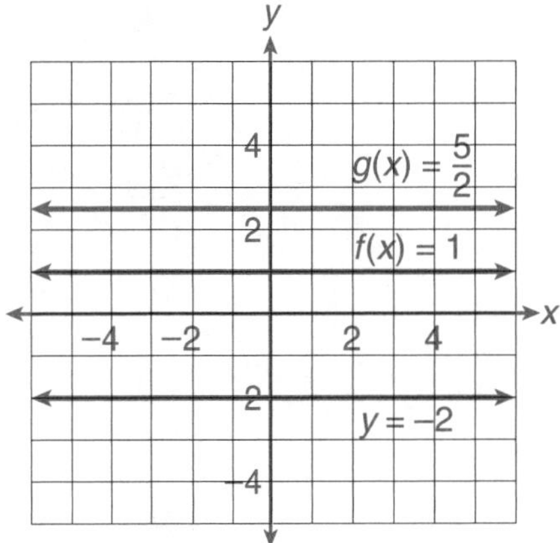

A graph in which y is a constant or, equivalently, $f(x)$ is a constant is a **horizontal line.** The slope of the horizontal line is zero.

10. a. Compare the equation $x = -2$ with $Ax + By = C$ and identify the values of A, B, and C.

$A = 1, B = 0, C = -2$

b. Write three ordered pairs that satisfy the equation $x = -2$.

$(-2, 0), (-2, 2), (-2, -4)$

c. Use the points from part b to sketch a graph of $x = -2$.

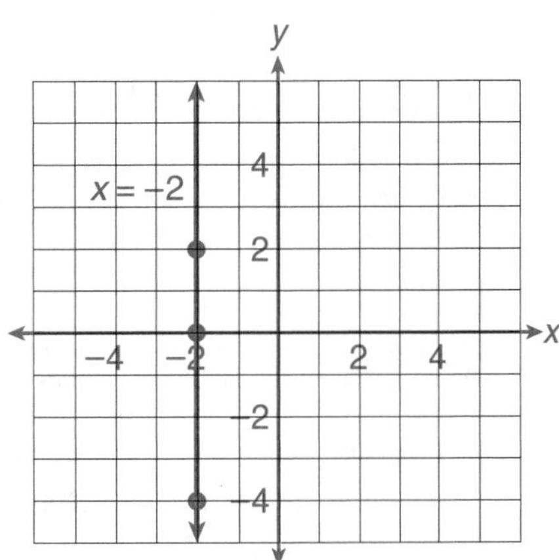

d. What are the intercepts (vertical and horizontal) of the line (if they exist)?

Vertical: none; Horizontal: $(-2, 0)$

e. Is it possible to write the equation of this line in function notation? Explain.

No, it is not possible because y is not a function of x.

f. Can you graph this equation with your grapher? What are the difficulties?

No, because there is no y value in the equation.

g. Choose two ordered pairs from part b and determine the slope m of the line, if possible.

This process will yield division by zero, which is undefined.

11. Sketch the graphs of the following equations.

a. $x = -2$ **b.** $x = 4$ **c.** $x = \frac{5}{2}$

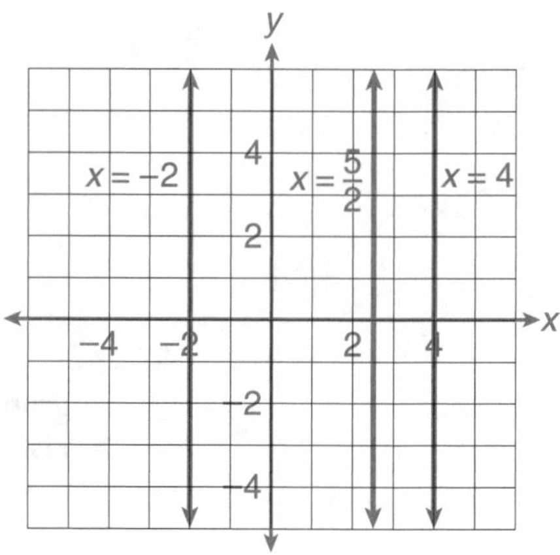

A graph in which x is a constant is a **vertical line.** The slope of a vertical line is undefined.

SUMMARY

- A linear function whose equation is in the form $Ax + By = C$, where A, B, and C are constants is said to be written in general form.
- The graph of $y = c$ or $f(x) = c$ is a horizontal line. In this case, f is called a constant function. Every point on this line has a y-coordinate equal to c. A horizontal line has slope of zero.
- The graph of $x = a$ is a vertical line. Every point on this line has an x-coordinate equal to a. The slope of a vertical line is undefined.

EXERCISES

1. Write the following linear equations in slope-intercept form. Determine the slope and vertical intercept of each line.

a. $2x - y = 3$

$y = 2x - 3$, $m = 2$, $(0, -3)$

b. $x + y = -2$

$y = -x - 2$, $m = -1$, $(0, -2)$

c. $2x - 3y = 7$

$y = \frac{2}{3}x - \frac{7}{3}$, $m = \frac{2}{3}$, $(0, -\frac{7}{3})$

d. $-x + 2y = 4$

$y = \frac{1}{2}x + 2$, $m = \frac{1}{2}$, $(0, 2)$

e. $0x + 3y = 12$

$y = 4$, $m = 0$, $(0, 4)$

Exercise numbers appearing in color are answered in the Selected Answers section of this book.

2. a. Write the equation of a horizontal line through the point $(-2, 3)$.

$y = 3$

b. What is the slope of the line?

0

c. What are the vertical and horizontal intercepts of the line?

Vertical: (0, 3); Horizontal: none

3. a. Write the equation of a vertical line through the point $(-2, 3)$.

$x = -2$

b. What is the slope of the line?

no slope (undefined)

c. What are the vertical and horizontal intercepts of the line?

Vertical: None; Horizontal: $(-2, 0)$

d. Sketch the graph of this equation.

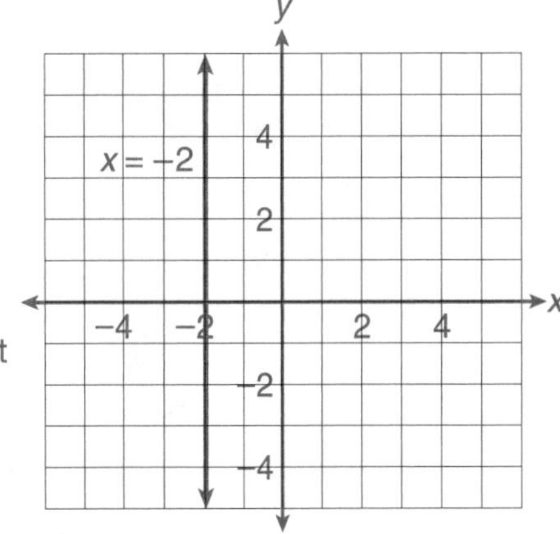

e. Is this a function? Explain.

This is not a function. It does not pass the vertical line test.

f. Explain the difference between a line with a zero slope and a line with an undefined slope.

A line with 0 slope is a horizontal line. It does represent a function. A line with undefined slope is a vertical line. It does not represent a function.

4. You are retained as a consultant for a major computer company. You receive $2000 per month as a fee no matter how many hours you work.

a. Using x to represent the number of hours you work each month, write a function f in symbolic form to represent the total amount received from the company each month.

$f(x) = 2000$

b. Complete the following table of values.

HOURS WORKED PER MONTH, x	15	25	35
FEE PER MONTH, $f(x)$	2000	2000	2000

c. Use your grapher to sketch the graph of this function.

d. What is the slope of the line? What is the practical meaning of the slope in this situation?

The slope is 0. This means the fee does not change.

e. Describe the graph of the function.

The graph is a horizontal line through (0, 2000)

5. You work in the purchasing department of an appliance retailer. This month you are stocking up on washers and dryers. Your supervisor informs you that your budget this month is $10,000. You know that the average wholesale cost of a washer over the past year has been $250, while the average wholesale cost of a dryer has been $200.

a. If w represents the number of washers you can purchase, write an expression that represents the amount spent on washers.

$250w$

b. If d represents the number of dryers you can purchase, write an expression that represents the amount spent on dryers.

$200d$

c. Write a linear equation in general form that relates the number of washers and dryers you can expect to purchase with your budget.

$250w + 200d = 10{,}000$

d. Solve your equation in part c for the variable d. In other words, express the number of dryers you can expect to purchase as a function of the number of washers you can expect to purchase.

$d = \frac{10{,}000 - 250w}{200} = 50 - \frac{5}{4}w$

e. What is the horizontal intercept for this function? What is its practical meaning in this situation?

(40, 0) The maximum number of washers I can purchase is 40.

f. What is the vertical intercept for this function? What is its practical meaning in this situation?

(0, 50) The maximum number of dryers I can purchase is 50.

g. What is the slope of this function? What is its significance in this situation?

The slope is $-\frac{5}{4}$. This means for every 5 dryers I purchase, that is 4 fewer washers I can purchase.

h. Use your grapher to produce a graph of the function in part d. What part of this graph is relevant to this situation?

The only relevant part is where both w and d are positive (quadrant I)

i. What are the practical domain and range for this situation?

Domain: $0 \le w \le 40$; Range: $0 \le d \le 50$

ACTIVITY 1.9

College Tuition

Topics: *Modeling a Line of Best Fit with a Straightedge, Goodness of Fit, Interpolation and Extrapolation*

The following graphic contains the average tuition and required fees for full-time matriculated students at private four-year colleges over the last two decades.

PAYING FOR COLLEGE

Year	Cost
1996	$12,990
1994	$11,480
1992	$10,290
1990	$11,380
1989	$10,350
1979	$3810

Source: National Center for Educational Statistics, U.S Department of Education.

1. Let t, the number of years since 1979, represent your input variable and c, the average cost, your output variable. Determine an appropriate scale, and plot the data points from the accompanying table. Therefore, $t = 0$ corresponds to the year 1979, $t = 1$ to 1980, $t = 2$ to 1981, and so on.

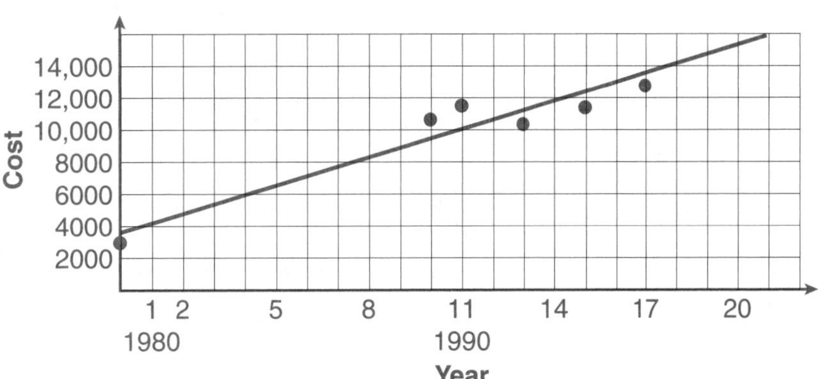

2. Does there appear to be a linear relationship between the year and the average cost of tuition? Explain.

The relationship is somewhat linear, but not exactly.

3. Using a straightedge (a taut string or dry strand of spaghetti is helpful in positioning the line), draw a line that will have as many data points as close to the line as possible. The line you are trying to draw is called the **line of best fit.**

4. Estimate the slope of your line. What is the practical meaning of the slope in this situation?

I estimate the slope to be 600. This means tuition increased at a rate of about $600 per year. (Answers will vary.)

5. What is the vertical intercept of your line of best fit? Does this number have any practical meaning in this situation?

The vertical intercept is about (0, 3800). This means tuition in 1979 was approximately $3800 per year.

6. What is the equation of your line of best fit? This is a **mathematical model** for the data.

My equation of best fit is $c = 600t + 3800$

7. To measure the goodness of fit of the line found in Problem 6, complete the following table.

Note: The fourth column is asking for absolute value of the difference between actual and model values.

INPUT, t	ACTUAL OUTPUT, c	MODEL'S PREDICTED OUTPUT	$\lvert$ACTUAL VALUE − MODEL VALUE$\rvert$
0	3810	3800	10
10	10,350	9800	550
11	11,380	10,400	980
13	10,290	11,600	1310
15	11,480	12,800	1320
17	12,990	14,000	1010

8. Determine the sum of the values in the last column. The sum measures the **error** in your model. The smaller the error, the better the fit of your line. Compare your error with those of your classmates.

My error is 5180.

The accepted method for determining the line of best fit to a set of data is called the *method of least squares*. This method is used to calculate a slope and y-intercept. The line with this slope and y-intercept is called the **regression line** for the data. Your graphing calculator is programmed with an algorithm that determines the regression line.

9. Enter the tuition data into your calculator and determine the regression line. Write the result, rounding coefficients to three decimal places. If necessary, see Appendix C for help operating the TI-83 graphing calculator.

$y = 517.865x + 4353.483$

10. a. Now use the regression equation you determined in Problem 9 to model the tuition data. What is the error measure for the regression line in Problem 9? (Proceed as you did in Problem 7.)

INPUT, t	ACTUAL OUTPUT, c	MODEL'S PREDICTED OUTPUT	|ACTUAL VALUE − MODEL VALUE|
0	3810	4353	543
10	10,350	9532	818
11	11,380	10,050	1330
13	10,290	11,086	796
15	11,480	12,121	641
17	12,990	13,157	167

b. Compare the error of your line of best fit, from Problem 8c, with the error of the regression line. Which is a better fit of the data?

The error is 4295, which is almost a thousand less than my error. The regression line is the better fit of the data.

11. a. Use the regression equation to predict the average tuition and fees at private four-year colleges in 1993 ($t = 14$).

The regression model predicts tuition of $11,603.59 for 1993.

Using a regression model to predict an output within the domain of the given input values is called **interpolation.** Using a regression model to predict an output outside the domain of the known input values is called **extrapolation.** In general, interpolation is more accurate than extrapolation.

b. Use the regression equation to predict the average tuition and fees at private four-year colleges in 2000. In 2010.

The regression model predicts $15,228.65 for 2000 and $20,407.30 for 2010.

c. Which prediction do you believe would be more accurate? Explain.

I have more confidence in the 2000 prediction because it is closer to the years included in the data.

d. Use the regression line to estimate the year in which average tuition and fees will be at least $20,000.

$20{,}000 = 517.865x + 4353.483$

So, $x = 30.21$

This means the model predicts tuition to exceed 20,000 for the first time in the year 1979 + 30, or 2009.

SUMMARY

- The linear regression equation is the linear equation that "best fits" a set of data.
- The regression line is a mathematical model for the data.
- Interpolation is the process of using a regression equation to predict a value of output for an input value that lies within the domain of the *original data*.
- Extrapolation is the process of using a regression equation to predict a value of output for an input value that lies outside the domain of the *original data*.

EXERCISES

1. **a.** Plot the following data.

x	0	3	6	9	12	15	18
y	−0.8	6.3	13.1	19.6	27.0	33.5	40.8

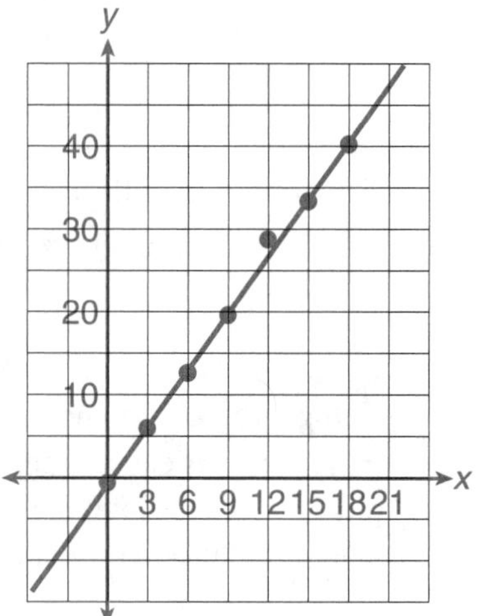

b. With a straightedge, draw a line that you think looks like the line of best fit. Determine the equation of the line you drew by estimating the slope and the y-intercept from the graph.

$y = 2x - 1$ (Answers will vary.)

c. Use your grapher to determine the equation of the regression line. Write the result here.

$f(x) = 2.299x - 0.761$

d. Use your equation from part b to predict the value of y when $x = 10$.

My value of y would be 19. (Answers will depend on part b.)

e. Use your regression equation from part c to predict the value of y when $x = 10$.

The value of y from the regression equation would be 22.229.

Exercise numbers appearing in color are answered in the Selected Answers section of this book.

f. Use your equations from parts b and c to predict the value of y when $x = 25$. Do you think your hand-drawn line of best fit is as good as the calculator's regression line? Explain.

For the x value of 25, my equation yields 49. The regression equation yields 56.714. I have more confidence in the regression equation.

2. Public debt increased at a relatively constant rate from 1986 to 1996. The following table gives the average debt per capita (in thousands of dollars) for selected years, where $t = 0$ corresponds to the year 1986.

t (YEARS)	0	2	4	6	8	10
d (IN THOUSANDS OF DOLLARS)	8.77	10.53	13.00	15.85	18.02	19.81

Source: Bureau of Public Debt, U.S. Department of the Treasury

a. Plot the data.

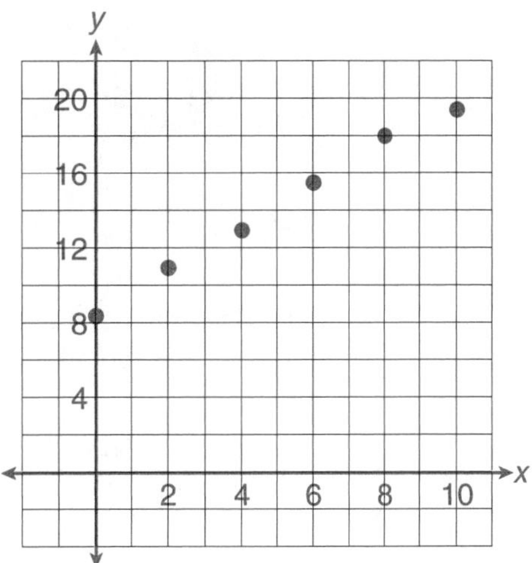

b. Use your grapher to determine the equation of the regression line. Write the result here.

$f(x) = 1.150x + 8.579$

c. What is the slope of the line? What is the practical meaning of slope in this situation?

The slope is 1.150. This means that the average debt per person is increasing at a rate of $1150 per year.

d. Use your regression line to determine the average debt of an individual in 1990 ($t = 4$). Compare your result with the actual value of $13,000 in 1990.

The regression line predicts an average debt of $13,179 in 1990. This is 179 above the actual 13,000, an error of slightly less than 1.4%.

e. Use the regression equation to predict the average debt of an individual in the year 2002.

The regression equation predicts an average debt of $26,979 in 2002.

3. Earth's rotational speed is gradually decreasing because of friction. This means that although one rotation of Earth now takes 24 hours, it previously took fewer hours. In other words, there were more rotations of Earth in a given period of time. We know that there are currently about 365 rotations, or days, in a year. From studies of daily and yearly growth rings in corals, geologist John Wells found that he could determine the number of days in a year at various times in history. Here is what he found:

MILLIONS OF YEARS AGO, t	DAYS PER YEAR, d
65 (Cenozoic)	371
136 (Cretaceous)	377
190 (Jurassic)	382
225 (Triassic)	385
280 (Permian)	390
345 (Mississippian/Pennsylvanian)	396
395 (Devonian)	401
435 (Silurian)	405
500 (Ordovician)	412
570 (Cambrian)	421

a. Enter the data in the table into your calculator. Determine the linear regression equation model and write the result here. Let t be the input and d the output.

$d = 0.097t + 363.433$

b. From the model, estimate how many days there are per year now. Does that agree with what you know to be true?

When $t = 0$, $d = 363.433$. This is very close to 365.25.

c. Estimate how many days per year there were 300 million years ago.

$d = 0.097(300) + 363.433 = 392.5$ days

d. Estimate the number of days per year 700 million years ago. Is this estimate likely to be as accurate as your estimate in part c? Give a reason for your answer.

$d = 0.097(700) + 363.433 = 431.3$ days The answer is not likely to be as accurate as part c because we are outside the range of the data.

e. Do you think this function is actually linear? Try to find at least two reasons for your answer.

The function probably is not linear, but over "short" time periods all functions are approximately linear. The length of the year may have been longer, but there are a lot of forces in the universe that we may not even have discovered yet.

PROJECT ACTIVITY 1.10

Reading a Movie

Topic: *Linear Regression*

In a course you are taking this semester, one of the requirements is to "read" a movie. You rent the movie at a local video store, keeping in mind that you'll need to note events of the movie for future reference. You decide to set up a double-check system that uses both time in minutes and the counter reading of your VCR to mark important events in the movie. You record the following data. Assume that the counter reading, n, is the input variable and that time in minutes, $t(n)$, is the output variable.

COUNTER READING, n	TIME (MIN), $t(n)$
0	0
100	1.1
280	3
400	4.5
800	9.5
900	10.75
990	12
1198	15
1300	16.5

1. a. Do you think that this relationship is linear?

Yes

b. Complete the following table.

COUNTER READING, n	TIME (MIN), $t(n)$	RATE OF CHANGE BETWEEN ADJACENT PAIRS OF DATA (ROUND TO FOUR DECIMAL PLACES)
0	0	—
100	1.1	(1.1 – 0)/(100 – 0) = 0.0110
280	3	(3 – 1.1)/(280 – 100) = 0.0110
400	4.5	(4.5 – 3)/(400 – 280) = 0.0125
800	9.5	(9.5 – 4.5)/(800 – 400) = 0.0125
900	10.75	(10.75 – 9.5)/(900 – 800) = 0.0125
990	12	(12 – 10.75)/(990 – 900) = 0.0139
1198	15	(15 – 12)/(1198 – 990) = 0.0144
1300	16.5	(16.5 – 15)/(1300 – 1198) = 0.0147

c. Do the rates of change in the table support or contradict your conjecture about whether or not the relationship is linear?

It may support the linear conjecture. The rate seems to be close to constant, but at the same time the rate seems to be constantly increasing.

2. Enter the data into your grapher and make a scatterplot. If you need help, see Appendix C. Look at the values in the table to determine an appropriate viewing window. Your scatterplot should resemble the following. The scatterplot indicates that the relationship may be strongly linear. Does this agree with your conjecture in Problem 1?

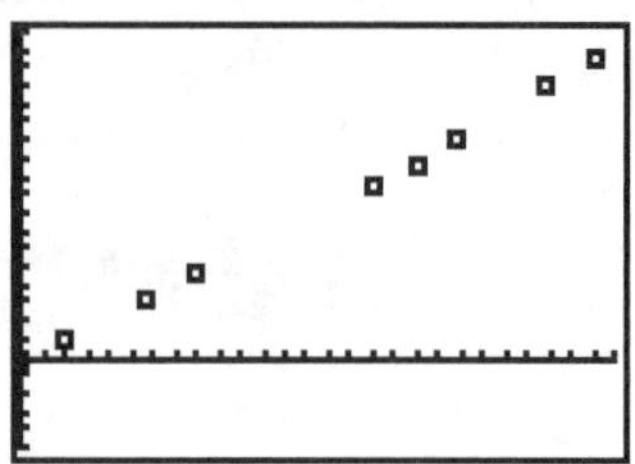

Yes.

3. **a.** Use your grapher to determine the equation of the regression line for the data. Write the result.

   $t(n) = 0.0126n - 0.3472.$

   b. What is the slope of the regression line?

   $m = 0.0126.$

   c. What is the practical meaning of the slope in this situation?

   The slope is the rate of change in time (minutes) per change in counter reading.

   d. What is the horizontal intercept of this line?

   $0 = 0.0126n - 0.3472$. This means $n = \frac{0.3472}{0.0126} = 27.6$ The horizontal intercept is (27.6, 0).

   e. What is the vertical intercept of this line?

   The vertical intercept is $(0, -0.3472)$.

   f. What is the practical domain over which the problem has meaning? Assume that the movie is approximately 2 hours long.

   Assuming that the function is linear and that the movie is 2 hours long, because 15 minutes corresponds to a counter reading of about 1200, two hours would have a counter reading of about 9600. Thus, the practical domain is $0 \leq n \leq 9600$.

   g. Use your grapher to graph the regression line in the same screen as the scatterplot. How well do you think the line fits the data?

   The regression line fits well.

4. Use the graph and the equation of the line to answer the following questions.

a. How much time has the movie run if the counter reads 2200?

$t(2200) = 0.0126(2200) - 0.3472 = 27.4$ minutes

b. If an important event takes place 30 minutes into the movie, what is the counter reading on your VCR to locate the event so that you can "read" this part of the movie again?

$30 = 0.012n - 0.3472$

$n = \frac{30.3472}{0.0126} = 2408.5$

What Have I Learned?

1. All points (x, y) on the line with slope m and vertical intercept $(0, b)$ satisfy the equation $y = mx + b$.

   a. The point (2, 3) is on the line whose equation is $y = 4x - 5$. Show how the point (2, 3) satisfies the equation $y = 4x - 5$.

   $3 = 4(2) - 5$
   $3 = 8 - 5$
   $3 = 3$

   b. Determine another point on the line whose equation is $y = 4x - 5$.

   $(0, -5)$

2. Given an input/output table that represents a function, how can you determine if the function is linear?

   To determine if a set of data is linear, calculate the ratio $\frac{\text{change in output}}{\text{change in input}}$ for each consecutive pair of ordered pairs. If the ratio is constant, the data set is linear.

3. Write a procedure for determining the equation of a line, given two points on the line.

   Step 1. Determine the slope of the line segment joining the two points, m.

   Step 2. Substitute the coordinates of one point and the value of m determined above in the equation $y = mx + b$. Then solve for b.

   Step 3. Substitute the values for m and b into $y = mx + b$.

4. Write a procedure for determining the horizontal intercept of a graph, given its equation.

   To find the horizontal intercept replace y in the equation with 0 and solve for x. The horizontal intercept is $(x, 0)$.

5. Consider two linear functions $f(x) = m_1x + b_1$ and $g(x) = m_2x + b_2$, whose graphs are distinct and parallel. What can you say about m_1 and m_2 and about b_1 and b_2? Explain.

   The lines are parallel. This means their rates of change are equal so, $m_1 = m_2$. Because they are distinct, they have no points in common, including their y-intercepts, thus, b_1 does not equal b_2.

6. If the graph of $Ax + By = C$ is a vertical line, what can you conclude about the values of A and B? Explain.

   If the graph is a vertical line $B = 0$. There is no y-value present in the equation.

7. **a.** Describe the graph of a line with a positive slope.

   The line rises to the right.

   b. Describe the graph of a line with a negative slope.

   The line falls to the right.

c. Describe the graph of a line with a slope of zero.

The line is horizontal.

d. Describe the graph of a line with an undefined slope.

The line is vertical.

8. Explain the difference between interpolation and extrapolation.

Interpolation uses the regression equation to predict values with the range of the known data points. Extrapolation uses the regression equation to predict values outside the range of the known data points.

How Can I Practice?

1. Match each of the following functions or equations with its corresponding graph.

$f(x) = -2x + 3$ $\quad g(x) = 2x - 3$ $\quad y = 2$

$h(x) = -2x - 3$ $\quad y = -2x$ $\quad x = 2$

a. 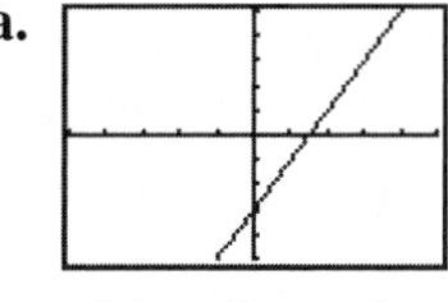

$g(x) = 2x - 3$

b. 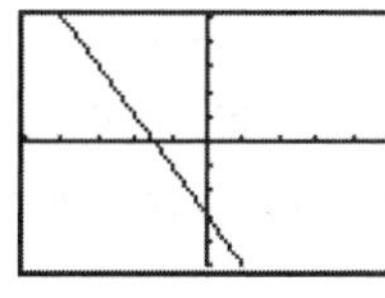

$h(x) = -2x - 3$

c. 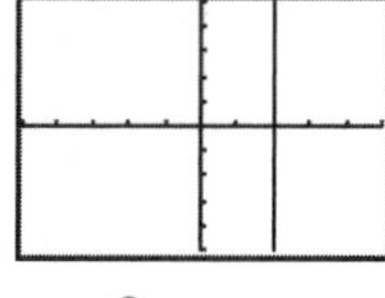

$x = 2$

d. 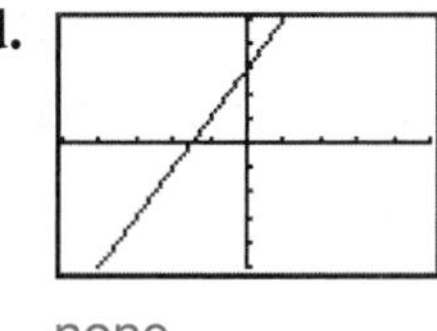

none

e. 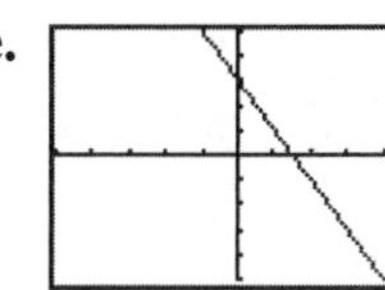

$f(x) = -2x + 3$

f. 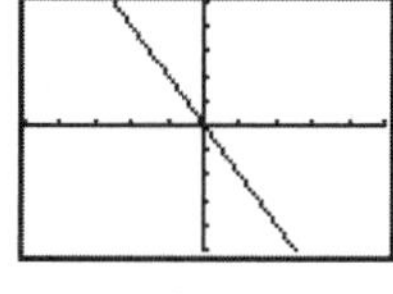

$y = -2x$

g. 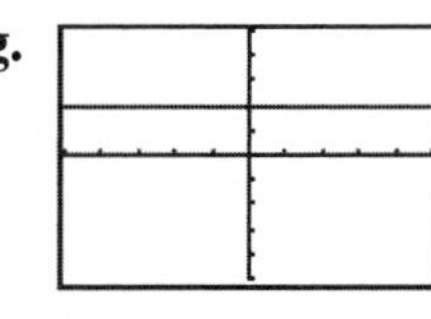

$y = 2$

h. 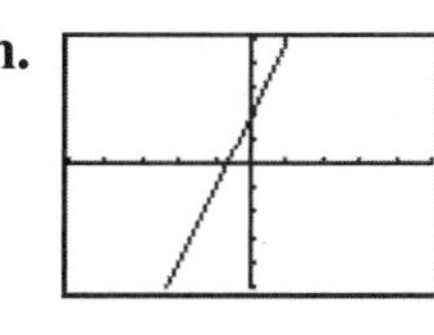

none

i. 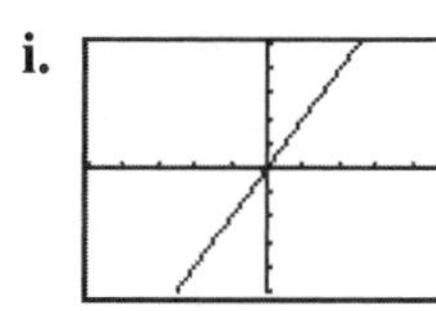

none

2. The cost of renting a grapher from the bookstore is \$20 plus \$4 per month for as long as you wish to rent.

a. Complete the table.

MONTHS, m	2	5	8	10	12
COST (\$), $c(m)$	28	40	52	60	68

b. Is the cost c a linear function of months m? If so, what is the slope?

Yes, it is linear. The slope is 4.

Exercise numbers appearing in color are answered in the Selected Answers section of this book.

c. Write the equation for the function.

$c = f(m) = 4m + 20$

d. Graph this function, and compare the results from your grapher.

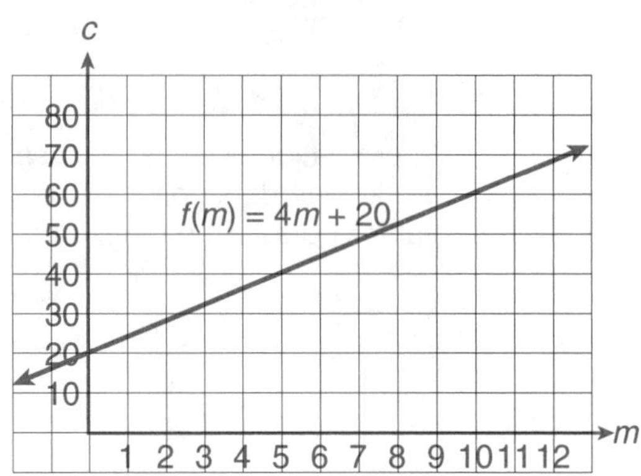

e. What is the slope? What is the meaning of the slope in this situation?

The slope is 4. This represents the monthly charge.

f. What is the vertical intercept of the graph of the function? What is the practical meaning of the vertical intercept in this situation?

The vertical intercept is (0, 20). It indicates that the initial rental cost is $20.

g. What is the horizontal intercept of the graph of the function? What practical meaning does this have in this situation?

The horizontal intercept is $(-5, 0)$. It has no practical meaning in this case.

h. Approximately how many months will you be able to keep your grapher if you have $65 budgeted for this expense?

$65 = 4m + 20$ or $45 = 4m$ or $m = 11.25$. I can keep the grapher for 11 months.

3. Consider the following table of values.

t	10	20	40
$s(t)$	0	15	45

a. Determine the rate of change from $t = 10$ to $t = 20$.

1.5

b. Determine the rate of change from $t = 20$ to $t = 40$.

1.5

c. Is $s(t)$ a linear function? Explain.

$s(t)$ is a linear function because the rate of change is constant.

4. Determine the slope of the line through the points (3, 8) and (−5, 12).

$m = \frac{12 - 8}{-5 - 3} = -\frac{1}{2}$

5. Determine the slope of the line represented by the equation $y = -4x + 2$.

$m = -4$

6. Determine the slope of the line having equation $2x - 5y = 9$.

$m = \frac{2}{5}$

7. Write an equation of a line with a slope of −7 and a vertical intercept of 4.

$y = -7x + 4$

8. Write an equation of a line that has a slope of 2 and goes through the point (0, 10).

$y = 2x + 10$

9. Write an equation of a line that has a slope of 0 and goes through the point (−4, 5).

$y = 5$

10. Write an equation of a vertical line that goes through the point (−3, −5).

$x = -3$

11. Write an equation of a line that goes through the points (2, −3) and (−4, 0).

$y = -\frac{1}{2}x - 2$

12. Write an equation of a line parallel to $y = \frac{1}{3}x - 7$ and through the point (6, −1).

$y = \frac{1}{3}x - 3$

13. Sketch a graph of the line through (2, −3) with slope of $\frac{1}{2}$.

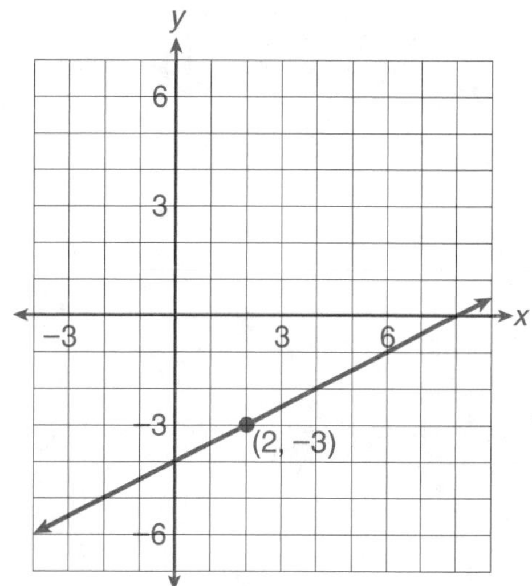

Graph each of the functions in Exercises 14–16 by hand. Then compare the results using your grapher.

14. $y = \frac{4}{5}x - 3$

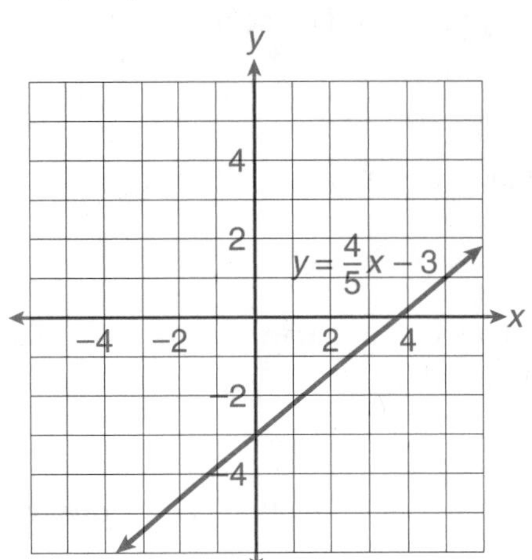

15. $4x - 5y = 20$

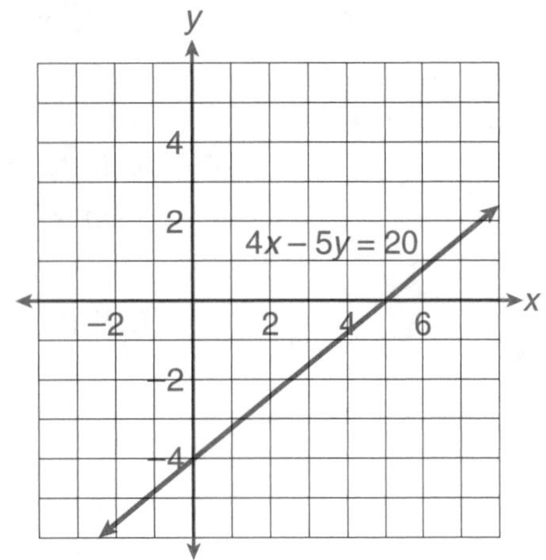

16. $y = -4$

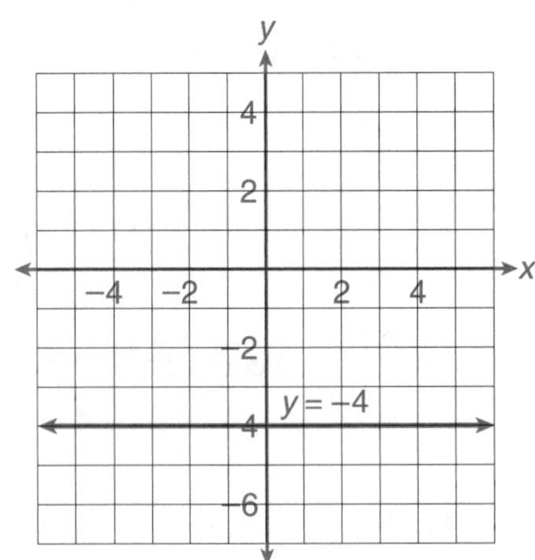

17. a. Plot the data on the following grid using an appropriate scale

x	0	2	4	6	8	10	12
y	23.76	24.78	25.93	26.24	26.93	27.04	27.93

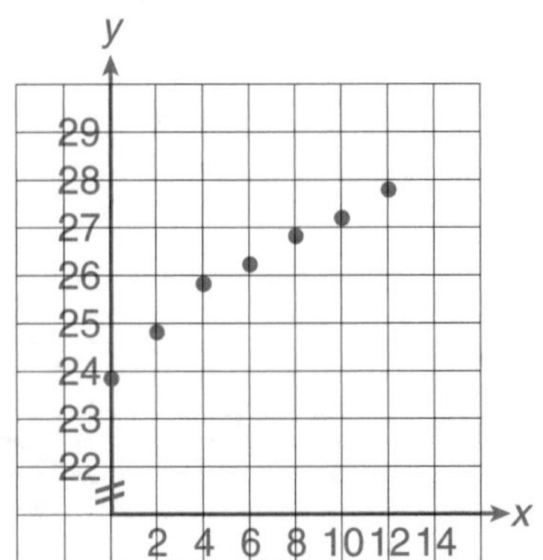

b. Use your grapher to determine the equation of the regression line. Write the result.

$f(x) = 0.322x + 24.156$

c. Use the result from part b to predict the value of y when $x = 9$.

$y = 27.054$

d. Use the result from part b to predict the value of y when $x = 20$.

$y = 30.596$

18. The following table shows the percentage of elected female state legislators from the years 1969 to 1997, as tabulated by the Center for American Women and Politics.

YEAR	1969	1973	1977	1981	1985	1989	1993	1997
PERCENTAGE OF FEMALE LEGISLATORS	6.6	7.6	9.9	10.5	13.3	14.3	22.2	25.4

Let x represent the number of years since 1969 and y represent the percentage of female state legislators.

a. Plot the data from the table on the following grid.

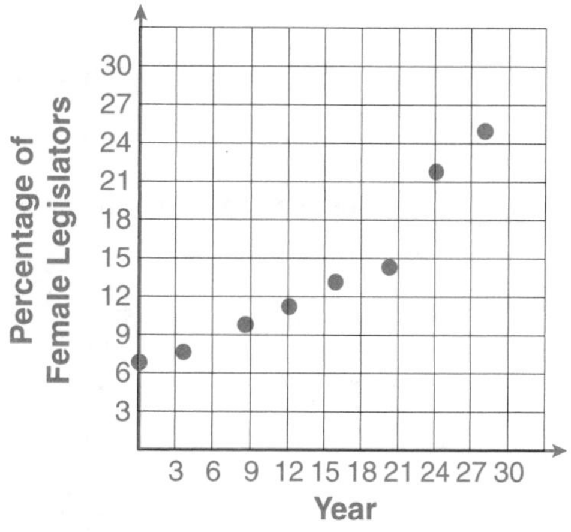

b. Use your grapher to produce the linear regression equation for the data in the graph, and record it here.

$f(x) = 0.657x + 4.533$

c. Use the equation from part b to estimate the percentage of state legislators in 1986 and 2010.

In 1986, $x = 17$. $f(17) = 15.7\%$. In 2010, $x = 41$. $f(41) = 31.5\%$

d. In which of the values found in part c do you have the most confidence? Explain.

I have more confidence in 1986 because it was interpolated from the data. The 2010 percentage was a result of extrapolation, which is always less accurate.

CLUSTER 3

Systems of Linear Equations and Absolute Value Functions

ACTIVITY 1.11

Car Speed Revisited

Topics: *2 × 2 Linear Systems—Solving Graphically, Numerically, and Algebraically*

You and your friend are traveling again. Recall from Activity 1.6, Car Speed, that your friend is 30 miles ahead of you when you both leave at the same time and in the same direction. Your speed is 60 mph. Her speed is 55 mph.

1. a. Complete the following table to show how far both of you are from your home.

t, TIME (hr)	$f(t) = 60t$, YOUR DISTANCE FROM HOME	$g(t) = 30 + 55t$, YOUR FRIEND'S DISTANCE FROM YOUR HOME
0	0	30
1	60	85
2	120	140
3	180	195
4	240	250
5	300	305
6	360	360
7	420	415

b. When will you catch up to your friend?

I will catch up in 6 hours.

c. Graph these two linear functions on the same coordinate axes.

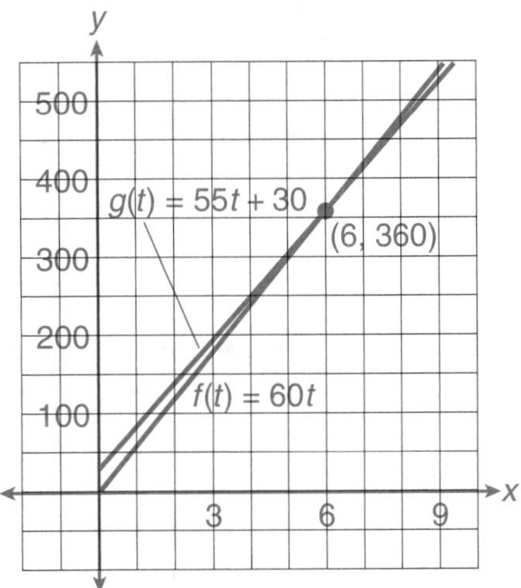

d. Determine the point where the two lines in part c intersect. What is the significance of this point?

The intersection point is (6, 360). This means I will catch up in 6 hours 360 miles from home.

e. Verify your results from part d using your graphing calculator. (See Appendix C for this procedure for the TI-83.)

C Appendix

This situation is an example of a 2×2 **system of linear equations.** Such a linear system of two equations in two variables can be written

$$y = ax + b$$
$$y = cx + d.$$

A **solution of the system,** if it exists, is the ordered pair of numbers (x, y) that makes both equations true. If the system has exactly one solution, the system is said to be **consistent.**

The system in this activity can be written

$$d = 60t$$
$$d = 55t + 30.$$

You first solved the system **numerically** by completing the table and noting the value of the input that produced the same output. You then solved this system **graphically** by locating the point of intersection of the two lines. The coordinates of the point of intersection were integers and could be determined exactly from the grid. If the solution to the system was not a pair of integers, you could only approximate the solution to the system using the graphing method.

To determine the solution to a system exactly, you can use **algebraic** methods. In this activity, you want d (the distance) to be the same for both functions. Because each expression is solved for d, you can set the expressions equal to each other. You are substituting an expression for d from one equation into the other equation. This method is called the **substitution method.**

2. Solve the system algebraically using the substitution method.

a. Because both equations are solved for d, set the two equations equal to each other.

$60t = 55t + 30$

b. Solve the linear in part a for t. What does this value for t represent in this situation?

$5t = 30$ or $t = 6$; t represents the input value of the point of intersection or the time required for you to catch up to your friend.

For additional practice solving linear equations, see Appendix B.

c. Determine the value of d by substituting the value of t into one of the original equations and solving for d.

$d = 60(6) = 360$

d. What does d represent in this situation?

d represents distance from home when you caught up to your friend.

e. Check to see if your solution satisfies both equations.

$60(6) = 360$ $\quad\quad$ $55(6) + 30 = 360$

Solve the following systems of equations algebraically and graphically. Verify with your graphing calculator.

3. a. $y = 2x + 3$
$y = x + 5$

$2x + 3 = x + 5$; $x = 2$;
$y = 2 + 5 = 7$ (2, 7)

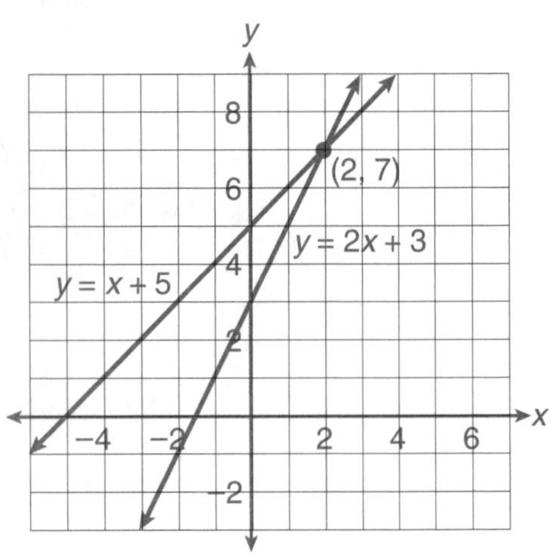

b. $x = y + 5$
$x = -5y - 7$

$y + 5 = -5y - 7$
$6y = -12$
$y = -2$
$x = -2 + 5 = 3$
(3, −2)

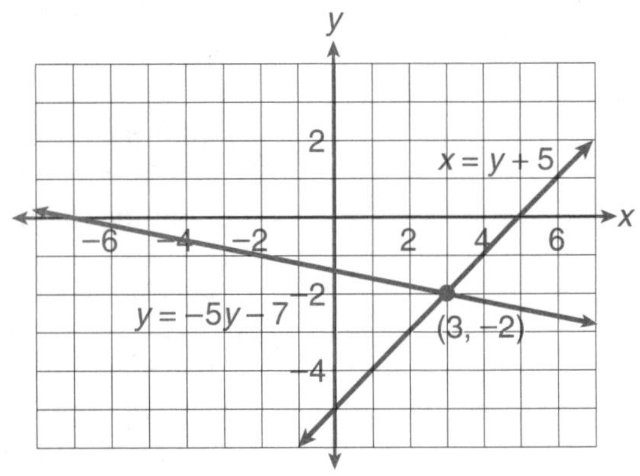

c. $-2x + 3y = 6$
$5x - 3y = -12$

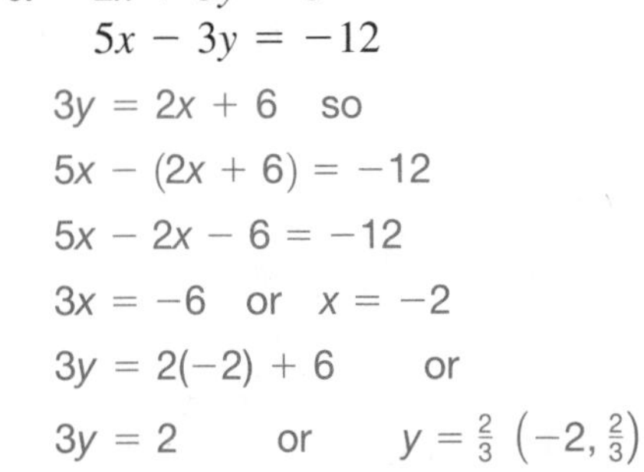

$3y = 2x + 6$ so
$5x - (2x + 6) = -12$
$5x - 2x - 6 = -12$
$3x = -6$ or $x = -2$
$3y = 2(-2) + 6$ or
$3y = 2$ or $y = \frac{2}{3}$ $\left(-2, \frac{2}{3}\right)$

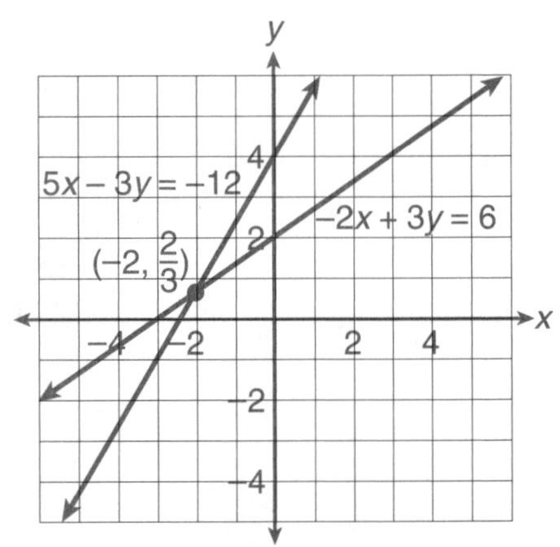

Sometimes it is more convenient to leave the system in general form rather than solving for one variable in terms of the other. Look again at the system in Problem 3c. If you apply the addition principle of algebra by adding the two equations (left side to left side and right side to right side), the y variable is eliminated.

$$\begin{array}{r} -2x + 3y = 6 \\ +\ 5x - 3y = -12 \\ \hline 3x + 0 = -6 \end{array}$$

Solving for x, you obtain the same solution as in Problem 3c.

This method of solving systems algebraically is called the **addition method.** In the previous example, the coefficients were very convenient. Not all systems have such convenient coefficients, and you may need to multiply one or both equations by a factor that will produce coefficients of the same variable that are additive inverses, or opposites.

For example, to solve this system

$$x - y = 5$$
$$4x + 5y = -7,$$

adding the equations will not eliminate a variable. But if you multiply the first equation by 5, the coefficients of y will be opposites.

$5(x - y = 5)$	$5x - 5y = 25$	
$4x + 5y = -7$	$+ \underline{4x + 5y = -7}$	Adding the corresponding
	$9x + 0 = 18$	sides of the equation

4. Finish solving this system.

$x = 2$

So, $4(2) + 5y = -7$

$8 + 5y = -7$

$5y = -15$

$y = -3$

5. Consider solving the following system using the addition method.

$$2x + 3y = 1$$
$$-4x + 6y = -14$$

a. Identify which variable you wish to eliminate. Multiply the appropriate equation by the appropriate factor so that the coefficients of your chosen variable are opposites. Show the two equations after you multiply by the factor. (Remember to multiply both sides of the equation by the factor.)

I want to eliminate x. Multiply the first equation by 2

$4x + 6y = 2$

$-4x + 6y = -14$

b. Add the two equations to eliminate the chosen variable.

$12y = -12$

c. Solve the resulting linear equation.

$y = -1$

d. Determine the complete solution. Remember to check by substituting into both of the original equations.

$4x - 6 = 2$ or $4x = 8$ so, $x = 2$ $(2, -1)$

e. Solve this same system again by eliminating the other variable at the start.

Multiply the first equation by -2

$-4x - 6y = -2$

$-4x + 6y = -14$

$-8x = -16$ or $x = 2$.

Substitute back to determine $y = -1$.

You and your friend are traveling again. She still has a 30-mile head start, but this time both of you are traveling at 55 mph. When will you catch up to your friend?

I will never catch up.

The answer is *never*! She will always be 30 miles ahead of you. If you look at the system just described, it could be written as

$$d = 55t + 30$$
$$d = 55t.$$

Graphically, the slopes of the lines are equal, but the vertical intercepts are different. Therefore, the graphs are parallel lines. The system is said to be **inconsistent,** and there is *no* solution.

6. Try to solve this system algebraically. What is the result from an inconsistent system if you attempt to solve it algebraically?

Setting the equations equal to each other

$55t + 30 = 55t$ or

$30 = 0$ The result is a false statement.

You and your friend are taking one last trip. This time she does not have a head start. You both leave from your house, both travel in the same direction, and both travel at 55 mph. When will you both be at the same point?

We will always be at the same point.

The two of you will always be at the same point. The system for this situation is

$$d = 55t$$
$$d = 55t.$$

This is an example of a **dependent** system. Graphically, in such a system, the equations represent the same line. The system has an infinite number of solutions.

7. Try to solve this system algebraically. What will be the result from a dependent system if you attempt to solve it algebraically?

$55t = 55t$

$0 = 0$ The result is a true statement.

Why do you even look at this case? Because sometimes dependent systems are disguised algebraically.

8. Show that the following system is dependent.

$$y = 2x + 3$$
$$4x - 2y = -6$$

Solving the second equation for y: $-2y = -4x - 6$ or $y = 2y + 3$

This is the first equation. The system is dependent.

SUMMARY

- A 2×2 system of linear equations consists of two equations with two variables. The graph of each equation is a line.
- A solution to a 2×2 system of equations is an ordered pair that solves both equations of the system.
- Solutions can be found in three different ways: numerically, by examining tables of values for both functions; graphically, by graphing each equation and finding the point of intersection; and algebraically, by combining the two equations to form a single linear equation in one variable, which can then be solved. Two distinct algebraic methods exist, the substitution method and the addition method.
- A linear system is consistent if there is at least one solution, the points of intersection of the graphs.
- A linear system is inconsistent if there is no solution; the lines are parallel.
- A linear system is dependent (also consistent) if there are infinitely many solutions; the equations represent the same line.

EXERCISES

1. You can run a 400-meter race at an average rate of 6 meters per second. Your friend can run the race at a rate of 5 meters per second. You give your friend a 40-meter head start. She then runs 360 meters.

   a. Write an equation for the distance, in meters, that you are from the starting point as a function of time in seconds.

   $d = 6t$

   b. Write an equation for the distance, in meters, that your friend is from the starting point as a function of time in seconds.

   $d = 5t + 40$

   c. How long does it take you to catch up to your friend?

   $6t = 5t + 40$

   $t = 40$ seconds.

   d. How far from the finish line do you meet?

   I am $6(40) = 240$ m from the starting point, so I am $400 - 240 = 160$ m from the finish line.

Exercise numbers appearing in color are answered in the Selected Answers section of this book.

Solve the following systems graphically. Use your grapher to check your results.

2. $y = 2x + 3$
$y = -x + 6$

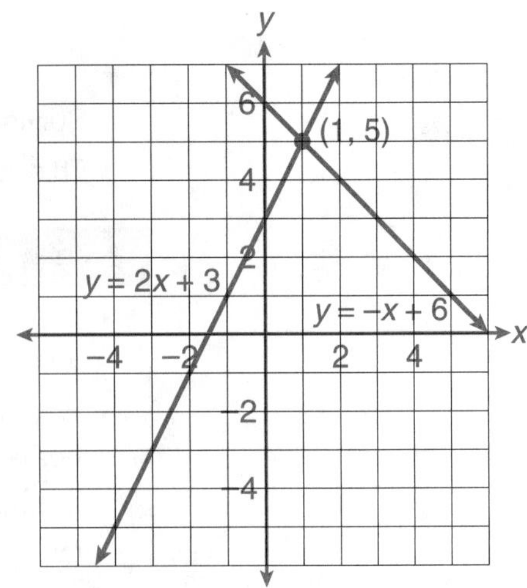

3. $2x + y = 1$
$-x + y = -5$

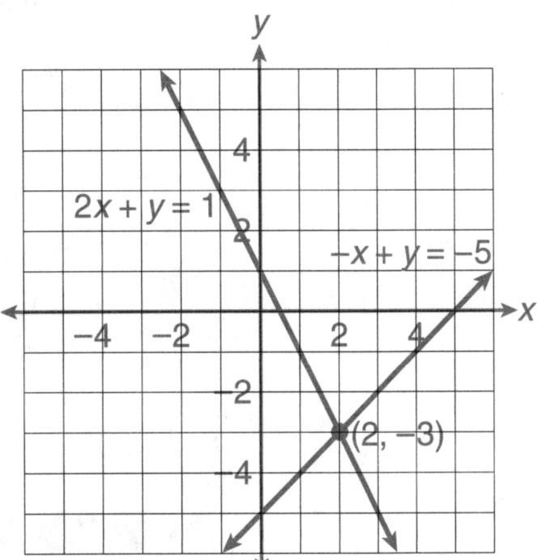

4. $2x + 5y = 1$
$3x - y = -7$

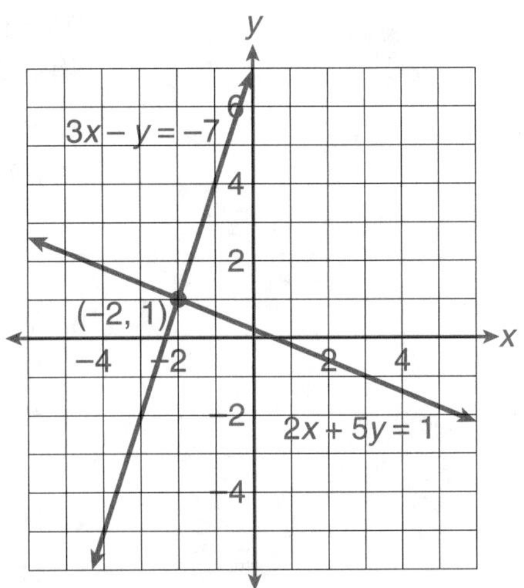

5. Use your grapher to determine the solution to the following system.

$$4x + 5y = 9$$
$$3x - y = 1$$

The solution is (0.7368, 1.2105)

6. What does a dependent linear system look like graphically?

Graphically, a dependent linear system consists of a single line.

7. Solve the following systems algebraically using the substitution method.

a. $y = 3x + 7$
$2x - 5y = 4$

$y = 3x + 7$

$2x - 5y = 4$

$2x - 5(3x + 7) = 4$

$2x - 15x - 35 = 4$

$-13x = 39$

$x = -3, y = -2 \quad (-3, -2)$

b. $2x + 3y = 5$
$-2x + y = -9$

$2x + 3y = 5$

$-2x + y = -9$ or $y = 2x - 9$

$2x + 3(2x - 9) = 5$

$2x + 6x - 27 = 5$

$8x = 32$

$x = 4, y = -1 \quad (4, -1)$

c. $4x + y = 10$
$2x + 3y = -5$

$4x + y = 10$ or $y = 10 - 4x$

$2x + 3y = -5$

$2x + 3(10 - 4x) = -5$

$2x + 30 - 12x = -5$

$-10x = -35$

$x = 3.5, y = -4 \quad (3.5, -4)$

d. $y = 3x + 1$
$6x - 2y = 1$

$y = 3x + 1$

$6x - 2y = 1$

$6x - 2(3x + 1) = 1$

$6x - 6x - 2 = 1$

$-2 = 1$

Inconsistent; No solution

8. Solve the following systems algebraically using the addition method.

a. $2x + y = 0$
$4x - y = 3$

$2x + y = 0$

$\underline{4x - y = 3}$

$6x = 3$

$x = \frac{1}{2}, \; y = -1 \; (\frac{1}{2}, -1)$

b. $2x + y = -2$
$-2x - 3y = -14$

$2x + y = -2$

$\underline{-2x - 3y = -14}$

$-2y = -16 \quad y = 8$

$2x + 8 = -2, \quad x = -5 \; (-5, 8)$

c. $3x + 2y = -1$
$5x - y = 20$

$3x + 2y = -1$

$2(5x - y = 20)$

$3x + 2y = -1$

$\underline{10x - 2y = 40}$

$13x = 39; x = 3$

$2y = -10; y = -5 \; (3, -5)$

d. $3x + 2y = -1$
$6x - 3y = 5$

$-2(3x + 2y = -1)$

$6x - 3y = 5$

$-6x - 4y = 2$

$\underline{6x - 3y = 5}$

$-7y = 7; y = -1$

$3x = 1; x = \frac{1}{3}, (\frac{1}{3}, -1)$

9. Solve the system both graphically and algebraically.

$3x + y = -18$
$5x - 2y = -8$

$6x + 2y = -36$
$5x - 2y = -8$
$11x = -44$
$x = -4, y = -6$
$(-4, -6)$

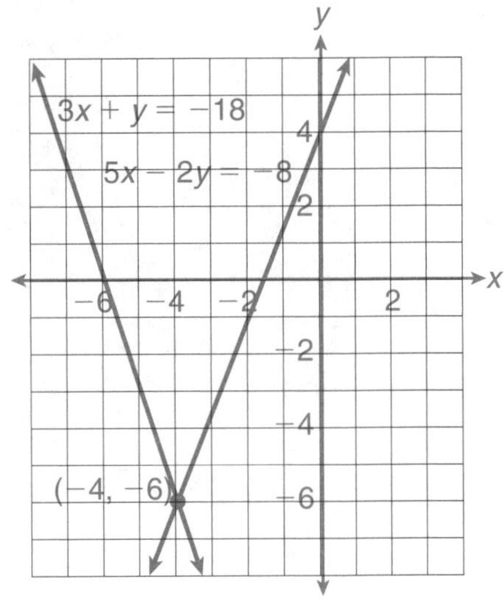

10. According to statistical data, in 1981, the supply curve for wheat was approximately given by the equation $S = 1800 + 240P$, where P is the price in dollars per bushel and S is the quantity in millions of bushels per year. According to these statistics, the demand for wheat in 1981 was given by the equation $D = 3550 - 266P$. According to economics, supply should equal demand.

a. At what price did supply equal demand in 1981?

$1800 + 240P = 3550 - 266P$
$506P = 1750$
$P = 3.46$

b. In 1985, the supply curve was almost the same as in 1981, but the demand curve changed. The new demand curve was given by $D = 2580 - 194P$. Find the price of wheat in 1985, for supply to equal demand.

$1800 + 240P = 2580 - 194P$
$434P = 780$
$P = 1.80$

ACTIVITY 1.12

Sam's Cafe

Topic: *Solving 3 × 3 Linear Systems of Equations*

In your job as buyer for Sam's Cafe, a nationwide coffee bar, you need to buy three grades of coffee bean. The different grades are blended with various flavors to make Sam's well-known coffee drinks. This week the three grades of beans are selling for \$0.80, \$1.20, and \$1.80 per pound. You want to know how much of each grade bean to buy, based on the following assumptions.

- The total weight of beans needed is 15,000 pounds.
- You wish to spend \$20,000.
- You need 2000 more pounds of the most expensive grade than the least expensive grade.

Use x, y and z to represent the weights of the three grades you are to buy, with x the weight of the least expensive and z the weight of the most expensive grade.

1. What is the equation for the total weight of coffee beans?

   $x + y + z = 15{,}000$

2. What is the equation for the total cost?

   $0.80x + 1.20y + 1.80z = 20{,}000$

3. What is the equation for the last of the three assumptions?

   $x + 2000 = z$

Taken together, the equations in Problems 1–3 form a **3 × 3 system of linear equations.**

The solution to this system is the ordered triple of numbers, (x, y, z) that solves all three equations. The strategy for solving such a system is typically to reduce the system to a 2 × 2 linear system, and then proceed to solve this smaller system.

4. One of the equations already has only two variables. Combine the two other equations (by either the substitution or addition method) to form a new equation with the same two variables.

   $$\begin{aligned} -1.2x - 1.2y - 1.2z &= -18{,}000 \\ \underline{0.8x + 1.2y + 1.8z} &= \underline{20{,}000} \\ -0.4x + 0.6z &= 2000 \quad \text{or} \quad 4x - 6z = -20{,}000 \end{aligned}$$

5. Now solve this new 2 × 2 system.

   $$\begin{aligned} x + 2000 &= z \\ 4x - 6z &= -20{,}000 \\ 4x - 6(x + 2000) &= -20{,}000 \\ 4x - 6x - 12{,}000 &= -20{,}000 \\ -2x &= -8000 \end{aligned}$$

   $x = 4000;\ z = 6000$

6. Substitute the solutions from Problem 5 into one of the *original* three equations. Now solve for the third variable.

$$4000 + y + 6000 = 15{,}000$$
$$y = 5000$$

7. How much of each grade of coffee should you order? Check to make sure your solution agrees with each of the three original assumptions.

4000 pounds of the least expensive grade, 5000 pounds of the middle grade and 6000 pounds of the expensive grade.

8. Explain why it is not possible to solve this 3×3 system by graphing on your calculator.

The graphing calculator will only graph functions of two variables, not three.

All of the equations in your 3×3 system are called *linear equations*, even though they cannot all be graphed as single lines. In this case, linearity refers to each variable being "linear"—that is, raised to the first power.

Note that an equation with three variables no longer has a single input and single output. Your cost equation can be considered the output of a function, since cost depends on the amount of each grade of bean. There are actually three input variables for the cost function! (This type of function is beyond the scope of this course.)

In general, each equation of a 3×3 system of equations will have three variables. The solution strategy remains the same—namely, to reduce the system to a 2×2 linear system of equations. This smaller system can then be solved by any of the methods learned in Activity 1.11.

9. Solve the following 3×3 linear system.

Equation I: $x - 2y + z = -5$

Equation II: $2x + y - z = 6$

Equation III: $3x + 3y - z = 11$

If you are not sure where to start, follow these steps.

a. Is it possible to add two of the equations (right side to right side and left side to left side) so that one of the variables is eliminated? (Add equation I to equation II.)

Yes,
$$\begin{array}{r} x - 2y + z = -5 \\ 2x + y - z = 6 \\ \hline 3x - y = 1 \end{array}$$

b. Is it possible to add a different pair of equations to eliminate the same variable? (Add equation I to equation III.)

$$\begin{array}{r} x - 2y + z = -5 \\ 3x + 3y - z = 11 \\ \hline 4x + y = 6 \end{array}$$

c. Notice that your equations from parts a and b form a 2 × 2 linear system. Solve this 2 × 2 system any way you can.

$3x - y = 1$

$y = 6 - 4x$

$3x - (6 - 4x) = 1$

$3x - 6 + 4x = 1$

$7x = 7; x = 1; y = 2$

d. Substitute your solution from part c into any one of the three original equations, and solve the resulting equation for the remaining variable.

$1 - 4 + z = -5; z = -2$

e. The final step is to substitute your potential solution into each of the three original equations. This is the only way you can be confident that your solution is correct.

Check: Equation I: $1 - 4 - 2 = -5$

Equation II: $2 + 2 + 2 = 6$

Equation III: $3 + 6 + 2 = 11$

Most 3 × 3 systems will not have coefficients that are quite so convenient as the ones you just encountered. The following application provides a case in point.

10. Your sister works for Sam's competitor, Java Works, and has a similar job. She needs to purchase the same three grades of coffee at the same prices you paid. But she must make the purchase under the following assumptions. Determine the equation that corresponds to each assumption.

x = least expensive; y = middle grade; z = most expensive

a. The total weight of beans needed is 11,400 pounds.

$x + y + z = 11{,}400$

b. She wishes to spend $13,000.

$0.8x + 1.2y + 1.8z = 13{,}000$

c. She needs 500 more pounds of the least expensive grade than the more expensive grades combined.

$x = y + z + 500$

11. Solve the system you determined in Problem 10. State your solution in terms of the application. Verify that all three assumptions are satisfied.

$$x + y + z = 11{,}400 \qquad -8x - 8y - 8z = -91{,}200$$

$$8x + 12y + 18z = 130{,}000 \qquad 8x + 12y + 18z = 130{,}000$$

$$x = y + z + 500 \qquad 4y + 10z = 38{,}800$$

$$(y + z + 500) + y + z = 11400 \qquad 2y + 5z = 19{,}400$$

$$2y + 2z = 10{,}900 \qquad -2y - 2z = -10{,}900$$

$$3z = 8500$$

$$x = 5950, \quad y = \frac{7850}{3}, \quad z = \frac{8500}{3}$$

Further examples and practice in solving 3 × 3 linear systems of equations can be found in Appendix A.

SUMMARY

- A 3 × 3 system of linear equations consists of three equations with a total of three variables.
- A linear equation in the three variables x, y and z is of the form $Ax + By + Cz = D$, where A, B, C, and D are any constants. The equation is linear because the variables are all raised to the first power.
- To solve a 3 × 3 system algebraically:
  1. Reduce the system in size to a 2 × 2 system.
  2. Solve the 2 × 2 system.
  3. Substitute the 2 × 2 solution into any original equation to solve for the third unknown.
  4. Check the solution by substituting into all three of the original equations.
- Note that 3 × 3 systems may also be **inconsistent** (no solution) or **dependent** (infinitely many solutions).

EXERCISES

In Exercises 1–4, solve the 3 × 3 linear systems. Be sure to check your solutions by substituting into all three of the original equations.

1. $x + y - z = -8$

$-x + y + z = 2$

$2x - y + z = 8$

$2y = -6 \quad y = -3$

$3x = 0 \quad x = 0$

$z = 5$

(0, −3, 5)

2. $2x - 3y + z = 7$

$x + 2y - 2z = -5$

$-2x + y + z = -1$

$-2y + 2z = 6 \qquad -6y + 6z = 18$

$5y - 3z = -11 \qquad 10y - 6z = -22$

$4y = -4$

$y = -1; z = 2; x = 1$ (1, 2, −1)

Exercise numbers appearing in color are answered in the Selected Answers section of this book.

3. $x + 2y - z = 0$
$3x + 2y + z = -8$
$2x + 3y + z = 0$

$4x + 4y = -8$
$3x + 5y = 0$
$12x + 12y = -24$
$-12x - 20y = 0$
$-8y = -24$
$y = 3; x = -5; z = 1$
$(-5, 3, 1)$

4. $x + 2y - 3z = 5$
$-x + y + 2z = 0$
$2x - y + z = -1$

$x + 2y - 3z = 5$
$-x + y + 2z = 0$
$3y - z = 5$
$-3y - 15z = 3$
$-16z = 8\ z = -\frac{1}{2}; y = \frac{3}{2}; x = \frac{1}{2}$
$(\frac{1}{2}, \frac{3}{2}, -\frac{1}{2})$

$-2x + 2y + 4z = 0$
$2x - y + z = -1$
$y + 5z = -1$

5. Recall that some 2×2 linear systems do not have unique solutions. Try to solve these 3×3 linear systems. Identify each system as either dependent or inconsistent.

a. $x + 2y + z = 4$
$2x - y + 3z = 2$
$3x + y + 4z = 6$

$x + 2y + z = 4$
$4x - 2y + 6z = 4$
$5x + 7z = 8$
$5x + 7z = 8$
$0 = 0$ dependent

b. $2x - y + 3z = 3$
$-x + 2y - z = 1$
$x + y + 2z = 2$

$4x - 2y + 6z = 6$
$-x + 2y - z = 1$
$3x + 5z = 7$
$3x + 5z = 5$
$0 = 2$ inconsistent

6. You are responsible for buying parts from a wholesale distributor. There are three types of comparable switches that are needed. The cost per switch is $1.20, $1.90, and $2.30. You need all three types and will place your order as dictated by the following facts.

Let x = number of first type of switch
y = number of second type of switch
z = number of third type of switch

i. You need a total of 12,000 switches in this order.

ii. Your budget will allow an expenditure of $23,400.

iii. You need three times as many of the most expensive switches as the least expensive switches.

a. Model this problem with a 3×3 linear system of equations.

$$x + y + z = 12{,}000$$
$$1.2x + 1.9y + 2.3z = 23{,}400$$
$$3x - z = 0$$

b. Solve the system.

$$-19x - 19y - 19z = -228{,}000$$
$$12x + 19y + 23z = 234{,}000$$
$$-7x + 4z = 6000$$
$$12x - 4z = 0$$
$$5x = 6000$$
$$x = 1200; z = 3600; y = 7200$$

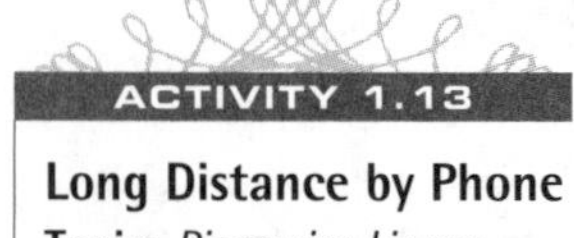

ACTIVITY 1.13

Long Distance by Phone
Topic: *Piecewise Linear Functions*

A certain long-distance telephone carrier offers the following rates for calls outside the state in which you live: \$0.15 per minute for the first 10 minutes and \$0.12 per minute for each minute thereafter. Also, whereas most companies round up to the next minute for any fraction of a minute, this company charges for the exact duration of your call.

1. Complete the following table for time t in minutes and cost c in dollars.

t (MIN)	1	2	5	10	15	20	30
c (t)	.15	.30	.75	1.50	2.10	2.70	3.90

2. a. Write a function rule that gives the cost of a call, c, if the call lasts 10 minutes or less.

$c(t) = 0.15t$

b. Write a function rule that gives the cost of a call, c, if the call lasts longer than 10 minutes. Remember, the input t is the total time of the call.

$c(t) = 0.12(t - 10) + 1.50$

3. The cost is determined in two different ways, depending on the length of the call. In other words, the cost function is defined in pieces. At what input value does the definition change from the first to the second piece?

$t = 10$

The resulting cost function is called a **piecewise function.** Let c be represented by $f(t)$. This function is written in the following way:

$$c = f(t) = \begin{cases} 0.15t, & t \leq 10 \\ 1.50 + 0.12(t - 10), & t > 10 \end{cases}$$

4. a. What is the cost of a 6-minute call?

$f(6) = 0.15(6) = \$0.90$

b. Determine $f(23)$ and interpret the result in the context of the situation.

$f(23) = 0.12(23 - 10) + 1.50$

$= 1.56 + 1.50 = \$3.06$

The cost is 1.50 for the first 10 minutes and 1.56 for the next 13 minutes.

5. Sketch the graph of the cost function over the domain 0 to 30 minutes.

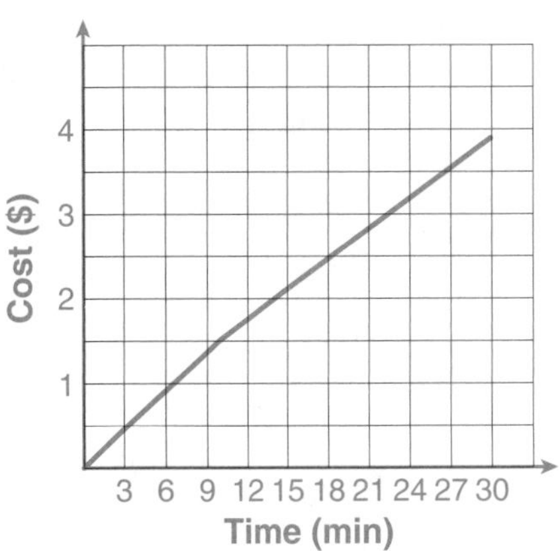

6. Use your grapher to graph the cost function. To accomplish this, you must enclose each piece of the function in parentheses with its domain also in parentheses. The pieces are connected by plus signs. To graph $f(t)$ you need to enter the following expression:

$$Y1 = (0.15x)(x \leq 10) + (1.5 + 0.12(x - 10))(x > 10).$$

To better see the pieces, also graph the linear function $Y2 = 0.15x$.

For more information on graphing piecewise functions, see Appendix C.

Compare the result on your grapher with your sketch in Problem 5. Your graph using the window Xmin $= -5$, Xmax $= 20$, Ymin $= -2$, Ymax $= 3$ should appear as follows;

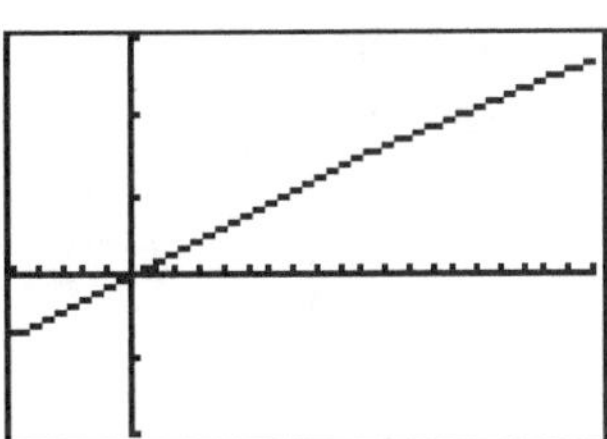

Let us investigate another situation that involves piecewise functions. In an upstate New York area, the utility bills for rural customers are calculated on readings taken every two months.

For residential customers, natural gas is billed in the following manner:

- \$31.36 for 0 to 5.8 therms
- 76.76 cents for each therm over 5.8 therms, but less than or equal to 96.7 therms
- 44.90 cents for each therm above 96.7 therms

You can write a function that represents the total cost of your natural gas usage. The output value will be calculated differently, depending on whether you use 5.8 therms or less, more than 5.8 therms but less than or equal to 96.7 therms, or more than 96.7 therms. This piecewise function is determined in Problems 7–10.

7. **a.** Let x represent the number of therms used. Write a function f to represent the cost if you use 5.8 therms or less.

   $f(x) = 31.36 \qquad 0 \le x \le 5.8$

   b. Write an expression g to represent the cost if the number of therms used is greater than 5.8 but less than or equal to 96.7. Remember x represents the number of therms used.

   $g(x) = 0.7676(x - 5.8) + 31.36 \qquad 5.8 < x \le 96.7$

   c. Write an expression h to represent the cost if the number of therms used is more than 96.7.

   $h(x) = 0.449(x - 96.7) + 101.13484 \qquad x > 96.7$

8. Use the expressions from Problem 7 to write a piecewise cost function C representing the total cost of using x therms, over the following three intervals: $0 \le x \le 5.8$, $5.8 < x \le 96.7$, and $x > 96.7$.

   $C(x) = (31.36)(x \le 5.8) + (0.7676(x - 5.8) + 31.36)(5.8 < x \le 96.7) + (0.449(x - 96.7) + 101.13484)(x > 96.7)$

9. Use your grapher to graph the piecewise function in Problem 8. To indicate $(5.8 \le x < 96.7)$, you must use two separate inequalities $x \ge 5.8$ and $x < 96.7$. Use the dot mode on the grapher. Your graph should appear as follows:

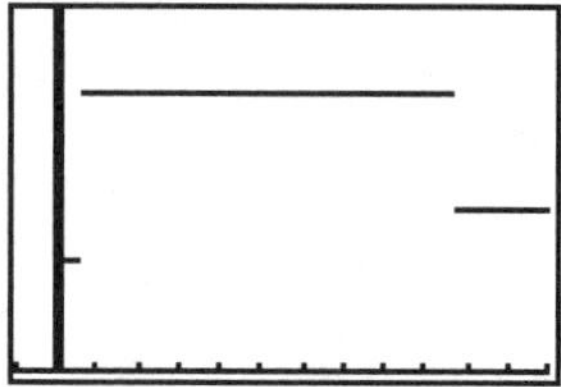

10. What is your total gas bill if you use 93 therms of gas in the two-month period?

    $C(93) = (0.7676(93 - 5.8) + 31.36) = \$98.29$

11. What will you pay if you use 110 therms during the two-month period?

    $C(110) = 0.449(110 - 96.7) + 101.13484 = \$107.11$

SUMMARY

A piecewise function is a function that is defined differently for certain "pieces" of its domain.

EXERCISES

1. To travel outside the city limits, a certain taxicab company charges \$1.20 for the first mile or less of travel. After the first mile, the charge is \$0.90 per mile (actual mileage, not rounded up).

   a. Write the piecewise function P that specifies the total cost of a taxicab traveling for x miles outside the city limits.

   $$P(x) = \begin{cases} 1.20 & 0 < x \leq 1 \\ 0.90(x - 1) + 1.20 & x > 1 \end{cases}$$

   b. Verify that the cost of a 15-mile taxi ride, all outside the city limits, is \$13.80.

   $P(15) = 0.90(15 - 1) + 1.2 = \$13.80$

   c. Sketch the graph of $P(x)$. Use the domain 0 to 20.

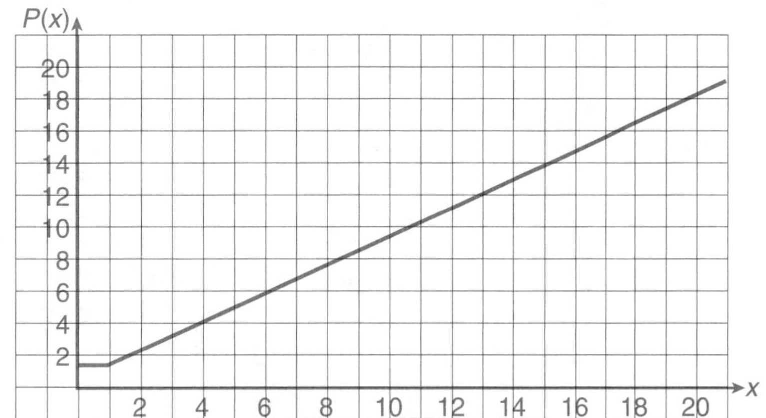

   d. Use your grapher to graph $P(x)$. Compare the result on your grapher with your sketch.

2. a. Sketch the graph of the piecewise function $H(x)$.

$$H(x) = \begin{cases} -2x + 3, & x < -2 \\ 4, & -2 \leq x < 1 \\ x - 1, & x \geq 1 \end{cases}$$

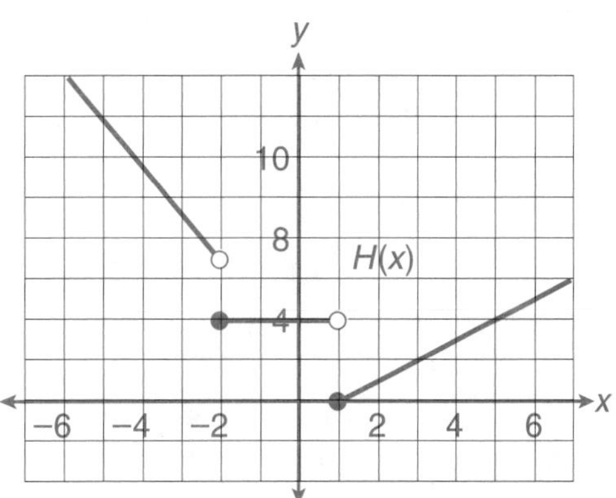

   b. Use your grapher and compare the result with your sketch.

Exercise numbers appearing in color are answered in the Selected Answers section of this book.

3. You are an author about to publish your first book, *Hockey in the '90s*. The book will sell for \$25. You will be paid royalties of 10% on the first 15,000 copies sold, 12% on the next 6000 copies, and 16% on any additional copies.

   a. Write a piecewise function f that specifies the total royalties if x copies are sold.

$$f(x) = \begin{cases} 2.5x & x \leq 15{,}000 \\ 3(x - 15{,}000) + 37{,}500 & 15{,}000 < x \leq 21{,}000 \\ 4(x - 21{,}000) + 55{,}500 & x > 21{,}000 \end{cases}$$

   b. Graph the function on your grapher.

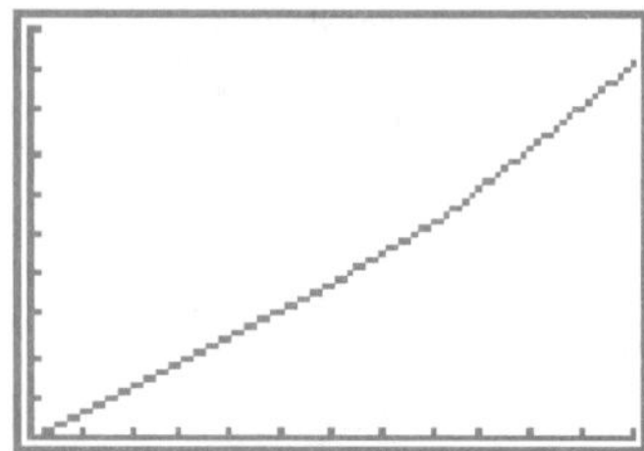

   c. Use your function from part a to confirm that the royalty paid on 18,000 copies sold is \$46,500 and that the royalty based on 25,000 copies sold is \$71,500. If your function does not yield these values then try to determine the source of your error.

$f(18{,}000) = 3(18{,}000 - 15{,}000) + 37{,}500 = 46{,}500$

$f(25{,}000) = 4(25{,}000 - 21{,}000) + 55{,}500 = 71{,}500$

   d. You would like to pay for your advanced degree in journalism. It will cost \$65,000. How many books will have to be sold for your royalty money to equal that amount?

$65{,}000 = 4(x - 21{,}000) + 55{,}500$

$9500 = 4x - 84{,}000$

$93{,}500 = 4x$

$x = 23{,}375$ books

ACTIVITY 1.14

How Much Can You Tolerate?

Topics: *Absolute Value Function, Inequalities*

"Gore is predicted to get 42% of the vote, with a 2% margin of error."

"Your allotted speaking time is 30 seconds, plus or minus 5 seconds."

"A bottle of soda must be filled to within 0.2 ounce of 16 ounces to be acceptable."

Measurements in the real world are usually approximations. In the preceding examples, you expect the end result to be within a range of values.

1. If Gore actually receives 40.5% of the vote, was the prediction a good one?

Yes

2. If you speak for 23 seconds, will you have satisfied your allotted time?

No

3. A soda bottle you choose to test has 15.81 ounces of soda. Is it acceptable?

Yes

In each statement, the allowable amount above or below the given (or predicted) value, also called the **tolerance,** lets you calculate the lowest and highest acceptable values in the range. For example, the Gore prediction is good if Gore gets from 40% to 44% of the vote. The tolerance is 2%. This is symbolically expressed as $40\% \leq \text{Gore} \leq 44\%$. Such an expression is called a **compound inequality** because both simple inequalities ($40\% \leq \text{Gore}$ and $\text{Gore} \leq 44\%$) must be true.

For work on solving inequalities algebraically, see Appendix A.

4. In each of the other statements (speaking time and ounces of soda), what inequality expresses the range of acceptable values? Identify the tolerance in each case.

$25 \leq \text{time} \leq 35$ $\quad 15.8 \leq \text{ounces} \leq 16.2$

5. **a.** In each of Problems 1–3, determine the difference between the actual value and the given value.

The error in 1 is -1.5%. The error in 2 is -7 seconds. The error in 3 is -0.19 ounces.

b. What does the difference represent?

The difference represents the difference between the predicted or known value and the actual value.

c. What does the sign of the difference represent?

The sign of the difference tells me whether the actual was above or below the known or predicted value.

> If you disregard the sign of the difference, then the number represents the **error** between the actual value and the predicted value.

To examine the error more fully, you can express the error as a function of the actual value. For example, if x represents Gore's actual percent of the vote, then $E = |x - 42|$ is the error in the prediction. Absolute value is used when you are only interested in the magnitude (size) of the error, not whether the actual value is above or below the predicted value. $E = |x - 42|$ is the distance between x and 42 on the number line.

6. Let x represent your actual speaking time. Write a symbolic rule for the error E as a function of x.

$E = |x - 30|$

7. Let x represent the actual fluid ounces of soda. Write a symbolic rule for the error E as a function of x.

$E = |x - 16|$

The lowest and highest acceptable values are determined when the error is equal to the tolerance (maximum error). In the Gore situation, the error is represented by $|x - 42|$. The tolerance is 2. The solutions to the equation $|x - 42| = 2$ represent the lowest and highest acceptable vote percentages.

8. What absolute value equation is solved to determine the upper and lower values for your speaking time?

$|x - 30| = 5$

9. What absolute value equation is solved to determine the upper and lower values for acceptable fluid ounces of soda?

$|x - 16| = 0.2$

You can picture the solutions to absolute value equations such as $|x - 42| = 2$ by interpreting $|x - 42|$ as the distance between x and 42 on the number line. If this distance must be 2 (the maximum error), then you can determine the solutions as follows:

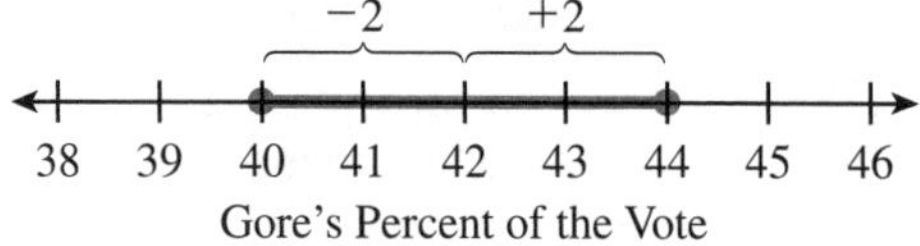

Therefore, the lowest and highest acceptable vote percentage is 40 and 44, respectively.

10. Solve the absolute value equations in Problems 8 and 9 on a number line.

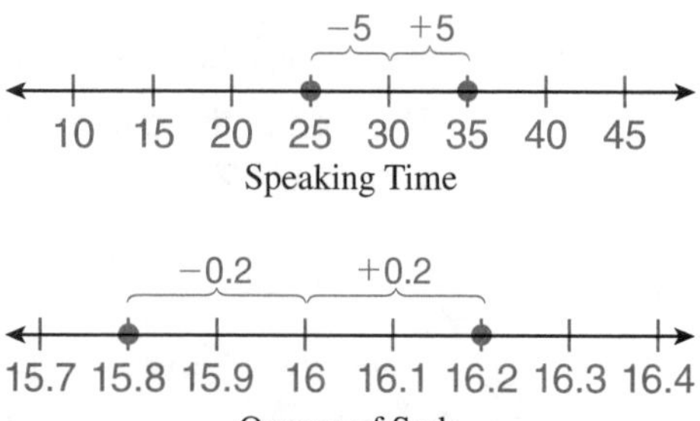

You are interested in *all* acceptable values—that is, all values between the lowest and highest acceptable values. These are all values where the error is less than or equal to the given tolerance. For example, the acceptable percentages of the vote for the Gore prediction are the solutions to the inequality $|x - 42| \leq 2$, pictured on the following number line.

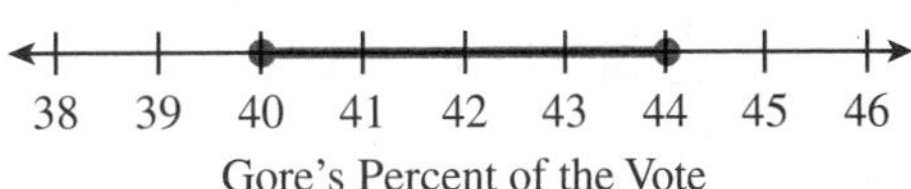

11. Write and solve the absolute value inequalities for the acceptable speaking time and ounces of soda tolerances.

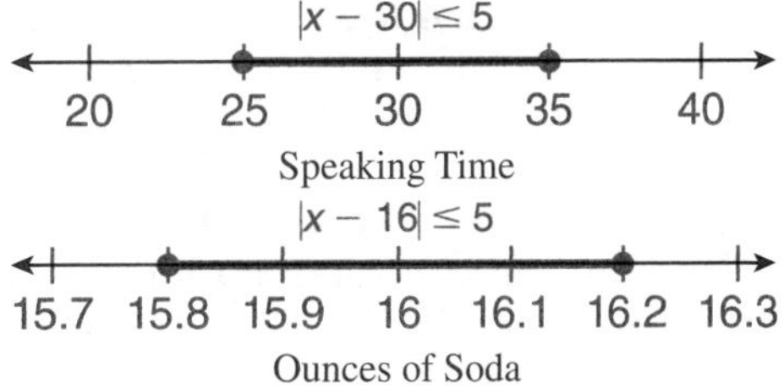

12. a. Consider again the error function for Gore's percent of the vote, $E = |x - 42|$. What is the domain and range?

The domain is $-\infty < x < \infty$. The range is $E > 0$.

b. What is the practical domain and range?

The practical domain is $0 \leq x \leq 100$. The practical range is $0 \leq E \leq 58$.

c. Use your grapher to produce the graph of $E = |x - 42|$, shown here, identifying the window you used.

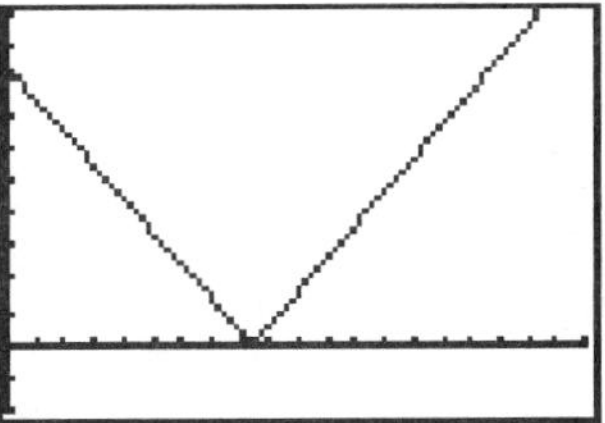

Xmin = 0, Xmax = 100, Ymin = −10, Ymax = 50 (Answers may vary slightly.)

> The **absolute value** function defined by $f(x) = |x - c|$, where c is a constant, will usually result in a V-shaped graph. The point at the bottom of the V is the **vertex.**

13. For the Gore percent of the vote error function, what is the practical interpretation of the vertex?

The vertex is (42, 0); this is the value of x for which the error is 0.

14. The solution to $|x - 42| = 2$ is the same as the solution to the following system of equations:

Tolerance function: $Y_1 = 2$

Error function: $Y_2 = |x - 42|$

Graph the two functions on your grapher.

You can see the solutions to $|x - 42| \leq 2$ by examining the graph of the system in Problem 14.

15. Describe how you can solve the inequality $|x - 42| \leq 2$ using the graphs of $y = |x - 42|$ and $y = 2$.

Locate the points of intersection of the two graphs. The x-values of these points are the boundary values of the solution set.

16. Use your grapher to graph the speaking time error function and the corresponding tolerance formula. Verify the solutions you found in Problem 11. Sketch the graph.

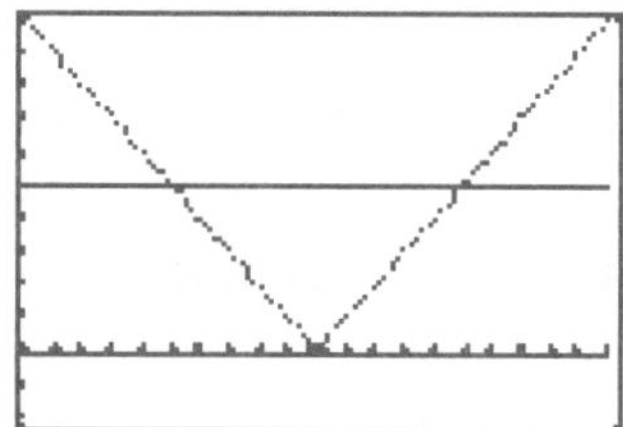

17. Use your grapher to graph the ounces of soda error function and the corresponding tolerance formula. Verify the solutions you found in Problem 11. Sketch the graph.

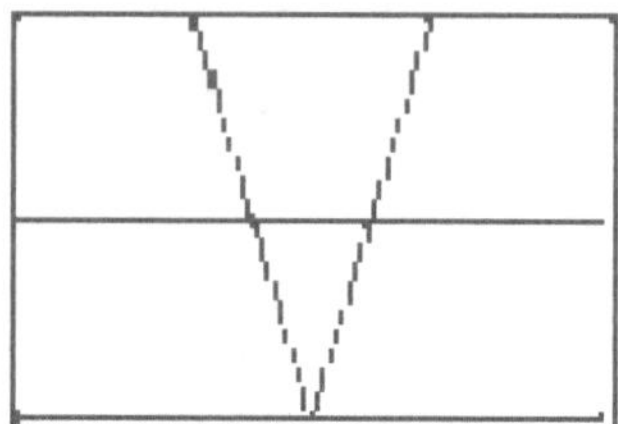

18. a. In some applications, you may be more interested in knowing when a value is farther than a tolerable amount from the target value. For example, in measuring the thickness of a precision part, the target thickness of 0.23 millimeter must be met to within 0.0015 millimeter (the tolerance). To find all thicknesses that are unacceptable, solve $|x - 0.23| > 0.0015$ graphically.

0.2290 0.2300 0.2310 0.2320

b. Because the unacceptable measurements are separated into two intervals (those too thick and those too thin), two inequalities are needed to express the solutions algebraically. What are they?

$x < 0.2285$ or $x > 0.2315$

You can determine the distance by subtracting in either direction, as long as you then take the absolute value.

For example, the distance between -4 and -10 on the number line is $|-4 - (-10)| = |-4 + 10| = |6| = 6$ or $|-10 - (-4)| = |-10 + 4| = |-6| = 6$. In general, the distance between any two real numbers is the absolute value of their difference.

The distance between a and b on the number line is $|a - b| = |b - a|$.

19. What is the distance between -3 and -15 on the number line?

12

20. a. Interpret $|x + 7|$ as a distance on the number line.

$|x + 7|$ represents the distance between some number x and -7.

b. Where is the vertex on the graph of $y = |x + 7|$?

$(-7, 0)$

c. Where is the vertex on the graph of $f(x) = |x + 7| + 3$?

$(-7, 3)$

SUMMARY

- $|a - b|$ is the distance between a and b on the number line.
- The basic absolute value function, $f(x) = |x| = |x - 0|$, is the distance from x to 0 on the number line.
- The absolute value of a linear function, $g(x) = |x + b|$, always has a V-shaped graph, with vertex at $(-b, 0)$.
- The maximum error (or tolerance or margin of error) determines the acceptable values for a measurement. If E is the maximum error, and a is the predicted or ideal measurement, then the acceptable values, x, are defined by $|x - a| \leq E$.

EXERCISES

1. The length of a screw must be within 0.25 centimeter of 8 centimeters.

a. What is the tolerance (or maximum error)?

0.25 cm

b. What inequality expresses the acceptable screw lengths?

$|x - 8| \leq 0.25$

Exercise numbers appearing in color are answered in the Selected Answers section of this book.

c. Solve your inequality graphically, expressing your solution algebraically in a compound inequality.

$7.75 \leq x \leq 8.25$

2. You are given a budget of $24,500 for the month. Your boss will tolerate your expenditures as long as they stay within 1% of your budget.

a. What is the tolerance for this budget problem?

Tolerance is $0.01(24{,}500) = \$245$.

b. What inequality expresses the acceptable expenditures for the month?

$|x - 24{,}500| \leq 245$

c. Solve this inequality, stating your solution within the context of the problem.

$-245 \leq x - 24{,}500 \leq 245$

$24{,}255 \leq x \leq 24{,}745$

Budget expenditures must be between $24,255 and $24,745

3. Express the following statements symbolically using absolute value.

a. The distance between 4 and -3 on the number line is 7.

$|4 - (-3)| = 7$

b. The distance between x and -3 on the number line is 5.

$|x - (-3)| = 5$

c. The distance between x and 4 on the number line is 3.

$|x - 4| = 3$

d. The weight must be within 5 grams of 175 grams.

$|x - 175| \leq 5$

e. The difference between x and 10 must be at least 3.

$|x - 10| \geq 3$

f. The difference between x and -20 is less than 5.

$|x - (-20)| < 5$

g. The actual score differed by 12 points from the predicted score of 83.

$|x - 83| = 12$

h. The predicted amount was more than $5 off from the actual $123 spent.

$|x - 123| > 5$

4. Solve each of the equations and inequalities of Exercise 3 graphically, both on a number line and on your grapher.

a.

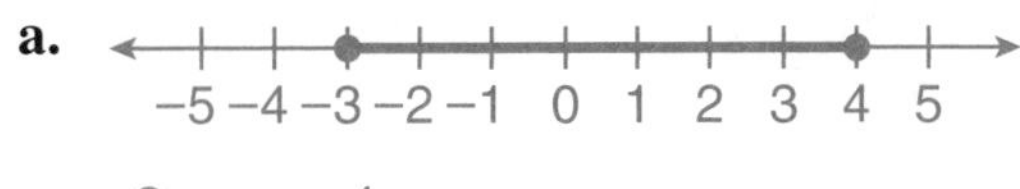

$-3 \le x \le 4$

b.

−8 −7 −6 −5 −4 −3 −2 −1 0 1 2 3 4

$x = -8$ or $x = 2$

c.

0 1 2 3 4 5 6 7

$x = 1$ or $x = 7$

d.

165 170 175 180 185 190

$170 \le x \le 180$

e.

7 10 13

$x \le 7$ or $x \ge 13$

f.

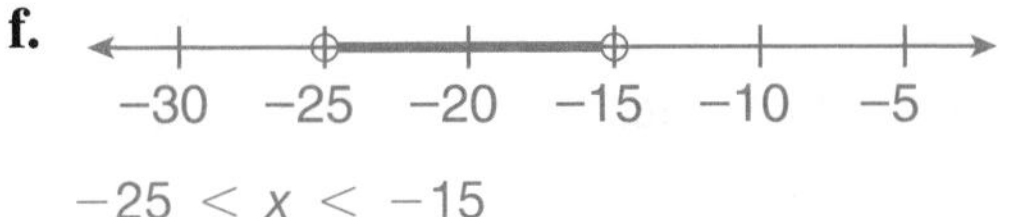

$-25 < x < -15$

g.

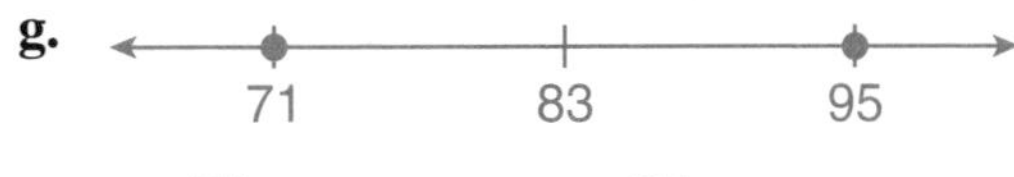

$x = 71$ or $x = 95$

h.

118 123 128

$x < 118$ or $x > 128$

5. Solve each equation graphically.

a. $|2x - 8| = 6$

1 2 3 4 5 6 7

b. $|3x + 9| = 15$

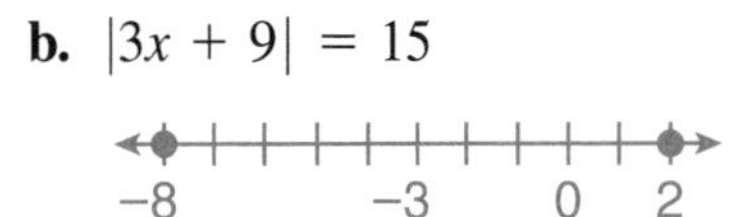

c. $|4x + 10| = 14$

−6 0 1

d. $|5 - 2x| = 0$

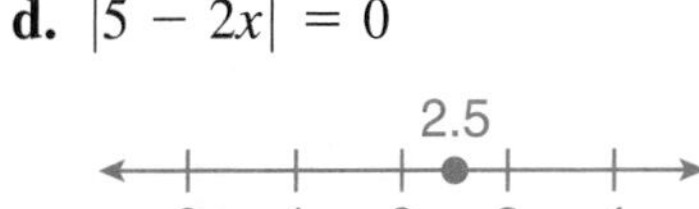

6. Solve each equation of Exercise 5 algebraically.

a. $2x - 8 = 6$ or $2x - 8 = -6$
$2x = 14$ $2x = 2$
$x = 7$ $x = 1$

b. $3x + 9 = 15$ or $3x + 9 = -15$
$3x = 6$ $3x = -24$
$x = 2$ $x = -8$

c. $4x + 10 = 14$ or $4x + 10 = -14$
$4x = 4$ $4x = -24$
$x = 1$ $x = -6$

d. $5 - 2x = 0$ or $5 - 2x = 0$
$5 = 2x$
$x = 2.5$

7. Solve each inequality graphically. (Utilize your solutions from Exercise 5.)

a. $|2x - 8| < 6$

1 2 3 4 5 6 7

b. $|3x + 9| \geq 15$

c. $|4x + 10| > 14$

d. $|5 - 2x| \leq 0$

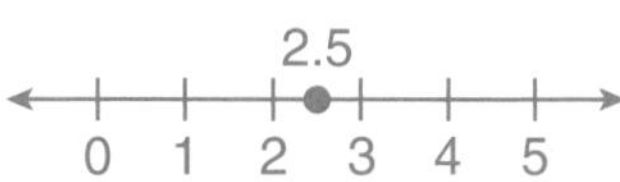

8. An absolute value function can be defined piecewise, or as pieces of two linear functions.

a. Graph the absolute value function $y = |x|$.

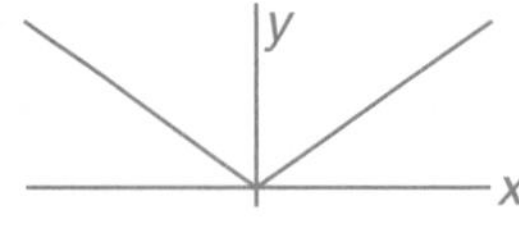

b. Sketch the graph of the piecewise function, $y = |x| = \begin{cases} x \text{ if } x \geq 0 \\ -x \text{ if } x < 0 \end{cases}$

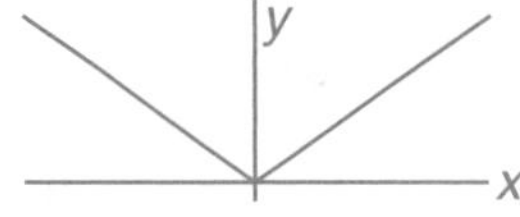

(Same graph as part a.)

c. How do the graphs in parts a and b compare?

The graphs are the same.

9. Rewrite $y = |x - 6|$ as a piecewise linear function.

$$y = |x - 6| = \begin{cases} x - 6 & x \geq 6 \\ -x + 6 & x < 6 \end{cases}$$

10. a. What is the equation for the absolute value function graphed here?

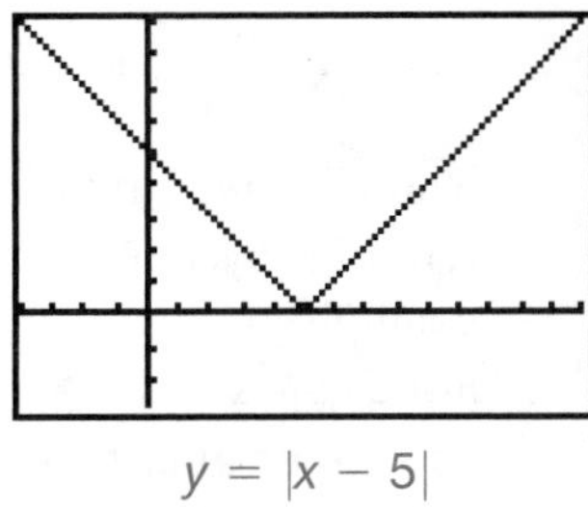

$y = |x - 5|$

b. Write your function in part a as a piecewise linear function.

$$y = |x - 5| = \begin{cases} x - 5 & x \geq 5 \\ -x + 5 & x < 5 \end{cases}$$

11. Once you have the piecewise definition, it might occur to you that solving an absolute value equation can be reduced to solving two linear equations. Simply set both linear pieces equal to the desired value, and solve each individually.

Determine the solutions to $|x - 3| = 5$ both graphically and algebraically.

$$x - 3 = 5 \quad \text{or} \quad x - 3 = -5$$
$$x = 8 \quad \text{or} \quad x = -2$$

What Have I Learned?

1. You are given two linear equations in slope-intercept form. How can you tell if the system is consistent, inconsistent, or dependent by inspection? Give examples.

   If the slopes are different, such as $y = 2x + 1$ and $y = 3x + 2$, then we can say immediately that the system is consistent and it has one solution. If the system is dependent, then the equations will be exactly the same. If the system is inconsistent, the slopes will be equal but the lines will possess different y-intercepts, i.e., $y = 2x + 1$ and $y = 2x + 3$.

2. In this cluster, you solved 2×2 linear systems four different ways. List them. Give an advantage of each approach.

   The four ways are graphically; numerically; and two algebraic methods, substitution and addition. The advantage to the graphical approach is that it is visual. The disadvantage is if the solutions are not integers, the solution may be hard to read accurately. Numeric can be relatively easy using the table function of the calculator, again if the solution is integral. But if it is not, the numeric approach can be cumbersome and time consuming. The advantages of an algebraic approach is accuracy. The disadvantage is it can be cumbersome.

3. Describe a procedure that will combine the following two linear equations in three variables to result in a single linear equation in two variables.

   $$2x + 3y - 5z = 10$$
   $$3x - 2y + 2z = 4$$

   Multiply the first equation by 2 and the second by 3. The result will be two equations in which the y-coefficients will be opposites. Adding the two equations will eliminate the y-variable from the system.

4. What number is its own opposite?

   0 is its own opposite.

5. The graphs of the absolute value functions in this cluster look like a V. What are the coordinates of the vertex of the V in the graph of $f(x) = |x - 10|$?

   (10, 0)

6. If the tolerance (maximum acceptable error) for some measurement is 3 centimeters, what is the width of the actual interval of acceptable values?

   The width of the actual interval of acceptable values is 6.

How Can I Practice?

Solve the following systems both graphically and algebraically.

1. $x + y = -3$
$y = x - 5$

$x + y = -3$
$y = x - 5$
$x + x - 5 = -3$
$2x = 2$ or $x = 1$
$y = 1 - 5$ or $y = -4$
$(1, -4)$

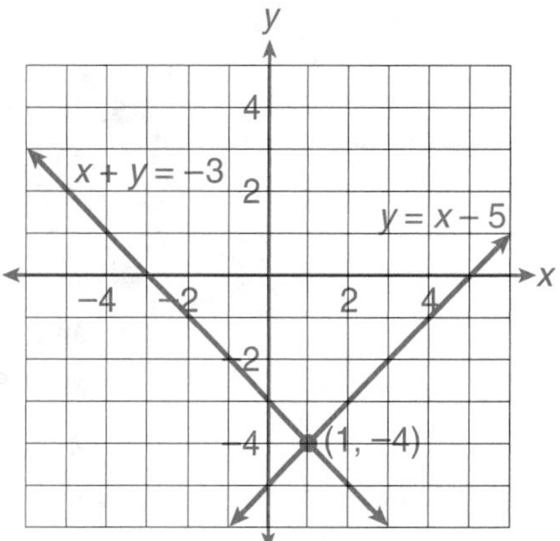

2. $x - 2y = -1$
$4x - 3y = 6$

$-4x + 8y = 4$
$4x - 3y = 6$
$5y = 10$ or $y = 2$
$x - 4 = -1$ or $x = 3$
$(3, 2)$

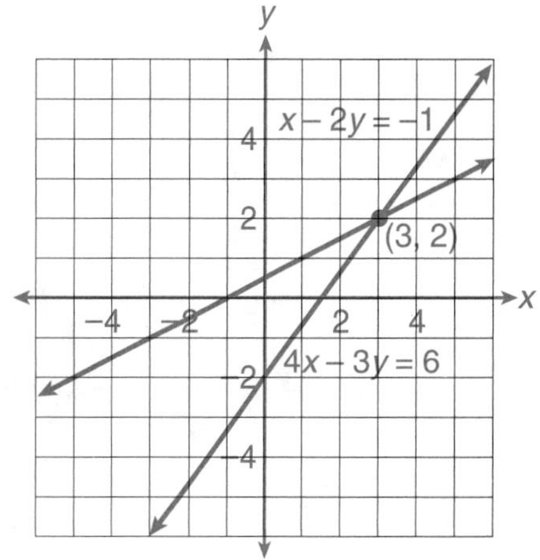

3. $2x - 3y = 7$
$5x - 4y = 0$

$8x - 12y = 28$
$-15x + 12y = 0$
$-7x = 28$ or $x = -4$
$-8 - 3y = 7$ or $y = -5$
$(-4, -5)$

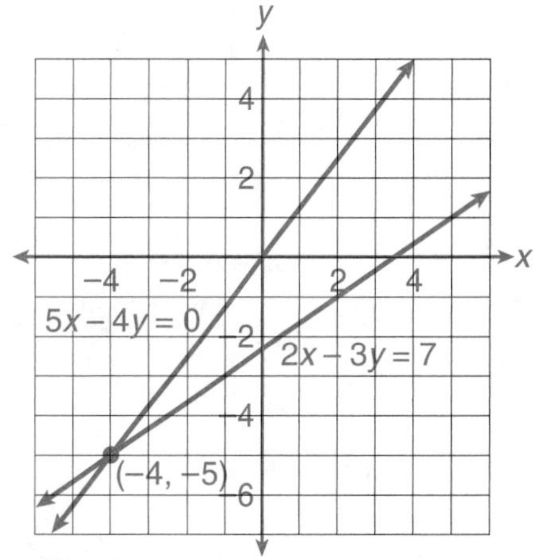

Exercise numbers appearing in color are answered in the Selected Answers section of this book.

4. $x - y = 6$
$y = x + 2$

$x - (x + 2) = 6$
$-2 = 6$
Inconsistent
No solution

5. Rewrite the systems in Problems 1–4 in the form

$$y = ax + b$$
$$y = cx + d$$

and check your solutions graphically or numerically using the table feature of your grapher.

6. Solve the following 3×3 system algebraically:

$$2x - y + z = -5$$
$$x - 2y + 2z = -13$$
$$3x + y - 2z = 12$$

$$\begin{array}{r} 2x - y + z = -5 \\ 3x + y - 2z = 12 \\ \hline 5x \quad - z = 7 \end{array} \qquad \begin{array}{r} x - 2y + 2z = -13 \\ 6x + 2y - 4z = 24 \\ \hline 7x \quad - 2z = 11 \end{array} \qquad \begin{array}{r} 7x - 2z = 11 \\ -10x + 2z = -14 \\ \hline -3x \quad = -3; x = 1 \end{array}$$

$5(1) - z = 7; z = -2$
$3(1) + y - 2(-2) = 12; y = 5$

$(1, 5, -2)$

7. Graph the following piecewise function.

$$f(x) = \begin{cases} 2x - 1, & x \leq 1 \\ 3 \quad , & 1 < x \leq 4 \\ -4x \quad , & x > 4 \end{cases}$$

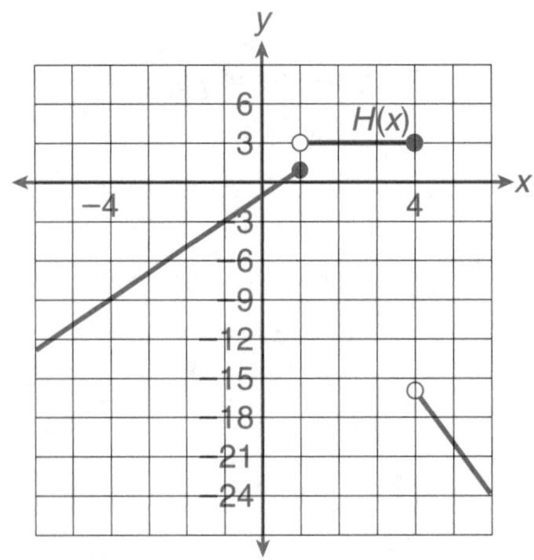

8. Solve the following graphically.

a. $|x - 4| = 7$

b. $|3x - 6| \leq 4$

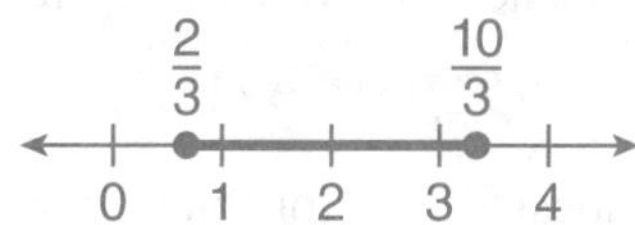

CLUSTER 4

Probability Functions and Statistical Reasoning

ACTIVITY 1.15

The Class Survey

Topics: *Organizing Data, Frequency Distributions, Measures of Central Tendency*

Decisions that are made in business, government, education, engineering, medicine, and many other professions depend on analyzing collections of data. As a result, data analysis has become an important topic in many undergraduate mathematics classes. In this activity, you will collect and organize data from your class.

Answers will vary with each class's data.

1. Record the requested data for your entire class.

GENDER	CREDIT HOURS THIS SEMESTER	MILES FROM CAMPUS	TIME STUDYING YESTERDAY (TO THE NEAREST HALF-HOUR)

2. Using the data collected in Problem 1, determine the following characteristics of your entire class.

a. The most common number of credit hours

b. The average number of miles from campus

c. More women or men

d. The most hours studied last night

The data can be organized in several different ways to help you arrive at your answers. One visual approach is to produce a **dotplot** for each category. To illustrate, consider the following data representing the size of 20 families.

Family sizes: 4, 6, 2, 8, 3, 5, 6, 4, 7, 2, 5, 6, 4, 6, 9, 4, 7, 5, 6, 3

The data values appear on the horizontal scale of the dotplot. The number of occurrences of each data value (called the **frequency**) is recorded on the vertical scale. Each dot represents one data value.

The following frequency table for these data shows how you can think of the frequency as a function of the data values.

FAMILY SIZE	2	3	4	5	6	7	8	9
FREQUENCY	2	2	4	3	5	2	1	1

3. Draw dotplots for each of the four data categories from Problem 1.

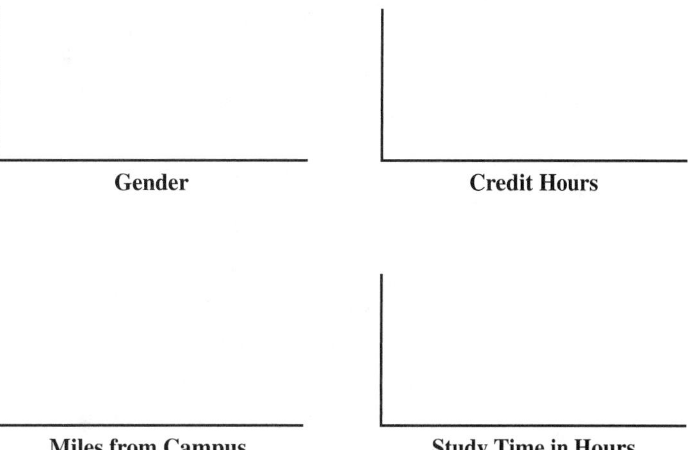

4. Explain how you can use the dotplots to answer each of the following questions.
   a. What is the most common number of credit hours?
   b. What is the average number of miles from campus?
   c. Are there more women or men in your class?
   d. What was the most number of hours studied?

5. Each dotplot in Problem 3 can be viewed as a function, where the input variable is the quantity being measured and the output variable is the frequency. For each of the four categories, find the domain and range for the frequency function.

CATEGORY	DOMAIN OF THE FUNCTION	RANGE OF THE FUNCTION
Gender		
Credit hours		
Miles from campus		
Time studying		

In the study of statistics, such frequency functions are usually called **frequency distributions.** They describe how the data are distributed over the domain of possible values.

6. Looking at your dotplots in Problem 3, describe in a few sentences how the frequency distributions compare with each other visually. Note any similarities and differences. (Answers will vary.)

7. Of the four frequency distributions, which one is really quite different because of the nature of the data values?

   The gender distribution is different because it only has two values and they are not numeric.

8. Look at the three frequency distributions with numerical data values. Estimate on each dotplot where you think the center of the frequency distribution lies. Record your estimates and compare with your classmates. (Answers will vary.)

FREQUENCY DISTRIBUTION	ESTIMATE OF THE CENTER
Credit hours	
Miles from campus	
Time studying	

Measuring the center of a frequency distribution is a basic starting point in many statistics applications. There are several different ways to measure the center. Each of the following is a statistic that measures the central tendency of a frequency distribution.

The **mean** is the usual average found by adding the data values and dividing by the number of values.

The **median** is in the exact middle of the numerically ordered data, half the data values lie above and half lie below the median. (If there is an even number of data values, the median is the mean of the two middle values.)

The **mode** is the data value that occurs most frequently.

The **midrange** is the exact midpoint between the lowest and highest data values.

9. Consider the sample data of 20 family sizes given in Problem 2. Verify the following.

Mean = 5.1 Median = 5 Mode = 6 Midrange = 5.5

a. Now determine these statistics for the class survey distributions, where possible.

DISTRIBUTION	MEAN	MEDIAN	MODE	MIDRANGE
Credit hours				
Miles from campus				
Time studying				

b. On your original dotplots in Problem 3, clearly mark with a vertical line each of the above statistics from the preceding table.

c. For each distribution, circle the statistic (mean, median, mode, midrange) that is closest to the estimate of the center that you made in Problem 8. Which type of statistic did you have in mind when you made your estimates?

10. Which statistic would you choose to best describe the "average" number of credit hours among your classmates, and why?

Most students will choose the mean, but depending on the particular data, median or mode could also be reasonably good answers, if they truly represent the center of the data.

11. Do any of these measurements of central tendency make sense for the gender distribution? Explain.

Only the mode makes sense because it does not depend upon numeric or ordinal data.

12. The table in Problem 9 should remind you of the input/output tables you have been using throughout this chapter. Each of the statistics that measure central tendency is determined by a well-defined rule. For example, consider the statistical mean of a distribution.

a. From your table, what is the input variable for the statistical mean?

The input is the set of data or the distribution.

b. Is there a unique output for every input?

Yes, there is a unique output for each particular set of data.

c. By definition, is the mean a function of the distribution?

Yes, since there is a unique output for each input.

d. What is the domain for the mean function?

The domain of the mean function is the collection of all finite sets of numeric data.

Statistical functions, such as the mean, median, and mode, are examples of functions whose domain is more than a collection of single numbers or values. In general, you should remember that functions can be defined with domains that may be collections of literally anything—that is, anything like frequency distributions, that may make for a useful function.

Your graphing calculator can also be used to generate a graph of a frequency distribution function and provide many statistics that describe the distribution. Using the sample family size data, the following **histogram** can be generated. The frequency of each data value (the output of the function) is represented by the height of a rectangle. So in a histogram, a rectangle replaces the column of dots in a dotplot. The rectangle also replaces a single point in the conventional graph of a function.

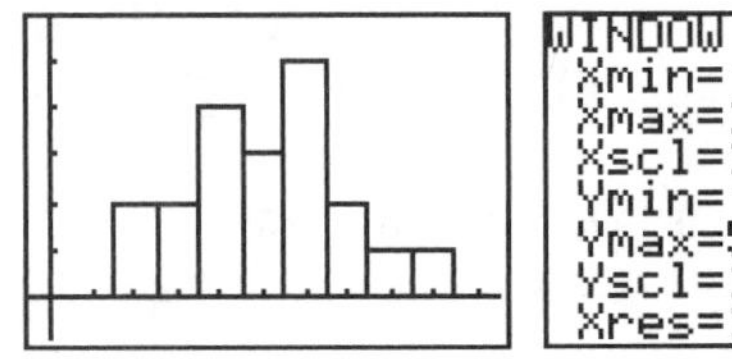

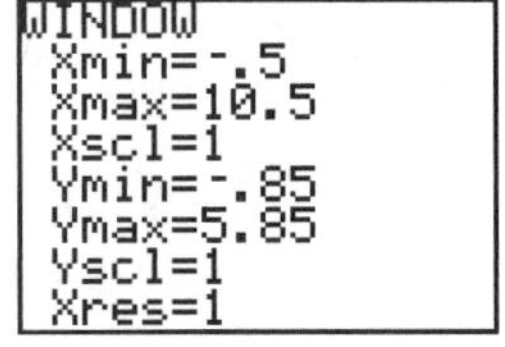

13. Use your grapher to produce the histogram for the class miles from the campus distribution. Refer to Appendix C for detailed instructions for the TI-83 calculator.

Answers will vary with each classmate's data.

Once the data are stored in your calculator, you can generate a variety of statistics for your data, including the measures of central tendency. For example, the following windows result from the sample family size data.

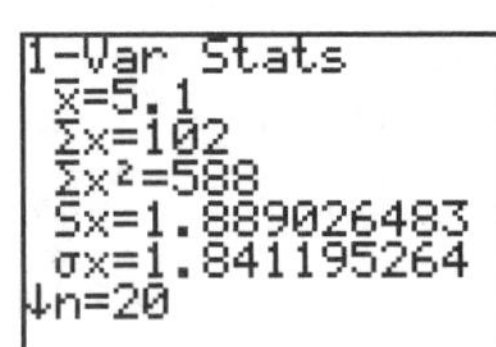

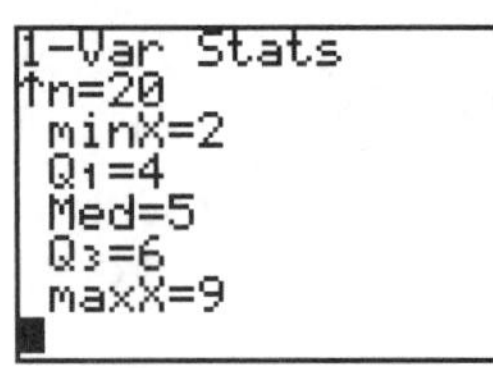

The mean $(\bar{x})$ and median (Med) are given, n is the number of data values, and minX and maxX are the smallest and largest data values respectively. From these you can calculate the midrange.

14. Use your grapher to produce the measures of central tendency for the class credit hours distribution. Refer to Appendix C for detailed instructions for the TI-83 calculator.

15. a. The three frequency distributions (functions) pictured here have the same domain. What is it? Domain: $2 \le x \le 8$

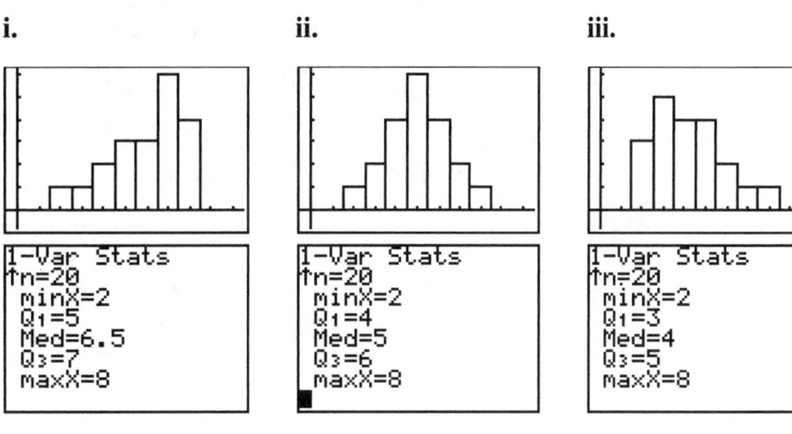

b. Describe in your own words the visual differences among the distributions in part a.

ii is symmetrical, i has the data shifted to the right, iii has the data shifted to the left.

c. The means for the distributions in part a are as follows:

$$\bar{x}_A = 6.0 \quad \bar{x}_B = 5.0 \quad \bar{x}_C = 4.2$$

Compare these to the median for each distribution.

In the symmetrical distribution, ii, the mean equals the median. When the data is shifted to the right (i), the mean is less than the median. When the data is shifted to the left (iii), the mean is greater than the median.

Some distributions are symmetrical (like distribution ii in Problem 15). Others are slightly "off," as if they have been stretched to one side or the other. Distribution i is **skewed to the left,** while distribution iii is **skewed to the right.**

16. a. If a distribution is perfectly symmetrical, what do you think will be true about the relationship between the mean and median?

The mean will equal the median.

b. Based on your results in part a, what is the relation between the mean and median of a skewed distribution?

If skewed to the right, the mean is greater than the median. If skewed to the left, the mean is less than the median.

c. Enter in your calculator a skewed distribution with ten data values. Record your data, sketch the histogram (or dotplot), and calculate the mean and median. Does this result help confirm your answer in part b?

EXERCISES

1. A large publishing company wants to review the ages of its sales representatives. The ages of a sample of 25 sales reps are as follows:

   50 42 32 35 41 44 24 46 31 47 36 32 30
   44 22 47 31 56 28 37 49 28 42 38 45

   a. Construct a histogram for the ages.

   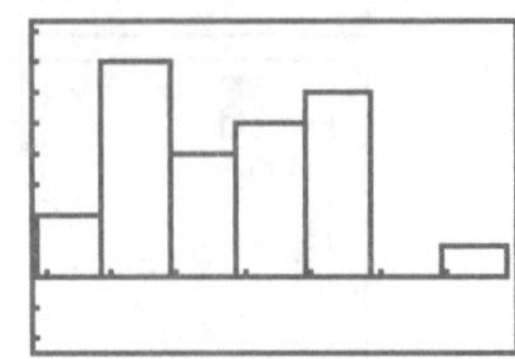

   b. How would you describe the shape of the distribution?

   The distribution is somewhat skewed to the right.

   c. Calculate the mean and median ages.

   Mean = 38.28, median = 38

   d. Describe in a single sentence how the mean and median are related to the shape of the distribution.

   Since the distribution is fairly symmetrical, the mean and median are very close.

   e. Determine the midrange.

   The midrange is (56 + 22)/2 = 39.

   f. Is there a mode for this distribution?

   No, there is no mode, several values appear twice, but none more than that.

2. Suppose the scores of seven members of a men's golf team are 68, 62, 60, 64, 70, 66, and 72. Find the mean, median, and midrange.

   Mean = 66, median = 66, midrange = 66.

3. The scores on the last math quiz are summarized in the following frequency table.

SCORE	10	9	8	7	6	5	4	3	2	1	0
FREQUENCY	5	7	6	4	2	0	1	0	0	0	0

Exercise numbers appearing in color are answered in the Selected Answers section of this book.

a. Construct a dotplot for the scores.

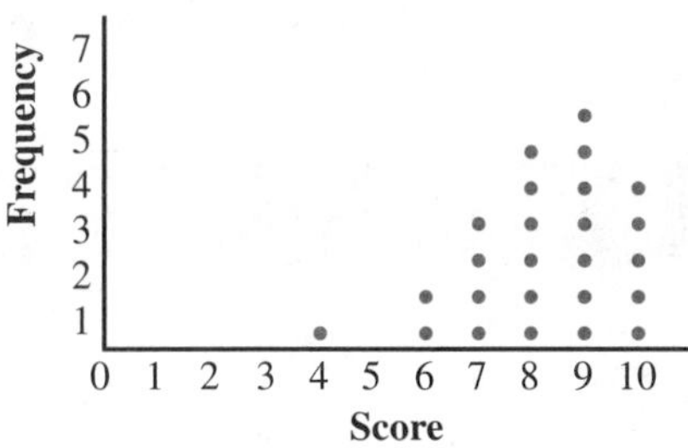

b. Construct a histogram on the same coordinate axes.

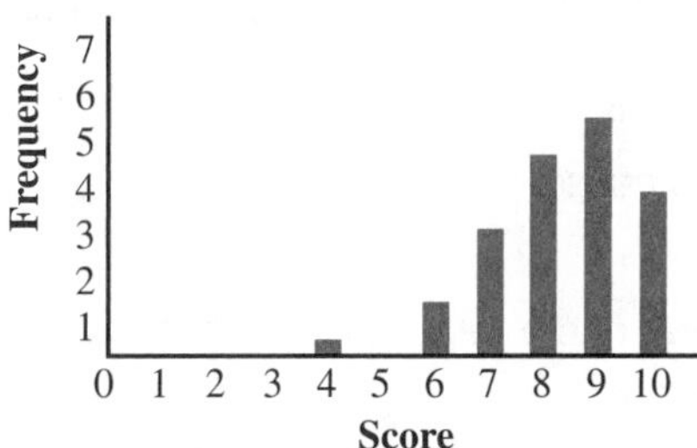

c. As defined in the table, what is the domain and range of this frequency distribution function?

The domain is {0, 1, 2, 3, 4, 5, 6, 7, 8, 9, 10}.

The range of the function is {0, 1, 2, 4, 5, 6, 7}.

d. Is this distribution skewed to the left or right?

The distribution is skewed to the left.

e. Calculate the mean, median, mode and midrange of this quiz distribution.

Mean = 8.2, median = 8, midrange = 7

4. a. Create a set of ten data values whose distribution is perfectly symmetrical.

Answers will of course vary.

b. Verify that the mean, median, and midrange are identical.

c. Change two data values so that the resulting distribution is skewed to the left.

d. Predict how this will change the mean and median. Then verify by doing the calculations.

5. A set of data has a mean of 32.4 and a median of 38.9. Would you expect the distribution for this data to be symmetrical, skewed to the left, or skewed to the right?

Skewed to the left.

6. Find a collection of at least 25 data values from a real-world source. Use your grapher to create a histogram, and calculate the four measures of central tendency.

(Answers will vary.)

ACTIVITY 1.16

Chances Are!

Topics: *Relative Frequency, Probability Functions, Simulation*

The following table gives the years of service of the 789 workers in your department at Regent's Manufacturing.

SENIORITY	LESS THAN ONE YEAR	BETWEEN ONE AND TEN YEARS	MORE THAN TEN YEARS	TOTAL
Male	82	361	47	490
Female	49	202	48	299
Total	131	563	95	789

1. **a.** Complete the table to display the total number of workers in each category.

   b. What is the total number of males?

   490 males

   c. What is the total number of workers having between one and ten years of service?

   563 workers

   d. Should the sum of the right-most column be the same as the sum of the bottom row?

   Yes, the 789 total workers.

2. Each of the numbers in the table can be considered a frequency for that category. If you consider this frequency a fractional part of the whole workforce, it becomes a **relative frequency.** For example, the relative frequency of male workers with less than one year of experience is $\frac{82}{789} \approx 0.104 = 10.4\%$. Calculate the relative frequency, expressed as a decimal, for each category.

SENIORITY	LESS THAN ONE YEAR	BETWEEN ONE AND TEN YEARS	MORE THAN TEN YEARS	TOTAL
Male	0.104	0.458	0.060	0.621
Female	0.062	0.256	0.061	0.379
Total	0.166	0.714	0.120	1.000

3. Now consider choosing one of the 789 workers by some random process, like drawing names out of a hat. The **probability** of picking a male worker with less than one year of experience is 0.104, the relative frequency for that particular outcome. A particular outcome is called an **event.**

   a. What is the probability of choosing a female with more than ten years of experience?

   P(female and more than 10 years) $= 0.061$

   b. What is the probability of choosing a male?

   P(male) $= 0.621$

c. What is the probability of choosing a worker with less than one year of experience?

P(less than 1 year) = 0.166

$$\text{Probability of event} = \frac{\text{number of outcomes for which the event is true}}{\text{total number of possible outcomes}}$$

For example, the probability of choosing a male is $\frac{490}{789} \approx 0.621$. The event is "choosing a male." Of the 789 possible outcomes, 490 of the outcomes make the event true.

One important assumption is necessary for this definition to hold true. All the possible outcomes must be equally likely to occur. Selecting one worker at random implies that each worker has the same likelihood, or probability, of being chosen.

4. a. As one of the 789 workers, what is the probability that you will be chosen?

P(you are chosen) = 1/789

b. What is the probability that one of the 789 workers will be chosen?

P(some worker) = 789/789 = 1

c. What is the probability that your uncle (who does not work in your department) will be chosen?

P(your uncle) = 0/789 = 0

5. Now consider a very random experiment, rolling a typical six-sided die.

a. What makes this experiment random?

Rolling a die is a random experiment because each outcome is equally likely to occur.

b. What is the probability of rolling a five?

P(five) = 1/6

c. What is the probability of rolling an even number?

P(even) = 3/6 = 1/2

d. For this experiment, think of an event that has a probability of zero.

P(seven) = 0 Many possible answers.

The probabilities are a function of the individual outcomes. The domain is the set of possible single outcomes. For probability functions, the domain is called the **sample space.**

e. Complete this input/output table for the die roll **probability function.**

OUTCOME	PROBABILITY
1	$\frac{1}{6}$
2	$\frac{1}{6}$
3	$\frac{1}{6}$
4	$\frac{1}{6}$
5	$\frac{1}{6}$
6	$\frac{1}{6}$

f. In function notation, let $P(x)$ be the probability of rolling x on the die. What does $P(3)$ equal?

$P(3) = \frac{1}{6}$

g. What is the sum of all the possible outputs for this function? Explain why this makes sense.

The sum of all the outputs is one. The probability is one that one of the numbers will occur.

6. Consider another random experiment, flipping a coin.

a. To be a random process, you must use a fair coin. What do you think is meant by a fair coin?

Equal chance of a head or tail coming up.

b. By definition, what is the probability of getting heads on a single flip of the coin?

$P(\text{head}) = \frac{1}{2}$

c. What is the sample space for this probability function?

sample space = domain = {head, tail}

The probability definition you used to answer the questions in Problem 6 is sometimes called the **theoretical probability** of an event.

Sometimes such probabilities are not possible to calculate. For example, suppose you want to estimate the probability of rain today or to predict the likelihood of living past the age of 80. There is another way to define probability that depends on experimental observation.

7. Suppose the weather forecaster claims that there is a 60% chance of rain tonight. How do you think such a probability could be calculated?

From past observations, when similar conditions occurred, it rained 60% of the time.

8. a. If you flip a coin ten times, how many heads would you expect to get?

Answers will vary, but most will say five, or a small range, like between four and six.

b. Would you be surprised to get ten heads in your ten flips?

Answer should be yes.

c. How about nine heads or only one head?

Answer should still be yes, but may vary. Fertile ground for discussion.

d. Have each member of the class flip a coin ten times. Summarize the results for the entire class in the following frequency table and histogram.

(Answers will vary.)

NUMBER OF HEADS	FREQUENCY
0	
1	
2	
3	
4	
5	
6	
7	
8	
9	
10	

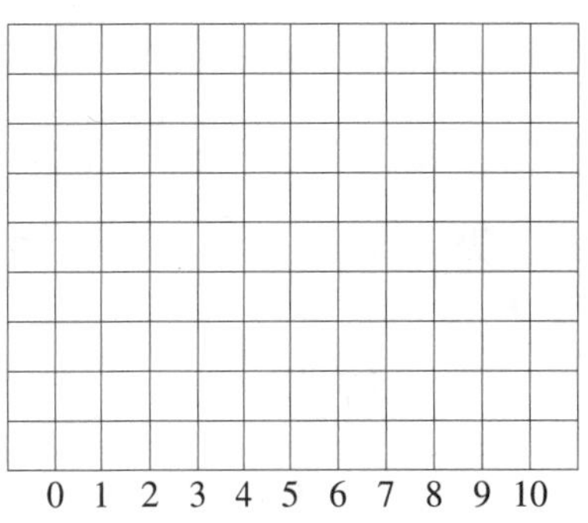

e. Does the frequency distribution confirm your answers in parts a–c?

Answers will vary.

f. You know that the theoretical probability of getting a head on a single coin flip is $\frac{1}{2}$. For this to be true, what assumption are you making?

The coin is fair, heads are as likely as tails.

9. When you flip a coin, you should expect to get heads approximately one-half the time. Determine the relative frequency of getting a head for the class experiment in Problem 8d. Would you be surprised if the relative frequency was not close to one half?

Answers will vary, but students should be surprised

You could use this relative frequency based on the results of the experiment to define the probability of getting a head, especially if you did not know the theoretical probability. This probability would be an **experimental probability.**

10. Repeat the coin-tossing experiment as a class, with each member of the class tossing the coin 20 times and recording the number of heads observed. How does the resulting relative frequency compare with the theoretical probability?

Answers will vary, but the new relative frequency should be closer to the theoretical probability.

If more is better, you could be flipping coins for a long time to get a truly large number of observations. You can accomplish this by employing technology. Your grapher or a computer can be used to **simulate** the flipping of a coin a very large number of times. This can be done by randomly generating a large number of zeros and ones (ones representing heads and zeros representing tails). The probability of getting a one must be 50%. (See Appendix C for TI-83 instructions.)

11. a. Use technology to simulate flipping a coin 100 times and then 500 times. Record your results in the following table. Then combine all your classmates' results to get as many observations as you can.

NUMBER OF FLIPS	NUMBER OF HEADS	RELATIVE FREQUENCY OF HEADS
100		
500		

b. What conclusion can you make about the relative frequency as the number of observations increases?

(Answers will vary.)

In Problems 9–11, as the number of coin flips increased, the closer the experimental probability of obtaining a head got to the theoretical probability of getting a head. This is usually called the **law of large numbers.** It is the law on which gambling casinos and state lotteries depend, as you will see later in this cluster.

SUMMARY

Theoretical Probability

$$\text{Probability of event} = \frac{\text{number of outcomes in event}}{\text{total number of possible outcomes}}$$

Experimental Probability

$$\text{Probability of event} = \frac{\text{number of observed occurrences of event}}{\text{total number of observations}}$$

Law of Large Numbers
The larger the number of observations, the closer the experimental probability of an event will get to the theoretical probability of that same event.

Properties of Probability Functions
If $P(x)$ is the probability that outcome x occurs, then the following special properties of probability functions must be true.

- The domain of all possible individual outcomes is called the **sample space** of P.
- $0 \leq P(x) \leq 1$ for all x in the sample space.
- If x is impossible, then $P(x) = 0$. If x is a certainty, then $P(x) = 1$.
- The sum of the probabilities of all x in the sample space must equal 1.

EXERCISES

1. A random survey of 100 teens in your community yields the following results.

	SMOKER	NONSMOKER	TOTAL
FEMALE	24	32	56
MALE	24	20	44
TOTAL	48	52	100

a. Complete the totals in the table.

b. Calculate the relative frequency for each category.

	SMOKER	NONSMOKER	TOTAL
FEMALE	0.24	0.32	0.56
MALE	0.24	0.20	0.44
TOTAL	0.48	0.52	1.00

c. Using these relative frequencies as the basis for defining probabilities, what is the probability that a teen in your community is a smoker?

P(teen smoker) = 0.48

d. If you choose one teen at random from your community, what is the probability that he or she is a female nonsmoker?

P(female nonsmoker) = 0.20

e. Given the fact that you have already chosen a female at random, what is the probability that she is a smoker?

Given that a female was chosen: *P*(smoker) = 24/44 = 0.545

f. Given the fact that you have already chosen a male at random, what is the probability that he is a smoker?

Given that a male was chosen: *P*(smoker) = 24/56 = 0.429

g. From your results in parts e and f, would you say there are more male or female teen smokers in your community? Explain.

There is a higher percentage of females that smoke.

2. Twenty uniformly shaped stones are placed in a vase. Five of the stones are white, eight of the stones are gray, and the remaining stones are black. One stone is drawn at random from the vase. The outcome of this experiment is to note the color of the selected stone.

a. What is the sample space for this probability function?

sample space = {white, gray, black}

Exercise numbers appearing in color are answered in the Selected Answers section of this book.

b. Make a table showing the probability of each individual outcome.

x	white	gray	black
$P(x)$	5/20 = 0.25	8/20 = 0.4	7/20 = 0.35

c. Find: P(white), P(gray), P(black), and P(red).

P(white) = 0.25, P(gray) = 0.4, P(black) = 0.35, P(red) = 0

3. If $P(x)$ is the probability of living to age x, interpret the statement $P(80) = 0.16$.

The probability of living to age 80 is 0.16. Or, there is a 16% chance of someone living to age 80.

4. State whether you think each of the following is a theoretical or experimental probability.

a. The chance of rain tonight is 35%.

b. The probability of living past 100 years of age is 0.03.

c. The probability of getting two tails on two flips of a coin is 0.25.

d. The probability that the sun will come up tomorrow is 1.

e. The probability of selecting a green stone from the vase of Exercise 2 is zero.

Theoretical probability: c, e Experimental probability: a, b, d

5. You are blindfolded and then throw a dart at a square dartboard, as illustrated. Assuming that the dart does hit the board, what is the probability that you will hit region II?

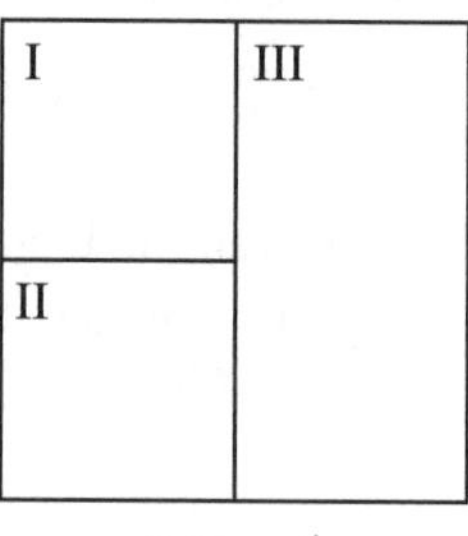

$P(\text{II}) = \frac{1}{4}$

6. If you and your friend separately choose a number between 1 and 10 at random, what is the probability that you will choose the same number?

P(same number) = $\frac{1}{10}$ (Whatever number you chose, there is a 1 in 10 chance your friend will choose the same number.)

7. The following functions are defined by their tables. Which functions could be probability functions? For those that cannot be probability functions, give a reason.

a.

x	1	2	3	4	5
$f(x)$	0.2	0.2	0.2	0.2	0.2

Yes, could be a probability function.

b.

x	3	4	5	6	7	8	9	10	11	12
$g(x)$	0.1	0.15	0.2	0.25	0.12	0.1	0.05	0.02	0.01	0.01

No, probabilities do not add up to one.

c.

x	blue	green	red	white	black	gray
$h(x)$	0.3	0.4	0.2	−0.3	0.2	0.2

No, every probability must be between zero and one, inclusive.

8. The spinner pictured at the right is used in a board game.

a. Assuming that it is a fair spinner, construct a table for the probability function, where the domain is the set of individual outcomes.

x	1	2	3	4
$P(x)$	0.25	0.25	0.25	0.25

b. What is the probability of getting a number greater than 1?

$P(x > 1) = 0.75$

c. What is the probability of getting an odd number?

$P(x \text{ is odd}) = 0.5$

9. In your class of 28 students, there are 12 smokers. Of these 12 smokers, only 3 are under 20 years old. There are 13 students in class that are 20 years old or older. This information is summarized in the following table.

	UNDER 20	20 OR OVER	TOTAL
SMOKERS	3	9	12
NONSMOKERS	12	4	16
TOTAL	15	13	28

(A student is selected at random.)

a. What is the probability that the student is a non-smoker?

$P(\text{nonsmoker}) = \frac{16}{28} = 0.57$

b. What is the probability that the student is a smoker who is also at least 20 years old?

$P(\text{smoker and 20 or over}) = \frac{9}{28} = 0.32$

c. What is the probability that the student is under 20 years old?

$P(\text{under 20}) = \frac{15}{28} = 0.54$

10. You flip a coin 500 times and get 500 heads. What conclusion would you make about this coin?

It either has two heads, or is otherwise completely unfair, i.e., weighted to always come up heads.

ACTIVITY 1.17

Choices

Topics: *Multiplication Principle of Counting, Tree Diagrams, Sample Space*

Suppose you are looking for a new car and have narrowed your decision down to a Mustang, but can't decide on the exact color, transmission, engine, or options package. There are three sizes of engine (3.0 liters, 3.8 liters, and 4.6 liters), two transmissions (standard and automatic), five colors you like (black, silver, red, yellow, and green), and three option packages (GL, Sport, and XL). With all these possible choices, you want to know how many different Mustangs there are from which you must choose.

1. From the choices given, how many different Mustangs are possible? (Solve this any way you can. A diagram or list may help.)

(3 engines)(2 trans)(5 colors)(3 options) = 90 different Mustangs

In solving the Mustang problem, you might have recognized a counting shortcut. If the outcomes you wish to count consist of a sequence of choices, it is possible to apply the **multiplication principle of counting**.

For example, suppose you have three sweaters: one cotton, one wool, and one alpaca. You also have four hats, colored red, green, black, and purple. If you want to wear one sweater and one hat, how many different combinations are possible?

Option 1: You could simply list all the possibilities:

cotton + red	wool + red	alpaca + red
cotton + green	wool + green	alpaca + green
cotton + black	wool + black	alpaca + black
cotton + purple	wool + purple	alpaca + purple

You could shorten the process with a **tree diagram** (and abbreviations), where each level of branching represents the next choice.

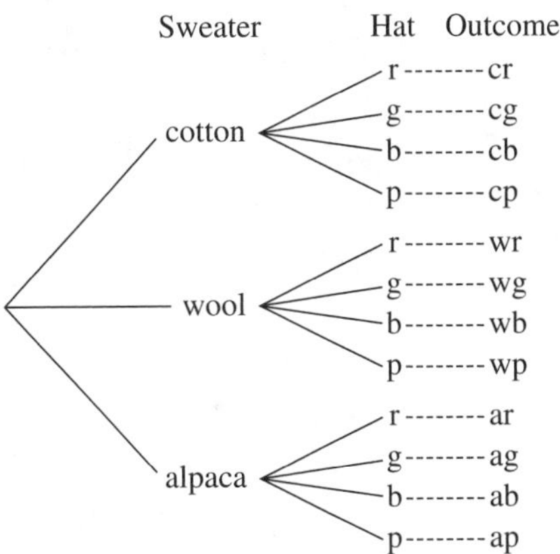

The total number of end points represents all the possibilities. Tracing each branch displays all the possible outcomes.

Option 2: You could use a table approach if there are only two levels of choices.

	RED	GREEN	BLACK	PURPLE
COTTON	cr	cg	cb	cp
WOOL	wr	wg	wb	wp
ALPACA	ar	ag	ab	ap

Option 3: You could multiply the 3 choices for a sweater by the 4 choices for a hat to get a total of 12 combinations. This is called the *multiplication principle of counting.*

THE MULTIPLICATION PRINCIPLE OF COUNTING

If some choice can be made in *M* ways and a subsequent choice can be made in *N* ways, then there are *M* times *N* ways these choices can be made in succession.

2. Apply the multiplication principle to the Mustang problem to verify your answer in Problem 1.

(3 engines)(2 trans)(5 colors)(3 options) = 90 different Mustangs

3. a. You want to create an ID code for all your customers based on three characters. The first character must be a letter of the alphabet, and the second and third must each be a digit between 1 and 9, inclusive. How many such codes are there? (Use the multiplication principle.)

$26 \times 9 \times 9 = 2106$ different codes

b. Would a list or tree diagram be practical in this case?

No, since there are way too many choices.

4. a. Suppose you flip a penny and a dime. Use a tree diagram or a table to display all possible outcomes.

penny	dime
head	head
head	tail
tail	head
tail	tail

b. If each single outcome is equally likely, you can use the tree diagram or table to help calculate probabilities. What is the probability of getting two heads?

P(2 heads) = 1/4

c. What is the probability of getting one head and one tail, on either coin?

P(1 head and 1 tail) = 2/4 = 1/2

d. If the input variable x is the number of heads, complete the table for this **probability function.**

x	$P(x)$
0	0.25
1	0.5
2	0.25

e. What must be true about the sum of the probabilities for this (and any other) probability function?

The sum of the probabilities must be one.

The collection of all the possible single outcomes displayed by the tree diagram is often called the **sample space** for the probability function.

5. Consider rolling two dice.

a. Display the sample space of all possible outcomes. You may use a tree diagram or a table. It may help to think of the dice as being different colors.

1, 1   1, 2   1, 3   1, 4   1, 5   1, 6
2, 1   2, 2   2, 3   2, 4   2, 5   2, 6
3, 1   3, 2   3, 3   3, 4   3, 5   3, 6
4, 1   4, 2   4, 3   4, 4   4, 5   4, 6
5, 1   5, 2   5, 3   5, 4   5, 5   5, 6
6, 1   6, 2   6, 3   6, 4   6, 5   6, 6

b. What is the probability of getting a total of two spots on the dice (snake eyes)?

$P(1, 1) = \frac{1}{36}$

c. If the input variable x is the total number of spots on the two dice, refer to your sample space to complete the table for this probability function.

x	2	3	4	5	6	7	8	9	10	11	12
$P(x)$	$\frac{1}{36}$	$\frac{2}{36}$	$\frac{3}{36}$	$\frac{4}{36}$	$\frac{5}{36}$	$\frac{6}{36}$	$\frac{5}{36}$	$\frac{4}{36}$	$\frac{3}{36}$	$\frac{2}{36}$	$\frac{1}{36}$

d. What must be the sum of all probabilities?

The sum must be one.

6. To win the jackpot in a large state lottery, the winner must pick correctly all six numbers from among 1 through 54. The theoretical probability of doing this is $\frac{1}{25827165} \approx .0000000387$. Stated another way, a single pick has a 1 in 25,827,165 chance to win the jackpot (and even then it might be shared with other winners). The theory of probability originated out of a desire to understand games of chance.

a. Show how the 25,827,165 is determined.

$54 \cdot 53 \cdot 52 \cdot 51 \cdot 50 \cdot 49 = 18{,}595{,}558{,}800$, which includes every possible arrangement of any specific six numbers. Divide by $6 \cdot 5 \cdot 4 \cdot 3 \cdot 2 \cdot 1 = 720$ to get the number of choices, since the order the numbers are selected does not matter.

7. Determine the probability of being dealt a royal flush (ten, jack, queen, king, and ace of the same suit) in poker.

There are $\frac{52 \cdot 51 \cdot 50 \cdot 49 \cdot 48}{5 \cdot 4 \cdot 3 \cdot 2 \cdot 1} = 2{,}598{,}960$ possible five card hands. Of these, only four are royal flushes, one for each suit. So the probability is $\frac{4}{2{,}598{,}960} = 0.00000154$.

8. What is the probability of getting ten heads on ten flips of a coin?

$P(10 \text{ heads}) = \left(\frac{1}{2}\right)^{10} = 0.00098$

EXERCISES

1. Phone numbers consist of a three-digit area code followed by seven digits. If the area code must have a 0 or 1 for the second digit, and neither the area code nor the seven-digit number can start with 0 or 1, how many different phone numbers are possible?

$8 \cdot 2 \cdot 10 \cdot 8 \cdot 10 \cdot 10 \cdot 10 \cdot 10 \cdot 10 \cdot 10 = 1{,}280{,}000{,}000$

2. You have four sweaters, five pairs of pants, and three pairs of shoes. How many different combinations can you make, wearing one of each?

$4 \cdot 5 \cdot 3 = 60$

3. If you flip a coin ten times, how many different sequences of heads and tails are possible?

$2^{10} = 1024$

4. If you roll a die three times, how many different sequences are possible?

$6^3 = 216$

5. You want to order a triple-scoop ice cream cone, with a different flavor for each scoop. If there are 23 flavors available, how many different cones are possible?

$23 \cdot 22 \cdot 21 = 10{,}626$ cones are possible, counting different orderings of the scoops.
$10{,}626/6 = 1771$ if the order doesn't matter.

Exercise numbers appearing in color are answered in the Selected Answers section of this book.

6. In a single experiment, a die is tossed and a spinner with the letters A, B, and C is spun. Each letter is equally likely .

   a. Find the resulting sample space.

1, A	1, B	1, C
2, A	2, B	2, C
3, A	3, B	3, C
4, A	4, B	4, C
5, A	5, B	5, C
6, A	6, B	6, C

   b. Find the probability of getting a 2 on the die *and* a B on the spinner.

   $P(2, B) = \frac{1}{18}$

   c. Find the probability of getting a B.

   $P(B) = \frac{1}{3}$

   d. Find the probability of getting a 2 or a B.

   $P(2 \text{ or } B) = \frac{8}{18} = \frac{4}{9}$

7. A computer is programmed to generate a sequence of three digits, where each digit is either 0 or 1, and each of these is equally likely to occur.

   a. Construct a sample space that shows all possible three-digit sequences of 0s and 1s.

   000, 001, 010, 011, 100, 101, 110, 111

   b. What is the probability that a sequence will contain exactly one 0?

   $P(\text{one } 0) = \frac{3}{8}$

   c. What is the probability that a sequence will contain at least one 0?

   (at least one 0) $= \frac{7}{8}$

8. Two teams are playing a best-of-seven series. For each game there are only two possible outcomes: One team wins or the other team wins. Construct a tree diagram showing all the possible outcomes for such a series. As soon as one team wins a fourth game, the series ends (and that branch of the tree ends also).

   (by hand)

9. You have ten pairs of socks, all a different color. They are mixed up in your drawer, and you select two socks at random.

   a. What is the probability that you will select a matched pair?

   There are $20 \cdot 19 = 380$ different ways of choosing two socks. Of these, ten will be matched pairs. So, $P(match) = \frac{1}{38}$.

   b. How many socks must you select to be sure you will have at least one matching pair?

   11

10. You roll two dice. Use the sample space you recorded in Problem 5 to find the probabilities of the following events.

a. P(a sum of 7)

$P(\text{a sum of } 7) = \frac{6}{36} = \frac{1}{6}$

b. P(both dice show an even number)

$P(\text{both even}) = \frac{9}{36} = \frac{1}{4}$

c. P(one die is even, the other odd)

$P(\text{one even, one odd}) = \frac{18}{36} = \frac{1}{2}$

d. P(one die is 1 more than the other)

$P(\text{one more than the other}) = \frac{10}{36} = \frac{5}{18}$

e. P(the sum is less than 6)

$P(\text{sum less than } 6) = \frac{10}{36} = \frac{5}{18}$

f. P(the product of the two numbers on the dice is even)

$P(\text{even product}) = \frac{27}{36} = \frac{3}{4}$

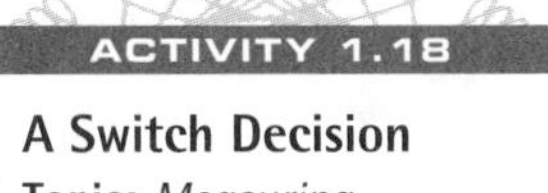

ACTIVITY 1.18

A Switch Decision

Topic: *Measuring Variability of a Distribution*

Statistical analysis is useful when important decisions need to be made. The following sets of data are the result of testing two different switches that can be used in the life-support system on a submarine. Two hundred of each type of switch were placed under continuous stress until they failed, the time recorded in hours. Switch A and switch B have approximately the same means and medians, as displayed by the following histograms. (The displays are from a TI-83.)

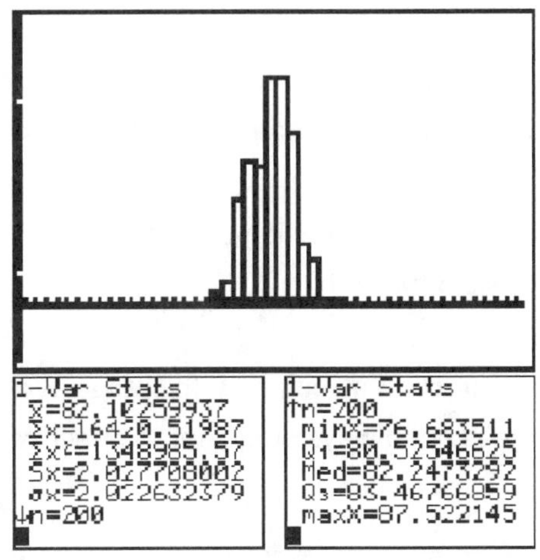

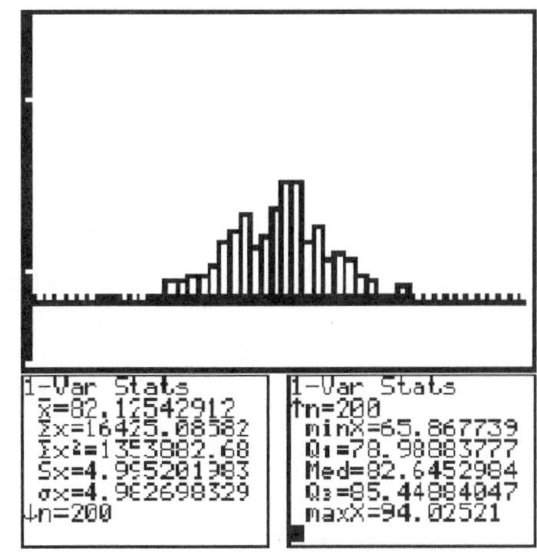

1. Verify that the means and medians for both switches are approximately the same. What does this tell you about the general shapes of the distributions?

   The distributions are approximately symmetrical about their centers.

2. Which distribution is the most spread out?

   Distribution B is more spread out.

3. Which distribution is packed more closely around its center?

   Distribution A is packed more closely around its center.

4. Based on these tests, which switch would you choose to use and why?

   Switch A, since its lifetime is more predictable and uniform.

Like the central tendency of a distribution, the spread, or **variability,** of a distribution is also measured several different ways. The **range** (not to be confused with the range of a function) is simply the difference between the minimum and maximum data values. As a statistical measure, the range is a function of the data values that form the distribution.

5. Determine the range for each set of switch data to the nearest hour. Do these ranges confirm your answers to Problems 2 and 3?

   Range of $A = 87.52 - 76.68 = 10.84$

   Range of $B = 94.03 - 65.87 = 28.16$, Yes, the more spread out the greater the range.

6. The range is of limited value in describing the variability (or spread) of a distribution. Consider these two data sets.

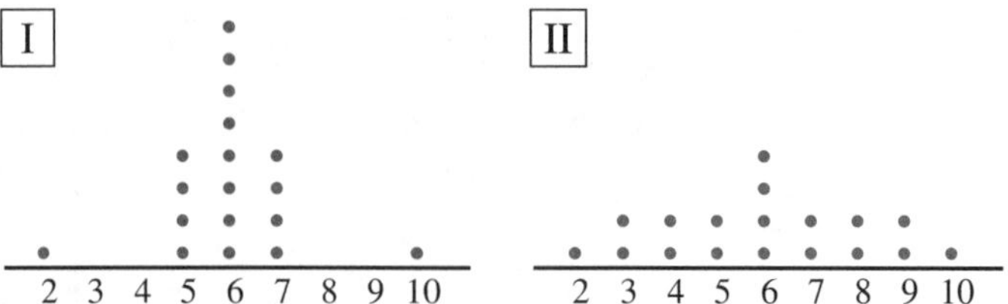

a. Which distribution has greater variability?

Distribution II has the greater variability, it's more spread out.

b. Calculate the range for each distribution.

The range is 8 for both.

c. What is your conclusion about the range as a measure of variability?

The range is not always sufficient to describe variability.

> The most common measure of spread is the **standard deviation** (symbol σ, the Greek lowercase letter sigma). It measures how much the data deviates from the mean.

7. Calculate the mean for distributions I and II of Problem 6.

Mean of I $= 6.0$, Mean of II $= 6.0$

Deviation refers to how far a data value is from the mean. For example, if the mean is 7, then a data value of 10 is a distance of 3 from the mean, and you would say that the data value 10 has a deviation of 3 from the mean. If the data value is 4, it is still a distance of 3 from the mean, but its deviation is -3, indicating that it is below the mean.

8. **a.** Calculate the deviations for every data value in both distributions I and II of Problem 6. Then add all the deviations for each distribution. Round your results in the last two columns of the following tables to three decimal places, if necessary.

DISTRIBUTION I

x	$x - \bar{x}$	$(x - \bar{x})^2$
2	−4	16
5	−1	1
5	−1	1
5	−1	1
5	−1	1
6	0	0
6	0	0
6	0	0
6	0	0
6	0	0
6	0	0
6	0	0
6	0	0
7	1	1
7	1	1
7	1	1
7	1	1
10	4	16
Total	0	40

DISTRIBUTION II

x	$x - \bar{x}$	$(x - \bar{x})^2$
2	−4	16
3	−3	9
3	−3	9
4	−2	4
4	−2	4
5	−1	1
5	−1	1
6	0	0
6	0	0
6	0	0
6	0	0
7	1	1
7	1	1
8	2	4
8	2	4
9	3	9
9	3	9
10	4	16
Total	0	88

b. Is the sum of the deviations, denoted by $\sum (x - \bar{x})$, a good measure of the spread of the data? Explain.

The sum of the deviations is 0 in both cases, because the mean is the center of the distribution. Therefore, it is not necessarily a good measure of the spread of the data.

To overcome the deficiency of the total deviation, you could simply take the absolute value of each deviation. The more conventional method to calculate the standard deviation of a distribution involves summing the squares of the deviations, denoted by $\sum (x - \bar{x})^2$.

9. For each distribution, calculate the standard deviation using the following procedure.

a. Square each deviation in both of the tables of Problem 8. (Complete the column $(x - \bar{x})^2$

	Distribution I	Distribution II

b. Add the squares of all the deviations: 40 88

c. Divide by the number of data values: $\frac{40}{18}$ $\frac{88}{18}$

d. Take the square root: 1.49 2.21

In a single formula, the standard deviation is $\sigma = \sqrt{\frac{\sum (x - \bar{x})^2}{n}}$, where σ is the standard deviation, $\sum$ is short for "the sum of," x is a single data value, $\bar{x}$ is the mean, and n is the number of data values.

e. Does distribution I or distribution II have greater variability? Explain using the standard deviation of each distribution.

Dist. II has the greater variability, which is measured by the larger standard deviation.

10. Verify that your standard deviations in Problem 9d agree with those in the following display, from the TI-83. (The TI-83 uses σx for σ.)

Distribution I

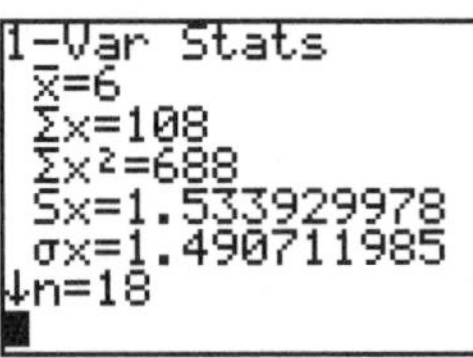

Distribution II

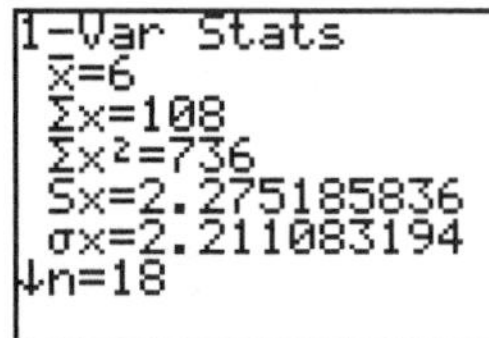

11. What do you think a standard deviation of zero would mean?

A standard deviation of zero means there is no variability. Every number is the same.

12. a. Return to the testing of switches A and B. The standard deviations of each distribution are given by the TI-83 output box. Record the standard deviations here.

Std. dev. of A = 2.02, Std. dev. of B = 4.98

b. Which distribution has the greater variability? Explain using the standard deviation of each distribution.

B has the greater std. dev., hence the greater variability.

Another type of statistical graph, the **boxplot,** helps you to visualize the variability of a distribution. Five statistics form a boxplot: the minimum data value, the **first quartile (Q_1)**, the median, the **third quartile (Q_3)**, and the maximum data value, in order from smallest to largest. These are often referred to as the **five-number summary** for the distribution.

Quartiles refer to values that separate the data into quarters. The lowest 25% of all the data falls between the minimum and the first quartile. The next lowest 25% of the data falls between the first quartile and the median. Hence, 75% of the data is above the first quartile.

13. a. How much of the data is below the third quartile?

75% of the data is below the third quartile.

b. How much of the data is between the first and third quartiles?

50%

The five-number summaries are displayed here for the switch A and B data.

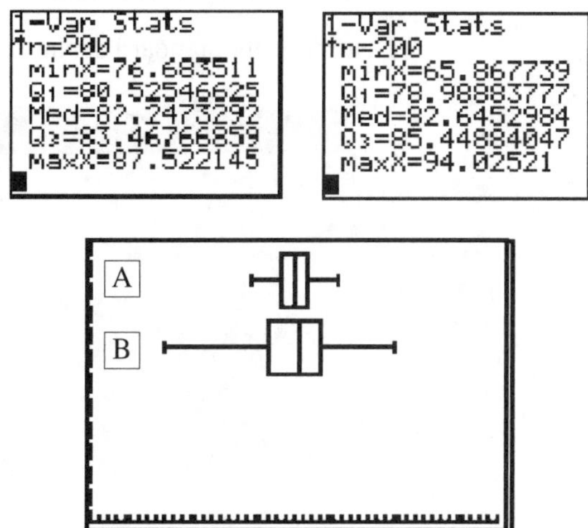

Sometimes called box-and-whisker plots, the preceding boxplots show visually how the quartiles for the switch data compare. The box represents the middle 50% of the data. The whiskers represent the extent of the lower and upper quarters of the data.

14. Consider the following boxplots for three distributions.

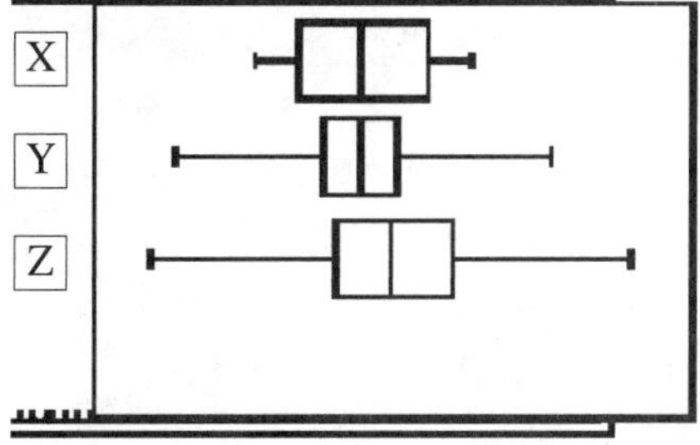

a. Compare the minimum, first quartile, median, third quartile, and maximum for the three distributions.

min Z < min Y < min X, Q1 X < Q1 Y < Q1 Z, med X = med Y = med Z
Q3 Y < Q3 X < Q3 Z, max X < max Y < max Z

b. Compare the ranges for each of the three distributions.

range X < range Y < range Z

c. Which distribution do you think has the least variability? Explain.

X has the smaller range, hence appears less variable over the entire data. Y has the least variability over its middle 50%, but without the standard deviation it is difficult to decide.

EXERCISES

Work the following exercises. Then check your work by using the statistics features of your calculator.

1. Consider the following data: 5 8 2 1 7 1

Determine the standard deviation by filling in the table as part of your calculation.

x_i	$\bar{x}$	$x - \bar{x}$	$(x - \bar{x})^2$
5	4	1	1
8	4	4	16
2	4	−2	4
1	4	−3	9
7	4	3	9
1	4	−3	9

$$\sigma = \sqrt{\frac{\Sigma(x - \bar{x})^2}{n}} = \sqrt{\tfrac{48}{6}} = \sqrt{8} = 2.83$$

2. Eight adults are surveyed and asked how many credit cards they possess. Their responses are 4, 0, 3, 1, 5, 2, 2, and 3. Determine the standard deviation for these data. Fill in the table as part of your calculation.

x_i	$\bar{x}$	$x - \bar{x}$	$(x - \bar{x})^2$
4	2.5	1.5	2.25
0	2.5	−2.5	6.25
3	2.5	0.5	0.25
1	2.5	−1.5	2.25
5	2.5	2.5	6.25
2	2.5	−0.5	0.25
2	2.5	−0.5	0.25
3	2.5	0.5	0.25

$$\sigma = \sqrt{\frac{\Sigma(x - \bar{x})^2}{n}} = \sqrt{\tfrac{18}{8}} = \sqrt{2.25} = 1.5$$

Exercise numbers appearing in color are answered in the Selected Answers section of this book.

3. A student takes ten exams during a semester and receives the following grades: 90, 85, 97, 76, 89, 58, 82, 102, 70, and 67. Find the five-number summary.

58, 70, 83.5, 90, 102

4. In a two-semester music course, you are required to attend 12 concerts. Last season, the lengths of the concerts were 92, 101, 98, 112, 80, 119, 92, 90, 116, 106, 78, and 65 minutes. Find the five-number summary for these data. Decide on a scale and draw a boxplot.

65, 85, 95, 109, 119

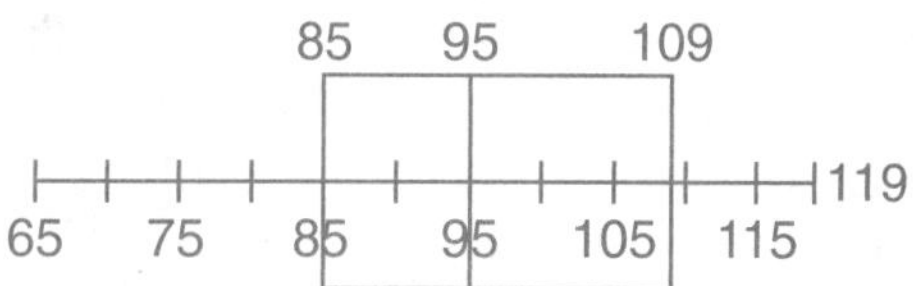

5. The weights, in pounds, of a group of workers are as follows:

173 123 171 175 188 120 177 160 151 169 162 128 145
140 158 132 202 162 154 180 164 166 157 171 175

Find the five-number summary for these data. Decide on a scale and draw a boxplot.

120, 148, 162, 174, 202

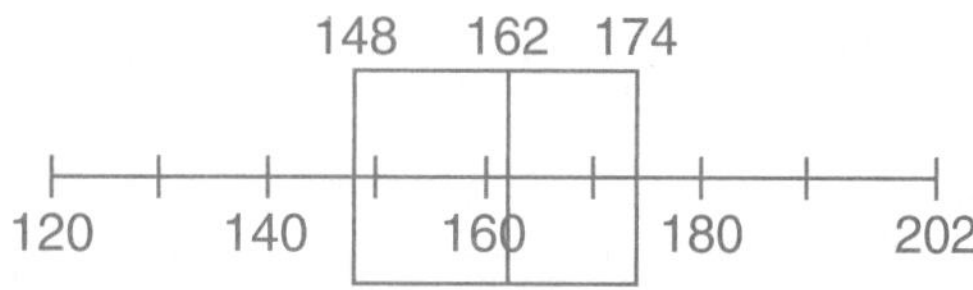

6. The following speeds of 21 cars are recorded as they pass a concealed marker on an interstate highway that has a legal speed limit of 65 mph: 73, 67, 69, 65, 64, 77, 59, 74, 71, 67, 70, 58, 67, 69, 71, 70, 69, 64, 85, 67, and 64. Find the five-number summary.

58, 64.5, 69, 71, 85

7. Joe DiMaggio played center field for the New York Yankees for 13 years. Mickey Mantle, who played for 18 years, succeeded him. Here is the number of home runs by DiMaggio and Mantle.

DiMaggio: 29, 46, 32, 30, 31, 30, 21, 25, 20, 39, 14, 32, 12

Mantle: 13, 23, 21, 27, 37, 52, 34, 42, 31, 40, 54, 30, 15, 35, 19, 23, 22, 18

a. Compute the five-number summary for each player.

	Min	Q_1	Median	Q_3	Max
DiMaggio:	12	20.5	30	32	46
Mantle:	13	21	28.5	37	54

b. Using the same scale, draw a box-and-whisker plot for each player. (Draw one boxplot above the other.)

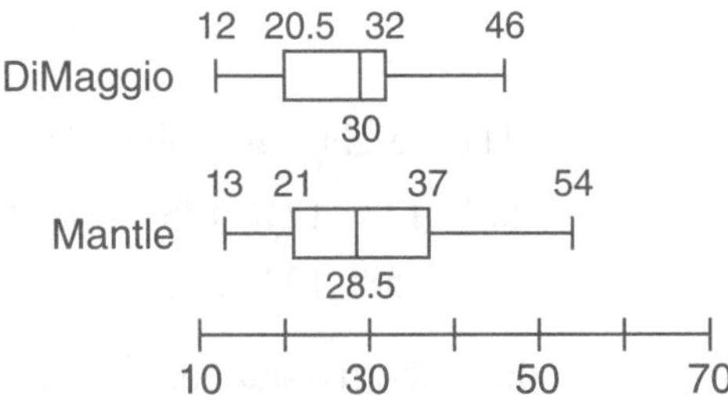

c. Discuss the similarities or differences of the two boxplots.

Mantle's home run distribution is more variable and more evenly spread out.

8. Given the following boxplots of three distributions, which do you think will have the smallest standard deviation?

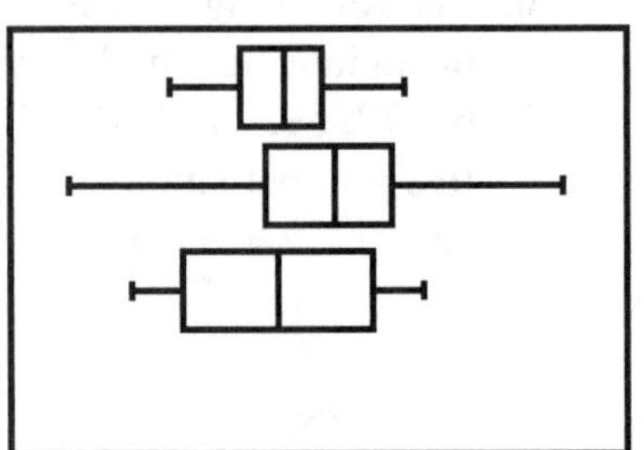

The first distribution has the smallest standard deviation since it is less spread out both in its range and over the middle 50%.

What Have I Learned?

1. What are the four common measures of central tendency for a frequency distribution?

   mean, median, mode, and midrange

2. If the mean is greater than the median for a frequency distribution, what would you conclude about the shape of the distribution?

   The distribution is probably skewed to the right.

3. If you flip a coin 50 times and get 22 tails, should you assume that the probability of getting tails with this coin is 0.44? Explain.

   No, since in only 50 flips 22 tails is fairly likely even if the coin is fair. 0.44 is close to 0.5.

4. What does the law of large numbers say about the relationship between theoretical and experimental probabilities?

   As an experiment is repeated more and more times, the experimental probability should get closer to the theoretical probability.

5. If a random experiment consists of rolling a six-sided die ten times, how many individual outcomes make up the sample space, and what is the probability of getting all sixes?

   By the multiplication principle, there are 6^{10} possible outcomes, only one of which is all sixes. So the probability of getting all sixes is $\left(\frac{1}{6}\right)^{10} = 0.0000000165$.

6. Could the function defined by this table be a probability function? Explain.

   No, because the sum of the probabilities is more than one.

x	1	2	3	4	5
$P(x)$	0.2	0.3	0.4	0.1	0.05

7. In calculating the standard deviation of a distribution, what is the reason for squaring the deviations from the mean?

Squaring the deviations is necessary so the negative deviations don't cancel out the positive deviations.

8. What characteristics of a five-number summary help describe the variability of a distribution?

The range and subranges between quartiles are readily seen.

How Can I Practice?

1. The following table displays the annual salaries and years of education for a cross section of the population. Complete the totals for each category. Then calculate the relative frequency for each entry.

EDUCATION	LESS THAN $20,000		$20,000 < SALARY < $50,000		$50,000 < SALARY < $100,000		MORE THAN $100,000		TOTAL	
12 years	130	0.079	146	0.081	41	0.025	4	0.002	321	0.195
14 years	105	0.064	198	0.120	52	0.032	10	0.006	365	0.221
16 years	31	0.019	252	0.153	187	0.113	24	0.015	494	0.300
More than 16	6	0.004	161	0.098	241	0.146	60	0.036	468	0.284
Total	272	0.165	757	0.459	521	0.316	98	0.059	1648	

a. If an individual is selected at random, use the corresponding relative frequencies to estimate the probability that the person has:

i. 12 years of education and makes more than $100,000.

P(12 yrs and more than $100,000) = 0.002

ii. 14 years of education and makes less than $20,000.

P(14 yrs and less than $20,000) = 0.064

iii. more than 16 years of education and makes more than $50,000.

P(more than 16 yrs and more than $50,000) = 0.146 + 0.036 = 0.182

b. Given that the individual chosen has 14 years of education, what is the probability that he or she makes more than $50,000?

Given 14 years, P(more than $50,000) = 62/365 = 0.17

c. Given that the individual chosen has 16 or more years of education, what is the probability that she or he makes more than $50,000?

Given 16 or more years,

$$P(\text{more than } \$50{,}000) = \frac{187 + 24 + 241 + 60}{494 + 468} = \frac{512}{962} = 0.532$$

Exercise numbers appearing in color are answered in the Selected Answers section of this book.

2. A vase contains 35 marbles: 10 blue, 8 green, 7 yellow, 5 red, and 5 white. One marble is selected at random. Find the following probabilities.

a. *P*(red)

$P(\text{red}) = \frac{5}{35} = \frac{1}{7}$

b. *P*(not blue)

$P(\text{Not blue}) = \frac{25}{35} = \frac{5}{7}$

c. *P*(green or white)

$P(\text{green or white}) = \frac{13}{35}$

d. *P*(black)

$P(\text{black}) = 0$

e. *P*(not black)

$P(\text{Not black}) = 1$

3. If a six-sided die is rolled four times, how many different four-digit sequences are possible?

$6^4 = 1296$

4. If a six-sided die is rolled three times, how many branches will be in the tree that displays the sample space?

$6^3 = 216$

5. If a coin is flipped four times, determine the probability function for the number of tails.

x, THE NUMBER OF TAILS	0	1	2	3	4
P(*x*)	$\frac{1}{16}$	$\frac{4}{16}$	$\frac{6}{16}$	$\frac{4}{16}$	$\frac{1}{16}$

6. If a license plate consists of three letters (excluding I and O) followed by three digits (excluding 0 and 1), how many different plates are possible?

$24^3 8^3 = 7{,}077{,}888$

7. You have ten books to arrange on your bookshelf. How many different orderings of all ten books are possible?

$10! = 3{,}628{,}800$

8. Consider the following data: 12, 8, 9, 10, 12, 9

Determine the standard deviation by filling in the table as part of your calculation.

x	$\bar{x}$	$x - \bar{x}$	$(x - \bar{x})^2$
12	10	2	4
8	10	−2	4
9	10	−1	1
10	10	0	0
12	10	2	4
9	10	−1	1

$$\sigma = \sqrt{\frac{\Sigma(x - x)^2}{n}} = \sqrt{\tfrac{14}{6}} = 1.53$$

9. The following speeds of 21 cars are recorded as they pass a concealed marker on an interstate highway that has a legal speed limit of 65 mph: 73, 67, 69, 65, 64, 77, 59, 74, 71, 67, 70, 58, 67, 69, 71, 70, 69, 64, 85, 67, and 64. Find the five-number summary and produce the boxplot.

58, 64.5, 69, 71, 85

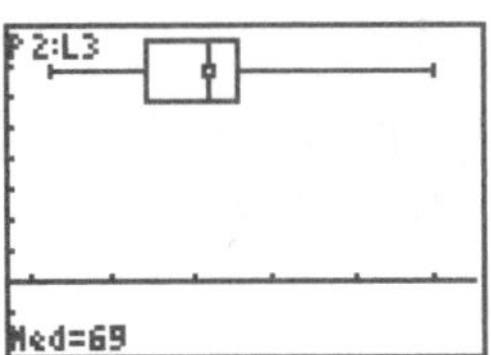

Xmin = 58
Q_1 = 64.5
Med = 69
Q_3 = 71
Xmax = 85

CHAPTER 1

Gateway Review

1. Determine whether each of the following is a function.

   a. The loudness of the stereo system is a function of the position of the sound dial.

   Yes, it is a function.

   b. $\{(2, 9)\ (3, 10)\ (2, -9)\}$

   No, it is not a function. There are two different outputs paired with 2.

   c. 

   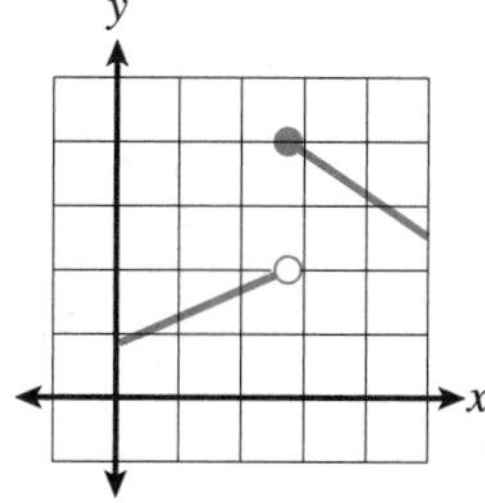

   Yes, it is a function.

2. For an average yard, the fertilizer costs \$20. You charge \$8 per hour to do yard work. If x represents the number of hours worked on the yard and $f(x)$ represents the total cost, including fertilizer, complete the following table.

x	0	2	3	5	7
$f(x)$	20	36	44	60	76

   a. Is the total cost a function of the hours worked? Explain.

   Yes, for each input there is one output.

   b. Which variable represents the input?

   The input is x, the number of hours worked.

   c. Which is the dependent variable?

   The dependent variable is $f(x)$, the total cost.

   d. Which value(s) of the domain would not be realistic for this situation? Explain.

   Negative values would not be realistic domain values. A negative number of hours worked does not make sense.

   e. What is the rate of change from 0 to 3?

   The rate of change is 8.

   f. What is the rate of change from 5 to 7?

   The rate of change is 8.

g. What can you say about the rate of change between any two of the points?

The rate of change between any two points is 8.

h. What kind of relationship exists between the two variables?

The relationship is linear.

i. Write this relationship in symbolic form.

$f(x) = 8x + 20$

j. What is the practical meaning of the slope in this situation?

The slope is the hourly rate I charge.

k. What is the vertical intercept? What is the practical meaning of this point?

(0, 20) is the vertical intercept. This represents the fertilizer cost.

l. Find $f(4)$.

$f(4) = 8(4) + 20 = 52$

m. For what value(s) of x does $f(x) = 92$? Explain.

$8x + 20 = 92$ or $8x = 72$ or $x = 9$

3. Let $f(x) = x^2 - 5x$ and let $g(x) = -3x + 4$. Evaluate each of the following.

a. $f(-2)$ and $g(-2)$

$f(-2) = 14$, $g(-2) = 10$

b. $f(3) + g(3)$

$-6 + (-5) = -11$

c. $f(-3) - g(-4)$

$24 - 16 = 8$

d. $f(-4) \cdot g(2)$

$36(-2) = -72$

4. Which of the following sets of data represent a linear function?

a.

x	0	2	4	6	8
f(x)	14	22	30	38	46

Linear.

b.

x	5	10	15	20	25
y	4	2	0	−2	−4

Linear.

c.

x	1	3	4	6	7
g(x)	10	20	30	40	50

Not linear.

d.

t	0	10	20	30	40
d	143	250	357	464	571

Linear.

5. **a.** Determine the slope of the line through the points (5, −3) and (−4, 9).

$m = \frac{9 + 3}{-4 - 5} = \frac{12}{-9} = -\frac{4}{3}$

b. From the equation $3x - 7y = 21$, determine the slope.

$7y = 3x - 21 \qquad m = \frac{3}{7}$

c. Determine the slope of the line from the graph.

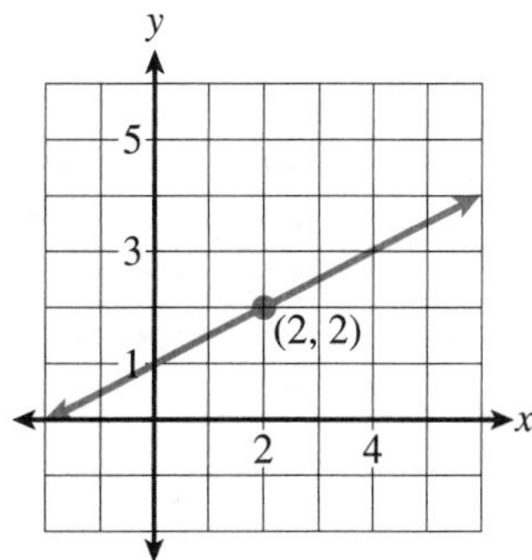

$m = \frac{1}{2}$

6. Write the equation of the line described in each of the following.

a. A slope of 0 and passing through the point (2, 4)

$y = 4$

b. A slope of 2 and a vertical intercept of (0, 5)

$y = 2x + 5$

c. A slope of −3 and passing through the point (6, −14)

$-14 = -3(6) + b,\ b = 4,\ y = -3x + 4$

d. A slope of 2 and passing through the point (7, −2)

$-2 = 2(7) + b,\ b = -16,\ y = 2x - 16$

e. A line with no slope passing through the point (2, −3)

$x = 2$

f. A slope of −5 and a horizontal intercept of (4, 0)

$0 = -5(4) + b,\ b = 20,\ y = -5x + 20$

g. A line passing through the points (−3, −4) and (2, 16)

$m = \frac{16 + 4}{2 + 3} = \frac{20}{5} = 4;\ 16 = 4(2) + b,\ b = 8,\ y = 4x + 8$

h. A line parallel to $y = -\frac{1}{2}x$ and passing through the point (0, 5)

$y = -\frac{1}{2}x + 5$

7. Given the following graph of the function, determine the equation of the line.

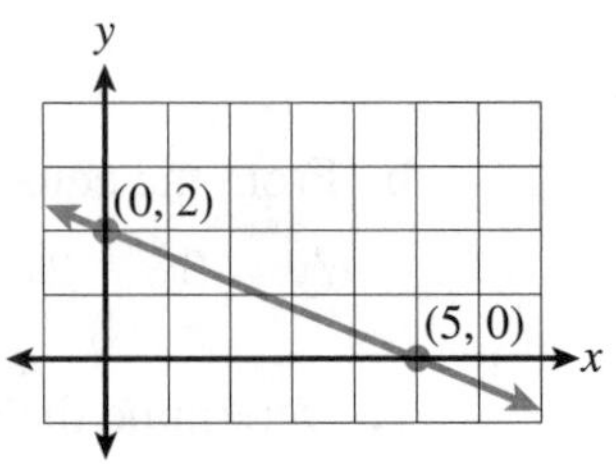

$y = -\frac{2}{5}x + 2$

8. **a.** The building where your sweet shop is located is ten years old and has a value of \$200,000. When the building was one year old, its value was \$290,000. Assuming that the building's depreciation is linear, express the value of the building as a function *f* of its age, *x*, in years.

   $f(x) = 300{,}000 - 10{,}000x$

   b. What is the slope of the line? What is the practical meaning of the slope in this situation?

   $m = -10{,}000$. The building depreciates \$10,000 per year.

   c. What is the vertical intercept? What is the practical meaning of the vertical intercept in this situation?

   (0, 300,000) The original value is \$300,000.

   d. What is the horizontal intercept? What is the practical meaning of the horizontal intercept in this situation?

   (30, 0) It takes 30 years for the building to fully depreciate.

9. Determine the vertical intercept of the following functions. Solve for *y* if necessary.

   a. $y = 2x - 3$

   $(0, -3)$

   b. $y = -3$

   $(0, -3)$

   c. $x - y = 3$

   $(0, -3)$

   d. What relationship do the graphs of these functions have to one another?

   The graphs all intersect at the point $(0, -3)$.

   e. Use your grapher to graph the functions in parts a–c on the same coordinate axes. Compare your results with part d.

   The results are the same.

10. Determine the slopes and y-intercepts of each of the following functions. Solve for y if necessary.

a. $y = -2x + 1$

$m = -2$; (0, 1)

b. $2x + y = -1$

$m = -2$; (0, −1)

c. $-4x - 2y = 6$

$m = -2$; (0, −3)

d. What relationship do the graphs of these functions have to one another?

The graphs are parallel lines.

e. Use your grapher to graph the functions in parts a–c on the same coordinate axes. Compare your results with part d.

11. Determine the slopes and y-intercepts of each of the following functions. Solve for y if necessary.

a. $y = -3x + 2$

$m = -3$, (0, 2)

b. $3x + y = 2$

$m = -3$, (0, 2)

c. $6x + 2y = 4$

$m = -3$, (0, 2)

d. What relationship do the graphs of these functions have to one another?

The graphs are all the same.

e. For two lines to be parallel to each other, what has to be the same?

The slopes.

f. For two lines to lie on top of each other (coincide), what has to be the same?

The slopes and the y-intercepts.

g. Use your grapher to graph the functions in parts a–c on the same coordinate axes. Compare your results with part d.

The results are the same.

12. a. Graph the function defined by $y = -2x + 150$. Indicate the vertical and horizontal intercepts. Make sure to include some negative values of x.

(0, 150) (75, 0)

b. Using your grapher, verify the graph you have drawn in part a.

c. Using the graph, determine the domain and range of the function.

The domain and range are all reals.

d. Assume that a 150-pound person starts a diet and loses 2 pounds per week for four weeks. Write the equation modeling this situation.

$w(t) = -2t + 150$

e. Compare the equation you found in part d with the one given in part a.

They are the same.

f. What is the practical meaning of the vertical and horizontal intercepts you found in part a?

The vertical intercept is (0, 150). It indicates the person's initial weight of 150 pounds. The horizontal intercept (75, 0) indicates that after 75 weeks of weight loss, the person weighs nothing.

g. What is the practical domain and range of this function for the situation given in part d?

The practical domain is $0 \leq t \leq 15$. The practical range is $120 \leq w(t) \leq 150$.

13. a. You pay a flat fee of $5 per month for your trash to be picked up, and it doesn't matter how many bags of trash you have. Use x to represent the number of bags of trash, and write a function f in symbolic form to represent the total cost of your trash for the month.

$f(x) = 5$

b. Sketch the graph of this function.

Horizontal line through (0, 5).

c. What is the slope of the line?

The slope is 0.

14. Sketch the graph of the following piecewise function.

$$f(x) = \begin{cases} 4x, & x < -2 \\ -x + 3, & -2 \leq x < 1 \\ 5, & x \leq 1 \end{cases}$$

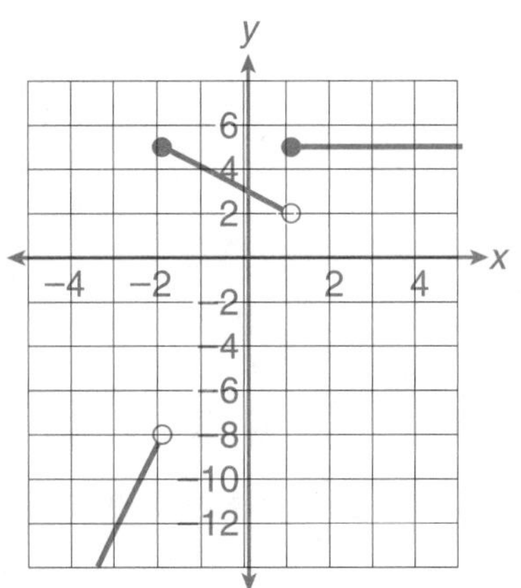

15. You work as a special events salesperson for a golf course owned by your city. Your salary is based on the following. You receive a flat salary of \$1500 per month for sales of \$10,000 or less; for the next \$30,000 of sales, you receive your salary plus 2% of the sales; and for any sales exceeding \$40,000, you receive your salary and your commission changes to 4% of sales.

a. Write a piecewise function *f* that specifies the total monthly salary when *x* represents the amount of sales for the month.

$$f(x) = \begin{cases} 1500 & x \le 10{,}000 \\ 1500 + 0.02x & 10{,}000 < x \le 40{,}000 \\ 1500 + 0.04x & x > 40{,}000 \end{cases}$$

b. Graph the function on your grapher.

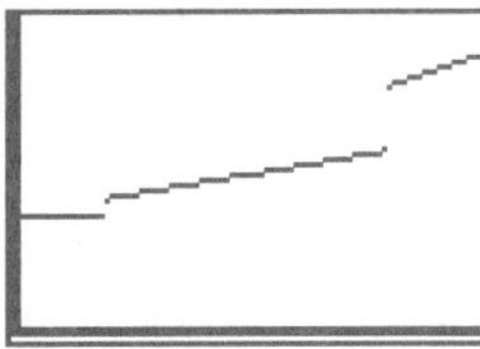

Xmin = 0, Xmax = 50, 000, Ymin = 0, Ymax = 4000, Xscl = 100

c. What is your salary if your sales are \$25,000?

$f(25, 000) = 1500 + 0.02(25, 000) = 2000$

d. You need to make \$3150 to cover your expenses this month. What will your sales have to be for your salary to be that amount?

$1500 + 0.04x = 3150,\ 0.04x = 1650,\ x = 41, 250$

16. During the years 1994–1998, the number of finishers in the top 30 marathons worldwide has increased. The following table gives the total number of finishers (to the nearest hundred) each year, where $t = 0$ represents the year 1994.

t	0	1	2	3	4
NUMBER OF FINISHERS, *n*	7800	9100	10,000	10,900	12,100

a. Enter the data from your table into your calculator. Determine the linear regression equation model and write the result.

$y = 1040x + 7900$ or $t(n) = 1040n + 7900$

b. What is the slope of the regression line? What is the practical meaning of the slope in this situation?

1040; The number of finishers increased at a rate of 1040 per year.

c. What is the vertical intercept? What is the practical meaning of the vertical intercept in this situation?

(0, 7900) The model indicates there were 7900 finishers in the year 1994.

d. Use your grapher to graph the regression line in the same screen as the scatterplot. How well do you think the line fits the data?

Pretty good.

e. Use your regression model to determine the number of finishers worldwide in the year 2000.

14,140

f. Did you use interpolation or extrapolation to determine your result in part e? Explain.

I used extrapolation because I am predicting outside the original data.

g. Do you think that the prediction in the year 2024 will be as accurate as that in 2000? Explain.

No, 2024 is farther from the data than 2000. The farther removed we are from the data, the more likely our prediction is incorrect.

17. Solve the systems of equations. Solve at least one algebraically and at least one graphically.

a. $3x - y = 10$

$5x + 2y = 13$

$3x - 10 = y$

$5x + 2(3x - 10) = 13$

$5x + 6x - 20 = 13$

$11x = 33, x = 3$

$y = 9 - 10 = -1$

$(3, -1)$

b. $4x + 2y = 8$

$x - 3y = -19$

$x = -19 + 3y$

$4(-19 + 3y) + 2y = 8$

$-76 + 12y + 2y = 8$

$14y = 84, y = 6$

$x = -19 + 18 = -1$

$(-1, 6)$

c. $2x + y = 10$

$y = -2x + 13$

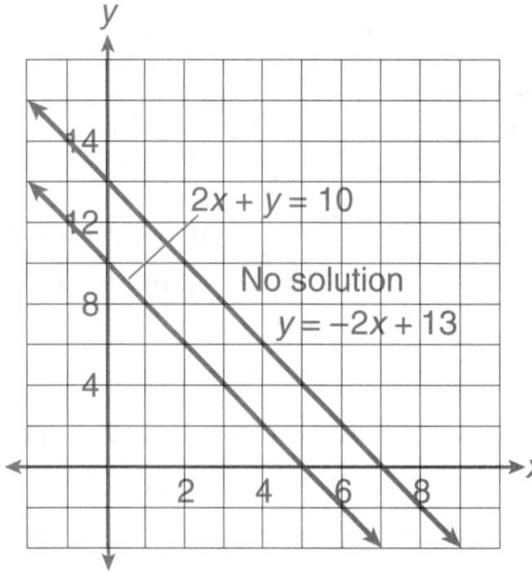

d. $2x + 6y = 4$

$x + 3y = 2$

$x = -3y + 2$

$2(-3y + 2) + 6y = 4$

$-6y + 4 + 6y = 4$

$4 = 4$

Dependent system.

18. The employees of a beauty salon order lunch two days in a row from the corner deli. Lunch on the first day consists of 5 small pizzas and 6 cookies for a total of \$27. On the second day, 8 pizzas are ordered along with 4 cookies, totaling \$39. To know how much money to pay, employees have to determine how much each pizza and each cookie cost. How much does the deli charge for each pizza and each cookie?

$x =$ cost of one pizza

$y =$ cost of one cookie

$5x + 6y = 27$

$8x + 4y = 39$

$40x + 48y = 216$
$-40x - 20y = -195$
$28y = 21$
$y = 0.75$

$5x + 4.50 = 27$
$5x = 22.50$
$x = 4.50$

19. Solve these 3×3 systems of linear equations.

a. $x + y + z = 3$
$2x - y + 2z = 3$
$3x + 2y - z = 0$

$3x + 3z = 6$
$x - 3z = -6$
$4x = 0; x = 0$
$(0, 1, 2)$

$y + z = 3$
$-y + 2z = 3$
$3z = 6$
$z = 2; y = 1$

b. $2x + 4y - z = -2$
$x - 2y + z = -5$
$-2x + y + 2z = 7$

$3x + 2y = -7$
$2x + 9y = 3$
$6x + 4y = -14$
$-6x - 27y = -9$
$-23y = -23; y = 1$
$-3 - 2 + z = -5$
$(-3, 1, 0)$

$3x + 2 = -7$
$3x = -9$
$x = -3$

c. $4x - 2y + z = 1$
$2x + 6y - z = 3$
$-3x + 4y + z = -1$

$6x + 4y = 4$
$-x + 10y = 2$
$-15x - 10y = -10$
$-16x = -8; x = 0.5$
$(0.5, 0.25, -0.5)$

$3 + 4y = 4$
$4y = 1; y = 0.25$
$2 - 0.5 + z = 1$
$z = -0.5$

d. $3x - 4y - z = -1$
$4x + y - 5z = 10$
$-x + 2y + z = 11$

$2x - 2y = 10$
$-x + 11y = 65$
$x - y = 5$
$10y = 70; y = 7; x = 12; z = 9$
$(12, 7, 9)$

20. Your favorite photography studio advertises a family portrait special in the newspaper. There are three different print sizes available: small (3 by 5), medium (5 by 7) and large (8 by 10). There are three different packages that can be ordered.

Number of Prints

PACKAGE	SMALL	MEDIUM	LARGE	TOTAL COST
A	4	2	1	\$6
B	6	4	2	\$11
C	10	6	4	\$19

a. Normally, small prints sell for \$0.65 per print, medium for \$1.10, and large for \$2.50. Decide whether you are getting a good deal by determining the cost per print of each size print.

x = cost of a small print
y = cost of a medium print
z = cost of a large print

$$-8x - 4y - 2z = -12$$
$$6x + 4y + 2z = 11$$
$$-2x = -1$$

$$2y + z = 4$$
$$6y + 4z = 14$$

$$4x + 2y + z = 6$$
$$6x + 4y + 2z = 11$$
$$10x + 6y + 4z = 19$$

$$-8y - 4z = -16$$
$$x = 0.50$$
$$2 + 2y + z = 6$$
$$5 + 6y + 4z = 19$$

$$-2y = -2$$
$$y = 1, z = 2$$

Yes, this is a good deal.

b. Will you take advantage of the special? Explain.

Answers will vary. I would not take advantage of this. I don't give away many pictures.

21. a. Sketch the graph of $f(x) = |x + 2|$.

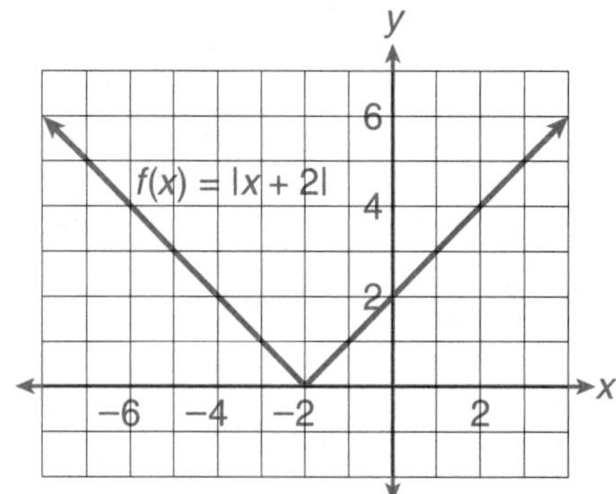

b. Determine the interval over which the function is increasing. Over which interval is the function decreasing?

Increasing $x > -2$, decreasing $x < -2$

c. Determine the domain of the function.

Domain is all real numbers.

d. Determine the range of the function.

Range is $y \geq 0$

e. Graph $g(x) = -|x + 2|$. How does the graph compare with the graph in part a?

g is the reflection through the x-axis.

f. Let $h(x) = |x| + 2$. Explain what makes the functions $f(x)$ and $h(x)$ similar. How are the functions different?

f shifts the graph of $y = |x|$ two units to the left. h shifts the graph of $y = |x|$ two units up.

22. Solve the following equations.

a. $|x - 23| = 5$

$x - 23 = 5$ or $x - 23 = -5$
$x = 28$ or $x = 18$

b. $|x + 12| = 7$

$x + 12 = 7$ or $x + 12 = -7$
$x = -5$ or $x = -19$

c. $|2x - 5| = 6$

$2x - 5 = 6$ or $2x - 5 = -6$
$x = \frac{11}{2}$ or $x = -\frac{1}{2}$

d. $|3 - 5x| = 2$

$3 - 5x = 2$ or $3 - 5x = -2$
$x = \frac{1}{5}$ or $x = 1$

23. Solve the following inequalities graphically. Express your solutions both as inequalities and graphically on a number line.

a. $|x - 2.5| \le 0.2$

$2.3 \le x \le 2.7$

2.3 2.7

b. $|x + 5| > 2$

$x > -3$ or $x < -7$

−7 −3

c. $|2x - 9| < 3$

$3 < x < 6$

3 6

d. $|18 + 3x| \le 2$

$-\frac{20}{3} \le x \le -\frac{16}{3}$

$\frac{-20}{3}$ $\frac{-16}{3}$

24. To pass inspection, a bag of strawberry twists must be within 8 grams of the target weight of 453 grams.

a. Express this statement in symbolic form using absolute value.

$|x - 453| \le 8$

b. Determine the solution to the inequality in part a.

$445 \le x \le 461$

25. The weights, in pounds, of a group of workers are as follows:

173	123	171	175	188	120	177	160	151	169
162	128	145	140	158	132	202	162	154	180
164	166	157	171	175					

Determine the mean, standard deviation, and five-number summary for these data. Decide on a scale and draw a boxplot. Check your answers with your grapher.

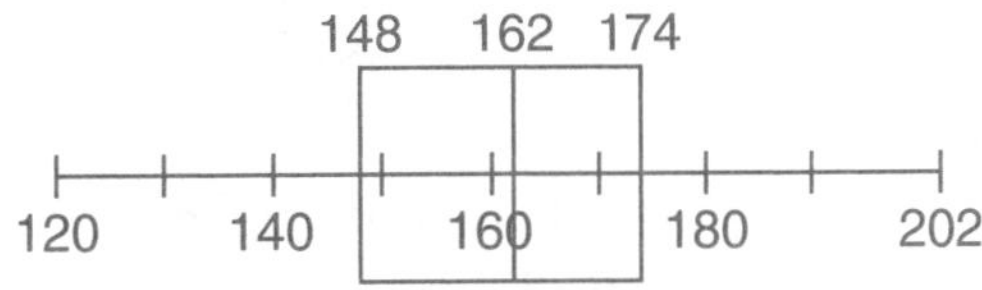

Mean is 160.12; Standard deviation is 19.8. min is 120, $Q_1 = 148$, median $= 162$, $Q_3 = 174$, max $= 202$

26. **a.** Determine the mean, median, mode, and midrange for this collection of class test scores:

88	82	97	76	79	92	65	84	79
90	75	82	78	77	93	88	95	73
69	89	93	78	60	95	88	72	80
94	88	74						

Mean is 82.4, median is 82, midrange is 78.5.

b. From these measures of central tendency, would you guess that the distribution is symmetrical, skewed to the left, or skewed to the right? Check your answer by displaying the histogram and/or boxplot on your grapher.

The distribution is skewed to the right.

27. The following table summarizes characteristics of registered voters in a small town district.

	REPUBLICAN	DEMOCRAT	REFORM	UNAFFILIATED	TOTAL
FEMALE	156	192	23	41	412
MALE	177	160	45	28	410
TOTAL	333	352	68	69	822

If one voter is selected at random, determine the following probabilities.

a. *P*(Democrat)

$\frac{352}{822} = .43$

b. *P*(male)

$\frac{410}{822} = .50$

c. *P*(female Republican)

$\frac{156}{822} = .19$

d. *P*(male Reform)

$\frac{45}{822} = .05$

e. *P*(not Republican)

$1 - \frac{333}{822} = \frac{489}{822} = .59$

f. Given the person selected is male, *P*(Reform)

$\frac{45}{410} = .11$

28. A box of candies contains 25 red, 40 green, 30 yellow, and 50 brown candies. If one candy is selected at random, determine the following probabilities.

a. P(red)

$\frac{25}{145} = .17$

b. P(yellow or brown)

$\frac{80}{145} = .55$

c. P(not green)

$\frac{105}{145} = .72$

d. P(blue)

0

29. A fair coin is flipped three times.

a. Display the sample space for this experiment.

{*HHH, HHT, HTH, HTT, THH, THT, TTH, TTT*}

b. Let the input variable x be the number of heads. Complete this table for the corresponding probability function.

NUMBER OF HEADS, x	$P(x)$
0	$\frac{1}{8}$
1	$\frac{3}{8}$
2	$\frac{3}{8}$
3	$\frac{1}{8}$

30. You have narrowed your vacation reading list to ten books. But you really only have time to read three of them. In how many ways can you choose the three books, assuming that you will also pick the order in which you will read them?

$10 \cdot 9 \cdot 8 = 720$

31. How many eight-digit serial numbers are possible if they cannot start with 0 or 1?

$8 \cdot 10 \cdot 10 \cdot 10 \cdot 10 \cdot 10 \cdot 10 \cdot 10 = 8 \cdot 10^7 = 80{,}000{,}000$

CHAPTER 2

The Algebra of Functions

CLUSTER 1

Addition, Subtraction, and Multiplication of Functions

ACTIVITY 2.1

Spending and Earning Money

Topic: *Addition, Subtraction, and Constant Multiples of Functions*

You are planning a trip with friends and are going to rent a van. The van you want rents for \$75 per day. You are given 100 free miles each day and are charged \$0.20 per mile for extra miles. The dealer claims that you can expect to average 25 miles per gallon. The Auto Club says that you can expect to pay an average of \$1.35 per gallon for gas on your trip. You plan to be gone for eight days, and you have been assigned the job of estimating the total cost of operating the van for the trip. You know that you will be traveling at least 1000 miles.

1. Determine a function rule for the cost $f(m)$ of renting the van as a function of the miles m traveled over the eight-day period. (Note that with 100 free miles each day, you have 800 free miles for the trip.)

$f(m) = 0.2(m - 800) + 600 = 0.2m + 440$

The cost of the fuel also depends on the total number of miles m traveled. The rental agency will start you with a full tank, but expects a full tank when you return.

2. Determine a function rule for the cost $g(m)$ of the fuel as a function of the miles m traveled over the eight-day period. (Be careful. Analyze your units.)

$g(m) = 1.35\left(\frac{m}{25}\right) = 0.054m$

3. a. Combine the equations in Problems 1 and 2 to define the total cost $C(m)$ of using the van as a function of the miles traveled.

$C(m) = f(m) + g(m) = 0.254m + 440$

b. What is the practical domain of your function?

$1000 \leq m \leq 2000$. The 2000 value may vary.

This situation involves the addition of functions. The total cost function found in Problem 3 is called the **sum function.** The notation is

$$C(m) = (f + g)(m) = f(m) + g(m)$$

IMPORTANT NOTE: The notation $(f + g)(m)$ does *not* represent multiplication by m. The notation $(f + g)(m)$ is another way of writing $f(m) + g(m)$.

4. a. Using f, g, and C as defined in the first three problems, complete the following table.

m	$f(m)$	$g(m)$	$C(m) = (f + g)(m)$
1000	640	54	694
1200	680	64.8	744.8
1400	720	75.6	795.6
1600	760	86.4	846.4
1800	800	97.2	897.2

b. Based on the table, what is the relationship between $f(m)$, $g(m)$, and $C(m)$?

$C(m) = (f + g)(m) = f(m) + g(m)$

c. Use your grapher to plot all three functions, f, g, and C. Use the trace or table feature to complete the following table for four input values not used in part a. Answers will vary depending on choices of m.

m	$f(m)$	$g(m)$	$C(m)$
1250	690	67.50	757.50
904	620.80	48.82	669.62
1303	700.60	70.36	770.96
1675	775.00	90.45	865.45

d. Are the results in the table consistent with your conjecture in part b? Explain.

Yes, $f(m) + g(m) = (f + g)(m) = C(m)$.

You have returned from your trip, and now it's back to work. You are the owner of a small pet kennel. Your kennel can accommodate at most 20 dogs. Your current charge for boarding a dog is $12 per day. Utility bills are approximately $15 per day. The cost of feeding each dog, cleaning its stall, and exercising the animal is approximately $7.15 per day.

5. a. Suppose you let the number of dogs being boarded on a given day be represented by the input variable d. Determine an equation that expresses the total revenue R as a function of the number of dogs d boarded on a given day. Call this function f.

$R = f(d) = 12d$

b. Complete the following input/output table for the revenue function f.

d	0	5	10	15	20
$R = f(d)$	0	60	120	180	240

6. a. Determine an equation that expresses the total daily cost C involved in operating the kennel. Call this function g.

$C = g(d) = 15 + 7.15d$

b. Complete the following table for the daily cost function g.

d	0	5	10	15	20
$C = g(d)$	15	50.75	86.50	122.25	158

7. a. Use the output values from Problems 5b and 6b to complete the following table for the profit. Recall that profit = revenue − cost.

d	0	5	10	15	20
$P(d)$	−15	9.25	33.50	57.75	82

b. Using the function rules for revenue R and cost C in Problems 5a and 6a, determine a rule for the profit P as a function of d. Use the new function rule to verify some of the entries in the table in part a.

$P = (f - g)(d) = f(d) - g(d) = 4.85d - 15$

This situation involves the subtraction of functions. The profit function determined in Problem 7b is called the **difference function.** The notation is

$$P(d) = (f - g)(d) = f(d) - g(d)$$

8. Sketch the graphs of the functions R, C, and P on the following grid. Label the axes with the appropriate scales.

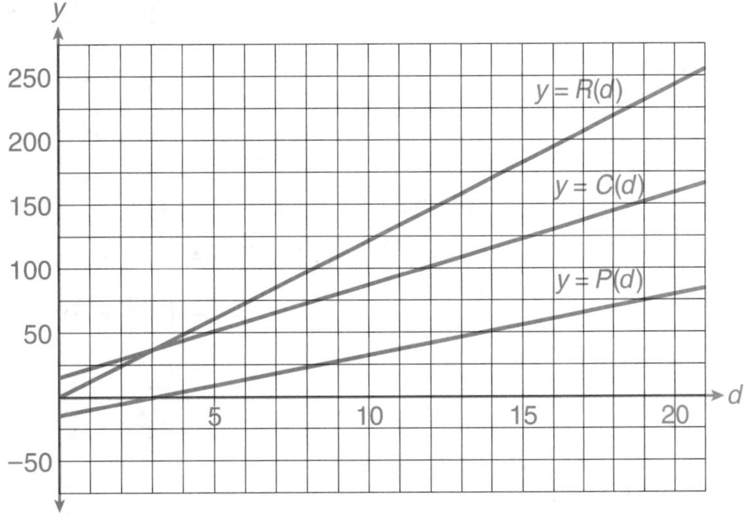

9. How many dogs need to be boarded to obtain a profit of at least \$50?

$$4.85d - 15 \geq 50$$
$$4.85d \geq 65$$
$$d \geq 13.4$$

At least 14 dogs are needed.

10. Determine the break-even point for your pet kennel business. That is, determine the number of dogs necessary for the profit to equal \$0.

$$4.85d - 15 = 0$$
$$4.85d = 15$$
$$d = 3.09$$

You will nearly break even with 3 dogs, but you need four dogs to break even.

SUMMARY

Given two functions f and g, the sum function $f + g$ is defined by

$$(f + g)(x) = f(x) + g(x)$$

and the difference function $f - g$ is defined by

$$(f - g)(x) = f(x) - g(x).$$

Similarly, for a constant c,

$$(c \cdot f)(x) = c \cdot f(x)$$

For example, suppose that f and g are defined as follows:

$$f(x) = 2x^2 + 3x - 5 \quad \text{and} \quad g(x) = -x^2 + 5x + 1.$$

Then

$$\begin{aligned}(f + g)(x) &= f(x) + g(x) \\ &= (2x^2 + 3x - 5) + (-x^2 + 5x + 1) \\ &= 2x^2 + 3x - 5 - x^2 + 5x + 1 \\ &= x^2 + 8x - 4.\end{aligned}$$

Similarly,

$$\begin{aligned}(f - g)(x) &= f(x) - g(x) \\ &= (2x^2 + 3x - 5) - (-x^2 + 5x + 1) \\ &= 2x^2 + 3x - 5 + x^2 - 5x - 1 \\ &= 3x^2 - 2x - 6\end{aligned}$$

and

$$\begin{aligned}(-5 \cdot f)(x) &= -5 \cdot f(x) \\ &= -5 \cdot \left(2x^2 + 3x - 5\right) \\ &= -10x^2 - 15x + 25.\end{aligned}$$

The functions f, g, $f + g$, $f - g$, and $-5 \cdot f$ are examples of a special family of functions called **polynomial functions.**

Any expression formed by adding or subtracting terms of the form ax^n, where a is a real number and n is a nonnegative integer, is called a **polynomial expression.**

A polynomial function is any function defined by an equation of the form $y = f(x)$, where $f(x)$ is a polynomial expression.

The addition, subtraction, and constant multiple of polynomial functions involve operations with polynomial expressions. For additional practice with adding and subtracting polynomials, see Appendix A.

EXERCISES

1. Jackie is a financial planner. In an effort to attract new customers, she sponsors a dinner at a local restaurant. The restaurant will charge \$100 for the banquet room plus \$12.50 per person for each meal. Jackie will pay these expenses herself. From past experience, Jackie knows that she can expect to make sales to approximately 15% of the people attending. She also knows that the average in sales she can expect from each new client is \$750, for which she receives a 13% commission. It is clear that Jackie's personal financial success depends on how many people she can attract to this dinner.

   a. Complete the following table.

x, NUMBER OF PEOPLE ATTENDING	COST OF BANQUET HALL	TOTAL MEAL COST	TOTAL COST
20	100	250	350
40	100	500	600
60	100	750	850
80	100	1000	1100
100	100	1250	1350

   b. Determine a formula for the total cost C of restaurant expenses as a function of x the number of attendees. Call this function f.

   $C = f(x) = 12.50x + 100$

Exercise numbers appearing in color are answered in the Selected Answers section of this book.

c. Complete the following table.

x, NUMBER OF PEOPLE ATTENDING	NUMBER OF NEW CUSTOMERS	TOTAL SALES	JACKIE'S COMMISSION
20	3	2250	292.50
40	6	4500	585
60	9	6750	877.50
80	12	9000	1170
100	15	11,250	1462.50

d. Determine a formula for the revenue R that Jackie can expect to generate from this dinner as a function of x the number of attendees. Call this function g.

$R = g(x) = 0.13(750)(0.15x) = 14.625x$

e. Combine the formulas in parts b and d to define a new function for the profit P that Jackie can expect from her dinner. A basic business equation is: profit = revenue − cost.

$P = R - C = (f - g)(x) = f(x) - g(x) = 14.625x - (12.50x + 100)$
$= 2.125x - 100$

f. What is the practical domain of this new function?

$0 \le x \le$ the number of people the banquet room will accommodate.

g. Using your new function, determine how many people must attend for Jackie to break even. Explain how you arrive at your answer.

Set $P(x) = 0$ and solve for x

$0 = 2.125x - 100$

$100 = 2.125x$

$x = 47.06$

48 people must attend.

h. Jackie hopes to make a profit of $500 on the dinner. How many people must attend for her to meet this goal? Explain.

Set the profit equal to 500 and solve for x:

$500 = 2.125x - 100$

$600 = 2.125x$

$x = 282.35$

283 must attend.

2. Suppose that f and g are defined by the following tables.

x	0	2	4	6	8	10
$f(x)$	3	−5	0	7	−1	4

x	0	2	4	6	8	10
$g(x)$	1	−1	1	−1	3	4

Complete the following table for $f + g$ and $f - g$.

x	0	2	4	6	8	10
$(f + g)(x)$	4	−6	1	6	2	8
$(f - g)(x)$	2	−4	−1	8	−4	0

3. **a.** Suppose that $f(x) = 4x + 1$ and $g(x) = -2x + 4$. Determine an algebraic expression for $(f - g)(x)$ by subtracting $g(x)$ from $f(x)$ and combining like terms.

$(f - g)(x) = (4x + 1) - (-2x + 4) = 4x + 1 + 2x - 4 = 6x - 3$

b. Complete the following table for f and g in part a.

x	$f(x)$	$g(x)$	$(f - g)(x)$
0	1	4	−3
2	9	0	9
4	17	−4	21
6	25	−8	33

c. Use your grapher to plot all three functions, f, g, and $f - g$. Use the trace or table feature to complete the following table for four input values not used in part b. Answers will vary depending on the choices of x.

x	$f(x)$	$g(x)$	$(f - g)(x)$
1	5	2	3
−1	−3	6	−9
2.5	11	−1	12
3.2	13.8	−2.4	16.2

d. Do the results in part c agree with your understanding of $f - g$? Explain.

Yes, $f(x) - g(x) = (f - g)(x)$

4. The algebraic skills needed for determining the algebraic form of the new functions are those of simplifying expressions and combining like terms. Simplify the following.

a. $(2x + 3) + (3x - 5)$

$5x - 2$

b. $(2x^2 - 3x + 1) - (x^2 - 6x + 9)$

$x^2 + 3x - 8$

c. $2(x + 9) - 3(x - 4)$

$-x + 30$

d. $14x - 9 - 3(x^2 + 2x - 2)$

$-3x^2 + 8x - 3$

e. $4(3x - 2) - (7 - 3x)$

$15x - 15$

f. $6x + 5 + 3(2 - 2x)$

11

g. $2x^2 + 5x - 3(3 - x^2)$

$5x^2 + 5x - 9$

h. $(5x - 2) - 2(3x^2 - 5x + 1)$

$-6x^2 + 15x - 4$

5. Given $f(x) = 3x - 5$ and $g(x) = -x^2 + 2x - 3$, determine a formula, in simplest form, for each of the following.

a. $(f + g)(x)$

$-x^2 + 5x - 8$

b. $(f - g)(x)$

$x^2 + x - 2$

c. $2f(x) + 3g(x)$

$-3x^2 + 12x - 19$

d. $f(x) - 2g(x)$

$2x^2 - x + 1$

6. Given $h(x) = 6$, $p(x) = 3 - 4x$ and $r(x) = 4x^2 - x - 6$, determine an expression, in simplest form, for each of the following.

a. $(r + h)(x)$

$4x^2 - x$

b. $(p + r)(x) - h(x)$

$4x^2 - 5x - 9$

c. $(h - p)(x)$

$3 + 4x$

d. $(r + p + h)(x)$

$4x^2 - 5x + 3$

ACTIVITY 2.2

Viewing the Algebra of Functions

Topic: *Adding and Subtracting Functions Graphically*

In Activity 2.1, Spending and Earning Money, you added and subtracted functions both algebraically and numerically. In this activity, you will explore the addition and subtraction of functions graphically.

Consider two functions defined by $f(x) = x - 3$ and $g(x) = 2$. If you enter these functions into your grapher with the standard window: Xmin $= -10$, Xmax $= 10$, Xscl $= 1$, Ymin $= -10$, Ymax $= 10$ and Yscl $= 1$, the graphs should resemble the following.

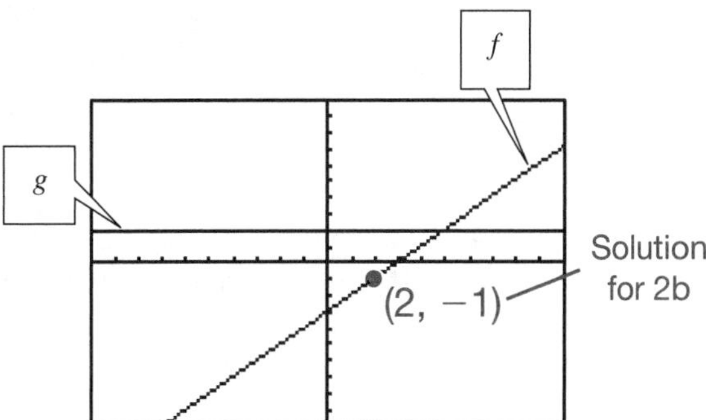

1. Determine the sum function $(f + g)(x)$ algebraically, and then graph it on your grapher with the graphs of f and g just shown. Your results should resemble the following.

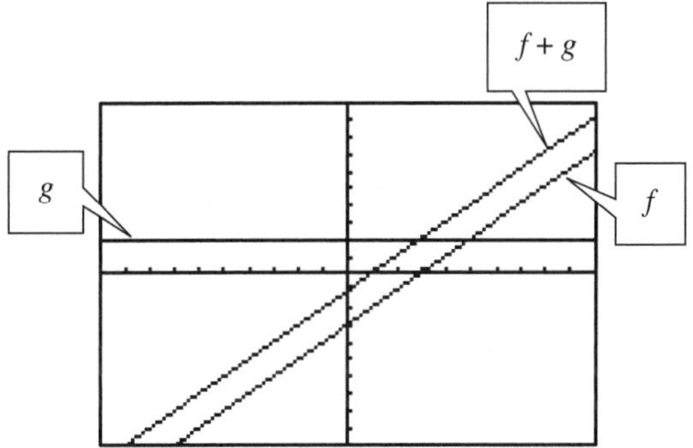

$(f + g)(x) = x - 1$

Let us investigate how the graph of the sum function $f + g$ can be determined from the graphs of f and g.

2. a. Using the definitions of f and g, determine each of the following.

$f(2) = 2 - 3 = -1$

$g(2) = 2$

$(f + g)(2) = f(2) + g(2) = -1 + 2 = 1$

b. What does the statement $f(2) = -1$ represent in the graph of f? Plot the point on the graph of f in Problem 1.

$f(2) = -1$ means that the point $(2, -1)$ is on the graph of f.

c. Plot $g(2) = 2$ and $(f + g)(2) = 1$ as points on the appropriate graph of f in Problem 1.

d. Explain how $(f + g)(2)$ can be determined using the graphs of f and g?

From the graph of f, the output at $x = 2$ is -1. From the graph of g the output at $x = 2$ is 2. The sum of these two values, 1, is the output for the sum function $f + g$ at $x = 2$.

3. Use the trace feature of your grapher and jump from f to g to $f + g$ for several specific values of x. What do you observe?

The conjecture given in Problem 2d is verified.

4. Use the table feature of your grapher to investigate f, g, and $f + g$ for several different values of x. What relationship do you observe between the output values of each of the three functions?

The same relationship as stated in Problem 3.

5. How do your observations in Problem 3 and 4 compare with your conjecture in Problem 2d?

The conjecture is the same.

> When you add two functions, you add the range (output) values for each different value of the domain (input).

6. a. Now suppose that $f(x) = 1.5x + 1$ and $g(x) = 1.5$. Determine an equation for $(f - g)$.

$(f - g)(x) = f(x) - g(x) = 1.5x - 0.5$

b. Graph all three functions on the following grid. Label the axes with the appropriate scales.

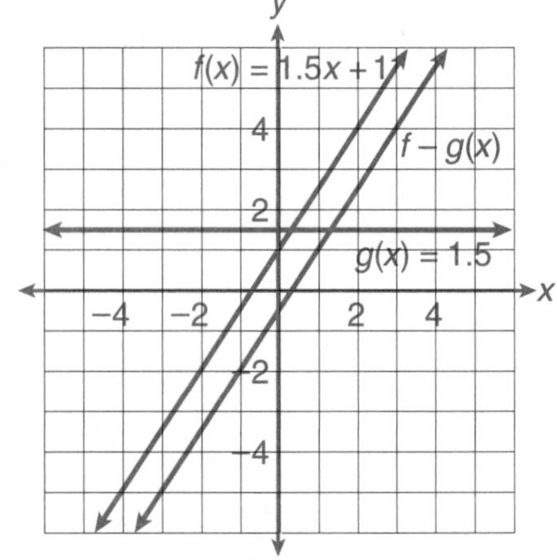

c. Is the graph of $f - g$ what you expected? Explain.

The graph, as expected, is 1.5 units below the graph of f.

7. The graphs of f and g are given in the following diagram.

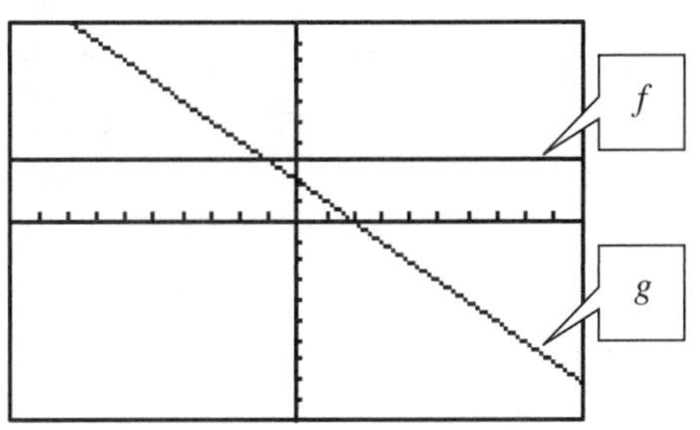

Which of the following graphs—a, b, or c—best represents the graph of $f + g$? Explain why you chose the graph you did.

a. 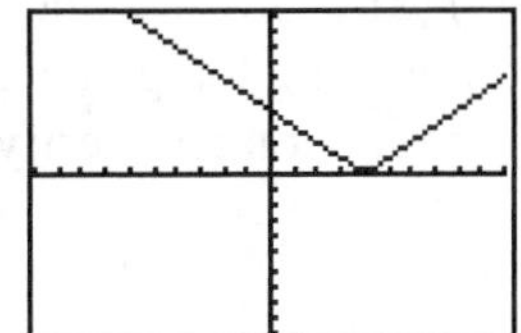

b. 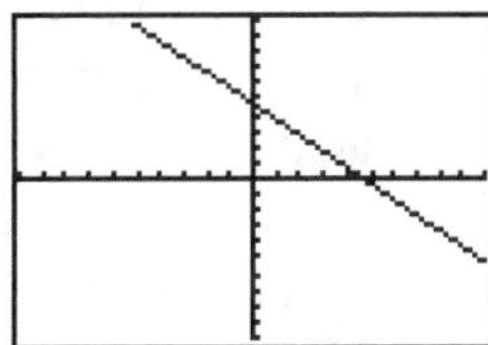

c. 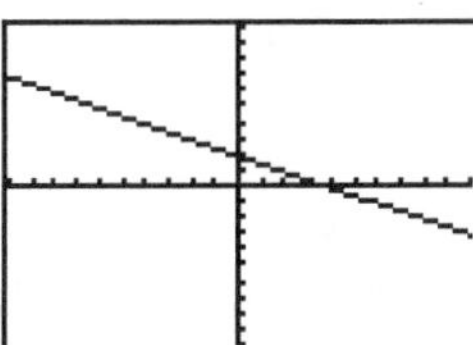

The best choice is b because it is 3 units above the graph of g.

SUMMARY

When adding or subtracting two functions f and g graphically, for each input value x, add or subtract the output values (vertical displacements) represented by $f(x)$ and $g(x)$ to obtain the value of $(f + g)(x)$ or $(f - g)(x)$.

EXERCISES

1. Consider the functions $f(x) = -x - 2$ and $g(x) = 3$. Sketch the indicated sum or difference function using the given graphs of f and g. Then determine an equation for the given function and verify your sketch using your grapher.

   a. $(f + g)(x) =$ $-x + 1$

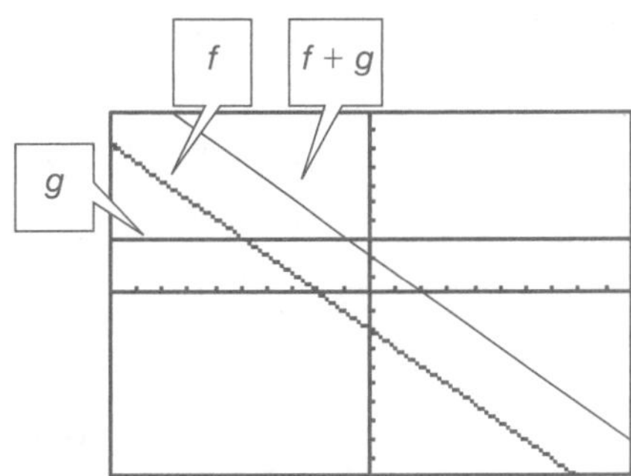

   b. $(f - g)(x) =$ $-x - 5$

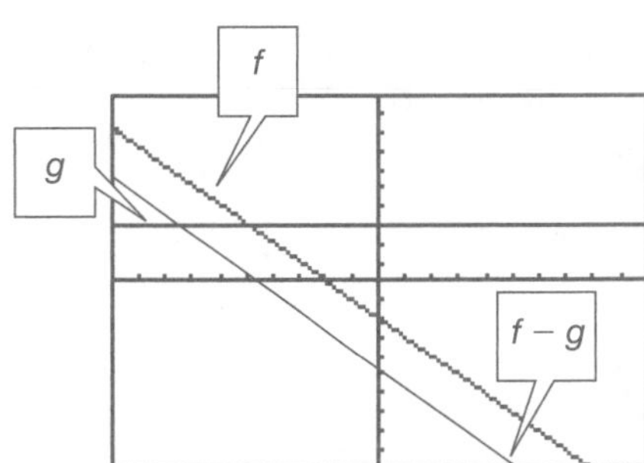

Exercise numbers appearing in color are answered in the Selected Answers section of this book.

c. $(g - f)(x) =$ x + 5

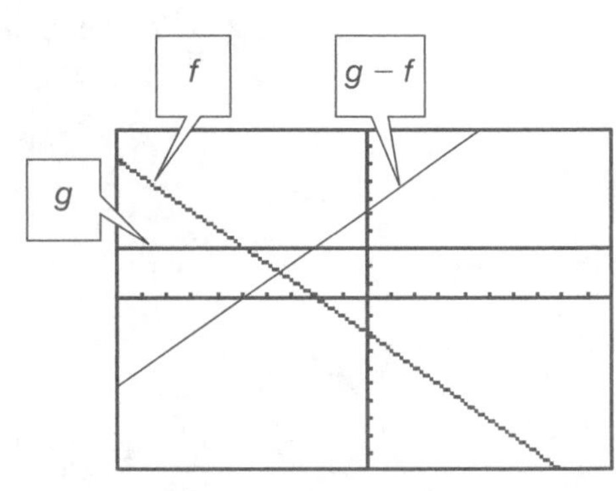

2. Consider the functions $f(x) = 2x - 3$ and $g(x) = -2$. Sketch the indicated sum or difference function using the given graphs of f and g. Then determine an equation for the given function and verify your sketch using your grapher.

a. $(g + f)(x) =$ 2x − 5

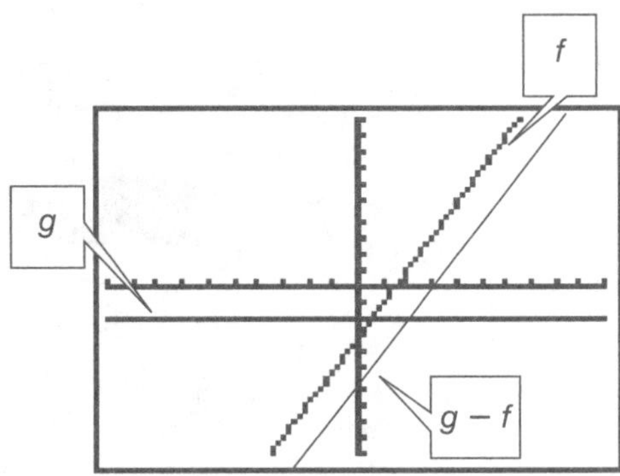

b. $(g - f)(x) =$ −2x + 1

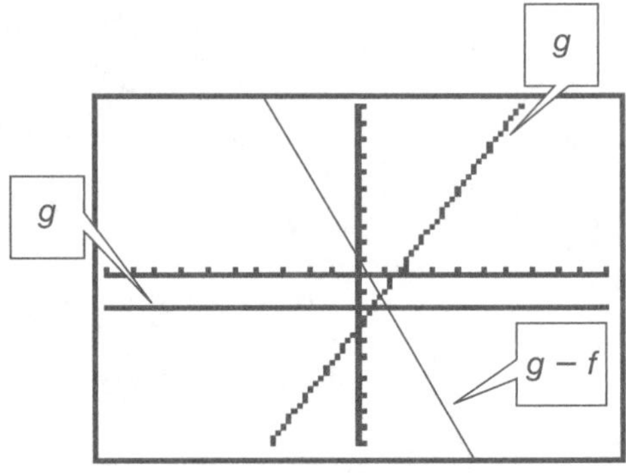

3. For the following graphs of f and g, sketch a possible graph of $f + g$.

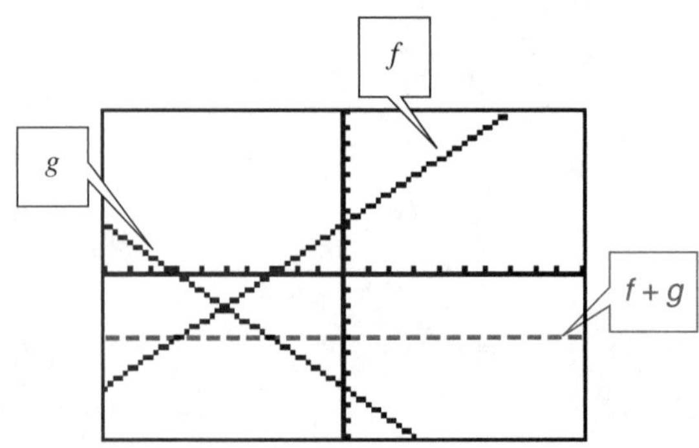

ACTIVITY 2.3

How Does Your Garden Grow?

Topics: *Product of Functions, Multiplication of Polynomials*

Last spring you planted your first garden. Since you were taking a course load of 19 hours, you decided to start small and staked out a plot 5 feet long by 3 feet wide.

1. What was the area of last spring's garden?

   15 ft^2

2. a. In general, your garden can be represented using l to represent length and w to represent width. Label the length and width on the following diagram.

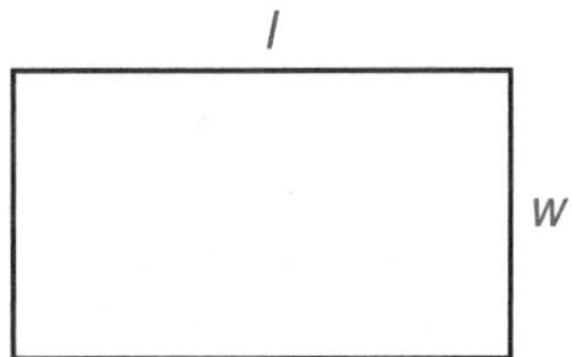

   b. Write the expression for area A using l and w.

   $A = l \cdot w$

This year you are taking only 15 credits of course work. You now want to expand your garden. You decide to add 4 feet to the length and 2 feet to the width.

Starting with a geometric representation of last spring's plot (5 by 3 feet), extend the length by 4 feet and the width by 2 feet to obtain a geometric model of the new plot.

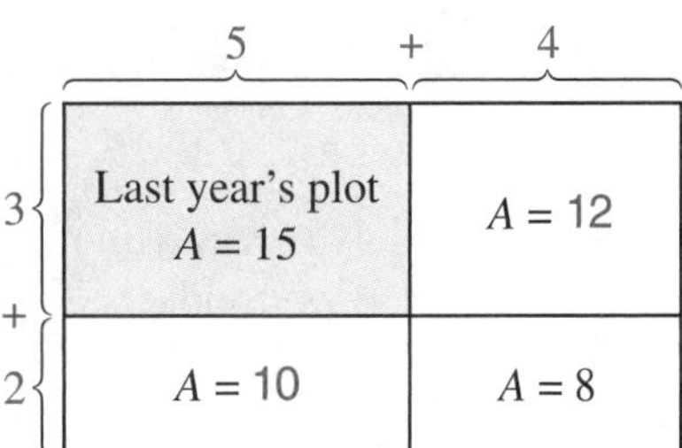

3. Determine the area of each section of this plot diagram, then record the area in the appropriate place in the diagram.

4. Determine the total area in two different ways.

   a. Sum the areas of the sections.

   $15 + 12 + 10 + 8 = 45$ ft^2

   b. Multiply the total length by the total width.

   $9 \cdot 5 = 45$ ft^2

Next year the requirements for your degree will be just about finished. Your garden will definitely get larger, but you are not sure by how much because you are concerned about expenses such as fertilizer and lime. Nevertheless, you decide to expand the length and width of your garden by the same number of feet, x.

5. Starting with a geometric representation of the current plot (9 by 5 feet), extend both the length and the width by x to obtain a geometric model of the new plot. Determine the area of each section, and fill in each area in your geometric model.

	9	+ x
5	Current plot $A = 45$	$A = 5x$
+ x	$9x$	x^2

6. Determine an algebraic expression for the total area by summing the areas of the sections. Combine like terms, and write your answer in descending order of the exponents.

   $x^2 + 14x + 45$

Another way of representing the area of your new garden is to multiply the length and width. Starting with the formula $A = lw$, replace l with $9 + x$ and w with $5 + x$ as follows:

$$A = lw$$
$$A = (9 + x)(5 + x).$$
$$A = f(x) = (9 + x)(5 + x) \text{ using function notation}$$

Note that the two factors on the right-hand side are polynomials.

> To multiply two polynomials, multiply each term of the first polynomial by each term of the second.

This rule is illustrated as follows:

$$\begin{aligned} f(x) &= (9 + x)(5 + x) \\ &= 9 \cdot 5 + 9 \cdot x + x \cdot 5 + x \cdot x \\ &= 45 + 9x + 5x + x^2 \\ &= 45 + 14x + x^2 \end{aligned}$$

In this situation, you are multiplying a binomial times a binomial. In such cases, the multiplication process is often referred to as the FOIL method. To review the FOIL method, see Appendix A.

Summarizing, if $l = g(x) = 9 + x$ is the length, and $w = h(x) = 5 + x$ is the width, then the area is given by $f(x) = g(x) \cdot h(x) = (9 + x)(5 + x) = 45 + 14x + x^2$.

> $f(x) = g(x) \cdot h(x)$ is called a **product function.** The notation is $(g \cdot h)(x) = g(x) \cdot h(x)$.

7. a. Evaluate $(g \cdot h)(3)$ using length $g(x) = 9 + x$ and width $h(x) = 5 + x$.

$(g \cdot h)(3) = (9 + 3)(5 + 3) = 12 \cdot 8 = 96$

Using the FOIL method:

$(9 + 3)(5 + 3) = 9 \cdot 5 + 9 \cdot 3 + 3 \cdot 5 + 3 \cdot 3 = 96$

b. What is the practical meaning of $(g \cdot h)(3)$ in this context?

If you increase the width and length of the garden by three feet, the area of the new garden is 96 square feet.

8. a. Given $f(x) = x + 7$ and $g(x) = x + 5$, determine a single expression for $(f \cdot g)(x)$. Write your answer as a sum of terms.

$(x + 7)(x + 5) = x^2 + 12x + 35$

b. Using f and g as defined in part a, complete the following table.

x	$f(x)$	$g(x)$	$(f \cdot g)(x)$
0	7	5	35
1	8	6	48
2	9	7	63
3	10	8	80
4	11	9	99

c. For a given input value, what is the relationship between the output values of the three functions f, g, and $f \cdot g$?

$(f \cdot g)(x) = f(x) \cdot g(x)$

d. Use your grapher to plot the functions, f, g, and $f \cdot g$. Use the trace or table feature to complete the following table for four input values not used in part b.

Answers will vary depending on choices of x.

x	$f(x)$	$g(x)$	$(f \cdot g)(x)$
5	12	10	120
6	13	11	143
7	14	12	168
8	15	13	195

e. Are the results in the table consistent with your conjecture in part c? Explain.

Yes, $f(x)$ times $g(x)$ equals $(f \cdot g)(x)$.

f. When you determine the product function, what do you multiply: domain values, range values, or both? Explain.

You multiply the range values for any given domain value, x.

Often the first terms of the product of two polynomials are not x and x as in $(x + 7)(x + 5)$. You may have to multiply $(x^3 + 7)$ by $(x^2 + 5)$. In this case the product of the first two terms is $x^3 \cdot x^2$. The term $x^3 = x \cdot x \cdot x$ and $x^2 = x \cdot x$. Therefore, $x^3 \cdot x^2 = (x \cdot x \cdot x) \cdot (x \cdot x) = x^5$. The product of 3 factors of x and 2 factors of x is 5 factors of x. Note that this result can be found equivalently by $x^3 \cdot x^2 = x^{3+2} = x^5$. You can determine the product of two powers of the same base by adding the exponents.

PROPERTY OF EXPONENTS

To multiply powers with the same base, keep the base and add the exponents: $a^m \cdot a^n = a^{m+n}$.

9. a. Expressions for $p(x)$ and $q(x)$ are given in the following table. Fill in the last column of the table with a single power of x for the product function, $p \cdot q$.

$p(x)$	$q(x)$	$(p \cdot q)(x)$
x^2	x^4	x^6
$2x^3$	x	$2x^4$
$-3x^5$	$4x^2$	$-12x^7$
$5x^4$	$3x^4$	$15x^8$

b. Multiply $(-2x^5)(8x^3)(3x^2)$.

$-48x^{10}$

c. Is a^2b^4 equal to ab^6? Explain.

No, if $a = 1$ and $b = 2$, $a^2b^4 = 16$, $ab^6 = 64$.

10. Given $f(x) = x + 2$, and $g(x) = x^2 - 4x + 3$, determine $(f \cdot g)(x)$. Remember to multiply each term of the first polynomial by each term of the second and then collect like terms.

$(f \cdot g)(x) = (x + 2)(x^2 - 4x + 3) = x^3 - 4x^2 + 3x + 2x^2 - 8x + 6 =$
$x^3 - 2x^2 - 5x + 6$

If you need more work on multiplication of polynomials, see Appendix A.

EXERCISES

1. You are the manager of a retail clothing store. It is time to stock up on dress shirts. Your wholesaler has the shirts you want at \$7.50 each for up to 50 shirts. However, if you order more than 50, each shirt will cost \$0.05 less for every shirt over 50 that you order, up to 100 shirts. So 60 shirts will cost \$7.00 each, 70 shirts will cost \$6.50 each, and so on.

   a. Let x be the number of *additional* shirts ordered over 50. Write an expression for the total number of shirts purchased. Assume that you are going to purchase at least 50 shirts.

   $50 + x$

   b. Write an expression for the cost per shirt.

   $7.50 - 0.05x$

   c. Determine an equation for the total cost of the shirts, $C(x)$, as a function of the number of shirts x you purchase in excess of 50.

   $C(x) = (50 + x)(7.50 - 0.05x)$

   d. What is the domain of the cost function if you know that you will not purchase more than 100 shirts? (Be careful.)

   Domain is $0 \leq x \leq 50$

   e. Using an appropriate window, graph the cost function using your grapher.

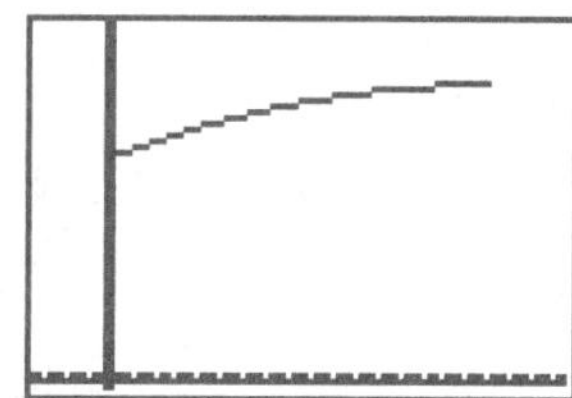

   f. Rewrite the cost function by multiplying the factors and combining like terms.

   $C(x) = (50 + x)(7.50 - 0.05x) = 375 - 2.50x + 7.50x - 0.05x^2 =$
   $-0.05x^2 + 5x + 375$

   g. Graph the new function from part f in the same window as part e. What do you see? Compare this graph to the graph in part e.

   The graphs are the same.

2. Use the property of exponents $a^m \cdot a^n = a^{m+n}$ to determine the following products.

   a. $3^5 \cdot 3^7$

   3^{12}

   b. $t^4 \cdot t$

   t^5

   c. x^2y^5

   x^2y^5

   d. $(2z^4)(3z^8)$

   $6z^{12}$

   e. $(-2x)(3x)^4(-5x^2)$

   $810x^7$

Exercise numbers appearing in color are answered in the Selected Answers section of this book.

f. $(a^2b^2)(a^3b^4)$

a^5b^6

g. $x^{2n} \cdot x^n$

x^{3n}

Use the geometric model as outlined in Problems 5 and 6 in this activity to determine the products in Exercises 3 and 4. Although the individual sections do not represent area, the general process can still be applied.

3. Multiply $(x + 3)(x^2 + 3x - 5)$. Determine the appropriate products to complete the chart. Combine like terms, and write the final answer for this multiplication in descending order of the exponents.

	x^2	$3x$	-5
x	x^3	$3x^2$	$-5x$
3	$3x^2$	$9x$	-15

$(x + 3)(x^2 + 3x - 5) = x^3 + 3x^2 - 5x + 3x^2 + 9x - 15 = x^3 + 6x^2 + 4x - 15$

4. Multiply $(x^2 + 2x - 3)(2x^2 + 3x - 4)$. Determine the appropriate products to complete the chart. Combine like terms, and write the final answer for this multiplication in descending order of the exponents.

	$2x^2$	$3x$	-4
x^2	$2x^4$	$3x^3$	$-4x^2$
$2x$	$4x^3$	$6x^2$	$-8x$
-3	$-6x^2$	$-9x$	12

$2x^4 + 7x^3 - 4x^2 - 17x + 12$

5. Determine each product, and simplify the result.

a. $(x + 2)(x + 3)$

$x^2 + 5x + 6$

b. $(x - 2)(x - 3)$

$x^2 - 5x + 6$

c. $(x + 2)(x - 3)$

$x^2 - x - 6$

d. $(x - 2)(x + 3)$

$x^2 + x - 6$

6. Compare your results for Exercises 5a and b; also for 5c and d. What is the effect on the product of changing the operation in each factor?

The operation of the middle term of the product changes.

7. Determine the following products and simplify the result.

a. $(x + 2)(x^2 + 4x - 3)$

$x^3 + 4x^2 - 3x + 2x^2 + 8x - 6$

$= x^3 + 6x^2 + 5x - 6$

b. $(4 - 3x + x^2)(2x^2 + x)$

$8x^2 - 6x^3 + 2x^4 + 4x - 3x^2 + x^3$

$= 2x^4 - 5x^3 + 5x^2 + 4x$

c. $(x - 3)(2x^2 - 5x + 1)$

$2x^3 - 5x^2 + x - 6x^2 + 15x - 3$

$= 2x^3 - 11x^2 + 16x - 3$

d. $(x - 4)(4 - x^2)$

$4x - x^3 - 16 + 4x^2$

$-x^3 + 4x^2 + 4x - 16$

e. $(x^2 - 3x + 1)(3x^2 - 5x + 2)$

$3x^4 - 5x^3 + 2x^2 - 9x^3 + 15x^2 - 6x + 3x^2 - 5x + 2$

$= 3x^4 - 14x^3 + 20x^2 - 11x + 2$

f. $(2x^2 + 5x)(6 - 2x)$

$12x^2 - 4x^3 + 30x - 10x^2 = -4x^3 + 2x^2 + 30x$

8. **a.** Given $f(x) = x + 1$ and $g(x) = 2x - 3$, determine a single expression $(f \cdot g)(x)$ by multiplying and combining like terms.

$(f \cdot g)(x) = 2x^2 - x - 3$

b. Using f and g as defined in part a, complete the following table.

x	$f(x)$	$g(x)$	$(f \cdot g)(x)$
0	1	−3	−3
1	2	−1	−2
2	3	1	3
3	4	3	12
4	5	5	25

c. Use your grapher to plot all three functions, f, g, and $f \cdot g$. Use the trace or table feature to complete the following table for four input values not used in part b. Answers may vary depending on the choices of x.

x	$f(x)$	$g(x)$	$(f \cdot g)(x)$
6	7	9	63
7	8	11	88
8	9	13	117
9	10	15	150

d. Are the results in the table consistent with your expectations? Explain.

Yes, the output of the product function is the product of the outputs of f and g.

What Have I Learned?

1. The graphs of functions f, g, and h appear in the accompanying figure.

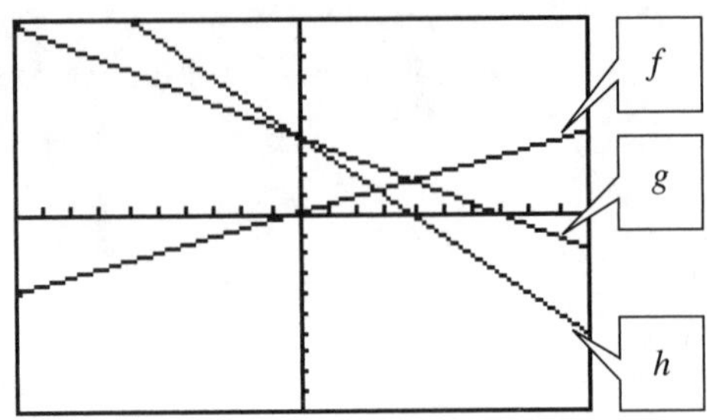

   a. Which function represents the sum of the other two functions?

   $g(x) = f(x) + h(x)$

   b. Which function represents the difference between the other two functions?

   $f(x) = g(x) - h(x)$ or $h(x) = g(x) - f(x)$

2. If the output of the function $(f - g)$ is constant, what must be true about the graphs of the functions f and g?

   The graphs are parallel.

3. Given $f(x) = 2x - 3$ and $g(x) = 4$, for what values of x is $(f + g)(x) = (f \cdot g)(x)$?

   $(f + g)(x) = 2x + 1$ and $(f \cdot g)(x) = 8x - 12$

   $2x + 1 = 8x - 12$

   $13 = 6x$

   $x = \frac{13}{6}$

4. Given the defining equations for two functions, describe how to determine the output of the product function for a particular input value.

   Graphically, for any given x value multiply the values of the vertical displacements of $f(x)$ and $g(x)$ to find the product $f(x)g(x)$.

How Can I Practice?

1. a. The Snowbelt Quilters Guild is planning a holiday dinner. A banquet room has been reserved, and catering arrangements have been made for a total of $600, a fixed fee not dependent on the number of persons who attend. The planning committee decides that a price of $20 per couple is the most they will charge for tickets. What is the *least* number of tickets they need to sell to break even?

$20x - 600 = 0$

$20x = 600$

$x = 30$

b. The committee also decides that once they have met their expenses, they will reduce the ticket charge by $0.50 per couple for each additional ticket (couple) above the break-even point you found in part a. Suppose you let t represent the *additional* tickets sold. Then the charge per ticket can be represented by the function $C = g(t)$. Write a symbolic rule for the total number N of couples attending the banquet (i.e., the number of tickets sold) as a function of t. Call this function f. Also write a rule for the charge per ticket, C.

$N = f(t) = 30 + t$ $\quad$ $C = g(t) = 20 - 0.5t$

c. Complete the following table for each of the functions $N = f(t)$ and $C = g(t)$.

t	0	2	4	6	8	10
$N = f(t)$	30	32	34	36	38	40
$C = g(t)$	20	19	18	17	16	15

d. The total revenue obtained from the ticket sales is the total number of tickets sold multiplied by the charge per ticket. Use the output values from part c to complete the following table for the total revenue function $R(t) = N \cdot C = f(t) \cdot g(t)$.

t	0	2	4	6	8	10
$R(t)$	600	608	612	612	608	600

e. Rewrite the symbolic description of the revenue function by multiplying the factors.

$R(t) = f(t) \cdot g(t) = (30 + t)(20 - 0.5t) = -0.5t^2 + 5t + 600$

Exercise numbers appearing in color are answered in the Selected Answers section of this book.

f. Use your grapher to graph the total revenue function on the accompanying grid. What window values Xmin, Xmax, and so on, did you use?

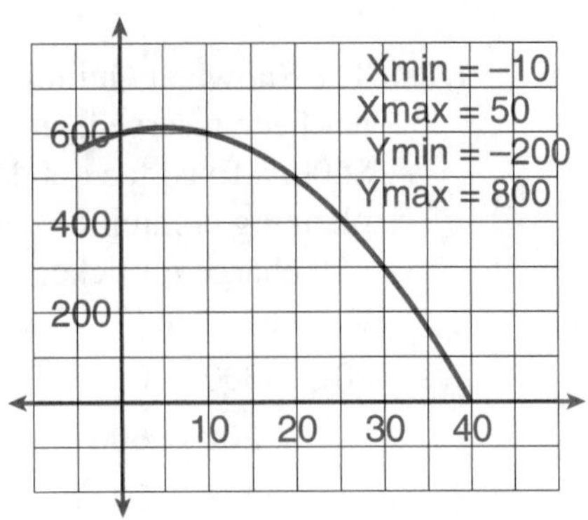

g. Determine the maximum revenue that can be obtained.

\$612.50 is the maximum revenue if 35 couples attend.

h. What is the total number of tickets that must be sold to obtain this maximum revenue? (Be careful.)

35 tickets must be sold to obtain the maximum revenue.

2. If $f(x) = x + 2$ and $g(x) = 2x - 3$, determine the following.

a. $(f + g)(x)$

$3x - 1$

b. $(f - g)(x)$

$-x + 5$

c. $(f \cdot g)(x)$

$2x^2 + x - 6$

d. $(f - g)(3)$

2

e. $(f \cdot g)(-2)$

0

f. $(3 \cdot f)(x)$

$3x + 6$

3. If $f(x) = x^2 - 2x + 1$ and $g(x) = x^2 + x - 4$, determine each of the following.

a. $(f - g)(x)$

$-3x + 5$

b. $(f \cdot g)x$

$x^4 - x^3 - 5x^2 + 9x - 4$

c. $(f + g)(-1)$

0

d. $2 \cdot f(x) - 3 \cdot g(x)$

$-x^2 - 7x + 14$

4. Perform the indicated operations and simplify.

a. $(4x + 5) + (x - 7)$
$5x - 2$

b. $(x^2 - 3x + 1) + (x^2 + x - 9)$
$2x^2 - 2x - 8$

c. $(x + 4) - (3x - 8)$
$-2x + 12$

d. $(3x^2 - 4x - 5) - (x^2 + 9x + 3)$
$2x^2 - 13x - 8$

e. $(5x^2 + 6x - 1) - (7x - 3)$
$5x^2 - x + 2$

5. Perform the indicated operations and simplify.

a. $x \cdot x^3$
x^4

b. $x^4 \cdot x^5$
x^9

c. $(2x^6)(3x^2)$
$6x^8$

d. $(xy^3)(x^4y^3z)$
x^5y^6z

e. $(2x^4y^5z^7)(5x^2z)$
$10x^6y^5z^8$

f. $(-3a^2b)(-2a)(-5a^2b^2)$
$-30a^5b^3$

6. Perform the indicated operations and simplify.

a. $(x - 2)(x - 5)$
$x^2 - 7x + 10$

b. $(4x - 3)(x + 7)$
$4x^2 + 25x - 21$

c. $(3 - x)(1 + x)$
$-x^2 + 2x + 3$

d. $(x - 2)(x^2 + 3x - 5)$
$x^3 + x^2 - 11x + 10$

e. $(2x + 1)(x^2 - x + 2)$
$2x^3 - x^2 + 3x + 2$

f. $3(x - 7) - 2(x^2 + 4x)$
$-2x^2 - 5x - 21$

g. $2x(x + 5) - 3x(4 - 3x)$
$11x^2 - 2x$

h. $3x^2 - (x^3 + 1) - x(x^4 - 2)$
$-x^5 - x^3 + 3x^2 + 2x - 1$

CLUSTER 2

Composition and Inverse of Functions

Inflated Balloons

Topic: *Composition of Functions*

The volume of an inflated balloon increases as the air temperature rises. The following table shows the data from experimental measurements for a particular balloon.

TEMPERATURE (°F)	32	39	42	45	50	58	63	68
VOLUME (cu in.)	35.1	36.5	37.1	37.7	38.7	40.3	41.3	42.3

1. Treating volume as a function of temperature, is this relationship a linear function? Describe how you determined your answer.

   $\frac{37.1 - 35.1}{42 - 32} = \frac{2}{10} = 0.2$, $\frac{38.7 - 37.7}{50 - 45} = \frac{1}{5} = 0.2$, $\frac{42.3 - 40.3}{68 - 58} = \frac{2}{10} = 0.2$

   The relationship appears to be linear since the rate of change appears to be a constant.

2. Use your grapher to sketch a scatterplot of these data points. Does your plot verify your answer to Problem 1? Refer to Appendix C for procedures to plot a set of data on the TI-83.

   Yes

3. Use the table of values and/or your grapher to determine the equation for this function. Use V for the output variable and F for the input variable. Call the function f, so that $V = f(F)$.

   $V = f(F) = 0.2F + 28.7$

4. Use your grapher to sketch the graph of the volume function f that you determined in Problem 3. Explain how you can be reasonably sure your function is correct.

   Trace to find values in the table and make sure the line goes through them.

5. Use your function f from Problem 3 to determine the volume of the balloon when the temperature is 55°F.

   $V = 0.2(55) + 28.7 = 39.7$ cu in.

6. Suppose you only have a Celsius thermometer, and you want to know the volume of the balloon when the temperature is 10°C. You need to first convert degrees Celsius to degrees Fahrenheit to use your function from Problem 3.

   a. To convert from degrees Celsius to degrees Fahrenheit, use the function defined by $F = 32 + 1.8C$, where C represents degrees Celsius. Call the function g so that $F = g(C)$. Use this function g to determine the Fahrenheit temperature equivalent to 10°C.

      $F = g(10) = 32 + 1.8(10) = 50$

b. Use the result from part a to determine the volume for 10°C.

$V = f(50) = 0.2(50) + 28.7 = 38.7$

7. Complete the following table using a combination of functions defined by $V = f(F) = 0.2F + 28.7$ and $F = g(C) = 32 + 1.8C$.

TEMPERATURE (C°)	0	10	20	30	40
VOLUME (cu in.)	35.1	38.7	42.3	45.9	49.5

In calculating the volumes in Problem 7, you followed a two-step calculation. First you used the degrees Celsius, C, as the input to $F = g(C) = 32 + 1.8C$ to convert the temperature to degrees Fahrenheit. Then you used this output, degrees Fahrenheit, as the input to the function $V = f(F) = 0.2F + 28.7$, from Problem 3, to obtain the volume V. To shorten this calculation, you can combine the two functions in a special way, as described in Problem 8.

8. a. Substitute the expression $32 + 1.8C$ for F in $V = 0.2F + 28.7$, and simplify. You have just found a symbolic rule for V as a function of C.

$V = 0.2F + 28.7$

$= 0.2(32 + 1.8C) + 28.7$

$= 6.4 + 0.36C + 28.7$

$= 0.36C + 35.1$

Symbolically, you started with $F = g(C)$. Then, substituting $g(C)$ for F in the second function $V = f(F)$, you then have

$$V = f(F) = f(g(C)).$$

This function of a function is called the **composition** of f and g.

b. Using the symbolic rule for the composition of f and g from part a, use your grapher to verify the table of values in Problem 7.

It agrees.

9. a. If $f(x) = x^2 + 2x + 1$ and $g(x) = x + 3$, determine a symbolic rule for $f(g(x))$.

$f(g(x)) = f(x + 3) = (x + 3)^2 + 2(x + 3) + 1$

$x^2 + 6x + 9 + 2x + 6 + 1$

$= x^2 + 8x + 16$

b. Use the result from part a to determine $f(g(3))$.

$f(g(3)) = 3^2 + 8 \cdot 3 + 16 = 9 + 24 + 16 = 49$

COMPOSITION OF FUNCTIONS

If x is the input of a function g, the output is $g(x)$. If $g(x)$ is then used as the input of a function f, the output is $f(g(x))$. Let $h(x) = f(g(x))$. The function h is the composition of the functions f and g. The notation is

$$h(x) = (f \circ g)(x) = f(g(x)).$$

$f(g(x))$ is read as f of g of x.

EXERCISES

1. Oil is leaking from a tanker and is spreading outward in the shape of a circle. The area A of the oil slick is a function of its radius r (in feet) and is given by $A = f(r) = \pi r^2$. The input r for the area function is itself a function of time t (in hours) since the oil began leaking.

a. If $r = g(t) = 100t$, determine $g(2)$ and interpret its meaning in this situation.

$g(2) = 200$. The radius of the slick is 200 ft 2 hours after the spill.

b. Determine $f(g(2))$ and interpret its meaning in this situation.

$f(g(2)) = f(200) = \pi(200)^2 = 40{,}000\pi \approx 125{,}663$ sq ft.

The area of the oil slick is 125,663 sq ft 2 hours after the spill.

c. Determine $f(g(10))$ and interpret its meaning in this situation.

$f(g(10)) = f(1000) = \pi(1000)^2 = 1{,}000{,}000\pi = 3{,}141{,}592$ sq ft.

This is the area of the slick after 10 hours.

d. Determine a general expression for $f(g(t))$.

$f(g(t)) = f(100t) = \pi(100t)^2 = 10{,}000\pi t^2$

e. Determine the area of the circular oil spill after 10 hours using the new composite area function found in part d, and compare the result with your answer to part c.

$f(g(10)) = 10{,}000\pi(10)^2 = 1{,}000{,}000\pi t^2$. The formulas are the same.

2. If $V = g(r) = \frac{4}{3}\pi r^2$, and $r = f(t) = t + 1$, determine $g(f(t))$.

$g(f(t)) = g(t + 1) = \frac{4}{3}\pi(t + 1)^2 = \frac{4}{3}\pi(t^2 + 2t + 1)$

3. If $s = u(t) = -2t^2 + 2t + 1$, and $t = v(x) = 3x - 1$, determine each of the following.

a. $(u \circ v)(x)$

$$u(v(x)) = u(3x - 1) = -2(3x - 1)^2 + 2(3x - 1) + 1$$
$$= -2(9x^2 - 6x + 1) + 6x - 2 + 1 = -18x^2 + 12x - 2 + 6x - 1$$
$$= -18x^2 + 18x - 3$$

b. $(v \circ u)(t)$

$$v(u(t)) = v(-2t^2 + 2t + 1) = 3(-2t^2 + 2t + 1) - 1$$
$$= -6t^2 + 6t + 3 - 1$$
$$= -6t^2 + 6t + 2$$

4. Use the first two tables to complete the third.

x	1	2	3	4	5	6
f(x)	2	−1	5	7	19	4

x	−1	2	4	5	7	19
g(x)	0	−3	4	1	5	12

x	1	2	3	4	5	6
g(f(x))	−3	0	1	5	12	4

ACTIVITY 2.5

Finding a Bargain

Topic: *Composition of Functions*

You have been waiting for the best price for a winter coat and see the following advertisement.

This is it! The time is right! Last week the coat was on sale for 25% off the original price, and now you can get the coat for 40% less than last week's sale price.

1. **a.** Complete the following table.

ORIGINAL COST OF THE COAT, x	LAST WEEK'S PRICE	TODAY'S PRICE
80	60	36
100	75	45
120	90	54
140	105	63

b. What percent of the original price would you have paid for the coat during last week's sale?

75%

c. Express last week's sale price as a function of the original price. Use $y = f(x)$, where x is the original price and y is the sale price.

$y = f(x) = 0.75x$

2. The ad indicates that you can now save an additional 40%.

a. What percent of last week's sale price would you now have to pay?

60%

b. Express this week's sale price as a function of last week's sale price. Use $z = g(y)$, where y is last week's sale price and z is this week's sale price.

$z = g(y) = 0.6y$

3. a. The original price of the coat was \$160. Use the function f from Problem 1c to determine the price after the first reduction.

$y = 0.75(160) = 120$

b. Use the function g from Problem 2b to determine the price after the second reduction.

$z = 0.6(120) = 72$

c. What percent of the original \$160 price will you pay?

$\frac{72}{160} = 45\%$

d. What is the total discount as a percent off the original price?

The total discount is 55%.

4. The salesclerk can't get her register to accept your credit card. The manager tells her to use a different register. In her frustration, the salesclerk enters the discount as a 65% reduction.

a. Why does she take a 65% reduction?

The clerk is thinking 25% + 40% = 65%.

b. Is this okay with you? Explain.

Yes, because I am getting a bigger discount than I should.

c. Would this be okay with the manager of the department? Explain.

No, because I should be getting a 55% discount.

To determine the final sale price of the coat requires a sequence of two calculations:

First:	$y = f(x) = 0.75x$	(With 25% off, you pay 75% of the cost.)
Second:	$z = g(y) = 0.60y$	(With 40% off, you now pay 60% of the reduced price.)

5. a. Substitute the expression for $f(x)$ into your formula for $g(y)$ to determine the single-step formula for this composition function. Symbolically, this is written as $z = g(y) = g(f(x))$.

$z = g(0.75x) = 0.60(0.75x) = 0.45x$

b. Your answer to part a should imply a savings of 55% from the original price. Does it? Explain.

Yes, since $0.45x$ means I pay 45% of the original price.

EXERCISES

1. **a.** Covert 5 miles to an equivalent number of feet.
   5280(5) = 26,400 ft.

   b. Convert the number of feet from part a to an equivalent number of inches.
   12(26,400) = 316,800 in.

   c. Convert 5 miles to an equivalent number of inches by combining the computations from parts a and b.
   12(5280)(5) = 316,800 in.

   d. Let x represent the number of miles. Write a function rule that converts x miles to an equivalent number of feet. Call this function f.
   $f(x) = 5280x$

   e. Write a function rule that converts w feet to an equivalent number of inches. Call this function g.
   $g(w) = 12w$

   f. Determine $g(f(5))$. Interpret your answer.
   $g(f(5)) = g(5280(5)) = g(26{,}400) = 12(26{,}400) = 316{,}800$

   g. Determine $g(f(x))$.
   $g(f(x)) = g(5280x) = 12(5280x) = 63{,}360x$

2. Function f gives the approximate percent increase in harmful ultraviolet rays for an x percent decrease in the thickness of the ozone layer.

x	0	1	2	3	4	5	6
$f(x)$	0	1.5	3.0	4.5	6.0	7.5	9.0

Function g gives the expected percent increase in cases of skin cancer for a p percent increase in ultraviolet radiation.

p	0	1.5	3.0	4.5	6.0	7.5	9.0
$g(p)$	0	5.25	10.5	15.75	21.0	26.25	31.5

Exercise numbers appearing in color are answered in the Selected Answers section of this book.

In Exercises a–d, determine the output value and interpret your answer.

a. $f(3)$

4.5

b. $g(4.5)$

15.75

c. $g(f(3))$

$g(4.5) = 15.75$

d. $g(f(6))$

$g(9.0) = 31.5$

e. What does $g(f(x))$ determine? That is, what does the output for $g(f(x))$ represent in this situation?

$g(f(x))$ determines the expected percent increase of skin cancer for an x percent decrease in the thickness of the ozone layer.

f. Complete the following table.

x	0	1	2	3	4	5	6
$g(f(x))$	0	5.25	10.5	15.75	21.0	26.25	31.5

3. A car dealership advertises a factory rebate of \$1500 and a 10% discount.

a. Let x represent the price of a car. Let $f(x)$ represent the price of a car after rebate. Determine a rule for $f(x)$.

$f(x) = x - 1500$

b. If $g(x)$ represents the price of the car after the discount, determine a rule for $g(x)$.

$g(x) = 0.9x$

c. Determine $g(f(20{,}000))$ and interpret your answer.

$g(f(20{,}000)) = g(20{,}000 - 1500) = g(18{,}500) = 0.9(18{,}500) = \$16{,}650$

The price of a \$20,000 car with a \$1500 rebate and a 10% discount is \$16,650.

d. Suppose the price of a car is \$20,000. Determine $f(g(\$20{,}000))$ and interpret your answer.

$f(g(20{,}000)) = f(0.9(20{,}000)) = f(18{,}000) = 18{,}000 - 1500 = 16{,}500$

The price of a \$20,000 car with a 10% discount and a \$1500 rebate is \$16,500.

e. Compare the sale price obtained by subtracting the rebate first and then taking the discount, with the sale price obtained by taking the discount first and then subtracting the rebate.

Taking the discount first is better for the consumer. Taking the rebate first is better for the dealership.

4. You drop a pebble off a bridge. Ripples move out from the point of impact as concentric circles. The radius (in feet) of the outer ripple is given by

$$R = f(t) = 0.5t,$$

where t is the number of seconds after the pebble hits the water. The area A of a circle is a function of its radius and is given by

$$A = g(r) = \pi r^2$$

a. Determine a formula for $g(f(t))$.

$g(f(t)) = g(0.5t) = \pi(0.5t)^2 = 0.25\pi t^2$

b. What is the input and output for the function defined in part a?

The input is the number of seconds after the pebble hits with water. The output is the area of the outer ripple in square feet.

5. The functions f and g are defined by the following tables.

Determine the values for each of the following.

x	−3	−2	0	1	4	5	8	10	12
f(x)	8	6	3	2	5	8	11	15	20

x	0	2	3	4	5	8	9	11	15
g(x)	1	3	5	10	4	2	0	−2	−5

a. $f(g(3))$

8

b. $g(f(4))$

4

c. $f(g(4))$

15

d. $g(f(-3))$

2

ACTIVITY 2.6

The Square of a Cube

Topics: *Properties of Exponents, Fractional Exponents*

Suppose that one function squares the input x: $f(x) = x^2$. Further suppose that a second function cubes the input x: $g(x) = x^3$.

1. a. Determine each of the following.

i. $f(3)$ $3^2 = 9$

ii. $g(4)$ $4^3 = 64$

iii. $g(f(2))$ $g(f(2)) = g(2^2) = g(4) = 64$

b. The general composition function in part a is written $g(f(x))$. Write the expression for $g(f(x))$ as a single power of x.

$g(f(x)) = g(x^2) = (x^2)^3 = x^6$

c. Use the expression from part b to determine $g(f(2))$, and compare the result to your answer from part a.

$g(f(x)) = x^6$. Therefore, $g(f(2)) = 2^6 = 64$. The results are the same.

d. Now determine $f(g(x))$.

$f(g(x)) = f(x^3) = (x^3)^2 = x^6$

The composition functions you determined in Problems 1b and 1d illustrate an important property of exponents.

PROPERTY OF EXPONENTS

If a and b are real numbers and m and n are integers, then

$$(a^m)^n = a^{m \cdot n}$$

For example, $(2^2)^3 = 2^{2\cdot 3} = 2^6$, and $(2^3)^2 = 2^{3\cdot 2} = 2^6$. In general, $(x^2)^3 = x^6$ and $(x^3)^2 = x^6$.

2. If $f(x) = x^4$ and $g(x) = x^5$, determine each of the following.

a. $f(g(x))$

$(x^5)^4 = x^{20}$

b. $g(f(x))$

$(x^4)^5 = x^{20}$

3. If $h(x) = 4x^3$ and $k(x) = x^2$, determine each of the following:

a. $k(h(2))$

$k(4(2)^3) = k(4(8)) =$

$k(32) = 32^2 = 1024$

b. $k(h(x))$

$k(4x^3) = (4x^3)^2$

In Problem 3b, you obtain the expression $(4x^3)^2$, which can be written as

$$\underset{\substack{\uparrow \\ \text{base}}}{(4x^3)^2} = 4x^3 \cdot 4x^3 = 16x^6.$$

The expression $(4x^3)^2$ is also equivalent to

$$(4x^3)^2 = 4^2(x^3)^2 = 16x^6.$$

Note that each factor in the base $4x^3$ (namely 4 and x^3) were each raised to the second power. This illustrates another important property of exponents.

> If a and b are real numbers, and n is an integer, then
>
> $$(ab)^n = a^n \cdot b^n.$$

For example, $(x^2y^3)^4 = (x^2)^4(y^3)^4 = x^8y^{12}$.

4. a. If $h(x) = 3x^2$ and $k(x) = x^3$, determine each of the following:

$h(k(x)) =$

$h(x^3) = 3(x^3)^2 = 3x^6$

$k(h(x)) =$

$k(3x^2) = (3x^2)^3 = 3^3(x^2)^3 = 27x^6$

b. Does changing the order of the composition result in the same output? That is, does $h(k(x)) = k(h(x))$?

The order does make a difference. $h(k(x)) \neq k(h(x))$.

> Composition of functions is not commutative. That is, changing the order of the compositions may change the result. In general,
>
> $$f(g(x)) \neq g(f(x)).$$

5. a. Apply the properties of exponents to simplify the following.

i. $y = (5x^3)^2$

$y = 25x^6$

ii. $y = (-x^4)^3$

$y = -x^{12}$

b. Determine $f(g(x))$ if $f(x) = x^4$ and $g(x) = -3x^2$.

$f(g(x)) = f(-3x^2) = (-3x^2)^4 = 81x^8$

What does $a^{\frac{1}{2}}$ represent? The properties of exponents allow you to adopt a reasonable definition for rational (fractional) exponents. Let us begin by reviewing the definition of square root.

Let a represent a non-negative number, symbolically written as $a \geq 0$. The square root of a, denoted by $\sqrt{a}$, is defined as the non-negative number that when squared produces a. That is, $(\sqrt{a})^2 = a$.

For example, $\sqrt{9} = 3$, since $(\sqrt{9})^2 = 3^2 = 9$.

To write $\sqrt{a}$ as a power of a, you need to determine the value of m such that

$$a^m = \sqrt{a}$$

Squaring both sides of this equation, you have

$$(a^m)^2 = (\sqrt{a})^2$$

Since $(a^m)^2 = a^{2m}$ and $(\sqrt{a})^2 = a^1$, you now have

$$a^{2m} = a^1.$$

Since the bases are equal, exponents must be equal. Therefore,

$$2m = 1$$
$$m = \tfrac{1}{2}$$

It follows that $a^{\frac{1}{2}} = \sqrt{a}$, where $a \geq 0$.

This result leads to another important property of exponents.

PROPERTY OF EXPONENTS

- If $a \geq 0$, $\sqrt{a} = a^{\frac{1}{2}}$, the square root of a.
- Similarly, $\sqrt[3]{a} = a^{\frac{1}{3}}$, the cube root of a,

  and $\sqrt[4]{a} = a^{\frac{1}{4}}$, the fourth root of a.
- In general, $\sqrt[n]{a} = a^{\frac{1}{n}}$, the nth root of a.

For example, $36^{\frac{1}{2}} = \sqrt{36} = 6$. Confirm this on your calculator (make sure to use parentheses when inputting the exponent $\frac{1}{2}$). This makes sense, since $6^2 = (36^{\frac{1}{2}})^2 = 36^1 = 36$.

6. a. Compute $81^{\frac{1}{4}}$ on your calculator, and explain why your answer is reasonable.

$81^{\frac{1}{4}} = \sqrt[4]{81} = 3$. It is reasonable because $3^4 = 81$.

b. Try to compute $(-81)^{\frac{1}{4}}$ on your calculator. Explain what happens.

It tells me to quit. There is no real number n such that $n^4 = -81$.

7. **a.** Compute $(1000)^{\frac{1}{3}}$ on your calculator, and explain why your answer is reasonable.

   10, It is reasonable because $10^3 = 1000$.

   b. Try to compute $(-1000)^{\frac{1}{3}}$ on your calculator. Does the answer seem reasonable? Explain.

   -10 It is reasonable because $(-10)^3 = -1000$.

These properties of exponents can be expanded to include rational exponents where the numerator is different from 1. For example;

$$8^{\frac{2}{3}} = 8^{2\left(\frac{1}{3}\right)} = \left(8^2\right)^{\frac{1}{3}} = 64^{\frac{1}{3}} = 4$$

or

$$8^{\frac{2}{3}} = 8^{\frac{1}{3}\cdot 2} = \left(8^{\frac{1}{3}}\right)^2 = 2^2 = 4.$$

Use your calculator to confirm these results.

PROPERTY OF EXPONENTS

$$a^{\frac{p}{q}} = \left(a^p\right)^{\frac{1}{q}} = \sqrt[q]{a^p} \quad \text{or} \quad a^{\frac{p}{q}} = \left(a^{\frac{1}{q}}\right)^p = \left(\sqrt[q]{a}\right)^p$$

8. Compute $25^{\frac{4}{2}}$ as written (do not simplify the exponent). Then compute $25^{\frac{4}{2}}$ by first simplifying the exponent. Compare the two results.

   $25^{\frac{4}{2}} = \left(\sqrt{25}\right)^4 = 5^4 = 625$

   $25^{\frac{4}{2}} = 25^2 = 625$

   The results are the same.

9. Compute $7^{\frac{2}{3}}$ on your calculator and explain why your answer is reasonable.

   3.65930571 It is reasonable because when I raise it to the $\frac{3}{2}$ power it is 7.

10. Write each of the following using fractional exponents.

    a. $\sqrt[3]{x}$

    $x^{\frac{1}{3}}$

    b. $\sqrt[5]{x^3}$

    $x^{\frac{3}{5}}$

    c. $\sqrt[4]{x+1}$

    $(x+1)^{\frac{1}{4}}$

    d. $\sqrt{xy}$

    $(xy)^{\frac{1}{2}} = x^{\frac{1}{2}}y^{\frac{1}{2}}$

For additional work with expressions using fractional exponents, see Appendix A.

11. Determine the domain of each of the following.

a. $f(x) = \sqrt{x}$

$x \geq 0$

b. $g(x) = \sqrt[3]{x}$

All real numbers

12. If $f(x) = \sqrt{x + 2}$, then determine each of the following.

a. $f(-2)$

0

b. $f(0)$

$\sqrt{2}$

c. $f(7)$

3

d. $f(-6)$

Undefined

13. If $g(x) = \sqrt[3]{x - 5}$, then determine each of the following.

a. $g(5)$

0

b. $g(13)$

2

c. $g(-3)$

-2

EXERCISES

1. Given $f(x) = 2x + 8$ and $g(x) = x - 3$, determine each of the following.

a. $f(g(2))$

$f(g(2)) = f(-1) = -2 + 8 = 6$

b. $g(f(2))$

$g(f(2)) = g(12) = 12 - 3 = 9$

c. $f(g(x))$

$f(g(x)) = f(x - 3) =$

$2(x - 3) + 8 =$

$2x - 6 + 8 = 2x + 2$

d. $g(f(x))$

$g(f(x)) = g(2x + 8) = 2x + 8 - 3 =$

$2x + 5$

2. Simplify each expression by applying the properties of exponents.

a. $(x^3)^6$

x^{18}

b. $(2x^5)^2$

$4x^{10}$

c. $(-3x^2)^3$

$-27x^6$

3. Determine $f(g(x))$ and $g(f(x))$ if $f(x) = x^6$ and $g(x) = -x^3$.

$f(g(x)) = f(-x^3) = (-x^3)^6 = x^{18}$

$g(f(x)) = g(x^6) = -(x^6)^3 = -x^{18}$

4. Using the accompanying graph, estimate each of the following.

a. $f(g(4))$

1

b. $g(f(4))$

3

c. $f(g(0))$

1

Exercise numbers appearing in color are answered in the Selected Answers section of this book.

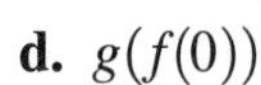

d. $g(f(0))$ 3 **e.** $f(g(2))$ 1 **f.** $g(f(2))$ 1

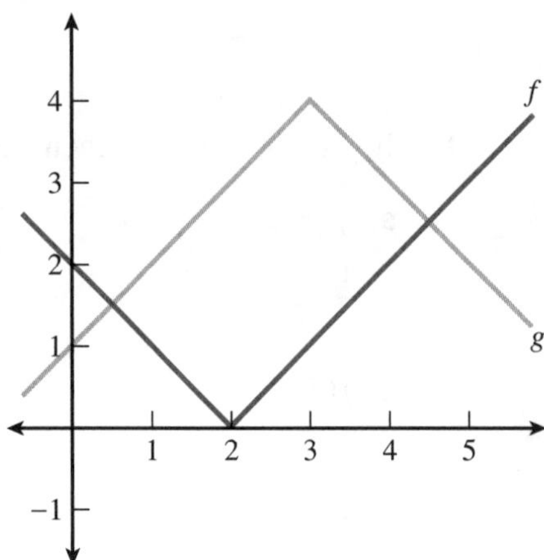

5. Compute each of the following quantities and explain why your answers are reasonable.

a. $100^{\frac{1}{2}}$

10

b. $144^{\frac{1}{2}}$

12

c. $64^{\frac{1}{3}}$

4

d. $64^{\frac{4}{3}}$

256

e. $5^{\frac{2}{5}}$

1.90365

f. $(-8)^{\frac{2}{3}}$

4

6. Write each of the following using fractional exponents.

a. $\sqrt{x}$

$x^{\frac{1}{2}}$

b. $\sqrt[4]{x^3}$

$x^{\frac{3}{4}}$

c. $\sqrt[3]{x + y}$

$(x + y)^{\frac{1}{3}}$

d. $\sqrt[5]{a^2b^3}$

$(a^2b^3)^{\frac{1}{5}} = a^{\frac{2}{5}}b^{\frac{3}{5}}$

7. If $f(x) = \sqrt{x - 3}$, determine each of the following:

a. $f(28)$

$\sqrt{25} = 5$

b. $f(3)$

0

c. $f(-1)$

Undefined

8. If $g(x) = \sqrt[3]{x + 10}$, determine each of the following:

a. $g(-74)$

$\sqrt[3]{-64} = -4$

b. $g(-10)$

0

c. $g(17)$

$\sqrt[3]{27} = 3$

ACTIVITY 2.7

Study Time

Topic: *Introduction to Inverse Functions*

You are interested in taking 16 credits this semester to complete your program, but you are concerned about the amount of time per week you will need for studying. The Academic Advising Center provides you with the information given in the following table.

FUNCTION *h*

NUMBER OF CREDITS TAKEN (INPUT)	NUMBER OF HOURS OF STUDY TIME (OUTPUT)
12	22
13	24
14	26
15	28
16	30
17	32
18	34

Notice that the number of hours of study time is a function of the number of credits taken. Call this function h.

1. Determine $h(14)$, and explain its meaning in practical terms.

$h(14) = 26$ The Advising Center recommends 26 hours of study time per week if your credit hour load is 14 hours.

2. Use the information from the table to construct another table in which the number of hours of study time is the input and the number of credits taken is the output.

FUNCTION *c*

NUMBER OF HOURS OF STUDY TIME (INPUT)	NUMBER OF CREDITS TAKEN (OUTPUT)
22	12
24	13
26	14
28	15
30	16
32	17
34	18

3. Is the number of credits taken a function of the number of hours of study time? Explain.

Yes, for each value of input there is one value of output.

4. Call this new function c and determine $c(30)$. Explain its meaning in practical terms.

$c(30) = 16$

If you have 30 hours per week to study you can handle 16 credit hours.

5. a. What is the domain of h and the range of h?

$D = \{12,13,14,15,16,17,18\}$

$R = \{22,24,26,28,30,32,34\}$

b. What is the domain of c and the range of c?

$D = \{22,24,26,28,30,32,34\}$

$R = \{12,13,14,15,16,17,18\}$

c. How are the domain and range of h related to the domain and range of c?

The domain and range are interchanged.

6. Determine each of the following. Refer to the appropriate table.

a. $h(15)$

28

b. $c(28)$

15

Notice that in Problem 6, the output of h—namely, 28—was used as the input of c. Recall that this is the composition of h and c and can be written as $c(h(15))$.

7. Determine each of the following. Use the table given at the beginning of this activity.

a. $c(h(18))$

18

b. $h(c(34))$

34

c. $c(h(13))$

13

d. $h(c(32))$

32

8. a. Let x represent the input for the function h. What is the result of the composition $c(h(x))$?

$c(h(x)) = x$

b. Let x represent the input for the function c. What is the result of the composition $h(c(x))$?

$h(c(x)) = x$

When the input of the composition of two functions is the same as the output of the composition, the two functions are **inverses** of each other. One function "undoes" the other. Symbolically, if functions f and g are inverses, then $f(g(x)) = x$ and $g(f(x)) = x$.

c. Are the functions h and c inverses? Explain.

Yes, because $c(h(x)) = h(c(x)) = x$.

In general, the inverse of a function f is written f^{-1}. Using this notation, $h = c^{-1}$ and $c = h^{-1}$.

INVERSE FUNCTIONS

- Two functions f and g are inverses if $f(g(x)) = x$ and $g(f(x)) = x$.
- The notation for the inverse of f is f^{-1}.
- The domain of f is the range of f^{-1}, and the range of f is the domain of f^{-1}.

IMPORTANT NOTE ABOUT NOTATION

The notation for the inverse function is potentially confusing. The -1 in $f^{-1}(x)$ is not an exponent! The notation is derived from the fact that the inverse function undoes the arithmetic operations of the original function. You may have seen -1 used as an exponent to denote the reciprocal of a number: $2^{-1} = \frac{1}{2}$. However, $f^{-1}(x) \neq \frac{1}{f(x)}$.

An important property of inverse functions is that the domain and range values are interchanged. For example, from the table on page 193,

$$h = \{(12, 22), (13, 24), (14, 26), \text{etc.}\}.$$

If the input and output values of each ordered pair are interchanged, you have

$$\{(22, 12), (24, 13), (26, 14), \text{etc.}\},$$

which match the (input, output) pairs of the function c, the inverse of h. See the table in Problem 2.

9. Given the function $p = \{(2, 4), (-5, 6), (0, 1), (7, 8)\}$, determine the following.

a. The inverse function, p^{-1}.

$p^{-1} = \{(4, 2), (6, -5), (1, 0), (8, 7)\}$

b. $p(2)$

4

c. $p^{-1}(4)$

2

d. $p(p^{-1}(4))$

4

e. $p^{-1}(p(2))$

2

10. The function q is defined by the following table, where $s = q(t)$.

t (INPUT)	s (OUTPUT)
1	2
2	3
3	5
4	3

a. Interchange the input and output values and record the results in the following table.

s (INPUT)	t (OUTPUT)
2	1
3	2
5	3
3	4

b. Does the table in part a represent a function? Explain.

No, there are two different outputs for the input value 3.

c. As a result of part b, the function q does not have an inverse. Could you have predicted that the function q does not have an inverse from the original table? Explain.

Yes, q would not have an inverse function because the output value of 3 was repeated.

EXERCISES

1. The functions f and g are defined by the following tables.

x	$f(x)$
2	3
4	5
6	7
8	9

x	$g(x)$
3	2
5	4
7	6
9	8

Determine each of the following.

a. $f(g(7))$
7

b. $g(f(4))$
4

c. $f(g(x))$
x

d. $g(f(x))$
x

2. The function h is defined by the following set of ordered pairs.

$$h = \{(2, 3),(3, 4),(4, 5),(5, 6)\}$$

a. Write h^{-1} as a set of ordered pairs.

$h^{-1} = \{(3, 2), (4, 3), (5, 4), (6, 5)\}$

b. Determine $h(3)$ and $h^{-1}(h(3))$.

$h(3) = 4;\ h(h^{-1}(3)) = 3$

c. Determine $h^{-1}(5)$ and $h\left(h^{-1}(5)\right)$

$h^{-1}(5) = 4;\ h(h^{-1}(5)) = h(4) = 5$

3. The function r is defined by the following table.

x	$r(x)$
0	2
1	3
2	4
3	2

a. Determine r^{-1}.

x	$r^{-1}(x)$
2	0
3	1
4	2
2	3

b. Does the table in part a represent a function? Explain.

No, because the input value 2 is paired with two different output values, 0 and 3.

c. Does the function $r(x)$ have an inverse? Explain.

The function does have an inverse, but the inverse is not a function.

ACTIVITY 2.8

Temperature Conversions

Topics: *Determining Inverse Functions, Graphs of Inverse Functions*

In Activity 2.4, Inflated Balloons, you used the function defined by $F = 32 + 1.8C$ to convert from a temperature measured in degrees Celsius to a temperature measured in degrees Fahrenheit. Call this function T.

1. a. Identify the input and output variables for the function T.

The input is C. The output is F or $T(C)$.

b. Determine $T(-5)$ and explain its meaning in this situation.

$T(-5) = 32 - 9 = 23$

A Celsius temperature of $-5°$ is equivalent to a Fahrenheit temperature of 23°.

2. When the temperature is 70°F; what is the temperature in degrees Celsius?

$70 = 32 + 1.8C$

$38 = 1.8C$

$C = 21.1$

70°F is equivalent to 21.1°C.

3. If you need to determine the temperature in Celsius for several Fahrenheit temperatures, it is easier to have a single formula (in fact, a new function) in which Celsius is the output and Fahrenheit is the input. Solve $F = 32 + 1.8C$ for C to find this new function. Call this function H.

$$H(F) = C = \frac{F - 32}{1.8}$$

4. a. Identify the input and output variables for the function H.

The input is F. The output is C.

b. Determine $H(62)$ and explain its meaning in this situation.

$$H(62) = \frac{62 - 32}{1.8} = \frac{30}{1.8} = 16.7$$

A Fahrenheit temperature of 62 degrees is equivalent to a Celsius temperature of 16.7 degrees.

5. Determine each of the following.

a. $T(10)$ **b.** $H(T(10))$

$T(10) = 32 + 1.8(10) = 50$ 10

6. Determine each of the following.

a. $T(H(95))$ **b.** $H(T(0))$ **c.** $T(H(212))$

95 0 212

7. a. Write a general expression for $H(T(x))$ and simplify the result.

$$H(T(x)) = H(32 + 1.8x) = \frac{32 + 1.8x - 32}{1.8} = x$$

b. Write a general expression for $T(H(x))$ and simplify the result.

$$T(H(x)) = T\left(\frac{x - 32}{1.8}\right) = 32 + 1.8\left(\frac{x - 32}{1.8}\right) = x$$

c. Based on your results in parts a and b, what can you conclude about the functions H and T?

H and *T* are inverse functions.

INVERSE FUNCTION ALGORITHM

Given an equation for a function f whose input is x and whose output is y, you can determine the equation for the inverse function, f^{-1}, as follows:

1. Exchange x and y in the given equation. (This switches input and output.)
2. Solve the resulting equation for y.
3. Write y as $f^{-1}(x)$.

For example, given $y = f(x) = 4x + 5$, you can determine the equation for the inverse f^{-1} as follows:

1. Exchange x and y: $y = 4x + 5$ becomes $x = 4y + 5$.
2. Solve for y: $y = \dfrac{x - 5}{4}$
3. Write y as $f^{-1}(x)$: $f^{-1}(x) = \dfrac{x - 5}{4}$

8. Given $y = f(x) = 5 - 3x$, determine f^{-1}.

$x = 5 - 3y$

$3y = 5 - x$

$y = f^{-1}(x) = \dfrac{5 - x}{3}$

9. a. Rewrite the function T that appeared at the beginning of this activity as $y = T(x) = 32 + 1.8x$. Rewrite T^{-1} as $y = T^{-1}(x) = \frac{x - 32}{1.8}$. Then graph the two functions on the same coordinate system with domain $-50 \leq x \leq 250$ and range $-50 \leq y \leq 250$.

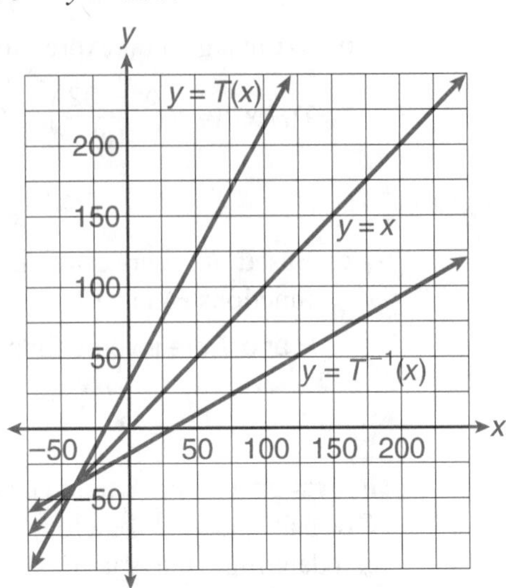

b. Draw the graph of the line $y = x$ on the coordinate system in part a. Describe the symmetry in the graphs of T and T^{-1}.

The graphs of T and T^{-1} are symmetric in the line $y = x$.

10. Determine the point of intersection of the graphs of T and T^{-1}. What is the significance of this point in this situation?

$32 + 1.8x = \frac{x - 32}{1.8}$ or $57.6 + 3.24x = x - 32$ or $2.24x = -89.6$ or $x = -40$

The Celsius and Fahrenheit scales are equivalent at -40 degrees.

GRAPHS OF INVERSE FUNCTIONS
The graphs of inverse functions are symmetric about the line $y = x$.

11. a. Determine the horizontal and vertical intercepts of the graphs of T and T^{-1}.

The intercepts of the graph of T are (0, 32) and (−17.7, 0).

The intercepts of the graph of T^{-1} are (0, −17.7) and (32, 0).

b. Write a sentence that describes the relationship between the intercepts of T and the intercepts of T^{-1}.

Using the intercepts of T, interchange the coordinates to obtain the intercepts of T^{-1}.

12. a. Determine the slopes of the graphs of T and T^{-1}.

The slope of T is 1.8 or $\frac{9}{5}$. The slope of T^{-1} is $\frac{5}{9}$.

b. Write a sentence that describes the relationship between the slope of T and the slope of T^{-1}.

The slopes of T and T^{-1} are reciprocals.

SUMMARY

- To determine the equation of the inverse of the function defined by $y = f(x)$:
  1. Exchange x and y in the given equation. (This switches input and output.)
  2. Solve the resulting equation for y.
  3. Write y as $f^{-1}(x)$.
- The graphs of inverse functions are symmetric about the line $y = x$.
- If two linear functions are inverses, the slopes of the graphs of the lines are reciprocals.

EXERCISES

1. You are a sales representative who is paid a base salary of $250 per week plus a 5% commission.

a. Determine a function for your weekly gross pay P (before taxes) as a function of S, your weekly sales in dollars.

$P(S) = 0.05S + 250$

b. Determine $P(6000)$ and interpret its meaning in this situation.

$P(6000) = 0.05(6000) + 250 = 550$. The weekly salary for $6000 worth of sales is $550.

c. Solve the equation $P = 0.05S + 250$ for S to determine the equation for a new function, $S(P)$, whose input is P and whose output is S.

$$S(P) = \frac{P - 250}{0.05}$$

d. Determine $S(400)$ and interpret its meaning in this situation.

$S(400) = \dfrac{400 - 250}{0.05} = 3000$. A weekly salary of $400 means I sold $3000 worth of merchandise.

e. Determine $S(P(8000))$.

$S(P(8000)) = 8000$

2. **a.** Complete the following table for the function $y = f(x) = 3x^2 - 2$.

x	-2	-1	0	1	2
y	10	1	−2	1	10

b. Describe how you know that f is a function by examining the table.

f is a function because for each input value there is one output value.

c. Use the table of values from part a to determine f^{-1}, if possible. If it is not possible, explain why.

This is not a function since two x-values are paired with two different y-values.

3. Determine the inverse of the given function.

a. $y = f(x) = 3x - 4$

$y = 3x - 4$ so, $x = 3y - 4$ or $y = f^{-1}(x) = \dfrac{x + 4}{3}$

b. $w = g(z) = \dfrac{z - 4}{2}$

$z = \dfrac{w - 4}{2}$ or $w = g^{-1}(x) = 2z + 4$

c. $s(t) = \frac{5}{t}$

$t = \frac{5}{s}$ or $s = \frac{5}{t}$.

4. a. Given $y = f(x) = 2x + 6$, determine f^{-1}.

$f^{-1}(x) = \dfrac{x - 6}{2}$

b. Add the sketch of the graphs of f and f^{-1} on the same coordinate system.

c. Add the sketch of the graph of $y = x$ to the sketches of f and f^{-1} in part b. Describe any symmetry in the graphs of f and f^{-1}.

The graphs of f and f^{-1} are symmetric with respect to the line $y = x$.

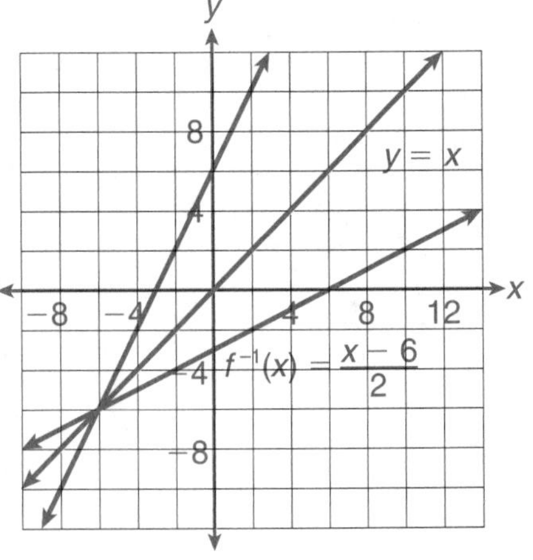

d. Determine the horizontal and vertical intercepts of the graphs of f and f^{-1}. Explain the relationship between the intercepts of f and the intercepts of f^{-1}.

The intercepts for f are (0, 6) and (−3, 0). The intercepts for f^{-1} are (6, 0) and (0, −3). The x and y coordinates of the intercepts of the inverse are interchanged from the coordinates of the intercepts of f.

e. Determine the slope of the graph of f and the slope of the graph of f^{-1}. What is the relationship between the slope of f and the slope of f^{-1}.

The slope of the graph of f is 2, the slope of the inverse is 1/2. The slopes are reciprocals.

5. Consider the graphs of functions g and h. Are the functions inverses of each other? Explain, using a symmetry argument.

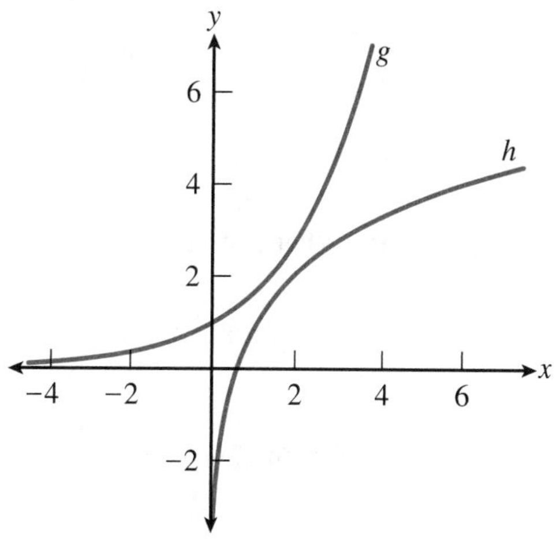

g and h are inverses. The graphs of g and h are symmetric with respect to the line $y = x$.

6. Consider the functions $f(x) = 3x + 6$ and $g(x) = \frac{1}{3}x - 2$.

a. Determine $f(g(x))$.

$f(\frac{1}{3}x - 2) = 3(\frac{1}{3}x - 2) + 6 = x$

b. Determine $g(f(x))$.

$g(3x + 6) = \frac{1}{3}(3x + 6) - 2 = x$

c. Are f and g inverse functions? Explain.

Yes, because $g(f(x)) = f(g(x)) = x$.

d. Complete the following tables for the given functions.

x	f(x)
−2	0
0	6
2	12
4	18

x	g(x)
0	−2
6	0
12	2
18	4

e. Do you notice anything about the ordered pairs of f and g?

The inputs and outputs have been interchanged.

f. Graph f and g on the following grid.

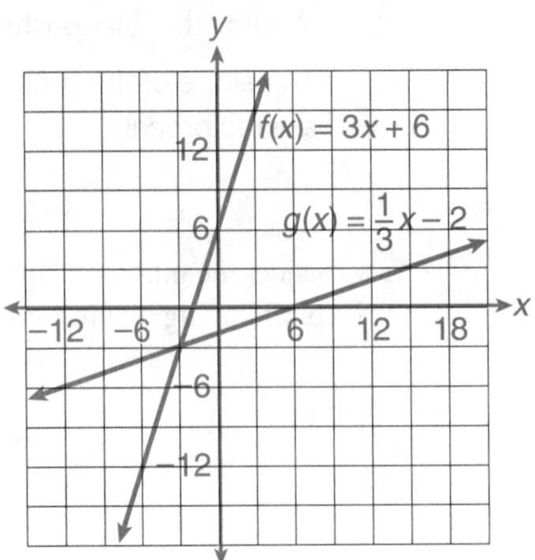

g. What can you say about the graphs of f and g with respect to the graph of $y = x$?

The graphs are reflections in the line $y = x$.

7. **a.** Given $g(x) = \dfrac{6 + 4x}{3}$, find an equation for $g^{-1}(x)$.

$g^{-1}(x) = \dfrac{3x - 6}{4}$

b. Sketch the graphs of g and g^{-1} on the following grid.

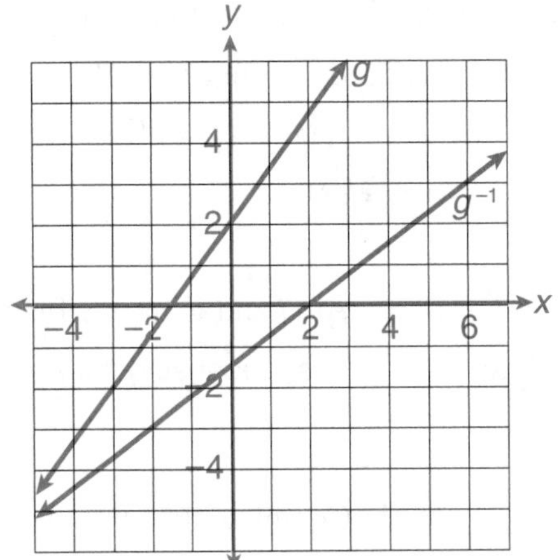

c. Do you believe that your equation for g^{-1} in part a is correct? Explain.

Yes, because the graphs are reflections in the line $y = x$.

d. Find $g^{-1}(g\ (x))$. Does your result support your answer in part c? Explain.

$g^{-1}\left(\dfrac{6 + 4x}{3}\right) = \dfrac{3\left(\frac{6 + 4x}{3}\right) - 6}{4} = \dfrac{4x}{4} = x$. Yes, because $g^{-1}(g(x)) = x$.

PROJECT ACTIVITY 2.9

Error Checking

Topic: *Composition of Functions*

In a computer, information is represented as strings of 0s and 1s, such as 0101110. When files of information are transmitted, you need ways to check for any errors or unwanted changes in the string that might occur. Such errors can be caused by noise in transmission, electrical interference, or human or machine error. Errors may also be introduced in data stored on old magnetic tape, because the condition of the tape degrades over time.

One way for you as a computer programmer to look for errors is to count the number of 1s in the string before it is transmitted. If you get an even number of 1s, put a 0 at the end of the string. If you get an odd number of 1s, put a 1 at the end of the string. This extra 0 or 1 is called a *parity check bit*. After the string is transmitted, you can check to see if there is an even or an odd number of 1s in the string.

1. **a.** If you define n to be the number of 1s before the check bit is added, you may consider n as a function of the string. So let s represent the input (the string), and $n = f(s)$. For example, when s is 0101110, then $n = f(s) = 4$. What is $f(1011)$?

   $f(1011) = 3$

   b. If you call the parity check bit p, you can write p as a function of the number of 1s in this way: $p = g(n)$. When n is 3, what is $g(n)$? What is $g(4)$?

   $g(n) = 1$ when $n = 3$; $g(4) = 0$

Another way of writing the function rule for finding the parity check bit is

$$g(n) = \begin{cases} 0 \text{ if } n \text{ is even} \\ 1 \text{ if } n \text{ is odd.} \end{cases}$$

The function g is an example of a piecewise function, where the function rule for determining the output is given separately, or in pieces, for different values of the input.

Because $n = f(s)$ and $p = g(n)$, you can replace n with $f(s)$ to get $p = g(f(s))$.

2. What are the independent and dependent variables for this composition function?

   The independent variable is s. The dependent variables are $f(s) = n$, and $g(n) = p$

Exercise numbers appearing in color are answered in the Selected Answers section of this book.

3. Complete the following table of values.

STRINGS, s	NUMBER OF 1s $n = f(s)$	PARITY CHECK BIT, $p = g(n) = g(f(s))$
100 100 100	3	1
100 100 101	4	0
100 100 110	4	0
100 100 111	5	1
100 101 000	3	1
100 101 001	4	0
100 101 010	4	0
100 101 011	5	1
100 101 100	4	0

4. What can you conclude if you use a parity check bit and the string received is 01110?

You can conclude that an error was made.

5. If you receive 111010, can you tell for sure if there were any errors in the transmission of this string?

No. Maybe the original string was 11101 and it was sent correctly or the original string was 111010 and the person forgot to add a 0 to the end of it.

6. In general, what is true about the number of 1s in every correctly transmitted string?

The number of 1s is even, or the final string will have an even number of 1s.

What Have I Learned?

1. For any two functions f and g, (i) determine which of the following equations are true, and explain why. Then (ii) determine which of the following equations are *not* always true and give an example to show why not.

a. $(f + g)(x) = (g + f)(x)$

b. $(f - g)(x) = (g - f)(x)$

c. $(f \cdot g)(x) = (g \cdot f)(x)$

d. $(f \circ g)(x) = (g \circ f)(x)$

e. $(f \circ f^{-1})(x) = (f^{-1} \circ f)(x)$

(i) Equation a is true because addition of functions is commutative. Equation c is true because multiplication of functions is commutative. Equation e is true because it is one of the properties of inverse functions.

(ii) Let $f(x) = 2x^2 + 1$ and $g(x) = x - 1$. I will use these to show that equations b and d are false.

$$(f - g)(x) = 2x^2 + 1 - (x - 1) = 2x^2 - x + 2$$

$$(g - f)(x) = x - 1 - (2x^2 + 1) = -2x^2 + x - 2$$

Clearly these are not equal.

$$(f \circ g)(x) = f(g(x)) = f(x - 1) = 2(x - 1)^2 + 1 = 2(x^2 - 2x + 1) + 1 = 2x^2 - 4x + 3$$

$$(g \circ f)(x) = g(f(x)) = g(2x^2 + 1) - 2x^2 + 1 - 1 = 2x^2$$

Again clearly not equal. (Answers will vary depending on choice of f and g.)

2. Describe how you would determine whether two functions are inverses of each other.

Given f and g, I would evaluate $f(g(x))$ and $g(f(x))$. If both expressions simplified to x I would conclude they are inverses. If they did not I would conclude they are not inverses. (Geometric or numeric arguments would also be considered here.)

3. Suppose that f is a nonconstant linear function.

a. Will f always have an inverse function?

Yes, it will.

b. What will always be true about the slopes of the lines representing the graphs of f and f^{-1}?

f and f^{-1} will have reciprocal slopes.

c. Why is it important to assume that f is nonconstant?

If f is constant, the slope of the graph is 0. The graph is a horizontal line. The graph of the inverse is a vertical line, which does not represent a function.

4. If $f(g(x)) = x^6$, determine at least three different ways to define f and g.

$f(x) = x$, $g(x) = x^6$, or $f(x) = x^2$, $g(x) = x^3$ or $f(x) = x^3$, $g(x) = x^2$.

5. It is possible to compose more than two functions. If $f(x) = 2x - 1$, $g(x) = 5 - 3x$, and $h(x) = 2x^2$, determine each of the following.

a. $f(g(h(1)))$

$f(g(h(1)) = f(g(2)) = f(-1) = -3$

b. $g(f(h(1)))$

$g(f(h(1)) = g(f(2)) = g(3) = -4$

c. $h(g(f(1)))$

$h(g(f(1)) = h(g(1)) = h(2) = 8$

d. $h(f(g(1)))$

$h(f(g(1)) = h(f(2)) = h(3) = 18$

How Can I Practice?

1. Given $f(x) = x^2 - 4$ and $g(x) = x + 2$, determine each of the following.

a. $f(g(-3))$

$f(-1) = -3$

b. $g(f(-3))$

$g(5) = 7$

c. $f(g(x))$

$f(x + 2) = (x + 2)^2 - 4 = x^2 + 4x$

d. $g(f(x))$

$g(x^2 - 4) = x^2 - 4 + 2 = x^2 - 2$

e. $f(f(x))$

$f(x^2 - 4) = (x^2 - 4)^2 - 4$

$= x^4 - 8x^2 + 12$

f. $g^{-1}(x)$

$x = y + 2$ or $y = g^{-1}(x) = x - 2$

2. Given $f(x) = x - 4$ and $g(x) = 4 + x - x^2$, determine each of the following.

a. $f(g(3))$

$f(-2) = -6$

b. $g(f(3))$

$g(-1) = 2$

c. $g(g(3))$

$g(-2) = -2$

d. $f(g(x))$

$f(4 + x - x^2) = (4 + x - x^2) - 4$

$= x - x^2$

Exercise numbers appearing in color are answered in the Selected Answers section of this book.

e. $g(f(x))$

$g(x - 4) = 4 + (x - 4) - (x - 4)^2$
$= x - (x^2 - 8x + 16)$
$= -x^2 + 9x - 16$

f. $f^{-1}(x)$

$x = y - 4$ or $y = f^{-1}(x) = x + 4$

3. Given the first two tables, complete the third table.

x	0	1	2	3	4
f(x)	6	−1	−3	0	2

x	−3	−1	0	2	6
g(x)	2	3	1	0	−1

x	0	1	2	3	4
g(f(x))	−1	3	2	1	0

4. Simplify the following.

a. $(x^2)^4$

x^8

b. $(xy)^3$

x^3y^3

c. $(2x^4y)^5$

$32x^{20}y^5$

d. $(3x^2)^3(2xy^4)$

$(27x^6)(2xy^4) = 54x^7y^4$

e. $25^{\frac{3}{2}}$

125

f. $64^{\frac{2}{3}}$

16

5. Given $f(x) = 3x^2$ and $g(x) = -2x^3$, determine each of the following.

a. $g(f(x))$ **b.** $f(g(x))$ **c.** $g(f(-4))$

a. $g(3x^2) = -2(3x^2)^3 = -54x^6$

b. $f(-2x^3) = 3(-2x^3)^2 = 12x^6$

c. $g(48) = -2(48)^3 = -221{,}184$

6. Given $s(x) = x^2 + 4x - 1$ and $t(x) = 4x - 1$, determine each of the following.

a. $s(t(x))$ **b.** $t(s(x))$ **c.** $t^{-1}(x)$

a. $s(4x - 1) = (4x - 1)^2 + 4(4x - 1) - 1 = 16x^2 - 8x + 1 + 16x - 4 - 1$
$16x^2 + 8x - 4$

b. $t(x^2 + 4x - 1) = 4(x^2 + 4x - 1) - 1 = 4x^2 + 16x - 5$

c. $x = 4y - 1$ or $y = t^{-1}(x) = \dfrac{x + 1}{4}$

7. Given $p(x) = \frac{1}{x}$ and $c(x) = \sqrt{x + 2}$, determine each of the following.

a. $p(c(x))$ **b.** $c(p(x))$ **c.** $p^{-1}(x)$

a. $p(\sqrt{x + 2}) = \dfrac{1}{\sqrt{x + 2}}$

b. $c(\frac{1}{x}) = \sqrt{\frac{1}{x} + 2}$

c. $x = \frac{1}{y}$ or $y = p^{-1}(x) = \frac{1}{x}$

8. The function q is defined by the following set of ordered pairs.

$$\{(4, 6), (7, -9), (-2, 1), (0, 0)\}$$

Determine q^{-1} as a set of ordered pairs.

$\{(6, 4), (-9, 7), (1, -2), (0, 0)\}$

9. Show that $f(x) = 2x - 3$ and $g(x) = \dfrac{x + 3}{2}$ are inverses of each other.

$f(g(x)) = f\left(\dfrac{x + 3}{2}\right) = 2\left(\dfrac{x + 3}{2}\right) - 3 = x$

$g(f(x)) = g(2x - 3) = \dfrac{(2x - 3) + 3}{2} = x$

Since $f(g(x)) = g(f(x)) = x$, f, and g are inverse functions.

10. **a.** Determine the inverse function of $f(x) = 4x + 3$.

$x = 4y + 3$ or $y = f^{-1}(x) = \dfrac{x - 3}{4}$

b. Sketch the graph of the function f and its inverse f^{-1} on the same coordinate system.

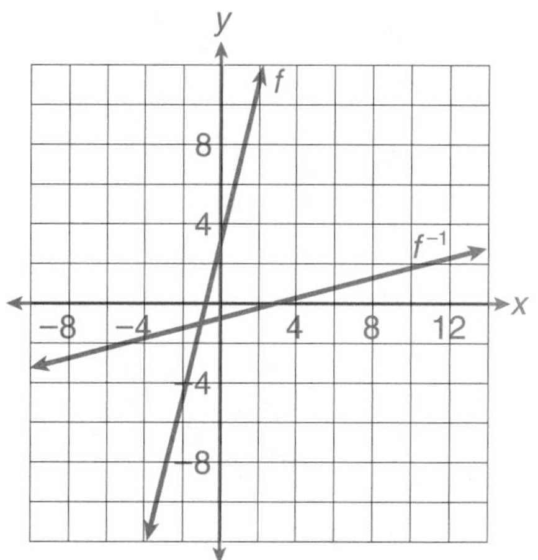

c. Determine the horizontal and vertical intercepts of the graphs of f and f^{-1}.

The intercepts of f are $(0, 3)$ and $(-\frac{3}{4}, 0)$. The intercepts of f^{-1} are $\left(0, -\frac{3}{4}\right)$ and $(3, 0)$.

d. Determine the slopes of the graphs of f and f^{-1}.

The slope of the graph of f is 4. The slope of the graph of the inverse is 1/4.

e. Sketch a graph of the line $y = x$ on the same coordinate system.

11. The volume of a rectangular box is equal to the area of the base times the height. Suppose that a particular box has a height of 10 inches and a square base.

a. Using V for the volume of the box, b for the area of the base, and x for the length of one side of the square base, express b as a function of x and V as a function of b.

$b = x^2 \quad V = 10b$

b. Show how the volume, $V(x)$, is the composition of these two functions.

$V = 10x^2$

12. Given $f(x) = 4x - 9$ and $g(x) = 10 - 3x$, what input to the composition function $f(g(x))$ will result in an output of 15?

$f(g(x)) = 15$ or $4(10 - 3x) - 9 = 15$

$40 - 12x - 9 = 15$

$31 - 12x = 15$

$-12x = -16$

$x = \frac{4}{3}$

Gateway Review

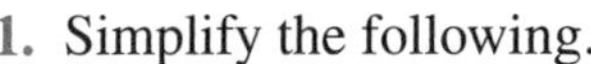

1. Simplify the following.

   a. $(x + 6) + (2x^2 - 3x - 7)$

   $2x^2 - 2x - 1$

   b. $(x^2 + 4x - 3) - (2x^2 - x + 1)$

   $-x^2 + 5x - 4$

   c. $(x - 3)(4x - 1)$

   $4x^2 - 13x + 3$

   d. $(x - 5)(x^2 - 2x + 3)$

   $x^3 - 7x^2 + 13x - 15$

   e. $4(x + 2) - 3(5x - 1)$

   $-11x + 11$

   f. $(2x^2 + x - 1)(x^2 - 3x + 4)$

   $2x^4 - 5x^3 + 4x^2 + 7x - 4$

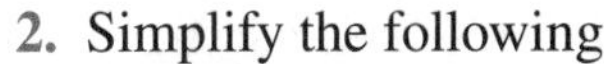

2. Simplify the following.

   a. $(3x^3)(2x^5)$

   $6x^8$

   b. $(4x^3y)^2$

   $16x^6y^2$

   c. $(xy)^2(-2x^3y)$

   $-2x^5y^3$

   d. $(5x^3y^4z)(-2x^2yz^3)$

   $-10x^5y^5z^4$

3. Given $f(x) = 6x - 2$ and $g(x) = -2x + 3$, determine each of the following.

   a. $f(-3)$

   -20

   b. $(f + g)(x)$

   $4x + 1$

   c. $(f - g)(3)$

   $f(3) - g(3) = 16 - (-3) = 19$

   d. $(f \cdot g)(x)$

   $(6x - 2)(-2x + 3)$

   $-12x^2 + 22x - 6$

Exercise numbers appearing in color are answered in the Selected Answers section of this book.

e. $f(g(x))$

$f(-2x + 3) = 6(-2x + 3) - 2$
$= -12x + 16$

f. $g(f(2))$

$g(10) = -2(10) + 3 = -17$

g. f^{-1} (Find the inverse of f.)

$x = 6y - 2$ or $y = f^{-1}(x) = \dfrac{x + 2}{6}$

4. Given $f(x) = x^2 - x + 3$ and $g(x) = 3x - 2$, determine each of the following.

   a. $(f - g)(x)$

   $x^2 - 4x + 5$

   b. $(f \cdot g)(x)$

   $3x^3 - 3x^2 + 9x - 2x^2 + 2x - 6$
   $= 3x^3 - 5x^2 + 11x - 6$

   c. $(f(g(x))$

   $f(3x - 2) = (3x - 2)^2 - (3x - 2) + 3$
   $= 9x^2 - 12x + 4 - 3x + 2 + 3$
   $= 9x^2 - 15x + 9$

   d. $(g(f(2))$

   $g(5) = 3(5) - 2 = 13$

5. Determine the value of each of the following.

   a. $49^{1/2}$ — 7

   b. $32^{2/5}$ — 4

   c. $(-27)^{4/3}$ — 81

   d. $7^{3/5}$ — 3.214

6. To ship the mail-order ceramic figures that you produce, you need to make square-bottomed boxes. For the size of the box to be proportional to the figurines, the height of the box must always be 3 times longer than the width. The cost of the material to make the top and bottom of the box molded to fit the figurine is \$0.01 per square inch, and the cost of the material for the sides of the box sells for \$0.004 per square inch.

   a. Write a function $f(x)$ to represent the cost of producing the top and the bottom of a box. Use x to represent the width of the bottom of the box in inches.

   $f(x) = 2(0.01)x^2 = 0.02x^2$

   b. Write a function $g(x)$ to represent the cost of producing the sides of the box.

   $g(x) = 4(0.004)(x)(3x) = 0.048x^2$

   c. Combine the functions in parts a and b to write one function that represents the total cost of making the box, $(f + g)(x)$. Write the equation in simplest form.

   $(f + g)(x) = 0.02x^2 + 0.048x^2 = 0.068x^2$

d. Using f, g and $f + g$ as defined in parts a, b, and c, complete the following table.

x (in.)	f(x)	g(x)	(f + g)(x)
2	0.08	1.92	2
4	0.32	7.68	8
6	0.72	17.28	18
8	1.28	30.72	32
10	2	48	50

e. Use your grapher to graph all three functions. Find $f(5)$, $g(5)$, and $(f + g)(5)$ from the graph. Explain the practical meaning of the values that you found.

$f(5) = 0.50$, $g(5) = 1.2$, $(f + g)(5) = 1.70$ For a box whose base is 5 in by 5 in, the cost of the top and bottom of the box is $.50, the cost of the 4 sides is $1.20, and the total cost of the box is $1.70.

7. You have a knitting machine in your home and your business is making ski hats. The fixed cost to run your knitting company is $300 per month and the cost to produce each hat averages approximately $12. The hats will sell for $25.95.

a. Write a function f to represent the cost of making the hats. Use x to represent the number of hats made per month.

$f(x) = 12x + 300$

b. Write a function g to represent the revenue from the sale of the hats.

$g(x) = 25.95x$

c. Write a function h to represent the profit for the month. Express this function in simplest form.

$h(x) = 25.95x - (12x + 300) = 13.95x - 300$

d. Graph the three functions on your grapher. How many hats must be sold in one month to break even?

22 hats must be sold, since 21 hats is not quite enough. The solution was obtained graphically.

e. Determine the value of $f(50)$, $g(50)$, and $h(f - g)(50)$. Explain the practical meaning of the values that you found.

$f(50) = 900$, the cost of producing 50 hats is $900. $g(50) = 1297.50$, the revenue from 50 hats is $1297.50. $h(50) = 397.50$, the profit from selling 50 hats is $397.50

f. Explain how the difference function $f(x) - g(x) = (f - g)(x)$ pertains to this situation.

The profit is the difference between the revenue and cost functions.

8. The manufacturer of a certain brand of computer printer prefers to sell her printers in lots of 60. Her wholesale price is \$110 per printer, based on selling 60 printers. Because the warehouse is overstocked and new high-speed printers are arriving, the manufacturer says on this order only that for every printer you purchase over 60, you will pay \$2 per printer less. The manufacturer will not let you purchase more than 90 with this order.

   a. Let x represent the number of printers in excess of 60 that you will purchase. Write a function for the total cost C of the printers as a function of the number of printers x. Call this function f.

   $f(x) = 60(110) + x(110 - 2x)$

   b. Rewrite the cost function by multiplying the factors and combining like terms.

   $f(x) = 6600 + 110x - 2x^2$

   c. What is the domain of the cost function?

   Integers $0 \le x \le 30$.

   d. If you decide that it is to your advantage to purchase 75 printers rather than 60 printers, explain the cost savings to you and your business.

   $f(15) = 7800$. At regular price the cost is \$8250, so the savings is \$450.

9. Functions f and g are defined by the following tables.

x	−1	0	1	2	4	5	8
$f(x)$	8	5	2	−1	−7	−10	−19

x	−1	0	1	2	4	5	8
$g(x)$	5	1	−1	−1	5	11	41

Determine the values for each of the following.

a. $f(g(4))$ −10 **b.** $g(f(-1))$ 41 **c.** $f(g(0))$ 2 **d.** $g(f(2))$ 5

10. You manufacture snowboards. You cannot produce more than 30 boards per day. The cost C of producing x boards is represented by the function $C = f(x) = 150x - 0.9x^2$.

   a. What is the domain of the function?

   Integers $0 \le x \le 30$

   b. What is the cost if 22 boards are produced?

   $f(22) = 2864.40$

c. The number of snowboards that can be produced in t hours is represented by the function $g(t) = 3.75t$. Your employees do not work more than 9 hours per day. Determine $f(g(t))$.

$f(3.75t) = 150(3.75t) - 0.9(3.75t)^2 = 562.50t - 12.65625t^2$

d. What is the input variable in the composition of the functions in part c?

The input variable is t.

e. Because of a blizzard, your employees work only 4 hours on a certain day. Find the production cost for that day.

$f(g(4)) = \$2047.50$

f. The company prefers to keep production costs at approximately \$3500. How many hours each day does the company have to operate to maintain this production cost?

$3500 = 562.50t - 12.65625t^2$

t is about 7.5 hours (determined graphically).

11. a. Determine the inverse of the function $f(x) = \dfrac{2x - 3}{5}$.

$\dfrac{2y - 3}{5} = x$ or $f^{-1}(x) = y = \dfrac{5x + 3}{2}$

b. What is the slope of the line for each function? What is the relationship between the slopes of the two functions?

The slope of f is 2/5. The slope of f^{-1} is 5/2. The slopes are reciprocals.

12. a. Show that $f(x) = -2x + 1$ and $g(x) = \dfrac{1 - x}{2}$ are inverse functions of each other.

Let $f(x) = -2x + 1$ and $g(x) = \dfrac{1 - x}{2}$

$f(g(x)) = f\left(\dfrac{1 - x}{2}\right) = -2\left(\dfrac{1 - x}{2}\right) + 1 = x$

$g(f(x)) = g(-2x + 1) = \dfrac{1 - (-2x + 1)}{2} = \dfrac{2x}{2} = x$

Since $f(g(x)) = g(f(x)) = x$, f, and g are inverses.

b. Sketch the graphs of the functions in part a on the same axis, and check the result with your grapher.

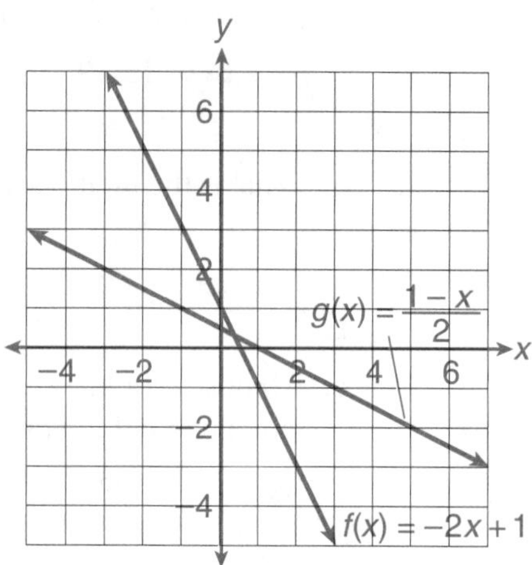

c. What can you say about the graphs of f and g with respect to the graph of $y = x$?

f and g are symmetric with respect to the line $y = x$.

13. You work in the box office of a movie theater. The system for purchasing tickets is automated. You enter the number of tickets you need for each category (adult, child, senior) and the output is the total cost. The following table is a sample from a computer screen that shows the cost for adult tickets only. The number of tickets represents the input and the total cost represents the output.

NUMBER OF ADULT TICKETS	TOTAL COST
2	$11.00
5	$27.50
7	$38.50
12	$66.00

a. Does this table represent a linear function? Explain.

Yes, the ratio (change in cost)/(change in number of tickets) is constant.

b. Write a function f to represent the total cost as a function of the number of tickets x that are purchased.

$f(x) = 5.5x$

c. Determine the cost of one ticket. What does this value represent in your function?

The cost of one ticket is $5.50. This is represented by the slope.

Often the customer approaches the window with the exact amount of cash for the tickets. In that case, you enter the total amount into the computer, press adult ticket, and out comes the number of tickets. In this case, the total cost is the input and the number of tickets is the output.

d. Fill in the table showing this situation.

TOTAL COST	NUMBER OF TICKETS
\$11.00	2
\$27.50	5
\$38.50	7
\$66.00	12

e. Write the function g that represents the total number of tickets purchased as a function of the total cost x.

$g(x) = \frac{2}{11}x$

f. What is the slope of this line? What is the relationship between the slopes of the two functions f and g?

The slope is 2/11. The slopes are reciprocals.

g. Determine $f(g(x))$ and $g(f(x))$. Are the functions inverses of each other? Explain.

$f(\frac{2}{11}x) = 5.5(\frac{2}{11})x = x$, $g(5.5x) = \frac{2}{11}(5.5x) = x$

The functions are inverses since $f(g(x)) = g(f(x)) = x$.

CHAPTER 3

Exponential and Logarithmic Functions

CLUSTER 1

Exponential Functions

ACTIVITY 3.1

The Summer Job
Topic: *Exponential Functions*

Your neighbor's son will be attending college in the fall, majoring in mathematics. On July 1, he comes to your house looking for summer work to help pay for college expenses. You are interested because you need some odd jobs done, but you don't have a lot of extra money to pay him. The young man says that he can start right away and will work all day July 1 for 2 cents. This gets your attention, but you wonder if there is a catch. He says that he will work July 2 for 4 cents, July 3 for 8 cents, July 4 (he even works holidays) for 16 cents, and so on, for *every* day of the month of July. He can't work after that because his family is planning a vacation in August.

1. Do you hire him?

   Yes, probably.

For problems 2–8, assume that you do hire him.

2. How much will he earn on July 5? July 6?

   July 5th, $2^5 = 32$ cents. July 6th, $2^6 = 64$ cents.

3. What will be his total pay for the first week of July (July 1 through July 7)?

   $2 + 4 + 8 + 16 + 32 + 64 + 128 = 254$ cents or \$2.54

4. a. Complete the following table.

DAY IN JULY (INPUT)	PAY IN CENTS (OUTPUT)
1	2
2	4
3	8
4	16
5	32
6	64
7	128
8	256

b. Do you notice a pattern in the output values? Describe how you can obtain the pay on a given day knowing the pay on the previous day.

Yes, the outputs are multiples of 2. Given yesterday's pay, multiply it by 2 to find today's pay.

c. Use what you discovered in part b to determine the pay on July 9.

The pay when $n = 9$ is 512 cents or $5.12.

5. a. The pay on any given day can be written as a power of 2. Write each pay entry in the output column of the table in Problem 4 as a power of 2. For example, $2 = 2^1$, $4 = 2^2$,

$8 = 2^3$, $16 = 2^4$, $32 = 2^5$, $64 = 2^6$, $128 = 2^7$, $256 = 2^8$

b. Describe how you can determine the young man's pay on a given day knowing the number of days he has worked.

The pay is 2^n cents, where n is the day of the month.

6. a. Let n represent the number of days worked. Write a symbolic rule for the daily pay $P = f(n)$ (in cents) as a function of n. Note that the number of days worked is the same as the July date.

$P = f(n) = 2^n$.

b. Use the rule from part a to determine how much your neighbor's son will earn on July 20. That is, determine the value of P when $n = 20$.

$P = f(20) = 2^{20} = 1{,}048{,}576$ cents or $10,485.76.

c. How much will he earn on July 31?

$P = f(31) = 2^{31} = 2{,}147{,}483{,}648$ cents or $21,474,836.48.

d. Was it a good idea to hire him?

No, it was not a good idea.

7. a. Determine the rate of change of P as n increases from $n = 3$ to $n = 4$.

$$\frac{\Delta P}{\Delta n} = \frac{16 - 8}{4 - 3} = 8$$

b. Determine the rate of change of P as n increases from $n = 7$ to $n = 8$.

$$\frac{\Delta P}{\Delta n} = \frac{256 - 128}{8 - 7} = 128$$

c. Is the function linear? Explain.

No, it is not linear. The rate of change is not constant.

8. a. What is the practical domain of the summer pay function defined by $P = f(n) = 2^n$?

The practical domain is the whole numbers from 1 to 31.

b. Sketch a scatterplot of ordered pairs of the form (n, P) from July 1 to July 6.

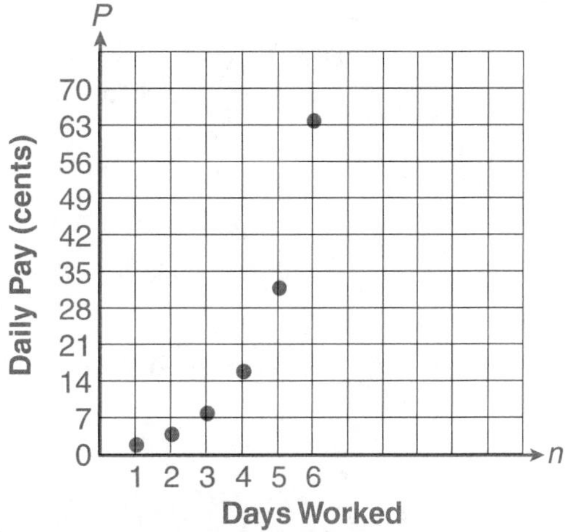

The function rule $P = f(n) = 2^n$ gives the relationship between the pay P (in cents) on a given day, n, worked. This function belongs to a family of functions called **exponential functions.**

> **Exponential functions** are defined by equations of the form $y = b^x$, where the base b is a constant such that $b > 0$ and $b \neq 1$. Such functions are called exponential functions because the independent variable (input) x is the exponent.

Some examples of exponential functions are $g(x) = 10^x$, $h(x) = 1.08^x$, and $F(x) = \left(\frac{1}{2}\right)^x$.

9. **a.** Use your graphing calculator to sketch a graph of $f(x) = 2^x$. Your screen should appear as follows if you use the window Xmin $= -10$, Xmax $= 10$, Ymin $= -2$, and Ymax $= 10$.

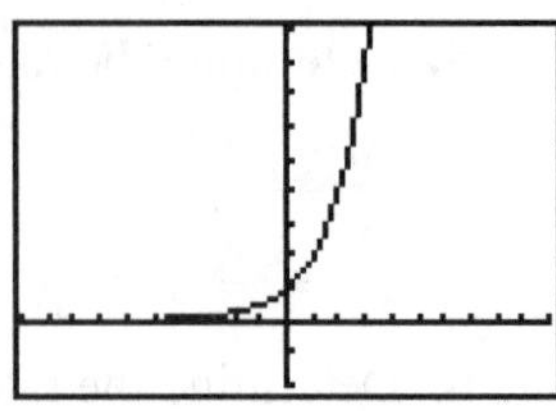

b. Because the graph of $f(x) = 2^x$ is continuous (no holes or breaks), what appears to be the domain of the function *f*?

The domain is all reals.

c. Determine the *y*-intercept of the graph of *f*. How is the *y*-intercept related to the value of *f*(0)?

$f(0) = 2^0 = 1$. The *y*-intercept is (0, 1).

d. Is the function *f* increasing or decreasing?

The function is increasing everywhere.

The base 2 of $f(x) = 2^x$ is called the **growth factor** because each time *x* is increased by 1, the corresponding output increases by a factor of 2.

e. Does the graph of *f* have an *x*-intercept?

The graph does not have an *x*-intercept.

f. Complete the following table. Use your calculator. Round to 4 decimal places.

x	-10	-8	-6	-4	-2	-1
$f(x) = 2^x$	0.0010	0.0039	0.0156	0.0625	0.25	0.5

Note: 2^{-10} is equivalent to $\frac{1}{2^{10}} \approx 0.0010$.

g. As the values of the input variable *x* get more and more negative, what happens to the output values?

Decrease.

h. Use the trace feature of your grapher to trace the graph of $f(x) = 2^x$ for $x < 0$. What do you observe?

The values of *f*(*x*) continue to decrease and get closer and closer to zero.

A horizontal line given by $y = c$ is called a **horizontal asymptote** if, as $|x|$ gets very large, the graph of the function gets closer and closer to the graph of $y = c$.

10. a. Sketch a graph of $g(x) = 10^x$ on the same coordinate axes as $f(x) = 2^x$ using your graphing calculator. If you use the window Xmin $= -5$, Xmax $= 5$, Ymin $= -2$, and Ymax $= 9$ your screen should resemble the following.

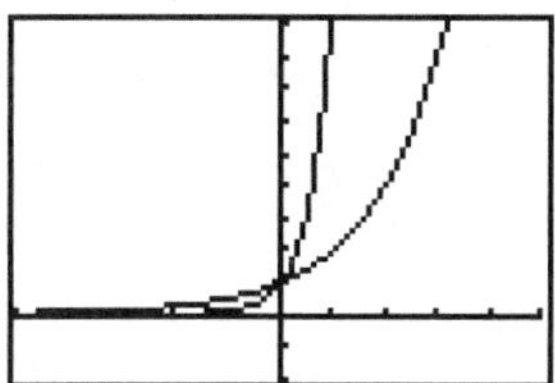

b. Describe how the graphs of $f(x) = 2^x$ and $g(x) = 10^x$ are similar and how they are different. Be sure to discuss if the graph of g increases faster or slower than the graph of f.

The graphs of f and g both increase for all values of x. Both graphs have the same y-intercept (0, 1). g increases more slowly than f for values of $x < 0$ and increases more quickly than f for values of $x > 0$.

11. a. Complete the following table.

x	−3	−2	−1	0	1	2	3	4	5
$f(x) = \left(\frac{1}{2}\right)^x$	8	4	2	1	0.5	0.25	0.125	0.0625	0.03125

b. Describe how you can obtain the output value for $x = 6$, using the output value for $x = 5$.

To obtain the value for $x = 6$ from the value for $x = 5$, multiply by 0.5.

c. Obtain a graph of $f(x) = \left(\frac{1}{2}\right)^x$ using your graphing calculator. If you use the same window settings as in Problem 10, your screen should appear as follows.

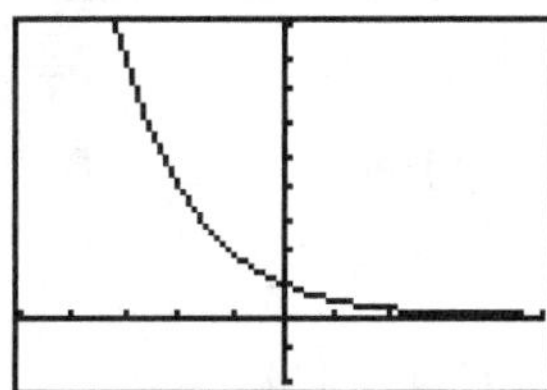

d. What is the domain of f?

The domain of f is all reals.

e. Determine the y-intercept. How does this compare with the value of $f(0)$?

$f(0) = (1/2)^0 = 1$. The y-intercept is (0, 1).

f. Is the function f increasing or decreasing?

The function f is decreasing everywhere.

The base $\frac{1}{2}$ in the function $f(x) = \left(\frac{1}{2}\right)^x$ is called the **decay factor** because each time x is increased by 1, the corresponding output decays by a factor of $\frac{1}{2}$.

g. Does the graph of f have an x-intercept?

f has no x-intercept.

h. Complete the following table:

x	1	3	5	7	10
$f(x) = \left(\frac{1}{2}\right)^x$	$\frac{1}{2}$	$\frac{1}{8}$	$\frac{1}{32}$	$\frac{1}{128}$	$\frac{1}{1024}$

i. As the values of the input variable x get larger and larger, what happens to the output values?

As x increases the output decreases getting closer and closer to 0.

j. Does the graph of f have a horizontal asymptote? Explain.

Yes, the graph of f has a horizontal asymptote of $y = 0$ because the output values approach 0, but never reach 0.

12. a. For each of the following exponential functions, identify the base b and then use your grapher to sketch a graph of each function. Use your graphs to complete the table.

FUNCTION	BASE, b	x-INTERCEPT	y-INTERCEPT	INCREASING OR DECREASING
$f(x) = 1.08^x$	1.08	None	(0, 1)	Increasing
$g(x) = 0.75^x$	0.75	None	(0, 1)	Decreasing
$h(x) = 3.2^x$	3.2	None	(0, 1)	Increasing
$r(x) = \left(\frac{1}{4}\right)^x$	$\frac{1}{4}$	None	(0, 1)	Decreasing

b. Without graphing, how might you determine which of the functions in part a increase and which decrease? Explain.

If the base, b, is greater than 1, the function is increasing. If the base b is $0 < b < 1$, then the function is decreasing.

13. Examine the output pattern to determine which one of the following data sets is linear and which one is exponential. For the linear set, determine the slope. For the exponential set, determine the growth or decay factor.

a.

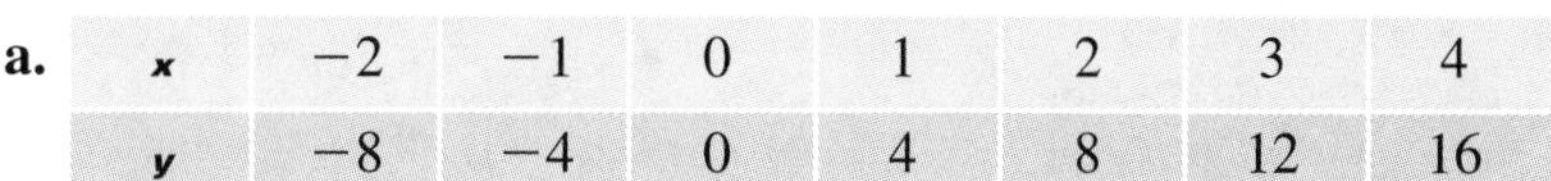

x	−2	−1	0	1	2	3	4
y	−8	−4	0	4	8	12	16

This function is linear because the change in output is constant for each unit increase in input.

The slope is 4.

b.

x	−2	−1	0	1	2	3	4
y	$\frac{1}{16}$	$\frac{1}{4}$	1	4	16	64	256

This function is exponential because the output increases by a constant factor for each unit increase in input.

The growth factor is 4.

SUMMARY

Functions defined by a rule of the form $y = b^x$, where $b > 0$, and $b \neq 1$, are called *exponential functions* and have the following properties:

1. The domain is all real numbers.
2. If $0 < b < 1$, the function is decreasing and has the following general shape.

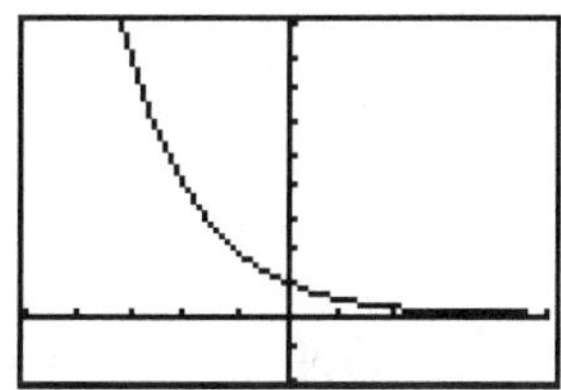

In this case, b is called the decay factor.

3. If $b > 1$, the function is increasing and has the following general shape.

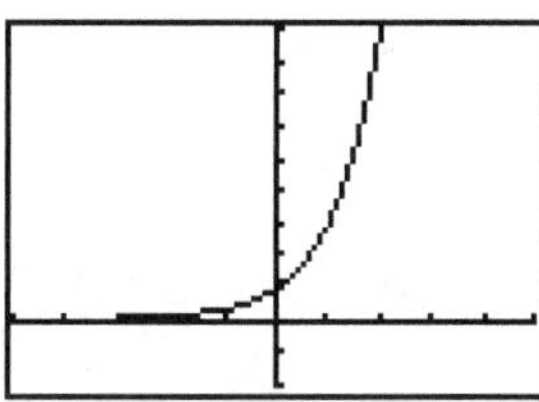

In this case, b is called the growth factor.

4. The vertical intercept (y-intercept) is (0, 1).
5. The graph does not intersect the horizontal axis.
6. The line $y = 0$ is a horizontal asymptote.

EXERCISES

1. **a.** Complete the following tables.

x	-2	-1	0	1	2
$h(x) = 5^x$	0.04	0.2	1	5	25

x	-2	-1	0	1	2
$g(x) = \frac{1}{5}^x$	25	5	1	0.2	0.04

b. Sketch graphs of h and g on the following grid.

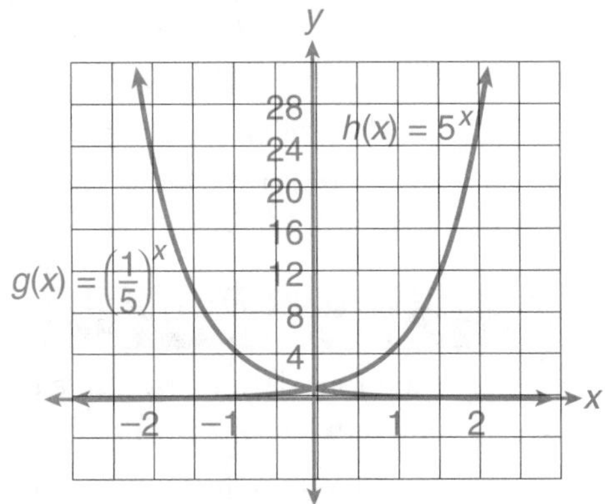

c. Describe any similarities and differences you observe in the graphs.

The graphs are reflections in the y-axis.

2. Sketch a graph of the following group of functions on your graphing calculator using the same set of coordinate axes and using a domain of $-3 \le x \le 3$. Describe any similarities and differences that you observe in the graphs.

a. $f(x) = 3^x$ **b.** $g(x) = x^3$ **c.** $h(x) = 3x$

All three graphs are increasing everywhere. g and h both pass through the origin, but f does not. As x increases, f grows faster than g and h, but g grows faster than h. As x gets very negative, f approaches the x-axis as an asymptote. Not true for either of the others.

3. Using your grapher, investigate the graphs of the following families (groups) of functions. Describe any relationships within each family.

a. $f(x) = 2^x$, $g(x) = 2^x + 1$, $h(x) = 2^x - 3$

All three functions have the same shape, but different y-intercepts.

b. $f(x) = \left(\frac{3}{4}\right)^x$, $g(x) = \left(\frac{4}{3}\right)^x$

The graphs intersect at (0, 1). They both have the x-axis as an asymptote. However, f is a decreasing function and g is an increasing function.

Exercise numbers appearing in color are answered in the Selected Answers section of this book.

c. $f(x) = 10^x$, $g(x) = -10^x$

The graphs are reflections over the x-axis.

d. $f(x) = 3^x$, $g(x) = (\frac{1}{3})^x$

The graphs are reflections in the y-axis.

4. Determine which of the following data sets are linear and which are exponential. For the linear sets, determine the slope. For the exponential sets, determine the growth factor or decay factor.

a.

x	−2	−1	0	1	2	3	4
y	$\frac{1}{9}$	$\frac{1}{3}$	1	3	9	27	81

The function is exponential with a growth factor of 3.

b.

x	−2	−1	0	1	2	3	4
y	2	2.5	3	3.5	4	4.5	5

The function is linear with slope 0.5.

c.

x	−2	−1	0	1	2	3	4
y	0.75	1.5	3	6	12	24	48

The function is exponential with a growth factor of 2.

5. Assume that y is an exponential function of x.

a. If the growth factor is 1.08, then complete the following table.

x	0	1	2	3
y	23.1	24.948	26.944	29.099

b. If the decay factor is 0.75, then complete the following table.

x	0	1	2	3
y	10	7.5	5.625	4.219

6. a. Would you expect $f(x) = 3^x$ to increase faster or slower than $g(x) = 2.5^x$ for $x > 0$? Explain. (*Hint:* You may want to use your grapher for help.)

I would expect f to grow faster because it has a larger growth factor.

b. Would you expect $f(x) = (\frac{1}{2})^x$ to decrease faster or slower than $g(x) = (0.7)^x$ for $x > 0$? Explain.

I would expect f to decrease faster because its decay factor is closer to 0.

ACTIVITY 3.2

Investment Clubs

Topics: *Exponential Functions of the Form $y = ab^x$, Recognizing Exponential Functions Using Tables*

There is a growing national increase in the number of investment clubs. An investment club is a group of people who meet on a regular basis to invest in the stock market. By joining a club, members are able to share in a diverse portfolio and therefore reduce the risk of losing money.

The following table shows the rapid growth in the number of clubs in recent years (figures for the number of clubs are approximate). Note that the input variable (year) increases in steps of 1 unit.

TABLE 1

YEAR	NUMBER OF CLUBS AS OF JAN. 1
1990	5820
1991	7180
1992	8860
1993	10,930
1994	13,480
1995	16,630
1996	20,510

1. Is this a linear function? How do you know?

   No, the function is not linear, because the rate of change is not constant.

2. **a.** If the data are not linear, is there some method you can use to determine if the function is exponential?

   b. Evaluate the indicated ratios to complete the following table.

TABLE 2

$\frac{\text{Clubs in 1991}}{\text{Clubs in 1990}}$	$\frac{\text{Clubs in 1992}}{\text{Clubs in 1991}}$	$\frac{\text{Clubs in 1993}}{\text{Clubs in 1992}}$	$\frac{\text{Clubs in 1994}}{\text{Clubs in 1993}}$	$\frac{\text{Clubs in 1995}}{\text{Clubs in 1994}}$	$\frac{\text{Clubs in 1996}}{\text{Clubs in 1995}}$
1.23	1.23	1.23	1.23	1.23	1.23

   c. What do you notice about the values in the table?

   The values in the table agree to two decimal places.

In an exponential function, equally spaced input values yield output values whose successive ratios are constant. If the input values increase by increments of 1, then the common ratio is called the *growth* or *decay factor.* This common ratio is the base, b, for the exponential function.

   d. Does the relationship in Table 1 represent an exponential function?

   Yes, the relationship is exponential.

   e. What is the growth factor?

   The growth factor is approximately 1.23.

3. As a consequence of the result found in Problem 2, you can start with 5820, the number of clubs in 1990, and obtain the number of clubs in 1991 by multiplying by the growth factor $b = 1.23$. You can then determine the number of clubs in 1992 by multiplying the number of clubs in 1991 by $b = 1.23$, and so on. Verify this with your calculator. Note that the results will vary slightly from the actual number of clubs given in Table 1.

Once you know the growth factor ($b = 1.23$), you can determine the equation that gives the number of clubs as a function of t, the number of years since 1990. Note that $t = 0$ corresponds to 1990, $t = 1$ to 1991, and so on.

4. Complete the table.

t	CALCULATION FOR NUMBER OF CLUBS	EXPONENTIAL FORM	NUMBER OF CLUBS
0	5820	$5820(1.23)^0$	5820
1	(5820)1.23	$5820(1.23)^1$	7159
2	$(5820 \cdot 1.23) \cdot 1.23$	$5820(1.23)^2$	8805
3	$(5820 \cdot 1.23 \cdot 1.23) \cdot 1.23$	$5820(1.23)^3$	10,830

5. a. Use the pattern in the preceding table to help you write the symbolic rule of the form $N = f(t) = a \cdot b^t$ that gives the number or clubs N as a function of t, the number of years since 1990.

$N(t) = 5280 \cdot 1.23^t$

Many exponential functions can be represented symbolically by $f(x) = a \cdot b^x$, where a is the value of f when $x = 0$ and b is the growth or decay factor.

b. Graph this function.

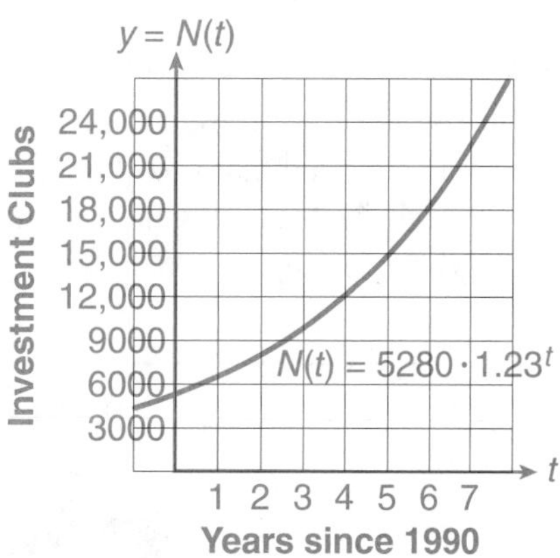

c. What is the vertical intercept (N-intercept)? What is the practical meaning of this intercept in this situation?

(0, 5820) 5820 is the number of clubs in 1990. ($t = 0$)

d. Determine $f(-1)$. Does this value have any meaning in this situation? Explain.

$N(-1) = 5820 \cdot (1.23)^{-1} = 4732.$

This could represent the number of clubs in 1989.

e. What is the practical domain of this function?

The practical domain is made up of integers probably from about -10 to 20.

6. Use your function rule in Problem 5 to estimate the number of clubs in the year 2000. Do you think this is a good estimate? Explain.

The number of investment clubs in 2000 is $N(10) = 5820 \cdot 1.23^{10} = 46{,}129$. This may be a fairly good estimate since we are extrapolating fairly close to the known data.

7. a. Use the graph of the exponential function $N = 5820(1.23)^t$ and the trace or table feature of your grapher to estimate the number of years it takes for the number of clubs to double from 5820 to 11,640.

3.35 years.

b. Estimate the time necessary for the number of clubs to double from 11,640 to 23,280. Verify using your calculator.

3.35 years.

c. How long will it take for any given number of clubs to double?

About 3.35 years.

> The **doubling time** of an exponential function is the time it takes for an output to double. The doubling time is determined by the growth factor and remains the same for all output values.

You have just purchased a new automobile for $16,000. Much to your dismay, you have learned that you should expect the value of your car to depreciate by 30% per year! The following table shows the retail value of the car for the next several years, where V is the value in thousands of dollars.

DEPRECIATION: TAKING ITS TOLL

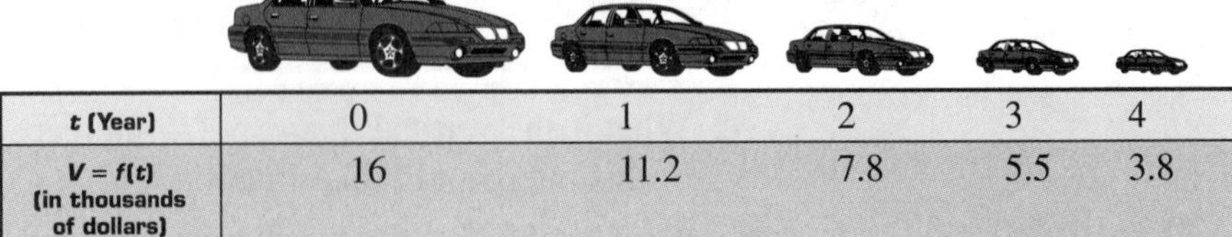

t (Year)	0	1	2	3	4
$V = f(t)$ (in thousands of dollars)	16	11.2	7.8	5.5	3.8

You may notice that each entry in the table for the value of the car can be obtained by multiplying the previous entry by a constant factor. This is another example of an exponential function. However, because the value of the car is decreasing, the constant factor is called a *decay factor*. Its value will be between 0 and 1.

8. Calculate the decay factor b in this situation. Show the calculations you performed to determine the factor.

$\frac{11.2}{16} = 0.7$

9. You can now start with 16, the initial value of the car (in thousands of dollars), and obtain the value after 1 year by multiplying by the decay factor, $b = 0.70$. The value of the car after 2 years is the value of the car after 1 year times the decay factor. Verify this on your calculator and compare your results with the entries in Table 3.

10. Complete the following table.

t	CALCULATION OF THE VALUE OF THE CAR	EXPONENTIAL FORM	VALUE, $V = f(t) = ab^t$ (IN THOUSANDS OF DOLLARS)
0	16	$16(0.70)^0$	16
1	(16)0.70	$16(0.70)^1$	11.2
2	$(16 \cdot 0.70)0.70$	$16(0.70)^2$	7.84
3	$(16 \cdot 0.70 \cdot 0.70)0.70$	$16(0.70)^3$	5.49

11. a. Use the pattern in the preceding table to help you write a symbolic rule of the form $V = f(t) = ab^t$, where V represents the value of the car as a function of time t.

$V = 16(0.70)^t$

b. What is the practical domain of this function?

The practical domain would be whole numbers from 0 to 7 or so.

c. Sketch a graph of this function using your grapher.

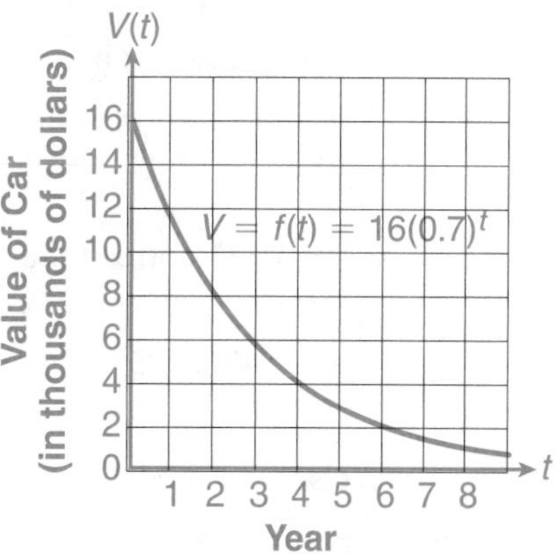

d. What is the vertical intercept (V-intercept)? What is the practical meaning of the intercept in this situation?

The vertical intercept is (0, 16,000). $16,000 is the initial value of the automobile.

12. a. Using your grapher, estimate the number of years it takes to halve the value of the automobile from $16,000 to $8000 using your grapher.

About 2 years.

b. Estimate the time necessary to halve the value from $8000 to $4000? Verify using your grapher

About 2 years.

c. How long will it take for any specific value of the car to halve?

About 2 years.

SUMMARY

- For exponential functions defined by $f(x) = ab^x$, a is the value of f when $x = 0$ (sometimes called the *initial value*) and b is the growth or decay factor.
- The vertical intercept of these functions is $(0, a)$.
- In an exponential function, equally spaced input values yield output values whose successive ratios are constant.
- The doubling time of an exponential function is the time it takes for an output to double. The doubling time is set by the growth factor and remains the same for all output values.

EXERCISES

1. The population of Russia in selected years can be approximated by the following table.

YEAR	1994	1995	1996	1997
POPULATION (IN MILLIONS)	148.3	148.0	147.6	146.9

a. Does this table seem to indicate that the population of Russia can be reasonably modeled with an exponential function? Explain.

Yes, because the ratios of consecutive outputs are fairly close: 0.998, 0.997, and 0.995 respectively.

b. Let 1994 correspond to $t = 0$. Determine an exponential function of the form $y = ab^t$ to represent the population of Russia symbolically.

$p = 148.3(0.997)^t$.

c. Use your model in part b to predict the population of Russia in the year 2004.

$p = 148.3(0.997)^{10} = 143.9$ million.

Exercise numbers appearing in color are answered in the Selected Answers section of this book.

2. Without using your grapher, match each graph with its equation. Then check your answers using your grapher.

a. $f(x) = 0.5(0.73)^x$ **b.** $g(x) = 3(1.73)^x$ **c.** $h(x) = -2(1.73)^x$

i.

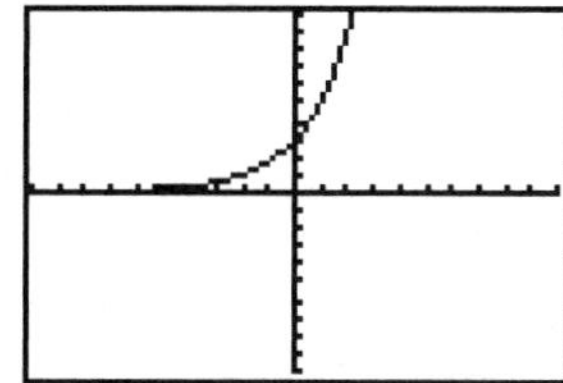

ii.

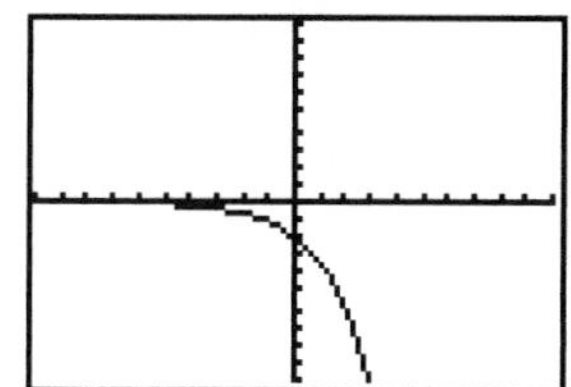

iii.

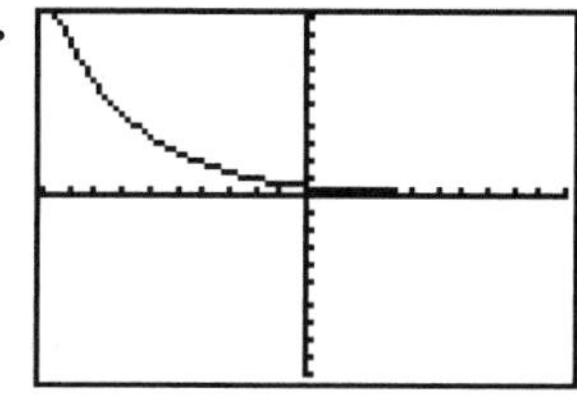

The graph of *f* is iii. The graph of *g* is i. The graph of *h* is ii.

3. Which of the following tables represent exponential functions? Explain. If the set is exponential, determine the growth or decay factor.

a.

x	0	1	2	3	4
y	0	2	16	58	128

This is not exponential because the output ratio is not constant even though the input changes by 1 at each step.

b.

x	0	1	2	3	4
y	1	4	16	64	256

This is exponential. The growth factor is 4.

c.

x	1	3	5	7	9
y	31	93	155	217	279

This is not exponential because the output ratio is not constant even though the input changes by 2 at each step.

d.

x	1	3	5	7	9
y	1750	858	420	206	101

This is exponential. The decay factor is 0.49.

4. a. Sketch the graphs of $f(x) = 2^x$, $g(x) = 3 \cdot 2^x$, and $h(x) = -3 \cdot 2^x$ on the same coordinate axes.

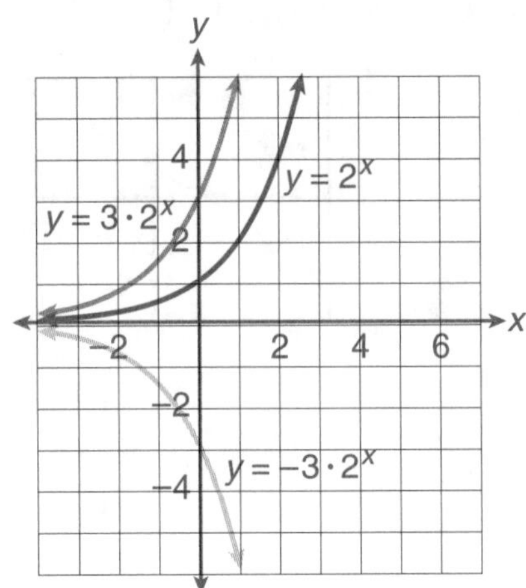

b. Describe how the graphs of *f* and *g* are similar and how they are different.

The graphs of *f* and *g* are very similar with *g* rising a little faster.

c. Describe how the graphs of *g* and *h* are related to each other.

The graphs of *g* and *h* are reflections in the *x*-axis.

5. If $f(x) = 3 \cdot 4^x$, determine the exact value of each of the following, when possible. Otherwise, use your calculator to approximate the value to the nearest hundredth.

a. $f(-2)$

$f(-2) = \frac{3}{16}$

b. $f\left(\frac{1}{2}\right)$

$f\left(\frac{1}{2}\right) = 6$

c. $f(2)$

$f(2) = 48$

d. $f(1.3)$

$f(1.3) = 18.189$

6. In 1995, the U.S. emitted approximately 1400 million tons of carbon into the atmosphere. The U.S. emissions were increasing at about 1.3% per year. Let *t* represent the number of years since 1995 and *A* represent the amount of carbon (in millions of tons) emitted in a given year.

a. Complete the following table.

T, NUMBER OF YEARS SINCE 1995	0	1	2	3	4	5
A, AMOUNT OF U.S. CARBON EMISSIONS (IN MILLIONS OF TONS)	1400	1418.2	1436.6	1455.3	1474.2	1493.4

b. Determine the growth factor for carbon emissions.

1.013

c. Write an equation, which represents A as an exponential function of t.

$A = f(t) = 1400(1.013)^t$

d. Sketch a graph of this exponential equation. Use $0 \leq t \leq 25$ and $0 \leq A \leq 2500$.

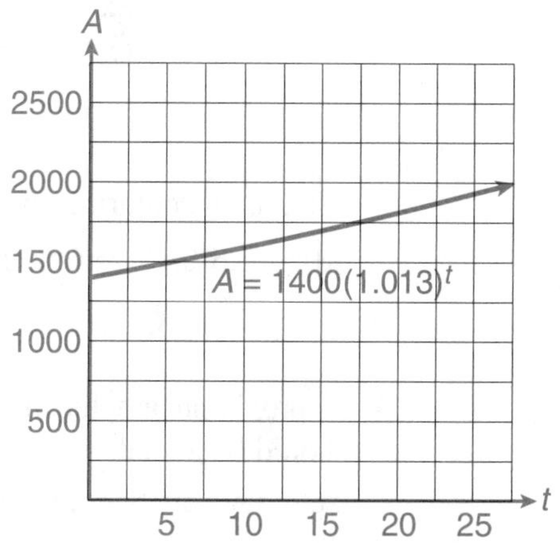

e. Using the equation, determine the amount of carbon emission in the year 2010.

$A = 1400(1.013)^{15} = 1699.3$ million tons

f. Using the graph and trace features of your grapher, approximate the year in which carbon emissions in the U.S. will exceed 2000 million tons.

It will happen in the 27th year after 1995 or 2022.

7. Chlorine is used to disinfect swimming pools. The chlorine concentration should be between 1.5 and 2.5 parts per million (ppm). On sunny, hot days, 30% of the chlorine can dissipate into the air or combine with other chemicals. The chlorine concentration, A, (in parts per million) in a pool after x days can be modeled by $A = f(x) = 2.5(0.7)^x$.

a. What is the initial concentration of chlorine in the pool?

2.5 parts per million

b. Sketch a graph of the chlorine concentration function.

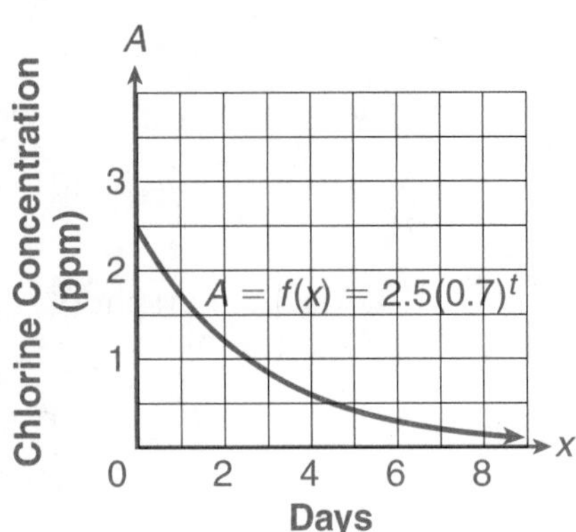

c. What is the chlorine concentration in the pool after 3 days?

$f(3) = 2.5(0.7)^3 = 0.86$ parts per million.

d. Approximate graphically and numerically the number of days before chlorine should be added.

If the days are hot and sunny then chlorine should be added every 1.4 days.

ACTIVITY 3.3

Population Growth

Topics: *Exponential Functions of the Form $y = a(1 + r)^t$, Growth Rate versus Growth Factor*

The city of Charlotte, North Carolina, had a population of approximately 396,000 in the 1990 census.

1. a. Assuming that the population increases at a constant percent rate of 2.3% per year, determine the population (in thousands) in 1991.

$y = 396 + 0.023(396) = 405.12$

b. Determine the population (in thousands) in 1992.

$y = 405.12 + 0.023(405.12) = 414.43$

c. The population of Charlotte can be modeled as a function of time using an exponential function. Divide the population in 1992 by the population in 1991 and record this ratio.

1.023.

d. Divide the population in 1991 by the population in 1990 and record this ratio.

1.023.

e. What do you notice about the ratios in parts c and d? What do these ratios represent?

They are equal to the growth factor.

Linear functions represent quantities that change at a constant rate (slope). Exponential functions represent quantities that change at a constant percent rate. Population growth, sales and advertising trends, compound interest, spread of disease, and concentration of a drug in the blood are examples of quantities that increase or decrease at a constant percent rate.

2. Let t represent the number of years since 1990 ($t = 0$ corresponds to 1990). Use the results from Problem 1 to complete the following table.

t, Years (since 1990)	0	1	2	3	4	5
P, Population (in thousands)	396	405	414	424	434	444

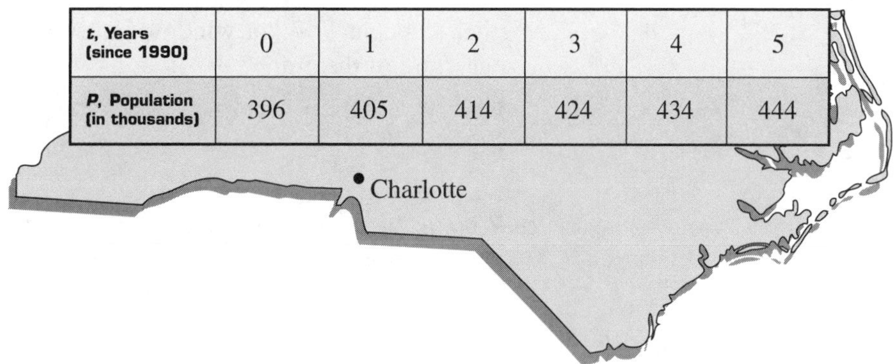

Once you know the growth factor ($b = 1.023$), you can determine the exponential model that describes the population of Charlotte as a function of t, where $t = 0$ corresponds to the year 1990.

3. a. Complete the following table.

t	CALCULATION FOR POPULATION (IN THOUSANDS)	EXPONENTIAL FORM	P, POPULATION (IN THOUSANDS)
0	396	$396(1.023)^0$	396
1	(396)1.023	$396(1.023)^1$	405
2	$(396 \cdot 1.023) \cdot 1.023$	$396(1.023)^2$	414
3	$(396 \cdot 1.023 \cdot 1.023) \cdot 1.023$	$396(1.023)^3$	424

b. Use the pattern in the table in part a to help you write the symbolic rule for P, the population of Charlotte, using t, the number of years since 1990, as the input value.

$P(t) = 396(1.023)^t$

c. Using the function rule developed in part b, determine the population in 1996. That is, determine P when $t = 6$.

$P(6) = 396(1.023)^6 = 453.888$ thousand

The equation $P = f(t) = 396(1.023)^t$ has the general form $P = f(t) = P_0(1 + r)^t$, where r is the annual *growth rate,* $(1 + r)$ is the *growth factor* (base of the exponential function), t is the time in years, and P_0 is the initial population (when $t = 0$).

4. a. Graph this function with your grapher, adjusting the window to show the population between 1990 and 2000 ($t = 0$, $t = 10$). Do you see anything you did not expect?

No

b. Is the function linear? Describe how you can adjust the window of your grapher to be sure. What window intervals did you use to see the upward curvature of the graph?

No, the function is not linear. Xmin = −10, Xmax = 35, Ymin = 350, Ymax = 600.

c. What is the P-intercept? What is the practical meaning of this intercept in this situation?

(0, 396) This represents the population of Charlotte (in thousands) in 1990.

5. a. Use this function to predict Charlotte's population in the year 2000.

$f(32) = 396(1.023)^{10} = 497.109$

b. Verify your prediction by using the trace feature of your grapher.

6. Use the graph to estimate when Charlotte's population will reach 600,000, assuming it continues to grow at the same rate.

2008.

7. Evaluate $f(32)$ and describe what it means.

$f(32) = 819.814$ The population of Charlotte will be 819,814 in 2022 if the current growth rate continues.

8. In which prediction would you be more confident, the population in the year 2000 or the population in the year 2012? Give a reason for your answer.

I am extrapolating less in 2000 than in 2022, so I am more confident in the 2000 prediction.

9. a. Assuming the growth rate and factor remain constant, how long will it take for the population of Charlotte to double its 1990 population?

30 years.

b. Explain how you reached your conclusion in part a.

I traced the graph.

You are working at a waste-water treatment facility. Presently you are treating water contaminated with 18 micrograms of pollutant per liter. Your process is designed to remove 20% of the pollutant during each treatment. Your goal is to reduce the pollutant to less than 3 micrograms per liter.

10. After each treatment, 20% of the contaminants are removed. However, exponential decay functions always model the percent that remains. Therefore, the decay factor applied to successive outputs is 80%, or 0.8.

a. Complete the following table.

n, NUMBER OF TREATMENTS	0	1	2	3	4	5
C, CONCENTRATION OF POLLUTANT (μ/ℓ), TO NEAREST HUNDREDTH	18	14.4	11.52	9.216	7.373	5.898

b. Write an equation for the concentration C of the pollutant as a function of the number of treatments n.

$C = 18(0.8)^n$.

11. Use the function rule from Problem 10b to predict the concentration after 7 treatments.

$C = 18(0.8)^7 = 3.775$.

12. a. Using your grapher, sketch a graph of the concentration function. Does the graph look like you expected it would? Explain.

Yes, it is a decay curve.

b. What is the C-intercept? What is the practical meaning of the intercept in this situation?

(0, 18) This represents the initial concentration.

c. Does the graph have a horizontal asymptote? Explain what this means in this situation.

Yes, as n gets large the C values approach 0, so the x-axis is a horizontal asymptote.

13. Use the table or trace feature of your grapher to estimate the number of treatments necessary to bring the concentration of pollutant below 3 micrograms per liter.

9 treatments are necessary to bring the concentration below 3.

SUMMARY

- Exponential functions are used to describe phenomena that grow or decay by a constant percent over time.
- If r represents the annual growth rate, the exponential function that models the quantity, P, can be written as

$$P = f(t) = P_0(1 + r)^t,$$

where P_0 is the initial amount and t represents the number of elapsed years and $1 + r$ is the growth factor.

- If r represents the annual percent that decays, the exponential function that models the amount remaining can be written as

$$P = f(t) = P_0(1 - r)^t, \text{ where } 1 - r \text{ is the decay factor.}$$

EXERCISES

1. a. If the growth rate is 2%, what is the growth factor?

If $r = 0.02$, the growth factor $1 + r = 1.02$

b. If the decay rate is 23%, what is the decay factor?

If $r = .23$, the decay factor $1 - r = 0.77$

c. If the growth factor is 1.029, what is the growth rate?

If the growth factor $1 + r = 1.029$, then $r = 0.029$ or 2.9%

d. If the decay factor is 0.32, what is the decay rate?

If the decay factor $1 - r = 0.32$, then $r = 0.68$ or 68%

2. The 1990 U.S. Census reports the populations of Bozeman, Montana, as 22,660 and Butte, Montana, as 33,336. Since the 1990 census, Bozeman's population has been increasing at approximately 0.46% per year. Butte's population has been decreasing at approximately 1.09% per year. Assume that the growth rates stay constant.

Exercise numbers appearing in color are answered in the Selected Answers section of this book.

a. Let P represent the population x years since 1990. Determine the exponential functions that model the populations of both cities.

Bozeman $P = 22{,}660(1.0046)^x$

Butte $P = 33{,}336(0.9891)^x$

b. Use your models to predict the populations of both cities in the year 2002.

Bozeman $P(12) = 22{,}660(1.0046)^{12} = 23{,}943$

Butte $P(12) = 33{,}336(0.9891)^{12} = 29{,}228$

c. Estimate the number of years for the population of Bozeman, Montana, to double.

Bozeman's population will double in about 150 years.

d. Using the table and/or graphs for these functions, predict when the populations will be equal.

The populations will be about equal in 24.8 years or 2015.

3. You have just taken over as the city manager of a small city. The personnel expenses were \$8,500,000 in 1995. Over the past 5 years, the personnel expenses have increased at a rate of 3.2% annually.

a. Assuming that this rate continues, write an equation describing personnel costs C in millions of dollars, where $t = 0$ corresponds to 1995.

$C = 8.5(1.032)^t$.

b. Sketch a graph of this function up to the year 2010 ($t = 15$).

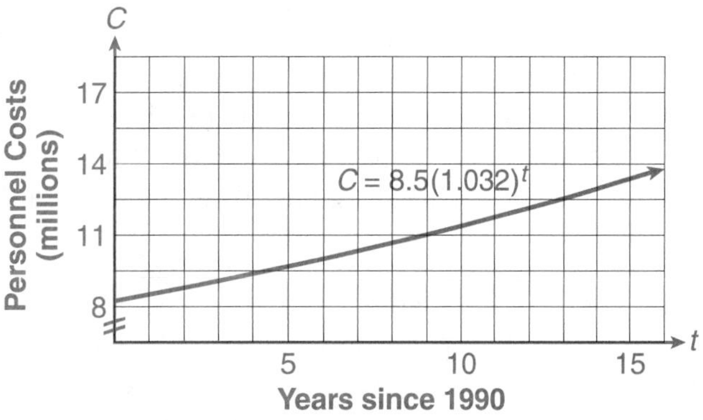

c. What are your projected personnel costs in the year 2005?

$C = 8.5(1.032)^{10} = 11.65$ million.

d. What is the C-intercept? What is the practical meaning of the intercept in this situation?

The C-intercept is (0, 8.5) This represents personnel expenses in 1995.

e. In what year will the personnel expenses be double the 1995 personnel expenses?

Personnel expenses will be double the 1995 level in 2017.

4. The population of the United States from 1930 to 1980, according to the U.S. Department of Census, is given by the following table.

YEAR, t	1930	1940	1950	1960	1970	1980
POPULATION, P (IN MILLIONS)	122.8	131.7	151.3	179.3	203.3	226.6

a. Plot these points on the following grid.

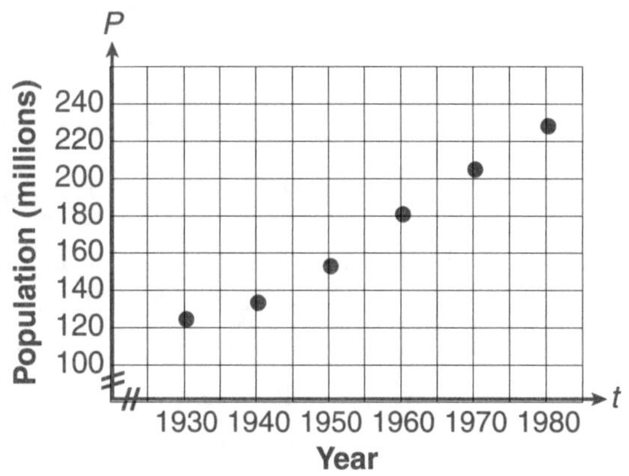

b. Is the annual growth rate approximately constant over this period? Explain.

Yes, the ratios are close.

c. You can develop a function for U.S. population by assuming that the annual growth rate has been constant. For convenience, let $t = 0$ correspond to the year 1930, and assume that the initial U.S. population was 122.8 million. Also, let the variable t represent the number of years since 1930 ($t = 0$ corresponds to 1930). Determine an equation for P in terms of t.

$P = 122.8(1.0125)^t$

d. Use your function rule from part c to determine the U.S. population (in millions) in 1980. How does your answer compare with the actual population of 226.6 million?

$P(50) = 122.8(1.0125)^{50} = 228.5$ million

5. You have recently purchased a new car for $20,000, by arranging financing for the next 5 years. You are curious about what your new car will be worth when the loan is completely paid off.

   a. Assuming that the value depreciates at a constant rate of 15%, write an equation that represents the value V of the car t years from now.

   $V = 20{,}000(0.85)^t$

   b. What is the decay rate in this situation?

   15%

   c. What is the decay factor in this situation?

   0.85

   d. Use the equation from part a to estimate the value of your car 5 years from now.

   $V(5) = 20{,}000(0.85)^5 = 8874$

   e. Use the trace and table features of your grapher to check your results in part d.

   They agree.

   f. Use the trace or table features of your grapher to determine when your car will be worth $10,000.

   4.3 years from purchase time.

PROJECT ACTIVITY 3.4

Photocopying Machines

Topics: *Exponential Functions, Growth Factor, Decay Factor, Doubling and Halving Time*

Most photocopy machines allow for enlarging or reducing the size of the original. Suppose you have a chart you wish to photocopy for a report you need to submit to your supervisor. The chart is 10 inches wide by 7 inches high. To reduce the size of the copy 20% you set the machine to take 80% of the original dimensions.

1. What will be the dimensions of your photocopy?

   8 inches by 5.6 inches.

2. What is the percentage reduction in *area* of the photocopy?

   Original area: 70 in.^{2}; New area: 44.8 in.^{2}; Reduction 25.2 in.^{2}, 25.2/70 = 36% reduction in area.

3. If your chart must fit in a space only 4 inches high in your report, how many times would you need to reduce the original? (Assume that the photocopier is set at 80% reduction.)

   3 times

4. a. Complete the following table showing the dimensions of the chart after x 80% reductions (photocopies of photocopies). Record each measurement to the nearest hundredth of an inch.

x, NUMBER OF 80% REDUCTIONS	0	1	2	3	4	5	6	7	8	9	10
$h(x)$, HEIGHT (in.)	7	5.6	4.48	3.58	2.86	2.29	1.83	1.46	1.17	0.94	0.75
$w(x)$, WIDTH (in.)	10	8	6.40	5.12	4.10	3.28	2.62	2.10	1.68	1.34	1.07

(Answers may vary slightly depending on rounding.)

   b. If you actually performed ten 80% reductions (photocopies of photocopies), what do you think your results would look like?

   It would be small and probably impossible to read.

5. Use the data from your table to plot points for two curves on separate axes. Use the number of reductions x versus the heights of the reduced copies for one curve and the number of reductions versus the widths of the reduced copies for a second curve. Describe how the two graphs are similar and how they are different.

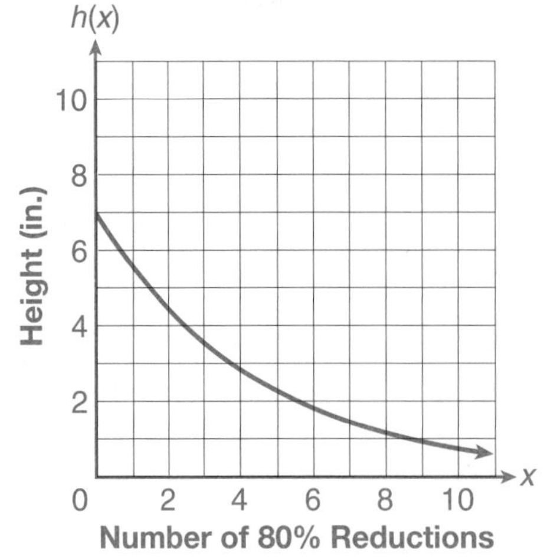

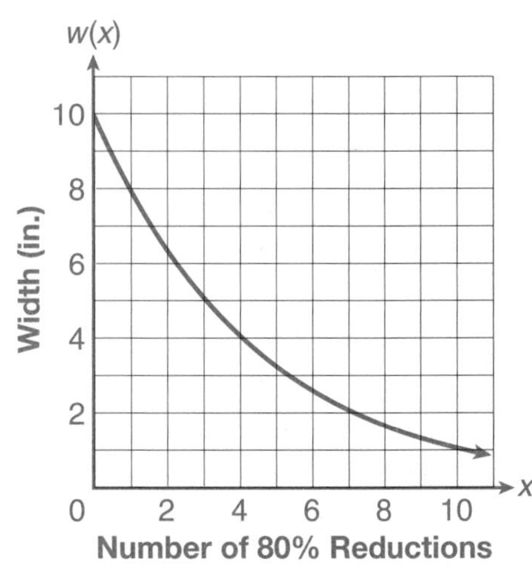

6. a. Notice that each entry in the table for $h(x)$ or $w(x)$ can be obtained by multiplying the previous entry by a constant factor. What is the constant factor in this situation?

0.80

b. What is the practical meaning of the constant factor in this situation?

Each copy has length and width of 80% of the original.

7. Find the equations that define the functions h and w, where x is the number of 80% reductions. Enter these functions on your grapher to verify your work in Problems 4 and 5.

$h(x) = 7(0.8)^x$

$w(x) = 10(0.8)^x$

8. The 80% reduction resulted in a decreasing function. What kind of percentage would you need to enter on the photocopier to result in an increasing function?

A percentage greater than 100%.

9. a. Complete the following table showing the width of a 10-inch-wide chart in which x represents the number of 20% enlargements.

x, NUMBER OF 20% ENLARGEMENTS	0	1	2	3	4	5
$w(x)$, WIDTH (in.)	10	12	14.4	17.28	20.74	24.88

b. What is the constant factor? What is the practical meaning of the constant factor in this situation?

The constant factor is 1.2, which represents the 120%.

c. Write a function rule for w in terms of x, where x is the number of 20% enlargements.

$w(x) = 10(1.2)^x$

d. Use your grapher to graph the function.

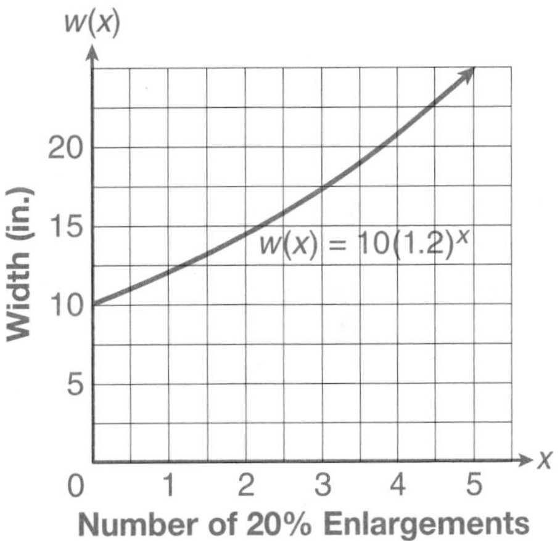

10. **a.** If the machine you are using will only enlarge at 20%, how many times would you need to copy the 10-inch width to make it at least 20 inches wide?

4 times

b. Will it ever be exactly 20 inches wide?

No

c. Describe in detail how you determined your answers.

I used the table in Exercise 9.

11. Assuming a constant 20% enlargement, how many copies would it take to get your original 10-inch width to grow to at least 40 inches? At least 80 inches?

8 times

12 times

12. Complete the following table of your results from Problems 10 and 11.

x, NUMBER OF 20% ENLARGEMENTS	0	4	8	12
WIDTH (in.)	10	20	40	80

13. What is the doubling time for this increasing function?

The doubling time is 4 times.

14. Examine the decreasing functions in Problem 7. How many copies are needed to halve the output for each function?

The halving time is 3 times.

15. Use the graphs (or the table feature) on your grapher to get a better estimate of the doubling or halving time for each of the exponential functions you displayed in Problems 7 and 9.

PERCENT REDUCTION OR ENLARGEMENT	NUMBER OF TIMES TO HALVE OR DOUBLE THE OUTPUT
80	3
120	4

ACTIVITY 3.5

Compound Interest

Topics: *Exponential Growth, Continuous Growth Rate, Natural Base e*

Suppose you deposit \$100 in the bank at a 6.5% annual interest rate. After one year, your balance is

$$\underbrace{100}_{\text{Balance}} + \underbrace{0.065(106.50)}_{\text{Interest}} = 100 + 6.5 = \underbrace{106.50}_{\text{New balance}}$$

Note that the interest, \$6.50, earned during the year becomes part of the new balance. At the end of the second year, your balance is

$$\underbrace{106.50}_{\text{Balance}} + \underbrace{0.065(106.50)}_{\text{Interest}} = 106.50 + 6.92 = \underbrace{113.42}_{\text{New balance}}$$

Note that you made interest on the original deposit plus interest on the first year's interest. In this situation, we say that interest is compounded. Usually, the compounding occurs at fixed intervals of time (typically at the end of every year, quarter, month, or day). In this introductory situation, interest is compounded annually.

If interest is compounded, then the current balance is given by the formula

$$A = P\left(1 + \tfrac{r}{n}\right)^{nt},$$

where A is the current amount, or balance, in your account

P is your principal (the original amount deposited)

r is the annual interest rate (annual percentage rate in decimal form)

n is the number of times per year that interest is calculated

t is the time in years that your money has been invested.

1. a. Suppose you deposit \$400 in an account that has a 9% annual interest rate (usually referred to as APR, for annual percentage rate). Interest is compounded annually. Therefore, $n = 1$ in the preceding formula. Rewrite the formula for the current balance A using the given information as a function of time, t.

$A = 400(1.09)^t$.

b. What will be your balance at the end of the first year?

\$436

c. What will be the amount of interest earned in the first year?

\$36

d. Use the formula developed in part a to complete the following table.

COMPOUNDED ANNUALLY, $n = 1$

t, YEAR	0	1	2	3	4
A, BALANCE	400	436	475.24	518.01	564.63

e. Is this an exponential function? Explain.

Yes, the ratios are the same.

2. a. Now consider your $400 being deposited in an account that has the same interest rate (APR) of 9%, but is compounded quarterly. In other words, interest is calculated and compounded four times each year ($n = 4$). Write a new formula for your current balance A as a function of time.

$A = 400\left(1 + \frac{0.09}{4}\right)^{4t} = 400(1.0225)^{4t}$.

b. What would your balance be after the first year?

$437.23

c. Use the table feature of your calculator to determine the balance at the end of each year for 10 years, and record the values in the table in Problem 3 under $n = 4$ (compounded quarterly).

d. Is the function exponential? Explain.

Yes, the ratios are the same.

3. Consider your $400 being deposited into a 9% APR account, but with *monthly* compounding ($n = 12$) and then with *daily* compounding ($n = 360$). (Assume 360 days in a year, as most banks do.) Use your grapher and the appropriate formula to complete the table.

COMPARISON OF $400 PRINCIPAL IN 9% APR ACCOUNTS WITH VARYING COMPOUNDING PERIODS

t	$n = 4$	$n = 12$	$n = 360$
0	400	400	400
1	437.23	437.52	437.66
2	477.93	478.57	478.88
3	522.42	523.46	523.97
4	571.05	572.56	573.31
5	624.20	626.27	627.29
6	682.31	685.02	686.36
7	745.82	749.28	750.99
8	815.24	819.57	821.70
9	891.13	896.45	899.07
10	974.08	980.54	983.73

(Answers in the table may vary depending on rounding.)

4. In Problem 3, you calculated the balance on a deposit of $400 at an annual interest rate of 9% that was compounded at different time intervals. Which account had the higher balance after 10 years? Does this seem reasonable? Explain.

Compounded daily. This seems reasonable because the number of compounding periods is the greatest.

You could extend this problem so that interest is compounded every hour or every minute or even every second. However, compounding more frequently than every hour does not increase the balance very much. Try it.

To discover why this happens, take a closer look at the exponential functions in Problems 1–3.

$$A = 400\left(1 + \tfrac{0.09}{1}\right)^{1t} = \underline{400\left[\left(1 + 0.09\right)^{1}\right]^{t}}$$
$$A = 400\left(1 + \tfrac{0.09}{4}\right)^{4t} = \underline{400\left[\left(1 + \tfrac{0.09}{4}\right)^{4}\right]^{t}}$$
$$A = 400\left(1 + \tfrac{0.09}{12}\right)^{12t} = \underline{400\left[\left(1 + \tfrac{0.09}{12}\right)^{12}\right]^{t}}$$
$$A = 400\left(1 + \tfrac{0.09}{360}\right)^{360t} = \underline{400\left[\left(1 + \tfrac{0.09}{360}\right)^{360}\right]^{t}}$$

Can you discover a pattern in the form of the underlined expressions?

Each formula can be expressed as $A = 400b^t$, where $b = \left(1 + \frac{0.09}{n}\right)^n$ for $n = 1, 4, 12$, and 360. The number b is the growth factor and n is the number of compounding periods.

5. Determine the value of b in the following table. Round to five decimal places.

***n*, NUMBER OF COMPOUNDING PERIODS**	1	4	12	360
***b*, GROWTH FACTOR**	1.09	1.09308	1.09381	1.09416

Note that each of the values for b in the table is of the form $1 + r$, where r represents the **effective annual growth rate** resulting from the compounding effect.

6. a. If there were 1000 compounding periods ($n = 1000$), determine the effective annual growth rate.

$1 + r = b = \left(1 + \frac{0.09}{1000}\right)^{1000} = 1.09417$

$r = 1.09417 - 1 = 0.09417$

b. Compare the rate for $n = 1000$ with that for 360 periods ($n = 360$).

$1 + r = b = \left(1 + \frac{0.09}{360}\right)^{360} = 1.09416$

$r = 1.09416 - 1 = 0.09416$

The rate for $n = 1000$ is only 0.00001 greater than the rate for $n = 360$.

Note that there isn't much of a difference in this rate as the number of compounding periods n increases.

If the compounding periods become shorter and shorter (compounding every hour, every minute, every second), n gets larger and larger. If you consider the period to be so short that it's essentially an instant in time, you have what is called **continuous compounding.** Some banks use this method for compounding interest. In such situations, the following formula is used to determine the balance A:

$$A = Pe^{rt},$$

where A is the current amount, or balance, in your account

P is your principal

r is the annual interest rate (annual percentage rate in decimal form)

t is the time in years that your money has been invested

e is the base of the continuously compounded exponential function.

7. The number e is an example of an irrational number. Another well-known irrational number is π. Using your calculator, approximate e and π to six decimal places.

a. $e \approx$

$e = 2.718282$

b. $\pi \approx$

$\pi = 3.141593$

8. a. Suppose you invest $400 in an account at 9% annual interest rate compounded continuously. Use the formula $A = Pe^{rt}$ to determine the balance after 10 years.

$A = 400e^{(0.09)(10)} = 983.84$

b. Compare the result from part a to the balance of the account after 10 years of compounding daily ($n = 360$).

Continuous compounding yields slightly more than daily compounding.

SUMMARY

- Compound interest formula: $A = P\left(1 + \frac{r}{n}\right)^{nt}$
- Continuous compounding formula: $A = Pe^{rt}$
- If the number of compounding periods is large, $A = P\left(1 + \frac{r}{n}\right)^{nt} \approx Pe^{rt}$.

9. a. Complete the following table.

x	−2	−1	0	2	4	6
$y = e^x$	0.1353	0.3679	1	7.3891	54.5982	403.4288

b. Sketch a graph of $y = e^x$ using your grapher.

c. Is this function increasing or decreasing?

This function is increasing.

d. Determine the vertical and horizontal intercepts (if any).

The vertical intercept is (0, 1); no horizontal intercept.

e. Does the graph of $y = e^x$ have a horizontal asymptote? Explain.

The x-axis is a horizontal asymptote the graph of $y = e^x$ because as x grows large in the negative direction, the graph approaches the x-axis.

10. *Escherichia coli* (*E. coli*) bacteria is capable of very rapid growth, doubling in number approximately every 49.5 minutes. The number N of *E. coli* bacteria per milliliter after x minutes can be modeled by the equation $N = 500{,}000e^{0.014x}$.

a. What is the initial number of bacteria?

500,000

b. How many *E. coli* bacteria would you expect after 99 minutes? (*Hint:* There will be two doublings.) Verify your estimate using the equation.

2,000,000 The equation yields 1,999,411, which is equivalent to 3 significant digits.

c. Use a graphing or numerical approach to determine the elapsed time when there would be 20,000,000 *E. coli* bacteria.

About 263 minutes.

Whenever growth (or decay) is continuous at a constant rate, the exponential model used is $y = y_0e^{rt}$, where r is the constant growth (or decay) rate, y_0 is the amount present initially (when $t = 0$), and e is the constant irrational number 2.71828182845904523. . . .

EXERCISES

1. You deposit $2000 in an account that earns 5% compounded monthly.

a. What will your balance be after 2 years?

$A = 2000\left(1 + \frac{.05}{12}\right)^{12(2)} = 2209.88$

b. Estimate how long it will take for your investment to double.

About 14 years.

c. Identify the growth rate and growth factor.

The growth rate is 0.0511619. The growth factor is 1.0511619.

2. Your friend deposits $1900 in an account that earns 6% compounded continuously.

a. What will her balance be after 2 years?

$2142.24.

Exercise numbers appearing in color are answered in the Selected Answers section of this book.

b. Estimate how long it will take for your friend's investment to double.

11.6 years

3. Strontium 90 is a radioactive material that decays according to the function $y = y_0e^{-0.0244t}$, where y_0 is the amount present initially and t is the time in years.

a. If there are 20 grams of strontium 90 present today, how much will be present in 20 years?

$y = 20e^{-0.0244(20)} = 12.277$ grams

b. Use the graph of the function to approximate how long it will take for 20 grams to decay to 10 grams, 10 grams to decay to 5 grams, and 5 grams to decay to 2.5 grams. The number you have found is called the *half-life* for strontium 90. In general, half-life is the time required for half of a radioactive substance to decay.

20 to 10 about 28 years, 10 to 5 about 28 years, 5 to 2.5 about 28 years.

c. Identify the decay rate and decay factor.

The growth (decay) rate is 2.44%. The decay factor is 0.9759.

4. When drugs are administered into the bloodstream, the amount present decreases continuously at a constant rate. The amount of a certain drug in the bloodstream is modeled by the function $y = y_0e^{-0.35t}$, where y_0 is the amount of the drug injected (in milligrams) and t is the time elapsed (in hours). Suppose that 10 milligrams is injected at 10:30 A.M.

a. How much of the drug is still in the bloodstream at 2:00 P.M.?

$y = 10e^{-0.35(3.5)} = 2.938$ mg

b. If another dose needs to be administered when there is 1 milligram of the drug present in the bloodstream, approximately when should the next dose be given (to the nearest quarter hour)?

6.5 hours or at 5 P.M.

5. The amount of credit card spending from Thanksgiving to Christmas has increased by 14% per year since 1987. The amount A, in billions of dollars, of credit card spending during the holiday period in a given year can be modeled by $A = f(x) = 36.2e^{0.14x}$, where x represents the number of years since 1987.

a. How much was spent using credit cards from Thanksgiving to Christmas in 1996?

$f(9) = 36.2e^{0.14(9)} = 127.62$ billion

b. Sketch a graph of the credit card function.

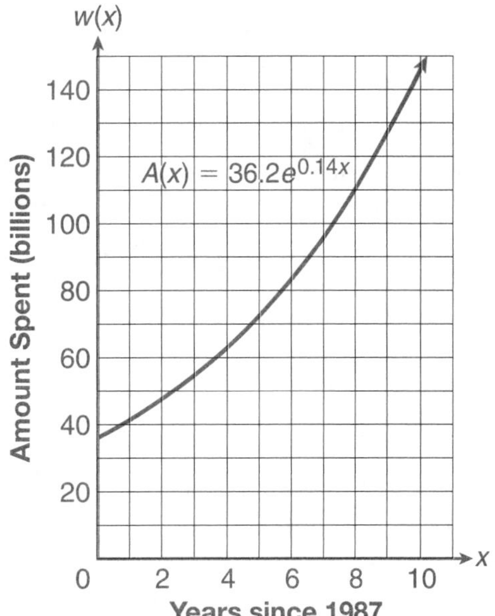

c. What is the vertical intercept of the graph? What is the practical meaning of the intercept in this situation?

(0, 36.2) This indicates the 36.2 billion spent in 1987.

d. Determine, graphically and numerically, the year when credit card spending will reach $75 billion.

1992

e. What is the doubling time?

The doubling time is about 5 years.

6. Use your grapher to sketch a graph of each of the following.

a. $f(x) = e^x + 2$

b. $g(x) = e^{x^2}$

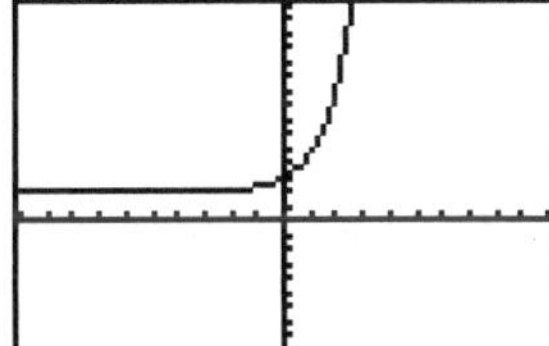

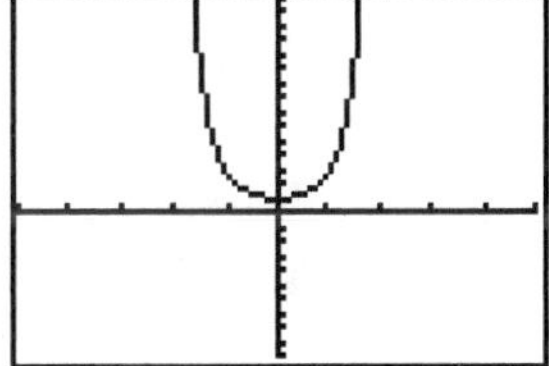

a. Window Xmin = −10, Xmax = 10, Ymin = −10, Ymax = 15

b. Window Xmin = −5, Xmax = 5, Ymin = −10, Ymax = 15

c. $h(x) = e^{-x}$

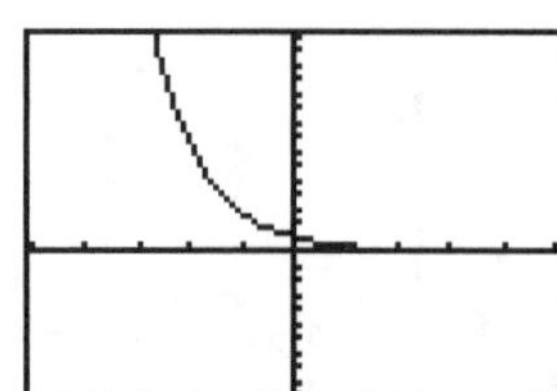

d. $F(x) = 3e^{x+1}$

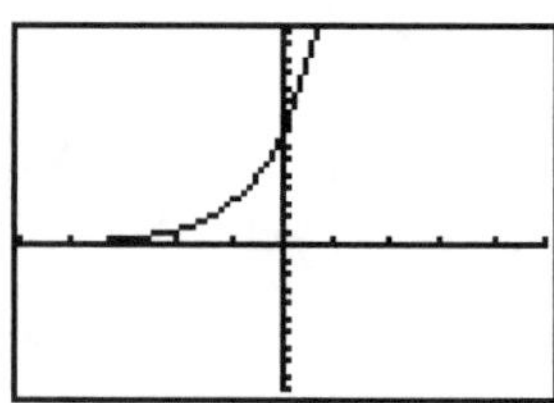

c. Window Xmin = −5, Xmax = 5, Ymin = −10, Ymax = 15

d. Window Xmin = −5, Xmax = 5, Ymin = −10, Ymax = 15

Lab Exercise:

7. Being irrational, the number e cannot be expressed as the ratio of two integers. Its significance in higher mathematics is unmatched by any other real number, with the possible exception of π, another irrational number. Research the following questions.

   a. Why is the letter e used to represent this important number?

   The number e is named for the Swiss mathematician Leonhard Euler.

   b. Give examples of additional numbers that are irrational.

   Additional irrational numbers are π, 2π, $\sqrt{3}$, $-2\sqrt[3]{7}$.

   c. How many decimal places do mathematicians and scientists know for either e or π?

   Well over 100.

   d. Since it has been proven that irrational numbers never have a repeating pattern of decimals, why would anyone want to find so many digits for either e or π?

   When they were looking, they were not absolutely sure that a pattern did not exist.

ACTIVITY 3.6

College Graduates

Topics: *Fitting Data to an Exponential Model, Regression Equations*

According to the U.S. Department of Education, the number of college graduates has increased significantly during the twentieth century. The following table gives the number (in thousands) of college degrees awarded from 1900 through 1990.

YEAR	1900	1910	1920	1930	1940	1950	1960	1970	1980	1990
NUMBER OF COLLEGE GRADUATES (IN THOUSANDS)	30	54	73	127	223	432	530	878	935	1017

1. Let t represent the number of years since 1900 ($t = 0$ corresponds to 1900, $t = 10$ to 1910, etc.). Let N represent the number of college graduates (in thousands) at time t. Sketch a scatterplot of the given data on your grapher. Your scatterplot should appear as follows.

2. What window settings did you use to obtain the graph in Problem 1?

Xmin = −10 Ymin = 0

Xmax = 100 Ymax = 1050

3. It appears that all of the data points do not exactly lie on a single curve. You want to determine a function whose graph best fits the set of data.

   a. How well would a linear function fit the data? Explain.

   A line would fit rather well, but the data is clearly not 100% linear.

   b. How well would an exponential function fit the data? Explain.

   The increasing exponential might hit more points.

4. Using your grapher, determine the equation of an exponential function that best fits the given data. Appendix C demonstrates how to determine a linear function of best fit. Use option 0 ExpReg rather than option 4 LinReg(ax+b).

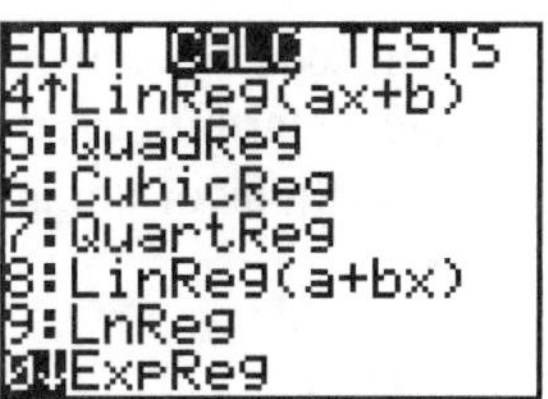

$y = 36.536(1.0427)^x$

5. a. Using the exponential regression equation of best fit, determine the number of college graduates in the year 1970 ($t = 70$).

From the graph, 683.96 thousand. (Answers will vary depending on rounding.)

b. Determine the percent error in the actual number of graduates in 1970 (see table on page 257) and the predicted number from part a.

Error $= 878 - 683.96 = 194.04$

Percent error $= \frac{194.04}{878} = 22.1\%$.

(Answers may vary depending on rounding.)

6. a. According to the exponential model, what is the growth factor for the number of college graduates per year? What is the significance that the growth factor is greater than 1?

The growth factor is 1.0427. Since greater than 1, the function is increasing.

b. What is the annual percent rate of growth?

4.27%

7. a. According to your exponential model, in what year will there be 2 million college graduates? Use the trace feature of your grapher to approximate your answer, recalling that the number of college graduates is measured in thousands.

1996

b. What equation did you solve in part a to answer the question?

$2000 = 36.536(1.0427)^x$

8. What is the doubling time for your exponential model? That is, approximately how many years will it take for a given number of college graduates to double?

Approximately 16.5 years.

EXERCISES

1. The total amount of money spent on health care in the United States is increasing at an alarming rate. The following table gives the total health care expenditures in billions of dollars in five-year intervals from 1970 through 1995.

YEAR	1970	1975	1980	1985	1990	1995
TOTAL SPENT (BILLIONS OF DOLLARS)	74.4	132.9	250.1	422.6	675	1205

Exercise numbers appearing in color are answered in the Selected Answers section of this book.

a. Does the table indicate that the data would be better modeled by a linear model, $y = mx + b$, or by an exponential model, $y = a \cdot b^x$? Explain.

The exponential model seems to be better since the rate of change appears to be increasing.

b. Sketch a scatterplot of the data.

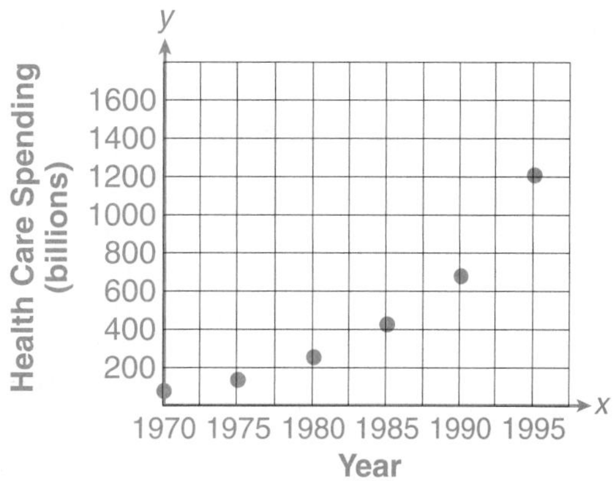

c. Does the graph reinforce your conclusion in part a? Explain.

The scatterplot reinforces part a because the points seem to be an increasing exponential curve.

d. Use your grapher to determine the exponential regression equation that best fits the health care data in the table.

$C(t) = 77.41(1.1167)^t$ t = Number of years since 1970.

e. Using the regression equation from part d, determine the predicted total health care expenditures for the year 1990.

703.93 billion

f. Determine the percent error in the actual total health care costs (see table) and the predicted total cost from part e.

Error $= 703.93 - 675 = 28.93$ Percent error $\frac{28.93}{675} = 4.3\%$

g. According to the exponential model, what is the growth factor for the total health care costs per year?

1.1167 billion dollars

h. According to the exponential model, in what year did the total heath care costs exceed $1 trillion for the first time?

$t = 23$ or 1993

i. What is the doubling time for this exponential model?

Doubling time is about 6.3 years.

2. a. Consider the following data set for the variables x and y.

x	5	8	11	15	20
y	70.2	50.7	35.1	22.6	9.5

Plot these points on the following grid.

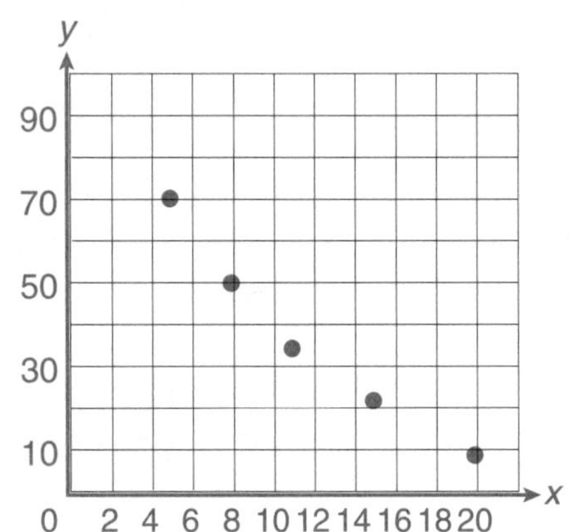

b. Use your grapher to determine both a linear regression and an exponential regression model of the data. Record the equations for these models here.

Linear: $y = -3.94726x + 84.19769$

Exponential: $y = 144.212(0.87688)^x$

c. Which model appears to fit the data better? Explain.

The exponential model appears to be closer to more points and, thus, the better model.

d. Use the better model to find y when $x = 13$ and when $x = 25$.

When $x = 13$, $y = 26.135$

When $x = 25$, $y = 5.401$

e. For the exponential model, what is the decay factor?

The decay factor is 0.87688.

f. What is the significance that the decay factor is between 0 and 1?

This means that the function is decreasing.

g. What is the halving time for the exponential model?

The halving time is 5.5.

3. Using the graph of $y = 2^x$ as a check, summarize the properties of the exponential function $y = a \cdot b^x$, where $a > 0$.

a. What is the domain?

All reals.

b. What is the range?

$y > 0$

c. When is $y = a \cdot b^x$ positive?

Since $b > 0$, the function is always positive.

d. When is $y = a \cdot b^x$ negative?

If $a < 0$, the function is always negative.

e. What is the vertical intercept of the graph of $y = a \cdot b^x$?

$(0, a)$

What Have I Learned?

1. Discuss the characteristics of an exponential function, and contrast them with similar characteristics of a linear function.

   f is increasing if $b > 0$.

   g is increasing if $m > 0$.

   f is decreasing if $0 < b < 1$ and *g* is decreasing if $m < 0$.

2. Suppose you have an exponential function of the form $f(x) = ab^x$, where $a > 0$, and $b > 0$, $b \neq 1$. By inspecting the graph of *f*, can you determine if $b > 1$ or if $0 < b < 1$? Explain.

   Yes, if $b > 1$, the function is increasing. If the function is decreasing, $0 < b < 1$.

3. You are given a function defined by a table and the input values are evenly spaced. By looking at the table, can you determine if the function can be approximated by an exponential model? Explain.

   Yes, if the ratio between consecutive output values is roughly constant, the function can be approximated by an exponential function.

4. Explain the difference between growth rate and growth factor.

   If the growth rate is *r*, the growth factor is $1 + r$. The growth rate is the increase in output per unit increase in input. The growth factor is the common factor that produces the next output (per unit of input).

5. An exponential function $y = ab^x$ passes through the point (0, 2.6). What can you conclude about the values of *a* and *b*?

   $a = 2.6$ Nothing can be concluded about the value of *b* without further information.

6. You have just received a substantial tax refund of *P* dollars. You decide to invest the money in a CD for 2 years. You have narrowed your choices to two banks. Bank A will give you 6.75% interest compounded quarterly. Bank B offers you 6.50% compounded continuously. Where do you deposit your money? Explain.

   The growth factor for Bank A is $\left(1 + \frac{0.0675}{4}\right)^4 = 1.06923$. The growth factor for Bank B is $e^{0.065} = 1.06716$. Therefore, I deposit in Bank A because the growth factor is larger.

How Can I Practice?

1. You are planning to purchase a new car and you have your eye on a specific model. You know that new car prices are projected to increase at a rate of 4% per year for the next few years.

   a. Write an equation that represents the projected cost C of your dream car t years in the future, given that it costs $17,000 today.

   $A = 17{,}000(1.04)^t$

   b. Identify the growth rate and growth factor.

   The growth rate is 0.04, the growth factor is 1.04.

   c. Use your equation in part a to project the cost of your car 3 years from now.

   $A = 17{,}000(1.04)^3 = 19{,}122.69$

   d. If the price continues to increase at 4% per year, use your grapher to approximate how long it will take for your dream car to cost $30,000.

   14.5 years

2. Without using your grapher, match the graph with its equation.

   a. $f(x) = -3(1.47)^x$ b. $g(x) = 2.5(0.47)^x$ c. $h(x) = 1.5(1.47)^x$

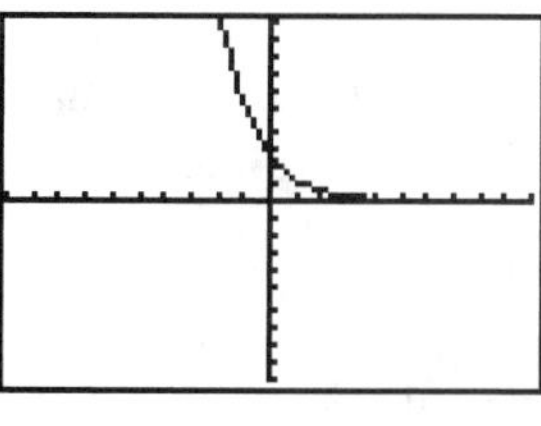

i.

graph i is function b

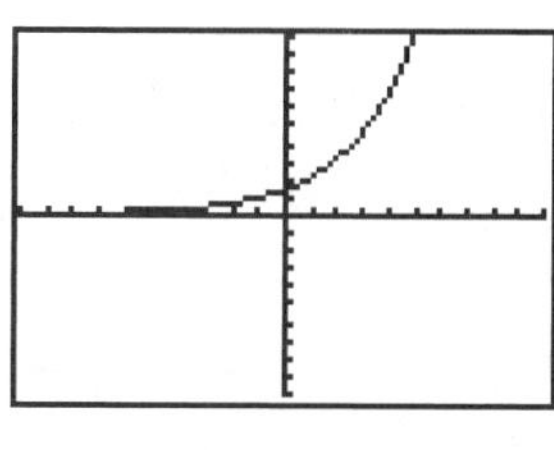

ii.

graph ii is function c

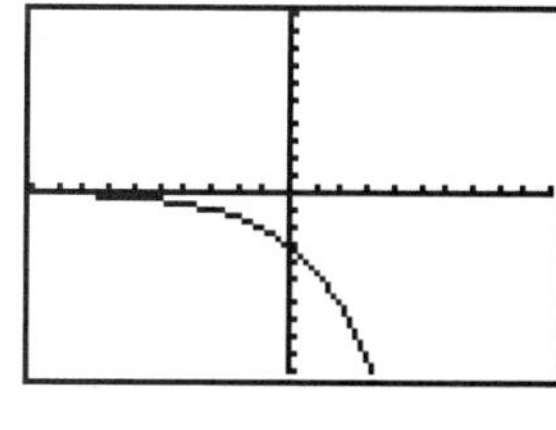

iii.

graph iii is function a

3. Explain the reasons for your choices in Problem 2.

   i is function b because it is decreasing and the only growth factor between 0 and 1 is function b's 0.47.

   ii is function c because it is positive and increasing with the growth factor of 1.47.

   iii is function a because it is the only one that will yield negative output.

Exercise numbers appearing in color are answered in the Selected Answers section of this book.

4. Complete each of the following tables representing exponential functions. Round calculations to two decimal places whenever necessary.

a.

x	0	1	2	3	4
y	2.00	5.10	13.01	33.18	84.61

b.

x	0	1	2	3	4
y	3.50	2.10	1.26	0.76	0.46

c.

x	0	2	4	6	8
y	7.10	12.78	23.00	41.50	74.7

5. Write the symbolic rule for each table in Problem 4.

a. $y = 2(2.55)^x$

b. $y = 3.5(0.6)^x$

c. $y = 7.1(1.8)^x$

6. Without graphing, classify each of the following functions as increasing or decreasing, and determine $f(0)$. (Use your grapher to verify.)

a. $f(x) = 1.3(0.75)^x$

$f(0) = 1.3$; decreasing

b. $f(x) = 0.6(1.03)^x$

$f(0) = 0.6$; increasing

c. $f(x) = 3(\frac{1}{5})^x$

$f(0) = 3$; decreasing

7. **a.** Given the following table, do you believe that the data can be approximately modeled by an exponential function? Yes

x	0	1	2	3	4	5	6
y	2	5	12.5	31.3	78.1	195.3	488.3

b. If you answered yes to part a, what is the constant ratio of successive output values?

The constant ratio is 2.5 or $\frac{5}{2}$.

c. Determine an exponential equation that models the data.

$A = 2(2.5)^x$

8. Your current salary is $22,000 per year. You are offered two options for salary increases:

Plan 1: an annual increase of $1000 per year

Plan 2: an annual percentage increase of 4% of your salary

Which plan would you choose? Explain.

The answer is, it depends. If I plan to be with the company 10 years or less, I would take Plan 1, because it takes Plan 2 about 9 years to catch up. If I expect to be with the company for a long time, say 20 years, I would choose Plan 2 because by then I am over $6000 per year better off.

9. The number of victims of a flu epidemic is increasing at a rate of 7.5% per week.

a. If 2000 people are currently infected, write an exponential model of the form $N = f(t) = N_0 e^{rt}$, where

N is the number of victims in thousands

N_0 is the initial number infected in thousands

r is the weekly percent rate expressed as a decimal

t is the number of weeks

$N = f(t) = 2e^{0.075t}$

b. Use the exponential model to predict the number of people infected after 8 weeks.

$N = f(8) = 2e^{0.075(8)}$

$= 3.6442$

c. Sketch the graph of the flu function.

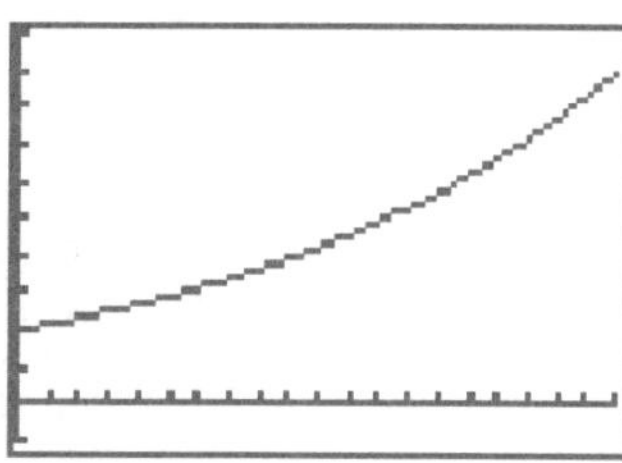

Xmin = 0, Xmax = 20, Ymin = −1, Ymax = 10

d. Predict when the number of victims of the flu will triple. Use a graphing approach.

14.6482 or 15 weeks

CLUSTER 2

Logarithmic Functions

ACTIVITY 3.7

The Foolish King
Topic: *Logarithmic Functions*

The humble knave, who had just saved the king's son from certain death, was asked by the king what he would like for his reward. An astute observer of the mathematical world around him, the knave requested what he suspected the king would quickly grant. "Simply place two grains of rice on the first square of a chessboard, four on the second square, eight on the next, and so on, doubling the number of grains as you go until all 64 squares of the board are counted." The king, thinking the knave a fool for requesting such a meager reward, quickly agreed to this request.

1. Have you seen a problem similar to this before?

   Yes, in Activity 3.1.

2. Who was the fool, and why?

   The king is the fool. He is giving away a lot more rice than he realizes.

3. How many grains of rice would need to be placed on the last square?

   $2^{64} = 1.84467 \cdot 10^{19}$

4. a. Express the number of grains on a square as a function of the square's number.

   The number of grains of rice on the nth square is $g(n) = 2^n$.

   b. What is the base of this exponential function?

   The base is 2.

   c. What is the practical domain for this application?

   The practical domain is integers from 1 to 64.

   d. Graph this function on your grapher, using the window Xmin $= -2$, Xmax $= 10$, Ymin $= 0$, and Ymax $= 750$.

   Xmin $= 0$, Xmax $= 64$, Ymin $= 0$, Ymax $= 1.9 \cdot 10^{19}$.

   e. Using the table or trace features of your calculator, estimate the first square for which there are at least 500 grains of rice.

   The first square with at least 500 grains of rice is the 9th.

5. a. For what inequality did you determine an approximate solution to help answer Problem 4e?

   $2^n \geq 500$

   b. Why is it difficult to determine the exact solution to this inequality?

   The solution is not an integer, and we have not yet solved equations with unknowns as an exponent.

Your goal is now to determine a way to solve exponential equations such as $2^x = 500$ and their associated inequalities exactly using an algebraic approach. For the equation $2^x = 8$, you are looking for the value of the variable x, an exponent in this case, that makes the statement true. Can you find the value that satisfies this equation? By inspection, the solution is $x = 3$. The difficulty is that until this point you have no algebraic technique or principle that allows you to isolate x whenever it appears as an exponent. Mathematicians have already invented a function to help you; it is called the **logarithm function.**

The notation $\log_2 8 = 3$ means exactly the same as $2^3 = 8$. Notice that the expression $\log_2 8 = 3$ is read "the logarithm, base 2, of 8" is equal to the exponent 3. In other words, a logarithm is really an exponent.

For any base $b > 0$, $b \neq 1$, and $N > 0$,

$$\underbrace{\log_b N = E}_{\textbf{Logarithmic form}} \text{ is equivalent to } \underbrace{b^E = N}_{\textbf{Exponential form}}$$

6. Determine the logarithm of the number to the given base in each of the following. Remember, your answer is the exponent that the base must be raised to to obtain the number.

a. $\log_2 16 =$ 4

(*Hint*: $2^? = 16$)

b. $\log_9 3 =$ 2

(*Hint:* $9^? = 3$)

c. $\log_5 25 =$ 2

d. $\log_{10} 1000 =$ 3

e. $\log_3\left(\frac{1}{3}\right) =$ −1

f. $\log_2\left(\frac{1}{8}\right) =$ −3

g. $\log_{10} 1 =$ 0

h. $\log_3 1 =$ 0

Parts g and h of Problem 6 demonstrate an important property of logarithms.

For any base $b > 0$, $b \neq 1$, $\log_b 1 = 0$.

7. Write each of the following as an equivalent statement in logarithmic form.

a. $10^2 = 100$

$\log_{10} 100 = 2$

b. $5^3 = 125$

$\log_5 125 = 3$

c. $2^{-1} = \frac{1}{2}$

$\log_2 \frac{1}{2} = -1$

d. $16^{1/2} = 4$

$\log_{16} 4 = \frac{1}{2}$

8. a. Write the equation $2^x = 500$ in logarithmic form.

$x = \log_2 500$

b. What is the solution (in logarithmic form) to the equation $2^x = 500$?

$x = \log_2 500$

c. Use the graph of $y = 2^x$ to approximate the value of $\log_2 500$. (*Hint:* See Problem 4e.)

x is approximately 8.97.

9. a. Can you determine $\log_2 500$ exactly? You may have noticed that there is a log key on your calculator. But the base of this particular logarithmic function is not indicated! See if you can discover what the base is. First, determine the value of each of the following logarithms.

i. $\log_2 2 =$ __1__ **ii.** $\log_3 3 =$ __1__ **iii.** $\log_4 4 =$ __1__

b. What is the value of $\log_b b$ for any value of b when $b > 0, b \neq 1$?

1.

c. Now use the property of logarithms from part b to experiment with your calculator and determine the base of the log key function on your calculator.

10.

Base 10 logarithms are called **common logarithms.** The notations $\log x$ and $\log_{10} x$ are equivalent.

d. Use your calculator to approximate the value of $\log_{10} 50$. Does your answer seem reasonable? Explain.

1.69897

Yes, because $10^{1.69897} = 50$.

Throughout the remainder of this activity, you will be using your calculator to approximate base ten logarithms. You will learn how to determine the value of $\log_2 500$ *in Activity 3.10.*

10. a. Try to evaluate $\log_{10}(-100)$ using your calculator. What do you observe? Does it seem reasonable? Explain.

Error. Yes it seems reasonable because 10 raised to any power will never be negative.

b. What is the domain for the function defined by $y = \log x$?

$x > 0$.

11. a. For which of the following can you determine an exact value without using your calculator?

i. log 100 — i. Yes

ii. log 35 — ii. No

iii. log 8.75 — iii. No

iv. $\log\left(\frac{1}{100}\right)$ — iv. Yes

v. log 0.5 — v. No

b. Use your calculator to evaluate the logarithms in part a, rounding to three decimal places.

i. 2 ii. 1.544 iii. 0.942

iv. −2 v. −0.301

12. Suppose you need to solve the equation $10^x = 500$ rather than $2^x = 500$.

a. Write the equation $10^x = 500$ in logarithmic notation.

$\log 500 = x$

b. Is there an exact solution to the equation?

No, there is not an exact solution.

c. Use your calculator to determine an approximate solution (to three decimal places).

$x = 2.699$

13. The exponential function defined by $f(x) = 10^x$ has a special relationship with the corresponding logarithmic function defined by $g(x) = \log_{10} x = \log x$.

a. Complete the following tables for $f(x) = 10^x$ and $g(x) = \log x$.

x	$f(x) = 10^x$
−2	0.01
−1	0.1
0	1
1	10
2	100

x	$g(x) = \log x$
0.01	−2
0.1	−1
1	0
10	1
100	2

b. Sketch the graphs of $y = 10^x$ and $y = \log_{10} x$ using your grapher. For the window Xmin $= -3.8$, Xmax $= 3.8$, Ymin $= -2.5$, and Ymax $= 2.5$ your screen should appear as follows.

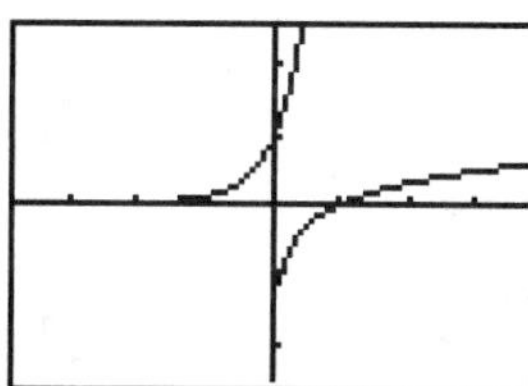

c. The two graphs are symmetric. Describe in a sentence or two the symmetry you observe in your graphs. (*Hint:* Sketch the line $y = x$.)

The graphs are reflected over the line $y = x$.

Recall the concept of an inverse function from Chapter 2. The inverse function interchanges the domain and range of the original function. You can determine the equation of the inverse by interchanging the x- and y-values of the equation and solving the new equation for y. The graph of an inverse function is the reflection of the original function about the line $y = x$.

14. Are $y = \log x$ and $y = 10^x$ inverse functions? Explain.

Yes, the graphs are reflections in the line $y = x$, and the input values of the exponential function are the output values of the logarithmic function and vice versa.

SUMMARY

- For any base $b > 0$, $b \neq 1$, the functions defined by $y = b^x$ and $y = \log_b x$ are inverse functions.
- For any base $b > 0$, $b \neq 1$, $\log_b 1 = 0$.
- For any base $b > 0$, $b \neq 1$, $\log_b b = 1$.
- The domain of $y = \log_b x$ is $x > 0$.
- The range of $y = \log_b x$ is all real numbers.

EXERCISES

1. Use the definition of logarithm to determine the exact value of each of the following.

a. $\log_2 32$ — 5

b. $\log_3 27$ — 3

c. $\log 0.1$ — -1

d. $\log_2 \left(\frac{1}{64}\right)$ — -6

e. $\log_5 1$ — 0

f. $\log_{1/2} \left(\frac{1}{4}\right)$ — 2

g. $\log_7 \sqrt{7}$ (*Hint:* $\sqrt{7} = 7^{1/2}$) — $\frac{1}{2}$

h. $\log_{100} 10$ — $\frac{1}{2}$

2. Because base 10 logarithms appear so frequently, it is a good idea to become familiar with the following base 10 logarithms. Evaluate each logarithm without the use of a calculator.

a. $\log \left(\frac{1}{1000}\right) = \underline{-3}$

b. $\log \left(\frac{1}{100}\right) = \underline{-2}$

c. $\log \left(\frac{1}{10}\right) = \underline{-1}$

d. $\log 1 = \underline{0}$

e. $\log 10 = \underline{1}$

f. $\log 100 = \underline{2}$

Exercise numbers appearing in color are answered in the Selected Answers section of this book.

g. $\log 1000 =$ ___3___

3. Rewrite the following equations in logarithmic form.

a. $3^2 = 9$

$\log_3 9 = 2$

b. $\sqrt{121} = 11$

$\log_{121} 11 = \frac{1}{2}$

c. $4^x = 27$

$\log_4 27 = x$

d. $y^3 = 19$

$\log_y 19 = 3$

4. Rewrite the following equations in exponential form.

a. $\log_3 81 = 4$

$3^4 = 81$

b. $\frac{1}{2} = \log_{100} 10$

$100^{\frac{1}{2}} = 10$

c. $\log_9 x = 12$

$9^{12} = x$

d. $y = \log_7 x$

$7^y = x$

5. Estimate between what two integers the solution to each equations falls. Then solve each equation exactly by first changing to log form. Use your calculator to approximate your answer to 3 decimal places.

a. $10^x = 3.25$

$0 < x < 1$

$x = \log 3.25$

$x = 0.5119$

b. $10^x = 590$

$2 < x < 3$

$x = \log 590$

$x = 2.771$

c. $10^x = 0.0000045$

$-6 < x < -5$

$x = \log 0.0000045$

$x = -5.347$

6. Explain why $\log_b 1 = 0$ for any base $b > 0$, $b \neq 1$.

If $\log_b 1 = x$, then $b^x = 1$. Since $b \neq 1$, the only solution is $x = 0$.

7. Using the graph of $y = \log x$ as a check, summarize the following properties of the common logarithmic function.

a. What is the domain?

$x > 0$

b. What is the range?

All real numbers.

c. For what values of x is $\log x$ positive?

$x > 1$

d. For what values of x is $\log x$ negative?

$0 < x < 1$

e. For what values of x does $\log x = 0$?

$x = 1$.

f. For what values of x does $\log x = 1$?

10.

g. If you replace base 10 with any other base $b > 1$, which of the preceding answers will change?

Only *f* will change. $\log_b x = 1$ when $x = b$.

h. If you replace base 10 with any other base $0 < b < 1$, which of the preceding answers will change?

c, *d*, and *f* will change.

c and *d* will be interchanged.

8. a. Complete the following table using your calculator. Round your answers to the nearest whole number.

x	0.001	0.01	0.1	0.25	0.5	1
$y = \log x$	−3	−2	−1	−1	0	0

b. As the input values take on values closer and closer to zero, what happens to the corresponding output values?

The output values approach $-\infty$.

9. The exponential function defined by $y = 2^x$ has an inverse. Determine the inverse function. Write your answer in logarithmic form.

$y = \log_2 x$.

10. The number of years n for a piece of equipment to depreciate to a known salvage value V is given by the formula

$$n = \frac{\log V - \log C}{\log (1 - r)}$$

where C is the initial cost of the piece of equipment and r is the annual rate of depreciation expressed as a decimal. If a computer costs \$34,000, has a life expectancy of 5 years, and a salvage value of \$1000, how old is the computer if its current value is \$10,000?

$$5 = \frac{\log (1000) - \log (34{,}000)}{\log (1 - r)}$$

$$\log (1 - r) = \frac{\log (1000) - \log (34{,}000)}{5} = -0.106$$

so

$$n = \frac{\log (10{,}000) - \log (34{,}000)}{-.106} = 1.7 \text{ years.}$$

ACTIVITY 3.8

The National Pastime

Topics: *Graphs of Logarithmic Functions, Modeling Data*

In his column dated July 19, 1996, Rocky Landsverk of *Sports Collector's Digest*, cited the following statistics regarding the number of participants in Little League baseball.

A LEAGUE OF THEIR OWN

Year	1991	1992	1993	1994	1995
t	1	2	3	4	5
$N(t)$ (in millions)	1.88	2.29	2.36	2.45	2.50

Data: Sports Collector's Digest

1. Using your grapher, construct a scatterplot of $N(t)$ versus t, where t represents the number of years since 1990 and $N(t)$ represents the number of participants in Little League baseball (in millions). Using Xmin $= -1$, Xmax $= 6$, Ymin $= -0.5$, and Ymax $= 3$, your scatterplot should resemble the following.

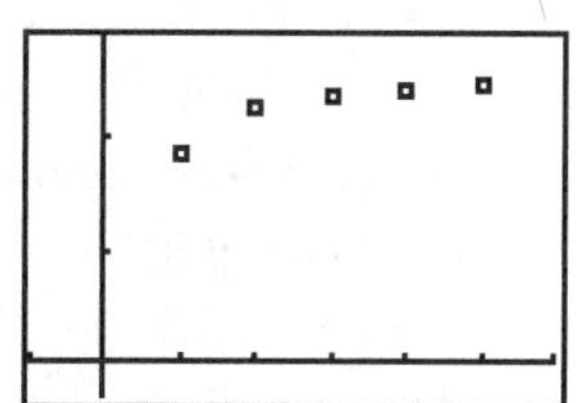

2. From the scatterplot, do the data points appear linear? Do the data points appear exponential? How would you describe the scatterplot?

   No. It is increasing, but tending towards horizontal.

The data on Little League baseball participants can be approximated by

$$N(t) = 1.94 + 0.867 \log (t)$$

(Remember, t is the number of years since 1990.)

3. a. Enter this function into your grapher. Verify visually that the preceding equation is a good model for your data.

   b. Using your graph, which year shows the largest difference between the prediction of the model and the actual number of participants?

   1992.

   c. Use the equation from Problem 2 to predict the number of participants in the year 1999.

   $N(9) = 1.94 + 0.867\log (9) = 2.77$ million.

d. Do you believe that this is a good prediction? Explain.

It is consistent with the model, but extrapolation is always risky.

Throughout the rest of the activity, you will try to discover the relationships between the logarithmic (log) function and other functions you have already investigated.

4. a. Using the data on the number of Little League participants, complete the following table.

YEAR	1992	1993	1994	1995
RATE OF CHANGE IN NUMBER OF PARTICIPANTS FROM THE PREVIOUS YEAR	0.41	0.07	0.09	0.05

b. What can you say in general about the rate of change in the number of participants from year to year?

All are positive. The rate of change was much higher in 1992. Later, it dropped off and seemed to level off.

You should have discovered that the rate of change is always positive. This means that the number of participants is increasing each year. Nevertheless, in general, the increase gets smaller as the years go by. This is characteristic of logarithmic functions.

- As the input of a logarithmic function increases, the output increases at a slower rate (the graph becomes less steep).
- For an increasing linear function, as the input variable increases, the output increases at a constant rate (the steepness remains the same).
- For an increasing exponential function, as the input increases, the output increases at a faster rate (the graph becomes steeper).

The inverse of the function defined by $y = 2^x$ is $y = \log_2 x$. (See Exercise 9 in Activity 3.7.) The inverse of $y = e^x$ is determined in the following way.

Interchange x and y: $x = e^y$

Write in logarithmic form: $y = \log_e x$

If the base of a logarithm is the number e, the logarithm is called a **natural logarithm** and is written as $\log_e x = \ln x$.

5. a. Your calculator has an ln key. Using your calculator, complete the following table. Round your answers to three decimal places.

x	0.1	0.5	1	5	10	20	50
$y = \ln x$	−2.303	−0.693	0	1.609	2.303	2.996	3.912

b. Sketch a graph of $y = \ln x$ using your grapher. Using the window Xmin $= -1$, Xmax $= 4$, Ymin $= -2.5$, and Ymax $= 2.5$, your screen should appear as follows.

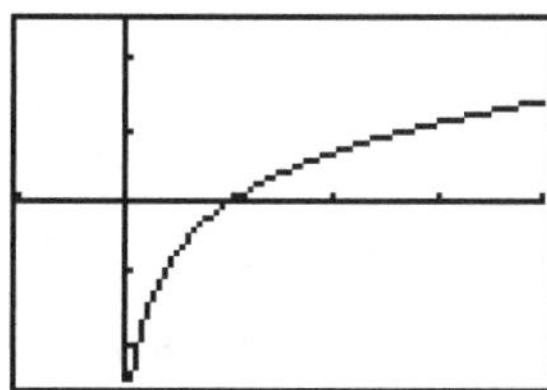

c. Sketch a graph of $y = e^x$ on the same set of coordinate axes using the window Xmin $= -7.5$, Xmax $= 7.5$, Ymin $= -5$, and Ymax $= 5$. Describe the symmetry that you observe.

It is a reflection over the line $y = x$.

The natural logarithmic function is so prevalent that on most graphing calculators it has its own built-in regression finder. The natural logarithmic function can be used to model a variety of scientific and natural phenomena. Consider the following example.

6. You are working on the development of an "elastic" ball for the IBF Toy Company. The question you are investigating is, If the ball is launched straight up, how far has it traveled vertically when it hits the ground for the tenth time?

Possibility for group discussion.

Your launcher will project the ball 10 feet into the air. This means that it will travel 20 feet (10 feet up and 10 feet down) before it hits the ground the first time. Assuming that the ball returns to 50% of its previous height, it will rebound 5 feet and travel 10 feet before it hits the ground again. A summary of this situation is found in the following table.

N, TIMES THE BALL HITS THE GROUND	1	2	3	4	5	6
DISTANCE TRAVELED SINCE LAST TIME	20	10	5	2.5	1.25	0.625
T, TOTAL DISTANCE TRAVELED	20	30	35	37.5	38.75	39.375

a. Using your grapher, create a scatterplot where N is the input and T be the output. Using the window Xmin $= 0$, Xmax $= 7$, Ymin $= 0$, Ymax $= 45$, your plot should resemble the following.

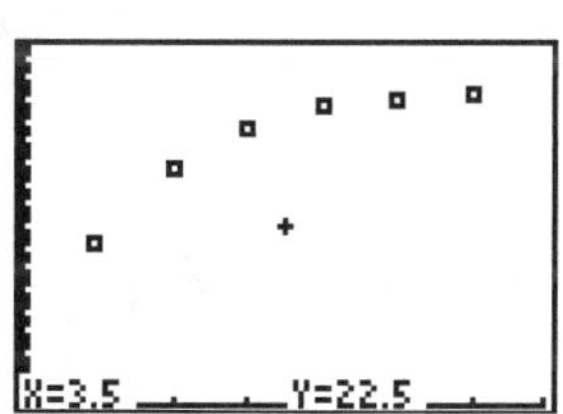

b. Do the table and scatterplot indicate that the data is linear, exponential, or logarithmic?

logarithmic

c. Use your grapher to produce linear, exponential, and natural log regression equations for the given data.

Linear:

Linear $y = 3.589x + 20.875$

Exponential:

Exponential $21.372 \cdot 1.128^x$

Natural log:

Natural log $y = 21.373 + 11.002 \ln x$

Graph each equation and determine which of the regressions appears to be the best fit.

d. Use the equation of best fit to predict the total distance traveled by the ball when it hits the ground for the tenth time.

The best fit equation is the logarithmic. When $x = 10$, $y = 46.7$

SUMMARY

- As the input of a logarithmic function increases, the output increases as well, but at a slower and slower rate.
- The graph of a logarithmic function defined by $\log_b x$, where $b > 1$, resembles the following graph.

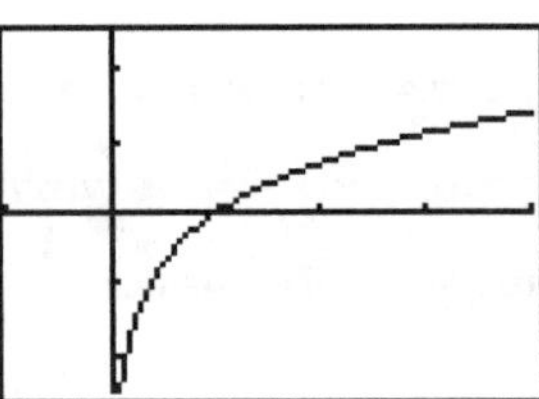

- The natural logarithmic function, denoted by ln, is defined by

$$y = \ln x = \log_e x.$$

EXERCISES

1. The following table indicates the deaths from AIDS in the United States for men from 1988 through 1993, as reported by the U.S. Centers for Disease Control and Prevention.

YEAR	1988	1989	1990	1991	1992	1993
AIDS DEATHS (IN THOUSANDS)	18	24	27	31	34	36

a. Plot the points on the following grid.

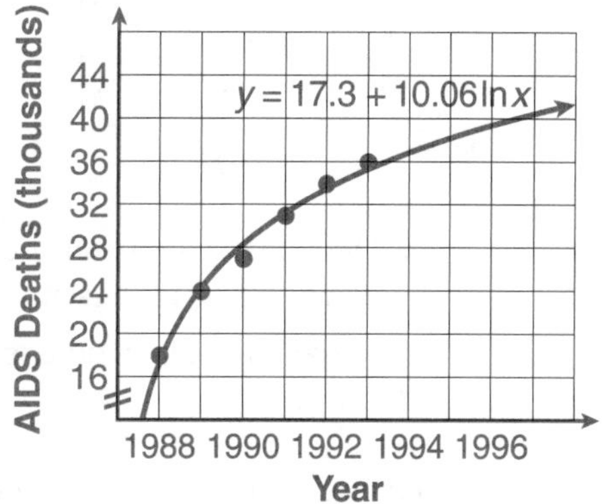

b. Does the graph indicate that the data are logarithmic? Explain.

Yes, it is increasing, but more and more slowly.

c. If you let x represent the number of years since 1987 and y represent the number of men dying of AIDS (in thousands), the data can be modeled by

$$y = 17.3 + 10.06 \ln x.$$

Sketch this function on the coordinate axes in part a.

d. Does this appear to be a good fit? Explain.

Yes, since all the points are close to the line. Some are above, some are below.

e. Use your model to predict the number of AIDS deaths among men in 1994.

36,900 deaths

f. The actual number of deaths among males in 1994 as reported by the Centers for Disease Control and Prevention was 37,360. How accurate was your model? Explain.

Quite accurate. The error is 460 or 1.2%.

2. a. Consider the following data set for the variables x and y.

x	1	4	7	10	13
$f(x)$	3.0	4.5	5.0	5.2	5.8

Plot these points on the grid.

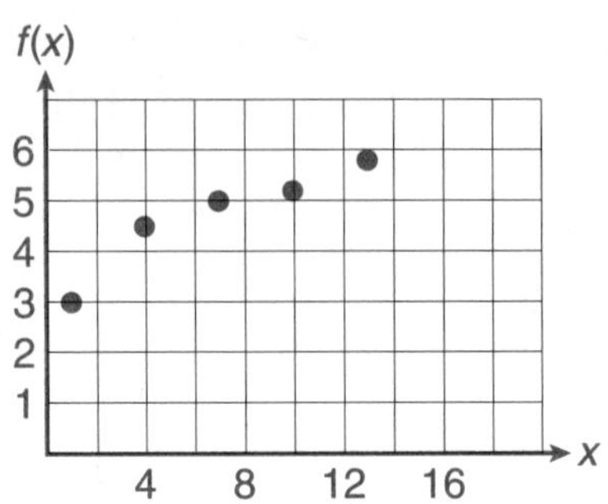

b. Does the scatterplot indicate that the data points are more likely linear, exponential, or logarithmic? Explain.

Logarithmic. It is increasing, but at continually lesser rates.

c. Use your grapher to determine a logarithmic regression model that represents the data.

$y = 3 + 1.033 \ln x$

d. Use your model to determine $f(11)$ and $f(20)$.

$f(11) = 5.48$

$f(20) = 6.1$

3. Using the graph of $y = \ln x$ as a check, summarize the following properties of the natural logarithmic function.

a. What is the domain?

$x > 0$

b. What is the range?

All real numbers.

c. For what values of x is $\ln x$ positive?

When $x > 1$

d. For what values of x is $\ln x$ negative?

$0 < x < 1$

e. When does $\ln x = 0$?

$x = 1$

f. When does $\ln x = 1$?

$x = e$

4. a. Complete the following table using your calculator. Round your answers to the nearest whole number.

x	0.001	0.01	0.1	0.25	0.5	1
$y = \ln x$	−6.908	−4.605	−2.303	−1.386	−0.6931	0

b. As the input values take on values closer and closer to zero, what happens to the corresponding output values?

Output becomes more and more negative without bound.

5. Determine each of the following without the use of a calculator.

a. $\ln 1$

0

b. $\ln e$

1

c. $\ln e^2$ $\left(Hint\text{: } \log_e e^2 = ? \text{ or } e^? = e^2.\right)$

2

6. The barometric pressure P in inches of mercury at a distance x miles from the eye of a moderate hurricane can be modeled by

$$P = f(x) = 0.48 \ln(x + 1) + 27.$$

a. Determine $f(0)$. What is the practical meaning of the value in this situation?

$f(0) = 27$ in. This is the pressure in the eye of the storm.

b. Sketch a graph of this function.

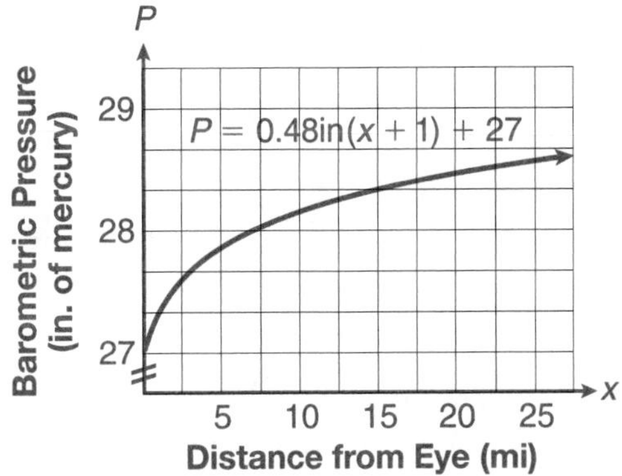

c. Describe how air pressure changes as you move away from the eye of the hurricane.

As you move away from the hurricane's eye, the pressure increases quickly at first and then more slowly.

7. The formula $R = 80.4 - 11 \ln x$ is used to approximate the minimum required ventilation rate R as a function of x the air space per child in a public school classroom. The rate R is measured in cubic feet per minute, and x is measured in cubic feet.

a. Sketch a graph of the rate function for $100 \leq x \leq 1500$.

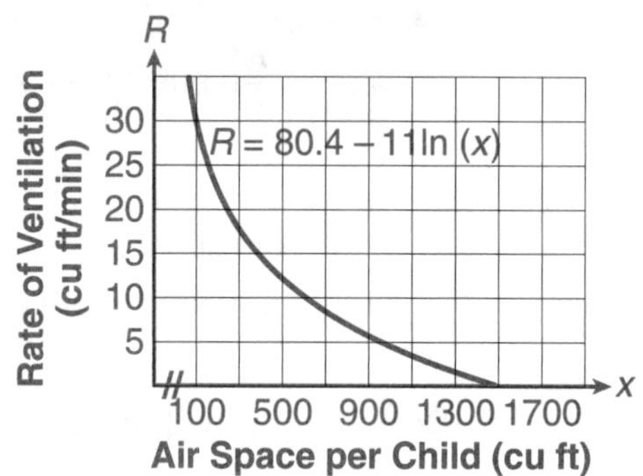

b. Determine the required ventilation rate if the air space per child is 300 cubic feet.

$f(300) = 17.66$

ACTIVITY 3.9

The Elastic Ball
Topic: *Properties of Logarithms*

You are continuing your work on the development of the elastic ball. You are still investigating the question, If the ball is launched straight up, how far has it traveled vertically when it hits the ground for the tenth time? However, your supervisor tells you that you cannot count the initial launch distance. You must only calculate the rebound distance. Using some physics properties, timers, and your calculator, you collect the following data.

N, NUMBER OF TIMES THE BALL HITS THE GROUND	1	2	3	4	5	6
T, TOTAL REBOUND DISTANCE (ft)	0	9.0	13.5	16.3	18.7	21.0

1. Do the data seem reasonable? Explain.

   Yes, it indicates that ball rebounds less with each successive bounce.

2. Use your grapher to construct a scatterplot of the data with N as the input and T as the output. Using a window of Xmin = 0, Xmax = 7, Ymin = 0, and Ymax = 25, your graph should resemble the following.

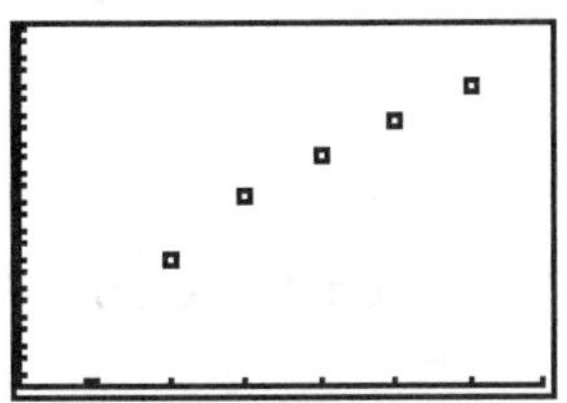

3. Do you believe that the data are logarithmic? Explain.

   Yes, it is growing, but it grows slower as x increases.

4. These data can be modeled by $T = 26.75 \log N$. Use your grapher to verify visually that this is a reasonable model for the given data.

5. **a.** Using your log model, complete the following table. Round values to the nearest hundredth.

N	2	5	10
$T = 26.75 \log N$	8.05	18.70	26.75

   b. What can you say about the relationship between the outputs of the table in part a?

   The third output is the sum of the first two outputs.

The results from Problem 5 can be written as follows.

$$26.75 \log 10 = 26.75 \log 2 + 26.75 \log 5$$

$$26.75 \log (2 \cdot 5) = 26.75 \log 2 + 26.75 \log 5$$

Dividing both sides by 26.75, you have

$$\log(2 \cdot 5) = \log 2 + \log 5$$

This result illustrates an important property of logarithms.

PROPERTY OF THE LOGARITHM OF A PRODUCT

$$\log_b(x \cdot y) = \log_b x + \log_b y$$

Expressed verbally, the logarithm of a product is the sum of the individual logarithms.

In particular, this tells you that the rebound distance of 10 bounces is the sum of the rebound distances after 2 bounces and 5 bounces.

6. Use the property of the logarithm of a product to write the following as the sum of two or more logarithms.

a. $\log_b 7 \cdot 13$

$\log_b 7 + \log_b 13$

b. $\log_3 xyz$

$\log_3 x + \log_3 y + \log_3 z$

c. $\log 15$

$\log 3 + \log 5$

d. $\ln 3xy$

$\ln 3 + \ln x + \ln y$

7. Write the following as the logarithm of a single expression.

a. $\ln a + \ln b + \ln c$

$\ln(abc)$

b. $\log_4 3 + \log_4 9$

$\log_4 27$

Note that the table in Problem 5 also indicates that the rebound distance after this ball has hit the floor twice is the total rebound distance when the ball has hit the ground 10 times minus the total rebound distance when the ball has hit the ground 5 times. To help clarify this point, do Problem 8.

8. Calculate 26.75 log 10 − 26.75 log 5, and compare this difference to 26.75 log 2.

Both equal 8.052552384.

If you divide out the factor of 26.75, you have

$$\log 10 - \log 5 = \log 2.$$

Because $\log\left(\frac{10}{5}\right) = \log 2$, then

$$\log\left(\frac{10}{5}\right) = \log 10 - \log 5.$$

This illustrates another important property of logarithms.

PROPERTY OF THE LOGARITHM OF A QUOTIENT

$$\log_b\left(\frac{A}{B}\right) = \log_b A - \log_b B$$

Expressed verbally, the logarithm of a quotient is the difference of the logarithm of the numerator and the logarithm of the denominator.

9. a. To demonstrate this property graphically, sketch graphs of $y = \log\left(\frac{x}{4}\right)$ and $y = \log x - \log 4$ on your calculator.

b. How do the graphs compare?

They are the same.

c. What do the graphs suggest about the relationship between $\log \frac{A}{B}$ and $\log A - \log B$?

$\log\frac{A}{B} = \log A - \log B$

10. Use the properties of logarithms to write the following as the sum or difference of logarithms.

a. $\log_6 \frac{17}{3}$

$\log_6 17 - \log_6 3$

b. $\ln \frac{x}{23}$

$\ln x - \ln 23$

c. $\log_3 \frac{2x}{y}$

$\log_3 2 + \log_3 x - \log_3 y$

d. $\log \frac{3}{2z}$

$\log 3 - (\log 2 + \log z)$

$\log 3 - \log 2 - \log z$

11. Write the following expressions as the logarithm of a single expression.

a. $\log x - \log 4 + \log z$

$\log \frac{xz}{4}$

b. $\log x - (\log 4 + \log z)$

$\log \frac{x}{4z}$

12. a. Use your calculator to sketch the graphs of $y = \log x + \log 4$ and $y = \log (x + 4)$.

b. How do these graphs compare?

The graphs have the same basic shape but they are definitely not the same.

c. What do the graphs suggest about the relationship between $\log (A + B)$ and $\log A + \log B$?

$\log (A + B) \neq \log A + \log B$

SUMMARY

Properties of the Logarithmic Function

If $A > 0, B > 0, b > 0$, and $b \neq 1$, then:

1. $\log_b (A \cdot B) = \log_b A + \log_b B$
2. $\log_b\left(\frac{A}{B}\right) = \log_b A - \log_b B$
3. $\log_b (A + B) \neq \log_b A + \log_b B$

EXERCISES

1. Use the properties of logarithms to write the following as the sum or difference of two or more logarithms.

 a. $\log_b 3 \cdot 7$
 $\log_b 3 + \log_b 7$

 b. $\log_3 3 \cdot 13$
 $1 + \log_3 13$

 c. $\log_7 \frac{13}{17}$
 $\log_7 13 - \log_7 17$

 d. $\log_3 \frac{xy}{3}$
 $\log_3 x + \log_3 y - 1$

2. Write the following expressions as the logarithm of a single number.

 a. $\log_3 5 + \log_3 3$
 $\log_3 15$

 b. $\log 25 - \log 17$
 $\log \frac{25}{17}$

 c. $\log_5 x - \log_5 5 + \log_5 7$
 $\log_5 \frac{7x}{5}$

 d. $\log(x + 7) - \log x$
 $\log \dfrac{x + 7}{x}$

3. a. Sketch the graphs of $y = \log (2x)$ and $y = \log x + \log 2$ on your graphing calculator.

 b. Are you surprised by the results? Explain.
 No, the graphs are the same because $\log (2x) = \log 2 + \log x$.

4. a. Sketch the graphs of $y = \log\left(\frac{3}{x}\right)$ and $y = \log x - \log 3$ on your graphing calculator.

 b. Are you surprised by your results? Explain.
 No, the graphs are reflected through the x-axis.
 $\log \left(\frac{3}{x}\right) = \log 3 - \log x = -(\log x - \log 3)$

Exercise numbers appearing in color are answered in the Selected Answers section of this book.

c. If your graphs were not identical for part a, can you modify the second function to make the graphs identical? Explain.

Multiply the right-hand side by -1.

5. You have been hired to handle the local newspaper advertising for a large used car dealership in your community. The owner tells you that your predecessor in this position used the formula

$$N(A) = 7.4 \log A$$

to decide how much to spend on newspaper advertising over a two-week period. The owner admitted that he didn't know much about the formula except that N represented the number of cars that the owner could expect to sell, and A was the amount of money that was spent on local newspaper advertising. He also indicated that the formula seemed to work well. You can purchase small ads in the local paper for \$15 per day, larger ads for \$50 per day, and giant ads for \$750 per day.

a. How many cars do you expect to sell if you purchase one small ad?

7.4 log (15) = 8.7 or 9 cars.

b. You decide to set up a table in an attempt to understand the relationship between the amount spent on advertising and the number of cars sold. Complete the following table.

AD COST, A	EXPECTED CAR SALES, N
15	9
50	13
750	21

c. How does the total of expected car sales from one small ad and one larger ad compare with the expected car sales from just one giant ad?

The sum of the sales from the smaller ads exceeds the sales from the larger ad by 1.

d. Are the results in the table consistent with what you know about the properties of logarithms? Explain.

Pretty close. 15 times 50 equals 750, so I would have expected the sum of the sales from the smaller ads to equal the sales from the largest. The error is due to rounding.

e. What are you going to advise the owner regarding the purchase of a giant ad?

Forget about the giant ad. It is a waste of money.

ACTIVITY 3.10

The Coroner's Office
Topics: *The Power Property of Logarithmic Functions, Change of Base Formula*

You have recently accepted a job in the coroner's office of a large city. Because of the large number of homicides, it has been very difficult for the coroners to complete all of their work. Your job is, in part, to assist them in the paperwork. On one particular day, you are working on a case in which you are attempting to establish the time of death. The coroner tells you that to establish the time of death, he uses the formula

$$t = 4 \ln \frac{98.6 - T_s}{T_b - T_s}, \qquad (1)$$

where t is the number of hours the victim has been dead

T_b is the temperature of the body when discovered

T_s is the temperature of the victim's surroundings

The coroner also tells you that the thermostat in the apartment in which the body was found was set at 68°F and the body temperature was 78°F.

1. a. Using formula (1), determine the number of hours the victim has been deceased. Use your calculator to approximate your answer to one decimal place.

4.5 hours

b. If the body was discovered at 10:07 P.M., what do you estimate for the time of death?

5:37 P.M.

Just as you are finishing this report, the assistant coroner gives you a second case. However, she gives you a different formula for determining the time of death:

$$t = \ln \left(\frac{98.6 - T_s}{T_b - T_s}\right)^4. \qquad (2)$$

Before you do the second report, you decide to redo the first case using the assistant coroner's formula.

2. a. Using formula (2), determine the number of hours the first body has been deceased.

4.5 hours

b. How does this compare with the results using the coroner's formula (1)?

They are exactly the same.

3. What do the results from Problem 2 suggest about the expressions $t = 4 \ln \frac{98.6 - T_s}{T_b - T_s}$ and $t = \ln \left(\frac{98.6 - T_s}{T_b - T_s}\right)^4$?

The expressions are equivalent.

4. a. Let $T_b = 78°F$ in each expression in Problem 3. Complete the following table using the table feature of your grapher. Be careful how you enter the functions into your calculator.

T_s	55	60	65	70	75
$t = 4\ ln \frac{98.6 - T_s}{78 - T_s}$	2.6	3.1	3.8	5.1	8.3
$t = ln\left(\frac{98.6 - T_s}{78 - T_s}\right)^4$	2.6	3.1	3.8	5.1	8.3

b. Are the expressions in part a equivalent? Explain.

They appear to be. The outputs are equivalent.

c. Sketch the graphs of $y = \ln\left(\frac{98.6 - x}{78 - x}\right)^4$ and $y = 4 \ln\left(\frac{98.6 - x}{78 - x}\right)$ on the same set of coordinate axes using your graphing calculator. How do the graphs compare? Are you surprised?

The graphs are equivalent for $x < 78$.

The results in Problem 4 illustrate another property of logarithms.

PROPERTY OF THE LOGARITHM OF A POWER

If $x > 0$ and k is any real number then

$$\log_b x^k = k \cdot \log_b x,$$

where $b > 0, b \neq 1$. In words, the logarithm of a power is equivalent to the exponent times the logarithm of the base.

5. Use the properties of logarithms to write the given logarithms as the sum or difference of two or more logarithms or as the product of a real number and a logarithm. All variables represent positive numbers.

a. $\log_3 x^{1/2}$

$\frac{1}{2}\log_3 x$

b. $\log_5 x^3$

$3 \log_5 x$

c. $\ln t^2$

$2 \ln (t)$

d. $\log \sqrt[3]{50}$ *Hint:* $\sqrt[3]{50} = 50^{1/3}$

$\frac{1}{3} \log 50 = \frac{1}{3} \log 10 \cdot 5$

$= \frac{1}{3} (\log 10 + \log 5)$

$= \frac{1}{3}(1 + \log 5)$

e. $\log_5 \frac{x^2y^3}{z}$

$2 \log_5 x + 3 \log_5 y - \log_5 z$

f. $\log_3 \frac{3x^2}{y^3}$

$1 + 2 \log_3 x - 3 \log_3 y$

6. Write each of the following as the logarithm of a single expression with coefficient 1.

a. $2 \log_3 5 + 3 \log_3 2$

$\log_3 200$

b. $\frac{1}{2} \log x^4 - \frac{1}{2} \log y^5$

$\log \sqrt{\frac{x^4}{y^5}}$

c. $3 \log_b 10 - 4 \log_b 5 + 2 \log_b 3$

$\log_b \frac{1000 \cdot 9}{5^4} = \log_b \frac{72}{5}$

d. $3 \log_b 10 - (4 \log_b 5 + 2 \log_b 3)$

$\log_b \frac{1000}{5^4 \cdot 9} = \log_b \frac{8}{45}$

Because the grapher has only the log base 10 and log base *e* keys, you cannot graph a logarithmic function such as $y = \log_2 x$ directly. Consider the following argument to rewrite the expression $\log_2 x$ as an equivalent expression using base 10 for the log. By definition of inverse, $y = \log_2 x$ is the same as $x = 2^y$. Taking the log of both sides of the second equation $x = 2^y$, you have

$$\log x = \log 2^y.$$

Using the property of the log of a power,

$$\log x = y \log 2.$$

Solving for *y*, you have

$$y = \frac{\log x}{\log 2}.$$

Therefore, the equation $y = \log_2 x$ is equivalent to $y = \frac{\log x}{\log 2}$.

7. Using the formula $\log_2 x = \frac{\log x}{\log 2}$, use your grapher to graph $y = \log_2 x$. Your graph should resemble the following.

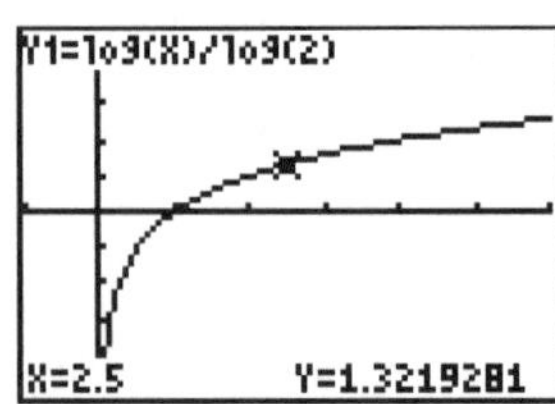

8. a. Write $y = \log_6 x$ in an equivalent way using base 10.

$y = \frac{\log x}{\log 6}$

b. Use the result from part a to graph $y = \log_6 x$.

c. What is the domain of the function?

$x > 0$

d. What is the x-intercept of the graph?

(1, 0)

The formula you developed for graphing log functions of different bases is a special case of the formula

$$\log_b x = \frac{\log_a x}{\log_a b}.$$

This is often called the **change of base formula,** where $b > 0$, $b \neq 1$. This formula is used to change from base b to base a. Because most calculators have log base 10 and log base e keys, you usually convert to one of those bases. Therefore,

$$\log_b x = \frac{\log x}{\log b} \quad \text{or} \quad \log_b x = \frac{\ln x}{\ln b}$$

9. Use each of the change of base formulas to approximate $\log_4 36$.

a. Using base 10:

$\log_4 36 = \frac{\log 36}{\log 4} = 2.585$

b. Using base e:

$\log_4 36 = \frac{\ln 36}{\ln 4} = 2.585$

10. If $f(x) = 17 + 2\log_5 x$, then determine each of the following.

a. $f(5)$

19

b. $f(17.5)$

20.56

EXERCISES

1. Use the properties of logarithms to write the given logarithms as the sum or difference of two or more logarithms or as the product of a real number and a logarithm simplify, if possible. All variables represent positive numbers.

a. $\log_3 3^5$

$5(\log_3 3) = 5 \cdot 1 = 5$

b. $\log_2 2^x$

$x \log_2 2 = x \cdot 1 = x$

Exercise numbers appearing in color are answered in the Selected Answers section of this book.

c. $\log_b \frac{x^3}{y^4}$

$3 \log_b x - 4 \log_b y$

d. $\ln \frac{\sqrt[3]{x}\sqrt[4]{y}}{z^2}$

$\frac{1}{3} \ln x + \frac{1}{4} \ln y - 2 \ln z$

e. $\log_3 (2x + y)$

$\log_3 (2x + y)$

2. Write each of the following as the logarithm of a single expression with coefficient 1.

a. $2 \log_2 7 + \log_2 5$

$\log_2 245$

b. $\frac{1}{4} \log x^3 - \frac{1}{4} \log z^5$

$\log \sqrt[4]{\frac{x^3}{z^5}}$

c. $2 \ln 10 - 3 \ln 5 + 4 \ln z$

$\ln \frac{100z^4}{5^3} = \ln \frac{4z^4}{5}$

d. $\log_5 (x + 2) + \log_5 (x + 1) - 2 \log_5 (x + 3)$

$\log \frac{(x + 2)(x + 1)}{(x + 3)^2}$

3. Given that $\log_a x = 6$ and that $\log_a y = 25$, find each numerical value.

a. $\log_a \sqrt{y}$

12.5

b. $\log_a x^3$

18

c. $3 + \log_a x^2$

15

d. $\log_a \frac{x^2 y}{a}$

$2\log_a x + \log_a y - \log_a a$

$= 12 + 25 - 1 = 36$

4. Use the change of base formula and your calculator to find a decimal approximation of each of the following to the nearest ten thousandth.

a. $\log_7 5$

0.8271

b. $\log_6 \sqrt{15}$

0.7557

c. $\log_{13} 47$

1.5011

d. $\log_5 \sqrt[3]{31}$

0.7112

5. The formula $P(t) = 95 - 30 \log_2 t$ gives the percentage P of students who could recall the important content of a classroom presentation as a function of time t, where t is the number of days that have passed since the presentation was given.

a. Sketch a graph of the function.

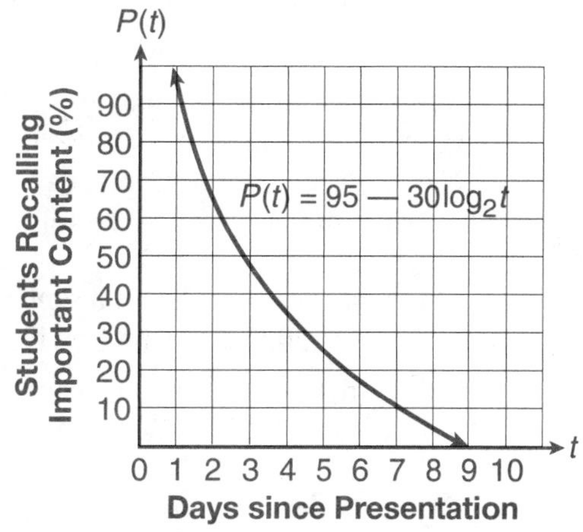

b. After 3 days, what percentage of the students could remember the important content of the presentation?

47.5%.

c. According to the model, after how many days did only half ($P = 50$) of the students remember the important features of the presentation? Use a graphing approach.

2.83 days.

ACTIVITY 3.11

Prison Growth

Topics: *Exponential Growth, Solving Exponential Equations*

You are a criminal justice major at the local community college. The following statistics appeared in one of your required readings relating to the inmate population of U.S. federal prisons.

	YEAR					
	1975	1979	1986	1990	1994	1998
TOTAL SENTENCED POPULATION, P_T (in thousands)	20.1	21.5	31.8	47.8	76.2	95.5
TOTAL SENTENCED DRUG OFFENDERS, P_D (in thousands)	5.5	5.5	12.1	25.0	46.7	56.3

You decide to do an analysis of the prison growth situation for a project in your criminology course. You notice that over the years, the number of drug offenders is becoming a bigger percentage of the total population. Therefore, you are interested in estimating answers to the following two questions.

- In what year can the total sentenced population in federal prisons be expected to exceed 120,000 for the first time?
- If current trends continue, in what year will the total sentenced drug offenders meet or exceed 75% of the total sentenced population?

1. Although the years in the table are not evenly spaced, you notice that the populations seem to grow rather slowly at first and more quickly later. Do you think the data will be better modeled by a linear or exponential function?

   exponential

2. Let t represent the number of years since 1970, and use your graphing calculator to produce scatterplots of the total inmate population P_T.

3. Use your graphing calculator to produce an exponential model of P_T where the input variable is t, the number of years since 1970. In your regression equation, $P_t = ab^t$, round the value for a to two decimal places and the value for b to three decimal places. Write your model here.

   $P_T = 12.00(1.075)^t$.

4. Use your grapher to visually check how well your equations fit your data. Using the window Xmin $= -3$, Xmax $= 40$, Ymin $= 0$, Ymax $= 140$, your screen should resemble the following.

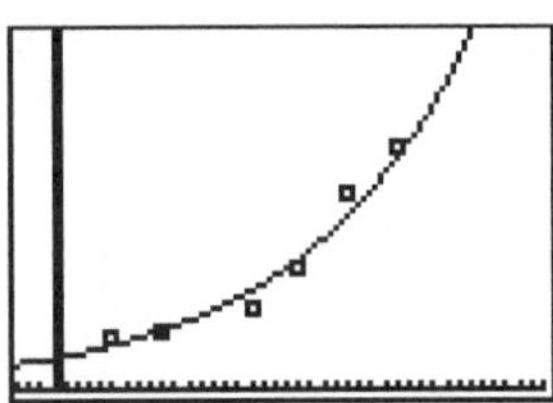

5. a. Using your model from Problem 3, write an equation that states that the total federal inmate population P_T is 120,000. Remember, the population is given in the model in thousands.

$120 = 12.00(1.075)^t$.

b. Solve this equation using a graphing approach. Your screen should resemble the following. What is the equation of the horizontal line in the graph?

$t = 31.83$ years

$P_T = y = 120$

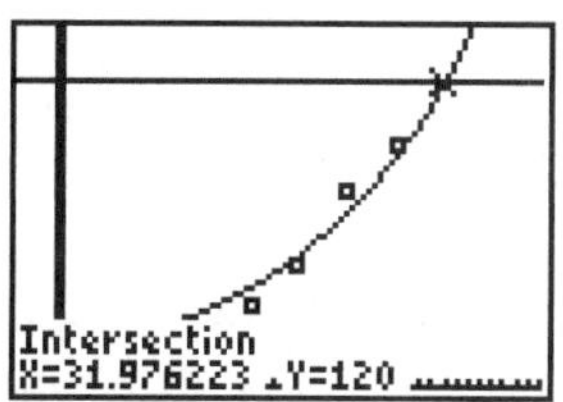

6. a. To solve the equation in Problem 5a for t using an algebraic approach, you must "remove" t as an exponent. This can be accomplished by taking the log (or ln) of each side of the equation, applying the appropriate properties of logarithms, and then solving for t. Solve for t using this approach.

$\log 120 = \log 12 + t \log (1.075)$, $t = \dfrac{\log 120 - \log 12}{\log(1.075)} = 31.83$.

b. How does your solution in part a compare with the solution in Problem 5b?

The solutions are the same.

7. Determine an exponential model for the number of total sentenced drug offenders P_D.

$P_D = 2.44(1.121)^t$

8. a. To determine the year in which you expect the total sentenced drug offenders to first equal 75% of the total sentenced population, what equation do you need to solve?

$2.44(1.121)^t = 0.75(12(1.075)^t)$

b. Solve this equation graphically.

$t = 31.15$ years, or the year is 2001.

Your equation in Problem 8 should have the variable as an exponent on both sides of the equation. To solve this equation, you need to use the properties of logarithms. Consider the equation

$$3 \cdot 2^x = 1.5 \cdot 3^x.$$

To solve this equation, you first take the logarithm of both sides and expand.

$$\log(3 \cdot 2^x) = \log(1.5 \cdot 3^x)$$
$$\log 3 + \log 2^x = \log(1.5) + \log 3^x$$
$$\log 3 + x\log 2 = \log(1.5) + x \log 3$$

Now this is just a linear equation in which your strategy is to isolate the variable.

$$\log 3 - \log 1.5 = x \log 3 - x \log 2$$
$$\log 3 - \log 1.5 = x (\log 3 - \log 2)$$
$$\frac{\log 3 - \log 1.5}{\log 3 - \log 2} = x$$
$$1.7095 = x$$

9. Use this algebraic approach to solve your equation in Problem 8.

$$\log 2.44 + t\log(1.121) = \log 9 + t \log(1.075)$$
$$t[\log(1.121) - \log(1.075)] = \log 9 - \log 2.44$$
$$t = \frac{\log 9 - \log 2.44}{\log(1.121) - \log(1.075)} = 31.15$$

10. As a summary, when do you expect the number of sentenced drug offenders to reach 75% of the total federal prison population, and how many sentenced drug offenders will there be?

The year is 2001 and the total number of sentenced drug offenders will be 85.6 thousand.

EXERCISES

Solve each of the following equations using an algebraic approach (taking the logarithm of both sides of the equation). Verify your answers graphically.

1. $2^x = 14$

$x \log 2 = \log 14$

$x = \frac{\log 14}{\log 2} = 3.81$

2. $3^{2x} = 8$

$2x \log 3 = \log 8$

$x = \frac{\log 8}{2 \log 3} = 0.946$

3. $1000 = 500(1.04)^t$

$\log 1000 = \log 500 + t \log(1.04)$

$t = \frac{\log 1000 - \log 500}{\log(1.04)} = 17.67$

4. $e^{0.05t} = 2$ (*Hint:* Take the natural log of both sides.)

$0.05t = \ln 2$

$t = \frac{\ln 2}{0.05} = 13.86$

5. $2^{3x+1} = 100$

$(3x + 1) \log 2 = \log(100)$

$3x + 1 = \frac{\log(100)}{\log 2}$

$x = 1.88$

6. $e^{-0.3t} = 2$

$-0.3t = \ln 2$

$t = \frac{\ln 2}{-0.3} = -2.31$

Exercise numbers appearing in color are answered in the Selected Answers section of this book.

7. $2 \cdot 3^x = 5^x$

$\log 2 + x \log 3 = x \log 5$

$\log 2 = x [\log 5 - \log 3]$

$$x = \frac{\log 2}{\log 5 - \log 3} = 1.36.$$

Radioactive substances such as uranium 235, strontium 90, iodine 131, and carbon 14 decay continuously with time. If P_0 represents the original amount of a radioactive substance, then the amount P present after a time t (usually measured in years) is modeled by

$$P = P_0 e^{kt},$$

where k represents the continuous decay rate. Use this information to solve Exercises 8 and 9.

8. Strontium 90 decays at a continuous constant rate of 2.44% per year. Therefore, the equation for the amount P of strontium 90 after t years is

$$P = P_0 e^{-0.0244t}.$$

a. If 10 grams of strontium 90 is present initially, determine the number of grams present after 20 years.

$P = 10e^{-0.0244(20)} = 6.1385$ g.

b. How long will it take for the given quantity to decay to 2 grams?

$2 = 10e^{-0.0244t}$ or $\ln\left(\frac{1}{5}\right) = -0.0244t$

$t = 65.96$ years.

c. How long will it take for the given amount of strontium 90 to decay to one-half its original size (called its half-life)? Round to the nearest whole number.

Graphically the solution is $t = 28.4$ years.

d. Do you think that the half-life of strontium 90 is 28 years regardless of the initial amount? Answer part c using P_0 as the initial amount. (*Hint:* Find t when $P = \frac{1}{2}P_0$.)

$\frac{1}{2}P_0 = P_0 e^{-0.0244t}$ or $\ln(.5) = -0.0244t$ or $t = 28.4$ years.

9. a. Iodine 131 disintegrates at a constant rate of 8.6% per day. Determine its half-life. Use the model

$$P = P_0 e^{-0.086t},$$

where t is measured in days. Round your answer to the nearest whole number.

$\ln(0.5) = -0.086t$

$t = 8$ days.

b. If dairy cows eat hay containing too much iodine 131, their milk will be unsafe to drink. Suppose that hay contains 5 times the safe level of iodine 131. How many days should the hay be stored before it can be fed to dairy cows? (*Hint:* Find t when $P = \frac{1}{5}P_0$.)

$\frac{1}{5}P_0 = P_0e^{-0.086t}$ or $t = \frac{\ln(0.2)}{-0.086} = 19$ days.

10. a. In a report by the U.S. National Academy of Sciences, it was estimated that a world population of 10 billion would be a maximum that Earth could reasonably support. The report was released in 1969. At that time, the world population was approximately 3.6 billion, with a continuous growth rate of 2% per year. If you assume that this growth rate remains constant, in what year will the world population reach 10 billion, referred to as Earth's carrying capacity? Use the model

$$P = P_0e^{kt},$$

where P is the population (in billions), $P_0 = 3.6$, $k = 0.02$, and t is the number of years since 1969.

$10 = 3.6e^{0.02t}$

$$t = \frac{\ln\left(\frac{10}{3.6}\right)}{0.02} = 51 \text{ years}$$

$1969 + 51 =$ the year 2020

b. According to your growth model, when would this 1969 population double?

$e^{0.02t} = 2$ or $t = \frac{\ln 2}{0.02} = 34.7$;

Sometime in the year 2003.

c. The world population in 1995 was approximately 5.7 billion. How does this compare with the population predicted by your growth model in part a?

$1995 - 1969 = 26$ years

$P(26) = 3.6e^{0.02(26)} = 6.06$ billion

The actual population was approximately 360 million below the prediction.

d. The growth rate in 1995 was 1.5%. Assuming that this growth rate remains constant, determine when Earth's carrying capacity will be reached. Use the model $P = P_0e^{kt}$.

$10 = 5.7e^{0.015t}$

$t = \frac{\ln(10/5.7)}{0.015} = 37.5$ The year would be 2032.

ACTIVITY 3.12

Frequency and Pitch
Topic: *Solving Logarithmic Equations*

Raising a musical note one octave has the effect of doubling the pitch, or frequency, of the sound. However, you do not perceive the note to sound "twice as high," as you might predict. Perceived pitch is given by the function

$$P = 2410 \log (0.0016f + 1),$$

where P is the perceived pitch in mels, and f is the frequency in hertz.

Let frequency (input) vary in value from 10 to 100,000 hertz, and let perceived pitch (output) vary from 0 to 6000 mels. Graph this equation on your grapher, using the following window: Xmin = 0, Xmax = 100,000, Ymin = 0, Ymax = 6000.

1. What is the perceived pitch P for the input value 10,000 hertz?
   $P(10{,}000) = 2410 \log (0.0016(10{,}000) + 1) = 2965.38$ mels.

2. **a.** What frequency f gives an output value of 1000 mels?
   $1000 = 2410 \log (0.0016f + 1)$
   $f = 999.87$ Hz

   b. Describe the method you used to determine your answer in part a.
   I graphed $P(f)$ and $P = 1000$, then I found their point of intersection.

To determine the exact answer in Problem 2, you can use an algebraic approach, which involves solving the corresponding logarithmic equation. You can convert the equation from logarithmic form to exponential form and solve the resulting system.

3. **a.** Write the equation that you need to solve to determine the frequency that gives a perceived pitch of 1000 mels.
   $1000 = 2410 \log (0.0016f + 1)$.

   b. Solve the equation in part a for $\log (0.0016f + 1)$. That is, isolate the log on one side of the equation. You should have an equation of the form $\log_b N = E$.
   $\log (0.0016f + 1) = \frac{1000}{2410}$.

   c. Write the equation from part b in exponential form, $b^E = N$.
   $10^{\frac{1000}{2410}} = 0.0016f + 1$.

4. **a.** In exponential form, the equation in Problem 3c should be

$$10^{1000/2410} = 0.0016f + 1.$$

Note: This is a linear equation that you need to solve for the variable f.

Of course, you will need to approximate a value of $10^{1000/2410}$ using your calculator. Solve the equation.

$0.0016f + 1 = 2.599787$ or $f = \frac{1.599787}{0.0016} = 999.87$ Hz

b. How does your answer to part a compare with your answer to Problem 2a?

It agrees.

5. a. Use an algebraic approach to determine the frequency f that produces a perceived pitch of 3000 mels.

$3000 = 2410 \log(0.0016f + 1)$

$(10^{\frac{3000}{2410}} - 1)/0.0016 = f = 10{,}357.30$ Hz

b. Verify your answer in part a using a graphing approach.

6. The formula $W = 0.35 \ln P + 2.74$ is a model for the average walking speed W in feet per second for a resident of a city with population P, measured in thousands.

a. Determine the walking speed of a resident of a small city having a population of 500,000.

$W = 0.35 \ln(500) + 2.74 = 4.92$ ft/sec

b. If the average walking speed of a resident is 4.5 feet per second, what is the population of the city? Round your answer to the nearest thousand.

$4.5 = 0.35 \ln P + 2.74$

$e^{\left(\frac{4.5-2.74}{0.35}\right)} = P = 153{,}000$

EXERCISES

In Exercises 1–7, solve each equation using an algebraic approach. Then verify your answer using a graphical approach.

1. $\log_2 x = 5$

$x = 2^5 = 32$

2. $\ln x = 10$

$x = e^{10} = 22{,}026$

3. $3 \log_5 (x + 2) = 5$

$x + 2 = 5^{5/3}$

$x = 5^{5/3} - 2 = 12.62$

4. $\log_5 (x - 4) = 2$

$x - 4 = 5^2$

$x = 29$

Exercise numbers appearing in color are answered in the Selected Answers section of this book.

5. $\log_3 7 + \log_3 (x + 2) = 4$

$\log_3 7(x + 2) = 4$

$7(x + 2) = 3^4$

$x = 81/7 - 2 = 9.57$

6. $\log_2 x + \log_2 (6 - x) = 3$

$\log_2 x(6 - x) = 3$

$x(6 - x) = 8$

$6x - x^2 = 8$

$0 = x^2 - 6x + 8,$

$0 = (x - 4)(x - 2)$

$x = 4$ or $x = 2$

7. $\ln (x + 4) - \ln x = 1$ (Let $e \approx 2.718$.)

$\ln\left(\frac{x + 4}{x}\right) = 1$

$\frac{x + 4}{x} = 2.718$

$x + 4 = 2.718x$

$4 = 1.718x$

$x = 2.328$

8. Stars have been classified into magnitude according to their brightness. Stars in the first six magnitudes are visible to the naked eye, but those of higher magnitudes require telescopes to be seen. The magnitude m of the faintest star that is visible with a telescope having lens diameter d, in inches, is modeled by

$$m = 8.8 + 5.1 \log d.$$

What is the highest magnitude of a star that is visible with the 200-inch diameter telescope at Mount Palomar, in California?

$m = 8.8 + 5.1 \log (200) = 20.5$

9. The acidity or alkalinity of any solution is determined by the concentration of hydrogen ions $[H^+]$, in the substance, measured in moles per liter. Acidity (or alkalinity) is measured on a pH scale, using the model

$$\text{pH} = -\log [H^+].$$

The pH scale ranges from 0 to 14. Values below 7 have progressively greater acidity, while values greater than 7 are progressively more alkaline. Normal unpolluted rain has a pH of about 5.6. The acidity of rain over the northeastern United States, caused primarily by sulfur dioxide emissions, has had very damaging effects. One of the most acidic rainfalls on record had a pH of 2.4. What was the concentration of hydrogen ions?

$2.4 = -\log [H^+]$

$[H^+] = 10^{-2.4} = 0.00398$ moles/liter

10. The Richter scale is a well-known method of measuring the magnitude of an earthquake in terms of the amplitude A (height) of its shock waves. The magnitude of any given earthquake is given by

$$m = \log\left(\frac{A}{A_0}\right),$$

where A_0 is a constant representing the amplitude of an average earthquake.

a. The magnitude of the 1906 San Francisco earthquake was 8.3 on the Richter scale. Write an equation that gives the amplitude A of the San Francisco earthquake in terms of A_0.

$8.3 = \log\left(\frac{A}{A_0}\right)$.

$10^{8.3} = \frac{A}{A_0}$, $A = A_0 \cdot 10^{8.3}$

b. An earthquake of magnitude 5.5 begins to cause serious damage. Write an equation that gives the amplitude A of a serious-damage earthquake in terms of A_0.

$A = A_0 10^{5.5}$

c. Determine the ratio of the amplitude for the San Francisco earthquake to the amplitude for a serious-damage (magnitude 5.5) earthquake. What is the significance of this number?

$$\frac{A_0 10^{8.3}}{A_0 10^{5.5}} = 10^{2.8} = 631$$

The amplitude of the San Francisco earthquake was 631 times greater than that of the smallest earthquake that causes serious damage.

What Have I Learned?

1. A logarithm is an exponent. Explain how this fact relates to the following basic properties of logarithms. (*Hint:* Write the properties of exponents with base b and exponents m and n.)

a. $\log_b (x \cdot y) = \log_b x + \log_b y$

$b^m \cdot b^n = b^{m+n}$

Multiplication of powers with the same base is accomplished by adding the exponents.

b. $\log_b \frac{x}{y} = \log_b x - \log_b y$

$\frac{bm}{bn} = b^{m-n}$

Division of powers of the same base is accomplished by subtracting the exponents.

c. $\log_b x^n = n \cdot \log_b x$

$(b^n)^m = b^{n \cdot m}$

Exponentiation of a power is accomplished by multiplying the exponents.

2. You have $20,000 to invest. Your broker tells you that mutual fund A has been growing exponentially for the past two years and that mutual fund B has been growing logarithmically over the same period. In which fund do you choose to invest your money? Explain.

I will choose fund A, because exponential growth results in more rapid growth over time. Logarithmic growth results in slower growth over time.

3. Study the following graphs showing various types of functions you have encountered in this course.

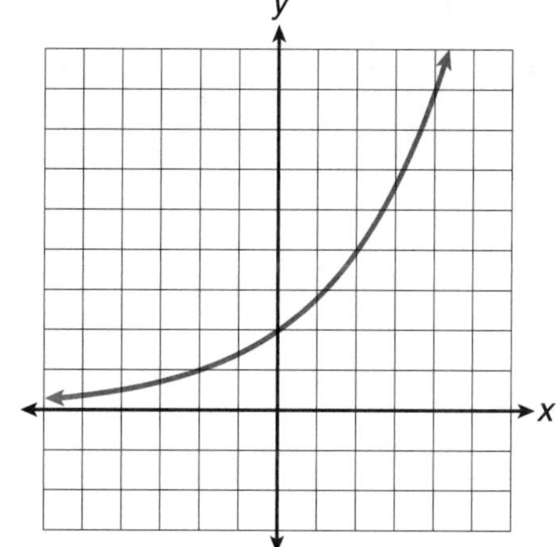

b.

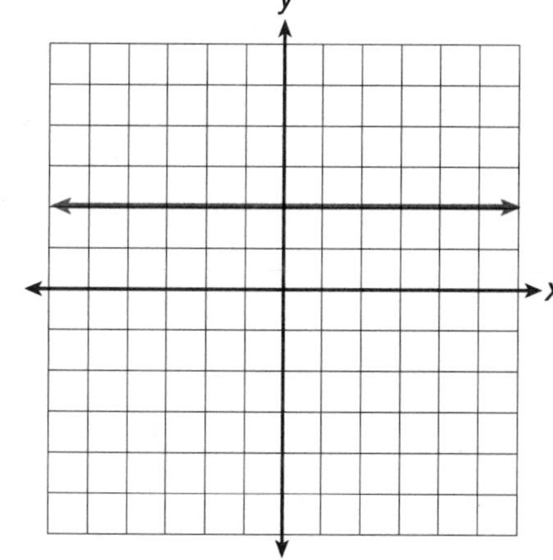

c.

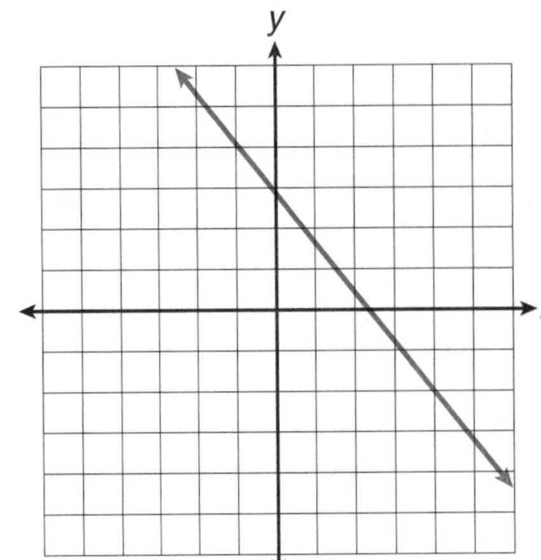

d.

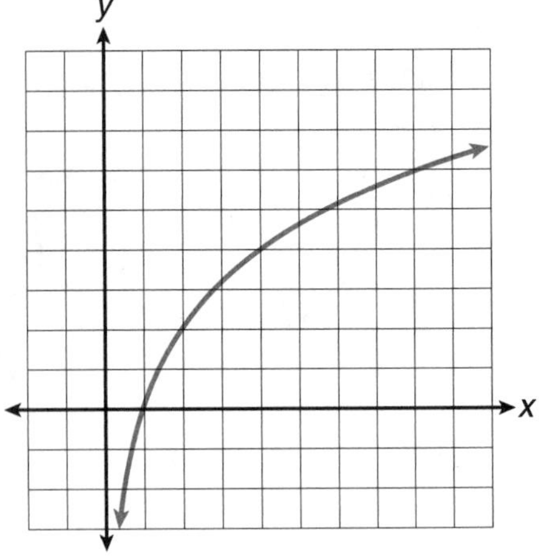

e.

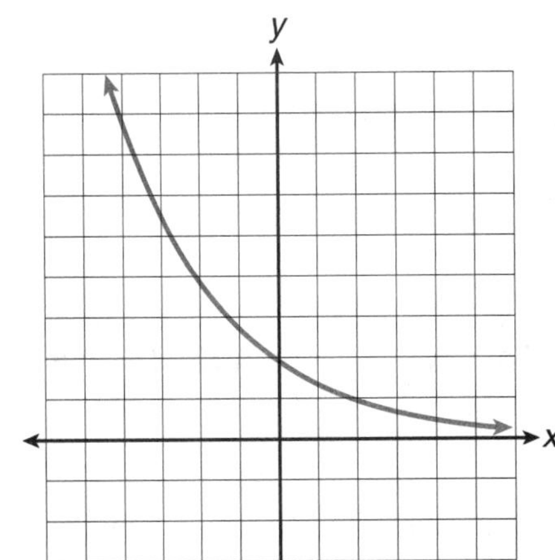

f.

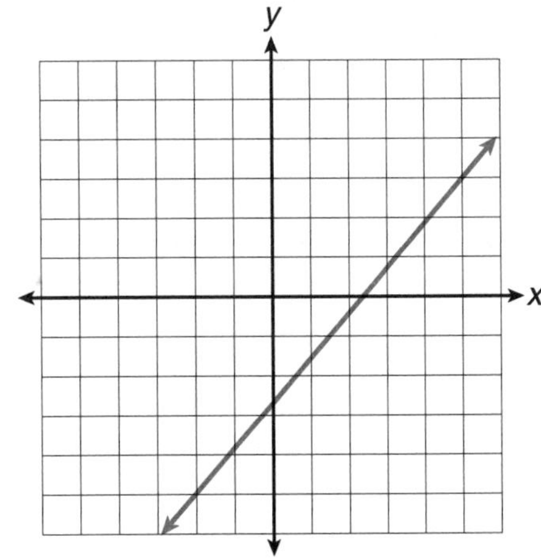

Complete the following table with respect to the previous graphs.

DESCRIPTION	GRAPH LETTER	GENERAL EQUATION
Constant Function	b	$y = a$
Linearly Decreasing Function	c	$y = mx + b; m < 0$
Logarithmically Increasing Function	d	$y = \log_b x; b > 1$
Exponentially Decreasing Function	e	$y = b^x; 0 < b < 1$
Exponentially Increasing Function	a	$y = b^x; b > 1$
Linearly Increasing Function	f	$y = mx + b; m > 0$

How Can I Practice?

1. Write each of the following as a sum, difference, or multiple of logarithms. Assume that x, y, and z are all greater than zero.

a. $\log_b \frac{xy^2}{z}$

$\log_b x + 2 \log_b y - \log_b z$

b. $\log_3 \frac{\sqrt{x^3 y}}{z}$

$\frac{3}{2}\log_3 x + \frac{1}{2}\log_3 y - \log_3 z$

c. $\log_5(x \cdot \sqrt{x^2 + 4})$

$\log_5 x + \frac{1}{2}\log_5 (x^2 + 4)$

d. $\log_4 \sqrt[3]{\frac{xy^2}{z^2}}$

$\frac{1}{3}\log_4 x + \frac{2}{3}\log_4 y - \frac{2}{3}\log_4 z$

2. Rewrite the following as the logarithm of a single quantity.

a. $\log x + \frac{1}{3}\log y - \frac{1}{2}\log z$

$\log \frac{x\sqrt[3]{y}}{\sqrt{z}}$

b. $3 \log_3 (x + 3) + 2 \log_3 z$

$\log_3 [(x + 3)^3 z^2]$

c. $\frac{1}{3}\log_3 x - \frac{2}{3}\log_3 y - \frac{4}{3}\log_3 z$

$\log_3 \sqrt[3]{\frac{x}{y^2 z^4}}$

3. Use the change of base formula and your calculator to approximate the following.

a. $\log_5 17$

$\frac{\log 17}{\log 5} = 1.76$

b. $\log_{13} \sqrt[3]{41}$

$\frac{1}{3} \cdot \frac{\log 41}{\log 13} = 0.4826$

4. Solve by converting the given equation to the exponential form and solving the resulting equation.

a. $1.5 \cdot \log_4 (x - 1) = 7$

$x - 1 = 4^{\frac{7}{1.5}}, x = 646.08$

b. $\log_7 6 + \log_7 (x - 1) = 13$

$6(x - 1) = 7^{13},$

$x = \frac{7^{13}}{6} + 1 = 1.6148 \times 10^{10}$

Exercise numbers appearing in color are answered in the Selected Answers section of this book.

5. Solve the following algebraically. Check your solution using graphs or tables.

a. $3^x = 17$

$x = \frac{\log 17}{\log 3} = 2.5789$

b. $2 \cdot 3^x = 4^x$

$\log 2 + x \log 3 = x \log 4$ or

$$x = \frac{\log 2}{\log 4 - \log 3} = 2.409$$

c. $1.5 \cdot 3^{2x+1} = 2 \cdot 1.5^{x-1}$

$$\log(1.5) + (2x + 1)\log 3 = \log 2 + (x - 1)\log(1.5)$$
$$\log(1.5) + 2x \log 3 + \log 3 = \log 2 + x \log(1.5) - \log(1.5)$$
$$x[2\log 3 - \log(1.5)] = \log 2 - 2\log(1.5) - \log 3$$
$$x = -0.6789$$

6. The following table shows per capita health care expenditures (in dollars) in the United States from 1988 to 1993.

YEAR	1988	1989	1990	1991	1992	1993
EXPENDITURES	2201	2422	2688	2902	3144	3331

a. Plot these data points on the following grid.

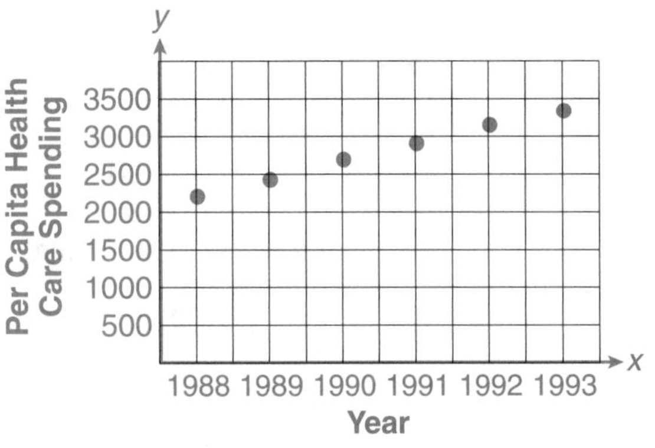

b. The logarithmic model that fits these data is $E = f(x) = 2090 + 630 \ln x$, where E represents the per capita health care expenditures and x is the number of years since 1987. Add a sketch of this model to the grid in part a.

c. Use this model to predict the per capita health care expenditures in the year 2005.

$E = f(18) = 2090 + 630 \ln(18) = 3910.93$

Gateway Review

1. **a.** Determine the output values for the function $f(x) = 8^x$ by completing the table.

x	-1	$-\frac{1}{3}$	0	1	$\frac{4}{3}$	2	3
$f(x) = 8^x$	$\frac{1}{8}$	$\frac{1}{2}$	1	8	16	64	512

b. Sketch the graph of the function.

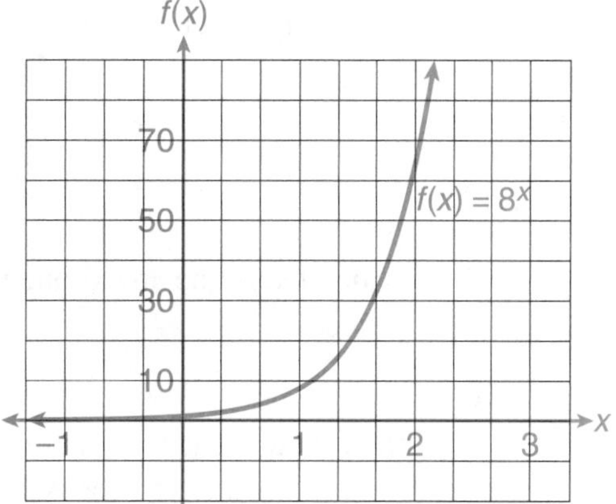

c. Is this an increasing or decreasing function? Explain how you know this by looking at the defining equation of the function.

Increasing, since $b = 8 > 1$.

d. What is the domain?

The domain is all real numbers.

e. What is the range?

The range is $y > 0$.

f. What are the x- and y-intercepts?

There is no x-intercept. The y-intercept is $(0, 1)$.

g. Are there any asymptotes? If yes, write the equations of the asymptotes.

There is one horizontal asymptote, the x-axis, $y = 0$.

h. Compare the graph $f(x)$ to the graph $g(x) = \left(\frac{1}{8}\right)^x$. What are the similarities and differences?

The domain and range are the same. The graphs are reflections in the y-axis. f is increasing, g is decreasing.

i. In what way does the graph $h(x) = 8^x + 5$ differ from $f(x) = 8^x$?

h is moved upward 5 units.

j. Write the equation of the function that is the inverse of the function $f(x)$.

$x = 8^y$ or $y = \log_8 x$.

2. **a.** Given the following table, determine whether it can be approximately modeled by an exponential function. If it can, what is the growth or decay factor between the output values?

The table is approximately exponential. The growth factor is about 1.55.

x	0	1	2	3	4
y	10	15.5	24	36	55.5

b. Determine an exponential equation that models these data.

$y = 10(1.55)^x$

3. **a.** Your salary has increased at the rate of 1.5% annually for the past 5 years and your boss projects this will remain unchanged for the next five years. You were making $10,000 annually in 1999. Create a table showing your yearly salary each year from 1999 to 2004.

Year	1999	2000	2001	2002	2003	2004
Salary	10,000	10,150	10,302	10,457	10,614	10,773

b. Write the exponential growth function that models your annual salary during this period of time. Let x represent the number of years since 1999.

$y = 10{,}000(1.015)^x$

c. If your increase in salary continues at this rate, how much will you make in the year 2005? Is this realistic?

$y = 10{,}000(1.015)^6 = 10{,}934.43$

This is reasonable if we assume that 10,000 is a reasonable starting salary.

d. You would like to double your salary. How many years will you have to wait before your salary will be double the salary you made in 1999?

$$20{,}000 = 10{,}000(1.015)^t$$

$$2 = (1.015)^t$$

$$t = \log_{1.015} 2 = \frac{\log 2}{\log (1.015)} = 46.6 \text{ years}$$

4. **a.** Your uncle just passed away and left you \$5000. In your bank, the money will compound continuously at 6.5%. In 8 years, your oldest child will be going to college. How much money will be in the bank for her education?

$A = 5000e^{0.065(8)} = 8410.14$

b. You actually need to have \$12,000 for the first year of college. How many years would you have to leave the money in the bank to have the \$12,000?

$12{,}000 = 5000e^{0.065t}$

$0.065t = \ln(12/5)$

$t = 13.5$ years.

5. Evaluate exactly without using your calculator.

a. $25^{3/2}$

125

b. $81^{3/4}$

27

c. $64^{-5/6}$

$\frac{1}{32}$

d. $\sqrt[3]{125^2}$

25

e. $\log_3 \frac{1}{9}$

-2

f. $\log_5 625$

4

g. $\log 0.001$

-3

6. Use the change of base formula and your calculator to approximate the following.

a. $\log_7 21$

$\frac{\log 21}{\log 7} = 1.56$

b. $\log_{15} \frac{8}{9}$

$\frac{\log (8/9)}{\log 15} = -4.35 \times 10^{-2}$

7. Write each of the following as a sum, difference, or multiple of logarithms. Assume that x, y, and z are all greater than zero.

a. $\log_2 \frac{x^3 y}{z^{1/2}}$

$3 \log_2 x + \log_2 y - 0.5\log_2 z$

b. $\log \sqrt{\frac{x^4 y^3}{z}}$

$2 \log x + \frac{3}{2} \log y - \frac{1}{2} \log z$

8. Rewrite the following as the logarithm of a single quantity.

a. $\log x + \frac{1}{4}\log y - 3\log z$

$\log \frac{x\sqrt[4]{y}}{z^3}$

b. $\frac{1}{3}(\log x - 2\log y - 5\log z)$

$\log \sqrt[3]{\frac{x}{y^2 z^5}}$

9. Solve the following algebraically.

a. $3^{3+x} = 7$

$3 + x = \frac{\log 7}{\log 3}$; $x = -1.23$

b. $3 \cdot 5^x = 4^{x+2}$

$\log 3 + x \log 5 = (x + 2) \log 4$

$\log 3 - 2\log 4 = x(\log 4 - \log 5)$; $x = 7.50$

c. $6^{x+2} = 3^{x-5}$

$(x + 2)\log 6 = (x - 5)\log 3$

$x \log 6 - x \log 3 = -5\log 3 - 2\log 6$

$x = -13.09$

d. $\log_2(4x + 9) = 4$

$4x + 9 = 2^4$; $x = 1.75$

e. $\log_4 x + \log_4(x - 6) = 2$

$\log_4 x(x - 6) = 2$; $x^2 - 6x - 16 = 0$, $x = 8$,

or $x = -2$, -2 is extraneous.

10. **a.** Given the following table, sketch the graph using the data from the table.

x	0.1	0.5	1	2	4	16
$f(x)$	−1.66	−0.5	0	0.5	1	2

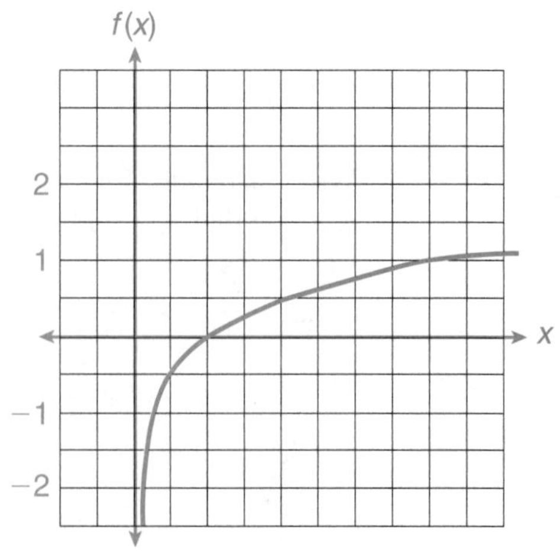

b. Using the information from the table and the graph, determine the function that is modeled by this data.

$f(x) = \log_2 \sqrt{x}$ or $f(x) = \frac{1}{2}\log_2 x$.

c. Using the function, determine the value of $f(54)$.

2.87744.

d. If $f(x) = 2.319$, determine the value of x.

$2.319 = \frac{\log x}{2 \log 2}$ $x = 24.9$ (by graphing).

e. Write the function $g(x)$, which is the inverse of the function $f(x)$.

$g(x) = 2^{2x}$, $(2^2)^x = 4^x$

11. The populations of New York State and Florida (in millions) can be modeled by the following:

$$\text{New York State:} \quad P_N = 18.2e^{0.001t}$$

$$\text{Florida:} \quad P_F = 14e^{0.0168t},$$

where t represents the number of years since 1994.

a. Determine the populations of New York and Florida in 1994 ($t = 0$).

New York 18.2 million; Florida 14 million.

b. Sketch a graph of each population function on the same coordinate axes.

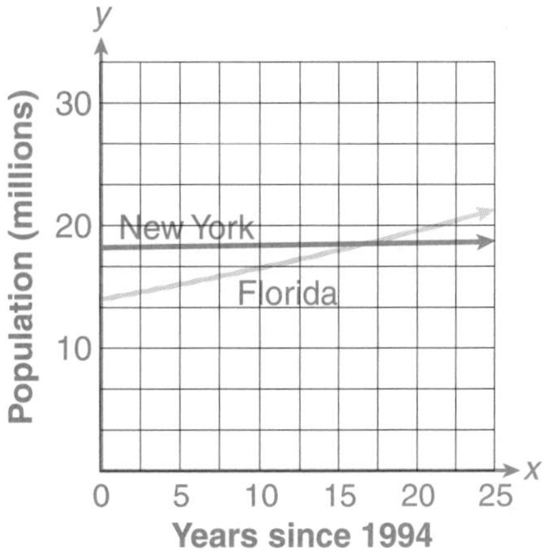

c. Determine algebraically the year when the population of Florida will equal the population of New York State. Verify this graphically.

$$18.2e^{0.001t} = 14e^{0.0168t}$$

$$\ln(18.2) + 0.001t = \ln 14 + 0.0168t$$

$$\ln(18.2) - \ln(14) = 0.0158t$$

$$t = 17$$

Florida's population will equal that of New York in the year 2011.

d. Determine algebraically the year when the population of Florida will exceed 25 million.

$$25 = 14e^{0.0168t}$$

$$\ln\left(\tfrac{25}{14}\right) = 0.0168t$$

$$t = 35$$

Florida's population will exceed 25 million in the year 2029.

e. Will the population of Florida ever exceed the population of New York? Explain. Assume that population growth given by both population models will continue.

This question is equivalent to when will the population of Florida exceed the population of New York.

$$14e^{0.0168t} > 18.2e^{0.001t}$$

$$\frac{e^{0.0168t}}{e^{0.001t}} > \frac{18.2}{14}$$

$$e^{0.0158t} > \tfrac{18.2}{14}$$

$$0.0158t > \ln\left(\tfrac{18.2}{14}\right)$$

$$t > 16.6$$

At current rates, the population of Florida exceeds the population of New York sometime in the year 2010.

CHAPTER 3 GATEWAY REVIEW

CHAPTER 4

Quadratic and Higher-Order Polynomial Functions

CLUSTER 1

Introduction to Quadratic Functions

ACTIVITY 4.1

Baseball throughout the Solar System

Topic: *Introduction to Quadratic Functions and Their Graphs*

Imagine yourself standing on top of a 100-foot-high tower on Earth, Mars, or Jupiter. When you release and drop a baseball from the tower, the ball's height H above the ground (in feet) can be described as a function of the time t (in seconds) since it was dropped.

$$H_{\text{Earth}}(t) = -16t^2 + 100 \quad H_{\text{Mars}}(t) = -6t^2 + 100 \quad H_{\text{Jupiter}}(t) = -40t^2 + 100$$

Complete the following table.

TIME (SEC)	$H_{Earth}(t) = -16^2 + 100$	$H_{Mars}(t) = -6^2 + 100$	$H_{Jupiter}(t) = -40^2 + 100$
0	100	100	100
0.5	96	98.5	90
1.0	84	94	60
1.5	64	86.5	10
2.0	36	76	−60
2.5	0	62.5	−150

1. How far does the baseball fall during the first second on Earth? On Mars? On Jupiter?

a. 16 ft b. 6 ft c. 40 ft

2. How far does it fall during the second second on Earth? On Mars? On Jupiter?

a. 48 ft b. 18 ft c. 60 ft Height cannot be < 0.

3. Using the Earth height function $H_{\text{Earth}}(t) = -16t^2 + 100$, determine the rate of change of H with respect to t over the given interval.

a. $0 \le t \le 1$

$\frac{H(1) - H(0)}{1 - 0} =$

$\frac{84 - 100}{1 - 0} = -16$

b. $1 \le t \le 2$

$\frac{H(2) - H(1)}{2 - 1} =$

$\frac{36 - 84}{2 - 1} = -48$

$$\text{Rate of change} = \frac{\text{change in output}}{\text{change in input}}$$

c. Is the graph of $H_{\text{Earth}}(t) = -16t^2 + 100$ a straight line? Explain.

No, the rates of change in the first and second second are not the same. A straight line must have a constant rate of change.

4. a. On which planet does the ball fall most quickly? Most slowly?

a. Jupiter b. Mars

b. How did you decide?

The decision is made by looking at the table to determine on which planet the ball reached 0 most quickly and most slowly.

5. What is the practical domain for each of the height functions?

Earth $[0 \le t \le 2.5]$ Mars $[0 \le t \le 4.08]$ Jupiter $[0 \le t \le 1.58]$

6. Graph these three functions together, using the window settings Xmin = −5 and Xmax = 5 for the input and Ymin = −20 and Ymax = 120 for the output.

The graph of each of the functions in this activity is called a **parabola.**

a. In your own words, describe the important features of the graph of $H_{\text{Earth}}(t) = -16t^2 + 100$.

The graph is shaped like a ∪, but a downward ∩. It is symmetric with respect to the y-axis. The y-intercept is (0, 100). The x-intercepts are (−2.5, 0) and (2.5, 0).

b. What similarities do you observe among the three graphs?

They are all ∩-shaped, and symmetric with respect to the y-axis. They all have (0, 100) as their y-intercept.

c. What differences do you note among the three graphs?

One difference is how wide or narrow the ∩ is. The x-intercepts are different for each graph.

d. Is the graph of the Earth height function the actual path of the object when the ball is dropped? Explain.

No. The graph is a "picture" of the height function with respect to time, not a graph of the path of the object.

7. a. What are the vertical intercepts of each graph?

All graphs have (0, 100) as a vertical intercept.

b. What is the practical meaning of the vertical intercept in this situation?

It is the ball's height above the ground before it is dropped.

c. Predict what the graph of $h(t) = -16t^2 + 100$ would look like if the constant term 100 was changed to 80. Verify your prediction by graphing $h(t) = -16t^2 + 80$ in the window setting of Problem 6.

The vertical intercept would be at (0, 80). The graph would still be ∩-shaped.

d. What does the constant term tell you about the graph of the parabola?

It tells you the height of the graph when the *x*-coordinate is zero. It tells you the vertical intercept.

8. a. Predict what the graph of $h(t) = -16t^2 + 100$ would look like if the coefficient of t^2 was changed to $+16$, as follows:

$$h(t) = 16t^2 + 100.$$

The graph would be shaped like a U, upward. The vertical intercept would still be at (0, 100).

b. Graph this function using the window settings in Problem 6 to check your prediction.

My prediction checks.

c. What effect does the sign of the coefficient of t^2 seem to have on the graph of the parabola?

The sign determines if the graph will be U-shaped or ∩-shaped. If the sign is negative the graph will be ∩-shaped. If the sign is positive the graph will be U-shaped.

The graph of a parabola is a U-shaped figure that opens upward U or downward ∩. If the sign is negative, the graph will be ∩-shaped. If the sign is positive, the graph will be U-shaped.

9. What effect does the magnitude of the coefficient of t^2 (namely, $|-16| = 16$, $|-6| = 6$, and $|-40| = 40$) have on the graph of that particular parabola?

It affects the width of the parabola. The greater the magnitude of the coefficient, the narrower the parabola.

10. Predict what the graph of each of the following functions will look like.

a. $f(t) = -16t^2 + 80$

∩-shaped; vertical intercept (0, 80) symmetric with respect to the y-axis

b. $g(t) = -60t^2 + 10$

∩-shaped; vertical intercept (0, 10) symmetric with respect to the y-axis

c. $k(t) = 2t^2 + 30$

∪-shaped; vertical intercept (0, 30) symmetric with respect to the y-axis

You will remain on Earth for the remainder of this activity. Instead of merely releasing the ball, suppose you *throw it down* with an initial velocity of 40 feet per second. Then the function describing its height above ground as a function of time is modeled by

$$H_{\text{down}}(t) = -16t^2 - 40t + 100.$$

If you tossed the ball *up* with an initial velocity of 40 feet per second, then the function describing its height above ground as a function of time is modeled by

$$H_{\text{up}}(t) = -16t^2 + 40t + 100.$$

11. a. Predict what features the graphs of H_{down} and H_{up} have in common with H_{Earth}.

All three graphs will open downward. The vertical intercept will be (0, 100) for all three graphs.

b. Graph the three Earth functions—$H_{\text{Earth}}(t)$, $H_{\text{down}}(t)$, and $H_{\text{up}}(t)$—using the same window settings you used in Problem 6.

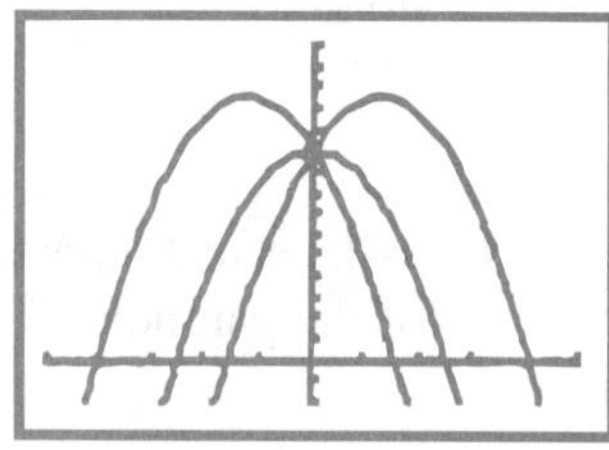

c. What effect do the $-40t$ and $40t$ terms seem to have on the graphs?

The graph shifts to the left for $-(40t)$ and shifts to the right for $(40t)$. The maximum height increases.

Any function defined by an equation of the form $y = ax^2 + bx + c$, where a, b, and c represent real numbers and $a \neq 0$, is called a **quadratic function.** In the example $h(t) = -16t^2 + 40t + 100$, $a = -16$, $b = 40$, and $c = 100$. Note that the output variable, $h(t)$, is defined by an expression having three terms: the **quadratic term,** $-16t^2$; the **linear term,** $40t$; and the **constant term,** 100. The numerical factor in each term, called the **coefficient** of the term, has an effect on the function and its graph. The effects of a, b, and c on the graph of the parabola will be discussed further in the next activity.

12. In each of the following quadratic functions, identify the value of a, b, and c.

QUADRATIC FUNCTION	a	b	c
$y = 3x^2$	3	0	0
$y = -2x^2 + 3$	−2	0	3
$y = x^2 + 2x - 1$	1	2	−1
$y = -x^2 + 4x$	−1	4	0

SUMMARY

The function that has a parabola as its graph is called a quadratic function. The equation of a quadratic function with x as the input variable and y as the output variable has the standard form

$$y = ax^2 + bx + c,$$

where a, b, and c represent real numbers and $a \neq 0$.

EXERCISES

1. a. Complete the following input/output table for $y = x^2$.

INPUT	2	1	0	−1	−3	−4
OUTPUT	4	1	0	1	9	16

b. Based on the data given in the table in part a, is the function linear? Explain.

No, the rate of change between any two points is not constant.

c. Is the function exponential? Explain.

No, there is not a constant growth or decay factor.

d. Sketch a graph of $y = x^2$. Verify using your grapher.

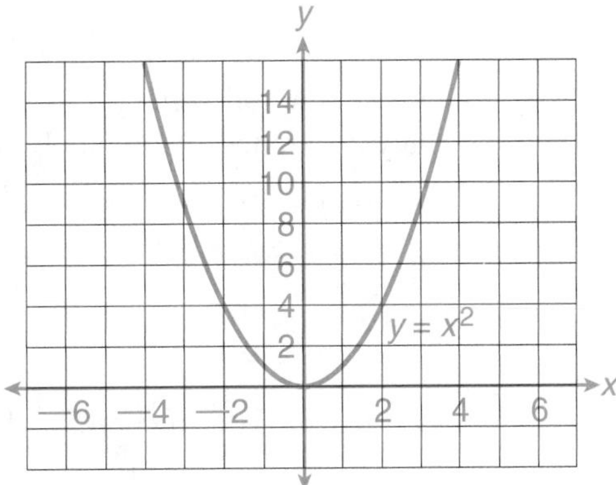

e. What is the coefficient of the term x^2?

The coefficient is 1.

2. a. Create a table similar to the one in Exercise 1a to show the output for $y = -x^2$.

INPUT	2	1	0	−1	−3	−4
OUTPUT	−4	−1	0	−1	−9	−16

b. Sketch the graph of $y = -x^2$. Verify using your grapher.

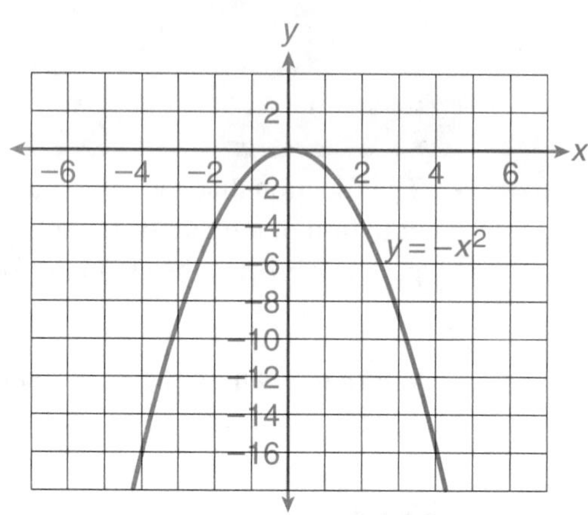

c. What is the coefficient of the term $-x^2$?

The coefficient is −1.

3. Predict what the graph of each of the following quadratic functions will look like. Use your grapher to verify your prediction.

a. $f(x) = 3x^2 + 5$

U-shaped; vertical intercept (0, 5) symmetric with respect to the y-axis.

b. $g(x) = -2x^2 + 1$

∩-shaped; vertical intercept (0, 1) symmetric with respect to the y-axis.

c. $h(x) = 0.5x^2 - 3$

U-shaped; vertical intercept (0, −3) symmetric with respect to the y-axis.

4. Graph the following pairs of functions and describe any similarities as well as any differences that you observe in the graphs.

a. $f(x) = 3x^2,\ g(x) = -3x^2$

f opens upward; *g* opens downward. Both pass through (0, 0).

b. $h(x) = \frac{1}{2}x^2,\ F(x) = 2x^2$

Both *F* and *h* open upward.

h is wider than *F*

c. $g(x) = 5x^2,\ h(x) = 5x^2 + 2$

h is *g* shifted up two units

Both open upward.

d. $F(x) = 4x^2 - 3,\ g(x) = 4x^2 + 3$

Both *F* and *g* open upward.

The low point of *F* is 3 units below the *x*-axis, the low point of *g* is 3 units above the *x*-axis.

e. $f(x) = 6x^2 + 1, \quad h(x) = -6x^2 - 1$

f opens upward with a vertical intercept at (0, 1)

h opens downward with a vertical intercept at (0, −1)

Both are symmetric with respect to the *y*-axis.

5. In each of the following functions, identify the value of *a*, *b*, and *c* in the standard form of the quadratic function, $y = ax^2 + bx + c$.

a. $y = -2x^2$ $a =$ −2 $b =$ 0 $c =$ 0

b. $y = \frac{2}{5}x^2 + 3$ $a =$ $\frac{2}{5}$ $b =$ 0 $c =$ 3

c. $y = -x^2 + 5x$ $a =$ −1 $b =$ 5 $c =$ 0

d. $y = 5x^2 + 2x - 1$ $a =$ 5 $b =$ 2 $c =$ −1

6. Use your grapher to graph the following two functions.

$$y_1 = 3x^2 - 2 \quad \text{and} \quad y_2 = 3x^2 + 2x - 2$$

a. What is the vertical intercept for the graph of each function?

y_1: (0, −2) y_2: (0, −2)

b. Compare the two graphs to determine the effect of the $2x$ term.

The $2x$ makes the graph shift to the left and down.

ACTIVITY 4.2

Galileo and the Quadratic Function

Topic: *The Roles of a, b, and c in* $y = ax^2 + bx + c$

The theory governing the motion of a free-falling object as it rises or falls near the surface of the Earth was developed by Galileo (1564–1642). He found that if you disregard air resistance, all bodies near the surface of the Earth fall toward the Earth with the same acceleration. The acceleration constant, usually denoted by g, is approximately 32 feet per second per second in the English system of measurement and 9.8 meters per second per second in the metric system. The acceleration due to gravity on the moon is 5.28 feet per second per second, or 1.617 meters per second per second.

The quadratic function that describes the distance from ground level of a free-falling object is

$$s(t) = -\tfrac{1}{2}gt^2 + v_0t + s_0,$$

where t is the time in seconds, g is the acceleration due to gravity, v_0 is the initial velocity of the object, and s_0 is the initial distance of the object from ground level.

In Activity 4.1, Baseball Throughout the Solar System, you stood on top of a 100-foot-high tower and threw the ball down with an initial velocity of 40 feet per second. In this situation,

$$g = 32, \quad v_0 = -40, \quad s_0 = 100,$$

and the equation for the height of the ball above ground level is

$$\begin{aligned} s(t) &= -\tfrac{1}{2}(32)t^2 + (-40)t + 100 \\ &= -16t^2 - 40t + 100. \end{aligned}$$

The function $f(x) = ax^2 + bx + c$ is the standard form of a quadratic function. Its graph, called a parabola, has the recognizable spreading U shape. The width and placement of the parabola in the coordinate plane depends entirely on the value of the numerical coefficients a, b, and c. One of your missions is to discover how a, b, and c influence the graph of the quadratic function. You will start with a and assume that b and c are zero for now.

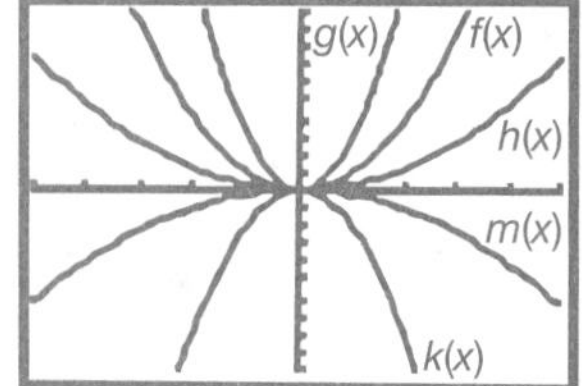

1. Set the window of your grapher to Xmin = −5, Xmax = 5, Ymin = −10, and Ymax = 10, and graph the parabolas defined by the following equations, noting the similarities and differences among the five parabolas.

   a. $f(x) = x^2$ **b.** $g(x) = 3x^2$

   c. $h(x) = 0.3x^2$ **d.** $k(x) = -2x^2$

   e. $m(x) = -0.25x^2$

   All parabolas have (0, 0) as their vertex, vertical and horizontal intercept. f, g, and h all open upward while k and m open downward. The larger the magnitude of a, the narrower the graph.

2. From your investigation in Problem 1, describe the effects of the coefficient a on the direction the parabola opens.

   If $a > 0$, the parabola opens upward.

   If $a < 0$, the parabola opens downward.

3. a. Is the graph of $h(x) = 0.3x^2$ wider or narrower than the graph of $f(x) = x^2$?

The graph of *h* is wider than the graph of *f*.

b. How do the output values of $h(x)$ and $f(x)$ compare for the same input value?

The output values of *h* are 0.3 times the output values of *f* for the same input values.

c. Is the graph of $g(x) = 3x^2$ wider or narrower than the graph of $f(x) = x^2$?

The graph of *g* is narrower than the graph of *f*.

d. How do the output values of $g(x)$ and $f(x)$ compare for the same input value?

The output values of *g* are 3 times the output values of *g* for the same input value.

e. Describe the effect of the magnitude of the coefficient *a* on the width of the graph of the parabola.

The larger the magnitude of *a*, the narrower the parabola.

f. Describe the effect of the magnitude the coefficient *a* on the output value.

For $a > 0$, the larger the value of *a*, the higher the output value. For $a < 0$, the larger the magnitude of *a*, the more negative the output value.

Now explore the role of the constant c.

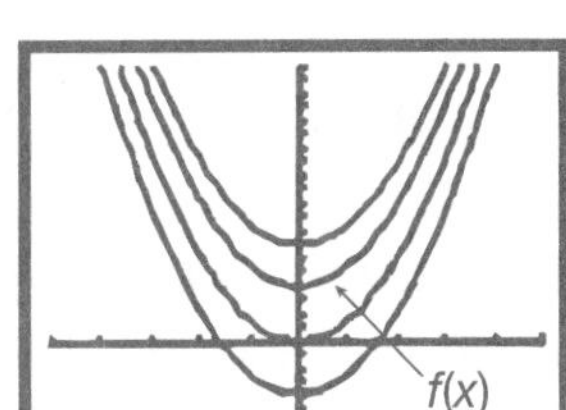

4. Graph the parabolas defined by the following equations. Once again, note the similarities and differences among the graphs. Be careful in your choice of a window.

a. $f(x) = 1.5x^2$

Vertical intercept (0, 0)

b. $g(x) = 1.5x^2 + 7$

g is *f* shifted up seven units

c. $q(x) = 1.5x^2 + 4$

q is *f* shifted up four units

d. $s(x) = 1.5x^2 - 4$

s is *f* shifted down four units.

All four graphs open upward and are symmetric with respect to the *y*-axis.

5. a. From your investigation in Problem 4, explain the effect of the constant term *c* on the graph of the quadratic function.

If $c > 0$, the graph shifts upward.

If $c < 0$, the graph shifts downward.

(0, *c*) is also the vertical intercept.

b. What relationship exists between the constant term, *c*, and the vertical intercept?

The vertical intercept is (0, *c*).

Finally, examine the role of the coefficient b.

6. Set the window of your grapher to Xmin = −8, Xmax = 8, Ymin = −20, and Ymax = 20, and graph the parabolas defined by the following equations. Note the differences among the graphs, paying careful attention to the signs of the coefficients a and b in each case.

a. $f(x) = x^2$ **b.** $g(x) = x^2 - 4x$ **c.** $h(x) = x^2 - 8x$

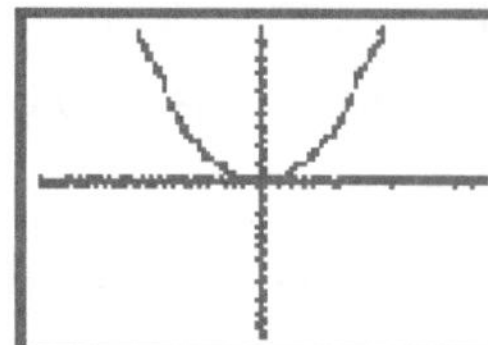
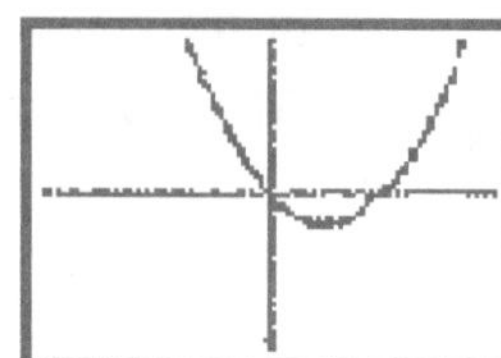
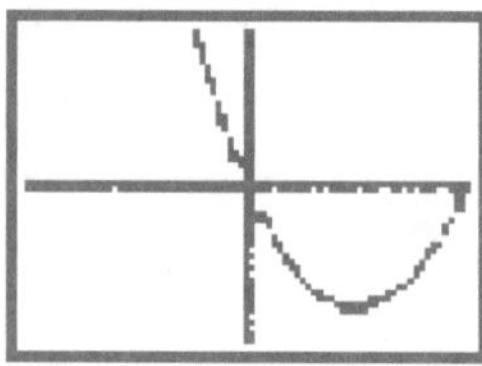

d. $p(x) = x^2 + 6x$ **e.** $q(x) = -x^2 + 6x$ **f.** $r(x) = -x^2 - 8x$

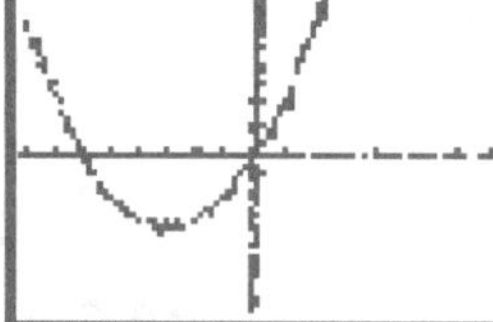
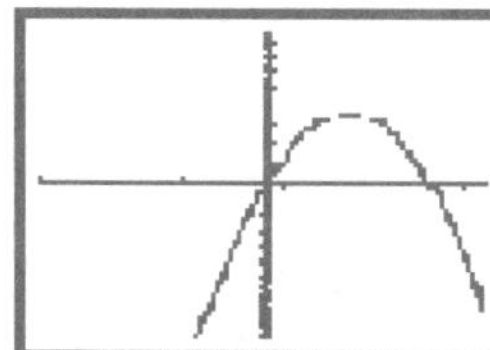
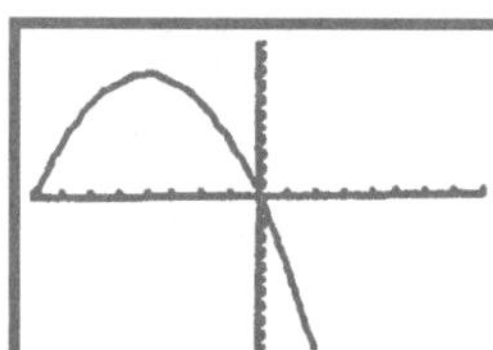

The role of the coefficient b is more complicated than that of a or c for the graph of $y = ax^2 + bx + c$ because both horizontal and vertical shifts of the graph are involved. Note that the general effect of having an x term ($b \neq 0$) is that the turning point of the parabola is not on the vertical axis.

7. From your investigation in Problem 6, explain the effects of the coefficient b on the graph of the quadratic function.

b shifts the graph of $y = x^2$ down to the right when $b < 0$ and down and to the left when $b > 0$. b shifts $y = -x^2$ up to the left when $b < 0$ and up to the right when $b > 0$.

8. Match each function with its corresponding graph. Then verify using your grapher.

i. $f(x) = x^2 + 4x + 4$ **ii.** $g(x) = 0.2x^2 + 4$ **iii.** $h(x) = -x^2 + 3x$

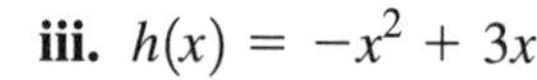

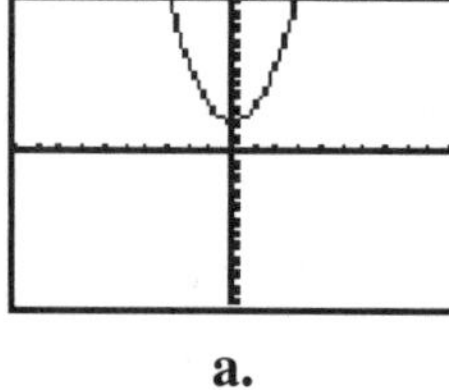
a.

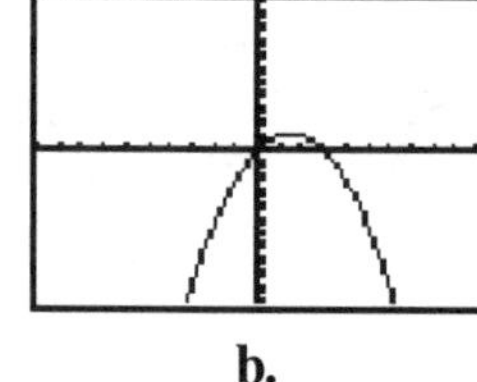
b.

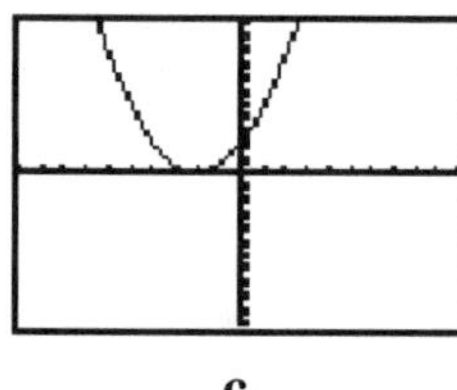
c.

ii is *a* iii is *b* i is *c*

SUMMARY

1. The graph of a quadratic function $f(x) = ax^2 + bx + c, a \neq 0$, is a parabola.
2. If $a > 0$, the parabola opens upward; if $a < 0$, the parabola opens downward. The magnitude of a affects the width of the parabola.
3. The constant term c will shift the parabola upward if $c > 0$ and downward if $c < 0$.
4. The coefficient b will shift the parabola both horizontally and vertically. The specific directions left/right and up/down depend on the signs of a and b.
5. The vertical intercept is $(0, c)$.

EXERCISES

For Exercises 1–5, determine the following characteristics.

a. Whether the parabola opens upward or downward.

b. The vertical intercept.

1. $f(x) = -5x^2 + 2x - 4$

   a. downward

   b. (0, −4)

2. $g(t) = \frac{1}{2}t^2 + t$

   a. upward

   b. (0, 0)

3. $h(v) = 2v^2 + v + 3$

   a. upward

   b. (0, 3)

4. $r(t) = 3t^2 + 10$

   a. upward

   b. (0, 10)

5. $F(x) = -x^2 + 6x - 7$

   a. downward

   b. (0, −7)

6. Does the graph of $y = -2x^2 + 3x - 4$ have any horizontal intercepts? Explain.

No, the graph does not cross the x-axis. Therefore, there can be no horizontal intercepts.

7. **a.** Is the graph of $y = \frac{3}{5}x^2$ wider or narrower than the graph of $y = x^2$?

   The graph of $y = \frac{3}{5}x^2$ is wider than the graph of $y = x^2$

   b. For the same positive input value, which graph would have a larger output value?

   $y = x^2$ would have a greater output value.

Exercise numbers appearing in color are answered in the Selected Answers section of this book.

8. Put the following in order from narrowest to widest.

a. $y = 0.5x^2$ **b.** $y = 8x^2$ **c.** $y = -2.3x^2$

b, *c*, *a* because $|0.5| < |-2.3| < |8|$.

9. a. Determine the values of x for which the functions defined by $y = 0.5x^2$ and $y = 8x^2$ are increasing.

The functions are increasing when $x > 0$.

b. Which graph is increasing more rapidly?

$y = 8x^2$ is increasing more rapidly than $y = 0.5x^2$.

ACTIVITY 4.3

The Shot Put

Topics: *Modeling Using the Quadratic Function, Special Features of Parabolas, the Vertex*

Parabolas are good models for a variety of situations that you encounter in everyday life. Examples include the path of a golf ball after it is struck, the arch (cable system) of a bridge, the path of a baseball thrown from the outfield to home plate, the stream of water from a drinking fountain, and the path of a cliff diver.

Consider the 1996 men's Olympic shot put event, which was won by the USA's Randy Barnes with a throw of 70 feet 11 inches. The path of his winning throw can be approximately modeled by the quadratic function

$$H(x) = -0.015294x^2 + x + 6,$$

where x is the horizontal distance in feet from the point of the throw and $H(x)$ is the vertical height in feet of the shot above the ground.

1. **a.** After inspecting the equation for the path of the winning throw, which way do you expect the parabola to open? Explain.

   The parabola will open downward. The coefficient $a = -0.015294$ is negative.

   b. What is the vertical intercept of the graph of the parabola? What practical meaning does this intercept have in this situation?

   The vertical intercept is (0, 6). Just before the shot was released the shot was 6 feet above the ground.

2. Use your grapher to produce a plot of the path of the winning throw. Be sure to adjust your window settings so that all of the important features of the parabola (including horizontal intercepts) appear on the screen. Your graph should resemble the following.

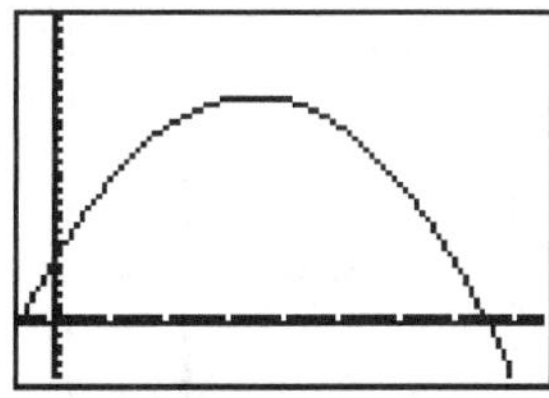

3. From your graph, what are the appropriate values for the input x (practical domain) and the output $H(x)$ (practical range)?

   Practical domain: $[0 \le x \le 70.9]$

   Practical range: $[0 \le H(x) \le 22.3]$

4. Use the table feature of your grapher to complete the following table. Round the output values to the nearest hundredth.

x	10	20	30	40	50
$H(x)$	14.47	19.88	22.24	21.53	17.77

An important feature of the graph of any quadratic function defined by $f(x) = ax^2 + bx + c$ is its **turning point,** also called the **vertex.** The turning point of a parabola that opens downward or upward is the point at which the parabola changes direction from increasing to decreasing or from decreasing to increasing.

5. Use your grapher to approximate the vertex of the function H.

   (32.7, 22.3)

6. The vertex is often very important in a situation. What is the significance of the coordinates of the turning point in this problem?

   When the shot was displaced approximately 32.7 feet horizontally from the thrower's feet the shot was at its maximum height, approximately 22.3 feet.

The turning point of a parabola having equation $y = ax^2 + bx + c$ lies on a vertical line given by

$$x = \frac{-b}{2a},$$

where a is the coefficient of the x^2-term and b is the coefficient of the x term. This line is called the **axis of symmetry** because it divides the parabola into two symmetrical parts that are mirror images in the line. For example, consider the following parabolas. Note that the line of symmetry passes through the vertex of each parabola. The axis of symmetry for the parabola on the left is $x = 1$. The axis of symmetry for the parabola on the right is $x = -1$.

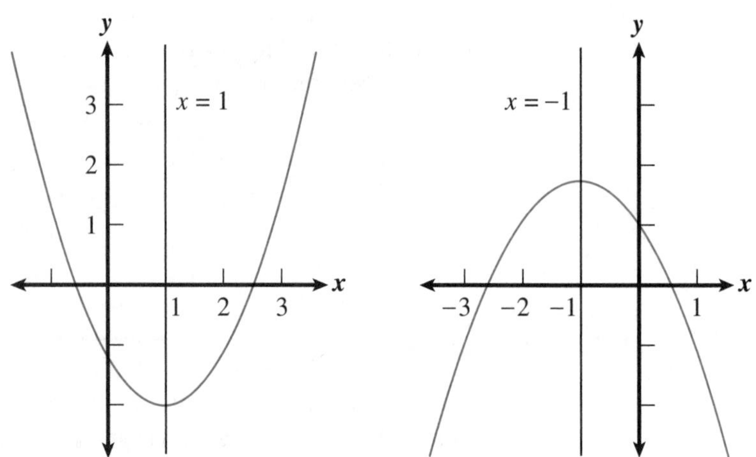

7. What is the axis of symmetry for the shot put function H?

   $x = \frac{-b}{2a}$: $x = \frac{-1}{2(-0.015294)} = 32.69256$

Because the turning point of a parabola lies on the axis of symmetry, you can determine the x-value of the vertex of a parabola by using the formula

$$x = \frac{-b}{2a}.$$

The y-value of the vertex is determined by substituting the computed x-value into the equation of the parabola and then evaluating.

8. **a.** Determine the vertex of the parabola having equation $H(x) = -0.015294x^2 + x + 6$ (the shot put function H).

(32.69256, 22.34628)

b. How do the coordinates you determined using your grapher (see Problem 5) compare with your results in part a?

The grapher results (32.7, 22.3) were an approximation. The algebraic results are more exact.

9. **a.** Use your grapher to determine the x-intercept(s) for the shot put function having equation $y = -0.01529x^2 + x + 6$.

(−5.5, 0) and (70.9, 0)

b. What is the relationship between the axis of symmetry of a parabola and the x-intercept(s) of the graph?

The axis of symmetry is halfway between the x-intercepts.

c. Are either of the x-intercepts found in part a significant to the problem situation? Explain.

Yes. $x = 70.9$ ft is the horizontal distance from the release point to where the shot hits the ground.

d. Does the graph of every parabola have x-intercepts? Explain.

No. If the graph is ∪-shaped and the vertex is above the x-axis then there are no x-intercepts. If the graph is ∩-shaped and the vertex is below the x-axis there are no x-intercepts.

10. **a.** Sketch the path of the winning throw of the shot put.

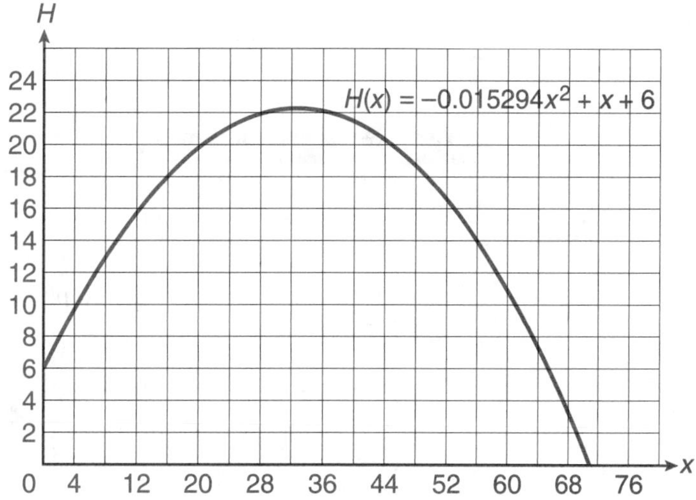

b. From the graph of the winning throw, over what horizontal distance (x-interval) was the height of the shot put increasing?

0 ft to 32.7 ft

c. Determine the x-interval over which the height of the shot put was decreasing.

32.7 ft to 70.9 ft.

11. Now consider the function $H(x) = -0.015294x^2 + x + 6$ as a general function that is not restricted by the physical situation in the activity.

a. For what x-interval does the general function increase?

$x < 32.7$

b. For what x-interval does the general function decrease?

$x > 32.7$

SUMMARY

The following characteristics are commonly used in analyzing the quadratic function $f(x) = ax^2 + bx + c$ and its graph.

1. *The direction in which the parabola opens.* For $a > 0$, the parabola opens upward; for $a < 0$, the parabola opens downward.
2. *The axis of symmetry.* This is a vertical line that separates the parabola into two mirror images. The equation of the vertical axis of symmetry is given by $x = \frac{-b}{2a}$.
3. *The vertex (turning point).* The vertex always falls on the axis of symmetry. The x-coordinate of the vertex is given by $x = \frac{-b}{2a}$. Its y-coordinate is determined by evaluating the function at this value. In other words, the y-coordinate of the vertex is given by $f\left(\frac{-b}{2a}\right)$.
4. *The y-intercept.* This point, where the parabola crosses the y-axis (i.e., where its x-coordinate is zero), is always given by $(0, c)$.
5. *The x-intercept(s).* This is the point or points (if any) where the parabola crosses the x-axis (i.e., where its y-coordinate is zero).

EXERCISES

For Exercises 1–8, determine the following characteristics of each quadratic function without graphing.

a. The direction in which the graph opens

b. The axis of symmetry

c. The vertex (turning point)

d. The y-intercept

1. $f(x) = x^2 - 3$

a. upward

b. $x = 0$

c. $(0, -3)$

d. $(0, -3)$

2. $g(x) = x^2 + 2x - 8$

a. upward

b. $x = -1$

c. $(-1, -9)$

d. $(0, -8)$

Exercise numbers appearing in color are answered in the Selected Answers section of this book.

3. $y = x^2 + 4x - 3$

a. upward

b. $x = -2$

c. $(-2, -7)$

d. $(0, -3)$

4. $f(x) = 3x^2 - 2x$

a. upward

b. $x = 1/3$

c. $(1/3, -1/3)$

d. $(0, 0)$

5. $h(x) = x^2 + 3x + 4$

a. upward

b. $x = -1.5$

c. $(-1.5, 1.75)$

d. $(0, 4)$

6. $g(x) = -x^2 + 7x - 6$

a. downward

b. $x = 3.5$

c. $(3.5, 6.25)$

d. $(0, -6)$

7. $y = 2x^2 - x - 3$

a. upward

b. $x = 0.25$

c. $(0.25, -3.125)$

d. $(0, -3)$

8. $f(x) = x^2 + x + 3$

a. upward

b. $x = -0.5$

c. $(-0.5, 2.75)$

d. $(0, 3)$

For Exercises 9–16, use your grapher to sketch the graphs of the functions and then determine each of the following.

a. The coordinates of the x-intercepts for each function, if they exist.

b. The domain and range for each function.

c. The x-interval over which each function is increasing.

d. The x-interval over which each function is decreasing.

9. $g(x) = -x^2 + 7x - 6$

a. $(1, 0)$ $(6, 0)$

b. D: (all real numbers)

R: $(g(x) \leq 6.25)$

c. $(x < 3.5)$

d. $(x > 3.5)$

10. $h(x) = 3x^2 + 6x + 4$

a. none

b. D: (all real numbers)

R: $(h(x) \geq 1)$

c. $(x > -1)$

d. $(x < -1)$

11. $y = x^2 - 12$

a. $(3.46, 0)$ $(-3.46, 0)$

b. D: (all real numbers) R: $(y \geq -12)$

c. $(x > 0)$

d. $(x < 0)$

12. $f(x) = x^2 + 4x - 5$

a. $(1, 0)$ $(-5, 0)$

b. D: (all real numbers) R: $(f(x) \geq -9)$

c. $(x > -2)$

d. $(x < -2)$

13. $g(x) = -x^2 + 2x + 3$

a. $(-1, 0)$ $(3, 0)$

b. D: (all real numbers) R:$(g(x) \leq 4)$

c. $(x < 1)$

d. $(x > 1)$

14. $h(x) = x^2 + 2x - 8$

a. $(2, 0)$ $(-4, 0)$

b. D: (all real numbers) R: $(h(x) \geq -9)$

c. $(x > -1)$

d. $(x < -1)$

15. $y = -5x^2 + 6x - 1$

a. (0.2, 0) (1, 0)

b. D: (all real numbers) R: ($y \le 0.8$)

c. ($x < 0.6$)

d. ($x > 0.6$)

16. $f(x) = 3x^2 - 2x + 1$

a. none

b. D: (all real numbers) R: $f(x) \geq \frac{2}{3}$

c. $x > \frac{1}{3}$

d. $x < \frac{1}{3}$

17. You shoot an arrow vertically into the air from a height of 5 feet with an initial velocity of 96 feet per second. The height h in feet above the ground at any time t in seconds is modeled by

$$h(t) = 5 + 96t - 16t^2.$$

a. Determine the maximum height the arrow will attain.

149 feet

b. Approximately when will the arrow reach the ground?

6.05 sec

c. What is the significance of the horizontal intercept?

It indicates when the arrow hits the ground.

What Have I Learned?

Recognizing the correspondence among situations, equations, and graphs is an important skill. Exercises 1–5 contain a description of a free-falling object. Match the description to the quadratic models the distance s that the object is above the ground. Then match each description (and equation) to the graph that represents the situation, selecting from graphs i–vii.

1. A rock is thrown straight up with a velocity of 20 meters per second from a building that is 50 meters high.

equation (f) graph (vi)

2. A model rocket is shot straight up into the air from a launch pad at ground level with a velocity of 70 feet per second.

equation (d) graph (vii)

3. A telephone repairperson drops her vice grips from a 50-foot tower.

equation (a) graph (iii)

4. A ball is thrown directly upward with a velocity of 100 feet per second from a height of 6 feet above the ground on the moon.

equation (c) graph (ii)

5. A bundle of shingles is thrown straight down with a velocity of 50 feet per second from the roof of a building that is 50 feet high.

equation (e) graph (iv)

---

a. $s(t) = -16t^2 + 50$

b. $s(t) = -4.9t^2 - 20t + 50$

c. $s(t) = -2.64t^2 + 100t + 6$

d. $s(t) = -16t^2 + 70t$

e. $s(t) = -16t^2 - 50t + 50$

f. $s(t) = -4.9t^2 + 20t + 50$

g. $s(t) = -16t^2 + 50t$

i.

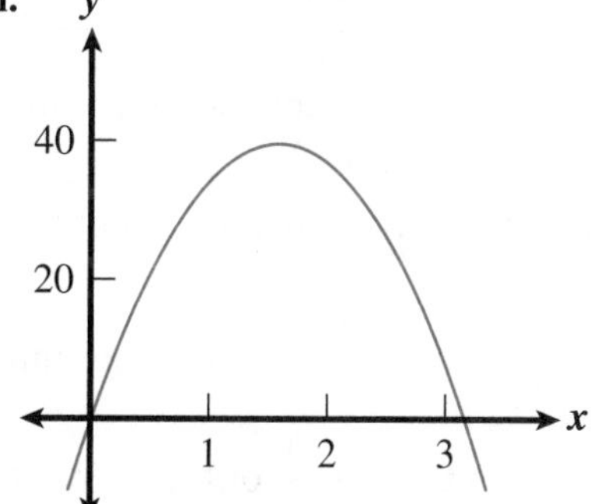

ii.

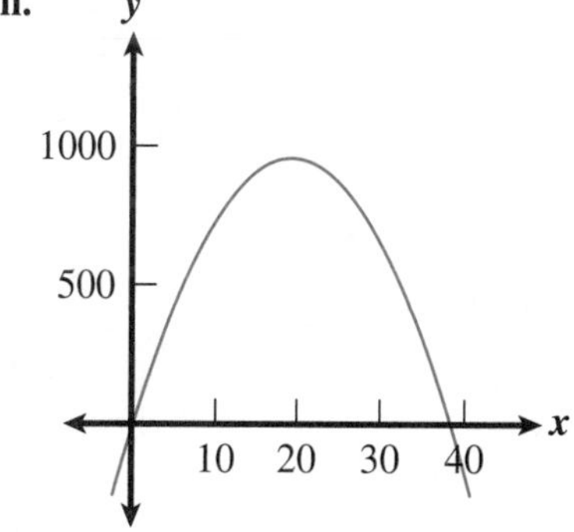

iii.

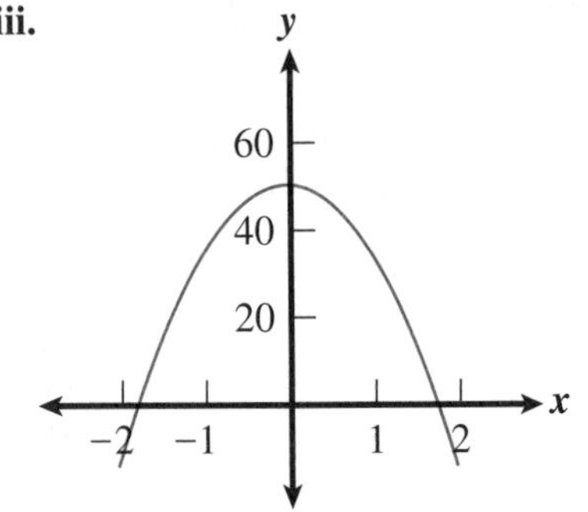

iv.

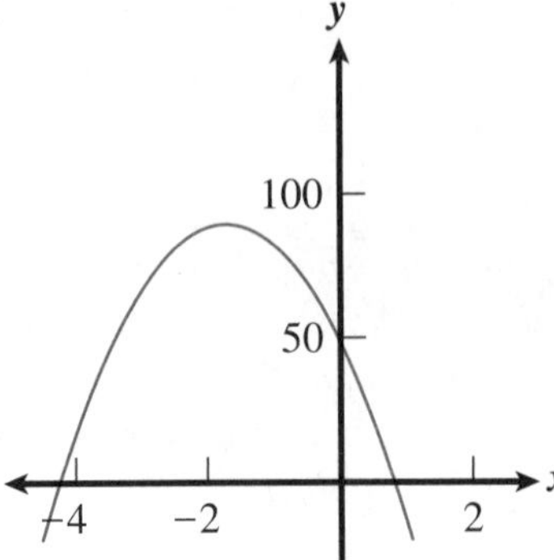

v.

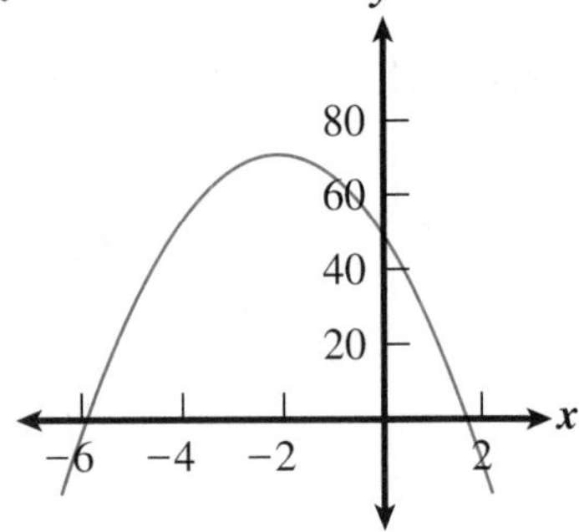

vi.

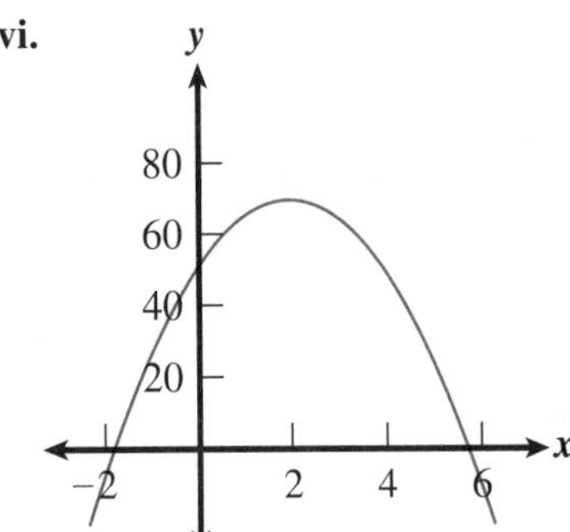

vii.

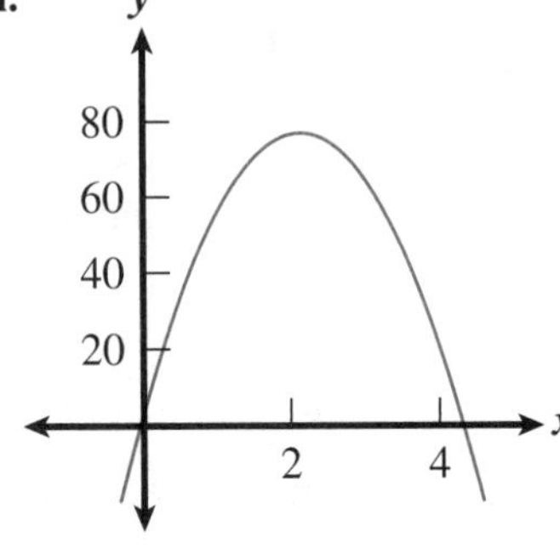

6. **a.** For the graph of the equation $y = ax^2 + bx + c$ to be a parabola, can the value of the coefficient of x^2 be zero? Explain.

   No, if $a = 0$, you would have $y = bx + c$ which is the equation of a line.

   b. What is the vertex of the parabola having an equation of the form $y = ax^2$?

   (0, 0)

   c. Describe the relationship between the vertex and the horizontal intercepts of the graph of $y = ax^2 + c$.

   The vertex is $(0, c)$. If there are two intercepts, then the vertex lies (horizontally) between the two intercepts. If $c = 0$, then the vertex is the x-intercept.

7. Determine if the vertex is the lowest point or the highest point of the graph of $y = ax^2 + bx + c$ for each of the following situations.

   a. $a < 0$

   Maximum

   b. $a > 0$

   Minimum

8. **a.** What are the possibilities for the number of vertical intercepts of the graph of a quadratic function?

   There is always one vertical intercept.

   b. What are the possibilities for the number of horizontal intercepts of a parabola?

   There may be 0, 1, or 2 horizontal intercepts.

9. What is the relationship between the vertex and the x-intercept of the graph of $y = x^2 - 4x + 4$?

They are the same, (2, 0).

10. a. The vertex of a parabola is (3, 1). Using this information, complete the following table.

x	1	2	3	4	5
y	5	2	1	2	5

b. If the vertex of a parabola is (2, 4), complete the following table.

x	−2	0	2	4	6
y	0	3	4	3	0

How Can I Practice?

1. Complete the following table.

EQUATION OF THE FORM $y = ax^2 + bx + c$	VALUE OF a	VALUE OF b	VALUE OF c
$y = 5x^2$	5	0	0
$y = \frac{1}{3}x^2 + 3x - 1$	$\frac{1}{3}$	3	−1
$y = x - 2x^2$	−2	1	0

For Exercises 2–7, determine the following characteristics for each graph.

a. The direction in which the parabola opens.

b. The equation of the axis of symmetry.

c. The vertex.

d. The y-intercept.

2. $y = -2x^2 + 4$

a. downward

b. $x = 0$

c. (0, 4)

d. (0, 4)

3. $y = \frac{2}{3}x^2$

a. upward

b. $x = 0$

c. (0, 0)

d. (0, 0)

4. $f(x) = -3x^2 + 6x + 7$

a. downward

b. $x = 1$

c. (1, 10)

d. (0, 7)

5. $F(x) = 4x^2 - 4x$

a. upward

b. $x = 1/2$

c. (1/2, −1)

d. (0, 0)

Exercise numbers appearing in color are answered in the Selected Answers section of this book.

6. $y = x^2 + 6x + 9$

a. upward

b. $x = -3$

c. $(-3. 0)$

d. $(0, 9)$

7. $y = x^2 - x + 1$

a. upward

b. $x = 1/2$

c. $(1/2, 3/4)$

d. $(0, 1)$

For Exercises 8–11, use your grapher to sketch the graph of each quadratic function and then determine the following for each function.

a. The coordinates of the x-intercepts (if they exist).

b. The domain and range of the function.

c. The x-interval over which the function is increasing.

d. The x-interval over which the function is decreasing.

8. $y = -x^2 + 4$

a. $(-2, 0)$ $(2, 0)$

b. D: (all real numbers) R: $(y \leq 4)$

c. $(x < 0)$

d. $(x > 0)$

9. $y = x^2 - 5x + 6$

a. $(2, 0)$ $(3, 0)$

b. D: (all real numbers) R: $(y \geq -0.25)$

c. $(x > 2.5)$

d. $(x < 2.5)$

10. $y = -3x^2 - 6x + 8$

a. $(0.91, 0)$ $(-2.91, 0)$

b. D: (all real numbers) R: $y \leq 11)$

c. $(x < -1)$

d. $(x > -1)$

11. $y = 0.22x^2 - 0.71x + 2$

a. none

b. D: (all real numbers) R: $(y \geq 1.427)$

c. $(x > 1.61)$

d. $(x < 1.61)$

12. Use your grapher to approximate the vertex of the graph of the parabola defined by the equation $y = -2x^2 + 3x + 25$.

(0.75, 26.125)

13. The height h (in feet) of a golf ball is a function of the time t (in seconds) it has been in flight. A golfer strikes a golf ball with an initial velocity of 80 feet per second. The flight path of the ball is a parabola. The approximate height that the ball is above the ground is modeled by

$$h(t) = -16t^2 + 80t.$$

a. Sketch a graph of the function. What is the practical domain in this situation?

Practical domain $[0 \leq t \leq 5]$

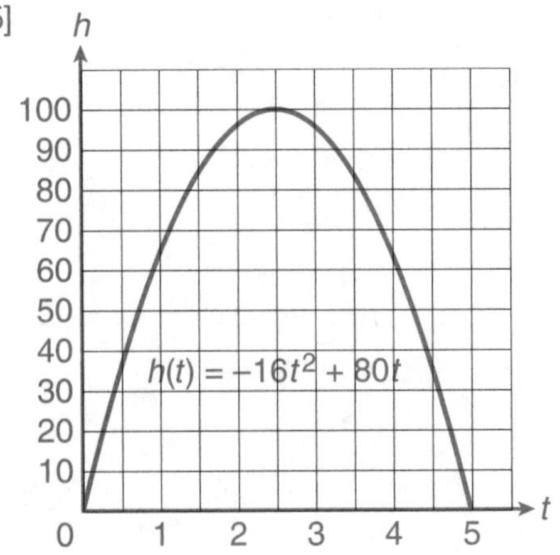

h
100
90
80
70
60
50
40
30
20
10
0
1 2 3 4 5
t
$h(t) = -16t^2 + 80t$

b. Determine the vertex of the parabola. What is the practical meaning of this point?

(2.5, 100) The ball reaches its highest level, 100 feet, 2.5 seconds after being struck.

c. What is the vertical intercept, and what is its practical meaning in this situation?

(0, 0) The ball is on the ground when the club makes contact.

d. Determine the horizontal intercepts. What is the significance of these intercepts?

(0, 0) and (5, 0) The ball is on the ground when the club makes contact, $t = 0$, and returns to the ground 5 seconds later.

e. What assumption are you making in this situation about the elevation of the spot where the ball is struck and the point where the ball lands?

We are assuming that the lift off point and the return point are at the same elevation.

14. A suspension bridge (shown in the accompanying figure) is 100 meters long from tower to tower. The bridge is supported by cables attached to the tops of 35-meter-high towers at each end of the bridge. The cables hang from the towers approximately in the shape of a parabola. The height h (in meters) of the cables above the surface of the roadway is modeled by

$$h(x) = 0.01x^2 - x + 35,$$

where x is the horizontal distance measured from the point where the tower and roadway meet.

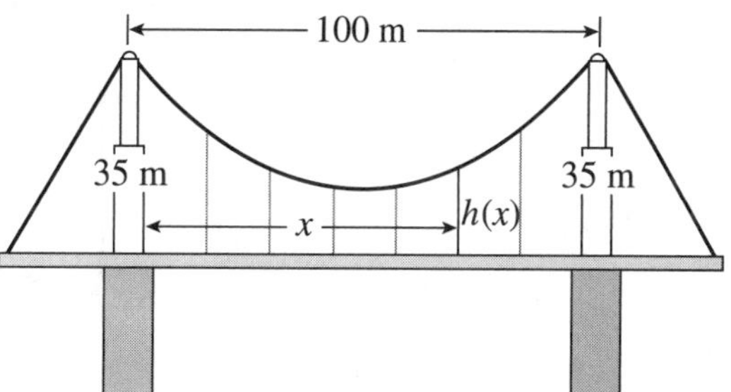

a. Use your grapher to graph the height function. What is the practical domain of this function?

$[0 \le x \le 100]$

b. What is the minimum distance of the cables from the roadway?

$h(50) = 0.01(50)^2 - 50 + 35 = 10$ feet.

CLUSTER 2

Problem Solving Using Quadratic Functions

ACTIVITY 4.4

Personal Computers

Topic: *Solving Quadratic Equations Graphically and Numerically*

The number of personal computers (in millions) sold to colleges and universities from 1981 to 1988 can be modeled by the equation

$$N(t) = 0.006t^2 + 0.041t + 0.025,$$

where t is the number of years since 1981, and $N(t)$ represents the number of computers sold in millions.

1. What is the practical domain for the model represented by the function N?

$0 \le t \le 7$ (years 1981–1988)

2. Let $t = 0$ correspond to the year 1981. Use your grapher to complete the following table of values for t, the number of years since 1981, and $N(t)$, the number of computers sold. Round your output to the nearest thousandth.

t	0	1	2	3	4	5	6	7	8	9	10
$N(t)$ (IN MILLIONS)	0.025	0.072	0.131	0.202	0.285	0.380	0.487	0.606	0.737	0.880	1.035

3. Sketch a graph of the function using your grapher using the window Xmin = −1, Xmax = 20, Ymin = −0.2, and Ymax = 3. Your graph should appear as follows.

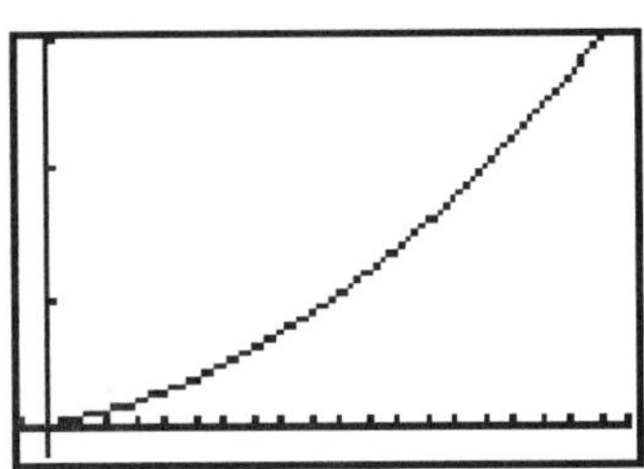

4. Estimate the number of personal computers sold to colleges and universities in the year 1989 ($t = 8$).

737,000

5. Suppose you want to determine in which year 1,035,000 personal computers were sold to colleges and universities. In other words, you want to determine for what value of t does $N(t) = 1.035$? Write an equation that you would need to solve to determine the value of t for which $N(t) = 1.035$.

$0.006t^2 + 0.041t + 0.025 = 1.035$

6. a. One method of approximating the solution to the equation in Problem 5 is a numerical approach, using a table of appropriate data points (see Problem 2).What is your approximation using this approach?

$t = 10$ corresponding to 1991.

b. Describe in your own words how to solve the quadratic equation $x^2 + 3x - 1 = 9$ numerically (using tables of data).

Create a table in which x is the input, $y = x^2 + 3x - 1$ is output. The solution is the x value corresponding to a y value of 9.

7. A second method of solving the equation in Problem 5 is a graphical approach.

a. Using the trace feature of your grapher, trace the graph obtained in Problem 3 to find the input for which the output is 1.035. Your graph should appear as follows.

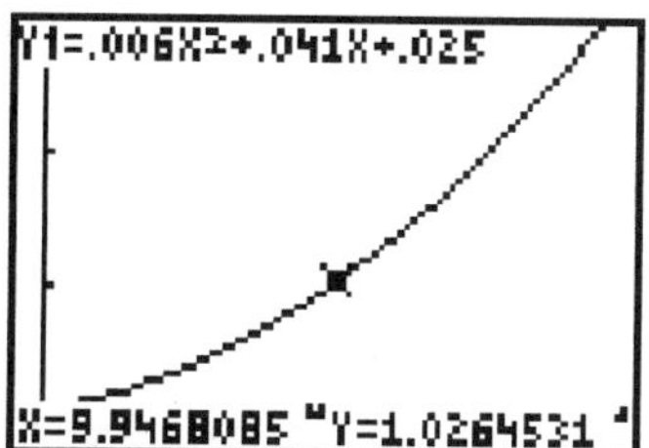

How does your answer compare with the result in Problem 6?

The results should be the same, but answers may vary slightly depending on the window used.

b. You can also solve the equation $1.035 = 0.006t^2 + 0.041t + 0.025$ by solving the following system of equations graphically on your calculator:

$$y_1 = 0.006x^2 + 0.041x + 0.025$$
$$y_2 = 1.035.$$

The expression for y_1 gives the number of computers sold in any given year. The value y_2 is the specific number of computers in which you are interested. You want to determine when $y_1 = y_2$. To do this, determine the point of intersection of these two graphs. If your calculator has an intersection command on its calculate menu, use it. The graph should appear as follows.

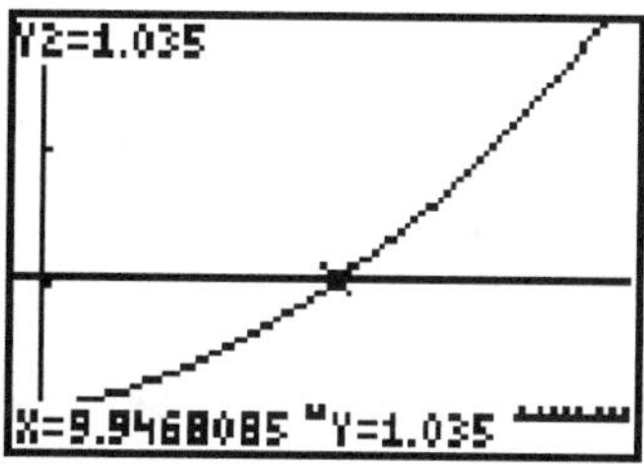

For help with using the TI-83, see Appendix C.

c. Still another graphical method for solving the problem is to rearrange the quadratic equation

$$1.035 = 0.006t^2 + 0.041t + 0.025$$

so that the left-hand side is equal to zero. Subtracting 1.035 from each side, you have

$$0 = 0.006t^2 + 0.041t - 1.010.$$

If you let $y = 0.006t^2 + 0.041t - 1.010$, then the solution to the equation consists of the x-intercepts of the graph, if they exist. Using your grapher, sketch a graph of $y = 0.006t^2 + 0.041t - 1.010$. The screen should appear as follows.

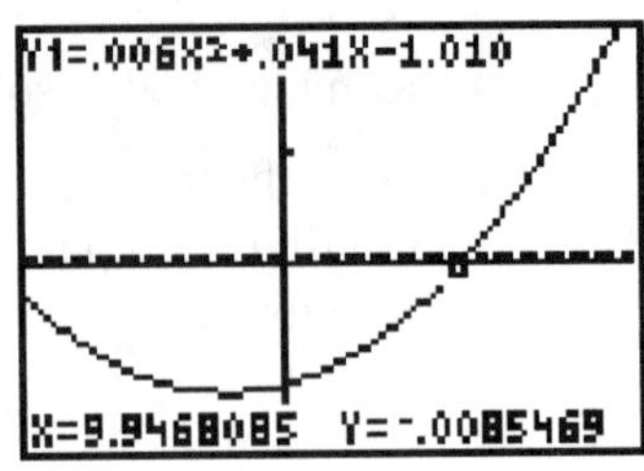

d. What are the x-intercepts of the new function defined by $y = 0.006t^2 + 0.041t - 1.010$? Are both of the values answers to the equation in Problem 5? Explain.

$t = 10$ and $t = -16.83$. They are both horizontal intercepts of the abstract function. But only $t = 10$ has a practical meaning in the context of the situation.

8. Describe in your own words three different ways to solve the equation $2x^2 - 4x + 3 = 2$ using a graphing approach. Solve the equation using each graphing method. How do your answers compare?

a. Graph $Y1 = 2x^2 - 4x + 3$ and $y2 = 2$. Use the intersection feature of your grapher.

b. Graph the function $y = 2x^2 = 4x + 3$ and use the trace and zoom features.

c. Write the equation in standard form $2x^2 - 4x + 1 = 0$.
Let $Y1 = 2x^2 - 4x + 1$ and find the x-intercepts of its graph. The solutions are approximately $x = 1.707$ and $x = 0.293$ in each case.

9. Suppose you are interested in determining in which years more than 1.5 million personal computers were sold to colleges and universities.

a. Write an inequality that you would need to solve to answer this problem.

$0.006t^2 + 0.041t + 0.025 > 1.5$

b. Solve the inequality using the graph of $N(t) = 0.006t^2 + 0.041t + 0.025$.

$N(t) > 1.5$ for $t > 12.6$. Thus, after 1993 more than 1.5 million PCs will be sold to colleges.

10. Solve the following quadratic inequalities using a graphing approach.

a. $x^2 - x - 6 < 0$

The graph of $y = x^2 - x - 6$ is below the x-axis for $-2 < x < 3$

b. $x^2 - x - 6 > 0$

The graph of $y = x^2 - x - 6$ is above the x-axis if $x < -2$ or $x > 3$.

SUMMARY

- To solve $f(x) = c$ numerically, construct a table and determine the x-values that produce c as an output.
- To solve $f(x) = c$ graphically:
  a. Graph $y = f(x)$, graph $y = c$, and determine the x-values of the points of intersection.
  b. Or graph $y = f(x) - c$ and determine the x-intercepts.
- To solve $f(x) > c$ graphically:
  a. Graph $y = f(x)$, graph $y = c$, and determine all x-values for which the graph of f is above the graph of $y = c$.
  b. Or graph $y = f(x) - c$ and determine all x-values for which the graph of $f(x) - c$ is above the x-axis.

EXERCISES

In Exercises 1–4, solve the quadratic equation numerically (using tables of x- and y-values). Verify your solution graphically.

1. $-4x = -x^2 + 12$
   $x = 6$ or $x = -2$

2. $x^2 + 9x + 18 = 0$
   $x = -3$ or $x = -6$

3. $2x^2 = 8x + 90$
   $x = 9$ or $x = -5$

4. $x^2 - x - 3 = 0$
   $x = 2.3$ or $x = -1.3$

In Exercises 5–8, solve the quadratic equation graphically using at least two different approaches. When necessary, give your solution to the nearest hundredth.

5. $x^2 + 12x + 11 = 0$
   $x = -11$ or $x = -1$

6. $2x^2 - 3 = 2x$
   $x = 1.82$ or $x = -0.82$

7. $16x^2 - 400 = 0$
   $x = \pm 5$

8. $4x^2 + 12x = -4$
   $x = 0.38$ or $x = -2.62$

In Exercises 9–12, solve the equation by using either a numerical or graphical approach.

9. $x^2 + 2x - 3 = 0$
   $x = -3$ or $x = 1$

10. $x^2 + 11x + 24 = 0$
    $x = -8$ or $x = -3$

11. $x^2 - 2x - 8 = x + 20$
    $x = 7$ or $x = -4$

12. $x^2 - 10x + 6 = 5x - 50$
    $x = 7$ or $x = 8$

In Exercises 13–14, solve the given inequality using a graphing approach.

13. **a.** $x^2 - 4x - 1 < 11$
    $-2 < x < 6$

    b. $x^2 - 4x - 1 > 11$
    $x < -2$ or $x > 6$

Exercise numbers appearing in color are answered in the Selected Answers section of this book.

14. a. $2x^2 + 5x - 3 < 0$

$-3 < x < \frac{1}{2}$

b. $2x^2 + 5x - 3 \geq 0$

$x \leq -3$ or $x \geq \frac{1}{2}$

15. The stopping distance d (in feet) for a car moving at a velocity (speed) of v mph is modeled by the equation

$$d(v) = 0.04v^2 + 1.1v.$$

a. What is the stopping distance for a velocity of 55 mph?

$d(55) = 181.5$ feet

b. What is the speed of the car if it takes 200 feet to stop?

$0.04v^2 + 1.1v = 200$; $v = 58$ mph

16. An international rule for determining the number of board feet (usable finished lumber) in a 16-foot log is modeled by the equation

$$n(d) = 0.22d^2 - 0.71d,$$

where d is the diameter of the log in inches, and $n(d)$ is the number of board feet.

a. How many board feet can be obtained from a 16-foot log with a 14-inch diameter?

$n(14) = 0.22(14)^2 - 0.71(14) = 33$ board feet

b. Sketch a graph of this function. What is the practical domain of this function?

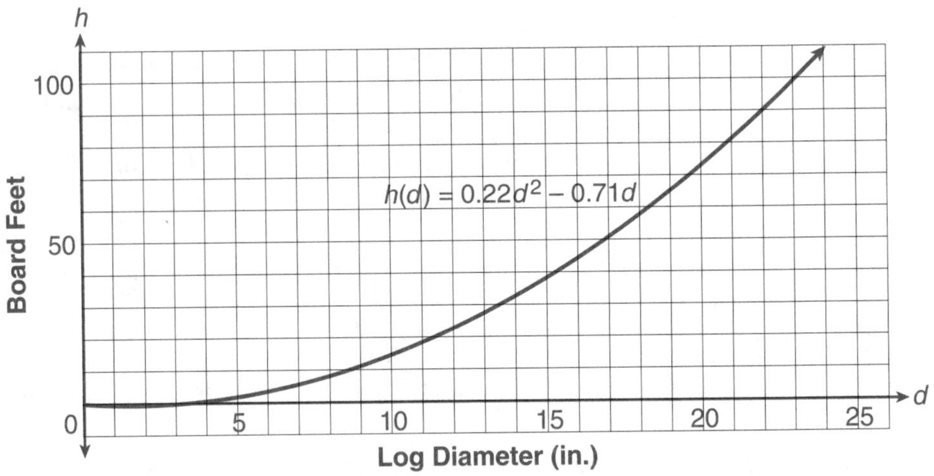

The practical domain is $3.2 < d < D$, where D is the maximum diameter of a log.

c. Use the graph to approximate the horizontal intercept(s). What is the practical meaning in this situation?

$d = 0$ and $d = 3.2$. The rule $n(d) = 0.22d^2 - 0.71d$ is valid only for logs whose diameters are greater than 3.2.

d. What is the diameter of a 16-foot log that has 2000 board feet?

$0.22d^2 - 0.71d = 2000$, d is approximately 97 feet.

ACTIVITY 4.5

Sir Isaac Newton XIV

Topics: *Solving Quadratic Equations by Factoring, the Quadratic Formula*

Sir Isaac Newton XIV, a descendant of the famous physicist and mathematician, takes you to the top of a building to demonstrate a physics property discovered by his famous ancestor. He throws your math book into the air. The book's distance s above the ground as a function of time t is modeled by

$$s = -16t^2 + 16t + 32.$$

1. When the book strikes the ground, what is the value of s?

$s = 0$

2. Write the equation that must be solved to determine when the book strikes the ground.

$-16t^2 + 16t + 32 = 0$

The equation in Problem 2 can be solved by using a numerical or graphical approach. However, an algebraic technique is efficient in this case and will give an exact answer. The algorithm is based on the algebraic principle known as the **zero product rule.**

If a and b are any numbers and $a \cdot b = 0$, then either a or b, or both, must be equal to zero.

Note that to apply the zero product rule, the equation must be written in the form

$$a \text{ product} = 0.$$

Because the equation in Problem 2 is already equal to zero, you need only factor the nonzero side of the equation, as follows:

$$\begin{aligned} 0 &= -16t^2 + 16t + 32 \\ 0 &= -16(t^2 - t - 2) \\ 0 &= -16(t - 2)(t + 1). \end{aligned}$$

The equation $0 = -16(t - 2)(t + 1)$ can only be true if $t - 2 = 0$ or $t + 1 = 0$. Solving each of these equations separately, you have

$t - 2 = 0$	$t + 1 = 0$
$t = 2$	$t = -1$

3. Are both solutions to the equation ($t = 2$ and $t = -1$) also solutions to the question, At what time does the book strike the ground? Explain.

Only $t = 2$ lies in the practical domain which starts at $t = 0$.

4. At what time is the book 32 feet above the ground? Solve the appropriate quadratic equation by factoring.

$-16t^2 + 16t + 32 = 32$

$-16t^2 + 16t = 0$ $\quad$ $t(t - 1) = 0$

$t^2 - t = 0$ $\quad$ $t = 0$ or $t = 1$

5. Solve each of the following quadratic equations by factoring.

a. $2x^2 - x - 6 = 0$
$(2x + 3)(x - 2) = 0$
$x = -\frac{3}{2}$ or $x = 2$

b. $3x^2 - 6x = 0$
$3x(x - 2) = 0$
$x = 0, 2$

c. $x^2 + 4x = -x - 6$
$x^2 + 5x + 6 = 0$
$(x + 3)(x + 2) = 0$
$x = -3, -2$

For a more extensive treatment of solving equations by factoring, see Appendix A.

6. a. What equation do you need to solve to determine when your math book is 5 feet above the ground?

$-16t^2 + 16t + 32 = 5$

b. To use the zero product rule, you need to put your equation in the form $F(x) = 0$, called **standard form.** Write the equation in part a in standard form.

$-16t^2 + 16t + 27 = 0$

c. Is the nonzero side of the equation factorable?

No

The technique of solving quadratic equations by factoring is very limited. In most real-world applications involving quadratic equations, the quadratic is not factorable. In those cases, you can use a formula to solve a quadratic equation of the form $ax^2 + bx + c = 0$.

Beginning with the standard quadratic function defined by $y = ax^2 + bx + c$, $a \neq 0$, set $y = 0$ to obtain the equation

$$0 = ax^2 + bx + c.$$

The equation $ax^2 + bx + c = 0$ has two solutions,

$$x_1 = \frac{-b + \sqrt{b^2 - 4ac}}{2a} \text{ and } x_2 = \frac{-b - \sqrt{b^2 - 4ac}}{2a}.$$

These solutions are often written as the single expression,

$$x = \frac{-b \pm \sqrt{b^2 - 4ac}}{2a}.$$

This formula is known as the **quadratic formula.**

The details of the solution of the equation $0 = ax^2 + bx + c$ by the quadratic formula are given in Appendix A.

7. a. Solve the equation $0 = -16t^2 + 16t + 32$ by using the quadratic formula. Because the equation is already written in standard form, you can begin the process by identifying the values of a, b, and c.

$a = -16$ $b = 16$ $c = 32$

b. Substitute these values into the quadratic formula and simplify the results as much as you can. Round the solutions to the nearest hundredth, if necessary.

$$t = \frac{-16 \pm \sqrt{256 - 4(-16)(32)}}{2(-16)} = \frac{-16 \pm \sqrt{2304}}{-32} = -1, \text{ or } 2$$

c. How do the solutions in part b compare with those determined by using the zero product rule in Problem 2?

The solutions are the same.

8. a. Sketch a graph of $y = 2x^2 + 9x - 5$. Write the equation that you would need to solve to determine the x-intercepts of the graph.

$2x^2 + 9x - 5 = 0$

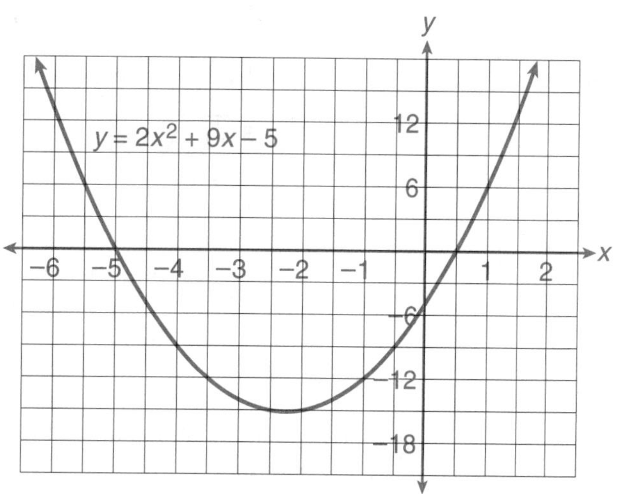

b. Solve the equation $0 = 2x^2 + 9x - 5$ using the quadratic formula.

$a = 2, b = 9, c = -5$

$$x = \frac{-9 \pm \sqrt{81 - 4(2)(-5)}}{2(2)} = \frac{-9 \pm \sqrt{121}}{4} = -5 \text{ or } 0.5$$

c. Approximate the x-intercepts of the graph using your grapher. How do these values compare with the results in part b?

The values should be identical.

If you write the quadratic formula in a slightly different form, you obtain

$$x = \frac{-b}{2a} \pm \frac{\sqrt{b^2 - 4ac}}{2a} \text{ or } x_1 = \frac{-b}{2a} + \frac{\sqrt{b^2 - 4ac}}{2a},\ x_2 = \frac{-b}{2a} - \frac{\sqrt{b^2 - 4ac}}{2a}$$

The next problem uses the rewritten form of the quadratic formula to help identify a relationship between the x-intercepts and the axis of symmetry of a parabola.

9. Consider the function $f(x) = 2x^2 + 9x - 5$.

a. Determine the equation of the axis of symmetry of the graph of f.

$x = \frac{-9}{2(2)} = -2.25$

b. What is the value of $\dfrac{\sqrt{b^2 - 4ac}}{2a}$?

$\dfrac{\sqrt{121}}{4} = \dfrac{11}{4} = 2.75$

c. Sketch a graph of the function f, and label the axis of symmetry. Show where the value computed in part b is located graphically. What are the x-intercepts of the graph?

The x-intercepts are $(-5, 0)$ and $(0.5, 0)$

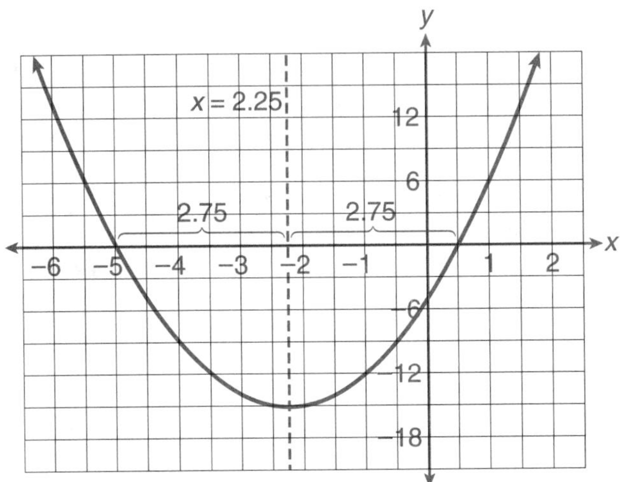

d. What is the relationship between the axis of symmetry and the x-intercepts of a parabola?

The axis of symmetry lies exactly midway between the x-intercepts.

10. For each of the following quadratic functions, write the equation that must be used to determine the x-intercepts of the graph. Solve the appropriate equation using the quadratic formula. Round your answers to the nearest hundredth.

a. $f(x) = 2x^2 - 6x - 3$

$2x^2 - 6x - 3 = 0$

$a = 2, b = -6, c = -3$

$x = \dfrac{6 \pm \sqrt{60}}{4} = 3.44 \text{ or } -0.44$

b. $h(x) = x^2 - 8x + 16$

$x^2 - 8x + 16 = 0$

$a = 1, b = -8, c = 16$

$x = \dfrac{8 \pm \sqrt{64 - 4(1)(16)}}{2} = \dfrac{8}{2} = 4$

11. Returning to Problem 6, use the quadratic formula to solve the appropriate equation. Round your answers to the nearest hundredth. Verify your solutions graphically.

$-16t^2 + 16t + 27 = 0$ $t = 1.89$ or $t = -0.89$

Only the first value lies in the practical domain.

SUMMARY

To solve a quadratic equation by factoring:

1. Set the equation equal to 0.
2. Factor the quadratic expression.
3. Employ the zero product rule.
4. Solve the resulting linear equations.

The quadratic formula, $x = \frac{-b \pm \sqrt{b^2 - 4ac}}{2a}$, can be used to solve any quadratic equation in the form $ax^2 + bx + c = 0,\ a \neq 0$.

EXERCISES

In Exercises 1–4, solve each of the following quadratic equations by factoring.

1. $3x^2 + 11x - 4 = 0$

$(3x - 1)(x + 4) = 0$

$x = \frac{1}{3}$ or $x = -4$

2. $3x^2 - 12x = 0$

$3x(x - 4) = 0$

$x = 0, 4$

3. $x^2 - 7x = 18$

$x^2 - 7x - 18 = 0$

$(x - 9)(x + 2) = 0$

$x = 9, -2$

4. $3x(x - 6) - 5(x - 6) = 0$

$(x - 6)(3x - 5) = 0$

$x = 6, \frac{5}{3}$

In Exercises 5–11, identify the value of a, b, and c and then solve the equation using the quadratic formula. Round your answers to the nearest hundredth. Verify your solutions graphically.

5. $x^2 + 6x - 3 = 0$

$a = 1, b = 6, c = -3$

$$x = \frac{-6 \pm \sqrt{36 - 4(1)(-3)}}{2}$$

$$= \frac{-6 \pm \sqrt{48}}{2}$$

$x = 0.46$ or $x = -6.46$

6. $4x^2 + 4x + 1 = 0$

$a = 4, b = 4, c = 1$

$$x = \frac{-4 \pm \sqrt{16 - 4(4)(1)}}{2(4)}$$

$$= -\frac{1}{2}$$

7. $x^2 + 5x = 13$

$a = 1, b = 5, c = -13$

$x^2 + 5x - 13 = 0$

$$x = \frac{5 \pm \sqrt{77}}{2} = 1.89 \text{ or } -6.89$$

8. $2x^2 - 6x + 3 = 0$

$a = 2, b = -6, c = 3$

$$x = \frac{6 \pm \sqrt{12}}{4} = 2.37 \text{ or } 0.63$$

Exercise numbers appearing in color are answered in the Selected Answers section of this book.

9. $2x^2 - 3x = 5$

$2x^2 - 3x - 5 = 0$

$a = 2, b = -3, c = -5$

$$x = \frac{3 \pm \sqrt{49}}{4} = 2.5, -1$$

10. $(2x - 1)(x + 2) = 1$

$2x^2 + 3x - 3 = 0$

$a = 2, b = 3, c = -3$

$$x = \frac{-3 \pm \sqrt{33}}{4} = 0.69, -2.19$$

11. $(x + 2)^2 + x^2 = 44$

$2x^2 + 4x - 40 = 0$

$x^2 + 2x - 20 = 0$

$a = 1, b = 2, c = -20$

$$x = \frac{-2 \pm \sqrt{84}}{2} = 3.58 \text{ or } -5.58$$

In Exercises 12–14, determine the x-intercept of the graph algebraically. Then check your results graphically.

12. $y = 3x^2 + 6x$

(0, 0) and (−2, 0)

13. $y = x^2 - x - 6$

(3, 0) and (−2, 0)

14. $f(x) = 2x^2 - x + 5$

There are no x-intercepts.

15. The number n (in millions) of cellular-phone subscribers in the United States from 1990 to 1994 is given in the following graphic.

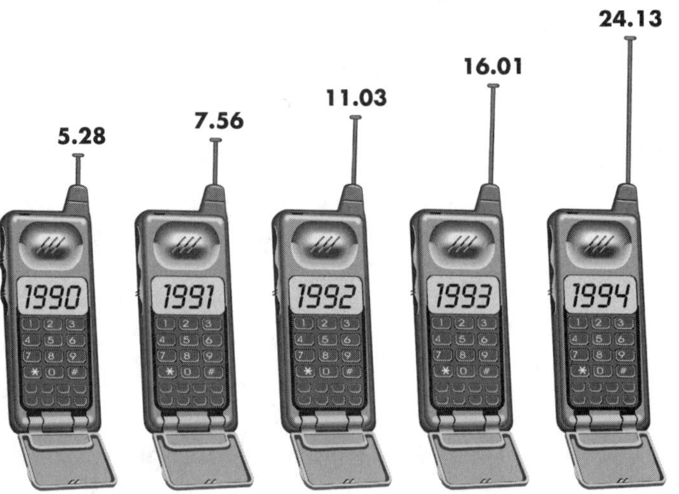

The data can be approximated by the quadratic model

$$n = 0.94t^2 + 0.84t + 5.45,$$

where $t = 0$ corresponds to the year 1990.

a. Use your grapher to sketch a graph of the function.

b. Use the graph to estimate the year in which there will be 40 million cell phone subscribers.

$t = 5.6$ Sometime in 1995.

c. Use the quadratic formula to answer part b. How does your answer compare to the estimate you obtained using a graphical approach?

The answers are the same.

d. How confident are you in your prediction? Explain.

We are only extrapolating a little, so I am fairly confident.

16. The quadratic function defined by the equation

$$d = 2r^2 - 16r + 34$$

gives the density d of smoke in millions of particles per cubic foot for a certain type of diesel engine. The input variable r represents the speed of the engine in hundreds of revolutions per minute.

a. Determine the density of smoke when $r = 3.5$ (350 revolutions per minute).

$d = 2.5$ million particles per cu ft

b. Determine the number of revolutions per minute for minimum smoke. What is the minimum output?

The minimum occurs at the vertex. $r = \frac{-b}{2a} = \frac{16}{4} = 4$

$d(4) = 2(4)^2 - 16(4) + 34 = 2$ million particles per ft^3

c. Suppose the density of smoke is determined to be 100 million particles per cubic foot. Determine the speed of the engine.

$2r^2 - 16r + 34 = 100$

$r^2 - 8r - 33 = 0$

$(r - 11)(r + 3) = 0$

$r = 11$ (1100 rpm)

Complex Numbers

Topic: *Introduction to Complex Numbers*

Recall that the solutions to $ax^2 + bx + c = 0$ correspond to the x-intercepts of the parabola $y = ax^2 + bx + c$.

Do all parabolas possess x-intercepts? Consider the graph of $y = 2x^2 + x + 5$. DERIVE is a computer algebra system with which you may be familiar. The accompanying DERIVE screen indicates that the parabola defined by this quadratic possesses no x-intercepts.

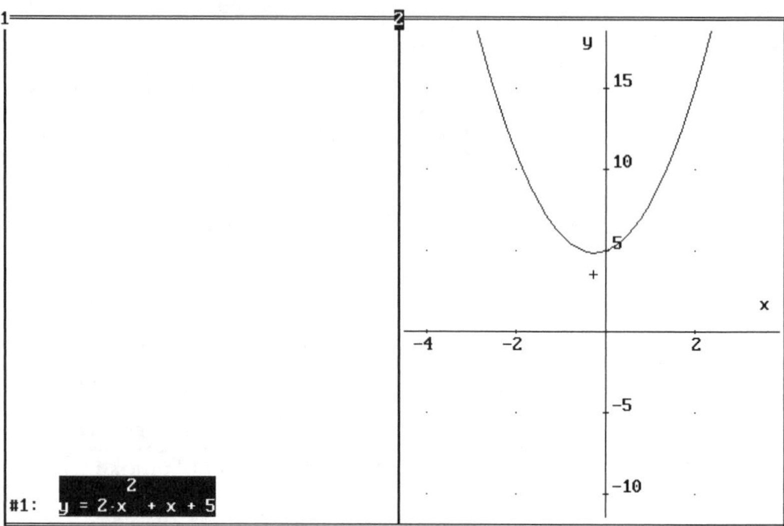

1. What can you say about the solutions to $2x^2 + x + 5 = 0$?

There are no real-number solutions.

If you ask the DERIVE program installed in the TI-92 graphing calculator to solve this equation, the following screen will appear.

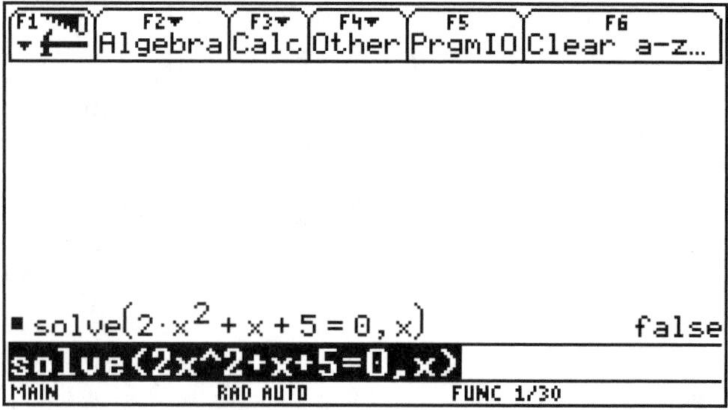

This is consistent with the graph. Because there are no x-intercepts for the graph of $y = 2x^2 + x + 5$, there are no real-valued solutions to the equation $2x^2 + x + 5 = 0$. One question at this point could be: Would you have discovered this if you had tried to solve the equation $2x^2 + x + 5 = 0$ algebraically using the quadratic formula?

2. Use the quadratic formula to solve $2x^2 + x + 5 = 0$. Where does the solution process break down? Explain.

   $b^2 - 4ac = 1 - 4(2)(5) = -39$ leads to a negative radicand.

Now return to the TI-92 and look at cSolve $(2x^2 + x + 5 = 0, x)$ rather than Solve $(2x^2 + x + 5 = 0, x)$.

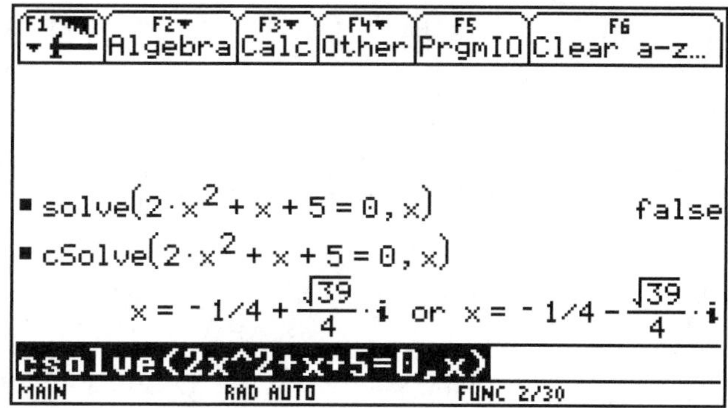

DERIVE gives you two solutions this time:

$$x = \frac{-1}{4} + \frac{\sqrt{39}}{4}i \text{ and } x = \frac{-1}{4} - \frac{\sqrt{39}}{4}i.$$

These are not **real numbers.** They are known as **complex numbers** (an extension of the real numbers). The distinguishing characteristic of the complex numbers is the **imaginary unit,** $i = \sqrt{-1}$.

The quadratic formula solution to $2x^2 + x + 5 = 0$ uses $a = 2, b = 1$, and $c = 5$. The solution is

$$x = \frac{-1 \pm \sqrt{1^2 - 4(2)(5)}}{2(2)} = \frac{-1 \pm \sqrt{1 - 40}}{4} = \frac{-1}{4} \pm \frac{\sqrt{-39}}{4}.$$

Note that the graph of $y = 2x^2 + x + 5 = 0$ has an axis of symmetry $x = -\frac{1}{4}$. The problem is that you cannot evaluate $\sqrt{-39}$ in the real-number system because any real number multiplied by itself is non-negative. Therefore, you introduce the imaginary unit, $i = \sqrt{-1}$, and interpret $\sqrt{-39}$ as

$$\sqrt{39(-1)} = \sqrt{39}\sqrt{-1} = \sqrt{39}i.$$

With this interpretation, the cSolve solution of the TI-92 now makes sense because you are solving the equation in the complex-number system.

3. Rewrite the following using the imaginary unit i.

   a. $\sqrt{-26}$

   $\sqrt{26}i$

   b. $\sqrt{-5}$

   $\sqrt{5}i$

   c. $\sqrt{-64}$

   $8i$

   d. $\sqrt{3 \cdot (-7)}$

   $\sqrt{21}i$

   e. $\sqrt{-18}$

   $3i\sqrt{2}$

   f. $\sqrt{-27}$

   $3i\sqrt{3}$

g. $\sqrt{-\frac{3}{4}}$

$\frac{\sqrt{3}}{2}i$

h. $\sqrt{\frac{-15}{27}}$

$\frac{\sqrt{5}}{3}i$

> Numbers of the form bi, where b is a real number and $i = \sqrt{-1}$, are called *pure imaginary numbers.* Numbers of the form $a \pm bi$, where a and b are real and $i = \sqrt{-1}$, are called *complex numbers.*

In the complex-number system, the quadratic equation $ax^2 + bx + c = 0$ has exactly two solutions. In the quadratic formula

$$x = \frac{-b \pm \sqrt{b^2 - 4ac}}{2a},$$

the expression $b^2 - 4ac$ is called the **discriminant** because its value determines the number and type of solutions of a quadratic equation $ax^2 + bx + c = 0$. There are three possible cases, depending on whether the value of the discriminant is positive, zero, or negative.

4. For each of the following quadratic functions, determine the sign of the discriminant and then sketch a graph using your grapher.

a. $y = 2x^2 - 7x - 4$

$a =$ 2

$b =$ −7

$c =$ −4

$b^2 - 4ac =$ 81

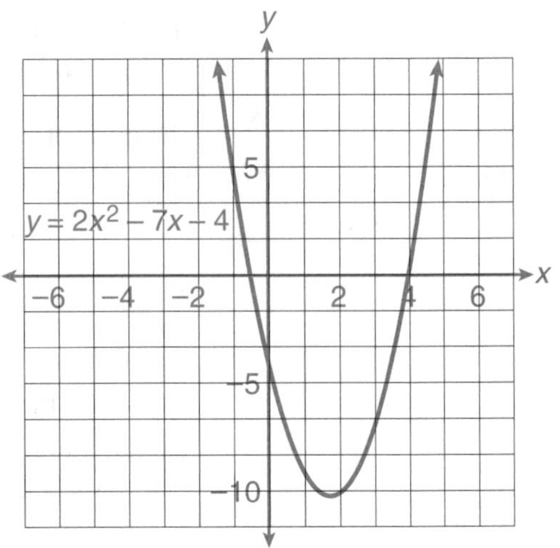

b. $y = 3x^2 + x + 1$

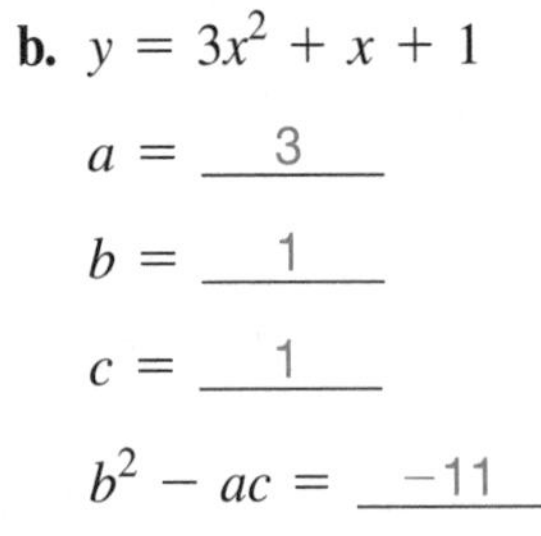

$a =$ 3

$b =$ 1

$c =$ 1

$b^2 - ac =$ −11

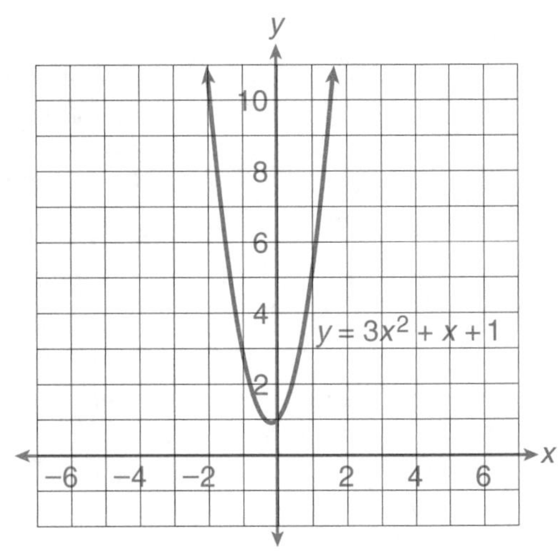

c. $y = x^2 + 2x + 1$

$a =$ 1

$b =$ 2

$c =$ 1

$b^2 - 4ac =$ 0

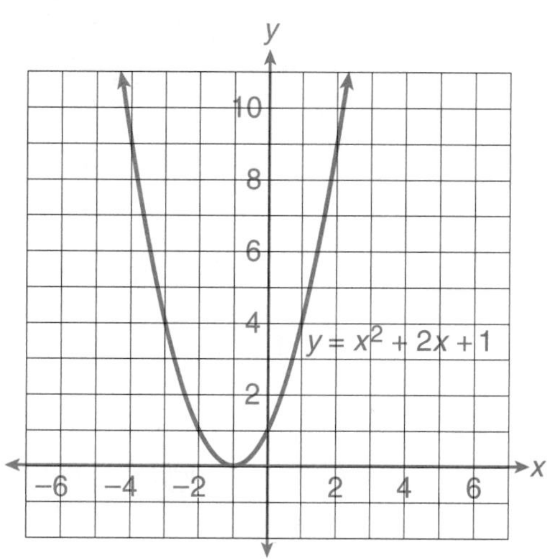

5. Recall that the real solutions to the equation $ax^2 + bx + c = 0$ and the x-intercepts of the graph of $y = ax^2 + bx + c$ are the same. Using the information from Problem 4, complete the following table.

SOLUTIONS TO $ax^2 + bx + c = 0$

$b^2 - 4ac$	NUMBER AND TYPE OF SOLUTIONS
Positive	2 distinct real solutions
Zero	1 repeated real solution
Negative	2 complex conjugate solutions

6. Determine the solutions to each of the following equations to verify your results in Problem 5.

a. $2x^2 - 7x - 4 = 0$

$x = 4, -1/2$

b. $3x^2 + x + 1 = 0$

$x = \frac{-1}{6} \pm \frac{\sqrt{11}}{6}i$

c. $x^2 + 2x + 1 = 0$

$x = -1, -1$

d. $3x^2 + 2x = -1$

$x = \frac{-1}{3} \pm \frac{\sqrt{2}}{3}i$

EXERCISES

Write each of the following using the imaginary unit i.

1. $\sqrt{-25}$

$5i$

2. $\sqrt{-20}$

$2i\sqrt{5}$

3. $\sqrt{-36}$

$6i$

4. $\sqrt{-10}$

$\sqrt{10}i$

Exercise numbers appearing in color are answered in the Selected Answers section of this book.

5. $\sqrt{-48}$

$4i\sqrt{3}$

6. $\sqrt{-80}$

$4i\sqrt{5}$

7. $\sqrt{-\frac{9}{16}}$

$\frac{3}{4}i$

8. $\sqrt{\frac{-20}{75}}$

$\sqrt{\frac{20}{75}}i = \sqrt{\frac{4}{15}}i = \frac{2}{\sqrt{15}}i$

Solve the following quadratic equations in the complex-number system using the quadratic formula.

9. $3x^2 - 2x + 7 = 0$

$x = \frac{1}{3} \pm \frac{\sqrt{80}}{6}i$

10. $x^2 + x = 3$

$x = \frac{-1 \pm \sqrt{13}}{2}$

11. $2x^2 + 5x = 7$

$x = 1, -3.5$

12. $0.5x^2 - x + 3 = 0$

$x = 1 \pm \sqrt{5}i$

Determine the type of solutions for each of the following equations by examining the discriminant.

13. $2x^2 + 3x - 5 = 0$

$b^2 - 4ac = 49$

2 distinct real solutions

14. $6x^2 + 7x - 5 = 0$

$b^2 - 4ac = 169$

2 distinct real solutions

15. $4x^2 - 4x + 1 = 0$

$b^2 - 4ac = 0$

1 repeated real solution

16. $9x^2 + 6x + 1 = 0$

$b^2 - 4ac = 0$

1 repeated real solution

17. $12x^2 = 4x - 3$

$12x^2 - 4x + 3 = 0$

$b^2 - 4ac = -128$

2 distinct complex solutions

18. $3x^2 = 5x + 7$

$3x^2 - 5x - 7 = 0$

$b^2 - 4ac = 109$

2 distinct real solutions

ACTIVITY 4.7

Airfare

Topics: *Building a Quadratic Model as a Product of Linear Models, Analyzing a Model Contextually*

You are an assistant to the president of a small commuter airline. You have been asked to develop a strategy for increasing the revenue from your primary route. The current fare for this route is \$160 per person, and each flight averages 40 passengers.

1. What is the average revenue from each flight?

$40(160) = 6400$

A recent marketing analysis suggests that each \$2 increase in fare will result in one less passenger per flight and that each \$2 reduction in fare will produce one additional passenger per flight. Your job is to use this information to set an airfare that maximizes the revenue from these flights.

You might first decide to adjust the fare up or down by \$2 increments and then determine the projected revenues. Do this by completing the accompanying table, where each positive value in the first column represents the number of upward fare adjustments and each negative value represents the number of downward fare adjustments (In other words, $n = -3$ means you have decreased the fare by \$6; $n = 2$ means you have increased the fare by \$4.)

NUMBER AND DIRECTION OF AIRFARE ADJUSTMENTS	AIRFARE (\$)	NUMBER OF PASSENGERS	ANTICIPATED REVENUE (\$)
−3	154	43	6622
−2	156	42	6552
−1	158	41	6478
0	160	40	6400
1	162	39	6318
2	164	38	6232
3	166	37	6142

2. a. Determine a rule for the airfare F as a function of x, where x represents the number and direction of the \$2 fare adjustments.

$F(x) = 160 + 2x$

b. Determine the value of $F(4)$. What is its practical meaning?

$F(4) = 168$ The airfare after 4 upward adjustments.

c. Determine the value of $F(-5)$. What is its practical meaning?

$F(-5) = 150$ The airfare after 5 downward adjustments.

3. a. Determine a rule for the average number of passengers P as a function of x.

$P(x) = 40 - x$

b. Determine the value of $P(4)$. What is its practical meaning?

$P(4) = 36$, the number of passengers after 4 upward adjustments.

c. Determine the value of $P(-5)$. What is its practical meaning?

$P(-5) = 45$, the number of passengers after 5 downward adjustments.

4. a. The revenue for the flight is the product of the airfare and the number of passengers. Determine a rule that represents the revenue R as a function of x.

$R(x) = (160 + 2x)(40 - x)$

b. Determine the value of $R(2)$. What is its practical meaning?

$R(2) = (164)(38) = 6232$, the revenue after 2 upward adjustments.

c. What is the largest value of x for which the revenue function has practical meaning?

$x = 40$. For values greater than 40, there are a negative number of passengers.

d. What is the smallest value of x for which the revenue function has practical meaning?

$x = -80$. For values less than -80, the airline will be paying passengers to ride the plane.

5. Use your algebraic model for the revenue function to answer the following.

a. What type of function describes the revenue?

$R(x) = -2x^2 - 80x + 6400$, is a quadratic function.

b. What is its vertical intercept? What does the intercept signify in terms of the flight revenue?

(0, 6400) This is the revenue with no airfare adjustments.

c. Where is the vertex of this function located? What is the significance of each coordinate of the vertex in terms of the flight revenue?

Vertex: $(-20, 7200)$ 20 downward adjustments will produce the maximum revenue.

d. What are the x-intercepts and how are they significant in terms of the revenue?

(40, 0) and $(-80, 0)$ The revenue will be zero.

6. Set the window of your grapher so that you can see all the features of the revenue function that you examined algebraically in Problems 4 and 5. Graphically confirm your results from Problem 5.

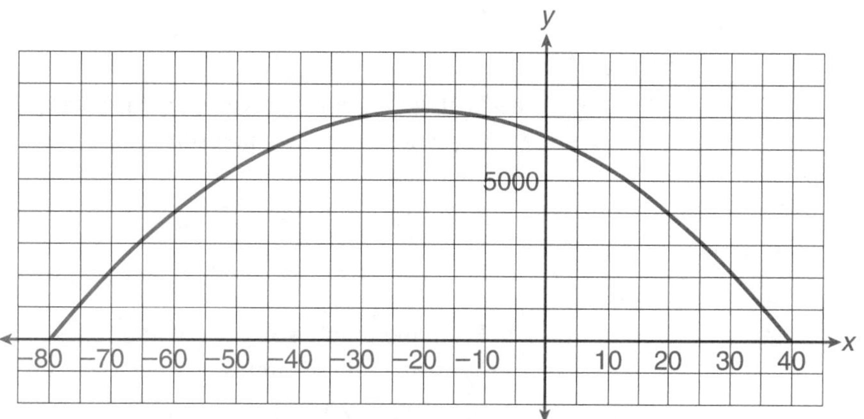

7. Using your graph, what airfares will result in revenue greater than $700?

Approximately $-77 < x < 37$ or airfares between 6 and 234 dollars

8. Summarize the strategy that you will recommend to your boss for maximizing the revenue from this flight.

Initially fare reductions will increase revenues, until the peak revenue occurs at $120. Any further reduction in fare will decrease the revenue.

EXERCISES

On your job as assistant to the foreman at a construction site, you have been asked to build an enclosure to store valuable materials and equipment. You have a single 500-foot roll of 10-foot-high heavy chain-link fencing. Your boss would like as much storage area as possible. Your job is to figure out the location of the corner posts for this enclosure.

1. a. Assuming that the enclosure will be rectangular and that you will use all of the fencing, make a table showing the dimensions (width and length) of some possible enclosures, with the resulting areas.

WIDTH	25	50	75	100	125	150	175	200	225
LENGTH	225	200	175	150	125	100	75	50	25
AREA	5625	10,000	13,125	15,000	15,625	15,000	13,125	10,000	5625

b. From your table, what would you choose for your dimensions to maximize the area?

125 feet by 125 feet

c. Letting w represent the width, express the length as a function of w. What expression using w will represent the area? Letting $f(w)$ equal this expression, you have found the area as a function of width.

$l = 250 - w$, $A = f(w) = w \cdot (250 - w)$

d. With your grapher, investigate the area function and determine the maximum possible area of the enclosure. What are the dimensions that yield this largest enclosure?

$w = 125$, $f(125) = 15{,}625$

e. From the graph, solve $f(w) = 0$. These are the w-intercepts of your graph. Why must these values be rejected in this situation?

$w \cdot (250 - w) = 0$ $w = 0$, or $w = 250$. There can be no rectangle constructed with these dimensions.

f. What are the practical domain and range for this function?

Domain: $0 < w < 250$, Range: $0 < A \leq 15{,}625$

2. What other practical things could you do that would alter your answer in Exercise 1d? In other words, would it be possible to get a larger area with this same fencing? Try some other possibilities, such as a triangle or circle, and try to determine which shape would produce the greatest area.

A circle with circumference 500 ft will enclose an area of approximately 19,894 ft^2.

3. The space used for an editorial in a college newspaper is in the shape of a rectangle. The height of the rectangle is 2 inches more than three times the base. If the area of the rectangle is 56 square inches, find its dimensions.

x = length of the base

$3x + 2$ = height

$x(3x + 2) = 56$

$3x^2 + 2x - 56 = 0$

$x = 4$ or $x = -4.7$

Reject the negative

length = 4 inches

height = 14 inches

4. A boat leaves Virginia Beach and sails due east for 1 hour and then due north for 2 hours. The boat is then at a location 10 miles from its departure point. If the average rate sailing east was 2 mph faster than the average rate sailing north, determine the rate of speed in each direction.

r = rate sailing north

$r + 2$ = rate sailing east

$(r + 2)^2 + (2r)^2 = 10^2$

$5r^2 + 4r + 4 = 100$

$5r^2 + 4r - 96 = 0$

$r = 4$ or -4.8 (reject)

4 mph north

6 mph east

PROJECT ACTIVITY 4.8

Chemical-Waste Holding Region

Topic: *Problem Solving Using Quadratic Functions*

Your architecture firm is designing a rectangular chemical-waste holding region for a local chemical manufacturing company. The holding area is to be located on a rectangular lot that is 200 meters wide and 80 meters long. Federal regulations require that the holding region be 10,000 square meters in area. A safety zone of uniform width around the perimeter of the holding area is also required.

Can these federal regulations be met if the chemical-waste holding region is constructed on the available rectangular lot? If so, what would be the width of the safety zone?

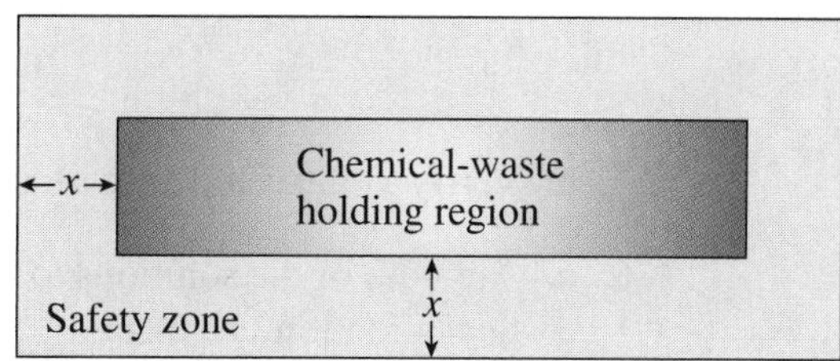

1. Let x represent the width of the safety zone. Do you know the dimensions of the rectangular lot? What do you know about the dimensions of the rectangular holding region?

   Entire lot is 200 m wide and 80 m long. Holding region would be $200 - 2x$ meters wide, $80 - 2x$ meters long.

2. **a.** Since the width of the lot is 200 meters, what is the width of the holding region in terms of x?

   $200 - 2x$

   b. Write an expression for the length of the holding region in terms of x.

   $80 - 2x$

3. What is the practical domain of the variable x in this situation? That is, what are the smallest and largest values of x for which the problem makes sense?

   $0 < x < 40$

4. The width and length of the waste holding region are both expressed in terms of x. Therefore, the area A of the holding region is a function of x. Using the results from Problem 2, write a symbolic rule for A as a function of x.

   $A(x) = (200 - 2x)(80 - 2x)$

5. In this situation, the area of the holding region is required to be 10,000 square meters.

a. Write an equation to determine the value of x that gives an output of 10,000. Solve the resulting equation using the quadratic formula. Approximate your solutions to the nearest hundredth.

$$(200 - 2x)(80 - 2x) = 10{,}000$$
$$4x^2 - 560x + 16{,}000 = 10{,}000$$
$$4x^2 - 560x + 6000 = 0$$
$$x^2 - 140x + 1500 = 0$$

$$x = \frac{140 \pm \sqrt{140^2 - 4(1)(1500)}}{2}$$
$$= \frac{140 \pm \sqrt{13{,}600}}{2} = 11.69,\ 128.31$$

b. Verify your results in part a graphically.

6. a. Are both of the solutions to the equation in Problem 5 solutions to the practical situation? Explain.

Only the smaller value, 11.69 meters, lies within the practical domain.

b. What are the dimensions of the chemical-waste holding region?

Width = 176.62 meters   length = 56.62 meters

c. What is the width of the safety zone?

11.69 meters

7. If federal regulations require a safety zone of width 15 meters around the perimeter of the holding region, can the holding region be built on the given rectangular lot? Explain.

The holding area would have an area of only 8500 m^2. It would be too small.

8. Consider the holding region area function developed in Problem 4.

a. What are the horizontal intercepts of the graph of this function? What practical meaning do these intercepts have in this situation?

(40, 0) (100, 0) They have no practical meaning. They lie outside the practical domain.

b. What is the vertex of the graph (a parabola) of the area function? Does the vertex have any significance in this situation?

Vertex (70, −3600) No practical meaning here.

What Have I Learned?

1. There are a variety of methods to solve quadratic equations. Make a list of the approaches that were presented in this cluster. In your own words, briefly describe each approach.

Factoring, quadratic formula, numerical table, intersection of graphs, x-intercepts of graphs.

2. a. Describe the relationship between the x-intercepts (if they exist) of the graph of $y = ax^2 + bx + c$ and the solutions to the equation $ax^2 + bx + c = 0$.

The solutions (real-valued) of $ax^2 + bx + c = 0$ are precisely the x-coordinates of the x-intercepts of the associated graphs.

b. Describe the relationship between the x-intercepts (if they exist) of the graph of $y = ax^2 + bx + c$ and the discriminant $b^2 - 4ac$.

If the x-intercepts exist, you can calculate $\sqrt{\text{discriminant}}$ and divide this value by 2a. This number represents the number of units on either side of the axis of symmetry that must be moved to locate the x-intercepts.

3. Review the steps in the following solution. Is the solution correct? Explain why or why not.

$$x^2 - 3x - 4 = 6$$
$$(x - 4)(x + 1) = 6$$
$$x - 4 = 6 \quad\Big|\quad x + 1 = 6$$
$$x = 10 \quad\Big|\quad x = 5$$

The conclusion is not correct. There is no 6-product rule, only a zero product rule.

4. Solve the following graphically using the graph of $y = 4x^2 - 8x + 7$.

a. $4x^2 - 8x + 7 = 0$

No solutions.

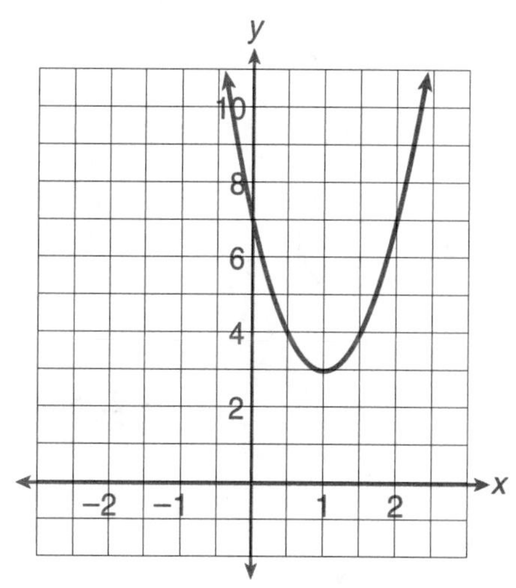

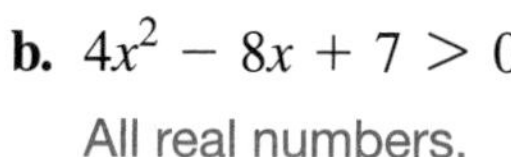

b. $4x^2 - 8x + 7 > 0$

All real numbers.

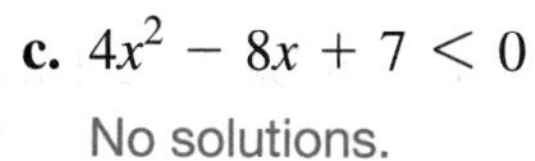

c. $4x^2 - 8x + 7 < 0$

No solutions.

5. Consider the quadratic equation $ax^2 + bx + c = 0$. If the quadratic expression $ax^2 + bx + c$ is factorable, what can you say about the sign of the discriminant, $b^2 - 4ac$?

$b^2 - 4ac$ must be non-negative.

6. For what values of c are the solutions to $2x^2 - 5x + c = 0$ imaginary?

The discriminant would be negative. $b^2 - 4ac = 25 - 8c < 0$; $c > \frac{25}{8}$

7. For what values of k does $x^2 - kx + k = 0$ have only one solution? (*Hint:* Examine the discriminant.)

The discriminant must be zero.

$$b^2 - 4ac = k^2 - 4k = 0$$
$$k(k - 4) = 0$$
$$k = 0, 4$$

How Can I Practice?

1. Solve each of the following quadratic equations numerically. That is, construct a table of (x, y) ordered pairs and estimate the value of x (input) that results in the required y-value (output).

a. $5x^2 = 7$ **b.** $x^2 - 7x + 10 = 5$ **c.** $3x^2 - 5x = 2$

a.

$x \approx 1.2$

$y = 5x^2$

x	1	1.1	1.2	1.3	1.4	1.5
y	5	6.05	7.2	8.45	9.8	11.25

b.

$x \approx 0.8$

$y = x^2 - 7x + 10$

x	0.5	0.6	0.7	0.8	0.9	1
y	6.75	6.16	5.59	5.04	4.51	4

c.

$x = 2$

$y = 3x^2 - 5x$

x	2					
y	2					

2. Solve each of the equations in Exercise 1 using a graphing approach. When necessary, round your solutions to the nearest tenth.

a. $x = 1.2, -1.2$

b. $x = 0.8, 6.2$

c. $x = -1/3, 2$

3. Solve the following inequalities using a graphing approach.

a. $x^2 + 6x - 16 < 0$

$-8 < x < 2$

b. $x^2 + 6x - 16 > 0$

$x < -8$ or $x > 2$

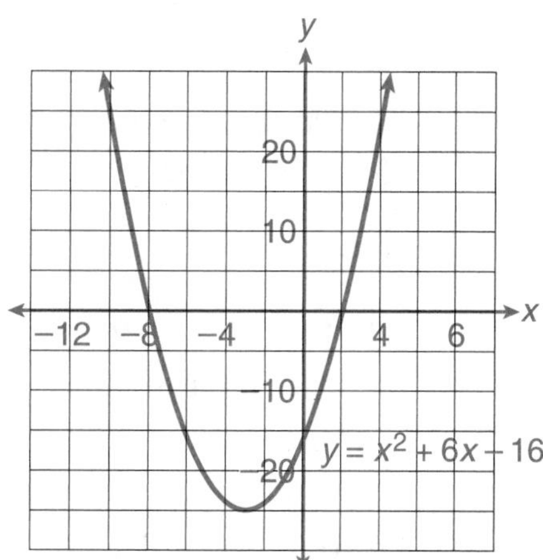

4. Solve each of the following equations by factoring.

a. $4x^2 - 8x = 0$

$4x(x - 2) = 0$

$x = 0, 2$

b. $x^2 - 6 = 7x + 12$

$x^2 - 7x - 18 = 0$

$(x - 9)(x + 2) = 0$

$x = 9, -2$

c. $2x(x - 4) = 6$

$2x^2 - 8x = -6$

$2x^2 - 8x + 6 = 0$

$x^2 - 4x + 3 = 0$

$(x - 3)(x - 1) = 0$

$x = 3, 1$

d. $x^2 - 8x + 16 = 0$

$(x - 4)(x - 4) = 0$

$x = 4, 4$

For Exercises 5–8, perform the following tasks.

- Identify the values of a, b, and c in $ax^2 + bx + c = 0$.
- Determine the type of solutions by examining the sign of the discriminant.
- Solve the given equation using the quadratic formula. If necessary, round your solutions to the nearest hundredth.
- Check your solutions by graphing as well as by substitution.

5. **a.** $3x^2 - x = 7$

$a = 3, b = -1, c = -7$

$b^2 - 4ac = 85$

two real solutions

$x = 1.70, -1.37$

b. $x^2 - 4x + 10 = 0$

$a = 1, b = -4, c = 10$

$b^2 - 4ac = -24$

two complex solutions

$x = 2 \pm \sqrt{6}i$

c. $2x^2 - 3x = 2x + 3$

$a = 2, b = -5, c = -3$

$b^2 - 4ac = 49$

two real solutions

$x = 3, -0.5$

d. $3x(3x - 2) + 1 = 0$

$a = 9, b = -6, c = 1$

$b^2 - 4ac = 0$

one real repeated solution

$x = 1/3$

6. A fastball is hit straight up over home plate. The ball's height h (in feet) from the ground is modeled by

$$h = -16t^2 + 80t + 5,$$

where t is measured in seconds.

a. What is the maximum height of the ball above the ground?

Vertex: $(2.5, h(2.5))$ or $(2.5, 105)$ 105 feet.

b. How long will it take for the ball to reach the ground?

Set $h = 0$; $t = 5.06$ seconds.

7. Safe automobile spacing (in feet) is modeled by

$$S(v) = \tfrac{1}{32}v^2 + v + 18,$$

where v is average velocity in feet per second, and $S(v)$ is the spacing (in feet).

a. Suppose a car is traveling at 44 feet per second. How far should it be from the car in front of it to be safe?

$s(44) = 122.5$ feet away.

b. If the car is following 50 feet behind a van, what is a safe speed for the car to be traveling? How fast is this in miles per hour? (Note that 60 mph $\approx$ 88 ft/sec.)

$\frac{1}{32}v^2 + v + 18 = 50$

$\frac{1}{32}v^2 + v - 32 = 0$

$v = -51.78$ or 19.78

Reject the negative

19.78 ft/sec 13.5 mph

CLUSTER 3

Curve Fitting and Higher-Order Polynomial Functions

ACTIVITY 4.9

The Population of Cleveland

Topic: *Curve Fitting*

The population of Cleveland, Ohio, from 1900 to 1980, according to the U.S. Census Bureau, is given by the following table.

YEAR	1900	1910	1920	1930	1940	1950	1960	1970	1980
POPULATION	381,768	560,663	796,841	900,429	878,336	914,808	876,050	750,879	573,822

1. Make a scatterplot of the data. Let t represent the number of years since 1900. Therefore, $t = 0$ corresponds to the year 1900. Do the data appear to be parabolic? Explain.

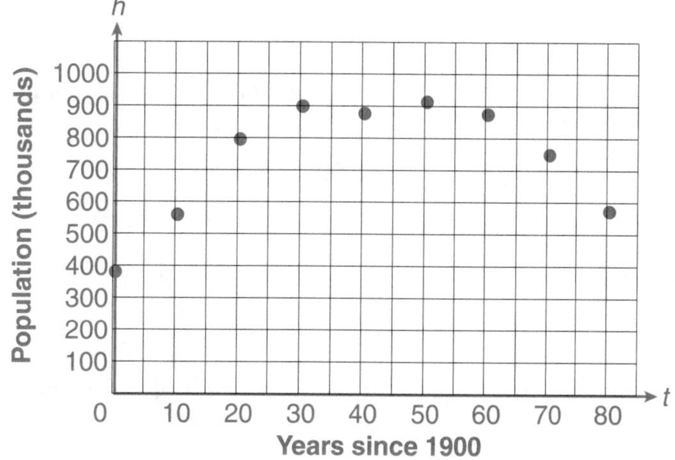

The data appear to be parabolic, forming an upside-down U-shaped curve.

2. Use the regression feature of your grapher to determine and plot a quadratic function that best fits these data. Your graph should appear as follows.

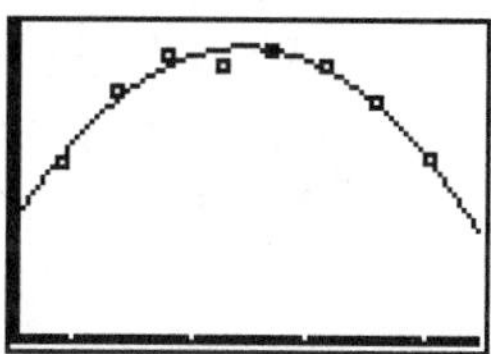

The quadratic function is $y = -280x^2 + 24{,}919x + 374{,}960$

3. How does the plot of this regression equation compare with your scatterplot of the data?

The regression plot looks like a parabola and fits the scatterplot.

4. What is the practical domain of this function?

$0 \le t \le 80$

5. Use the graph of the quadratic regression equation to estimate the population of Cleveland in 1955. In 1890. In 1990.

1955: About 900,000

1890: About 100,000

1990: About 350,000

Which of these estimates do you think is most reliable? Explain.

The estimate for "a" is the most reliable, since we have the real data before or after 1955. We have, for example, no actual data regarding the population before 1900.

6. Estimate the years in which the population of Cleveland was greater than or equal to 750,000 using each of the following methods.

a. The given table (numerical)

1915–1970

b. The graph of the regression equation (graphical)

1920–1970

7. Use the quadratic formula (algebraic) to estimate the year in which the population of Cleveland was equal to 750,000.

$$750{,}000 = -280x^2 + 24{,}919x + 374{,}960$$

$$0 = -280x^2 + 24{,}919x - 375{,}040$$

$$x = \frac{-b \pm \sqrt{b^2 - 4ac}}{2a} = 19.1869\ldots \approx 19$$

$$= 69.863\ldots \approx 70$$

So the population of Cleveland was at least 750,000 between 1919 and 1970 according to the regression equation.

8. Estimate graphically the years between 1900 and 1980 when the population of Cleveland was less than 500,000.

1900–1905

9. a. The population of Cleveland in 1996 was approximately 506,000. Does this agree with the prediction from the regression model?

No, the regression model predicts a population of only approximately 186,000.

b. Include the data for 1996 from part a in the original data set and then recalculate the regression equation.

The new regression equation is $y = -209x^2 + 20{,}077x + 417{,}902$

c. Predict the 1996 population from this new regression equation from part b. Are the results any better?

The new regression model predicts a 1996 population of approximately 193,000, still much lower than the actual value.

EXERCISES

1. Buffalo Bills punter Chris Mohr was called on to punt the ball eight times. On one of these punts, Mohr struck the ball at his own 30-yard line. The height h of the ball above the field in feet as a function of time t in seconds can be partially modeled by the following table.

t	0	0.6	1.2	1.8	2.4	3.0
h	2.50	28.56	43.10	46.12	37.12	17.60

a. Sketch a scatterplot of the data using your grapher.

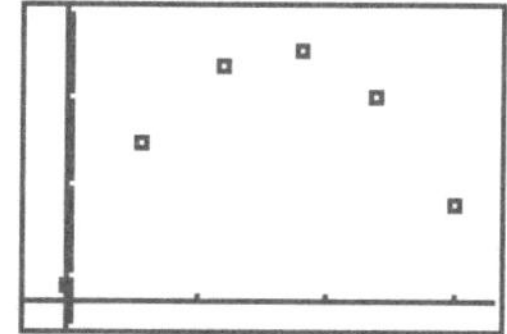

b. Use your grapher to obtain a quadratic regression equation for these data. Round the values of a, b, and c to four decimal places.

$y = -15.9752x^2 + 52.88875x + 2.5536$

c. Graph the equation from part b on the same coordinate axes as the data points. Does the curve appear to be a good fit for the data? Explain.

The curve is a great fit for the data, very close to all the points.

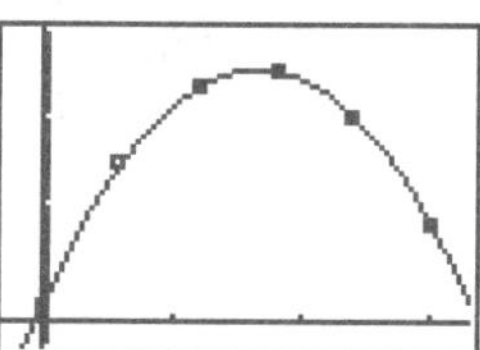

d. In this model, what is the practical domain for the regression function?

Time could be between 0 and approximately 3.3 seconds (when the ball hits the ground).

e. Estimate the practical range for this model.

The height of the ball above the field is between 0 and approximately 47 feet.

f. How long after the ball was struck did the ball reach 35 feet above the field? Explain.

You can trace the regression curve to find that the ball is 35 feet above the ground at approximately 0.8 seconds, on the way up.

g. How many results did you obtain for part f? Do you think you have all of the solutions? Explain.

The ball will also be at a height of 35 feet at about 2.5 seconds, on the way down (so, there are two solutions).

Exercise numbers appearing in color are answered in the Selected Answers section of this book.

2. Consider the following data set.

x	0	3	6	9	12
y	5	28	86	180	310

a. Determine an appropriate scale and plot these points.

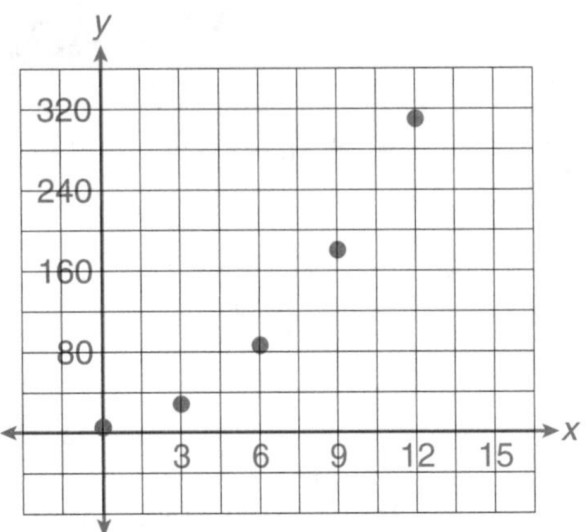

b. Use your grapher to determine the quadratic regression equation for this data set.

$y = 2x^2 + 1.6x + 5$

c. Graph the regression equation on the same coordinate axes as the data points in part a.

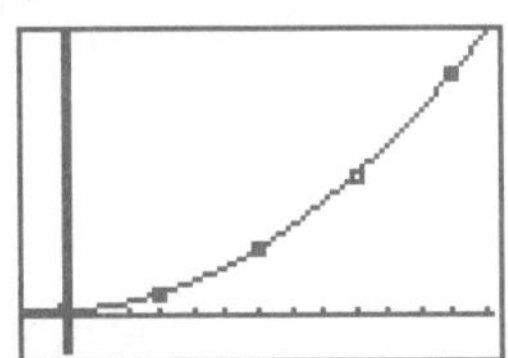

d. Use the regression equation to complete the following table.

x	0	3	6	9	12
y	5	27.8	86.6	181.4	312.2

e. How do the *y*-values resulting from the regression equation compare with the *y*-values of the data points (part a)?

The *y*-values are close.

f. Predict the output for $x = 15$.

479

3. The following table shows the stopping distance for a car at various speeds on dry pavement.

SPEED (mph)	25	35	45	55	65	75
DISTANCE (ft)	65	108	167	245	340	450

a. Use your grapher to determine a quadratic regression equation that represents these data.

$y = 0.086x^2 - 0.842x + 32.487$

b. Use this regression equation to predict the stopping distance at 90 mph.

Approximately 700 feet.

c. What speed would produce a stopping distance of 280 feet? (Round your answer to the nearest tenth.)

$280 = 0.086x^2 - 0.842x + 32.487$

$0 = 0.086x^2 - 0.842x - 247.513$

Using the quadratic formula, a speed of 58.87 mph would require a stopping distance of 280 feet.

ACTIVITY 4.10

The Power of Power Functions

Topics: *Power Functions, Combinations of Power Functions*

You are traveling in a hot-air balloon when suddenly a pair of binoculars drops from the edge of the basket. At that moment, the balloon is maintaining a constant height of 500 feet. The distance that the falling binoculars are from the edge of the basket is modeled by

$$s(t) = 16t^2.$$

The following table gives the distance s (in feet) from the drop point at various times t (in seconds).

t	0	1	2	3	4
s	0	16	64	144	256

As the input values (units of time) increase, the corresponding output values (units of distance) increase. Consider how this increase takes place.

Because $s(t) = 16t^2$, you can say that the output $s(t)$ varies directly as the square of the input t. Therefore, as t doubles in value from 1 to 2 or from 2 to 4, the corresponding output values become 4 times as large: 16 to 64 or 64 to 256.

1. a. As t triples from 1 to 3, the corresponding s-values become __9__ times as large.

   b. In general, if y varies directly as the square of x, then when x becomes n times as much, the corresponding y-values become __n^2__ times as large.

The volume V of a sphere is given by $V = \frac{4}{3}\pi r^3$. In this situation, you can say that the output V varies directly as the cube of the radius r.

2. a. Complete the following table. Leave your answers for V in terms of π.

r	1	2	3	4	8
V(r)	$\frac{4}{3}\pi$	$\frac{32}{3}\pi$	36π	$\frac{256}{3}\pi$	$\frac{2048}{3}\pi$

   Values for $V(r)$ are: $\frac{4}{3}\pi$, $\frac{32}{3}\pi$, 36π, $\frac{256}{3}\pi$, and $\frac{2048}{3}\pi$

   b. As r doubles from 2 to 4 or from 4 to 8, the corresponding V-values become __8__ times as large.

   c. In general, if y varies directly as the cube of x, then when x becomes n times as large, the corresponding y-values become __n^3__ times as large.

d. Sketch a graph of the volume function. What is the practical domain of this function?

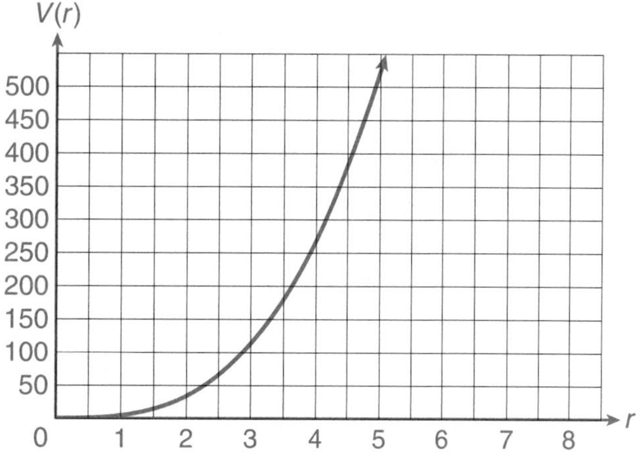

The value of r should be greater than 0 (a radius of 0 gives you a rather boring sphere).

CONSTANT OF VARIATION

The equation

$$y = kx^n,$$

where $k \neq 0$ and n is a positive integer, defines a direct variation function in which y varies directly as x^n. The constant k is called the **constant of variation** (or constant of proportionality).

3. a. What is the constant of variation k in the free-falling object situation defined by $s(t) = 16t^2$?

16

b. What is the constant of variation k for the direct variation function defined by $V = \frac{4}{3}\pi r^3$?

$\frac{4}{3}\pi$

4. For each table, determine the pattern and complete the table. Then write a direct variation equation for each table.

a. y varies directly as x.

$12 = 2k$, so $k = 6$.

x	1	2	4	8	12
y	6	12	24	48	72

b. y varies directly as x^3.

$32 = k2^3$, so $k = 4$.

x	1	2	3
y	4	32	108

c. y varies directly as x.

$3 = k3$, so $k = 1$.

x	1	2	3	4	5
y	1	2	3	4	5

5. The length l of skid marks left by a car varies directly as the square of the initial velocity v (in miles per hour) of the car.

a. Write a general equation for l as a function of v. Let k represent the constant of variation.

$l = kv^2$

b. Suppose a car traveling at 40 mph leaves skid marks of 60 feet. Use this information to determine the value of k.

$60 = k(40)^2$, $k = 0.035$

c. Use the function to determine the length of the skid marks left by a car traveling at 60 mph.

$l = 0.035(60)^2$, $l = 135$ feet

The direct variation functions having equations of the form $y = kx^n$, where n is a positive integer, are also called **power functions.** The graphs of this family of functions are very interesting and are useful in problem solving.

6. Use your grapher to graph each of the following power functions, and record your graph on the accompanying grid.

a. $y = x$

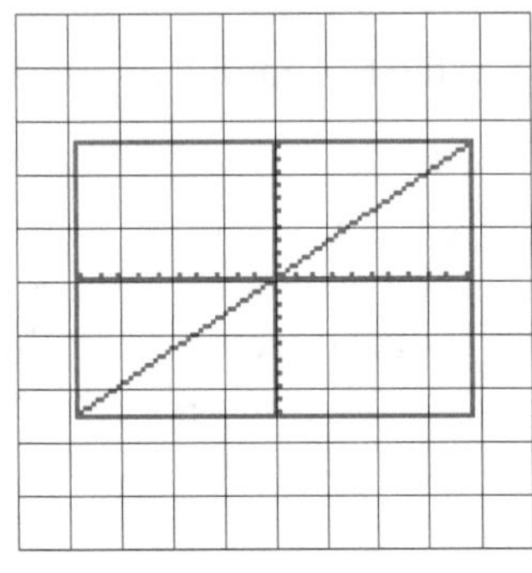

b. $y = x^2$

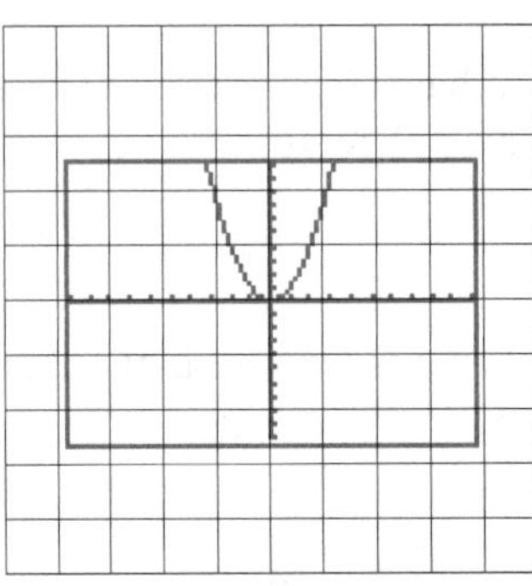

c. $y = x^3$

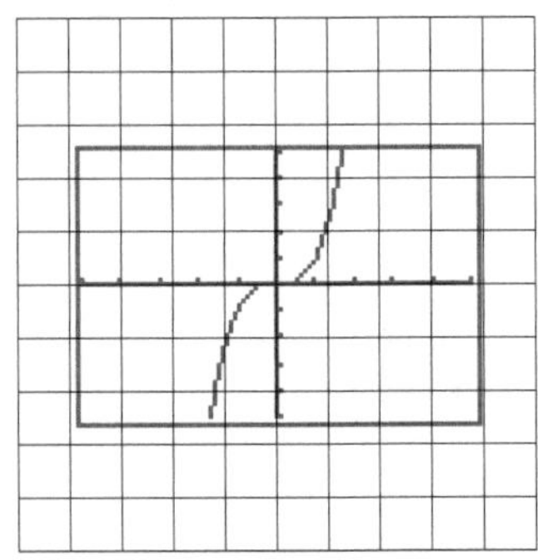

d. $y = x^4$

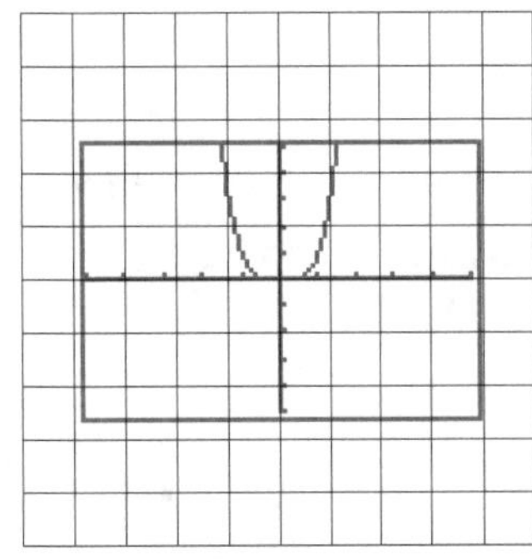

e. $y = x^5$

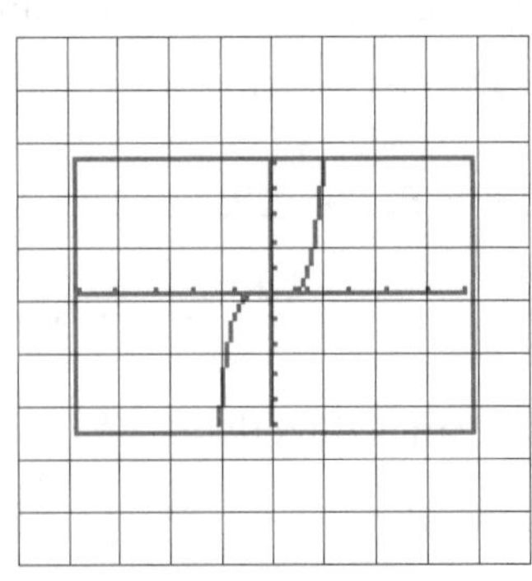

f. $y = x^6$

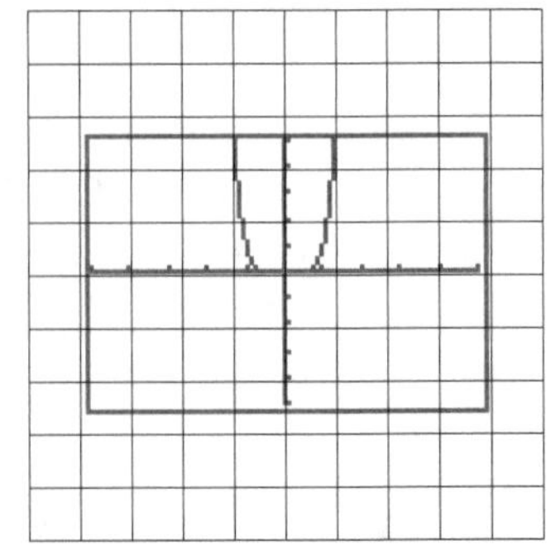

7. Carefully review the graphs in Problem 6. What patterns do you observe?

The graphs of $y = x^2$, $y = x^4$ and $y = x^6$ have similar shapes, like a U. The U shape becomes flatter at the bottom, with steeper sides, as the power increases. The graphs of $y = x$, $y = x^3$ and $y = x^5$ are all increasing. $y = x^3$ and $y = x^5$ have similar shapes, somewhat S like.

8. Use the patterns from Problem 7 in combination with graphing techniques you have learned previously to sketch a graph of each of the following without using a grapher.

a. $y = x^2 + 1$

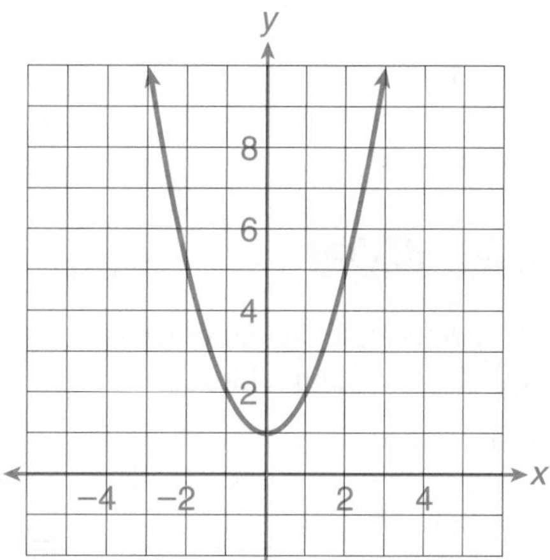

b. $y = -2x^4$

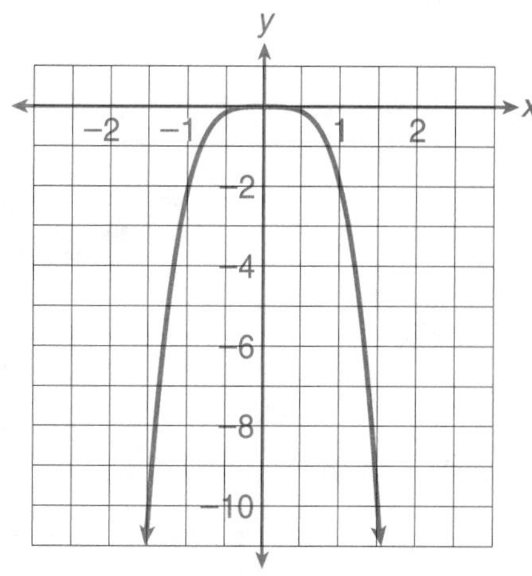

c. $y = 3x^8 + 1$

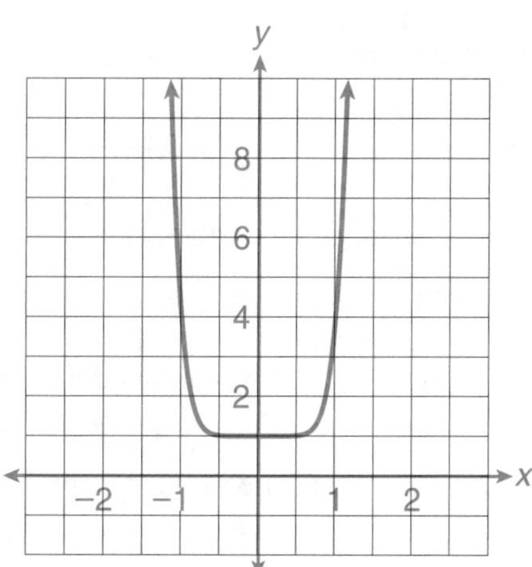

d. $y = -2x^5$

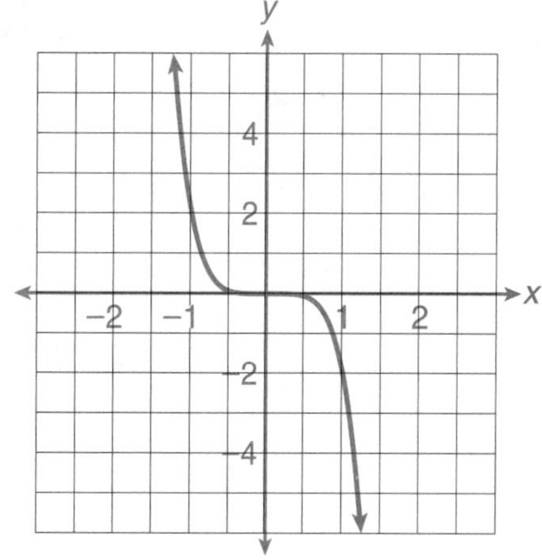

e. $y = x^{10}$

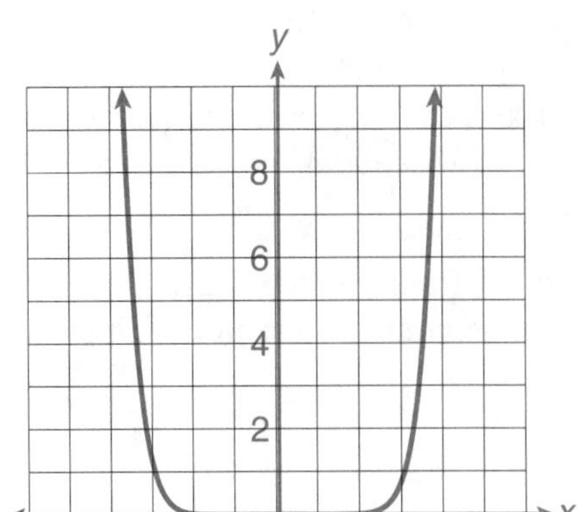

f. $y = 5x^3 + 2$

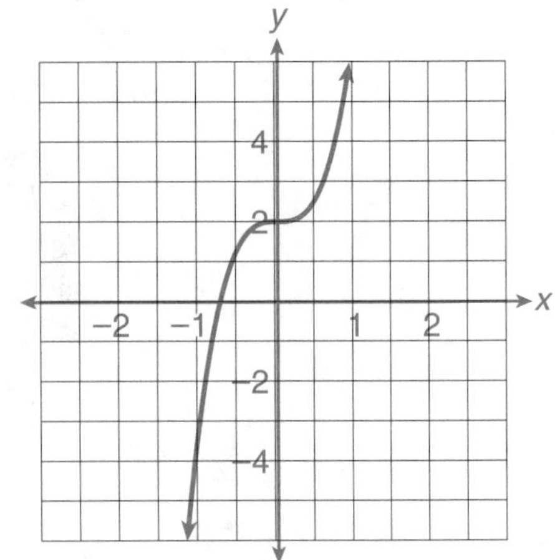

EXERCISES

1. For each table, determine the pattern and complete the table. Then write a direct variation equation for each table.

   a. y varies directly as x.

x	$\frac{1}{4}$	1	4	8
y	2	8	32	64

   $y = 8x$, $8 = k1$, so $k = 8$, or $y = 8x$

   b. y varies directly as x^3.

x	$\frac{1}{2}$	1	3	6
y	$\frac{1}{8}$	1	27	216

   $y = x^3$, $1 = k1^3$, so $k = 1$ or $y = x^3$

2. The area A of a circle is given by the function rule $A = \pi r^2$, where r is the radius of the circle.

   a. Does A vary directly as the radius? Explain.

   No, A varies directly as the square of the radius.

   b. What is the constant of variation k?

   $k = \pi$

3. Assume that y varies directly as the square of x, and when $x = 2$, $y = 12$. Determine y when $x = 8$.

   $12 = k2^2$, so $k = 3$. So $y = 3x^2$. When $x = 8$, $y = 3(8)^2 = 192$

Exercise numbers appearing in color are answered in the Selected Answers section of this book.

4. The distance d that you drive at a constant speed varies directly as the time t that you drive. If you can drive 150 miles in 3 hours, how far can you drive in 6 hours?

$d = kt$, $150 = k3$, so $k = 50$.

Now $d = 50t$, so in 6 hours you drive $d = 50(6) = 300$ miles.

5. The number of meters d that a skydiver falls before her parachute opens varies directly as the square of the time t that she is in the air. A skydiver falls 20 meters in 2 seconds. How far will she fall in 2.5 seconds?

$d = kt^2$, $20 = k(2)^2$, so $k = 5$.

Now $d = 5t^2$, so in 2.5 seconds you travel $d = 5(2.5)^2 = 31.25$ meters.

In Exercises 6–10, sketch a graph of the given power function. Verify using your grapher.

6. $y = -3x^2$

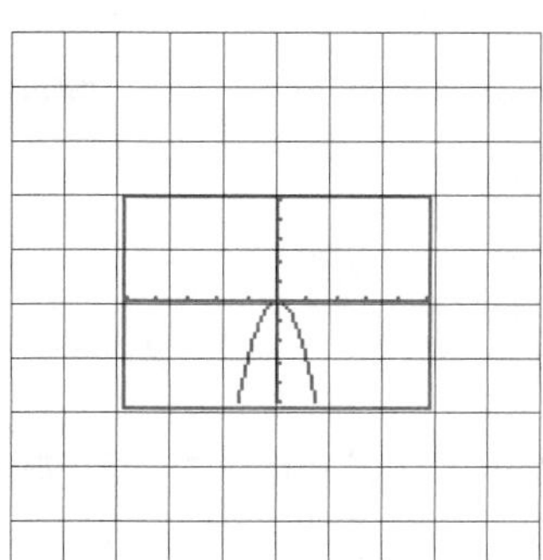

7. $y = x^4 + 1$

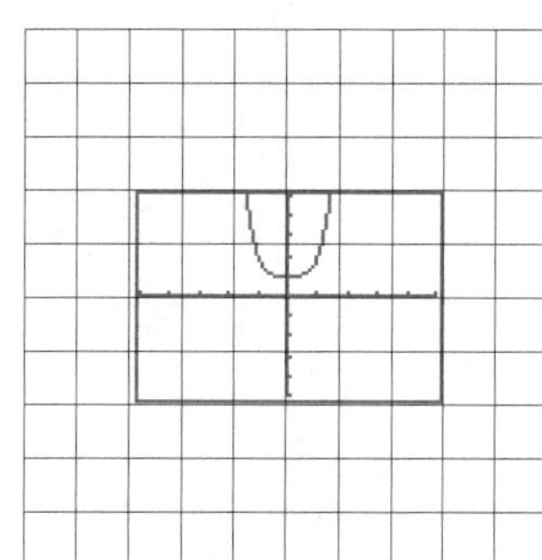

8. $y = -2x^5$

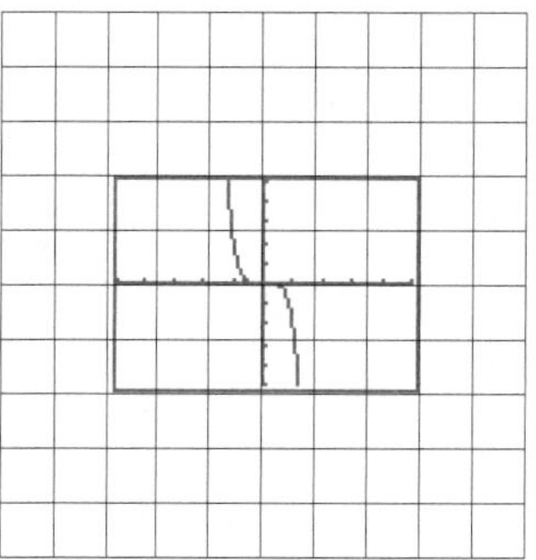

9. $f(x) = x^6$

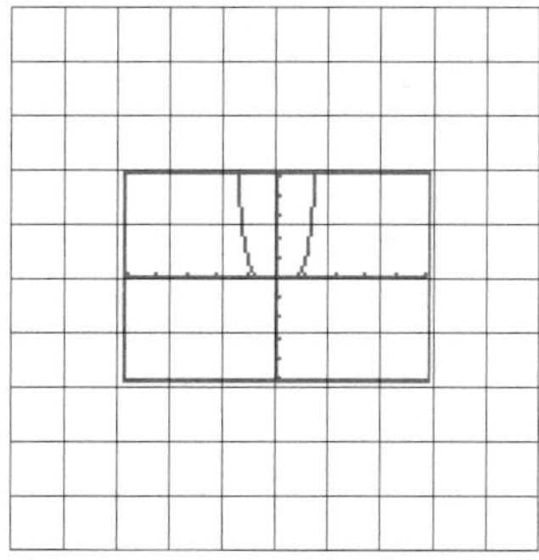

10. $g(x) = 3x^3 - 3$

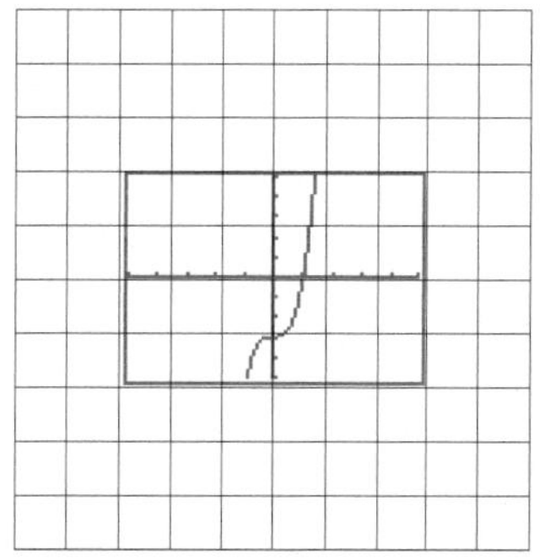

11. Determine the x-interval over which the function $f(x) = \frac{1}{2}x^4$ is increasing.

$f(x)$ is increasing for $x > 0$

12. Does the function $g(x) = -\frac{1}{2}x^6$ have a maximum or a minimum point? Explain.

$g(x)$ has a maximum point. The graph opens downward, with a upside down U shape, reaching the maximum at (0, 0).

13. For $x > 1$, is the graph of $y = x^2$ rising faster or slower than the graph of $y = x^3$? Explain.

$y = x^2$ is rising more slowly than $y = x^3$ for $x > 1$.

14. Is the graph of $y = \frac{3}{2}x^4$ wider or narrower than the graph of $y = x^4$?

Narrower

15. How are the graphs of $y = -2x^3$ and $y = 2x^3 + 1$ different? How are the graphs similar?

$y = -2x^3$ is decreasing and goes through (0, 0), while $y = 2x^3 + 1$ is increasing and does not pass through the origin. Both have a similar "S" like shape.

16. a. For $x > 0$, is the graph of $y = x^2$ rising faster or slower than the graph of $y = 2^x$? Explain.

The graphs are fairly close until $x > 4$, when $y = 2^x$ begins to grow much more quickly than $y = x^2$.

b. For $x > 0$, is the graph of $y = x^5$ rising faster or slower than the graph of $y = 2^x$? Explain.

The graph of $y = x^5$ is steeper than $y = 2^x$ until $x > 22$, when $y = 2^x$ begins to be steeper than $y = x^5$.

ACTIVITY 4.11

Hot-Air Balloons
Topic: *Polynomial Functions and Their Graphs*

Returning to the hot-air balloon situation, you are relieved because the binoculars you dropped did not strike anyone on the ground. As you continue your ride in the balloon, you enter into a conversation with the pilot concerning why the balloon rises. He says that because the hot air is lighter than the surrounding air, the balloon will rise if the upward lift (force) provided by the hot air is great enough to overcome the downward force on the balloon—its weight.

The upward force varies directly as the volume of the spherical balloon. Because $V = \frac{4}{3}\pi r^3$, the upward force varies directly as the cube of the radius.

1. Write a general symbolic rule that represents the upward force, denoted by U, as a function of the radius r of the sphere. Let k_1 represent the constant of variation.

$U = k_1 r^3$

The downward force is represented by the total weight of the balloon itself, the basket, and the heat generator. The weight of the basket and heat generator can be considered a constant, represented by C.

The weight of the balloon material is directly proportional to the surface area of the balloon when inflated. Because $S = 4\pi r^2$, the weight of the balloon varies directly as the square of the radius r.

2. a. Write a general symbolic rule that represents the weight of the balloon as a function of the radius r. Let k_2 represent the constant of variation.

$W = k_2 r^2$

b. The downward force, denoted by D, is the sum of the weight of the balloon material, denoted by w, and the weight of the basket and heat generator, denoted by C. Write a symbolic rule for D.

$D = W + C = k_2 r^2 + C$

The total force F acting on the balloon is given by

$$F = U - D.$$

Substituting your results from Problems 1 and 2b into this equation gives you

$$F = k_1 r^3 - (k_2 r^2 + C)$$

or

$$F = k_1 r^3 - k_2 r^2 - C.$$

This equation expresses the total force acting on the hot-air balloon as a function of r. Because the largest exponent on the input variable r is 3, this function is called a **third-degree polynomial function,** or a **cubic function.**

Polynomial functions are actually sums and differences of power functions. Other examples of polynomial functions are listed in the following table.

POLYNOMIAL FUNCTION	DEGREE OF THE POLYNOMIAL	NAME
$y = 3x - 2$	1	Linear
$y = 2x^2 + 3x - 4$	2	Quadratic
$y = 3x^2 - x - 4$	3	Cubic
$y = 0.2x^4 - 2x^2 + 7x - 1$	4	Quartic
$y = -2x^5 + 3x^4 + 2x - 6$	5	Quintic

Note that the cubic defined by $y = 3x^3 - x - 4$ can be written as $y = 3x^3 + 0x^2 - x - 4$.

3. Determine the horizontal intercepts of each of the following polynomial functions using an algebraic approach (factoring). Note that the zero product rule discussed in Activity 4.5, Sir Isaac Newton XIV, can be extended from $a \cdot b = 0$ to any finite number of factors $a \cdot b \cdot c \cdot \cdot \cdot f = 0$. Verify your results using a graphing approach.

   a. $2x^3 + 5x^2 = 12x$

   $x = 0, -4, \frac{3}{2}$

   b. $x^2(x^2 - 5) = -4$

   $x = -1, 1, -2, 2$

   c. $2x^5 - 18x^3 = 0$

   $x = 0, -3, 3$

4. Using your grapher, plot the following third-degree polynomials. Be careful of your choice of windows.

   a. $f(x) = x^3$

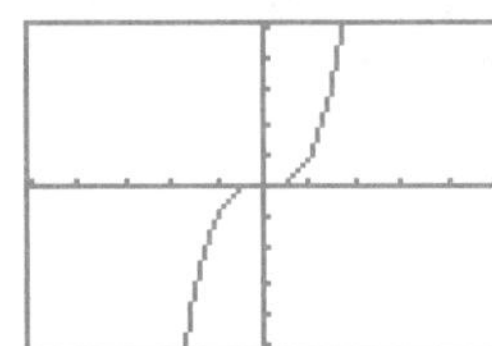

   b. $i(x) = 3x^3 - x - 4$

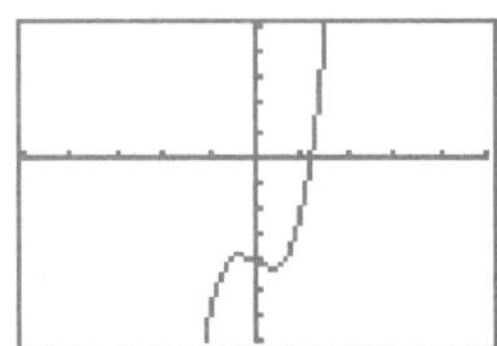

   c. $g(x) = 0.2x^3 - 2x + 7$

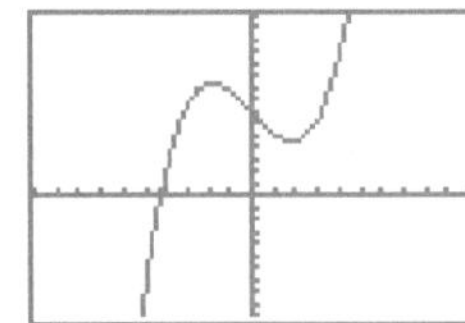

   d. $j(x) = -5x^3 + 1$

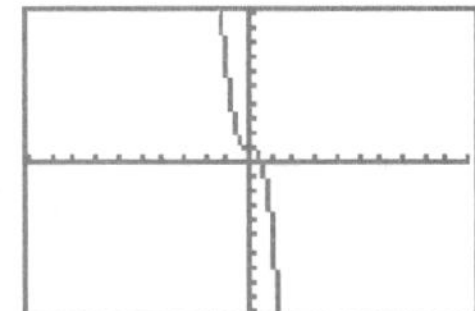

   e. $h(x) = -0.6x^3 + 2x^2 - 1$

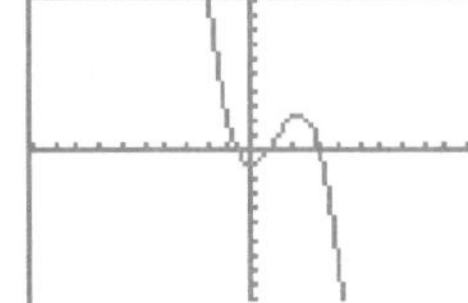

f. Use the graphs gathered in parts a through e to write a few sentences comparing and contrasting the graph of the general quadratic equation, $y = ax^2 + bx + c$, $a \neq 0$, and the general cubic equation, $y = ax^3 + bx^2 + cx + d, a \neq 0$. Include comments on turning points and general trends, such as increasing and decreasing intervals.

The graphs of cubics and quadratics, like those of all polynomial functions, are smooth curves. The graph of any quadratic has exactly one turning point, while the graph of a cubic may have zero or two turning points. A quadratic with $a > 0$ will decrease until it reaches its turning point, then it will increase (with $a < 0$, it will increase until the turning point, then decrease). A quadratic will always have a line of symmetry through the turning point. A quadratic will have a vertical intercept and either zero, one or two horizontal intercepts. A cubic may be increasing everywhere or decreasing everywhere with no turning points. However, when b and c are not both zero, the cubic will have two turning points. Any cubic with $a > 0$ will be increasing at the far right and far left of the graph. A cubic with $a < 0$ will decrease at the far right and far left. Cubics do not have any line of symmetry. Any cubic will have a vertical intercept and either one, two, or three horizontal intercepts.

5. Using your grapher, plot the following fourth-degree polynomials. Be careful of your choice of windows.

a. $f(x) = x^4$

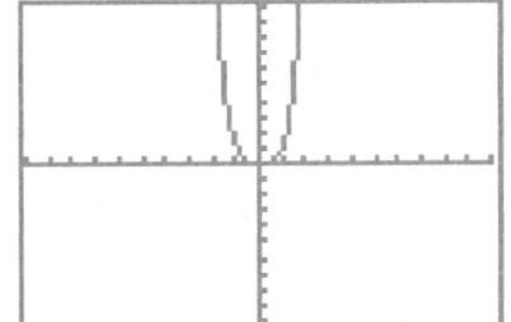

b. $i(x) = 3x^4 - x - 4$

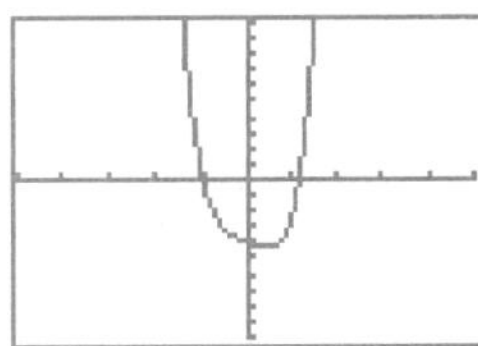

c. $g(x) = 0.2x^4 - 2x^2 + 7x - 1$

d. $j(x) = -5x^4 + 1$

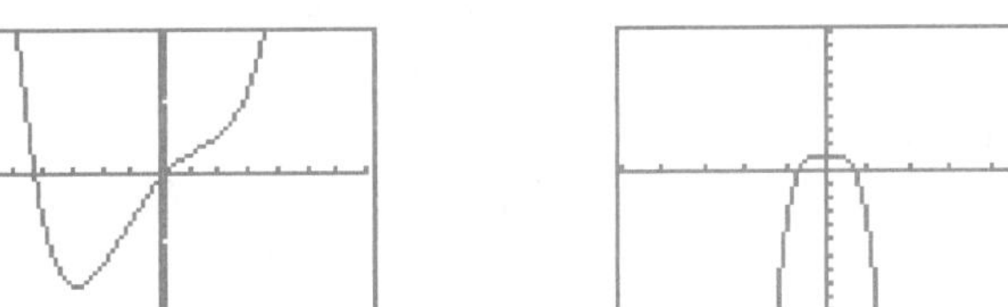

e. $h(x) = -0.6x^4 + 2x^3 - x + 1$

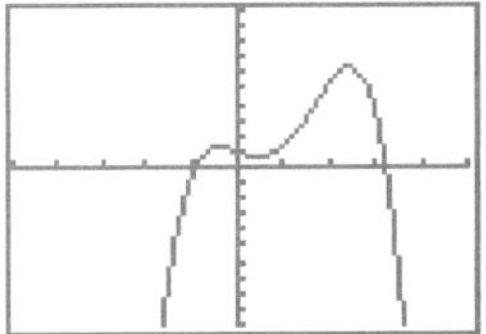

f. Use the graphs gathered in parts a through e to write a few sentences comparing and contrasting the graph of the general quadratic equation, $y = ax^2 + bx + c, a \neq 0$, and the general quartic equation, $y = ax^4 + bx^3 + cx^2 + dx + e, a \neq 0$. Include comments on turning points and general trends, such as increasing and decreasing intervals.

Quartics and quadratics are smooth-curved functions. The most basic quartic, $y = x^4$, and the most basic quadratic, $y = x^2$, are similar in their U shape, passing through the origin with symmetry on the y-axis. Any quartic will have a vertical intercept and from zero to four horizontal intercepts, while any quadratic will have a vertical intercept and from zero to two horizontal intercepts. A quadratic has exactly one turning point, but a quartic may have one or three turning points. For both quartics and quadratics, when $a > 0$, the graphs turn upwards on both ends. When $a < 0$, the graphs turn downward on the ends.

EXERCISES

In Exercises 1–3, determine the x-intercept(s) of the graph of each polynomial function using an algebraic approach (factoring). Verify your answer using your grapher.

1. $f(x) = x^3 + 3x^2 + 2x$

   $x = 0, -1, -2$

2. $g(x) = 2x^2(x^2 - 3)$

   $x = 0, \pm\sqrt{3}$

3. $h(x) = x^4 - 13x^2 + 36$

   $x = \pm 2, \pm 3$

4. Determine the vertical intercept of each of the functions in Exercises 1–3.

   (0, 0), (0, 0), (0, 36)

5. Sketch a graph of the function $f(x) = x^4 - 6x^3 + 8x^2 + 1$. Does the function have a maximum or a minimum point? If yes, determine these points.

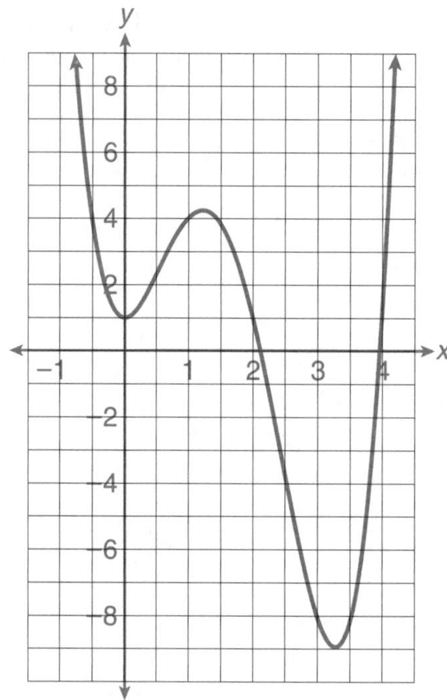

   No, maximum point; minimum point is (3.28, –8.91)

6. Describe any symmetry of the graph of $y = x^4 - 4x^2 - 2$.

   There is symmetry on the *y*-axis.

7. As the value of the input variable x increases without bound (say, 10 to 100 to 1000 and so on), do the output values decrease without bound for the function $y = x^3 + 3x^2 - x - 4$? Use a graph of the function to help answer the question.

   No, as *x* increases without bound, *y* increases without bound.

Exercise numbers appearing in color are answered in the Selected Answers section of this book.

8. Is the graph of $y = -x^3 - x + 3$ increasing or decreasing?

The graph is decreasing everywhere.

9. Consider the following graph of $y = f(x)$.

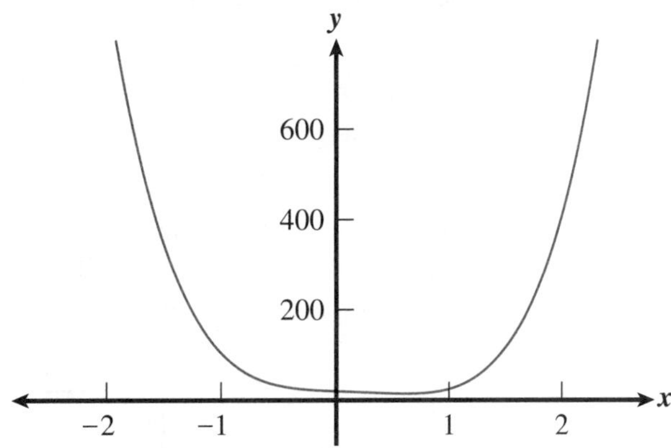

a. As x decreases without bound, the corresponding y-values increase.

b. Is the function f increasing or decreasing for $-2 < x < 0$?

Decreasing

c. How many turning points does the curve have?

One

10. Sketch a graph of $y = (x - 2)^4$. What is the relationship between the minimum point of the graph and its horizontal intercept?

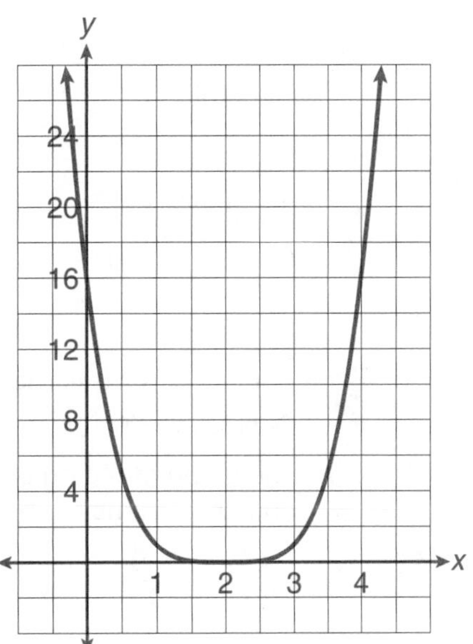

The minimum point is the same as the horizontal intercept.

ACTIVITY 4.12

Stolen Bases

Topics: *Curve Fitting, General Properties of Cubics and Quartics*

There is probably no sport in which more statistics are gathered and analyzed by nonparticipants than baseball. Numbers are generated in all kinds of offensive and defensive categories. Some of these categories provide numbers that can be related quite nicely to polynomial functions. Consider the following data on stolen-base leaders in the National League in the 1980s.

YEAR	1980	1981	1982	1983	1985	1987	1988	1989
BASES STOLEN	97	71	78	90	110	109	81	65

1. Let x represent the number of years since 1980. Let y represent the number of bases stolen by the National League individual champion. Plot these points on your grapher. Your scatterplot should resemble the following.

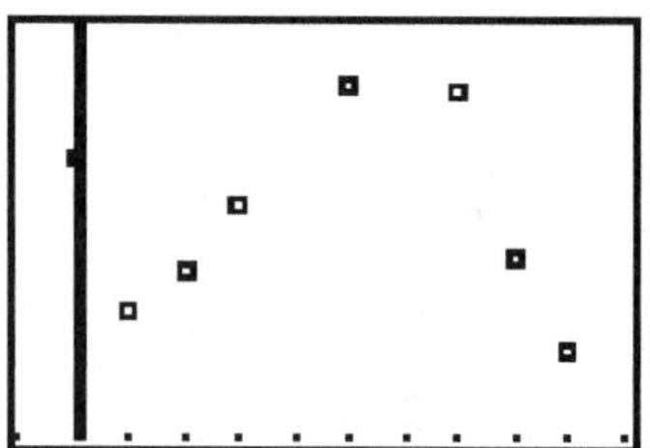

2. a. Using your grapher, determine the first-, second-, third-, and fourth-degree regression equations for the data. Which of these curves seems to best describe the data? Explain.

First degree (linear):

Linear: $y = -0.30x + 88.93$

Second degree (quadratic):

Quadratic: $y = -1.16x^2 + 10.22x + 76.63$

Third degree (cubic):

Cubic: $y = -0.66x^3 + 7.58x^2 - 18.63x + 91.60$

Fourth degree (quartic):

Quartic: $y = 0.12x^4 - 2.90x^3 + 19.99x^2 - 39.67x + 96.21$

The graph of the quartic equation fits closest to the points, so the quartic equation seems to best describes the data.

b. Graph each of these curves on the same coordinate axes as the scatterplot.

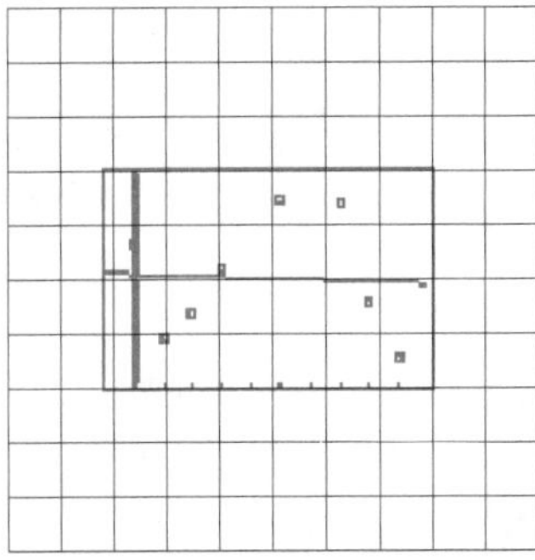

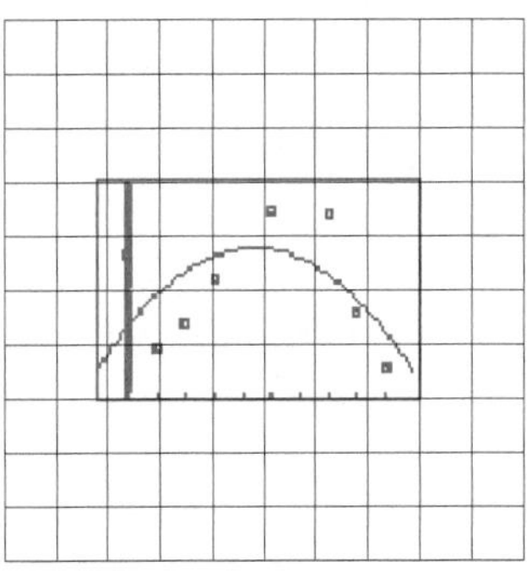

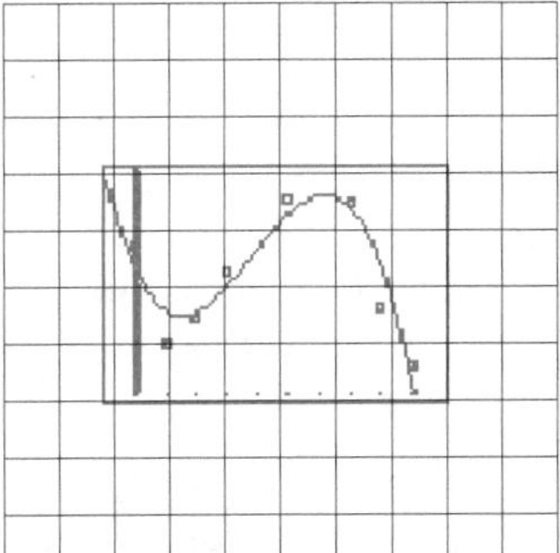

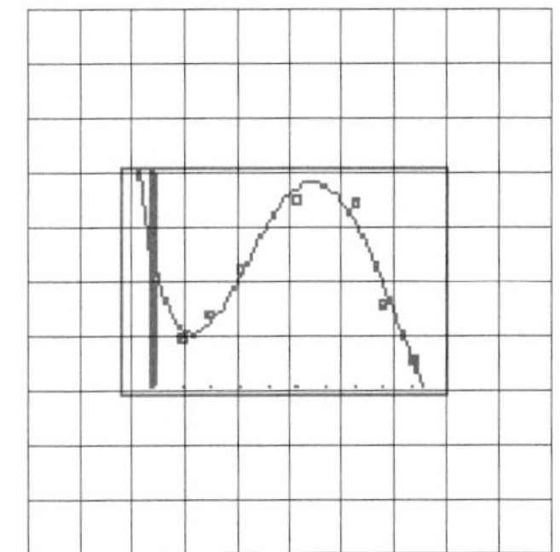

c. Which of the curves seems to be the best fit?

The quartic.

3. What is the practical domain of this problem? Would you consider this a discrete situation (consisting of separate, isolated points) or a continuous situation? Explain.

t can take on values from 0 to 9. Each data point represents the number of stolen bases per year by the National League champion. At any given time, there will be a number of bases stolen so far that year. So, although the outputs are given as the total number of stolen bases per twelve-month period, we may consider this as a continuous situation.

4. What is the practical range of this problem?

Practical range is 65 to 110.

5. In 1986, Vince Coleman led the National League in stolen bases with 107. Is this result consistent with the curve you chose as the best to describe the given data? Explain.

Yes, tracing to $t = 6$ gives bases stolen as approximately 107.

6. In 1984, Tim Raines led the National League in stolen bases with 75. Is this result consistent with the curve you chose as the best to describe the given data? Explain.

No, tracing to $t = 4$ gives bases stolen as approximately 103.

7. Add these two data points from Problems 5 and 6 to the lists in your grapher and recalculate the quartic regression equations. How does the new regression equation fit the data set?

The new quartic is $y = 0.05x^4 - 1.51x^3 + 12.92x^2 - 31.33x + 95.86$. This curve does not fit as closely to the points, which appear more scattered.

8. Using the function generated in Problem 7, estimate the number of stolen bases the National League will have this year. Is this a realistic estimate? Explain.

The number of bases stolen in 1999 is predicted by this model to be 392, not a realistic estimate. The model is not reliable for predicting the number of stolen bases outside the decade of the 1980s.

EXERCISES

1. Prior to the 1980s, sports card collectors were known as baseball card collectors because the vast majority of cards produced were related to baseball. The industry was monopolized by Topps Trading Card Company of Brooklyn, New York. Therefore, the number of card sets produced each year was hardly more than the number of major sports—four. (Those sports are baseball, football, basketball, and hockey.)

Once this monopoly was broken and people found that there was money to be made in trading cards, the number of licensed card sets grew. The December 8, 1996, issue of *Sports Collector's Digest* reported information regarding the number of licensed regular card sets produced for the four major sports during the years 1978 to 1995. The data are summarized in the following table.

YEAR	1978	1979	1981	1986	1988	1989	1990	1991	1992	1993	1994	1995
NUMBER OF SETS	5	5	7	7	8	12	24	35	46	58	81	111

Data: *Sports Collector's Digest*

a. Make a scatterplot of the data. Let t represent the number of years since 1978. Do the data appear to be linear? Explain.

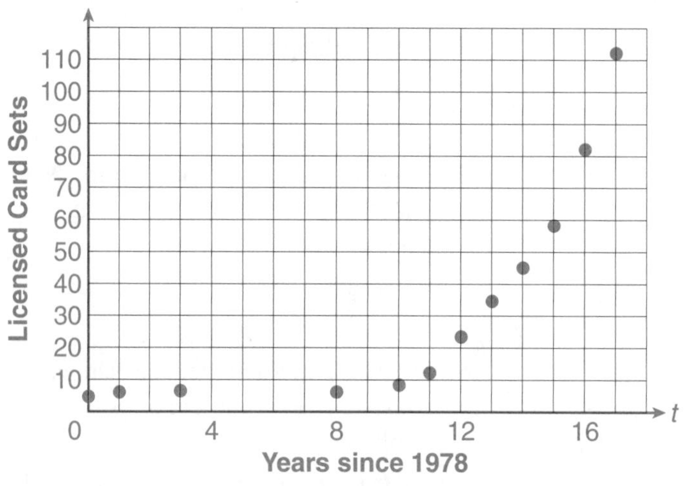

No, the data points do not form a straight line.

b. Use your grapher to determine and plot the quadratic, cubic, and quartic regression equations for the data. Which equation appears to be the best fit? Explain.

The quartic seems best. It fits very closely to the points.

2. a. Using the results from Exercise 1b, what is your equation for the number of sports card sets, $N(t)$, where t is the number of years since 1978?

$N(t) = 0.0017x^4 + 0.006x^3 - 0.32x^2 + 1.46x + 4.65$

b. What is the practical domain of this function?

Practical domain is $0 \leq t \leq 17$

c. What is the practical range of this function? Explain.

Practical range is $5 \leq N(t) \leq 111$

d. Use your equation to estimate the number of sports card sets produced in 1975. In 1985. In 1996. In which of these estimates do you have the most confidence? Explain.

i. −3 ii. 5 iii. 141

iv. The first estimate is not possible; we cannot have a negative number of card sets. The middle estimate seems roughly correct as we know that there were seven card sets in years near 1985. The estimate of 141 seems possible but I am not very confident in it, since we have no knowledge of the number of card sets after 1995.

e. *Sports Collector's Digest* projected the number of card sets produced in 1996 to be 100. Does this fit your model? Explain.

No, 100 is much lower than predicted by my model.

f. If you add the data point from part e and recalculate your regression equation, does it seem to affect how well your equation fits the data? Explain.

With the additional data point, the new regression equation does not fit as closely to the points.

3. The following graphic gives the annual consumption of cigarettes (in billions) in the United States for specific years.

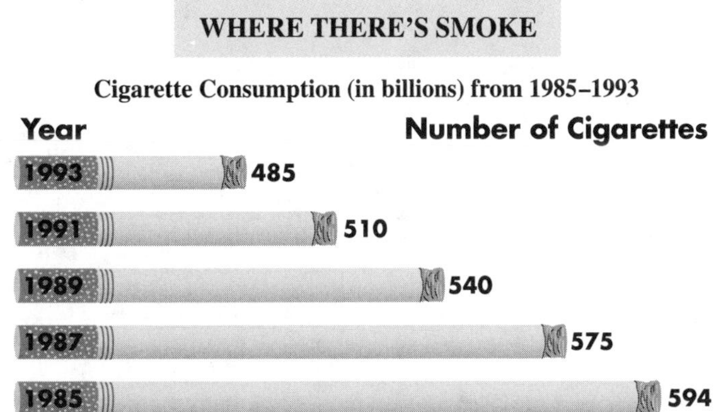

a. Let $t = 0$ correspond to the year 1985. Sketch a scatterplot of the data.

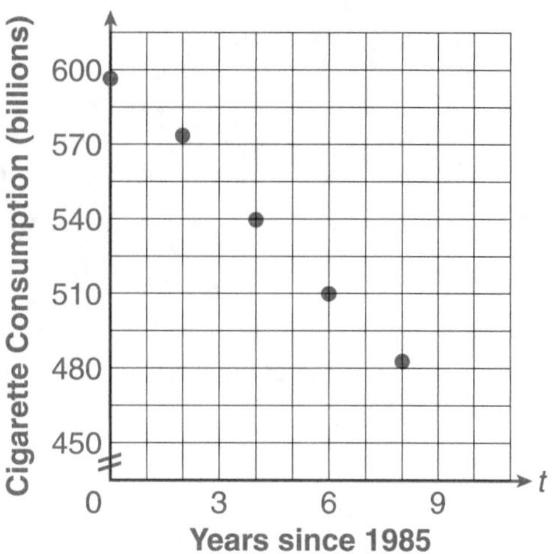

b. Determine a linear model (equation) for the data.

$y = -14.15x + 597.4$

c. Determine a quadratic model (equation) for the data.

$y = -0.125x^2 - 13.15x + 596.4$

d. Which model best represents the data? Explain.

There appears to be no difference between the two models. Both fit closely to the data.

e. Use each model to predict the consumption of cigarettes in the year 2005.

The linear model predicts 314.4 and the quadratic predicts 283.4.

f. How confident are you in your predictions? Explain.

We are predicting quite far outside our practical domain, so I am not very confident in either model's prediction.

PROJECT ACTIVITY 4.13

Finding the Maximum Volume

Topic: *Problem Solving Using Polynomial Functions*

You have an $8\frac{1}{2}$-by-11-inch piece of cardboard that you want to make into an open box (no top). To make the open box, you must cut out equal-sized squares from all four corners of the cardboard and then fold up the sides. Your goal is to obtain a box possessing maximum volume.

1. Before doing any cutting or calculating, estimate what size square you think needs to be cut out to make a box with the largest (maximum) volume.

2. Draw a sketch of the problem.

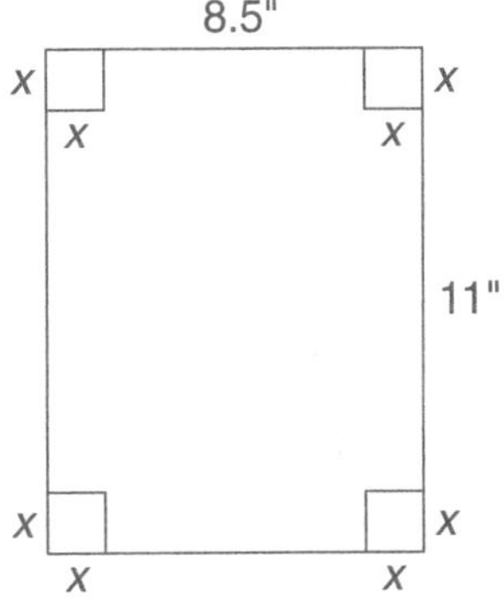

3. Cut out equal-size squares from each corner of an $8\frac{1}{2}$-by-11-inch piece of cardboard. Measure as carefully as you can to the size you chose in Problem 1. Fold and tape the sides to form your box. Measure the dimensions and calculate the volume of your box.

4. Make a table listing the size of the cut square, the other two dimensions of the box, and the volume of the box. Enter the data for your box in the first column, followed by the data from other persons in the class.

SQUARE (HEIGHT)	1"	2"	3"	1.5"	1.6"	1.59"
LENGTH	9"	7"	5"	8"	7.8"	7.82"
WIDTH	6.5"	4.5"	2.5"	5.5"	5.3"	5.32"
VOLUME	58.5	63	37.5	66	66.144	66.148

5. Use several other sizes for the cut square, calculate the resulting volume, and enter the results in your table.

6. From the data in your table, what do you think is the maximum volume? What size of cut square results in the largest box?

   Maximum volume: 66.148 cubic inches

   Square size: 1.59 in. × 1.59 in.

7. Let x represent the length of each side of the cut squares. Therefore, x is the height of the box. Write two expressions: one for the length of the box in terms of x and one for the width of the box in terms of x. Then use these expressions to write an expression for the volume $V(x)$.

   $L(x) = 11 - 2x$

   $W(x) = 8.5 - 2x$

   $V(x) = x(11 - 2x)(8.5 - 2x)$

8. Graph $V(x)$ on your grapher. Trace the graph to find the maximum volume. How closely does it agree with your answer in Problem 6? How close was your original estimate in Problem 1?

Maximum volume: 66.148235, when $x = 1.5854204$

The estimate was very close.

9. As accurately as you can, give the dimensions for the box with maximum volume. Could you reasonably cut out the size square needed to make the maximum volume? Explain.

Height: 1.585 in.

Width: 5.33 in.

Length: 7.83 in.

It would be difficult to cut a square of exactly the right size, but you can come close to a box with maximum volume by using height: $1\frac{9}{16}$ in., width: $5\frac{3}{8}$ in., length: $7\frac{7}{8}$ in.

10. What is the practical domain and range for this volume function?

Practical domain: $0 < x \leq 4.25$

Practical range: $0 < y \leq 66.148$

11. If you changed the length of your cardboard from 11 inches to 14 inches, would the maximum volume change? If so, what would be the value of the cut size needed to obtain the maximum volume? Explain the method you used to get your answer.

Yes, the maximum volume would change. The square cut size would be 1.714 in. for a maximum volume of 91.907 cubic inches.

Graph $V(x) = x(14 - 2x)(8.5 - 2x)$ using your grapher and trace to find the maximum.

What Have I Learned?

1. In a hurricane, the wind pressure varies directly as the square of the wind velocity (speed). If the wind speed doubles in value, what change in the wind pressure do you experience?

   The wind pressure is multiplied by 4.

2. Is the graph of $y = 3x^4$ narrower or wider than the graph of $y = x^2$? Explain.

   $y = 3x^4$ is narrower than $y = x^2$ because it grows more quickly.

3. The graph of any cubic function (third-degree polynomial function) must have one of the four following general shapes.

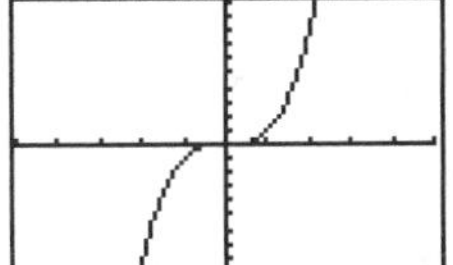
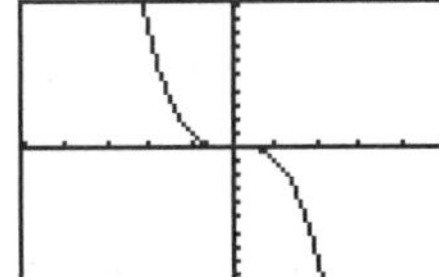
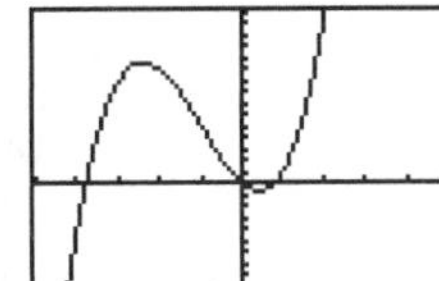
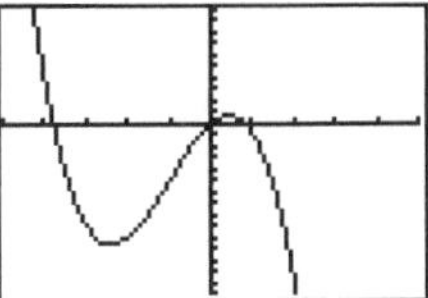

   a. Complete the following table, giving the maximum number of turning points for a given family of polynomial functions.

DEGREE OF POLYNOMIAL FUNCTION	MAXIMUM NUMBER OF TURNING POINTS
First: (Linear)	0
Second: (Quadratic)	1
Third: (Cubic)	2
Fourth: (Quartic)	3

   b. Write an expression that represents the maximum number of turning points for the graph of a polynomial of degree n.

   $n - 1$ will be the maximum number of turning points for a polynomial of degree n.

4. **a.** Use your grapher to sketch a graph of $y = x^4 - 4x^2$. Describe any symmetry that you observe.

   There is symmetry on the y-axis.

   b. Do all graphs of quartic (fourth-degree) functions have symmetry? Explain.

   No, a quartic will only have symmetry if its terms all have even powers.

5. **a.** Does the graph of any cubic function have a horizontal intercept? Can the graph have more than one horizontal intercept? Explain.

   Any cubic will have at least one horizontal intercept, possibly 2 or 3.

   b. Does the graph of any cubic function have at least one vertical intercept? Explain.

   Any cubic has one vertical intercept. Zero is always an element of the domain of a cubic function.

How Can I Practice?

1. Assume that y varies directly as x^2, and when $x = 3$, $y = 45$. Find y when $x = 6$.

   $y = kx^2$, $45 = k3^2$, so $k = 5$

   $k = 5(6)^2 = 180$

2. Have you ever noticed that during a thunderstorm, you see lightning before you hear the thunder? This is because light travels faster than sound. If d represents the distance (in feet) that the lightning is from the observer, then d varies directly as the time t (in seconds) it takes to hear the thunder. This relationship is modeled by

$$d = 1080t.$$

   a. As the time t doubles (say, from 3 to 6), the corresponding output values __double__.

   b. What is the value of k, the constant of variation, in this situation? What significance does k have in this problem?

   $k = 1080$; k represents the speed at which the sound of thunder travels.

3. The velocity v of a falling object is directly proportional to the time t of the fall. After 3 seconds, the velocity of the object is 60 feet per second. What will be its velocity after 4 seconds?

   $v = kt$, $60 = k3$, $k = 20$

   $v = 20(4) = 80$ ft/sec.

4. For each of the following pairs of functions, describe the differences and the similarities in the graphs. Verify your descriptions by graphing.

   a. $y = 3x^2$, $y = 3x^2 + 5$

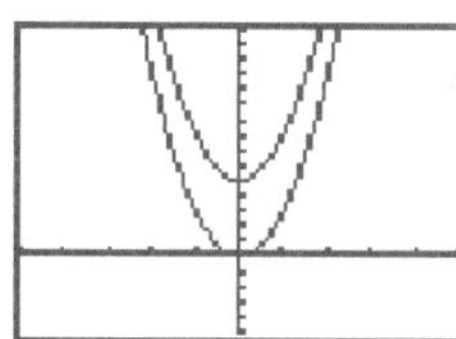

   These are the same shape and size, however, $y = 3x^2 + 5$ is shifted up by five units.

   b. $y = 5x^4$, $y = -5x^4$

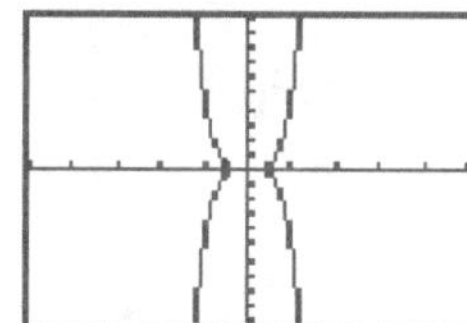

   These are the same shape but are reflections of each other in the x-axis.

Exercise numbers appearing in color are answered in the Selected Answers section of this book.

c. $y = 2x^3 + 1,\ y = 2x^3 - 4$

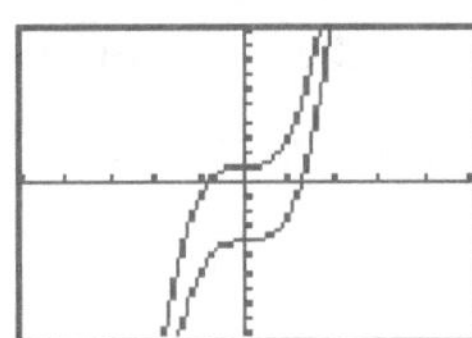

These are the same shape and size but are shifted vertically by five units.

d. $y = 4x^2,\ y = 4(x - 1)^2$

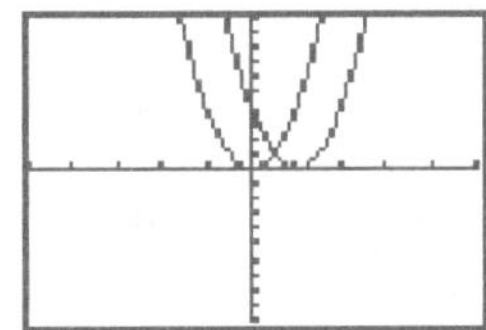

These are the same shape and size but are shifted horizontally one unit to the right.

5. Using your grapher, graph each of the following polynomial functions. For each graph, determine the vertical intercepts, approximate the horizontal intercepts (if they exist), and determine the coordinates of any turning points.

a. $y = x^3 + 2x^2 - 8x$

i. (0, 0)

ii. (0, 0),(−4, 0), (2, 0)

iii. (−2.4, 16.9), (1, −5)

b. $y = -x^4 + 2x + 3$

i. (0, 3)

ii. (−1, 0), (1.57, 0)

iii. (0.77, 4.2)

6. Using an algebraic approach (factoring), determine the x-intercepts of the graph of the function having the equation

$$F(x) = -x^4 + 4x^3 - 4x^2$$

Verify using your grapher.

(0, 0), (2, 0)

7. To use the regression feature of your calculator to determine the equation of a parabola, you need three distinct points. The stream of water flowing out of a water fountain is in the shape of a parabola. Suppose you let the origin of a coordinate system correspond to the point where the water begins to flow out of the nozzle. (See the accompanying figure.)

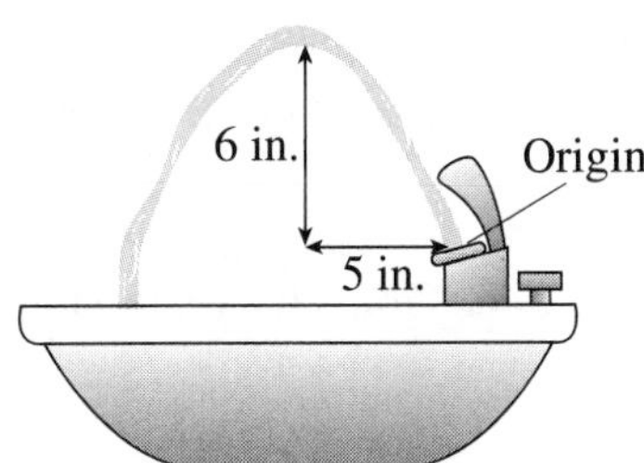

The maximum height of the water stream is approximately 6 inches measured vertically from the nozzle. This maximum height occurs above a point that is 5 inches, measured horizontally, from the nozzle.

a. What is the vertex of the parabola?

(−5, 6)

b. You already have two points that lie on the parabola. What are they? Use symmetry to obtain a third point.

(0, 0), (−5, 6), (−10, 0)

c. Using these three points, determine the regression equation of the stream of water.

$y = -0.24x^2 - 2.4x$

8. Consider the following data set.

x	0	1	3	5	7	8
y	10	4	−18	−54	−107	−145

a. Determine an appropriate scale and plot these points.

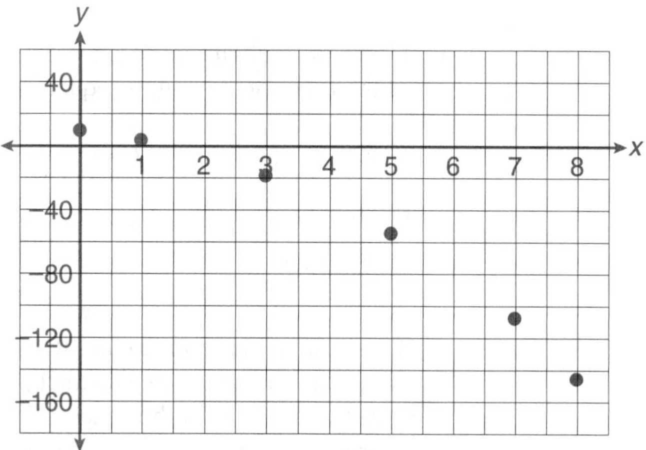

b. Use your grapher to determine the quadratic regression equation for this data set.

$y = -2.096153846x^2 - 2.25x + 9.038461538$

c. Graph the regression equation on the same coordinate axes as the data points.

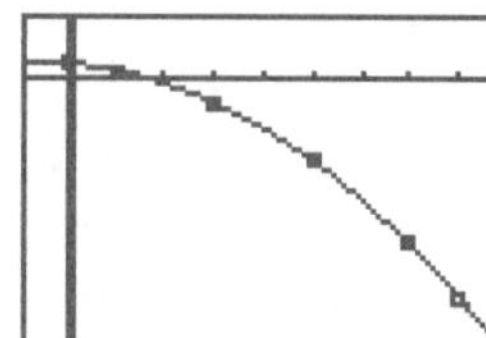

d. Compare the predicted outputs with the given outputs in the table.

Predicted values are very close to the actual values.

e. What is the predicted output for $x = 4$? For $x = 9$?

-33.5, -181

9. The average miles per gallon (mpg) for U.S. cars has steadily increased over the past several years. The following table gives the average miles per gallon for selected years.

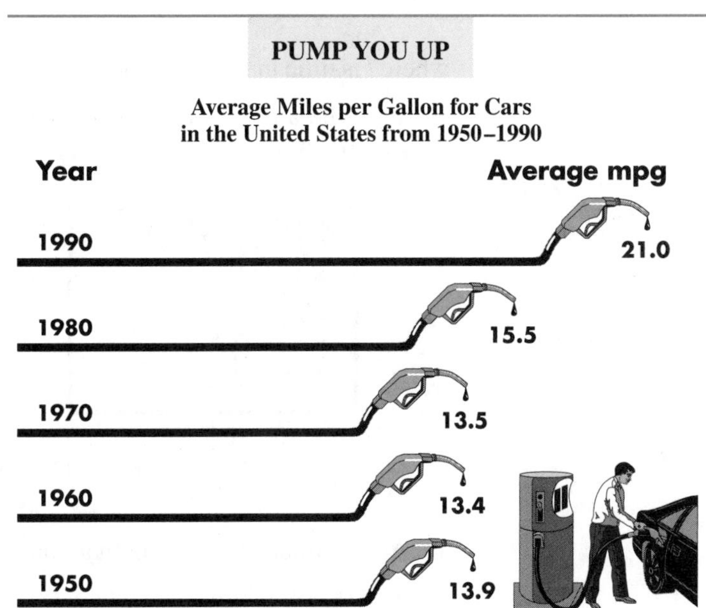

a. Draw a scatterplot of the data points. Let t represent the number of years since 1950.

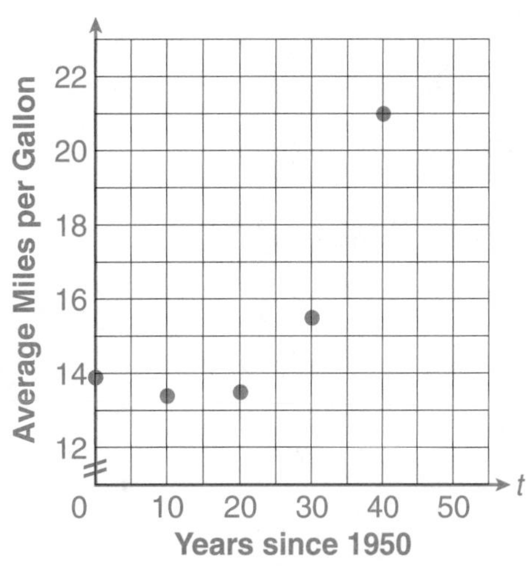

b. Determine the equation of a quadratic function that best fits the data.

$y = 0.0099285714x^2 - 0.2341428571x + 14.18571429$

c. Use the regression equation to predict the average miles per gallon in the year 2000.

27.3 mpg

d. Use your model to determine the year when the average miles per gallon is 30.

2003

10. The amount of water (in gallons) in a leaky bathtub is given by

$$W(t) = 10 + 7t^2 - t^3 \quad (t \geq 0),$$

where t is time in minutes, and $W(t)$ represents the amount of water (in gallons).

a. With the aid of your grapher, sketch the graph of $W(t)$. Don't go beyond $t = 10$. Why?

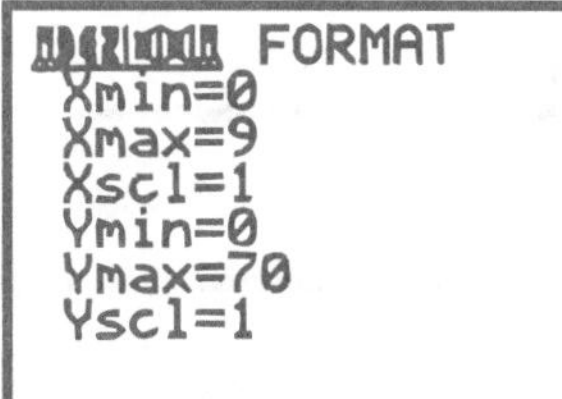

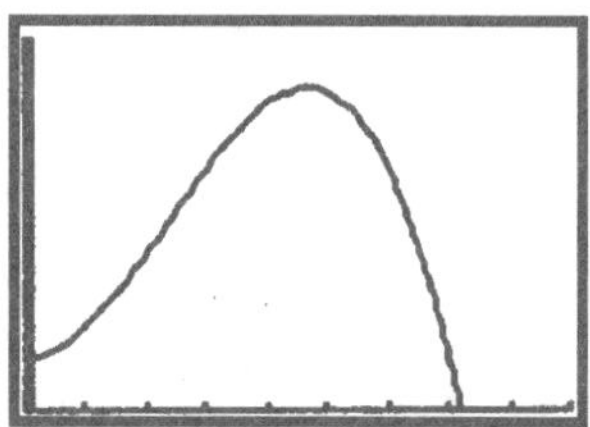

$W(t)$ becomes negative before ten minutes.

b. Approximate the maximum amount of water in the tub. Explain your result.

60.8 gallons, found by tracing on the grapher.

c. Use the trace and zoom features of your grapher to determine when the tub will be completely empty, to the nearest 0.01 minute.

7.19 minutes

CHAPTER 4

Gateway Review

In Exercises 1–8, determine the following characteristics of each quadratic function by inspecting its equation.

a. The direction in which the graph opens.

b. The equation of the axis of symmetry.

c. The vertex.

d. The y-intercept.

1. $f(x) = x^2 + 2$

a. up b. $x = 0$

c. (0, 2) d. (0, 2)

2. $y(x) = -3x^2$

a. down b. $x = 0$

c. (0, 0) d. (0, 0)

3. $g(x) = -3x^2 + 4$

a. down b. $x = 0$

c. (0, 4) d. (0, 4)

4. $f(x) = 2x^2 - x$

a. up b. $x = \frac{1}{4}$

c. $\left(\frac{1}{4}, -\frac{1}{8}\right)$ d. (0, 0)

5. $h(x) = x^2 + 5x + 6$

a. up b. $x = -\frac{5}{2}$

c. $(-2.5, -0.25)$ d. (0, 6)

6. $y(x) = x^2 - 3x + 4$

a. up b. $x = \frac{3}{2}$

c. (1.5, 1.75) d. (0, 4)

7. $f(x) = x^2 - 2x + 1$

a. up b. $x = 1$

c. (1, 0) d. (0, 1)

8. $g(x) = -x^2 + 5x - 6$

a. down b. $x = 2.5$

c. (2.5, 0.25) d. $(0, -6)$

In Exercises 9–15, sketch the graph of each quadratic function using your grapher. Then determine each of the following using the graph.

a. The coordinates of the x-intercepts, if they exist.

b. The domain and range of the function.

c. The horizontal interval in which the function is increasing.

d. The horizontal interval in which the function is decreasing.

9. 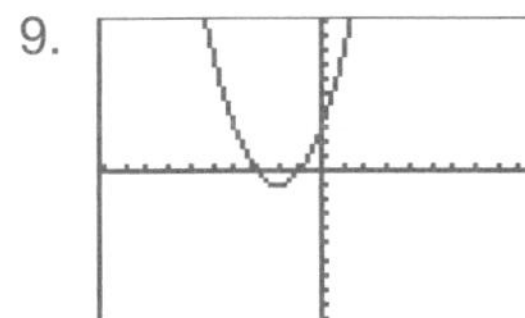

10. 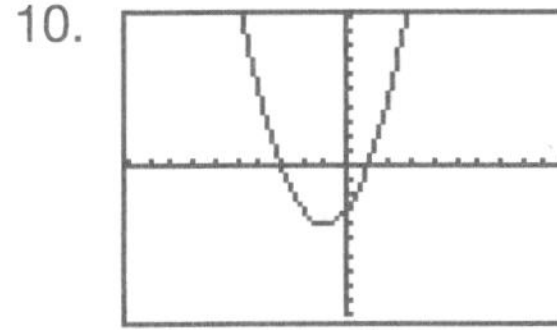

9. $g(x) = x^2 + 4x + 3$

a. $(-3, 0), (-1, 0)$

b. D: (all real numbers)
R: ($g(x) \geq -1$)

c. ($x > -2$) d. ($x < -2$)

10. $f(x) = x^2 + 2x - 3$

a. $(-3, 0), (1, 0)$

b. D: (all real numbers)
R: ($f(x) \geq -4$)

c. ($x > -1$) d. ($x < -1$)

CHAPTER 4 GATEWAY REVIEW

11. 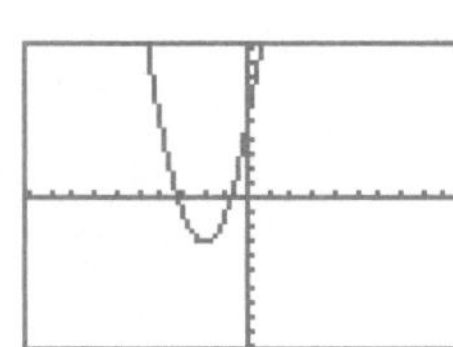

12. 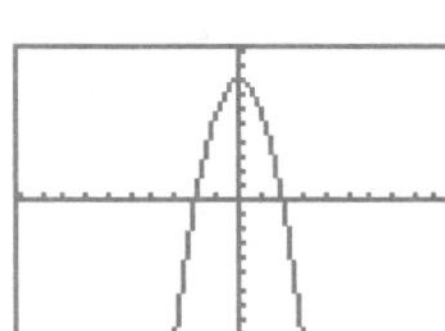

13. 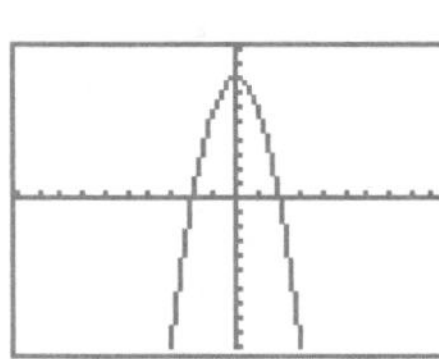

14. 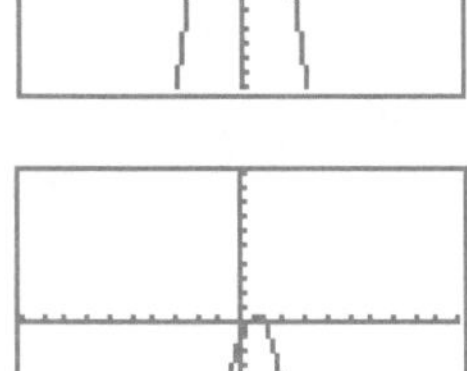

15. 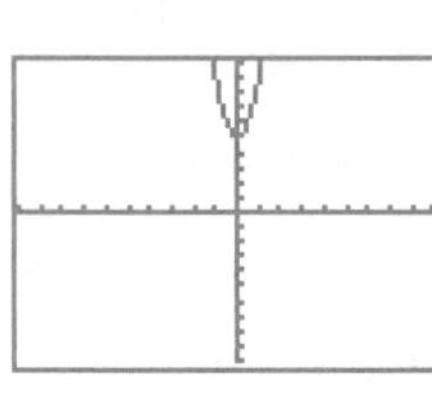

11. $y(x) = x^2 - 3x + 1$

a. (0.382, 0), (2.62, 0)

b. D: (all real numbers), R: ($y \geq -1.25$)

c. ($x > 1.5$) d. ($x < 1.5$)

12. $h(x) = 2x^2 + 8x + 5$

a. (−3.22, 0), (−0.775, 0)

b. D: (all real numbers), R: ($h(x) \geq -3$)

c. ($x > -2$) d. ($x < -2$)

13. $y(x) = -2x^2 + 8$

a. (−2, 0), (2, 0)

b. D: (all real numbers), R: ($y(x) \leq 8$)

c. ($x < 0$) d. ($x > 0$)

14. $f(x) = -3x^2 + 4x - 1$

a. ($\frac{1}{3}$, 0), (1, 0)

b. D: (all real numbers), R: ($f(x) \leq \frac{1}{3}$)

c. ($x < \frac{2}{3}$) d. ($x > \frac{2}{3}$)

15. $g(x) = 4x^2 + 5$

a. none b. D: (all real numbers), R: ($g(x) \geq 5$)

c. ($x > 0$) d. ($x < 0$)

In Exercises 16–19, solve the quadratic equation numerically (using tables). Verify your solutions graphically.

16. $x^2 + 4x + 4 = 0$

$x = -2$

17. $x^2 - 5x + 6 = 0$

$x = 2, 3$

18. $3x^2 = 18x + 10$

$x = -0.51, 6.51$

19. $-x^2 = 3x - 10$

$x = -5, 2$

In Exercises 20 and 21, solve each equation using two different approaches. Round your answer to the nearest tenth when necessary.

20. $8x^2 = 10$

$x = \pm 1.1$

21. $5x^2 + 25x = -5$

$x = -0.21, -4.79$

In Exercises 22–26, solve each equation by factoring. Verify your answer by the substitution method or graphically.

22. $x^2 - 9 = 0$

$x = \pm 3$

23. $-x^2 + 36 = 0$

$x = \pm 6$

24. $x^2 - 7x + 12 = 0$

$x = 3, 4$

25. $x^2 - 6x = 27$

$x = -3, 9$

26. $x^2 = -x$

$x = 0, -1$

In Exercises 27–31, write each of the equations in the form $ax^2 + bx + c = 0$. Then identify a, b, and c and solve the equation using the quadratic formula. Verify your solutions by substitution.

27. $x^2 + 5x + 3 = 0$

$a = 1, b = 5, c = 3$

$x = -0.7, -4.3$

28. $2x^2 - x = -3$

$a = 2, b = -1, c = 3$

$x = 0.25 \pm 1.2i$

29. $x^2 = 8$

$a = 1, b = 0, c = -8$

$x = \pm 2.83$

30. $3x^2 + 5x = 12$

$a = 3, b = 5, c = -12$

$x = -3, \frac{4}{3}$

31. $2x^2 = 3x + 5$

$a = 2, b = -3, c = -5$

$x = -1, 2.5$

32. For the quadratic function $f(x) = 2x^2 - 8x + 3$, determine the x-intercepts of the graph, if they exist. First, approximate the intercepts using your grapher. Second, solve the equation using the quadratic formula. Approximate your answers to the nearest hundredth.

From the grapher: (0.419, 0), (3.581, 0)

$$x = \frac{-(-8) \pm \sqrt{(-8)^2 - 4(2)(3)}}{2(2)} = \frac{8 \pm \sqrt{40}}{4} = 3.581, 0.419$$

33. Write each of the following using the imaginary unit i.

a. $\sqrt{-49}$

$= 7i$

b. $\sqrt{-48}$

$= 4\sqrt{3}i$

c. $\sqrt{-9}$

$= 3i$

d. $\sqrt{-23}$

$\sqrt{23}i$

e. $\sqrt{-\frac{5}{9}}$

$\frac{\sqrt{5}}{3}i$

f. $\sqrt{\frac{-17}{16}}$

$\frac{\sqrt{17}}{4}i$

In Exercises 34–37, determine the type of solutions to each of the equations by considering only the discriminant.

34. $2x^2 - 3x + 1 = 0$

Two real solutions.

35. $4x^2 + 16x = 0$

Two real solutions.

36. $x^2 - 9 = 0$

Two real solutions.

37. $3x^2 + 2x + 2 = 0$

Two complex solutions.

38. Solve the equation in Exercise 37 in the complex-number system using the quadratic formula. Verify your solution graphically.

$$x = \frac{-2 \pm \sqrt{2^2 - 4(3)(2)}}{2(3)} = \frac{-2 \pm \sqrt{-20}}{6} = \frac{-2 \pm 2\sqrt{5}i}{2(3)} = \frac{-1 \pm \sqrt{5}i}{3}$$

39. Solve the following inequalities using a graphing approach.

a. $x^2 - x - 6 < 0$

a. $-2 < x < 3$

b. $x^2 - x - 6 > 0$

$x < -2$ or $x > 3$

40. **a.** Suppose y varies directly as x. When $x = 3$, $y = 12$. Find y when $x = 5$.

$y = 20$

b. Suppose y varies directly as x^2. When $x = 4$, $y = 8$. Find y when $x = 8$.

$y = 32$

c. Suppose y varies directly as x^3. When $x = 1$, $y = 5$. Find y when $x = 2$.

$y = 40$

In Exercises 41–45, graph each function using your grapher. Then determine the following characteristics from your grapher.

a. The x-intercepts of the function (if it has any).

b. The domain and range of the function.

c. The x-interval over which the function is increasing and the x-interval over which the function is decreasing.

41. $y = x^3 - 8$

a. (2, 0)

b. D: (all real numbers),
R: (all real numbers)

c. inc (all real numbers)

42. $y = -2x^3 - 2$

a. $(-1, 0)$

b. D: (all real numbers),
R: (all real numbers)

c. decreasing (all real numbers)

43. $y = x^4 - 8$

a. $(-1.68, 0)$, $(1.68, 0)$

b. D: (all real numbers),
R: $y \geq -8$

c. inc: $(x > 0)$
dec: $(x < 0)$

44. $y = x^4 + 2x$

a. (0, 0), $(-1.26, 0)$

b. D: (all real numbers),
R: $(y \geq -1.19)$

c. inc: $(x > -0.8)$
dec: $(x < -0.8)$

45. $y = x^4 + 5$

a. none

b. D: (all real numbers), R: $(y \geq 5)$

c. inc: $(x > 0)$ dec: $(x < 0)$

CHAPTER 5

Rational and Radical Functions

CLUSTER 1

Rational Functions

ACTIVITY 5.1

Speed Limits

Topic: *Properties of Graphs of the Form* $y = \frac{k}{x}$

In recent years, there has been much discussion of federal legislation allowing the states to change interstate highway speed limits.

1. The speed limit on the New York State Thruway has been increased from 55 mph to 65 mph. If you travel at the speed limit, how much time will you save at the higher speed limit in making a 200-mile trip on the thruway?

Time at 55 mph $= \frac{200 \text{ mi}}{55 \text{ mph}} \approx 3.64$ hr; Time at 65 mph $= \frac{200 \text{ mi}}{65 \text{ mph}} \approx 3.08$ hr

Difference = 3.64 hr − 3.08 hr = 0.56 hr or 33.6 minutes.

2. Complete the following table, in which the input variable r represents the average speed in miles per hour and the output variable t represents the time in hours to complete a 200-mile trip.

r (mph)	20	30	40	50	60	70	80
t (hr)	10	6.67	5	4	3.33	2.86	2.5

3. Write a rule that defines t as a function of r.

$t = f(r) = \frac{200}{r}$

4. As the values of the input r increase, what happens to the values of the output t? What does this mean in practical terms?

As the values of r increase, the values of t decrease, but at a slower rate. Increasing the speed improves the time less at higher speeds than at lower speeds.

5. During a winter storm, a combination of drifting snow and icy conditions reduces your average speed to almost a standstill. Complete the following table for a 200-mile trip on the New York State Thruway.

r (mph)	1	2	3	5	7	10
t (hr)	200	100	66.7	40	28.6	20

6. As the values of the input r get closer to zero, what happens to the values of the output t? Explain what this means in practical terms.

   The values of r increase without bound. At very slow rates, the time of the trip is very, very long.

7. Can zero be used as an input value? Explain.

   No. Division by zero is undefined. If you average 0 mph, you will never get there.

8. What is the practical domain of the function given in Problem 3? Sketch a graph of this function.

   The practical domain is $r > 0$.

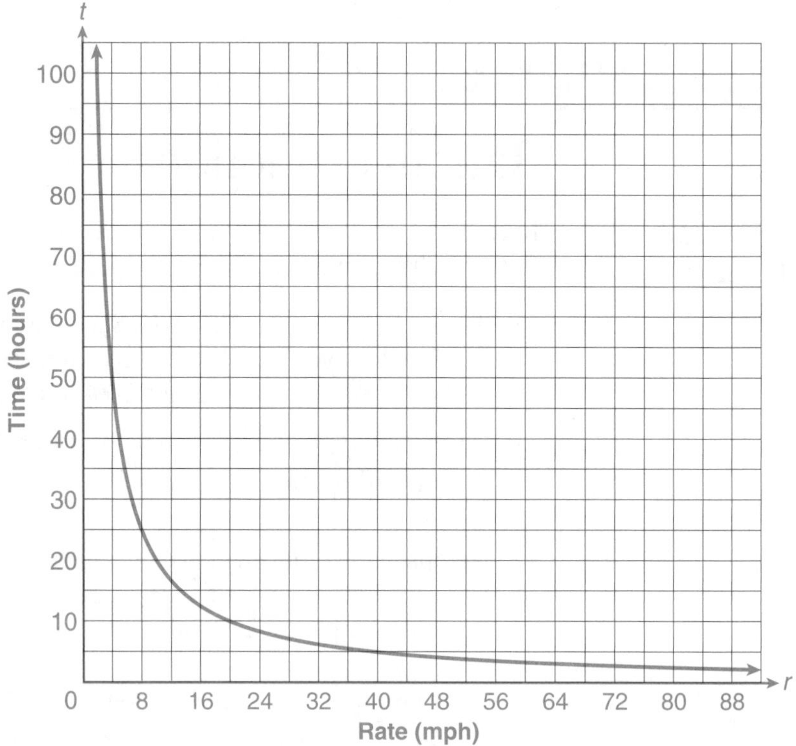

9. **a.** What are the horizontal and vertical intercepts of the graph?

   There are no intercepts.

   b. Describe the relationship between the horizontal axis ($y = 0$) and the graph of the function as the values of r get very large.

   As the input increases, the graph gets closer to the horizontal axis but never touches it.

In this situation, the horizontal line $y = 0$ is called a **horizontal asymptote.** A horizontal asymptote is a line that a graph approaches as the input values of x get very large in both positive and negative directions.

   c. Describe the relationship between the vertical axis, ($x = 0$) and the graph of the function as the values of r get close to zero.

   As the input gets close to zero, the graph approaches the vertical axis but never touches it.

In this situation, the vertical line $x = 0$ is called a **vertical asymptote.** A vertical asymptote is a line $x = a$ that the graph approaches as the input values of x get close to a.

10. Using the graph, approximate your average speed if the 200-mile trip takes 3.5 hours.

(Answers will vary.) $r \approx 57$ mph.

The function rule $t = \frac{200}{r}$ gives the relationship between the average speed r, the time t, and the given value for distance (200). This function belongs to a family of functions having a general rule of the form $f(x) = \frac{k}{x}$, where k represents some nonzero constant.

Examples of this type of function are $f(x) = \frac{1}{x}$, $g(x) = \frac{5}{x}$, and $h(x) = \frac{10}{x}$. Use these functions to answer Problem 11.

11. a. What is the domain of functions, f, g, and h?

All real numbers except zero.

b. Complete the following table.

x	−20	−10	−5	−1	−0.5	−0.1	0	0.1	0.5	1	5	10	20
$f(x)$	−0.05	−0.1	−0.2	−1	−2	−10	undef.	10	2	1	0.2	0.1	0.05
$g(x)$	−0.25	−0.5	−1	−5	−10	−50	undef.	50	10	5	1	0.5	0.25
$h(x)$	−0.5	−1	−2	−10	−20	−100	undef.	100	20	10	2	1	0.5

c. Sketch a graph of f, g, and h on the same coordinate system.

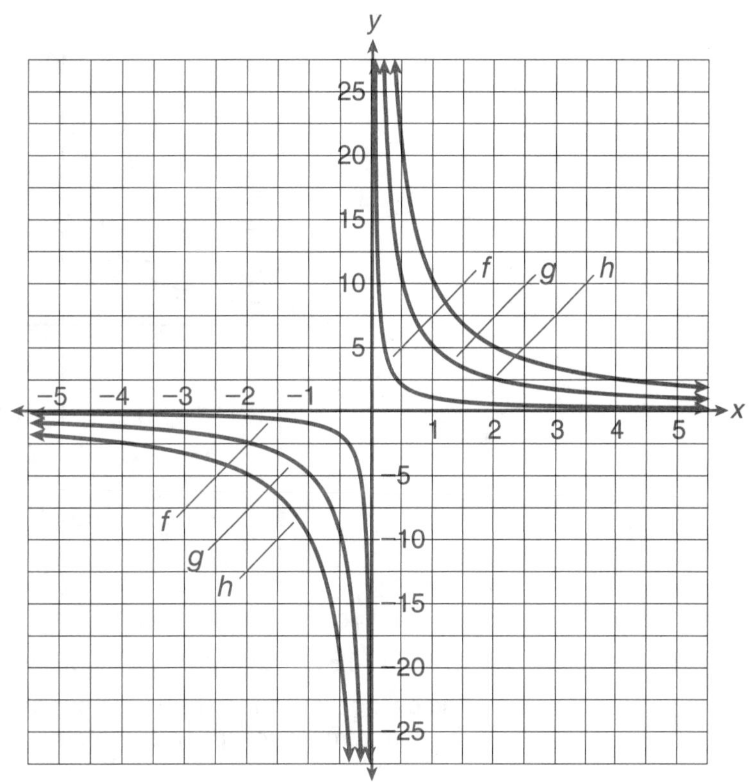

12. Using the table and graphs in Problem 11, answer each of the following questions.

    a. What happens to the output values as the input increases infinitely in both the positive and negative directions?

    The output values get closer and closer to zero.

    b. What is the horizontal asymptote for each graph?

    $y = 0$

    c. What happens to the output as the positive input values get closer to zero?

    The output values get very large (towards positive infinity).

    d. What happens to the output as the negative input values get closer to zero?

    The output values get very small (towards negative infinity).

    e. What is the vertical asymptote for each graph?

    $x = 0$.

13. Do the functions f, g, and h in Problem 11 have a maximum function value or a minimum function value? Explain.

    No, the functions have neither a minimum nor maximum value.

14. Complete the following table, and sketch a graph of $F(x) = \frac{-1}{x}$.

x	−10	−5	−1	−0.5	−0.1	0	0.1	0.5	1	5	10
$F(x)$	0.1	0.2	1	2	10	undef	−10	−2	−1	−0.2	−0.1

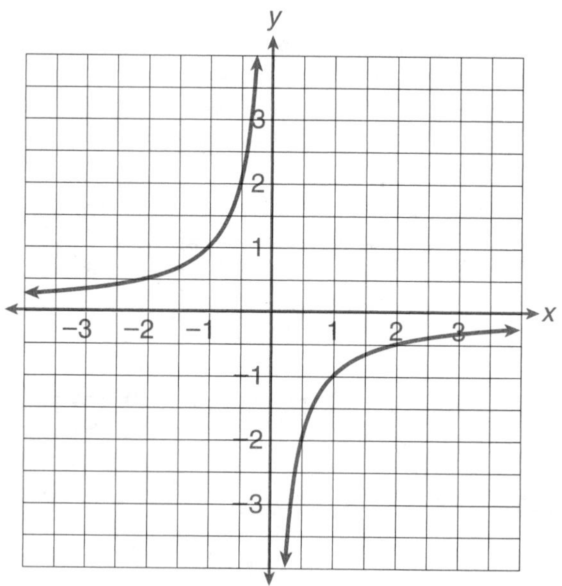

15. Describe the effect of the sign on the graphs of $f(x) = \frac{1}{x}$ and $F(x) = \frac{-1}{x}$.

    The change in sign results in the opposite output values. The graph of one is the mirror image reflection of the other, about the x-axis.

SUMMARY

Functions having the general form $f(x) = \frac{k}{x}$, where k represents some nonzero constant, have the following properties:

1. The domain and the range consist of all real numbers except zero.
2. If $k > 0$, the graph of $f(x)$ has the following general shape.

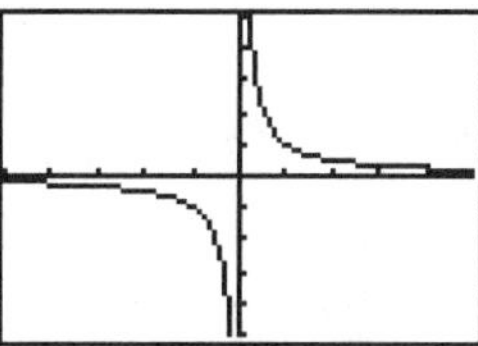

3. If $k < 0$, the graph of $f(x)$ has the following general shape.

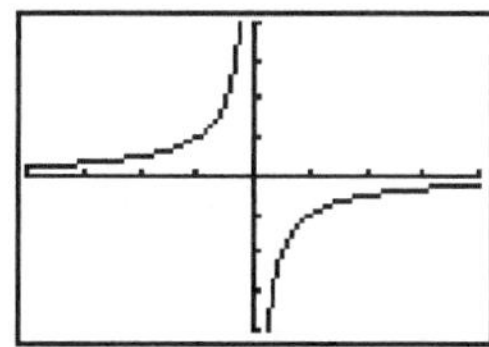

4. The vertical line $x = 0$ is the vertical asymptote.
5. The horizontal line $y = 0$ is the horizontal asymptote.
6. The graph does not intersect either axis (there are no intercepts).
7. There is no maximum or minimum output value.

EXERCISES

1. You are a member of a group of distance runners who compete in races ranging in length from 5 to 25 kilometers. In these races, each runner who finishes is told his or her time. Given the time and the length of the race, you can calculate your average running speed.

   a. If you finish a 20-kilometer race in 1 hour 15 minutes, what is your average speed?

   Average speed $= \frac{20 \text{ km}}{1 \text{ hr } 15 \text{ min}} = \frac{20 \text{ km}}{1.25 \text{ hr}} \approx 16$ km per hour.

   b. Complete the following table for a 20-kilometer race.

t (hr)	1.00	1.25	1.50	1.75	2.00	2.25	2.50
s (km/hr)	20	16	13.33	11.43	10	8.89	8

   c. Write a rule that expresses s as a function of t in a 20-kilometer race.

   $s = f(t) = \frac{20}{t}$

   d. **i.** What is the domain of the function?

   The domain is the set of all nonzero real numbers.

   ii. What is the practical domain?

   (Answers will vary.) $1 \leq t \leq 5$

Exercise numbers appearing in color are answered in the Selected Answers section of this book.

iii. Sketch a graph of the function.

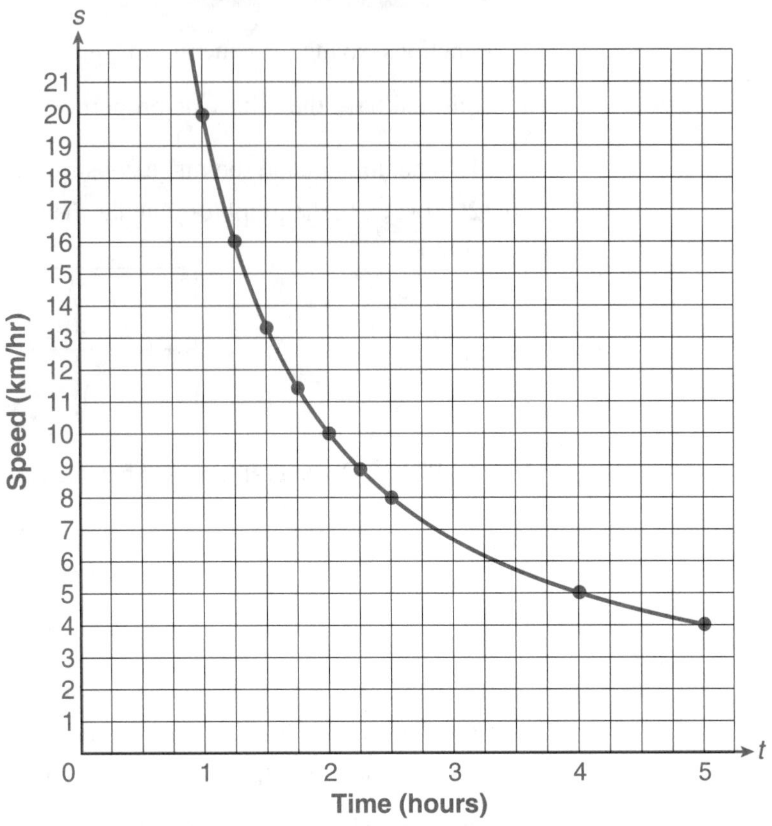

e. As t gets larger, what happens to the average speed s?

The average speed decreases, approaching zero.

f. As t is reduced (gets closer to zero), what happens to the average speed s?

The average speed increases without bound.

2. a. Sketch the graphs of the following pair of functions on the same coordinate system. Use a different color to differentiate the graphs.

$$f(x) = \frac{5}{x},\ g(x) = \frac{-5}{x}$$

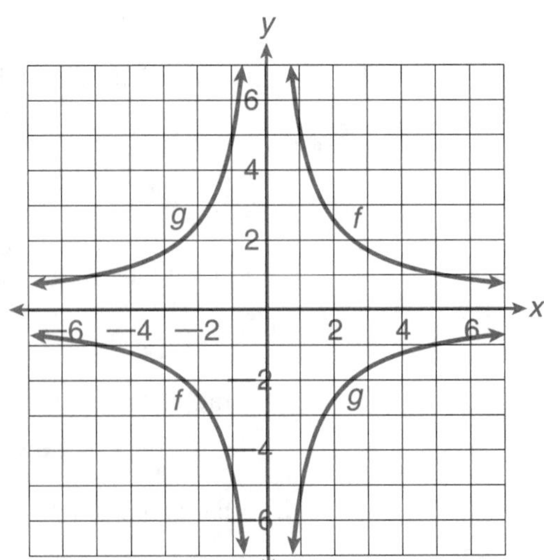

b. Describe the effect of the sign on the graphs of $f(x) = \frac{5}{x}$ and $g(x) = \frac{-5}{x}$.

The change in sign results in the opposite output values. The graph of one is the mirror image reflection of the other, about the *x*-axis.

3. A commercial refrigerator has an initial cost C and a scrap value V. If the life of the refrigerator is N years, then the amount D that can be depreciated each year is given by the formula

$$D = \frac{C - V}{N}.$$

a. If the initial cost is $1400 and the scrap value is $200, write a rule for D as a function of N.

$D = f(N) = \frac{1400 - 200}{N} = \frac{1200}{N}$

b. Sketch a graph of the function.

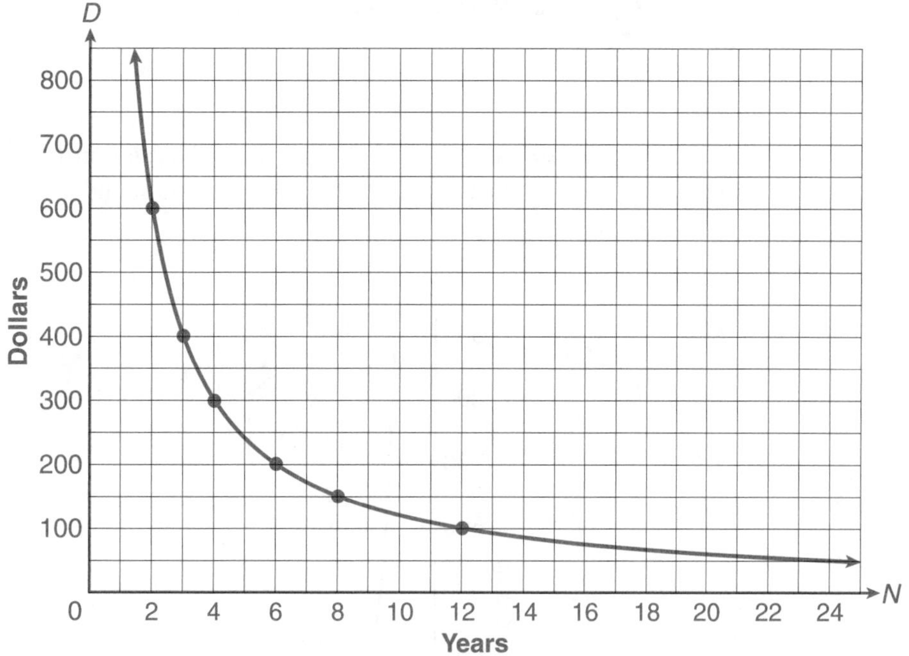

c. If the refrigerator is well constructed, it should have a long, useful life. Will an increase in the useful life of the refrigerator increase or decrease the amount D that can be depreciated each year? Explain.

Decrease. As N gets larger, D gets smaller.

ACTIVITY 5.2

Loudness of Sound

Topic: *Functions of the Form* $f(x) = \frac{k}{x^n}$

The loudness (or intensity) of any sound is a function of the listener's distance from the source of the sound. In general, the relationship between the intensity I and the distance d can be modeled by an equation of the form

$$I = \frac{k}{d^2},$$

where I is measured in decibels, d is measured in feet, and k is a constant determined by the source of the sound and the surroundings.

1. The intensity I of a human voice can be given by the formula $I = \frac{1500}{d^2}$. Complete the following table.

d (ft)	0.1	0.5	1	2	5	10	20	30
I (dB)	150,000	6000	1500	375	60	15	3.75	1.67

2. a. What is the practical domain of the function?

   $d > 0$

   b. Sketch a graph that shows the relationship between intensity of sound and distance from the source of the sound.

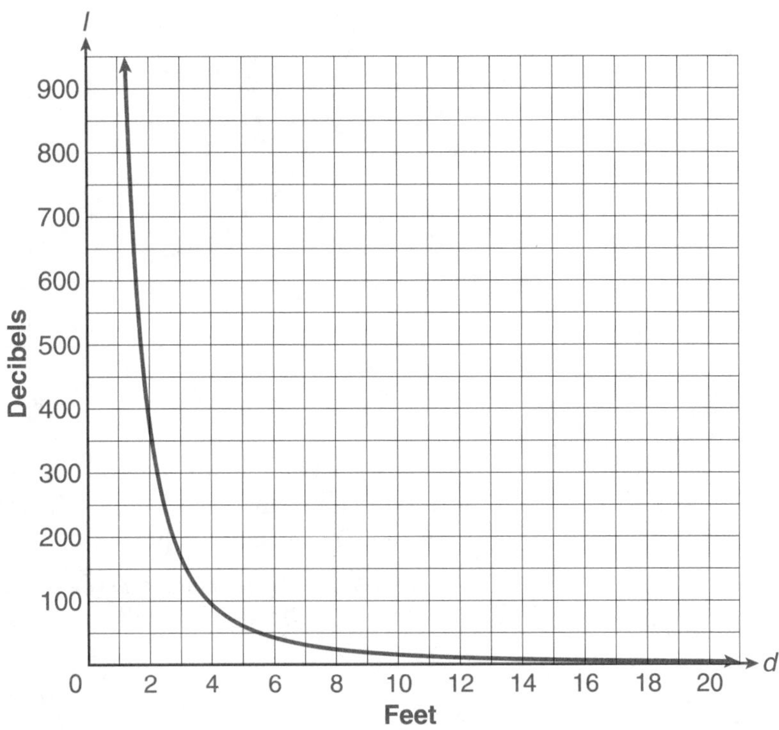

3. As you move closer to the person speaking, what happens to the intensity of the sound?

   It increases.

4. As you move away from the person speaking, what happens to the intensity of the sound?

It decreases.

The function defined by $I = \frac{1500}{d^2}$ belongs to a family of functions having a rule of the form $f(x) = \frac{k}{x^2}$, where k represents some nonzero constant. Examples of this type of function are $f(x) = \frac{1}{x^2}$ and $g(x) = \frac{10}{x^2}$. Use these functions to answer Problem 5.

5. a. What is the domain of functions f and g?

The domain is all nonzero real numbers.

b. Sketch the graphs of f and g on the same coordinate system.

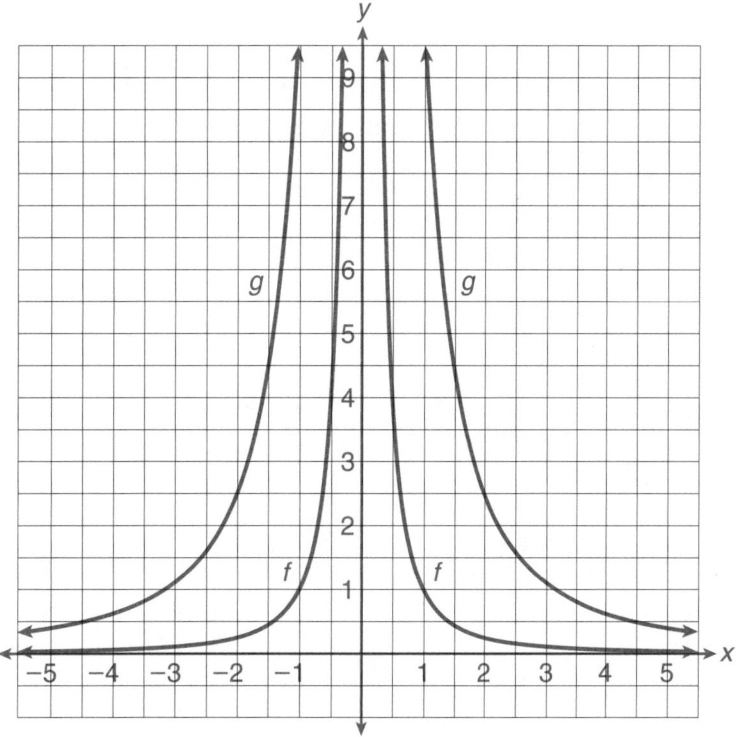

c. Explain why no part of each graph appears in the third or fourth quadrant.

The output is always positive.

d. What happens to the output values as the input increases infinitely in both the positive and negative directions?

Decrease, approaching zero.

e. What is the horizontal asymptote for each graph?

The x-axis, $y = 0$.

f. What happens to the output values as the positive input values get closer to zero?

They increase.

g. What happens to the output values as the negative input values get closer to zero?

They increase.

h. What is the vertical asymptote for each graph?

The y-axis, $x = 0$.

i. Do the functions have a maximum function value or a minimum function value?

No.

j. For a given input, how is the output of g related to the output of f? Describe this relationship graphically.

For the same input, the output of g is ten times the output of f.

6. Describe how the graphs of $y = \frac{1}{x}$ and $y = \frac{1}{x^2}$ are similar and how they are different.

The graphs have the same asymptotes. Neither has a max or min. $\frac{1}{x}$ is symmetric with respect to the origin; $\frac{1}{x^2}$ is symmetric with respect to the y-axis.

7. Sketch graphs of $g(x) = \frac{10}{x^2}$ and $h(x) = \frac{-10}{x^2}$ on the same coordinate system. Use different colors to differentiate the graphs. Describe the effect of the sign on the graphs of $g(x) = \frac{10}{x^2}$ and $h(x) = \frac{-10}{x^2}$.

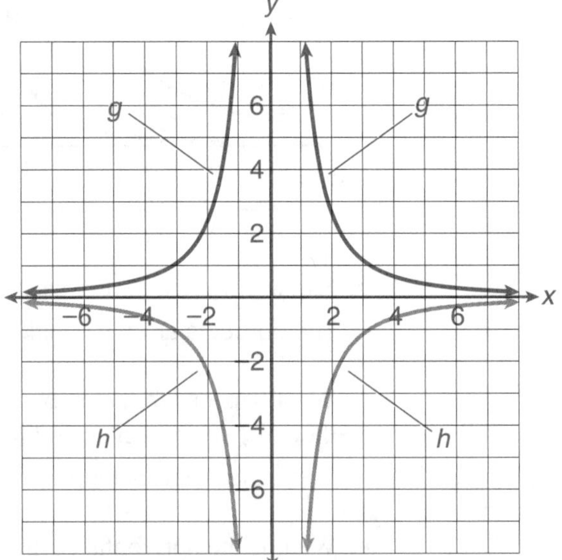

They have the same domain and same asymptotes. They have opposite ranges. h is a reflection of g in the x-axis.

The graph is similar to $f(x) = \frac{5}{x}$.

The graph is similar to $g(x)$.

8. Sketch a graph of $h(x) = \dfrac{1}{x^3}$. Is the graph similar to the graph of $f(x) = \dfrac{1}{x}$ or $g(x) = \dfrac{1}{x^2}$?

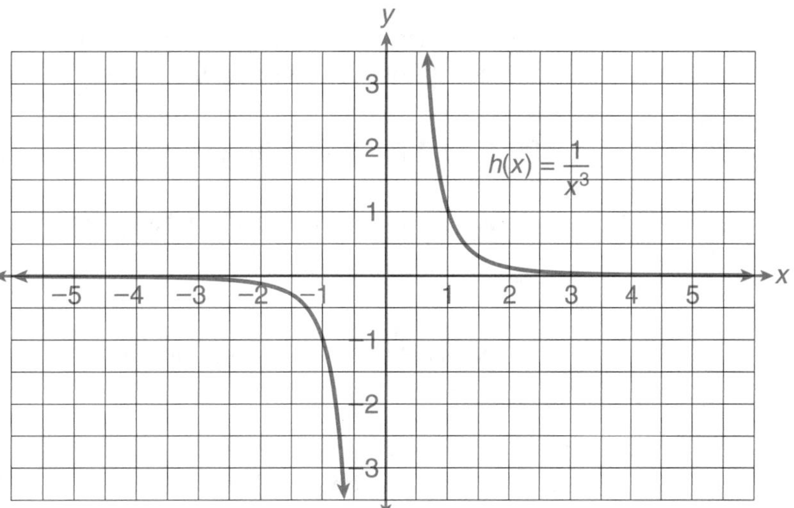

The graph is similar to $\frac{1}{x}$.

9. Sketch a graph $F(x) = \dfrac{1}{x^4}$. Is the graph similar to the graph of $f(x) = \dfrac{1}{x}$ or $g(x) = \dfrac{1}{x^2}$?

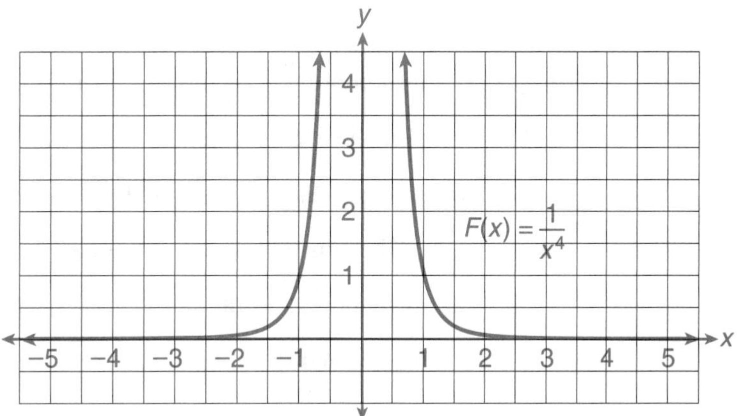

The graph is similar to $y = \dfrac{1}{x^2}$.

Functions of the form $y = \dfrac{k}{x^n}$ belong to the family of functions called **rational functions.** The rational functions of the form $y = \dfrac{k}{x^n}$ are also called **inverse variation functions.**

For example, for the function given by $y = \frac{10}{x}$, y varies inversely as x, or y is inversely proportional to x. The number 10 is called the constant of variation or the constant of proportionality. As x doubles in value, the corresponding y-values are reduced by half.

In this activity the intensity of sound I is inversely proportional to the square of the distance d from the source of the sound.

10. For the function defined by $f(x) = \dfrac{8}{x^2}$, answer the following questions.

a. $f(x)$ varies inversely as what quantity?

$f(x)$ varies inversely as x^2.

b. What is the constant of proportionality?

8

c. If x is doubled, what is the effect on $f(x)$?

If x is doubled, $f(x)$ is quartered.

11. Using the patterns of inverse variation, complete the following table if y is inversely proportional to the cube of x

x	0.5	1	2	6
y	64	8	1	0.037

12. In this activity, the relationship between the intensity I of a human voice and the distance d from the individual was given by $I = \dfrac{1500}{d^2}$, where I is measured in decibels, d is measured in feet, and 1500 is the constant of proportionality. The constant of proportionality depends on the source of the sound and the surroundings. If the source of the sound changes, the value of the constant of proportionality will also change.

a. The intensity of the sound made by a heavy truck 60 feet away is 90 decibels. Determine the constant of proportionality.

$$I = \frac{k}{d^2} \Rightarrow k = 90 \cdot 60^2 = 324{,}000$$

b. Determine the intensity of the sound made by the truck when it is 100 feet away.

$$I = \frac{324{,}000}{100^2} = 32.4 \text{ decibels}$$

EXERCISES

1. Sketch a graph of the functions $f(x) = \frac{3}{x^2}$ and $g(x) = \frac{-3}{x^2}$ on the same coordinate system. Describe how the graph of g is related to the graph of f.

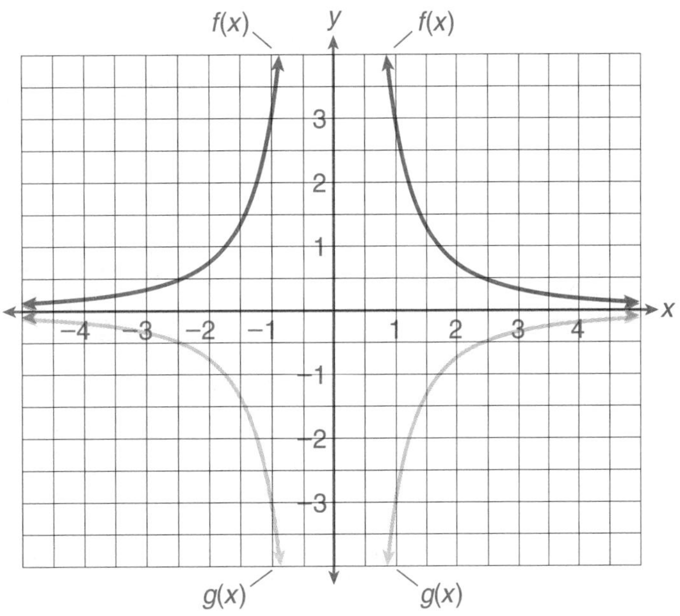

g is the reflection of *f* about the *x*-axis.

2. Match the following functions with the accompanying graphs.

i. $f(x) = \frac{10}{x^4}$ **ii.** $g(x) = \frac{100}{x^5}$ **iii.** $h(x) = \frac{-10}{x^3}$ 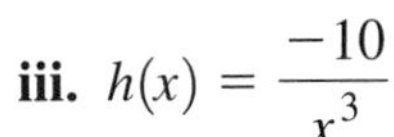 **iv.** $F(x) = \frac{-1}{x^2}$

a.

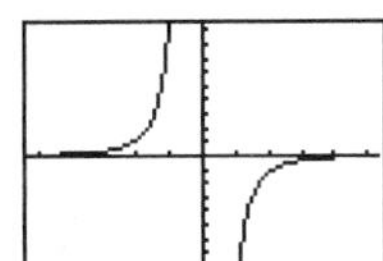

b.

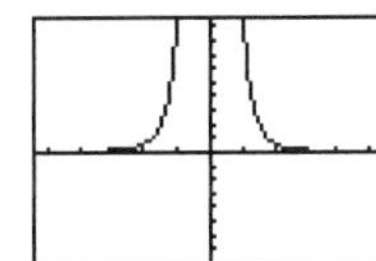

c.

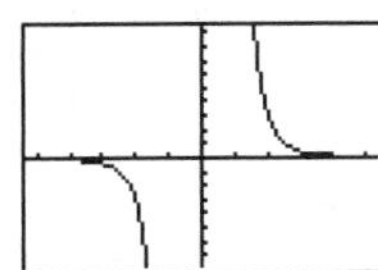

d.

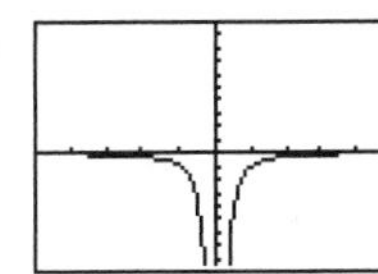

i. Choice b ii. Choice c iii. Choice a iv. Choice d

3. Describe how the graphs of $y = \frac{1}{x^2}$ and $y = \frac{1}{x^3}$ are similar and how they are different.

The graphs have the same asymptotes and the same domain. Neither has a max or a min. $\frac{1}{x^2}$ is symmetric with respect to the *y*-axis. $\frac{1}{x^3}$ is symmetric with respect to the origin.

Exercise numbers appearing in color are answered in the Selected Answers section of this book.

4. Consider the family of functions of the form $f(x) = \dfrac{k}{x^n}$ where k is a nonzero constant and n is a positive integer.

a. What is the domain of f?

All nonzero real numbers.

b. If $k > 0$ and n is an odd positive integer, use several different values of k and n to determine the general shape of the graph of f.

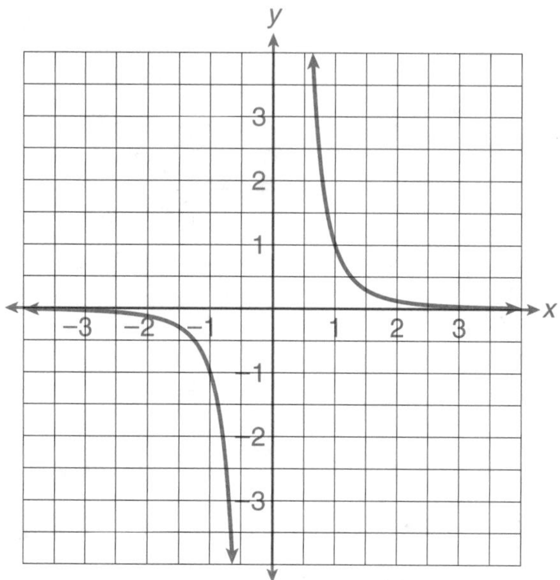

c. If $k > 0$ and n is an even positive integer, use several different values of k and n to determine the general shape of the graph of f.

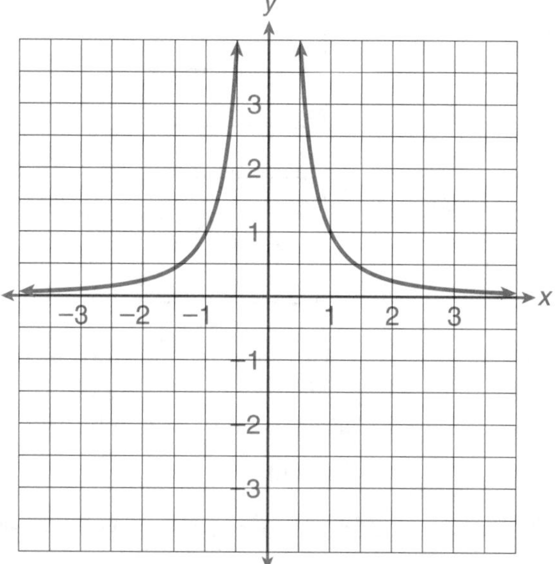

5. How will the general shapes of the graphs in Exercise 4 change if $k < 0$?

The output corresponding to a given input will be the opposite in sign. The graphs will be reflected in the x-axis.

6. Complete the following tables of ordered pairs for the given inverse variations.

a. y varies inversely as x $y = 2/x$

x	y
$\frac{1}{2}$	4
1	2
2	1
6	1/3

b. y varies inversely as x^3 $y = \frac{8}{x^3}$

x	y
$\frac{1}{2}$	64
1	8
2	1
6	1/27

7. If y varies inversely as the cube of x, determine the constant of variation if $y = 16$ when $x = 2$.

$y = \frac{k}{x^3}$ $16 = \frac{k}{2^3}$ or $k = 16 \cdot 2^3 = 128$

8. The amount of current I in a circuit varies inversely as the resistance R. A circuit containing a resistance of 10 ohms has a current of 12 amperes. Find the current in a circuit containing a resistance of 15 ohms.

$I = \frac{k}{R}$; $12 = \frac{k}{10}$ or $k = 12 \cdot 10 = 120$ $I = \frac{120}{R}$; $I = \frac{120}{15} = 8$ amps

9. The intensity I of light varies inversely as the square of the distance d between the source of light and the object being illuminated. A light meter reads 0.25 unit at a distance of 2 meters from a light source. What will the meter read at a distance of 3 meters from the source?

$I = \frac{k}{d^2}$; or $0.25 = \frac{k}{2^2}$ or $k = (0.25) \cdot 4 = 1$ $I = \frac{1}{d^2} = \frac{1}{3^2} \approx 0.11$ unit

10. You are investigating the relationship between the volume V and pressure P of a gas. In a laboratory, you conduct the following experiment: While holding the temperature of a gas constant, you vary the pressure and measure the corresponding volume. The data that you collect appear in the following table.

P (psi)	20	30	40	50	60	70	80
V (cu ft)	82	54	41	32	27	23	20

a. Sketch a graph of the data.

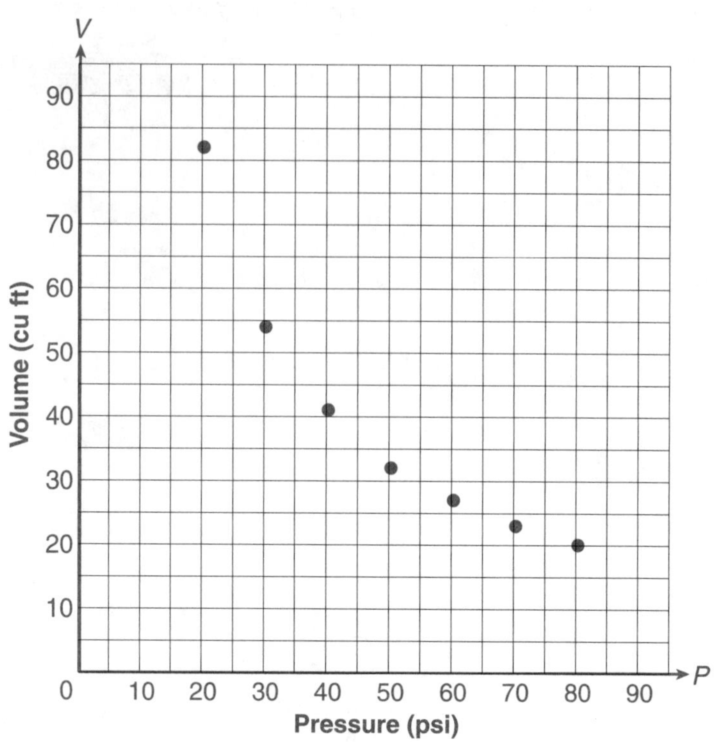

b. One possible model for the data is that V varies inversely as the square of P. Do the data fit the model $V = \frac{k}{P^2}$? Explain.

No. Using $P = 20$, $V = 82$; $k = 20^2(82) = 32{,}800$.

If $V = \frac{32{,}800}{P^2}$, then $P = 30$ would yield $V = \frac{32{,}800}{30^2} = 36.44$ (not very close).

c. Another possible model for the data is that V varies inversely as P. Does $V = \frac{k}{p}$ model the data? Explain.

Yes. Using $P = 20$, $V = 82$; $k = 20(82) = 1640$.

$V = \frac{1640}{30} = 54.67 \quad V = \frac{1640}{40} = 41$

d. Predict the volume of the gas if the pressure is 65 psi.

(Answers will vary if using the graph.) ≈ 25

ACTIVITY 5.3

Percent Markup

Topic: *Rational Functions of the Form* $f(x) = \dfrac{k}{ax + b}$

You are a buyer for a national chain of retail stores. You purchase merchandise at a wholesale cost. The merchandise is then sold at a retail price (called the selling price). The retailer's markup is the difference between the selling price (what the consumer pays) and the wholesale cost.

1. a. You acquire a line of sports jackets at a wholesale cost of \$80 per jacket. If the jackets sell for \$120 each at the retail level, what is the amount of the markup?

Markup = \$120 − \$80 = \$40

b. The markup is what percentage of the selling price? (This percentage is called the percent markup of the selling price.)

$\frac{40}{120} = \frac{1}{3} = 33\frac{1}{3}\%$

2. The relationship between the selling price S, the wholesale cost C, and the percent markup P of the selling price (expressed as a decimal) is given by

$$S = \frac{C}{1 - P}.$$

If the wholesale cost of a sports jacket is \$80, write a function rule for S in terms of P.

$$S = \frac{80}{1 - P}$$

3. a. Can the percent markup of the selling price be 100% (i.e., can $P = 1$)? Explain.

No. P cannot equal 1 because the denominator would become $1 - 1 = 0$.

b. What is the practical domain for this function?

$0 \le P < 1$

4. a. Complete the following table for $S = \dfrac{80}{1 - P}$.

P (PERCENT MARKUP)	0	0.01	0.05	0.10	0.25	0.50	0.75	0.95
S (SELLING PRICE)	80	80.81	84.21	88.89	106.67	160	320	1600

b. As the values of P approach 1, what happens to the values of S? What does this mean in practical terms?

The values of S increase. As the percent markup increases, the selling price increases.

5. Sketch a graph of the function.

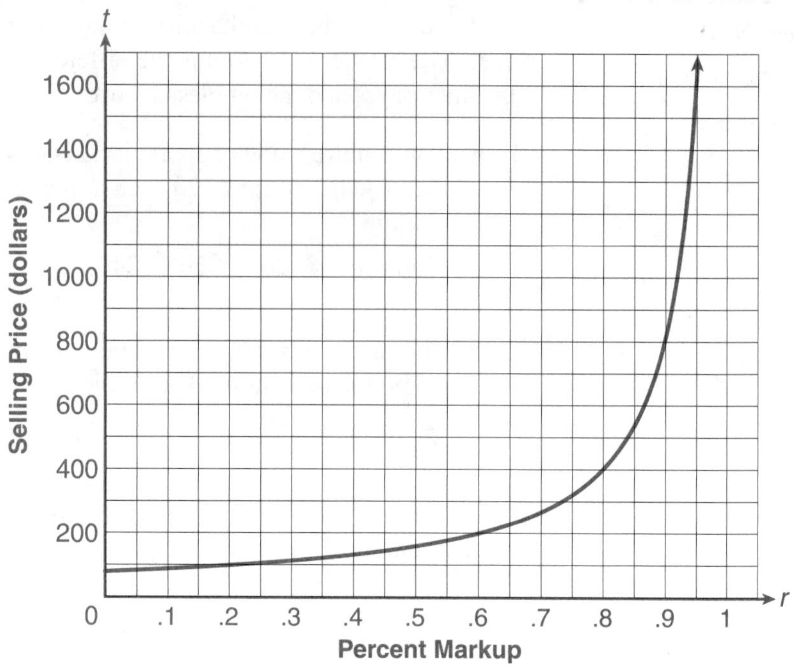

Because S and P represent real-world quantities, the practical domain limits our investigation of the function defined by $S = \frac{C}{1 - P}$.

6. Consider the general function f defined by $f(x) = \frac{80}{1 - x}$.

a. What is the domain of this function f?

All real numbers except $x = 1$.

b. Complete the following table.

x	−10	−5	0	0.50	0.75	0.90	1	1.10	1.25	1.50	2	5	10
$f(x)$	7.27	13.33	80	160	320	800	---	−800	−320	−160	−80	−20	−8.99

c. Does the graph of f have a horizontal asymptote? Explain why or why not. If you answered yes, what is the equation of the horizontal asymptote?

Yes. The horizontal asymptote is $y = 0$. As x gets larger in magnitude, $f(x)$ gets smaller (closer to zero).

d. Does the graph of f have a vertical asymptote? Explain why or why not. If you answered yes, what is the equation of the vertical asymptote?

Yes. The vertical asymptote is $x = 1$. f is not defined for $x = 1$ (denom $= 0$) but as x approaches 1 $|f(x)|$ gets very large.

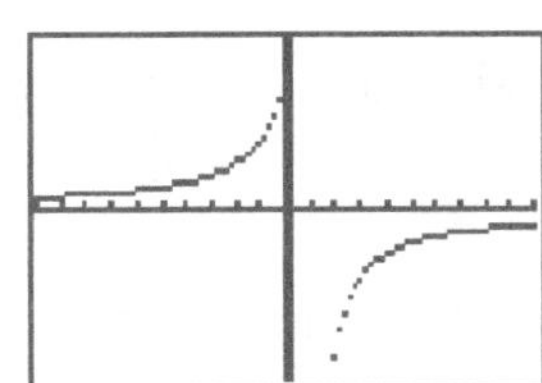

e. Sketch a graph of the function f using your grapher.

f. For what value of x is $f(x)$ maximum?

f has no maximum.

7. Consider the function defined by $g(x) = \dfrac{80}{x + 1}$.

a. What is the domain of g?

All real numbers except $x = -1$.

b. Construct a table of data points for g.

x	−4	−3	−2	−1	0	1	2
$g(x)$	−26.7	−40	−80	—	80	40	26.7

c. Sketch a graph of g.

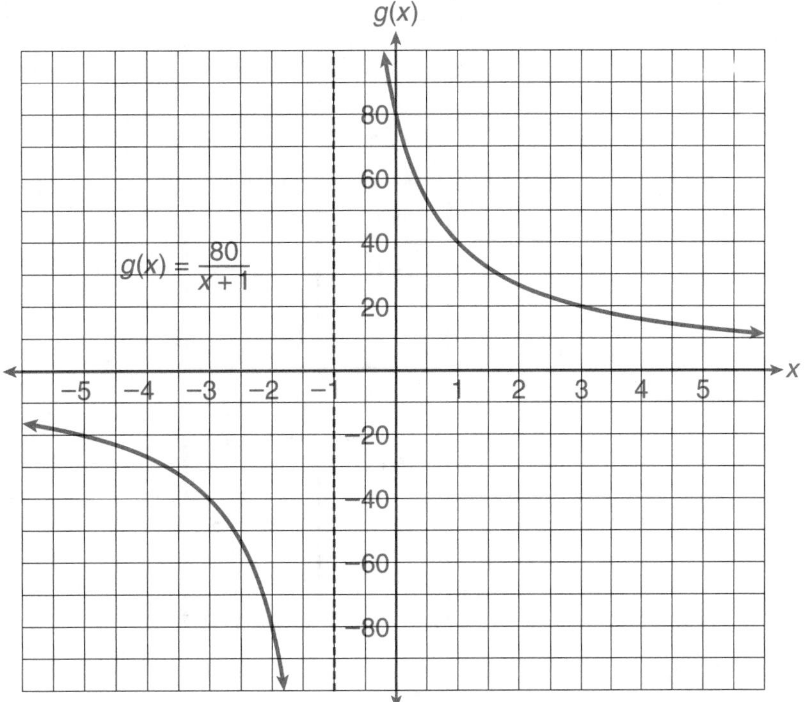

d. Determine the equation of the vertical asymptote.

$x = -1$

e. Determine the equation of the horizontal asymptote.

$y = 0$

8. How are the graphs of $f(x) = \dfrac{80}{1 - x}$ and $g(x) = \dfrac{80}{x + 1}$ similar? How are they different?

The graphs have the same horizontal asymptote and the same y-intercept and basic shape. The vertical asymptotes are different. The graphs are mirror images with respect to the y-axis.

9. Without using your grapher, match the following function rules with the accompanying graphs. Use your grapher to verify.

i. $f(x) = \dfrac{5}{x}$ **ii.** $g(x) = \dfrac{5}{x^2}$ **iii.** $h(x) = \dfrac{-5}{x}$

iv. $F(x) = \dfrac{5}{x + 2}$ **v.** $G(x) = \dfrac{5}{2x - 4}$

a.

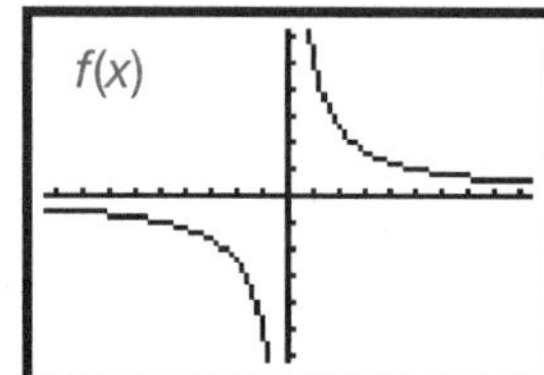

b.

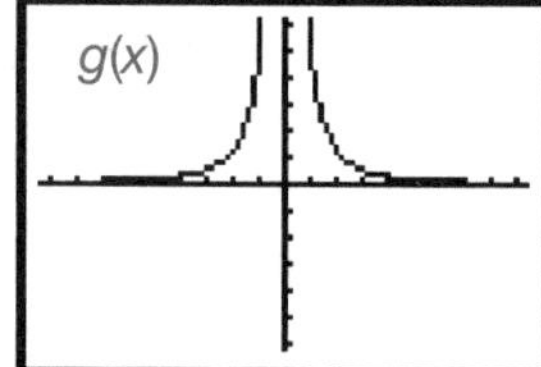

c.

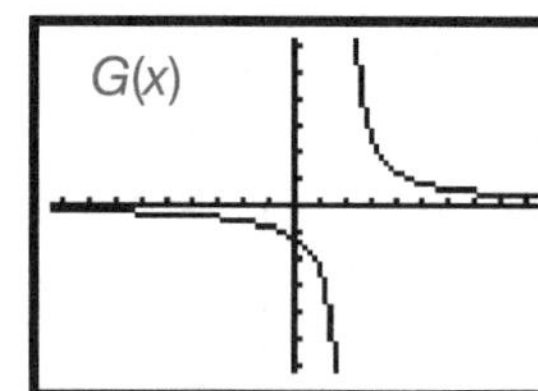

d.

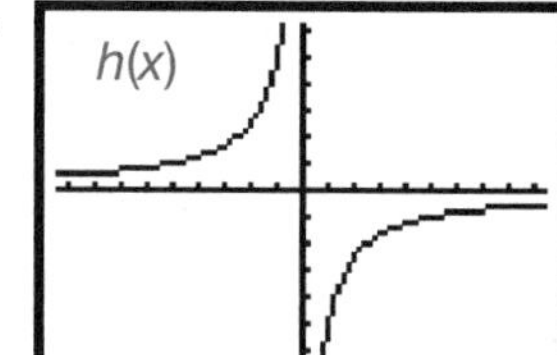

e.

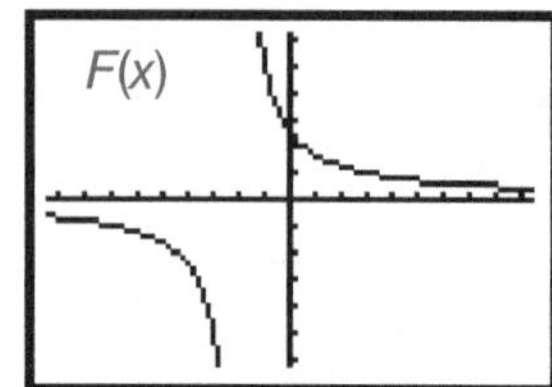

SUMMARY

A rational function Q is any function that can be defined by

$$Q(x) = \frac{f(x)}{g(x)},$$

where $f(x)$ and $g(x)$ are polynomials and $g(x) \neq 0$. This means that rational functions are quotients of polynomials, and the only values at which the function is not defined is any value for which the denominator is zero. If $g(a) = 0$ and $f(a) \neq 0$, then $x = a$ is a vertical asymptote of the graph of Q.

EXERCISES

1. To obtain an estimate of the required volume V of timber that must be harvested to break even, the following model is used:

$$V = \frac{Y + L}{P - S - F - T},$$

where: V is the required annual logging volume (in cubic meters)
Y is the yard cost (in dollars)
L is the loading cost (in dollars)
P is the selling price (in dollars per cubic meter)
S is the skidding cost (in dollars per cubic meter)
F is the falling cost (in dollars per cubic meter)
T is the transportation cost (in dollars per cubic meter)

a. Suppose a logging company estimates that the yard cost will be \$25,000, the loading cost will be \$55,000, the skidding cost will be \$1.50 per cubic meter, the falling cost will be \$0.40 per cubic meter, and the transportation cost will be \$0.60 per cubic meter. Write a rule for V as a function of P.

$$V = \frac{25{,}000 + 55{,}000}{P - 1.5 - 0.40 - 0.60} = \frac{80{,}000}{P - 2.5}$$

b. Complete the following table.

P ($)	2.50	3.00	5.00	10.00	25.00
V (m³)	—	160,000	32,000	10,667	3555.55

c. As the selling price per cubic meter increases, what happens to the corresponding required logging volume V?

It decreases.

d. Determine the value of V when $P = 2$. What is the practical meaning of the negative value of V?

$V(2) = -160{,}000$. A price of \$2 per cubic meter is not practical.

e. What is the practical domain of this function?

$P > 2.5$

Exercise numbers appearing in color are answered in the Selected Answers section of this book.

f. Sketch a graph of the function.

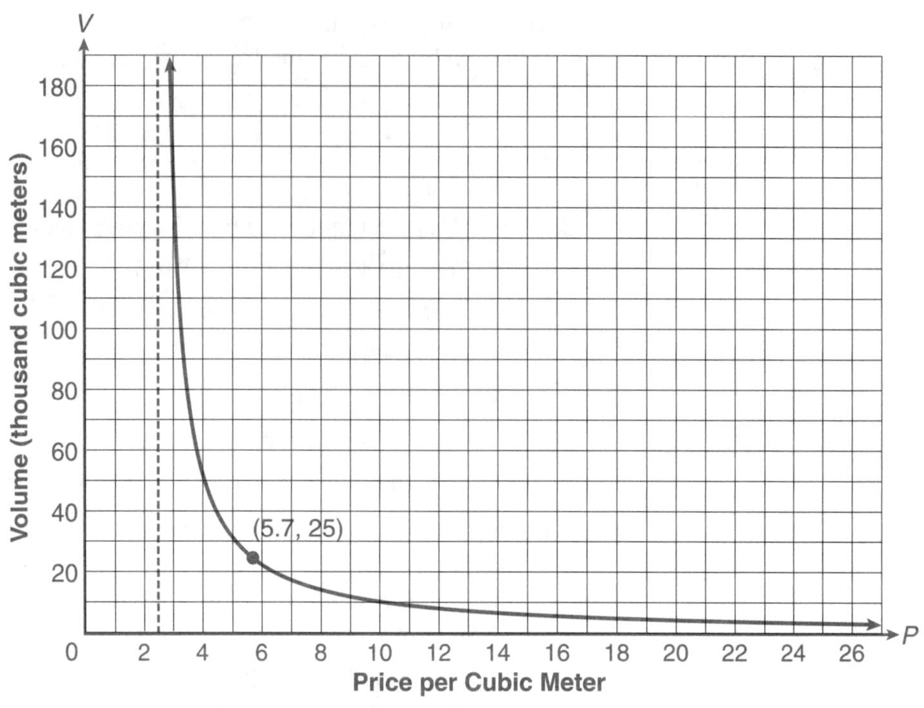

2. Two functions are defined by $f(x) = \dfrac{10}{x - 5}$ and $g(x) = \dfrac{10}{5 - x}$.

a. Describe how you can determine the vertical asymptote without graphing.

Set the denominator equal to zero and solve for x.

b. Determine the vertical asymptote for the graph of each function.

For both, vertical asymptote: $x = 5$; horizontal asymptote: $y = 0$.

c. Verify your answers by graphing each function on your grapher.

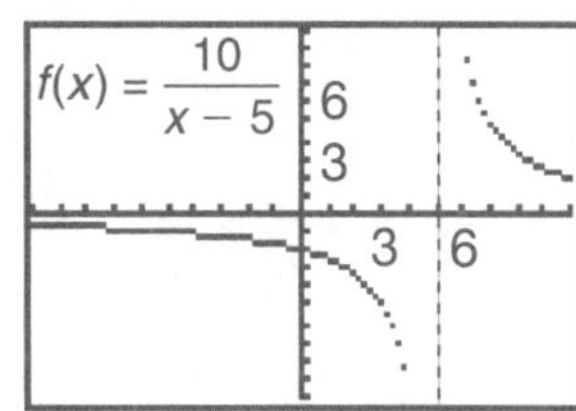

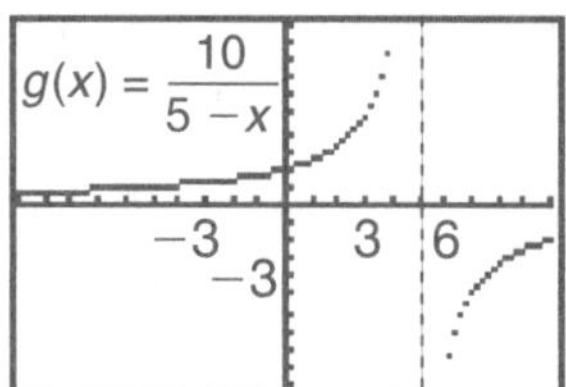

3. Without graphing, determine the domain of each of the following functions. Then determine the equation of the vertical asymptote for each function. Verify by using your grapher.

a. $f(x) = \dfrac{6}{x - 7}$

D: all real numbers except $x = 7$

Vert. asy: $x = 7$

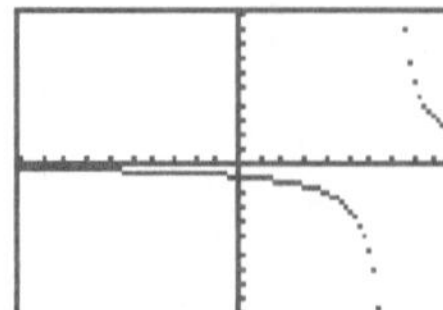

b. $g(x) = \dfrac{20}{25 - x}$

D: all real numbers except $x = 25$

Vert. asy: $x = 25$

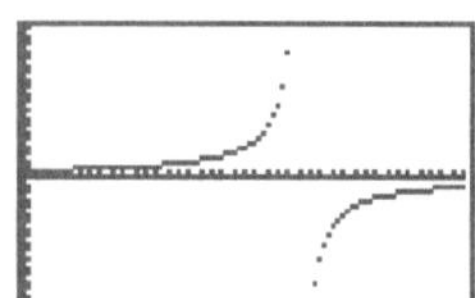

c. $h(x) = \dfrac{3}{2x - 10}$

D: all real numbers except $x = 5$

Vert. asy: $x = 5$

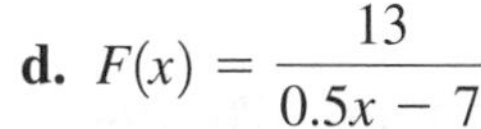

d. $F(x) = \dfrac{13}{0.5x - 7}$

D: all real numbers except $x = 14$

Vert. asy: $x = 14$

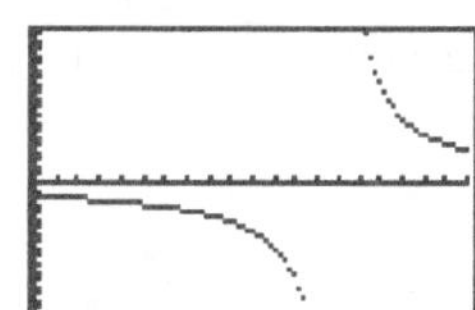

e. $G(x) = \dfrac{-4}{2x + 5}$

D: all real numbers except $x = -2.5$

Vert. asy: $x = -2.5$

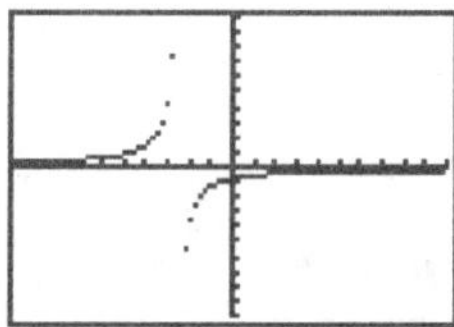

4. Give examples of two different rational functions that have a vertical asymptote at $x = 10$.

$y = \dfrac{k}{x - 10}$ and $y = \dfrac{k}{10 - x}$ for any nonzero k.

5. As the input value of a rational function gets closer to a vertical asymptote, the output becomes larger in magnitude, approaching either positive or negative infinity. Consider the functions $f(x) = \dfrac{1}{x - 5}$ and $g(x) = \dfrac{10}{5 - x}$.

a. Determine the equations of the vertical asymptotes for functions f and g.

$x = 5$

b. Describe what happens to the output value when x is near the right-hand side of the vertical asymptote but to the right of it.

$f(x)$ gets large, approaching infinity.

$g(x)$ gets small, approaching negative infinity.

c. Describe what happens to the output value when x is near the left-hand side of the vertical asymptote but to the left of it.

$f(x)$ gets small, approaching negative infinity

$g(x)$ gets large, approaching infinity.

6. How many vertical asymptotes do you expect for the rational function whose equation is $y = \dfrac{1}{(x + 12)(x - 2)(x - 20)}$? Determine the equation of each vertical asymptote.

3 vertical asymptotes; $x = -12$, $x = 2$, $x = 20$.

ACTIVITY 5.4

Blood-Alcohol Levels

Topics: *Solving Equations Involving Rational Expressions, Horizontal Asymptotes*

In 1992, the U.S. Department of Transportation recommended that states adopt 0.08% blood-alcohol concentration as the legal measure of drunk driving. If you assume that a regular 12-ounce beer is 5% alcohol by volume and that the normal bloodstream contains 5 liters (or 169 ounces) of fluid, your maximum blood-alcohol concentration can be approximately modeled by the equation

$$B = \frac{600n}{w(169 + 0.6n)},$$

where n is the number of beers consumed in one hour and w is your body weight in pounds.

1. Replace w with your body weight and complete the following table.

NUMBER OF BEERS, n	1	2	3	4	5	6	7	8	9	10
BLOOD ALCOHOL CONCENTRATION, B	0.018	0.035	0.053	0.070	0.087	0.104	0.121	0.138	0.155	0.171

(Answers will vary.) Above uses $w = 200$ lb.

2. According to this model, how many beers can you consume in 1 hour without exceeding the recommended legal measure of drunk driving?

   (Answers will vary.) For $w = 200$, the answer is 4.

3. a. A football player friend of yours weighs 232 pounds. What is his maximum blood-alcohol level if he drinks 4 beers in one hour?

   $B = 0.06$ percent blood-alcohol concentration

   b. Suppose your friend is given a breathalyzer test. The result is a blood-alcohol concentration of 0.05. Using the blood-alcohol concentration function, write an equation that can be solved to determine the number of beers your friend consumed in the previous hour.

   $$0.05 = \frac{600n}{232(169 + 0.6n)}$$

   c. Solve the equation in part b using a graphical approach. $n = 3.3$

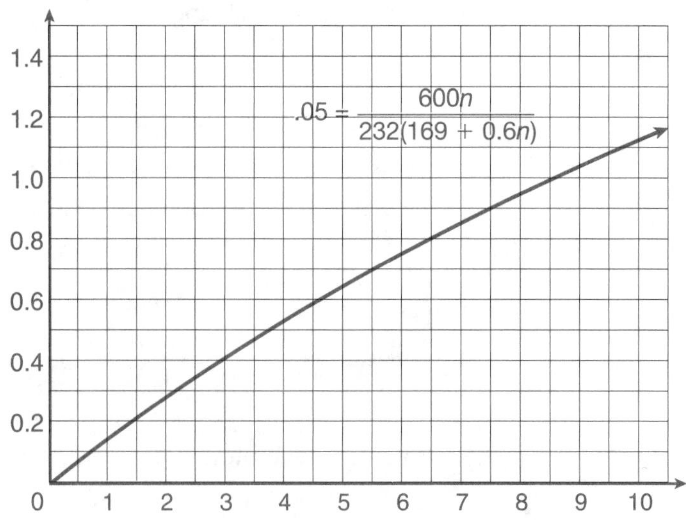

When applying algebraic techniques to solve equations, recall that you undo the operations in reverse order. If a variable appears in the denominator of a fraction, you need to multiply both sides of the equation by the denominator.

For example, to solve the equation $\frac{16}{x + 3} = 2$, you first multiply both sides of the equation by the denominator $x + 3$ as follows:

$$(x + 3) \cdot \frac{16}{x + 3} = 2(x + 3)$$
$$16 = 2x + 6$$

Solving for x, you have

$$10 = 2x$$
$$5 = x$$

Therefore, if $x = 5$, the equation $\frac{16}{x + 3} = 2$ is satisfied.

You can verify that 5 is a solution to the given equation by graphing $y_1 = \frac{16}{x + 3}$ and $y_2 = 2$.

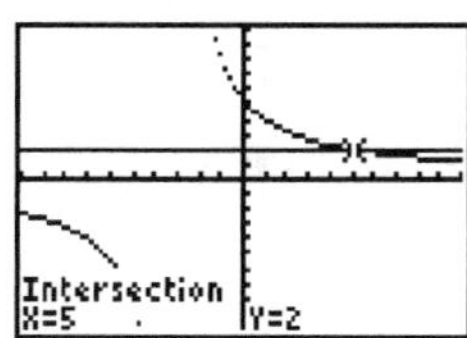

4. Solve each of the following equations using an algebraic approach. Verify your answer graphically.

   a. $\frac{45}{x} = 9$ $\quad x = 5$

   b. $\frac{23}{x + 2} = 15$ $\quad x = -7/15 \approx -.467$

   c. $\frac{13}{x} = \frac{2}{5}$ (Multiply both sides of the equation by the least common denominator (LCD).) $\quad x = 32.5$

   d. $\frac{16}{x^2} = \frac{1}{4}$ $\quad x = \pm 8$

For additional examples and practice using the LCD, the least common denominator, to solve equations involving rational expressions, see Appendix A.

5. **a.** Solve the equation in Problem 3b using an algebraic approach.

$$0.05 = \frac{600n}{232(169 + 0.6n)}$$
$$0.05(232)(169 + 0.6n) = 600n$$
$$0.05(232)(169) + 0.05(232)(0.6n) = 600n$$
$$1960.4 + 6.96n = 600n$$
$$1960.4 = 593.04n$$
$$3.306 \approx n$$

b. How does your solution compare with the result in Problem 3c using a graphical approach?

The same, but more accurate.

6. a. What is the practical domain of the blood-alcohol function of Problem 3?

(Answers may vary.) Generally between zero and ten beers.

b. Does the weight of a person have any impact on the practical domain? Explain.

Yes, because the lower the weight, the lower the upper limit of beers consumed.

c. What is the vertical intercept?

When $n = 0$, $B = 0$

d. Sketch the graph of your blood-alcohol function over the practical domain identified in part a.

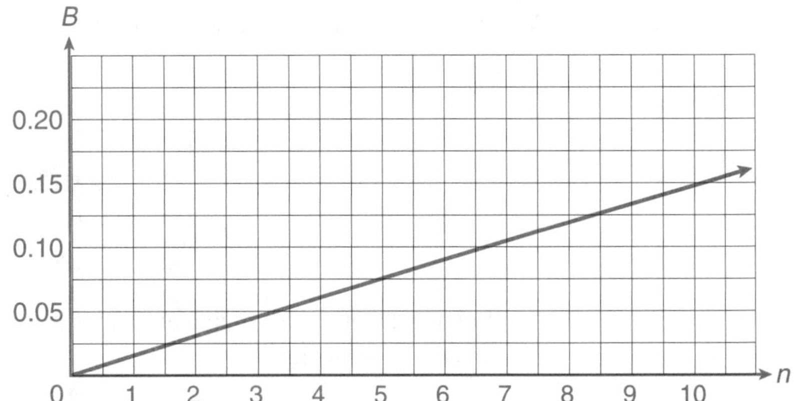

e. The graphs you have studied in this chapter so far have at least one feature in common. As the input values get larger and larger, the output values have always approached zero. In the blood-alcohol function, as the values of n get larger and larger, what happens to the corresponding values of B?

As n gets larger and larger, B also gets larger.

f. Extend the window of your grapher until you can see the graph leveling off (becoming horizontal) for large values of n. Estimate the equation of the horizontal asymptote of the graph of the blood-alcohol function.

Horizontal asymptote appears to be approximately $y = 4.25$.

More generally, $y = \frac{1000}{w}$ for any weight, w.

g. Does this asymptote have any practical significance for this application?

The horizontal asymptote has no practical significance, since there is a definite practical upper limit to the number of beers anyone can consume in one hour.

7. Consider a function defined by the equation $f(x) = \dfrac{2x}{x - 5}$.

a. What is the domain of this function?

The domain of f is all real numbers except 5.

b. Sketch a graph of this function.

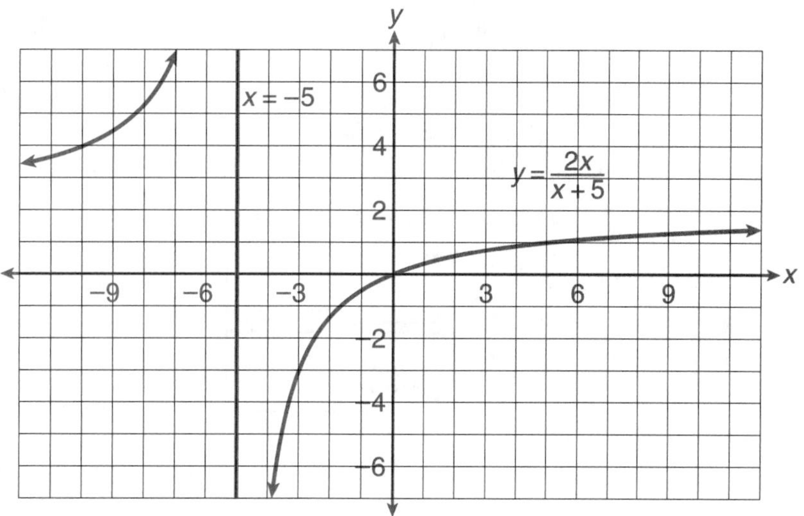

c. What are the equations of the vertical and horizontal asymptotes?

Vertical asymptote: $x = -5$ Horizontal asymptote: $y = 2$

EXERCISES

1. For each rational function
   i. determine the domain
   ii. determine the vertical asymptotes
   iii. graph the function using your grapher.
   iv. determine the horizontal asymptote by inspecting the graph of your function.

a. $y = \dfrac{4x}{x + 2}$

Domain: $x \neq -2$

H: $y = 4$; V: $x = -2$

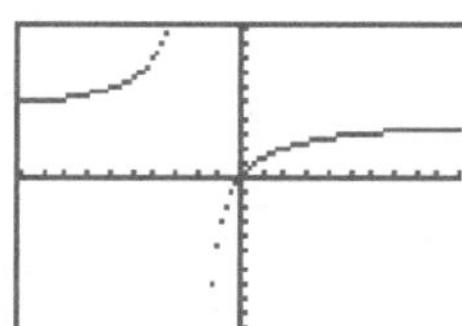

b. $y = \dfrac{1 - x}{x + 1}$

Domain: $x \neq -1$

H: $y = -1$; V: $x = -1$

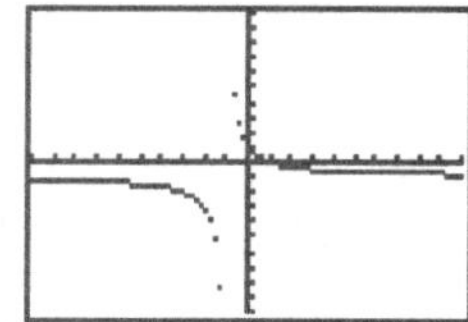

c. $y = \dfrac{3x}{x^2 - 4}$

Domain: $x \neq \pm 2$

H: $y = 0$; V: $x = \pm 2$

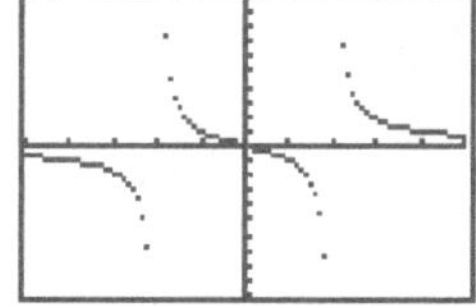

d. $y = 12 - \dfrac{6x}{1 - 2x}$

Domain: $x \neq \frac{1}{2}$

H: $y = 15$; V: $x = \frac{1}{2}$

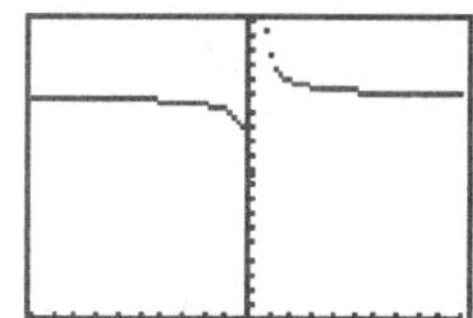

Exercise numbers appearing in color are answered in the Selected Answers section of this book.

2. Solve the following equations algebraically and by graphing.

a. $\dfrac{3x}{2x - 1} = 3$

$3x = 3(2x - 1)$

$3x = 6x - 3$

$-3x = -3$

$x = 1$

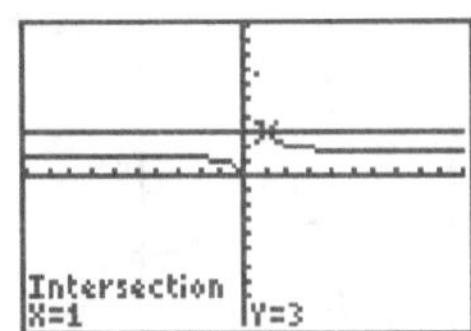

b. $\dfrac{x + 1}{5x - 3} = 2$

$x + 1 = 2(5x - 3)$

$x + 1 = 10x - 6$

$-9x = -7$

$x = \frac{7}{9} \approx 0.778$

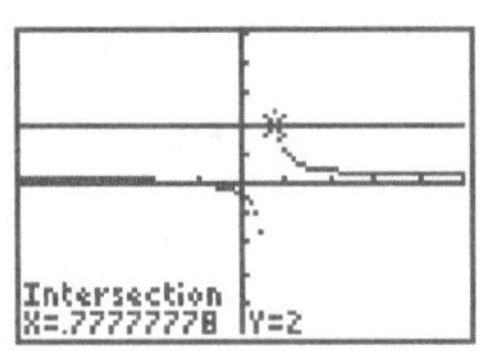

c. $\dfrac{-7x}{2.8 + x} = 3.1$

$-7x = 3.1(2.8 + x)$

$-7x = 8.68 + 3.1x$

$-10.1x = 8.68$

$x = -0.859$

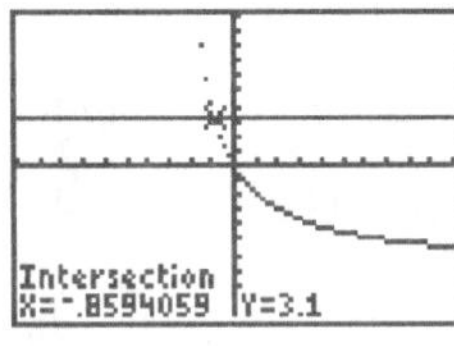

d. $\dfrac{6 - x}{x^2 + 2} = 2$

$6 - x = 2(x^2 + 2)$

$6 - x = 2x^2 + 4$

$0 = 2x^2 + x - 2$

$$x = \frac{-1 \pm \sqrt{1 - 4(2)(-2)}}{2(2)}$$

$$x = \frac{-1 \pm \sqrt{17}}{4} = 0.781, -1.281$$

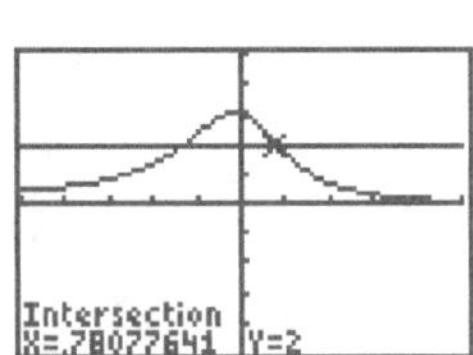

3. Solve the following inequalities by graphing.

a. $\dfrac{x + 2}{2x - 1} \le 5$

$x < 0.5, x \ge 0.778$

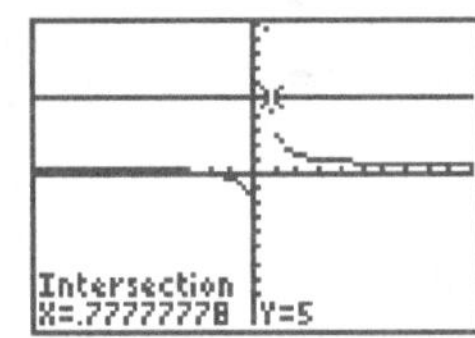

b. $\dfrac{3.9 - 2x}{0.2 + x} < 3$

$x < -0.2, x > 0.66$

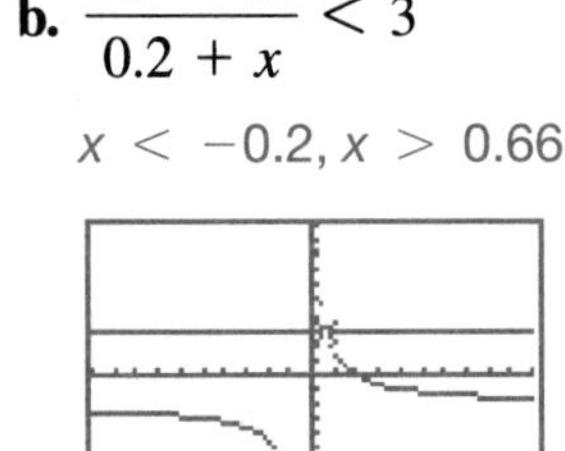

c. $\dfrac{x + 1}{6 - x} > 5x$

$x < 0.0345, 5.766 \le x < 6$

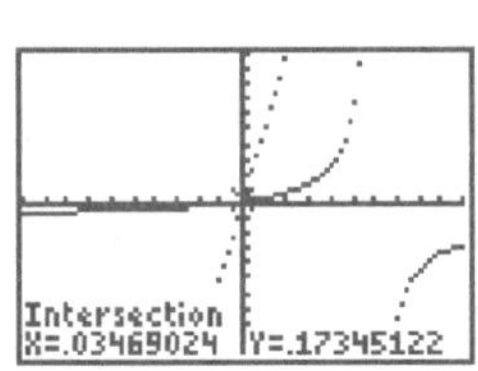

4. In a 20-kilometer race, the equation that expresses average speed (in kilometers per hour) as a function of time (in hours) is $s = \frac{20}{t}$.

a. Determine your time to complete the race if you average 16 kilometers per hour.

$16 = \frac{20}{t}$; $16t = 20$, $t = \frac{20}{16} = 1.25$ hr.

b. What is your time if you average 18 kilometers per hour?

$18 = \frac{20}{t}$; $18t = 20$; $t = \frac{20}{18} = 1.11$ hr.

5. The intensity of the human voice is inversely proportional to the square of the distance from the source. This is given by the formula from Activity 5.2, Loudness of Sound: $I = \frac{1500}{d^2}$, where I is in decibels and d is in distance in feet.

a. Determine the distance from the source when the intensity of the sound is 15 decibels.

$$15 = \frac{1500}{d^2}$$

$15d^2 = 1500$; $d^2 = 100$ $d = \pm 10$ ft, but only 10 makes sense

b. What is the distance from the source when the intensity is 8000 decibels?

$8000 = \frac{1500}{d^2}$; $8000d^2 = 1500$; $d^2 = 0.1875$; $d = 0.433$ ft

6. As a fund-raising project, the horticulture club at your college decides to publish and sell a calendar. The cost of photographs and typesetting is $450. It costs $3 to print and assemble each calendar.

a. What is the total cost of printing 200 calendars?

$450 + 3(200) = \$1050$

b. What is the average cost per calendar of printing the 200 calendars?

$\frac{1050}{200} = \$5.25$

c. Write an expression for the total cost of printing n calendars.

$C = 450 + 3n$

d. Let A represent the average cost per calendar. Write an equation that gives A as a function of n.

$$A = \frac{450 + 3n}{n}$$

e. Complete the following table.

n (NUMBER)	50	75	100	500	750	1000
A (AVERAGE COST)	12	9	7.50	3.90	3.60	3.45

f. As the input n gets larger and larger, what happens to the output A?

A gets closer and closer to 3.

g. What is the horizontal asymptote for this function?

$A = 3$

h. Verify your answer in part g graphically.

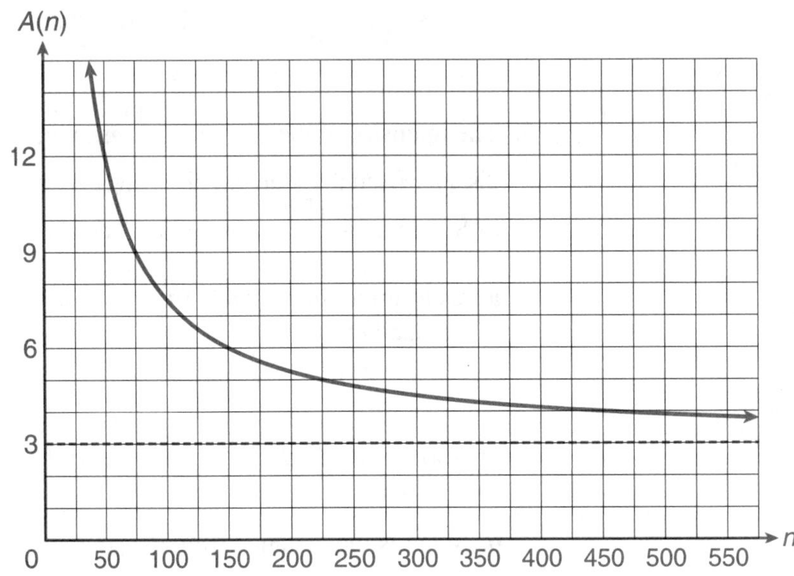

i. Interpret what the horizontal asymptote means.

The average cost will always be at least \$3 per calendar and gets closer to \$3 for larger numbers of calendars.

j. Suppose you want the average cost to be less than \$3.20. Model this problem with an inequality, solve algebraically for n, and verify graphically.

$$\frac{450 + 3n}{n} < 3.20$$

$450 + 3n < 3.20n$

$450 < 0.20n \Rightarrow n > 2250$

7. In a predator-prey model from wildlife biology, the rate R at which prey are consumed by one predator is approximated by the function

$$R = \frac{0.623n}{1 + 0.046n},$$

measured in prey per week, where n is the number of prey available per square mile.

a. If the number of prey available per square mile is 30, what is the rate R?

$$R(30) = \frac{0.623(30)}{1 + 0.046(30)}$$

$R(30) = 7.85$ prey per week.

b. Approximately how many prey must be available per square mile for the predator to consume 10 prey per week?

$$10 = \frac{0.623(n)}{1 + 0.046(n)}$$

$$10(1 + 0.046n) = 0.623n$$

$$10 + 0.46n = 0.623n$$

$$10 = 0.163n$$

$$61.3 = n$$

n is approximately 62 prey per square mile.

c. Suppose you want to maintain the prey population to ensure that a predator may obtain between 6 and 10 prey per week. State the inequality that must be solved, and then solve it.

$$6 \le \frac{0.623n}{1 + 0.046n} \le 10$$ The right-hand side was solved in part b.

$$6(1 + 0.046n) \le 0.623n$$

$$6 + 0.276n \le 0.623n$$

$$6 \le 0.347n$$

$$17.3 \le n$$

$$17.3 \le n \le 61.3$$

$$18 < n < 62$$

d. Use the graph of this function to illustrate your solutions to part c.

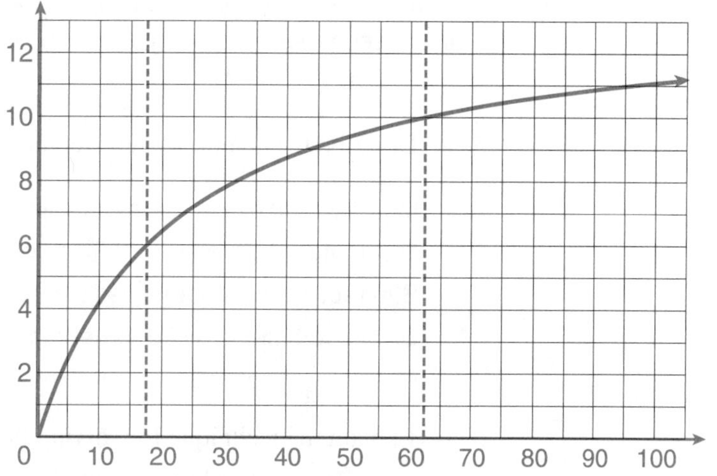

$$6 \le \frac{0.623n}{1 + 0.046n} \le 10$$

$$18 < n < 62$$

What Have I Learned?

1. Make a list of some of the special features of the graphs of rational functions.

Graphs have asymptotes. Vertical asymptotes where the denominator is zero, and horizontal asymptotes when the graph levels off as *x* gets larger and larger (to positive infinity) or as *x* gets smaller and smaller (to negative infinity).

2. Describe the connection, if any, between the domain of a rational function and the equation of its vertical asymptote.

The equation of a vertical asymptote gives a number where the denominator of the rational function is zero. In other words, where the function is not defined, and hence a number that is not in the domain.

3. Describe the algebraic steps required to determine the vertical asymptote(s) of the graph of a rational function.

A rational function must be expressed as a single simplified fraction. Any number that makes the denominator equal to zero will then be the location of a vertical asymptote.

4. For what values of k will the graph of $y = \frac{k}{x}$ be in the second and fourth quadrants?

When *k* is negative, *y* will have the opposite sign of *x*. This will place the graph in the second and fourth quadrants.

5. a. Describe the algebraic steps required to solve $10 = \frac{35}{1 + 5x}$.

Multiply both sides of the equation by $1 + 5x$

Distribute 10 to get $10 + 50x$ on one side of the equation.

Subtract 10 from both sides to get: $25 = 50x$.

Divide both sides by 50 to get the solution: $x = 0.5$

Check by substituting $x = 0.5$ into the original equation.

b. Explain the technique for solving the equation in part a graphically.

To solve graphically, enter two functions on the calculator, one for the left side and one for the right side of the equation. Graph both, adjusting the window to see any points of intersection. Use the intersect routine to approximate the coordinates of the point of intersection. The *x* coordinate is a solution to the equation.

6. Explain how you would determine the horizontal asymptote of the rational function $f(x) = \frac{6x + 1}{2 - 3x}$.

As *x* gets bigger, either by observing the graph or using a table, the values of the function appear to get closer and closer to -2. Also, by looking at the ratio of the *x* terms (the highest degree terms) in the numerator to denominator, we can see $y = -2$.

How Can I Practice?

1. Describe the relationship between the graphs of $f(x) = \frac{1}{x}$ and $g(x) = \frac{-1}{x}$.

   f and *g* are reflections of each other about the *x*-axis (and the *y*-axis!).

2. Describe the relationship between the graphs of $f(x) = \frac{1}{x}$ and $g(x) = \frac{1}{x - 5}$.

   The graph of *g* is the same as *f*, but shifted 5 units to the right.

3. Describe the relationship between the graphs of $f(x) = \frac{1}{x}$ and $g(x) = \frac{1}{x^3}$.

   They are similar, but the graph of *g* is closer to the *x*-axis, and the graph of *f* is closer to the *y*-axis.

4. **a.** Suppose you are taking a trip of 145 miles. Assume that you drive the entire distance at a constant speed. Express your time to take this trip as a function of your speed.

   T = time in hours, s = speed in mph

   $T = \frac{145}{s}$

   b. What is the practical domain for this function?

   $0 < s < 80$

   c. What is the domain based solely on the abstract formula for the function?

   Domain: all real numbers except 0.

5. Determine the domain for each of the following functions. Then give the equation of the vertical asymptote for each function.

   a. $g(x) = \frac{10}{x + 5}$

   D: all real numbers

   except $x = -5$

   Vert. asy.: $x = -5$

   b. $f(x) = \frac{5}{13 - 2x}$

   D: all real numbers

   except $x = 13/2$

   Vert. asy.: $x = 13/2$

   c. $g(x) = \frac{-3}{5x - 8}$

   D: all real numbers

   except $x = 8/5$

   Vert. asy.: $x = 8/5$

   d. $h(x) = \frac{0.02}{5.7x - 3.2}$

   D: all real numbers

   except $x = 0.5614$

   Vert. asy.: $x = 0.5614$

6. Give an example of a rational function that has exactly three vertical asymptotes.

   Answers will vary: three different linear factors in the denominator, not repeated in the numerator.

Exercise numbers appearing in color are answered in the Selected Answers section of this book.

7. The weight of a body above the surface of Earth varies inversely with the square of the distance from the center of Earth. If an object weighs 100 pounds when it is 4000 miles from the center of Earth, how much will it weigh when it is 4500 miles from the center?

$w = \dfrac{k}{d^2}$ $\qquad 100 = \dfrac{k}{4000^2}$ $\qquad 4000^2 \cdot 100 = k = 1.6 \cdot 10^9$

$$w = \frac{1.6 \cdot 10^9}{d^2} = \frac{1.6 \cdot 10^9}{(4500)^2} \approx 79.01 \text{ lbs}$$

8. A manufacturer of lawn mowers uses the function $C(x) = \dfrac{132x + 75{,}250}{x}$ to model the average cost per lawn mower, in dollars, where x is the number of lawn mowers produced.

a. What is the practical domain of this function?

Practical domain: all positive integers, with some realistic upper limit, depending on the specific situation.

b. What is the minimum number of lawn mowers that must be manufactured to bring the average cost per lawn mower down to $199? Solve algebraically and graphically.

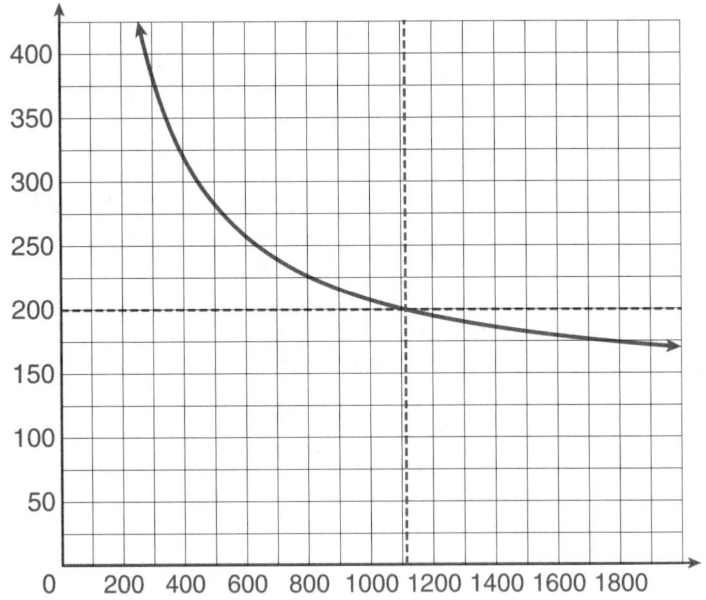

$$199 = \frac{132x + 75{,}250}{x}$$

$$199x = 132x + 75{,}250$$

$x = 1123$ mowers.

c. Suppose the manufacturer wants the average cost to be between \$145 and \$159. Write the inequality that models this situation. Sketch the graph of $C(x)$ and indicate the solutions to the inequality.

$$145 < \frac{132x + 75{,}250}{x} < 159$$

$2787 < x < 5788$, between 2787 and 5788 lawn mowers must be sold.

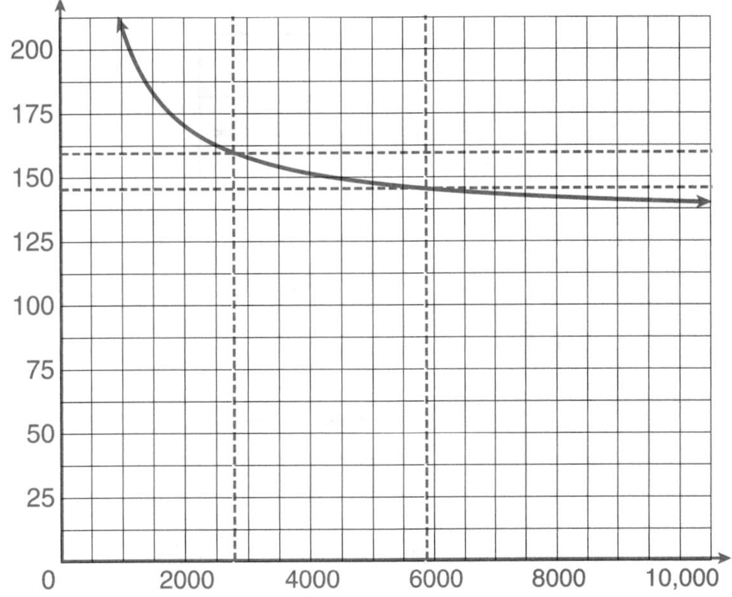

9. The concentration of a drug in the bloodstream, measured in milligrams per liter, can be modeled by the function

$$C = \frac{14t}{3t^2 + 2.5},$$

where t is the number of minutes after injection of the drug.

a. How long after injection will it take for the concentration to get below 0.05 milligrams per liter?

$$\frac{14t}{3t^2 + 2.5} < 0.05$$

$$14t < 0.05(3t^2 + 2.5)$$

$$14t < 0.15t^2 + 0.125$$

$$0 < 0.15t^2 - 14t + 0.125 \quad \text{Find roots of the related equation.}$$

$$t = \frac{-(-14) \pm \sqrt{14^2 - 4(0.15)(0.125)}}{2(0.15)} = 93.32 \text{ min or } 0.0089 \text{ min,}$$

only 93.32 is practical.

b. When will the drug be at its highest concentration?

The drug will be at its highest concentration 0.913 min after injection.

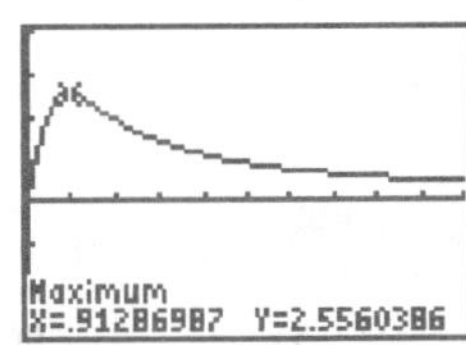

10. Solve each equation algebraically. Verify your answer graphically.

a. $\dfrac{3}{x+1} = 4$

$x = -0.25$

b. $\dfrac{3x}{2x-5} = 10$

$x = \frac{50}{17} \approx 2.94$

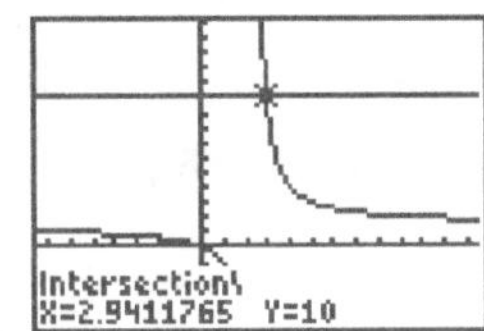

c. $\dfrac{4}{x+3} + 12 = 52$

$x = \frac{-116}{40} \approx -2.9$

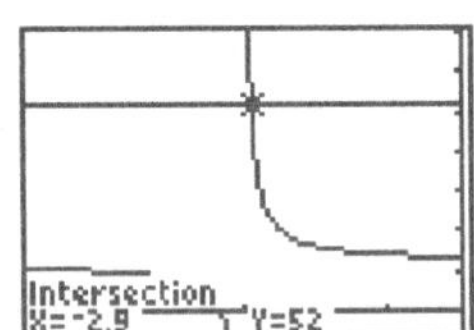

d. $\dfrac{2.4x}{1 + 0.3x} = 5.8$

$x = \dfrac{5.8}{2.4 - (0.3)5.8} = \dfrac{290}{33} \approx 8.788$

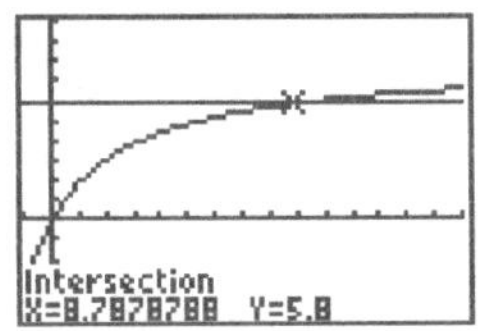

11. The weight of any object decreases as the distance from Earth's surface increases. As the object rises, the effect of Earth's gravitational pull on the object is reduced. The weightlessness that astronauts experience in the space shuttle as it orbits the earth is due to the distance of the shuttle above Earth's surface.

If an object weighs E kilograms at sea level on Earth's surface, then the weight W (also in kilograms) of the object at a distance of h kilometers above sea level is given by the function rule

$$W = \frac{E}{(1 + \frac{h}{6400})^2}.$$

a. Suppose you are flying in a commercial jetliner 15 kilometers above sea level. Replace E with your body weight, measured in kilograms (1 kg = 2.2 lb), and calculate your weight at 15 kilometers above sea level.

(Answers will vary.) 200-lb man ≈ 90.9 kg

$$W = \frac{90.9}{(1 + \frac{15}{6400})^2} = 90.475 \text{ kg}$$

b. If an astronaut weighs 70 kilometers at sea level, write a rule that expresses the astronaut's weight as a function of his or her distance above sea level.

$$W = \frac{70}{(1 + \frac{h}{6400})^2}$$

c. Complete the following table using the function rule from part b.

h	0	10	100	1000	1500	2000	10,000	20,000
W	70	69.78	67.86	52.36	45.94	40.64	10.66	4.11

d. As the height h of the space shuttle increases, what happens to the corresponding weight of the astronaut?

The weight decreases.

e. As the space shuttle reaches its orbiting altitude of 40,000 kilometers above sea level, what is the weight of the astronaut?

1.3317 kg.

f. What is the practical domain of the weight function?

(Answers will vary some at the upper end.)

Domain is $0 \leq h \leq 40{,}000$.

g. Use your grapher to sketch a graph of the weight function.

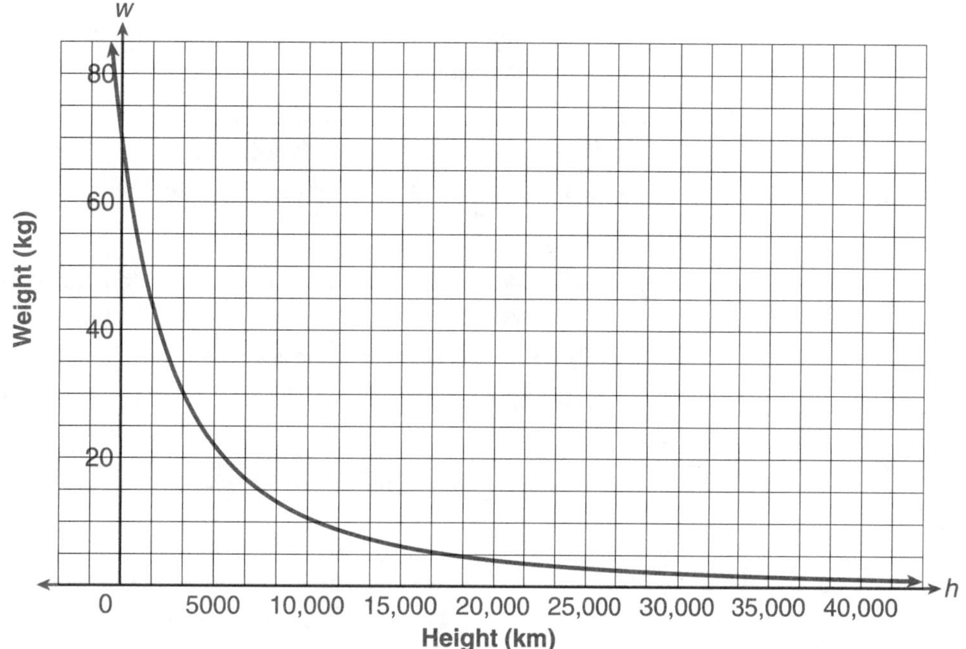

h. At what altitude does the astronaut's weight equal one-half of what it is at sea level?

Find the zero of $f(h) = \dfrac{70}{\left(1 + \frac{h}{6400}\right)^2} - 35$

$h = 2650.9668$

CLUSTER 2

Radical Functions and Equations

ACTIVITY 5.5

Hang Time

Topics: *Radical Functions, Roots, Fractional Exponents*

During the seventeenth century, many mathematicians were interested in projectiles, primarily for their military applications. More recently, studies have been done in the area of sports, where the shot put, the javelin, and a punted football are the projectiles of interest. Dr. Peter Brancazio, a physics professor at Brooklyn College, has spent considerable time studying one of the most famous human projectiles, Michael Jordan. In particular, Brancazio has been interested in Jordan's hang time, the length of time elapsed from the instant that Jordan leaves the floor to the instant that he touches it again. Using basic physics, Brancazio has discovered that the hang time T of any jump (in seconds) is related to the height H of that jump (in feet) by the formula

$$H = 4T^2, \ T \geq 0.$$

1. Using the formula with the table feature of your calculator, complete the following table.

T (sec)	0	0.2	0.4	0.6	0.8	1.0	1.2	1.4	1.6
H (ft)	0	0.16	0.64	1.44	2.56	4	5.76	7.84	10.24

2. In the formula $H = 4T^2$, the height H is a function of the hang time T. Determine the practical domain and range of this function.

The practical domain is probably about $0 \leq T \leq 1$.

The practical range would be $0 \leq H \leq 4$.

3. Sketch a graph of the function $H = 4T^2$.

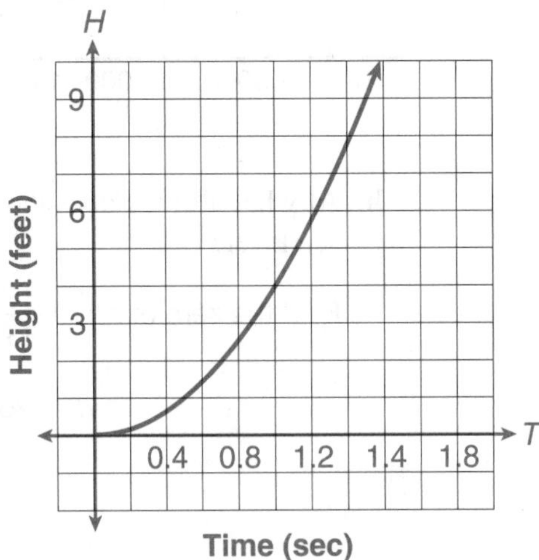

Although the formula $H = 4T^2$ is useful, the form of the equation is not entirely satisfactory. The formula implies that the height of the jump, H, depends on hang time T. The equation may be true in a relational sense, but it may be more logical to say that the hang time T depends on the height H of the jump. Therefore, it makes more sense to input values for H and find corresponding values of T.

4. Suppose you are able to measure the height of a jump and obtain a value of 1.44 feet. Determine the corresponding hang time T.

   $T = 0.6$ sec

5. The process of finding hang times for given jump heights would be greatly simplified if you had a formula that expressed T as a function of H.

   a. Solve the formula $H = 4T^2$ for T, where $T \geq 0$.

   $T^2 = \frac{H}{4}$; $T = \sqrt{\frac{H}{4}}$; $T = \frac{1}{2}\sqrt{H}$

   b. Complete the following table.

H (ft)	0	0.16	0.64	1.44	2.56	4	5.76	7.84	10.24
T (sec)	0	0.2	0.4	0.6	0.8	1.0	1.2	1.4	1.6

   c. What are the practical domain and range of your new function?

   The practical domain is probably $0 \leq H \leq 4$ feet. The practical range is probably $0 \leq T \leq 1$ sec.

6. a. How are the ordered pairs in the tables in Problems 1 and 5 related?

   They are interchanged.

   b. What is the relationship between the domains and ranges of the two functions defined by $H = 4T^2$ and $T = \frac{1}{2}\sqrt{H}$, where $T \geq 0$?

   The domain of one is the range of the other.

Recall that a fundamental characteristic of *inverse* functions is that their domains and ranges are interchanged. Therefore, these functions are inverses.

7. Sketch the graph of $T = \frac{1}{2}\sqrt{H}$, where H is the input, T is the output, and $0 \leq H \leq 4$.

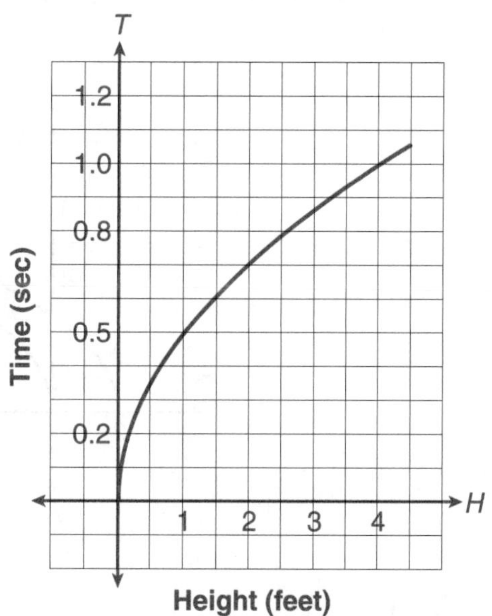

8. a. The investigation of the properties of the function defined by $T = \frac{1}{2}\sqrt{H}$ is somewhat limited because of the restrictions placed on the variables T and H, which represent real-world quantities. Consider the general function defined by $F(x) = \frac{1}{2}\sqrt{x}$. What is the domain of $F(x)$?

All non-negative real numbers.

b. Sketch a graph of F.

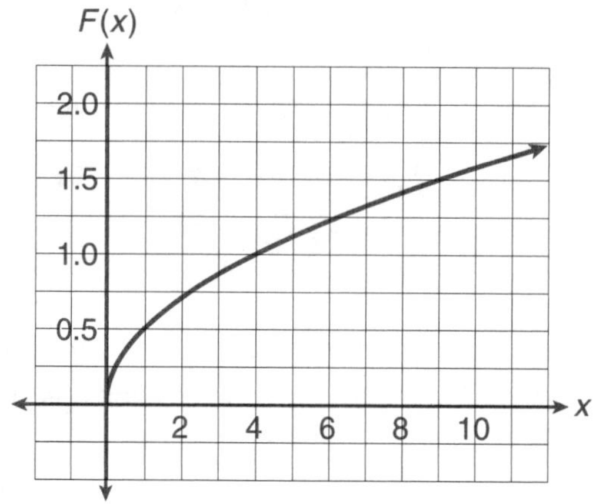

c. What is the range of F?

All non-negative real numbers.

9. Consider the functions defined by the following equations.

$$f(x) = \sqrt{x}, \quad g(x) = \sqrt{x + 2}, \quad h(x) = \sqrt{x - 3}.$$

a. Determine the domain of each function. Remember, the square root of a negative number is not a real number.

Domain of f is $x \geq 0$. Domain of g is $x \geq -2$. Domain of h is $x \geq 3$.

b. Sketch graphs of all three functions on the same coordinate system.

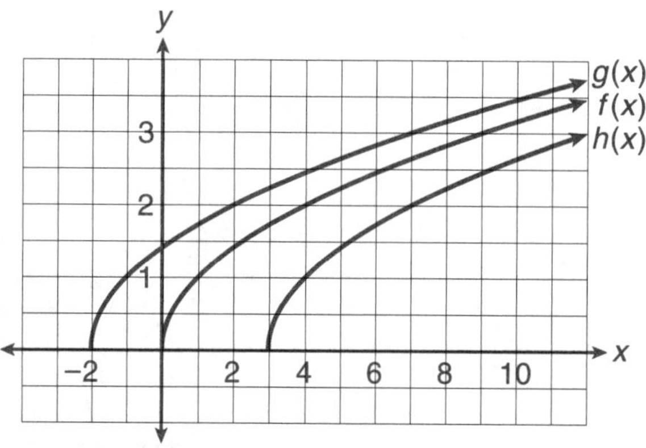

c. For what values of x is the following true?

i. $f(x) = 5$
If $f(x) = 5$, $x = 25$

ii. $g(x) = 5$
If $g(x) = 5$, $x = 23$

iii. $h(x) = 5$
If $h(x) = 5$, $x = 28$.

d. How would you obtain the graph of g from the graph of f?

Shift f two units to the left.

e. How would you obtain the graph of h from the graph of f?

Shift f three units to the right.

10. a. Determine the domain and range of the functions defined by $f(x) = \sqrt{x}$ and $g(x) = -\sqrt{x}$.

The domain of f is $x \geq 0$ and the range of f is $f(x) \geq 0$.

The domain of g is $x \geq 0$ and the range of g is $g(x) \leq 0$.

b. Sketch graphs of f and g on the same coordinate system.

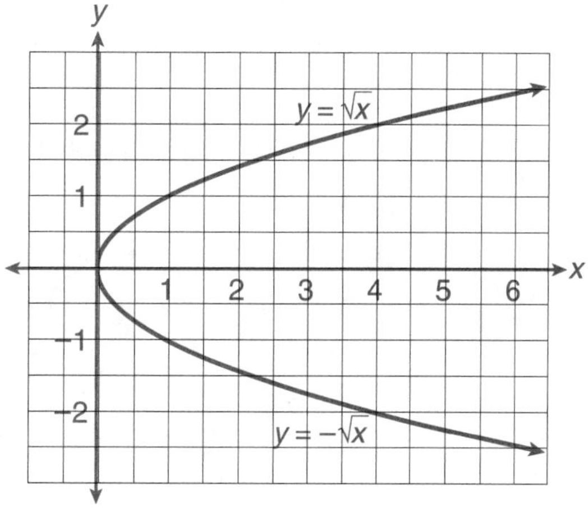

c. How would you obtain the graph of g from the graph of f?

Reflect the graph of f through the x-axis to obtain the graph at g.

The expression $\sqrt{x}$ can also be written as $x^{1/2}$. The fractional exponent means that you are taking the positive square root of x.

11. Verify that $x^{1/2} = \sqrt{x}$ by graphing $y_1 = x^{1/2}$ and $y_2 = \sqrt{x}$. Explain how your graph tells you that $x^{1/2}$ is indeed the same as $\sqrt{x}$.

The graphs are identical.

12. Sketch the graph of $y = (3x - 2)^{1/2}$. Use your grapher to verify that this is the same as $y = \sqrt{3x - 2}$. What is the domain?

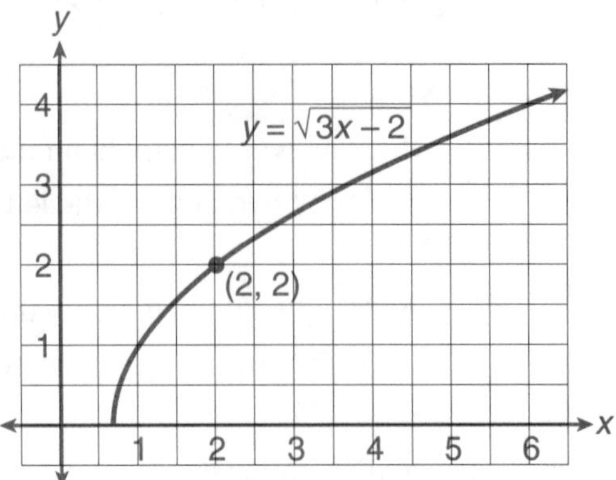

Domain is $x \geq \frac{2}{3}$.

SUMMARY

Notation and Terminology

- $\sqrt[2]{n}$, or simply $\sqrt{n}$, represents the square root of a nonnegative number n. The 2 is called the *index*. In general, when working with square roots, the 2 is omitted.
- The symbol $\sqrt{\ }$ is called the *radical sign*.
- $\sqrt{n} \geq 0$

Properties of Radical Functions

The function defined by $f(x) = \sqrt{x}$ has domain $x \geq 0$. Its range is all y-values such that $y \geq 0$. The function f is an increasing function over its entire domain.

Its output values are greater than x for $0 < x < 1$, and its output values are less than x for $x > 1$.

EXERCISES

1. Using your calculator, determine the value of each number to the nearest hundredth, if necessary.

a. $\sqrt{30}$
5.48

b. $6^{1/2}$
2.45

c. $(\sqrt{13})^4$
169

d. $(9^{1/2})^3$
27

2. Determine the domain of each function.

a. $f(x) = \sqrt{x - 5}$
$x \geq 5$

b. $g(x) = \sqrt{3x + 2}$
$x \geq -\frac{2}{3}$

Exercise numbers appearing in color are answered in the Selected Answers section of this book.

3. The function $f(x) = 13.2(\sqrt{x})^5 + 22{,}500$ can be used to approximate yearly income as a function of years of education.

   a. Determine $f(14)$ and interpret its meaning.

   $f(14) = 32{,}180$. The approximate income of an individual with 14 years of education is $32,180.

   b. What is the minimal number of years of education predicted by the function to expect a yearly income of $50,000?

   21 years of education.

4. Describe how to obtain the graph of the second function from the graph of the first.

   a. $g(x) = \sqrt{x},\ h(x) = \sqrt{x} + 1$

   The graph of h is obtained by shifting the graph of g up one unit.

   b. $f(x) = \sqrt{x},\ g(x) = -\sqrt{x}$

   The graph of g is obtained from the graph of f by reflecting the graph of f in the x-axis.

   c. $h(x) = 2\sqrt{x},\ H(x) = 2\sqrt{x + 1}$

   The graph of H is obtained by shifting the graph of h one unit to the left.

5. Sketch a graph of $f(x) = x^2$ and $g(x) = \sqrt{x}$ on the same coordinate system. Use the graphs to answer the following;

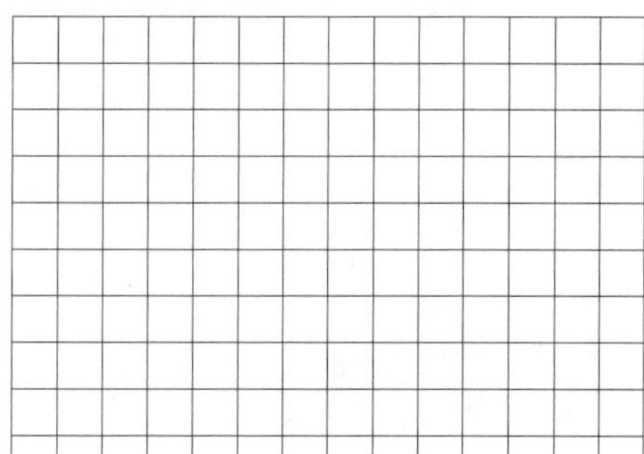

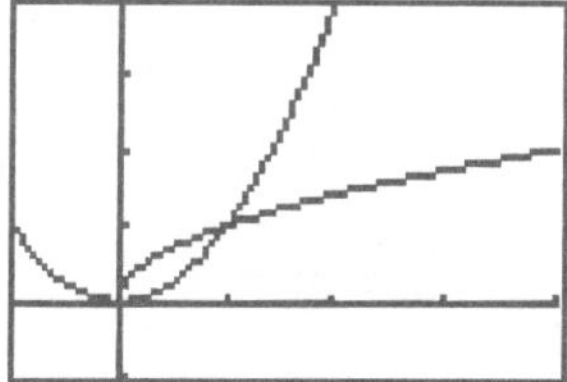

   a. Is $x^2 > \sqrt{x}$ for $0 < x < 1$? Explain.

   No, the graph of f is below the graph of g for $0 < x < 1$.

   b. Is $x^2 > \sqrt{x}$ for $x > 1$? Explain.

   Yes, the graph of f is above the graph of g for $x > 1$.

6. Which of the following functions increase most rapidly for $x > 1$: $f(x) = \sqrt{x}$ or $g(x) = \log(x)$?

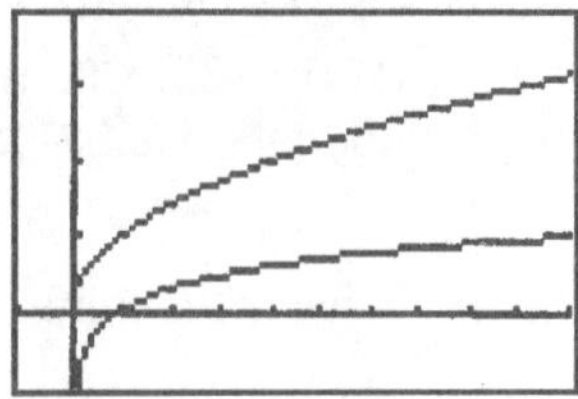

From viewing the graph, it appears that *f* grows more rapidly than *g*.

ACTIVITY 5.6

Falling Objects
Topic: *Radical Equations*

If a certain object is dropped from a tall building, the time t in seconds that it takes for the object to strike the ground is given by

$$t = \frac{\sqrt{d}}{4} = \frac{1}{4}\sqrt{d} = 0.25\sqrt{d},$$

where the input d is the distance traveled in feet. The time it takes for the object to hit the ground is directly proportional to the square root of the distance traveled. The number $\frac{1}{4} = 0.25$ is called the constant of proportionality.

1. **a.** How long will it take an object to fall from the top of the World Trade Center in New York City, a distance of 1368 feet? Round to the nearest hundredth of a second.

   Approximately 9.25 seconds.

   b. Sketch a graph of the given function.

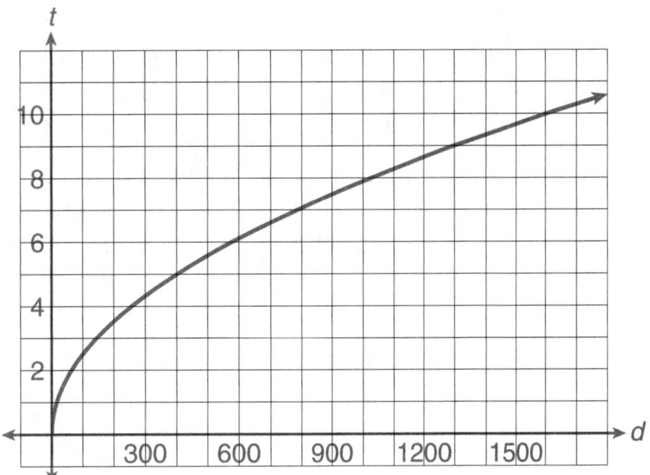

   c. How tall must a building be for the object to take 8.37 seconds to fall to the ground? Use the graph from part b to approximate your answer.

   Graph: about 1100 feet; $(0.25\sqrt{d})^2 = (8.37)^2$

   $0.0625d = 70.0569$

   $d \approx 1121$ feet

Suppose you are interested in determining the value of d for many different values of t. In such a situation, the process could be simplified if you had a rule for d as a function of t. The equation $t = \frac{\sqrt{d}}{4}$ gives t as a function of d. You need to solve the equation for d.

Solving an equation when the variable appears under a radical involves using the following two properties:

Property 1: If a and b are two quantities such that $a = b$, then $a^n = b^n$, where n is a positive integer.

Example   If $t = \sqrt{s}$, then $t^2 = (\sqrt{s})^2$.

Property 2: $(b^n)^m = b^{nm}$

Example: $(\sqrt{s})^2 = (s^{\frac{1}{2}})^2 = s^{\frac{1}{2}\cdot 2} = s^1 = s.$

2. a. Solve the equation $t = \frac{\sqrt{d}}{4}$ for d by first squaring both sides of the equation.

$t^2 = \frac{d}{16}$

$d = 16t^2$

b. How tall must a building be for the object to take 10 seconds to fall to the ground?

$d = 16(10)^2 = 1600$ feet.

3. Artificial gravity can be created in a space station by revolving the station. The number of revolutions required can be determined by

$$N = \frac{1}{2\pi}\sqrt{\frac{a}{r}},$$

where N is measured in revolutions per second, a is the artificial acceleration produced (measured in meters per second squared), and r is the radius of the space station in meters.

a. To produce an artificial acceleration simulating gravity on earth, a must equal 9.8 meters per second squared. If the space station must revolve at the rate of 1 revolution every 5 minutes, what must its radius be? Solve both algebraically and graphically. Be careful, N is measured in revolutions per second.

1 revolution per 5 min $= \frac{1}{300}$ revolution per sec; $N = \frac{1}{300}$, $a = 9.8$

$\frac{2\pi}{300} = \sqrt{\frac{9.8}{r}}$ $r = 22{,}341$ meters.

b. Solve the original formula for r.

$2\pi N = \sqrt{\frac{a}{r}}$; $4\pi^2 N^2 = \frac{a}{r}$

$$r = \frac{a}{4\pi N^2}$$

4. Suppose two different objects are dropped: a marble and a large beach ball. Because of air resistance, the beach ball will take longer than the marble to fall the same distance. Assume that the marble falls according to $t = 0.25\sqrt{d}$, as in Problem 1. The time for the beach ball to hit the ground is modeled by $t = k\sqrt{d}$, where the constant k is determined by experiment.

a. The beach ball is dropped from a height of 250 feet, and it takes 4.11 seconds to hit the ground. Determine the constant k accurate to the nearest hundredth.

$4.11 = k\sqrt{250}$ $\quad k = 0.26$

b. Now suppose the beach ball is dropped from a height 50 feet lower than the marble. Then $t = k\sqrt{d - 50}$ is the time for the beach ball to drop $d - 50$ feet, where d is the height the marble falls. From what height must the marble be dropped so that the beach ball and marble will hit the ground at the same time?

$$\begin{aligned}(0.25\sqrt{d})^2 &= (0.26\sqrt{d-50})^2\\ 0.0625d &= 0.0676(d-50)\\ -0.0051d &= -3.38\\ d &= 662.7\end{aligned}$$

5. Consider the following algebraic solution of the equation $\sqrt{x+3} + 5 = 0$.

$$\begin{aligned}\sqrt{x+3} + 5 &= 0\\ \sqrt{x+3} &= -5\\ (\sqrt{x+3})^2 &= (-5)^2\\ x + 3 &= 25\\ x &= 22\end{aligned}$$

a. It appears that $x = 22$ is a solution to the given equation. Check the solution by substituting 22 for x in the original equation. Does it check?

No. $\sqrt{22+3} + 5 = 10 \neq 0$

b. What happened in the solution process that caused an *extraneous solution* (an apparent solution that does not check) to appear?

Two quantities were squared and the results were seen as equal. This does not imply that the original two quantities were equal.

c. Does the equation $\sqrt{x+3} + 5 = 0$ have a solution? Include a graph to help support your answer.

No solution exists. Both terms on the left-hand side are positive. Thus, their sum is always greater than 0, never equal to zero.

SUMMARY

To solve an equation involving one radical expression:

1. Isolate the radical expression on one side of the equals sign.
2. Square both sides of the equation.
3. Solve the resulting equation.
4. Check your solutions in the context of the original problem.

EXERCISES

1. Without actually solving, which of the following equations does not have a solution? Explain your reasoning. Then verify by solving all three equations.

a. $\sqrt{2x+1} = 3$

Has a solution.
$x = 4$

b. $\sqrt{x+1} + 5 = 1$

No solution. The equation would be true only if the radical were negative.

Exercise numbers appearing in color are answered in the Selected Answers section of this book.

c. $\sqrt{2 - x} = -x$ Has a solution.

$2 - x = x^2$

$0 = x^2 + x - 2$

$0 = (x + 2)(x - 1)$

$x = -2 \quad x = 1;$ Reject

2. Solve each of following equations algebraically. Then verify graphically.

a. $\sqrt{x} = 2.5$

$x = 6.25$

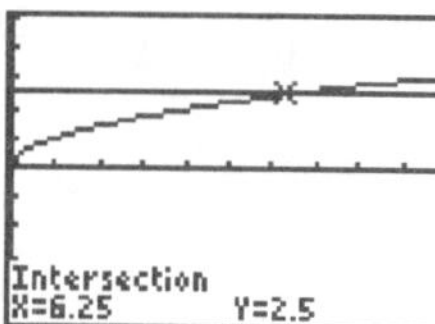

b. $\sqrt{x} - 3 = 0$

$x = 9$

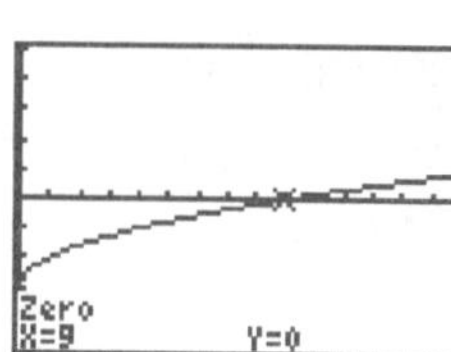

c. $\sqrt{2x} = 14$

$x = 98$

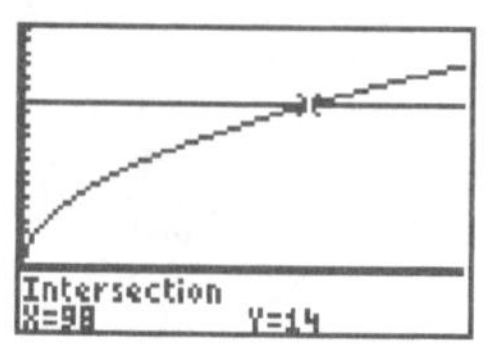

d. $3\sqrt{x} = 243$

$x = 6561$

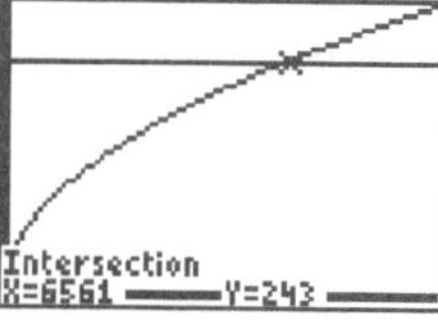

e. $4 - 5\sqrt{3x} = 1$

$x = 0.12$

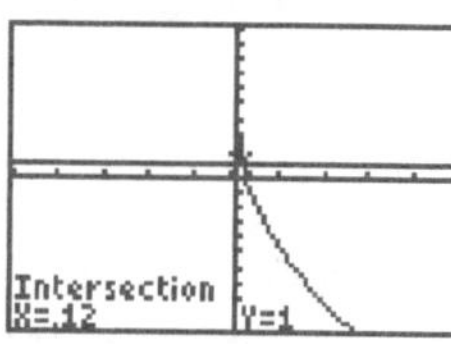

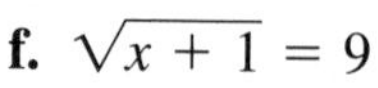

f. $\sqrt{x + 1} = 9$

$x = 80$

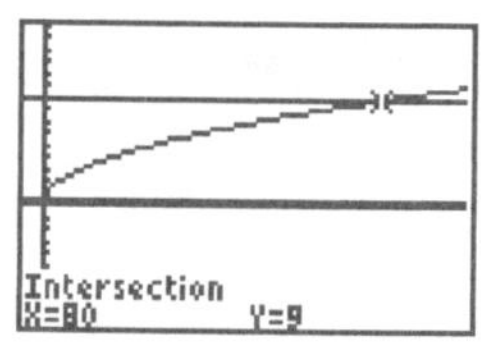

3. Solve each of the following equations algebraically and graphically.

a. $\sqrt{3x - 1} = 5$

$x = \frac{26}{3}$

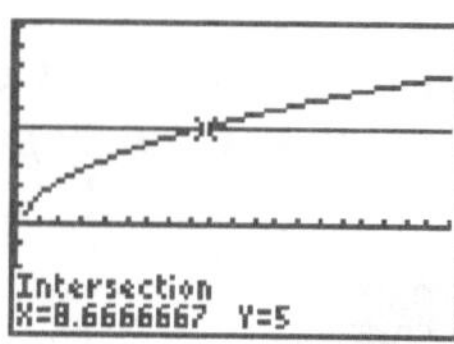

b. $\sqrt{4x + 13} = 8$

$x = 12.75$

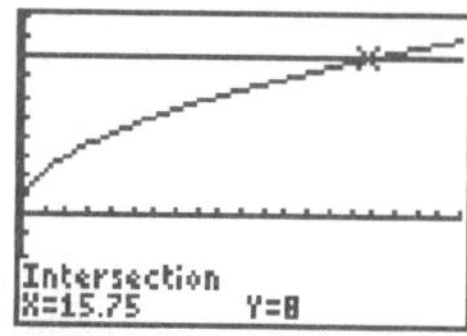

c. $\sqrt{5 - x} = x + 1$

$5 - x = (x + 1)^2$

$5 - x = x^2 + 2x + 1$

$0 = x^2 + 3x - 4$

$x = 1, -4$: Reject -4

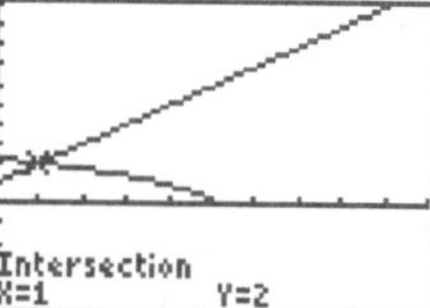

d. $\sqrt{1 - 2x} - 3 = x$

$\sqrt{1 - 2x} = x + 3$

$1 - 2x = x^2 + 6x + 9$

$0 = x^2 + 8x + 8$

$$x = \frac{-8 \pm \sqrt{64 - 4(8)}}{2}$$

$= -1.17, -6.83$

Reject -6.83

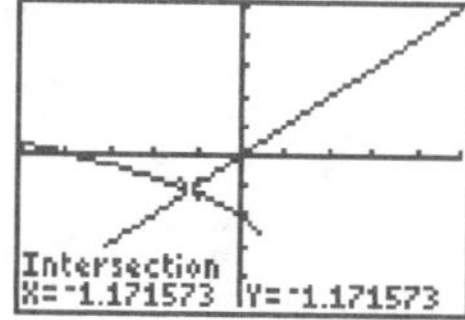

4. Solve each of the following equations algebraically and by graphing. Be aware of any extraneous roots.

a. $\sqrt{x + 5} = 1$

$x = -4$

b. $10\sqrt{x + 2} = 20$

$x = 2$

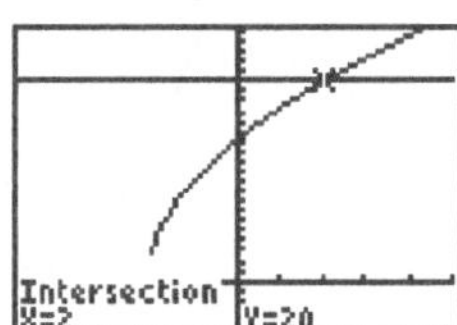

5. Solve algebraically and graphically: $\sqrt{1.4x + 3.2} = \sqrt{3.8x - 1}$.

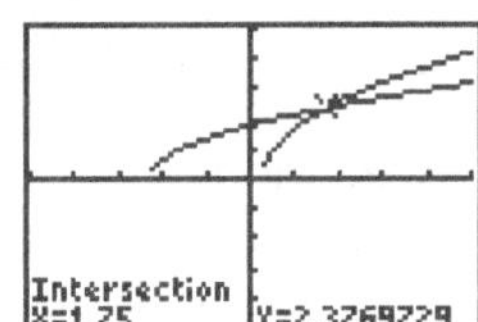

$$1.4x + 3.2 = 3.8x - 1$$
$$4.2 = 2.4x$$
$$1.75 = x$$

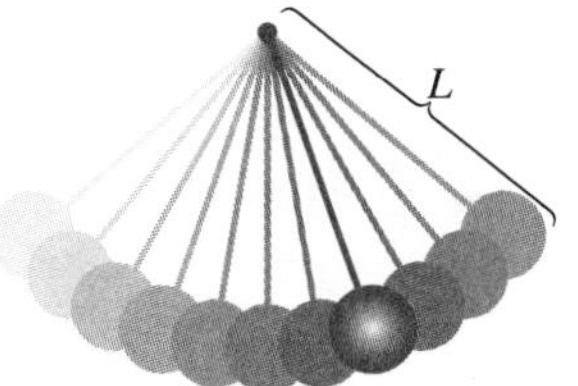

6. The time t in seconds that it takes for a pendulum to complete one complete period (to swing back and forth one time) is modeled by

$$t = 2\pi\sqrt{\frac{L}{32}},$$

where L is the length of the pendulum in feet. How long is the pendulum of a clock with a period of 1.95 seconds?

$t = 1.95$: $1.95 = 2\pi\sqrt{\frac{L}{32}}$: $L = 3.08$ feet.

7. In a certain population, there are 28,520 births on a particular day. The number N of these people surviving to age x can be modeled by the function $N = 2852\sqrt{100 - x}$.

a. According to this model, how many of the 28,520 babies will survive to age 5?

Approximately 27,798.

b. What is the practical domain of this function?

$0 \le x \le 100$

c. When only 5000 of this group are still alive, how old would you expect them to be?

$$2850\sqrt{100 - x} = 5000$$
$$\sqrt{100 - x} = 1.75$$
$$100 - x = 3.0625$$
$$x = 97 \text{ years}$$

d. How many years will it take for half of the 28,520 people to die?

$$2850\sqrt{100 - x} = 14260$$
$$\sqrt{100 - x} = 5$$
$$100 - x = 25$$
$$x = 75 \text{ years}$$

8. Suppose a pressure gauge on a bridge indicates a wind pressure P of 10 pounds per square foot. What is the velocity V of the wind if

$$V(P) = \sqrt{\frac{1000P}{3}},$$

where velocity is measured in miles per hour?

$P = 10$, $V(10) = \sqrt{\frac{10,000}{3}} \approx 58$ mph

ACTIVITY 5.7

Take a Hike

Topics: *Cube Root Functions, n^{th} Roots, Fractional Exponents*

Summer is here, and you and your friends plan to do some wilderness camping. You need to carry your drinking water. You buy a collapsible cube from a camping supply store that holds 4 liters $\left(4000 \text{ cm}^3\right)$ of water.

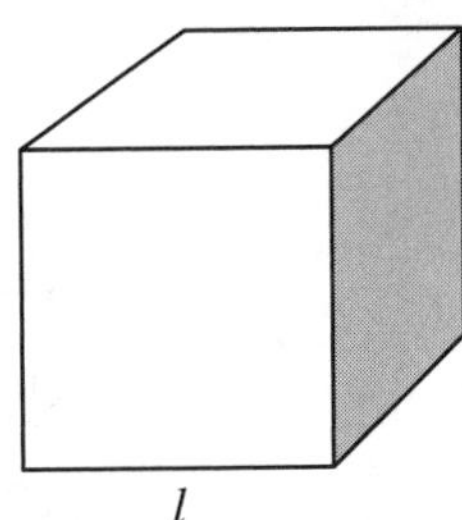

Recall that the formula for the volume of a cube is $v = l^3$, where l is the length of an edge.

1. a. Approximate, to the nearest tenth of a centimeter, the length l of an edge of the cube by guessing and then cubing your guess. Get as close to 4000 as you can.

15.9

b. The answer in part a is called the **cube root** of 4000. Because $\left(4000^{1/3}\right)^3 = 4000^{1/3 \cdot 3} = 4000^1 = 4000$, the cube root of 4000 can be written as $4000^{\frac{1}{3}}$. The number $4000^{\frac{1}{3}}$ is also written as $\sqrt[3]{4000}$. Use the exponent key on your calculator to approximate $\sqrt[3]{4000}$, or $4000^{1/3}$, to the nearest tenth. (Some calculators, like the TI-83, have a $\sqrt[3]{\ }$ function.)

$4000^{1/3} \approx 15.874$

c. How does your result in part b compare with your result in part a?

The results are very close.

2. Without using your calculator, determine each of the following.

a. $8^{1/3}$

2

b. $64^{1/3}$

4

c. $\sqrt[3]{1000}$

10

d. $\sqrt[3]{-27}$

3

Numbers such as 8, 64, 1000, and -27 that have exact cube roots are called **perfect cubes.**

3. Consider the functions $f(x) = x^3$ and $g(x) = \sqrt[3]{x}$.

a. Determine the domain of each function.

The domain of *f* and the domain of *g* are all real numbers.

b. Sketch a graph of f and g on the same coordinate system.

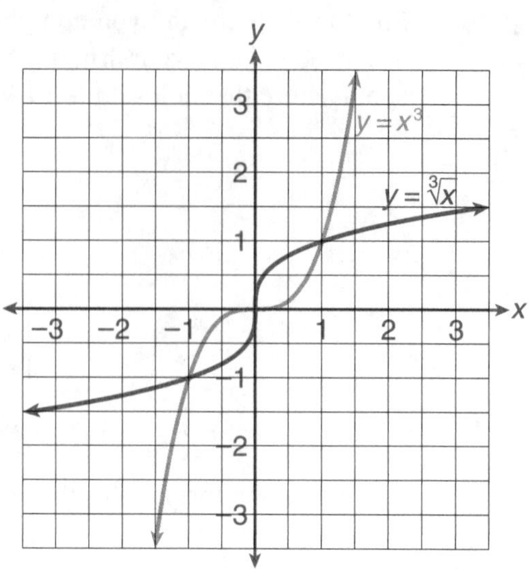

c. Are f and g inverse functions? Explain.

Yes. Their graphs are reflections about $y = x$. Their ordered pairs are interchanged.

d. Determine the composition of f and g. That is, determine $(f \circ g)(x)$ and $(g \circ f)(x)$.

$f \circ g(x) = f(g(x)) = f(\sqrt[3]{x}) = (\sqrt[3]{x})^3 = x$

$g \circ f(x) = g(f(x)) = g(x^2) = \sqrt[3]{x^3} = x$

4. a. The fourth root of x, denoted by $\sqrt[4]{x}$, is the number that when raised to the fourth power equals x. Determine the exact value of $\sqrt[4]{81}$.

$\sqrt[4]{81} = 3$

b. $\sqrt[4]{81}$ can also be expressed as $81^{1/4}$. Verify using your calculator.

$81^{1/4} = 3$

c. Determine the value of $\sqrt[4]{-16}$.

The value is not a real number.

d. What is the domain of the function given by $y = \sqrt[4]{x}$, also written $y = x^{1/4}$?

$x \geq 0$

For additional examples and practice with fractional exponents and radicals, see Appendix A.

If b is a real number and n is a positive integer, then $b^{1/n} = \sqrt[n]{b}$, read as "the nth root of b." If n is even, then $\sqrt[n]{b}$ is called an *even root.* If n is odd, then $\sqrt[n]{b}$ is called an *odd root.*

5. If possible, determine each of the following without the aid of a calculator.

a. $\sqrt[3]{125}$

5

b. $\sqrt[3]{-1}$

-1

c. $\sqrt[4]{10{,}000}$

10

d. $\sqrt[4]{256}$

4

e. $\sqrt[6]{0}$

0

f. $\sqrt[5]{-32}$

-2

g. $36^{1/4}$

$\sqrt{6}$

h. $\left(\frac{1}{8}\right)^{1/3}$

$\frac{1}{2}$

i. $16^{1/4}$

2

6. a. Explain why $(-1)^{1/4}$ and $\sqrt{-9}$ do not represent real numbers.

The even root of a negative number is not a real number.

b. If n is an even integer, what must be true about the value of b for $\sqrt[n]{b}$ to represent a real number?

$b \geq 0$

c. Are there any restrictions on the value of b if n is odd?

No.

7. a. Sketch a graph of each of the following on the same coordinate system.

$f(x) = \sqrt[3]{x}$, $g(x) = \sqrt[3]{x+1}$ and $h(x) = \sqrt[3]{x-2}$

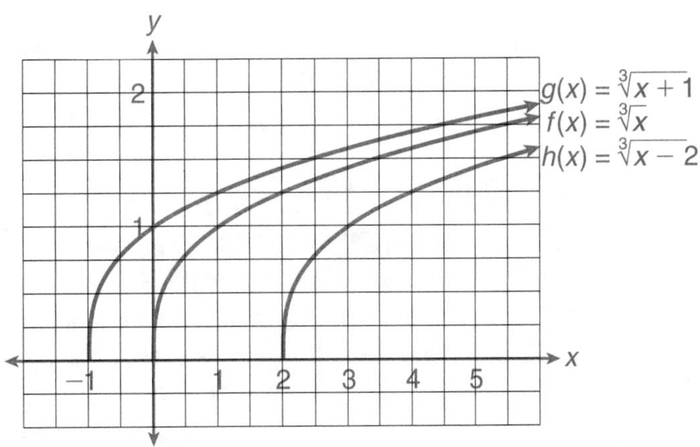

b. How are the graphs of f, g, and h similar, and how are they different?

They all have identical shapes and are shifted horizontally from one another. Graph of $g(x)$ is shifted 1 unit to the left of that of $f(x)$. Graph of $h(x)$ is shifted 2 units to the right of $f(x)$.

8. Solve the equation $V = I^3$ for I.

$V = I^3$

$\sqrt[3]{V} = \sqrt[3]{I^3}$

$\sqrt[3]{V} = 1$

9. The radius r of a sphere is given by

$$r = \sqrt[3]{\frac{3V}{4\pi}},$$

where V is the volume of the sphere.

a. Determine the radius of a sphere that has a volume equal to 40 cubic centimeters.

$V = 40$ $r = \sqrt[3]{\frac{3 \cdot 40}{4\pi}} \approx 2.12$ cm.

b. Determine the volume of a sphere that has a radius equal to 3.5 feet.

$V = 179.6$ cu ft

c. Solve the formula for V, expressing volume as a function of the radius.

$V = \frac{4}{3}\pi r^3$

10. Solve the equation $\sqrt[3]{x+1} = 4$ using an algebraic approach. Verify your solution graphically.

$x + 1 = 4^3$

$x + 1 = 64$

$x = 63$

11. a. Simplify the expression $(x^{3/4})^{4/3}$by using the appropriate laws of exponents.

$(x^{3/4})^{4/3} = x^{12/12} = x^1 = x$

b. Solve the equation $x^{3/4} = 8$ using an algebraic approach. Verify your solution graphically.

$(x^{3/4})^{4/3} = 8^{4/3}$

$x = 2^4 = 16$

SUMMARY

- If b is a real number and n is a positive integer, then $b^{1/n} = \sqrt[n]{b}$, read as "the nth root of b." If n is even, then $\sqrt[n]{b}$ is called an even root. If n is odd, then $\sqrt[n]{b}$ is called an odd root.
- If n is even, then b must be greater than or equal to zero for $\sqrt[n]{b}$ to represent a real number.
- If n is odd, then $\sqrt[n]{b}$ represents a real number for any real number b.

Solving an equation when the variable appears under a radical involves using the following two properties:

Property 1: If a and b are two quantities such that $a = b$, then $a^n = b^n$, where n is a positive integer.

Example If $t = \sqrt[n]{s}$, then $t^3 = \left(\sqrt[n]{s}\right)^3$.

Property 2: $\left(b^n\right)^m = b^{nm}$.

Example $\left(\sqrt[n]{s}\right)^n = \left(s^{\frac{1}{n}}\right)^n = s^{\frac{1}{n}\cdot n} = s^1 = s$.

EXERCISES

1. If possible, determine the exact value of each of the following.

a. $\sqrt[3]{64}$

4

b. $\sqrt[4]{16}$

2

c. $(-27)^{1/3}$

-3

d. $(625)^{1/4}$

5

e. $\sqrt{\frac{1}{36}}$

$\frac{1}{6}$

f. $(-81)^{1/4}$

Not a real number.

g. $(100{,}000)^{1/5}$

10

h. $(-1)^{1/6}$

Not a real number.

2. If the volume of a cube is 728 cubic centimeters, then what is the length of one edge to the nearest tenth of a centimeter?

Length is approximately 9 cm.

3. If the volume of a cube is decreased from 1450 cubic inches to 1280 cubic inches (and still remains a cube), by how much has the length of one edge decreased?

$l_1 = \sqrt[3]{1450}, \quad l_2 = \sqrt[3]{1280}, \quad l_1 - l_2 = 0.46$ inches

4. The volume of a sphere is 520 cubic meters. What is the diameter of the sphere?

$r = \sqrt[3]{\frac{3V}{4\pi}}\ V = 520, \quad r = 4.99, \quad$ so $d = 9.98$ m

5. What is the domain of each function?

a. $y = \sqrt[3]{x + 6}$

All real numbers

b. $f(x) = \sqrt[4]{x - 3}$

$x \geq 3$

c. $g(x) = \sqrt[5]{2 - x}$

All real numbers

d. $f(x) = (2 - x)^{1/6}$

$x \leq 2$

6. Solve each of the following algebraically and graphically.

a. $\sqrt[3]{x + 4} = 3$

$x = 23$

b. $\sqrt[4]{x + 5} = 2$

$x = 11$

c. $\sqrt[3]{2x - 3} + 4 = 3$

$x = 1$

d. $\sqrt[4]{2 - x} > 5$

$x < -623$

7. Solve each of the following algebraically and verify your results graphically.

a. $x^{2/3} = 16$

$(x^{2/3})^{3/2} = (16)^{3/2}$

$x = 4^3$

$x = 64$

Exercise numbers appearing in color are answered in the Selected Answers section of this book.

b. $2x^{3/4} = 54$

$$x^{3/4} = 27$$

$$(x^{3/4})^{4/3} = (27)^{4/3}$$

$$x = 3^4$$

$$x = 81$$

8. The diameter d of a sphere is given by the formula

$$d = \sqrt[3]{\frac{6v}{\pi}},$$

where v represents the volume of a sphere. Approximate the diameter of a sphere having a volume of 10 cubic inches.

$V = 10, \quad d = \sqrt[3]{\frac{60}{\pi}} \approx 2.67$ inches

What Have I Learned?

1. Explain the steps involved in solving the equation $\sqrt{2x + 3} = 5$ using an algebraic approach. Why must you be sure to check your solution?

Square both sides: $2x + 3 = 25$

Solve for x: $x = 11$

Check in the original: $\sqrt{2 \cdot 11 + 3} = \sqrt{25} = 5$

2. What is the the domain for the variable b in each of the following?

a. $\sqrt[n]{b}$, n an even positive integer

$b \geq 0$

b. $\sqrt[n]{b}$, n an odd positive integer

b can be any real number.

3. Is it possible for an extraneous solution to appear when solving the equation $\sqrt[3]{2x + 1} = -3$? Explain.

No, because a cube root can be negative.

4. Describe two ways to check for extraneous solutions when solving an equation by squaring both sides.

Check algebraically or check graphically.

5. Determine if the following statements are true or false. Explain your answer.

a. If two numbers are equal, then their squares are equal.

True.

b. If the squares of two numbers are equal, then the two numbers are equal.

False. The numbers may be opposites; that is, they may have opposite signs.

6. a. For a given value of x, which is greater, $\sqrt[5]{x}$ or $x^{1/3}$? Explain how you determined your answer.

You must know something about the value of x. The answer depends on whether $x < -1$, $x = -1$, $-1 < x < 0$, $x = 0$, $0 < x < 1$, $x = 1$, or $x > 1$.

b. In part a, did you assume that $x > 0$? Does your answer change if $x < 0$?

It depends on the interval in part a.

How Can I Practice?

1. Solve each of the following equations algebraically and graphically.

   a. $\sqrt{x+2} = 10$
   $x = 98$

   b. $(x-5)^{1/2} = 6$
   $x = 41$

   c. $\sqrt{2x+1} - 5 = 0$
   $x = 12$

   d. $\sqrt[2]{x^2+3} = 4$
   $x = \pm\sqrt{61}$

   e. $\sqrt{x} = \sqrt{x+2}$
   No solution.

   f. $(2-x)^{1/3} = -2$
   $x = 10$

   g. $\sqrt[4]{2x-5} = 2$
   $x = 10.5$

   h. $(2.3x + 1.9)^{1/3} = 1.6$
   $x \approx 0.95$

2. Solve the following inequalities by graphing.

   a. $\sqrt{x-3} > 2$

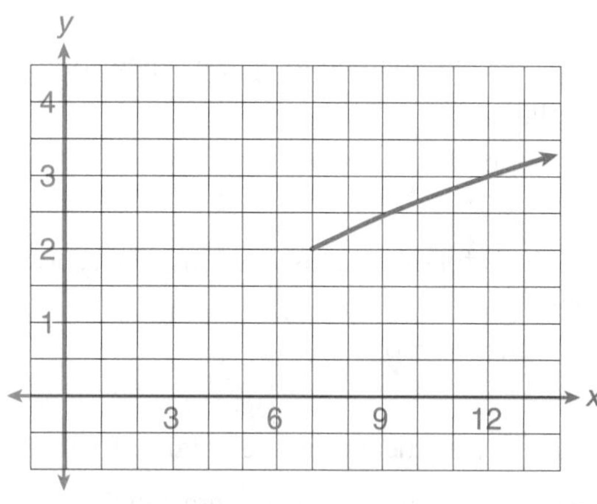

$x > 7$

   b. 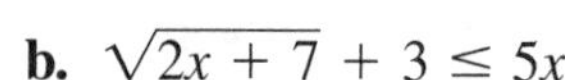 $\sqrt{2x+7} + 3 \le 5x$

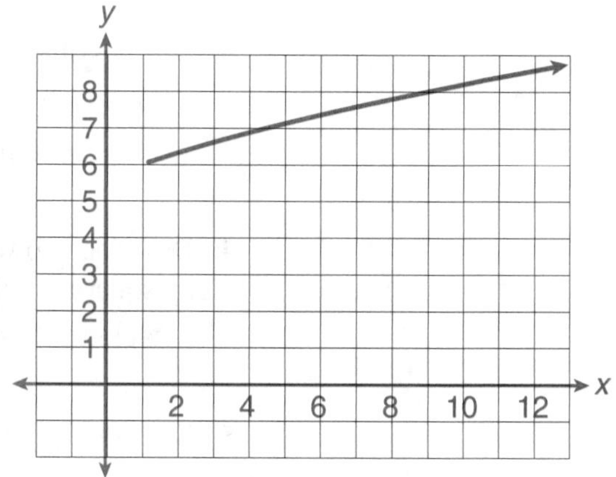

$x \ge 1.2141$

   c. $(5 + x^2)^{1/4} \ge 2 - x^2$

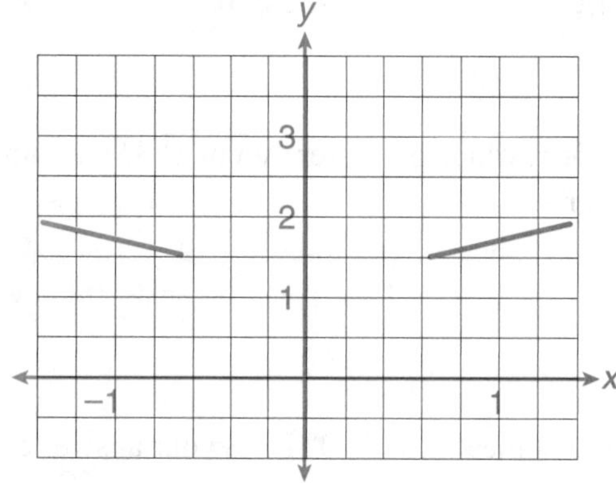

$x \le -0.686$ or $x \ge 0.686$

Exercise numbers appearing in color are answered in the Selected Answers section of this book.

3. Identify the domain for each of the following functions.

a. $f(x) = \sqrt{6 - x}$ **b.** $g(x) = (2x - 9)^{1/3}$ **c.** $h(x) = (x^2 - 4)^{1/4}$

$x \leq 6$ All real numbers. $x \geq 2$ or $x \leq -2$

4. If the volume of a cube is 458 cubic inches, what is the length of one edge? Determine the value to the nearest hundredth of an inch.

Length is approximately 7.71 inches.

5. If the volume of a sphere is 620 cubic centimeters, what is its radius?

$r = \sqrt[3]{\frac{3V}{4\pi}}$, $V = 620$, $r = 5.29$ cm

6. When a stone is dropped to the ground, its velocity is modeled by the function $v = \sqrt{64d}$, where d is the distance the stone has fallen, in feet, and v is its velocity in feet per second. If the stone hits the ground at 100 feet per second, from what height was it dropped?

$v = 100$, $100 = \sqrt{64d}$; $d = 156.25$

7. A cardboard box with a square bottom has a height of 10 inches and a volume of 422.5 cubic inches. What are the dimensions of the bottom of the box?

$10x^2 = 422.5$

$x = 6.5$ inches.

8. The speed of a car that produces skid marks in coming to a complete stop can be estimated by measuring the length of the skid marks. In examining an accident scene, investigators can model this situation with the function $s = \sqrt{24x}$, where x is the length of the skid mark in feet and s is the car's speed in miles per hour.

a. If the skid marks at an accident scene are 115 feet long, what is the estimated speed of the car?

$x = 115$; $s = \sqrt{24 \cdot 115} \approx 53$ mph

b. If a car is traveling at 80 mph when the driver hits the brakes, how long would you expect the skid marks to be?

$s = 80$

$80 = \sqrt{24x}$; $x \approx 267$ feet

c. What is the practical domain for this function?

Probably something like $0 \leq x < 600$.

9. Describe the similarities and differences between the graphs of $y = \sqrt{2 - x}$ and $y = \sqrt{x - 2}$.

The graphs are reflections about the line $x = 2$.

Gateway Review

1. According to the blueprint, the floor area of the stage in the new auditorium at your college must be rectangular and equal to 1200 square feet. The width of the stage is key to all of the theater productions. Therefore, the depth is a function of the width in this situation.

a. Write this function in symbolic form.

$d = \frac{1200}{w}$

b. Using widths of 30, 35, 40, 50, and 60 feet, create a table to determine the depth for each of these widths.

w	30	35	40	50	60
d	40	34.286	30	24	20

c. What is happening to the depth as the width increases?

As width increases, the depth decreases.

d. What happens if the width is 100 feet? Is this realistic? Explain.

The depth is 12 feet, not enough room for any theater set.

e. What do you think is the practical domain for this function?

(Answers may vary.) $40 \leq w \leq 60$

f. Can the width be zero? Explain.

No. Division by zero is undefined.

g. What type of a function do you have in this situation?

Rational function.

h. What is the domain of the general function?

All real numbers except 0.

i. What is the vertical asymptote?

$w = 0$

j. What is the horizontal asymptote? Explain in words how you determined it.

$d = 0$, as w increases d approaches 0.

Exercise numbers appearing in color are answered in the Selected Answers section of this book.

2. Sketch the following graphs without using your grapher.

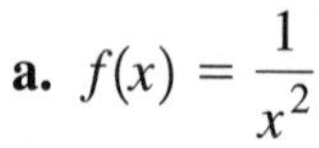

a. $f(x) = \dfrac{1}{x^2}$

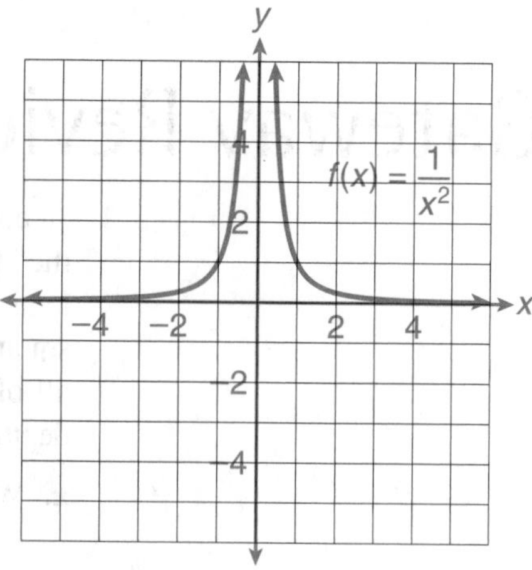

b. $f(x) = \dfrac{-1}{x^3}$

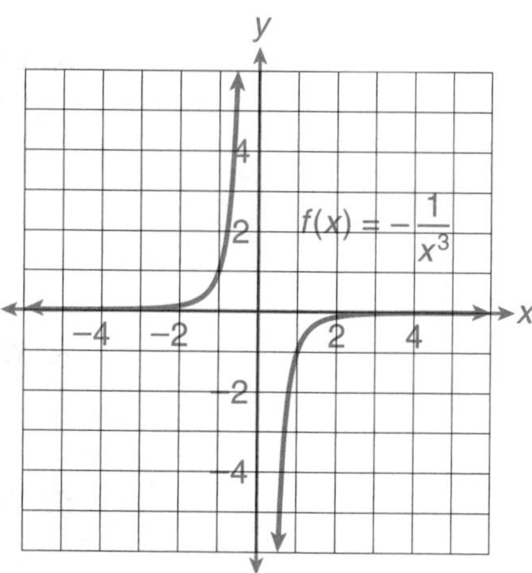

c. Describe how the graphs are similar and how they are different.

The graphs have the same horizontal and vertical asymptotes. $f(x) = \dfrac{1}{x^2}$ is symmetric with respect to the y-axis. $f(x) = -\dfrac{1}{x^3}$ is symmetric with respect to (0, 0) in quadrants II and IV.

3. **a.** If y varies inversely as x, and $x = 10$ when $y = 12$, then determine the value of y when $x = 30$.

$y = \frac{k}{x}$; $12 = \frac{k}{10}$; $k = 120$; $y = \frac{120}{30} = 4$

b. The loudness, in decibels, of a stereo is inversely proportional to the square of the distance from the speaker to the person listening. If the loudness is 32 decibels at a distance of 4 feet, then what is the loudness when the listener is 10 feet from the speaker?

$I = \dfrac{k}{d^2}$; $32 = \frac{k}{16}$; $k = 512$; $I = \frac{512}{100} = 5.12$ decibels

c. When the volume of a cylinder is constant, the height varies inversely as the square of the radius. If the radius is 2 inches when the height is 8 inches, determine the height when the radius is 5 inches.

$h = \dfrac{V}{r^2}$; $8 = \frac{V}{4}$; $32 = v$; $h = \dfrac{32}{25} = 1.28$ inches

4. Determine the horizontal and vertical asymptotes and the intercepts of each of the following. Then sketch a graph of each function.

a. $f(x) = \dfrac{-4}{x-3}$	**b.** $f(x) = \dfrac{2x}{x+2}$	**c.** $f(x) = \dfrac{x+1}{3x-2}$
H: $y = 0$	H: $y = 2$	H: $y = \frac{1}{3}$
V: $x = 3$	V: $x = -2$	V: $x = \frac{2}{3}$
$(0, \frac{4}{3})$	$(0, 0)$	$(0, -\frac{1}{2})$
No x-intercept	$(0, 0)$	$(-1, 0)$

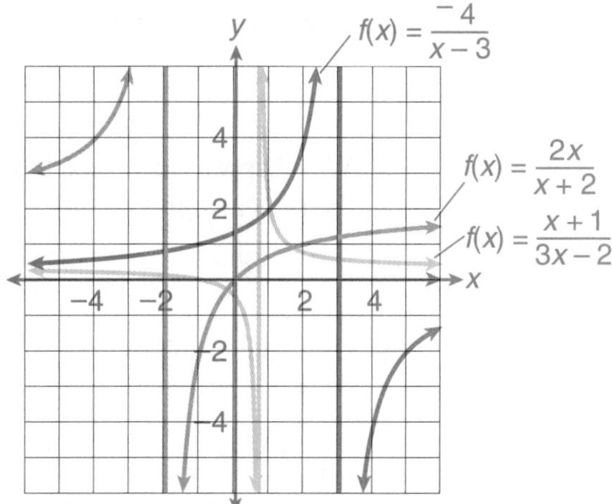

5. **a.** Solve the equation $\dfrac{4}{x-2} + 3 = 9$ using an algebraic approach. Verify your answer graphically.

$\dfrac{4}{x-2} = 6;\ 4 = 6x - 12;\ 16 = 6x;\ x = \frac{8}{3}$

b. When you graph the function $f(x) = \dfrac{4}{x-2} - 6$, what do you discover about the solution to the equation in part a and the x-intercept of the graph of the function f? Explain.

The solution is the x-coordinate of the x-intercept.

6. **a.** Sketch the graph of the function $f(x) = \sqrt{x+4}$.

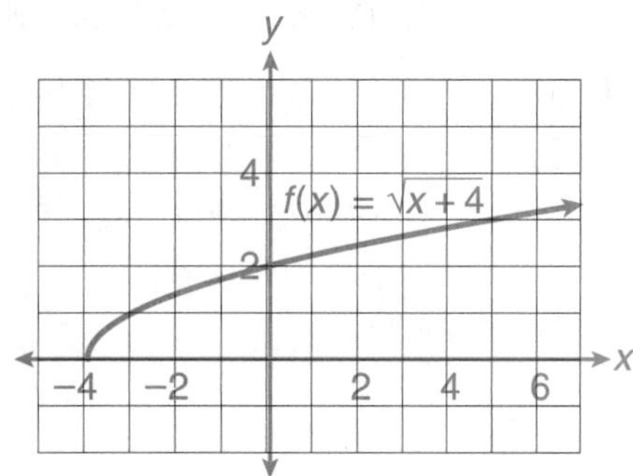

b. As the input gets larger, what is happening to the output values? The output is increasing.

c. What is the domain of this function?

$x \geq -4$

d. What is the range of this function?

$x \geq 0$

e. Are there any intercepts? If so, what are they?

The x-intercept is $(-4,0)$. The y-intercept is $(0,2)$.

f. How is the function f similar to the function $g(x) = \sqrt{x - 4}$?

g has the same shape, but is shifted 8 units to the right.

g. What happens to the graphs of $f(x)$ and $g(x)$ if a negative is placed before the radical sign?

The graphs are reflected through the x-axis

7. a. Draw the graph of $f(x) = \sqrt{x}$.

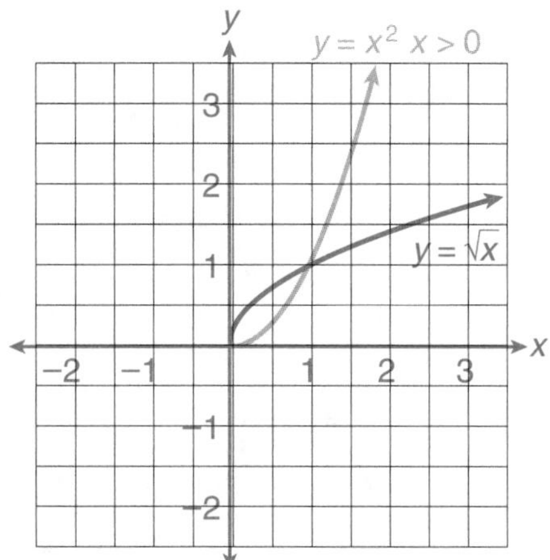

b. Determine the equation of the inverse of the function f.

$y = \sqrt{x}$; $x = \sqrt{y}$; $y = x^2$; $f^{-1}(x) = x^2$; $x \geq 0$

c. Sketch the graph of the inverse on the same axes as the graph of f.

d. From the graph, describe how you know that they are inverses.

The graphs are reflections in $y = x$.

e. Show f and f^{-1} are inverses algebraically.

$f(f^{-1}(x)) = f(x^2) = \sqrt{x^2} = x$

$f^{-1}(f(x)) = f^{-1}(\sqrt{x}) = (\sqrt{x})^2 = x$

8. Solve each of the following equations using an algebraic approach. Verify your solutions graphically.

a. $\sqrt{3x - 2} - 6 = -2$

$\sqrt{3x - 2} = 4$; $3x - 2 = 16$

$3x = 18 \quad x = 6$

b. $\sqrt{2x + 1} - \sqrt{x + 7} = 0$

$2x + 1 = x + 7$

$x = 6$

c. $\sqrt[3]{5x + 4} = 3$

$5x + 4 = 27$

$5x = 23$

$x = \frac{23}{5} = 4.6$

d. $\sqrt{4x + 8} - 3 = -5$

$\sqrt{4x + 8} = -2$

$4x + 8 = 4$ -1 does not check

$4x = -4$; $x = -1$

No solution.

e. $\dfrac{3}{x + 2} = 5$

$3 = 5(x + 2)$

$3 = 5x + 10$

$-7 = 5x$

$x = -\frac{7}{5} = -1.4$

f. $\dfrac{-2x}{3x - 4} = 2$

$-2x = 6x - 8$

$8 = 8x$

$8 = 8x$

$x = 1$

g. $x^{4/3} = 81$

$(x^{4/3})^{3/4} = 81^{3/4}$

$x = 3^3$

$x = 27$

h. $\dfrac{1}{x^2} + \dfrac{1}{2} = 1$

$\dfrac{1}{x^2} = \dfrac{1}{2}$

$2 = x^2$

$x = \pm\sqrt{2}$

CHAPTER 6

Introduction to the Trigonometric Functions

CLUSTER 1

Introducing the Sine, Cosine, and Tangent Functions

ACTIVITY 6.1

The Leaning Tower of Pisa
Topic: *Introduction to Right-Triangle Trigonometry*

During a trip to Italy, you visit a wonder of the world, the Leaning Tower of Pisa. Your guidebook explains that the tower now makes an 85° angle with the ground and measures 179 feet in length. If you drop a stone straight down from the top of the tower, estimate (without calculating) how far from the base it lands.

To answer this question more accurately, you need a branch of mathematics called **trigonometry.** Although its development is generally credited to the ancient Greeks, there is evidence that ancient Egyptian cultures used trigonometry in constructing the pyramids.

As you will see, the accurate answer to the Leaning Tower question requires some knowledge of **right triangles.** Consider the following right triangle with angles A, B, and C and sides a, b, and c.

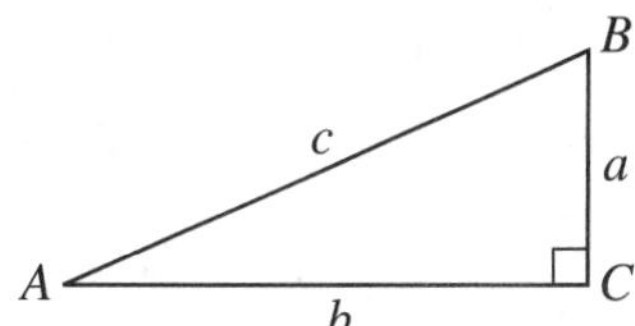

Angle C is the right angle—the angle measuring 90°. The side opposite the right angle, c, is called the **hypotenuse.** Side a is said to be **opposite** angle A because it is not part of angle A. Side b is said to be **adjacent** to angle A because it and the hypotenuse form angle A. Similarly, side b is the side opposite angle B and side a is the side adjacent to angle B.

1. Consider the following right triangle.

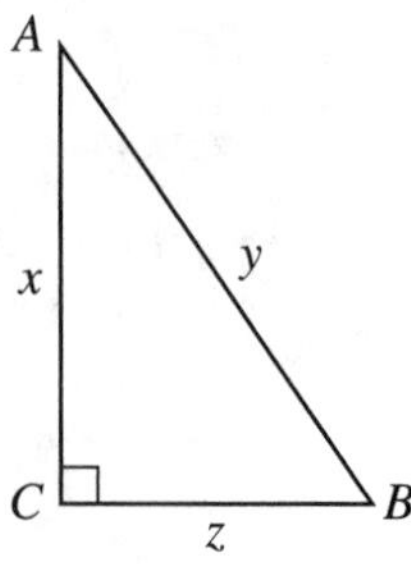

a. Which side is opposite angle *B*?

x is the side opposite of angle B.

b. Which side is adjacent to angle *B*?

z is the side adjacent to angle B.

c. Which side is opposite angle *A*?

z is the side opposite of angle A.

d. Which side is adjacent to angle *A*?

x is the side adjacent to angle A.

e. Which side is the hypotenuse?

Side y is the hypotenuse.

Consider the following right triangles whose angles are the same, but whose sides are different lengths. These three triangles are called **similar triangles.**

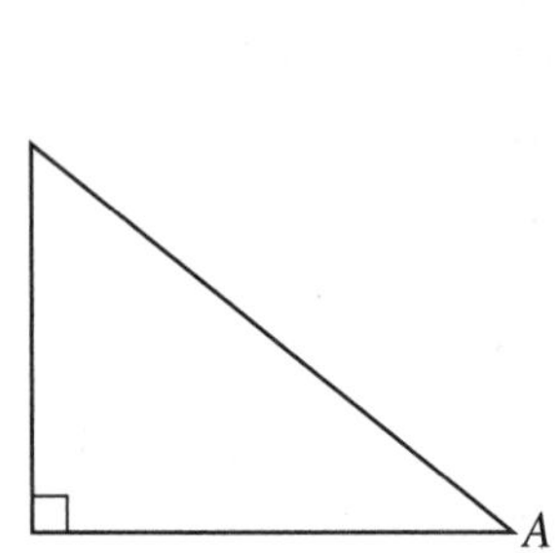

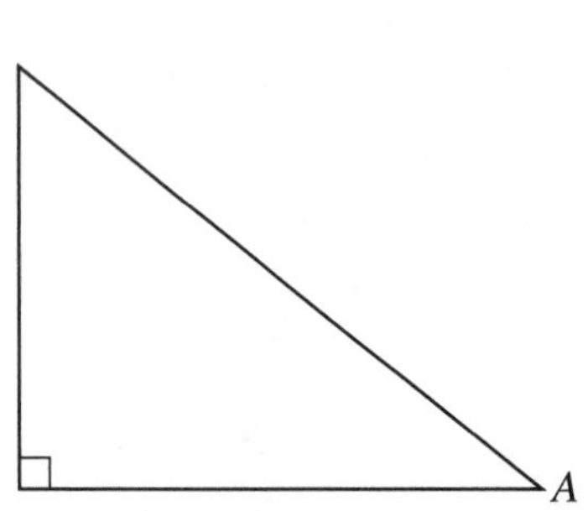

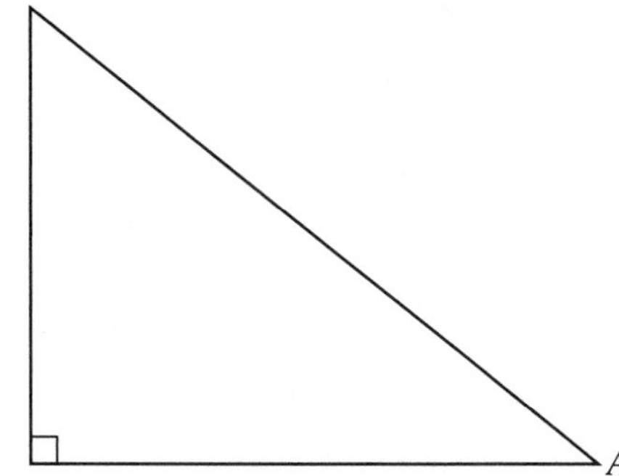

2. a. Using a protractor, estimate the measure of angle *A* to the nearest degree. For a review of angles measured in degrees, see Appendix B. Since $0° \leq A < 90°$, angle *A* is called an **acute angle.**

The measure of angle A to the nearest degree is approximately 38°.

b. Use a ruler, either metric or English, to complete the following table.

	Length of the Hypotenuse	Length of the side Opposite angle *A*	Length of the side Adjacent to angle *A*
SMALL TRIANGLE	1.7 in. or 4.3 cm	1 in. or 2.5 cm	1.3 in. or 3.3 cm
MIDSIZE TRIANGLE	2.1 in. or 5.4 cm	1.3 in. or 3.4 cm	1.7 in. or 4.3 cm
LARGE TRIANGLE	2.6 in. or 6.6 cm	1.6 in. or 4.1 cm	2.1 in. or 5.4 cm

3. a. Use the information in the preceding table to complete the ratios in the following table with respect to angle *A*. Write each ratio as a decimal rounded to the nearest tenth.

	Length of the side Opposite angle *A* / Length of the Hypotenuse	Length of the side Adjacent to angle *A* / Length of the Hypotenuse	Length of the side Opposite angle *A* / Length of the side Adjacent to angle *A*
SMALL TRIANGLE	0.6	0.8	0.8
MIDSIZE TRIANGLE	0.6	0.8	0.8
LARGE TRIANGLE	0.6	0.8	0.8

Recall that the ratios $\frac{a}{b}$ and $\frac{c}{d}$ are proportional if $\frac{a}{b} = \frac{c}{d}$.

b. What do you observe about the ratio $\dfrac{\text{Length of the side Opposite angle } A}{\text{Length of the Hypotenuse}}$ for each of the three right triangles?

The ratio is the same for each of the three right triangles, that is, they are all 0.6 to the nearest tenth.

The table in Problem 3a illustrates the geometric principle that the ratios of *corresponding sides of similar triangles are proportional.*

4. Consider another right triangle in which the measure of *A* is not the same as the measure of *A* in the three similar triangles from Problems 2 and 3.

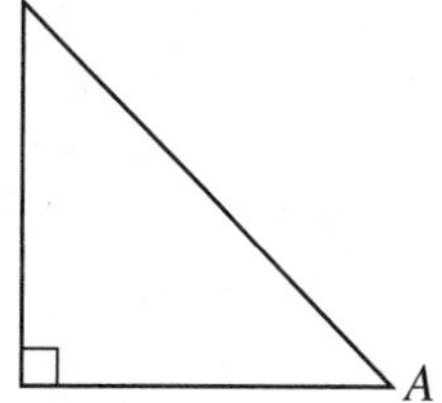

a. Using a protractor, estimate the measure of *A* to the nearest degree.

Angle *A* to the nearest degree is 45°.

b. For this new triangle, use your ruler to complete the following table with respect to angle *A*.

	Length of the side Opposite angle *A* / Length of the Hypotenuse Adjacent to angle *A*	Length of the side Adjacent to angle *A* / Length of the Hypotenuse	Length of the side Opposite angle *A* / Length of the side
NEW TRIANGLE	0.7	0.7	1.0

c. Are the ratios for the new triangle the same as the ratios for the three similar triangles?

The ratios here are different from the ones in the table on page 461.

d. What changed from the similar triangles to the new triangle to make the ratios change?

The measure of angle *A* changes from 38° to 45°.

The ratios of the sides of a right triangle are dependent on the size of the angle *A*. If the angle changes, the ratios change. This fact is fundamental to trigonometry.

The ratios of the sides of a right triangle are functions of the size of the acute angles.

The ratios are given special names and are defined as follows.

- Let *A* be an acute angle (less than 90°) of a right triangle. The **sine, cosine,** and **tangent** of angle *A* are defined as follows:

$$\text{Sine of } A = \sin A = \frac{\text{length of the side opposite } A}{\text{length of the hypotenuse}}$$

$$\text{Cosine of } A = \cos A = \frac{\text{length of the side adjacent to } A}{\text{length of the hypotenuse}}$$

$$\text{Tangent of } A = \tan A = \frac{\text{length of the side opposite } A}{\text{length of the side adjacent to } A};$$

where sin, cos, and tan are the standard abbreviations for sine, cosine, and tangent, respectively.

- Sine, cosine, and tangent are called **trigonometric functions.**
- Note that the input values for the trigonometric functions are angles, and the output values are ratios.

5. Consider the following triangle.

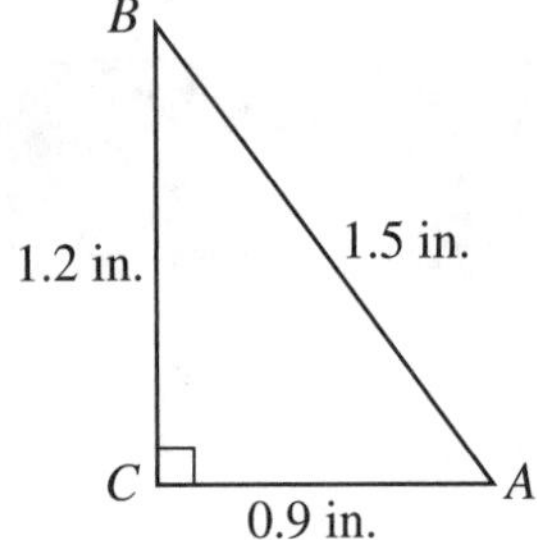

Calculate the following, writing your answer as a decimal rounded to four decimal places.

a. sin A

sin A = 0.8000

b. cos A

cos A = 0.6000

c. tan A

tan A = 1.3333

d. sin B

sin B = 0.6000

e. cos B

cos B = 0.8000

f. tan B

tan B = 0.7500

You are now ready to answer the original Tower of Pisa problem.

6. a. Recall that the tower makes an 85° angle with the ground and the tower is 179 feet in length. Construct a right triangle that satisfies these conditions.

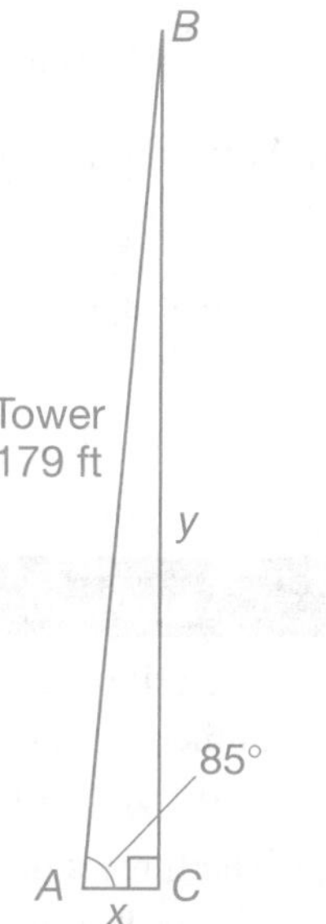

b. Is the height of the tower represented by the length of an opposite side, the length of an adjacent side, or the length of the hypotenuse of your triangle with respect to the 85° angle?

The length of the tower is represented by the hypotenuse with respect to the 85° angle. The height of the tower (distance from top of tower to base measured vertically) is measured by the length of the opposite side.

c. You want to determine how far from the base of the tower the stone hits the ground. Therefore, you want to determine the length of which side of the triangle with respect to the 85° angle?

I want to determine the side adjacent the 85° angle.

d. Which trigonometric function relates the side with length you know and the side with length you want to know?

The cosine function relates the 179-ft. side (hypotenuse) to the distance the tower leans from the vertical.

e. Write an equation using the information in parts a–d.

$\cos 85° = \frac{x}{179}$ where x is the side adjacent to the 85° angle in the diagram in part a.

f. Using your calculator to evaluate cos 85°, solve the equation in part e. Make sure the calculator is in degree mode. Press the key marked (COS), followed by (8), (5), ( )),and (ENTER).

$x = 15.6$ ft. Thus, the tower leans 15.6 feet from the vertical.

7. Solve the following equations. Round your answers to the nearest tenth.

a. $\sin 24° = \frac{x}{10}$ **b.** $\cos 63° = \frac{x}{23.5}$ **c.** $\tan 48° = \frac{16}{x}$

$x = 4.1$ $x = 10.7$ $x = 14.4$

SUMMARY

- The **trigonometric functions** are functions whose inputs are the measures of the acute angles of a right triangle and whose outputs are ratios of the lengths of the sides of the right triangle.
- The three sides of a right triangle are the **adjacent** side, the **opposite** side, and the **hypotenuse.** The hypotenuse is always the side opposite the right (90°) angle. The other two sides vary, depending on which angle is used as the input.
- The **sine, cosine,** and **tangent** of angle A are defined by

$$\sin A = \frac{\text{length of the side opposite } A}{\text{length of the hypotenuse}}$$

$$\cos A = \frac{\text{length of the side adjacent to } A}{\text{length of the hypotenuse}}$$

$$\tan A = \frac{\text{length of the side opposite } A}{\text{length of the side adjacent to } A}.$$

For additional practice working with trigonometric functions in right triangles and special triangles, see Appendix B.

EXERCISES

1. Triangle ABC is a right triangle.

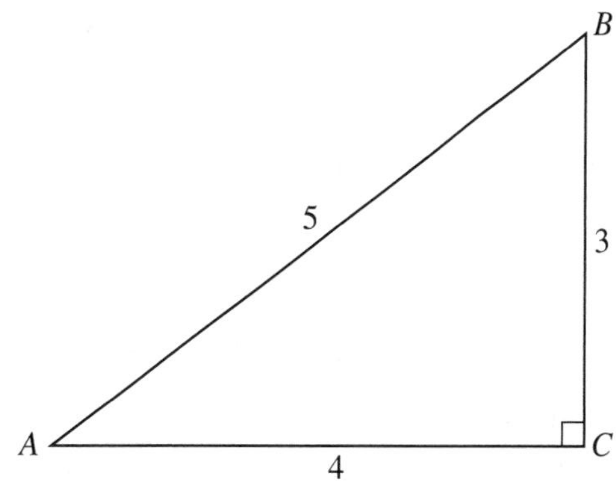

Calculate each of the following.

a. $\sin A$

$\sin A = 0.6000$

b. $\sin B$

$\sin B = 0.8000$

c. $\cos A$

$\cos A = 0.8000$

d. $\cos B$

$\cos B = 0.6000$

e. $\tan A$

$\tan A = 0.7500$

f. $\tan B$

$\tan B = 1.3333$

2. In a certain right triangle, $\sin A = \frac{24}{25}$.

a. Determine possible lengths of the three sides of a right triangle.

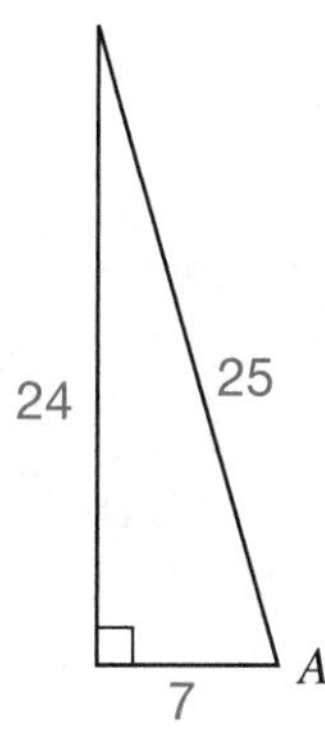

The side opposite angle A is 24; the hypotenuse is 25. Use the Pythagorean theorem to determine the side adjacent to angle A is 7.

b. Determine $\cos A$.

$\cos A = 7/25 = 0.2800$

c. Determine $\tan A$.

$\tan A = 24/7 = 3.4286$

Exercise numbers appearing in color are answered in the Selected Answers section of this book.

3. In a certain right triangle, $\tan B = \frac{7}{4}$.

a. Determine possible lengths of the three sides of a right triangle.

Given $\tan B = \frac{7}{4}$, the side opposite angle B is 7; the side adjacent to angle B is 4. Use the Pythagorean theorem to determine that the hypotenuse is $\sqrt{65}$.

b. Determine $\sin B$.

$\sin B = 7/\sqrt{65} = 0.8682$

c. Determine $\cos B$.

$\cos B = 4/\sqrt{65} = 0.4961$

4. Consider the following right triangle.

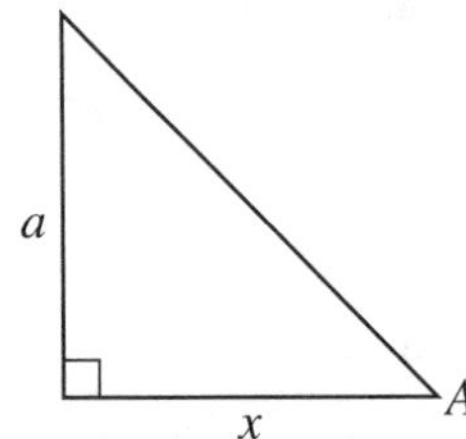

a. Which of the trigonometric functions relates angle A and sides a and x?

The tangent function relates angle A and sides a and x.

b. What equation involving angle A and side a would you solve to determine the value of x?

$\tan A = \frac{a}{x}$

5. Consider the following right triangle.

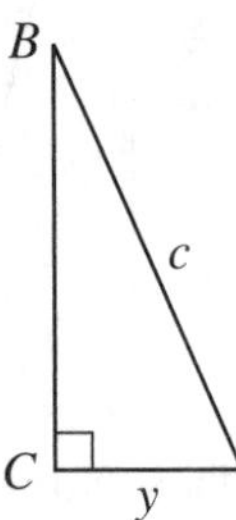

a. Which of the trigonometric functions relates angle B and sides c and y?

The sine function relates angle B and sides c and y.

b. What equation involving angle B and side c would you solve to determine the value of y?

$\sin B = \frac{y}{c}$

6. Consider the following right triangle.

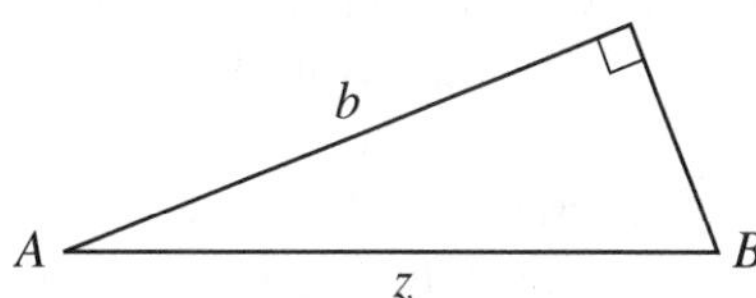

a. Which of the trigonometric functions relates angle A and sides b and z?

The cosine function relates angle A and sides b and z.

b. What equation involving angle A and side b would you solve to determine the value of z?

$\cos A = \frac{b}{z}$

7. Solve the following equations.

a. $\cos 49° = \frac{x}{12}$

$x = 12 \cos 49°$

$x = 7.9$

b. $\tan 84° = \frac{x}{9}$

$x = 9 \tan 84°$

$x = 85.6$

c. $\sin 22° = \frac{23}{x}$

$x = 23/\sin 22°$

$x = 61.4$

8. A friend asks you to help build a ramp at his mother-in-law's house. There are three 7-inch-high steps leading to the front door. Another friend will donate a 15-foot ramp. A local code officer informs you that a handicapped ramp can have an inclination no greater than 5°.

a. Sketch a diagram with the assumption that the landing in front of the steps is level and that a ramp will make a 5° angle with the top of the steps.

b. What is the increase in height from one end of the ramp to the other?

$3 \times 7 = 21$ inches. The increase in height from one end of the ramp to the top of the stairs is $21/12 = 1.75$ feet.

c. Would the donated ramp be long enough to meet the code? Explain.

$\sin 5° = 1.75/x$

$x = 1.75/\sin 5°$

$x = 20.1$ feet

The ramp needs to be at least 20.1 feet. Therefore, the donated ramp will not be long enough to meet the code.

Alternative approach: $15 \sin 5° = 1.3$ feet. The 3 steps must measure at most 1.3 feet in height so the 15-foot ramp satisfies the code.

Each solution suggests ways to think about modifications to either the ramp or the steps (or both) that could be used to meet the code.

ACTIVITY 6.2

A Gasoline Problem

Topic: *Cofunctions and Complementary Angles*

You and a friend take a camping trip to the great Southwest. On the way home, you realize that your Jeep is running low on gas, so you stop at a filling station. Unfortunately, the attendant informs you that his station has been without gas for several days. However, he is certain that there is a station with gas on a side road up ahead that should be able to help you.

After a quick phone call confirming this information, you ask the attendant about the exact location of the station. The attendant shows you a map of the area. You can continue along the main road that you are on and make a left at the intersection with the side road or you can drive through the desert at an angle of 35° with the main road for a distance of 10 miles.

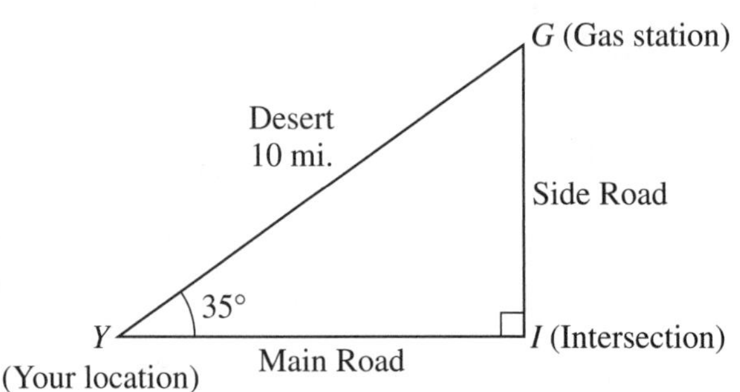

Your Jeep is equipped with a compass, so driving through the desert is not a big problem. However, you would prefer to stay on the road, if possible. You estimate that you have enough gas for 15 miles. Do you believe that you have enough gas to make it to the other station without going through the desert?

This problem can be solved using the given triangle and trigonometry. You need to determine the distance from you to the intersection, side *YI*, and the distance from the intersection to the gas station, side *IG*.

1. a. With respect to angle *Y*:

i. Side *YI* is called the side adjacent to angle *Y* (35°).

ii. Side *YG* is called the hypotenuse.

b. The function that relates *YI*, *YG*, and angle *Y* is the cosine function.

c. Write an equation using the trigonometric function determined in part b.

$\cos Y = \frac{YI}{YG}$

d. Solve the equation for the length of *YI*.

$\cos 35° = \frac{YI}{10}$

$YI = 10 \cos 35°$

$YI = 8.2$ miles

2. a. With respect to angle *Y*:

i. Side *IG* is called the side opposite to angle *Y* (35°).

ii. Side *YG* is called the hypotenuse.

b. The function that relates IG, YG, and angle Y is the sine function.

c. Write an equation using the function from part b.

$\sin Y = \frac{IG}{YG}$

d. Solve the equation for the length of IG.

$\sin 35° = \frac{IG}{10}$

$IG = 10 \sin 35°$

$IG = 5.7$ miles

3. Do you believe that you will have enough gas to make it to the second service station without driving through the desert? Explain.

I would have to travel 8.2 + 5.7 = 13.9 miles on the two roads to the other station. I should be able to make it without journeying through the desert.

Meanwhile, the attendant at the second service station is also making some calculations. He is aware of your situation and is trying to anticipate which option you will choose in case he has to go look for you.

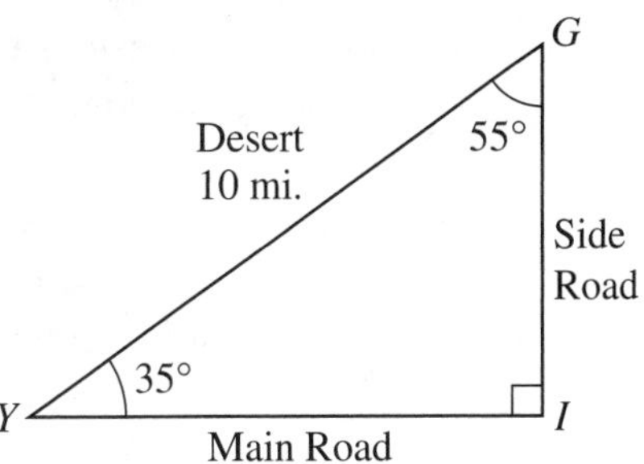

He knows that the angle that the line to the first station makes with the side road is 55°.

4. a. With respect to angle G:

i. Side YI is called the opposite side.

ii. Side YG is called the hypotenuse.

b. The function that relates YI, YG, and angle G is the sine function.

c. Write an equation using the function from part b.

$\sin G = \frac{YI}{YG}$

d. Solve the equation for the length of YI.

$\sin 55° = \frac{YI}{10}$

$YI = 10 \sin 55°$

$YI = 8.2$ miles

5. a. With respect to angle G:

i. Side IG is called the adjacent side.

ii. Side YG is called the hypotenuse.

b. The function that relates IG, YG, and angle G is the ___cosine function___.

c. Write an equation using the function from part b.

$\cos G = \frac{IG}{YG}$

d. Solve the equation for the length of IG.

$IG = 10 \cos 55°$

$IG = 5.7$

Although you used different angles of the triangle, the lengths of YI and IG that you calculated in each case should have been the same. The angles involved in these calculations were 35° and 55°. Their sum is 90°, and they are called complementary angles.

Two angles A and B whose measures sum to 90° are called **complementary angles.** In general, if x represents an acute angle, then its complement is represented by $90 - x$. (Note that the name *cosine* is derived from the words *sine* and *complement.*)

The sum of the measures of the 3 angles of a triangle is 180°. The two acute angles in a right triangle are complementary.

6. a. Compare your results in Problems 1d and 4d. Why did your calculations for YI result in the same value?

cos 35° = sin 55° in the respective equations, thus, the resulting values are equal.

b. Compare your results in Problems 2d and 5d. Why did your calculations for IG result in the same value?

sin 35° = cos 55° in the respective equations, thus, the resulting values are equal.

Sine and cosine are called **cofunctions.**

7. What have you observed about the cofunctions of complementary angles, such as sin 35° and cos 55° or cos 35° and sin 55°?

The cofunctions of complementary angles are equal.

8. Complete the following table using your grapher to verify your conjecture in Problem 7.

x (degrees)	90 − *x*	sin x	cos (90 − *x*)
0	90	0.0000	0.0000
15	75	0.2588	0.2588
30	60	0.5000	0.5000
45	45	0.7071	0.7071
60	30	0.8660	0.8660
75	15	0.9659	0.9659
90	0	1.0000	1.0000

SUMMARY

- Complementary angles are two angles whose measures sum to 90°.
- The *co* in *cosine* comes from the word *complement*. Sine and cosine are called cofunctions.
- Cofunctions of complementary angles are equal.

EXERCISES

1. You are in a rowboat on Devil Lake in Ontario, Canada. Your lakeside cabin has no running water, so you sometimes go to a fresh spring at a different point on the lakeshore. To reach the spring, you row in a direction 60° north of east for half a mile. You are not really tired yet and it is a lovely day.

a. How far would you now have to row if you returned to your cabin by rowing directly south and then directly west? Remember to start by drawing a diagram, including a right triangle.

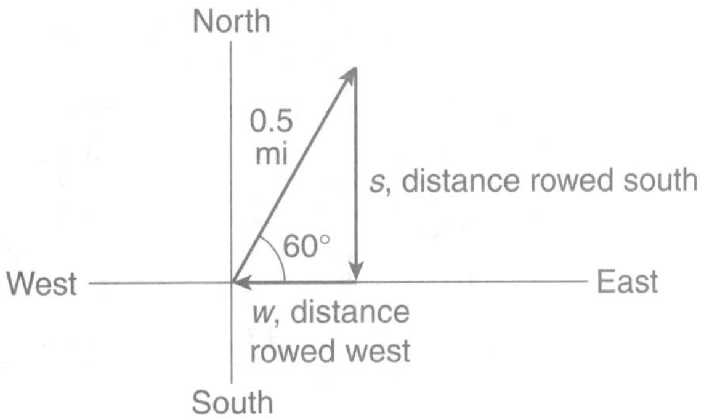

North
0.5 mi
s, distance rowed south
60°
West
East
w, distance rowed west
South

$s = 0.5 \sin 60° = 0.43$ miles

$w = 0.5 \cos 60° = 0.25$ miles

$s + w = 0.68$ miles

I would travel 0.68 miles going back directly south and then directly west.

b. Check your solution to part a using the complementary angle and cofunction of those used in part a.

$s = 0.5 \cos 30° = 0.43$ miles

$w = 0.5 \sin 30° = 0.25$ miles

These calculations confirm the result in part a.

Exercise numbers appearing in color are answered in the Selected Answers section of this book.

2. You aren't paying enough attention while rowing one afternoon. You row 20° off course, too far to the north, instead of directly west as you intended. You row 300 meters.

 a. Draw a diagram of this situation.

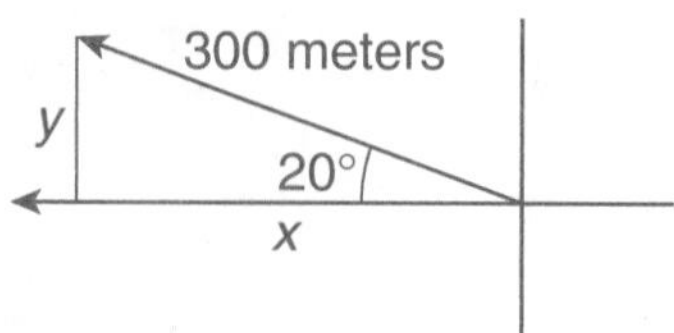

 b. How far west are you when you realize you are off course?

 Let x be the distance to the west when I realized I was off course.

 $x = 300 \cos 20° = 282$ meters

 I rowed 282 meters directly west.

 c. How far north are you from where you originally planned to be?

 Let y be the distance I rowed to the north when I realized I was off course.

 $y = 300 \sin 20° = 103$ meters

 I was 103 meters to the north when I realized I was off course.

 d. Check your solutions to parts b and c by using the complementary angle and cofunctions of those used in parts b and c.

 $x = 300 \sin(90° - 20°) = 300 \sin(70°) = 281$ meters

 $y = 300 \cos(90° - 20°) = 300 \cos(70°) = 103$ meters

 These calculations verify the results in b and c.

3. a. Complete the following table.

x (degrees)	90 − x	cos x	sin (90 − x)
7	83	0.9925	0.9925
17	73	0.9563	0.9563
24	66	0.9135	0.9135
33	57	0.8387	0.8387
48	42	0.6691	0.6691
67	23	0.3907	0.3907
77	13	0.2250	0.2250

 b. What trigonometric property does this table illustrate?

 The table in part a illustrates the property that cofunctions of complementary angles are equal.

The Sidewalks of New York

Topic: *Inverse Trigonometric Functions*

A friend of yours is having a party in her Manhattan apartment, which borders Central Park. She gives you directions from your place, which also borders the park:

i. If you are coming after dark, head east for three blocks, going around the park, and then go north for two blocks.

ii. If you can come early, you can cut through the park, a shorter route.

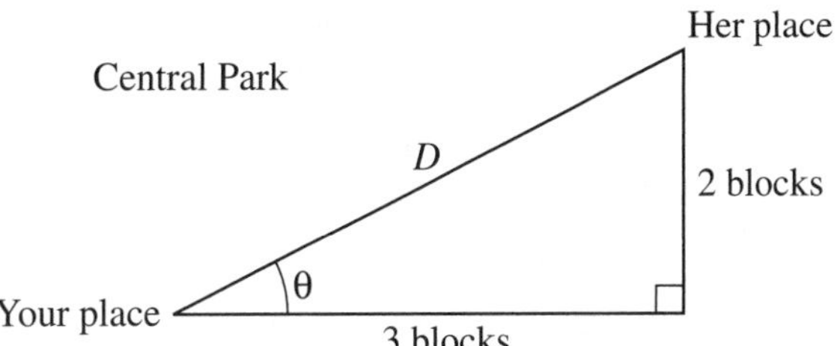

Suppose you leave your place early and decide to cut through the park. You want to compute the shortcut distance D (in blocks) between your apartments.

1. Using the Pythagorean theorem, $(c^2 = a^2 + b^2)$, determine the distance D, in blocks, across the park.

$\sqrt{2^2 + 3^2} = \sqrt{13} = 3.6$ blocks

The shortest distance between the two apartments is 3.6 blocks.

Now you want to determine the direction (angle) you need to go to get to your friend's place. You can represent the angle by θ, the Greek letter theta. Because you now have the lengths of all three sides of the right triangle, you can use any of the trigonometric functions to help determine θ. Begin with the tangent function.

Recall that the input for the tangent function is an angle, and the output is the ratio of the length of the side opposite to the length of the side adjacent to the angle.

$$\text{Tangent of an angle} = \frac{\text{opposite side}}{\text{adjacent side}}$$

2. Determine the value of the tangent of θ, written $\tan \theta$, for the given triangle.

$\tan \theta = \frac{2}{3} = 0.6667$

If you want to determine the tangent of a *known* angle you can use the button marked TAN on your calculator. From Problem 2, you know the value of the tangent of the angle, but do not know the value of the angle θ. That is, you know the output for the tangent function, but you do not know the input.

3. Use the table feature on your calculator to approximate θ from Problem 2. You should compute the tangent of several possible values of θ to get as close as possible to the desired answer. Complete the following table. Round your answers to five decimal places.

θ	TAN θ
30°	0.57735
40°	0.83910
35°	0.70021
34°	0.67451
33.7°	0.66692
33.69°	0.66666

You don't have to experiment every time to determine θ when you know the tangent of θ. There is a more direct method, using the inverse tangent function. Recall that with inverse functions, the inputs and outputs are interchanged.

The input of the **inverse tangent** function is the ratio of the length of the side opposite to the length of the side adjacent to the angle. The output is the acute angle. The inverse tangent function is denoted by $\mathbf{tan^{-1}}$ or **arctan** and defined by

$$\tan^{-1} x = \theta \textit{ if and only if } \tan\theta = x,$$

where x represents the *ratio* of the length of the opposite side to the length of the adjacent side.

The inverse tangent function is located on your calculator as second function to tangent. That is, you will need to press a special key (marked 2nd or shift) before you press the tangent key. Note your calculator uses the notation $\tan^{-1}$ rather that arctan.

4. Use your calculator to determine the inverse tangent of the answer to Problem 2. (Make sure your calculator is in degree mode.) Compare this answer with your approximation from Problem 3.

$\theta = \tan^{-1}(2/3) = 33.6901°$

Remember: $\tan^{-1}(\text{ratio}) = \text{angle}$
$\tan(\text{angle}) = \text{ratio}$

There are similar definitions for the inverse sine and inverse cosine functions.

INVERSE SINE AND INVERSE COSINE

The input of the **inverse sine** function is the ratio of the length of the side opposite the angle to the length of the hypotenuse of the triangle. The output is the acute angle. The inverse sine function is denoted by $\sin^{-1}$ or arcsin and defined by

$$\sin^{-1} x = \theta \text{ if and only if } \sin \theta = x.$$

The input of the **inverse cosine** function is the ratio of the length of the side adjacent to the angle to the length of the hypotenuse of the triangle. The output is the acute angle. The inverse cosine function is denoted by $\cos^{-1}$ or arccos and defined by

$$\cos^{-1} x = \theta \text{ if and only if } \cos \theta = x.$$

5. a. Use the inverse sine function to determine the value of θ in the Central Park situation.

$\theta = \sin^{-1}(2/\sqrt{13}) = 33.6901°$

b. Use the inverse cosine function to determine the value of θ in the Central Park situation.

$\theta = \cos^{-1}(3/\sqrt{13}) = 33.6901°$

c. Are you surprised by your answers to parts a and b? Explain.

No, since $\sin \theta = \dfrac{2}{\sqrt{13}}$ and $\cos \theta = \dfrac{3}{\sqrt{13}}$

6. The term used by highway departments when describing the steepness of a hill is **percent grade.** For example, a hill with a 5% grade possesses a slope of $\frac{5}{100}$, or $\frac{1}{20}$.

a. You are driving along Route 17 in the Catskill Mountains of New York State. Just before coming to the top of a hill, you spot a sign that reads "7% Grade Next 3 Miles. Trucks Use Lower Gear." Draw a triangle and label the appropriate parts to model this situation.

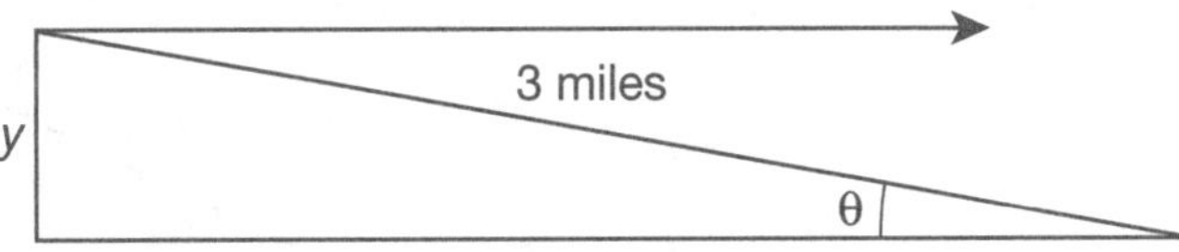

b. Use an inverse trigonometric function to determine the angle that the base of the hill makes with the horizontal.

$\theta = \tan^{-1}(7/100) = 4.004°$

c. Use trigonometry to determine how many feet of elevation you will lose from the top of the hill to the bottom.

$y = 3 \sin(4.004°) = 0.21$ miles

In three miles, the elevation drops 0.21 miles or 1106 ft.

SUMMARY

- The domain (inputs) of the inverse trigonometric functions is the set of ratios of the lengths of the sides of a right triangle.
- The range (outputs) of the inverse trigonometric functions is the set of angles.
- The inverse trigonometric functions are defined by

$$\sin^{-1} x = \theta \text{ if and only if } \sin \theta = x$$

$$\cos^{-1} x = \theta \text{ if and only if } \cos \theta = x$$

$$\tan^{-1} x = \theta \text{ if and only if } \tan \theta = x.$$

EXERCISES

1. For each of the following, use your calculator to determine θ to the nearest 0.01°.

a. $\theta = \arcsin \frac{1}{2}$

$\theta = 30°$

b. $\theta = \cos^{-1} \frac{3}{7}$

$\theta = 64.62°$

c. $\theta = \arctan 2.36$

$\theta = 67.04°$

d. $\theta = \sin^{-1} 0.8974$

$\theta = 63.82°$

e. $\tan \theta = \frac{7}{3}$

$\theta = 66.81°$

f. $\cos \theta = \frac{3}{7}$

$\theta = 64.62°$

g. $\sin \theta = 0.3791$

$\theta = 22.28°$

h. $\tan \theta = 0.3791$

$\theta = 20.76°$

2. Complete the table, which refers to the following right triangle.

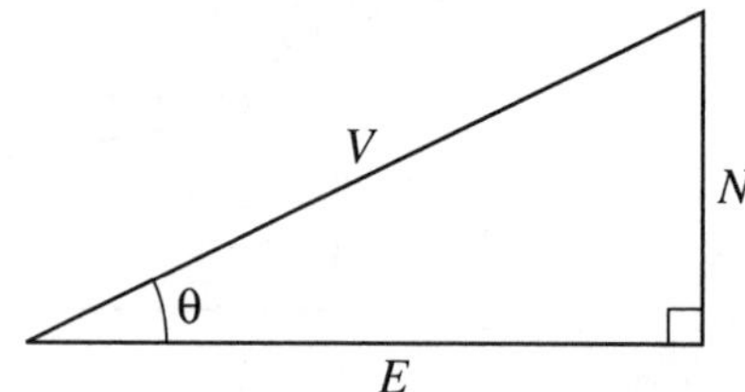

V	θ	E	N
32	65°	13.5	29.0
23.3	59.0°	12	20
4.1	54°	2.4	3.3
26	43.8°	18.8	18
4.5	45°	3.2	3.2

3. You are in a rowboat again, as in Exercise 2 in Activity 6.2. Recall that you went 300 meters in a direction 20° north of west, instead of going directly west. You turn to go directly south. At what angle must you turn your rowboat?

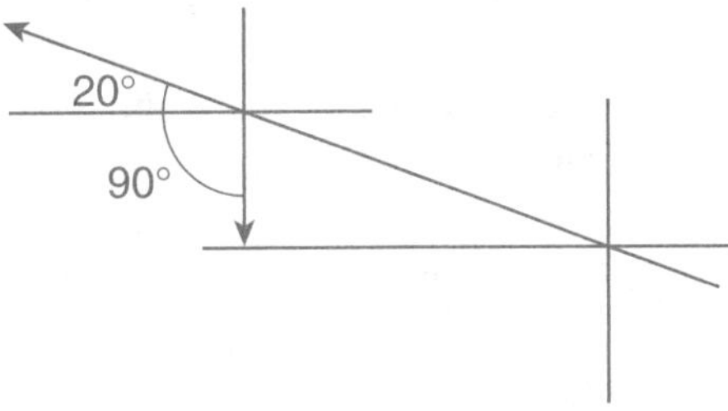

I must turn the rowboat 110° to head directly south.

4. While hiking you see an interesting rock formation on the side of a vertical cliff. You want to describe for a friend how he might see it when he walks down the path. If you stand on the path at a certain place, 50 feet from the base of the cliff, the rock formation is visible about 30 feet up the cliff. At what angle should you tell your friend to look?

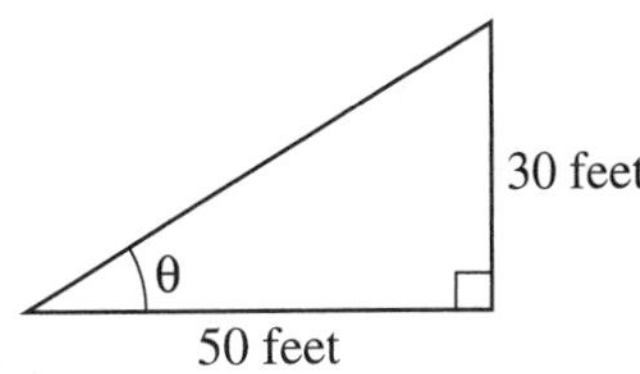

$\theta = \tan^{-1}(30/50) = 31°$

My friend should look up at an angle of approximately 31°.

5. A warehouse access ramp claims to have a 10% grade. The ramp is 15 feet long.

a. Draw a diagram of this situation.

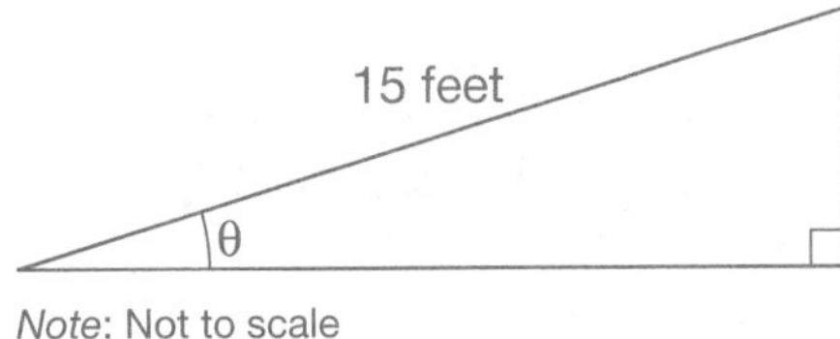

Note: Not to scale

b. What angle does the ramp make with the horizontal?

Since grade is rise over run, $\tan\theta = 0.1$.

$\theta = \tan^{-1}(0.1) = 5.7°$

The ramp makes an angle of 5.7° with the horizontal.

c. How much does the elevation change from one end of the ramp to the other?

$y = 15\sin(5.7°) = 1.5$ feet.

The elevation changes 1.5 feet from one end of the ramp to the other.

ACTIVITY 6.4

Solving a Murder
Topic: *Solving Right Triangles*

There has been a fatal shooting 110 feet from the base of a 25-story building. Each story measures approximately 12 feet. There are two likely suspects who live in the building, one on the seventh floor and one on the twentieth floor. Both suspects were in their apartments at the time of the murder. Forensic specialists report that the bullet was fired from somewhere in the building and entered the body at an angle of approximately 58° with the ground.

1. Draw a diagram that models this situation.

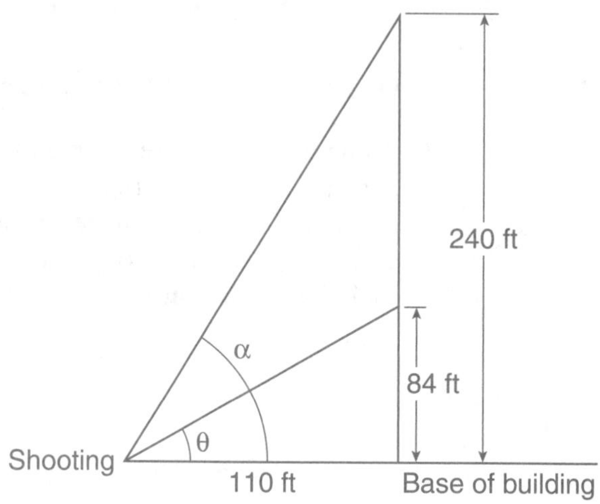

Based on the diagram, the question is now: Is α, or is θ equal to 58°?

2. Use the trigonometric functions to determine which of the two suspects could not have committed the murder.

$\alpha = \tan^{-1}(84/110) = 37°$

$\theta = \tan^{-1}(240/110) = 65°$

These calculations show that the suspect on the 7th floor could not have committed the murder.

3. On what other floors of the building should the police question additional possible suspects? Explain.

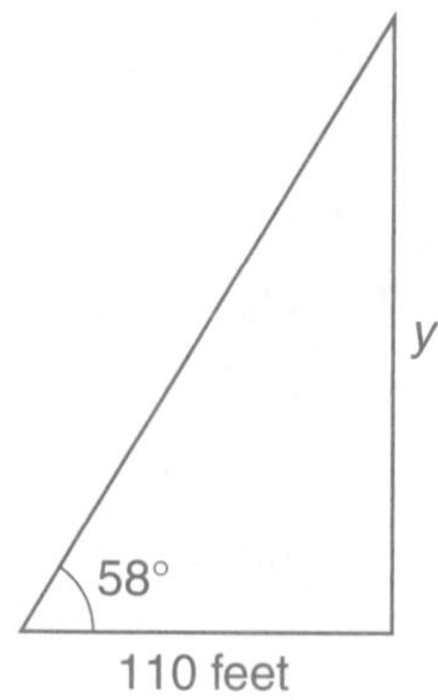

$y = 110 \tan 58° = 176$ feet or about 14.7 floors. Therefore, the police should question possible suspects on the 14th and 15th floors.

In this chapter, you have been solving problems related to right triangles.

To **solve a triangle** means to determine the measure of all sides and all angles of the triangle. This process can be especially useful for architects, surveyors, and navigators.

4. Using the given information, solve each of the following right triangles.

a.

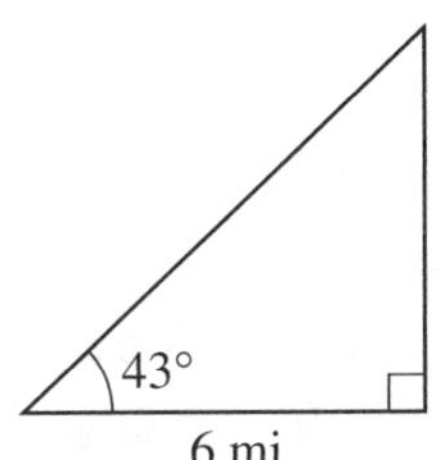

Side opposite the 43° angle $= 6 \tan 43° = 5.6$

Hypotenuse $= 6/\cos 43° = 8.2$

The other acute angle is $90 - 43 = 47°$

b.

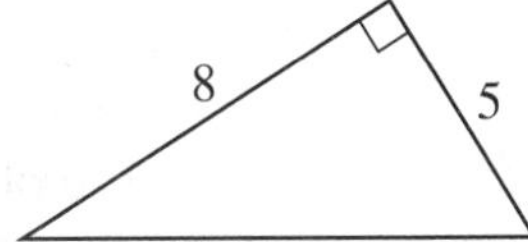

Hypotenuse $= 9.4$ by using the Pythagorean theorem.

The angle adjacent to side $8 = \tan^{-1}(5/8) = 32°$

The angle adjacent to side $5 = 58°$.

c.

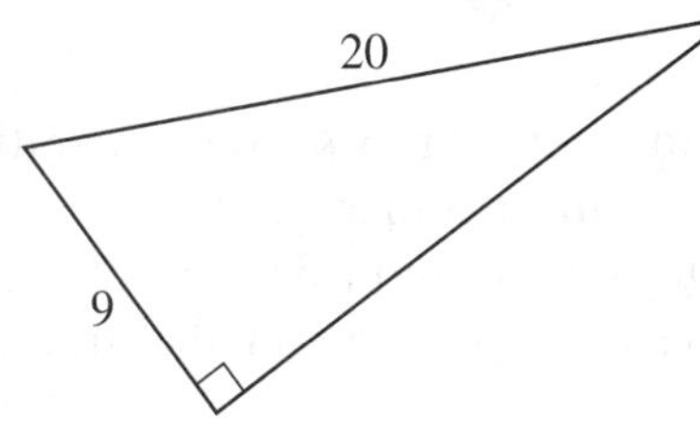

The other leg $= 17.9$

The angle adjacent to side $9 = \cos^{-1}(9/20) = 63°$

The other acute angle is 27°

SUMMARY

- Many trigonometric problems involve solving right triangles—that is, determining the measures of all sides and angles.
- Here is a trigonometric problem-solving strategy:

1. Draw a diagram of the situation using right triangles.

2. Identify all known sides and angles.

3. Identify the sides and/or angles you want to know.

4. Identify functions that relate the known and unknown.

5. Write and solve the appropriate trigonometric equation(s).

EXERCISES

1. Solve each of the following right triangles using the information given. (Round all approximations to the nearest tenth.)

a. 6.5 ft, 57°

The side adjacent to the 57° angle $= 4.2$ ft.

The hypotenuse is 7.8 ft.

The other acute angle is 33°.

b. 18, 6

The hypotenuse is 19.0

The angle adjacent to side 18 $= 18.4°$

The other acute angle is 71.6°

c.

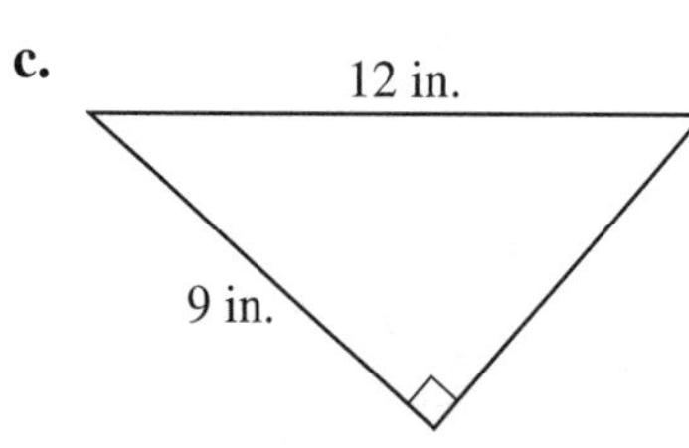

The other leg $= 7.9$ in.

The angle adjacent to side 9 in. is 41.4°

The other angle is 48.6°

2. You need to construct new steps for your deck and read that stringers are on sale at the local lumber company. Stringers are precut side supports to which you nail the steps; they are made in three-, four-, five-, six-, or seven-step sizes. The dimensions of the steps on the stringers are 7 inches on 12 inches.

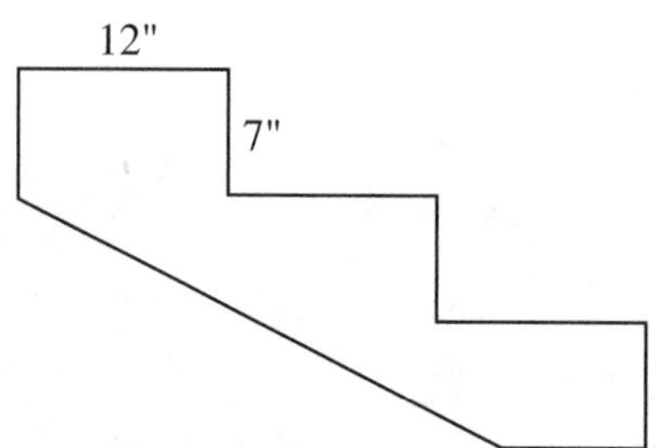

a. If you measure that the vertical rise of your deck is 3.5 feet, which size stringer should you buy? Explain.

The height of the staircase is $3.5 \times 12 = 42$ inches. The number of steps $= 42$ in./7 in. $= 6$. Therefore, I will need the 6-step increment.

b. How far out will your steps extend from the porch? Explain.

The steps will extend 6 steps $\times$ 12 in. $= 72$ inches or 6 feet from the porch.

Exercise numbers appearing in color are answered in the Selected Answers section of this book.

c. What angle will your steps make with the ground? Explain.

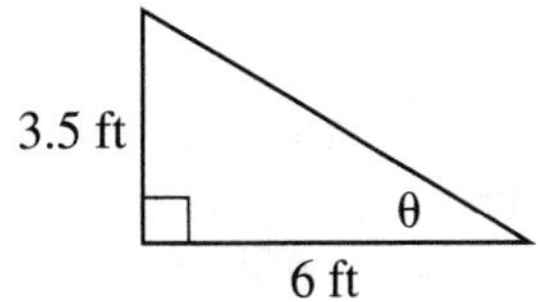

The height of the staircase is 3.5 ft. and the length is 6 feet.

$\theta = \tan^{-1}(3.5/6) = 30.3°$. The stairs make an angle of about 30° with the ground.

d. What angle will your steps make with the house?

60°

ACTIVITY 6.5

How Stable Is That Tower?

Topic: *Problem Solving with Right Triangle Trigonometry*

You are considering buying property near a communications tower and are concerned about your property value. You decide to do some reading about issues involving towers, such as aesthetics, safety, and stability. Of course, anyone living near the tower would like a guarantee that it could not blow down. Guy wires are part of that guarantee.

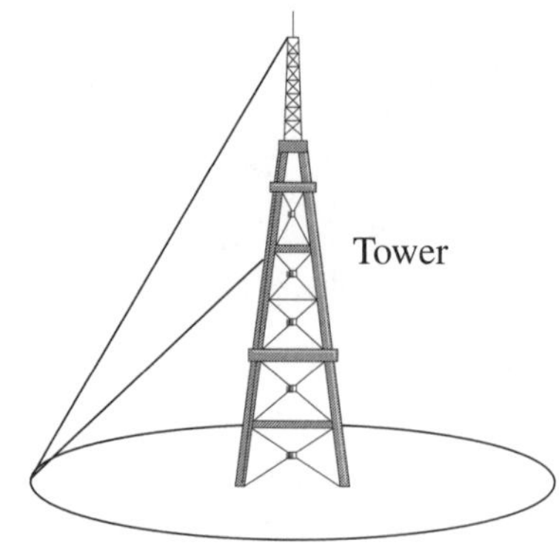

The tower rises 300 feet and is supported by several pairs of guy wires all attached on the ground at the same distance from the base of the tower. For each pair, one guy wire extends from the ground to the top of the tower and the other is attached halfway up. The accompanying diagram illustrates one pair of wires.

1. New guidelines for stability recommend that the angle the guy wires make with the line through the center of the tower (not the angle of elevation) must be at least 40°. Therefore, the existing guy wires may need to be replaced. Because you are concerned with how close the wires will come to your property, you need to compute the shortest distance from the tower at which the guy wires may be attached. Use trigonometry to compute this distance.

   Let x represent the distance of the guy wire from the center of the base of the tower.

   $\tan 40° = x/150$

   $x = 150 \cdot \tan 40° = 126$ ft

   Similarly, $x = 300 \cdot \tan 40° = 252$ ft

   Since the angle must be at least 40°, the minimum distance from the tower at which the guy wires may be attached is 252 ft.

2. To improve stability, the drafters of the guidelines propose increasing the minimum angle the guy wires make with the tower from 40° to 50°. What is the effect on the shortest distance from the tower at which the guy wires may be attached?

   The shortest distance increases from about 252 ft to about 358 ft., since 300*tan 50° = 357.52 ft.

EXERCISES

For Exercises 1 and 2, the following definitions are useful.

The **angle of elevation** is the angle formed by your horizontal line of sight and a straight line from you to the object you are viewing above you.

The **angle of depression** is the angle formed by your horizontal line of sight and a straight line from you to the object you are viewing below you.

The only difference between these two angles is that with elevation the object is above you and with depression the object is below you.

1. You are driving on a straight highway at sea level and begin to climb a hill with a 5% grade. (Recall that a grade is given in percent, but may be expressed as a fraction. In that way, a grade can be viewed as a slope.)

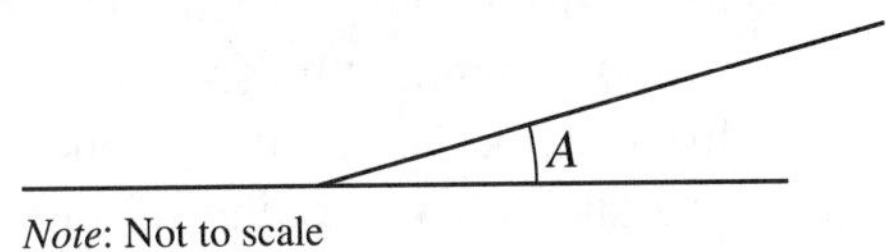

Note: Not to scale

   a. What is the slope of the highway with a grade of 5%?

   The slope is 5/100 or 1/20, or 0.05.

   b. What is the *angle of elevation A*? That is, what is the angle the highway makes with the horizontal? Explain.

   $A = \tan^{-1}(0.05) = 2.86°$ The highway makes an angle of 2.86° with the horizontal. This angle is called the angle of elevation.

   c. If you drive for 1 mile along the highway, how many feet above sea level are you? Explain.

   I would be 264 feet above sea level after 1 mile. 1 mile is equivalent to 5280 ft. If x represents the number of feet above sea level after climbing 1 mile, then $x = 5280 \cdot \sin(2.9) =$ approximately 264 ft.

2. You and some friends take a trip to the Grand Canyon of Pennsylvania and in particular Colton Point State Park. Some of your friends go white-water rafting, while the others join you for a hike. You reach the observation deck at the point in time to see the rest of your party battling the white water. Someone in the group asks you how close you think the rafts actually get to you as they pass by. You have no idea, and neither does the park ranger. However, she does tell you that the canyon is approximately 800 feet deep at Colton Point and the angle of depression to the creek (the angle formed by your horizontal line of sight and a straight line to the creek) is about 22°.

   a. Draw a diagram of this situation.

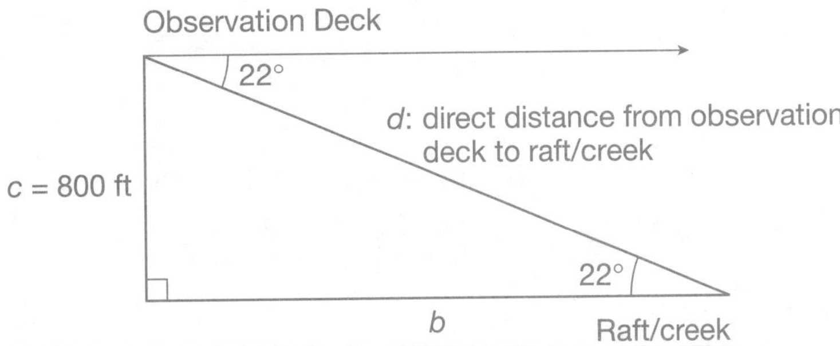

   b. Use trigonometry to estimate how close the rafters get to you as you stand on the observation deck.

   The direct distance, d, from the observation deck to the raft is approximately $800/\sin 22° = 2135$ feet.

   If you could walk straight down the cliff and straight across at the base of the cliff to the creek, the distance would be approximately $b + c = 2780$ ft., where $b = 800/\tan 22°$.

Exercise numbers appearing in color are answered in the Selected Answers section of this book.

ACTIVITY 6.6

Climbing a Mountain

Topics: *Right-Triangle Trigonometry, Algebraic Equation Solving, Problem-Solving Heuristics*

You are camping in the Adirondacks and decide to climb a mountain that dominates the local area. You are curious about the vertical rise of the mountain and recall from your mathematics course that surveyors can measure the angle of elevation of a mountain summit with a theodolite. You are able to borrow a theodolite from the local community college to gather some pertinent data. You find a level field and take a first reading of an angle of elevation of 23°. Then you walk 100 feet toward the mountain summit and take a second reading of 24° angle of elevation (see diagram).

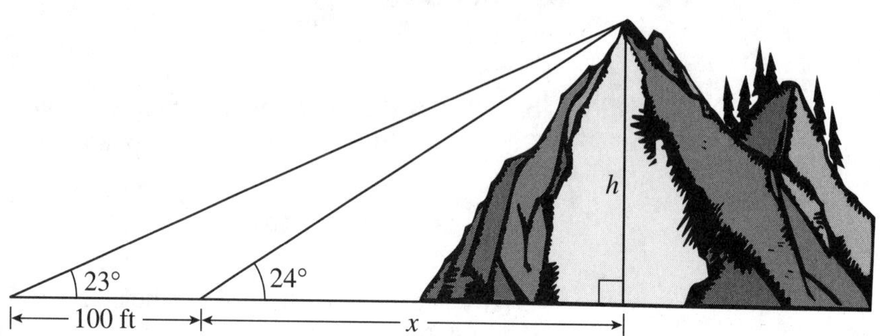

1. Use h to represent the vertical rise of the mountain, and write expressions for tan 23° and tan 24° in terms of h and x.

a. $\tan 23° = \dfrac{h}{100 + x}$ b. $\tan 24° = \dfrac{h}{x}$

2. a. Solve the system of equations in Problem 1 to determine x.

From 1a, $h = (\tan 23°)(100 + x)$

From 1b, $h = (\tan 24°)(x)$

$$100 \tan 23° + x \tan 23° = x \tan 24°$$
$$x \tan 24° - x \tan 23° = 100 \tan 23°$$
$$x(\tan 24° - \tan 23°) = 100 \tan 23°$$
$$x = \frac{100 \tan 23°}{\tan 24° - \tan 23°}$$
$$x = 2045.3 \text{ feet}$$

b. Use the value of x from part a to determine the vertical rise h of the mountain.

$h = 2045.3 \tan 24 = 910.6$. The vertical rise of the mountain is 911 feet. To check, $h = 2145.3 \tan 23 = 910.6$.

EXERCISES

1. You are standing at a distance of about 92 meters from the base of the CN Tower in Toronto, Canada. You are able to measure the angle of elevation to the top of the tower as 80.6°.

Exercise numbers appearing in color are answered in the Selected Answers section of this book.

a. Draw a diagram and indicate the angle of elevation.

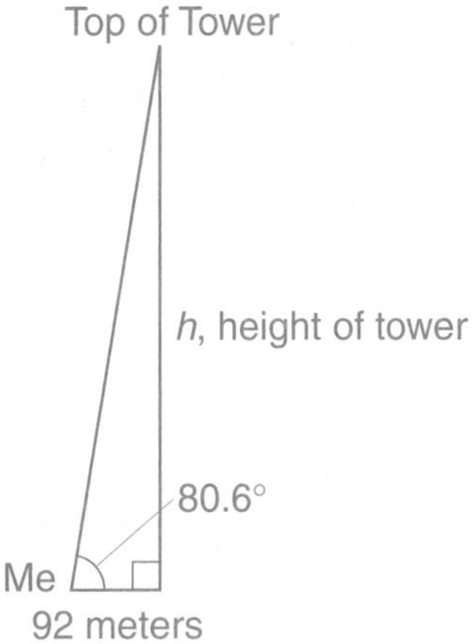

b. What is the height of the tower?

The height of the tower is 556 feet since $h = 92 \tan 80.6° = 555.7$ feet.

2. You are in a spy satellite, equipped with a measuring device like a theodolite, orbiting 5 miles above Earth. Your mission is to discover the length of a secret airport runway. Use techniques that worked successfully in this activity to describe for your supervisor how you are going to determine the desired length. Then, using some reasonable data (make up your own), determine the length.

Answers will vary. Here is a sample: The satellite is 5 miles above Earth and y miles from the start (A) of the runway as shown in the diagram. The problem is to determine the length of the runway, which is the distance between point A and point B, the end of the runway. I measured the angle of depression to point B to be 25° and the angle of depression for point A to be 30°.

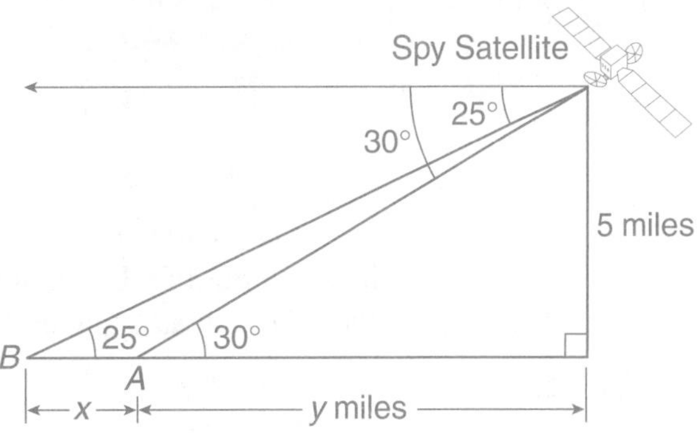

The two equations are (a) $\tan 25° = \dfrac{5}{x + y}$ and (b) $\tan 30° = \frac{5}{y}$. Solving equation (b), $y = 8.7$ miles.

Then equation (a) becomes $\tan 25° = \dfrac{5}{x + 8.7}$. Solve this equation for x.

$$(x + 8.7) \tan 25 = 5$$

$$x \tan 25 = 5 - 8.7 \tan 25$$

$$x = \frac{(5 - 8.7 \tan 25)}{\tan 25}$$

$$x = 2.0 \text{ miles}$$

The runway is approximately 2 miles long.

3. You are interested in constructing a feeding trough for your cattle that can hold the largest amount of feed. You buy a 15- by-50-foot piece of aluminum to construct a 50-foot-long trapezoidal trough with a base of 5 feet. You bend up the two 5-foot sides through an angle of $t°$ with the horizontal. Each cross section is a trapezoid (see diagram). You need to determine the angle t that produces the largest volume for the trough.

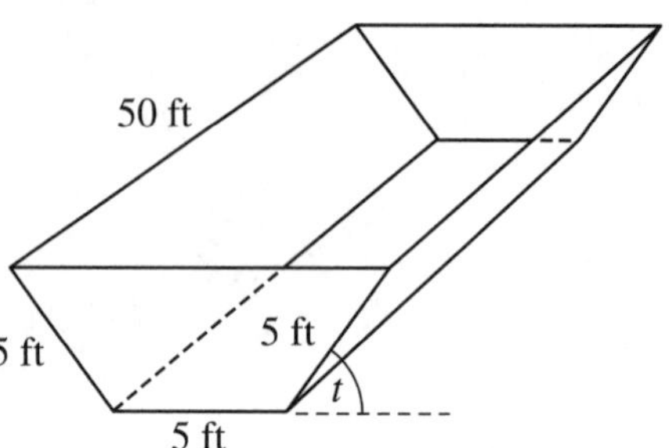

a. Recall the formula for the area of a trapezoid (see Appendix A, if necessary), and write the area of the trapezoidal cross section in terms of h and x (see diagram).

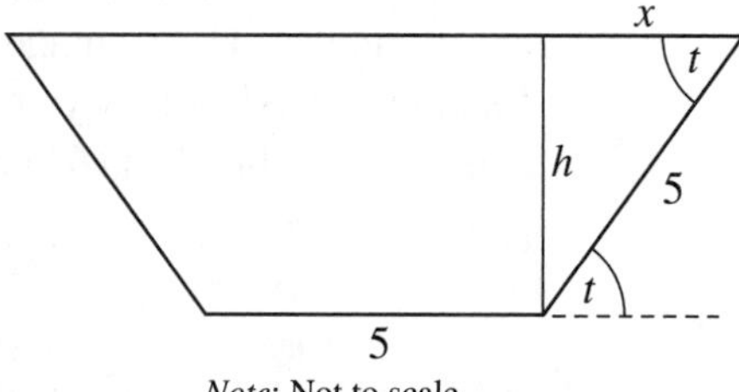

Note: Not to scale

Let A represent the area of the trapezoidal cross section. The height of the cross section is h, and the two bases are 5 and $5 + 2x$ respectively. The area is then determined by the formula $A = \frac{1}{2}h(10 + 2x)$ or simplifying, $A = h(5 + x)$ or $A = 5h + hx$.

b. Using right-triangle trigonometry, write h in terms of t. In a similar way, write x in terms of t. Using this information, write an expression for the area of the trapezoid as a function of t.

$h = 5 \sin t$

$x = 5 \cos t$

$A = 5(\sin t)(5 + 5 \cos t)$ or $A = 25 \sin t(1 + \cos t)$ or

$A = 25 \sin t + 25 \sin t (\cos t)$

c. Graph the area function you constructed in part b with $0° < t < 90°$. Label your axes and remember to indicate units.

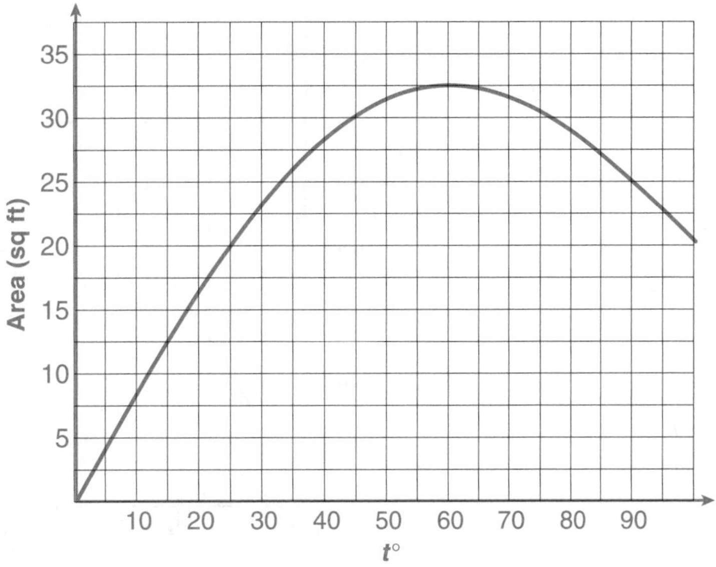

d. What is the angle that produces the largest area for the trapezoid? Explain.

The graph in part c indicates that the area of the trapezoidal cross section (output) is the greatest when the angle t is 60°.

e. What is that area? Explain.

The area is approximately 32.5 sq ft as read from the graph in part c.

f. Write the volume of the trough as a function of the angle t.

Let V represent the volume. Then,

$V = 50 \cdot A$ where A is the cross-section area.

In terms of t, the volume is

$V = 1250 \sin t(1 + \cos t)$

g. Graph the volume function you constructed in part f with $0° < t < 90°$. Label axes and show your units.

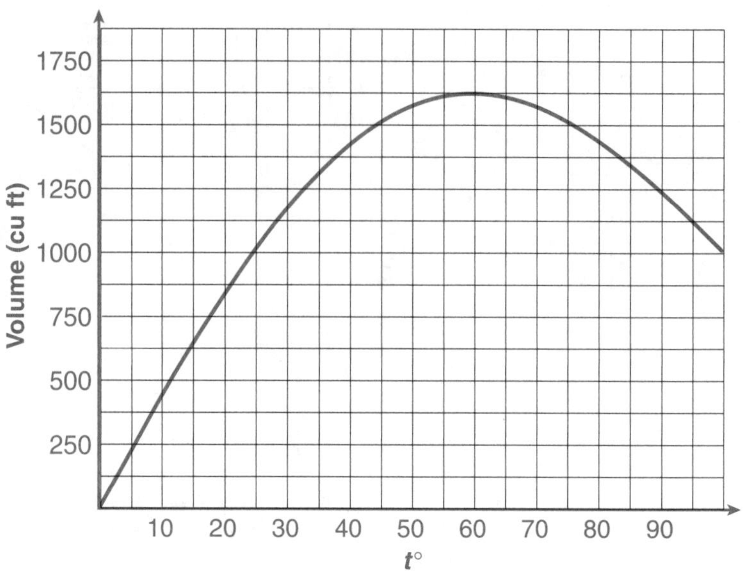

h. What is the angle that produces the largest volume, and what is that volume? Justify your conclusion.

The graph indicates the greatest value for the volume between 0° and 90° is 1625 cubic feet when the angle *t* is 60°.

i. What do you conclude about the angle that produces the largest cross-sectional area and the angle that produces the largest volume for the trough?

The angle is the same, namely 60° for this scenario.

ACTIVITY 6.7

Seeing Abraham Lincoln

Topics: *Right-Triangle Trigonometry, Inverse Trigonometric Functions, Geometric Drawing, Optimization by Analyzing Graphs and Tables*

You are traveling to South Dakota and plan to see Mount Rushmore. In preparation for your trip, you do some research and discover that from the observation center, the vertical rise of the mountain is approximately 500 feet and the height of Abraham Lincoln's face is 60 feet (see diagram). To get the best view, you want to position yourself so that your viewing angle of Mr. Lincoln's face is as large as possible.

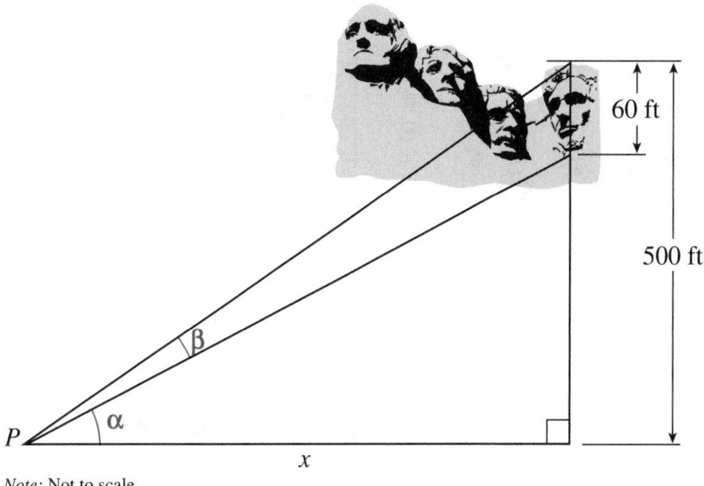

Note: Not to scale

1. a. Label your viewing angle if you are standing at point P on the diagram. Use trigonometric functions and their inverses to write an expression that defines the viewing angle as a function of the distance x that you are standing from the base.

$\tan(\alpha + \beta) = \frac{500}{x}$; $\alpha + \beta = \tan^{-1}\left(\frac{500}{x}\right)$

$\tan(\alpha) = \frac{440}{x}$; $\alpha = \tan^{-1}\left(\frac{440}{x}\right)$

$\beta = \tan^{-1}\left(\frac{500}{x}\right) - \alpha$

$\beta = \tan^{-1}\left(\frac{500}{x}\right) - \tan^{-1}\left(\frac{440}{x}\right)$

b. What is the practical domain for this function?

x is the distance in feet you are standing from the base of the mountain, so it must be positive and is limited by the size of the observation platform. A good practical domain to view the function seems to be $0 < x < 2000$. Other domains are possible.

2. Graph this function over its practical domain.

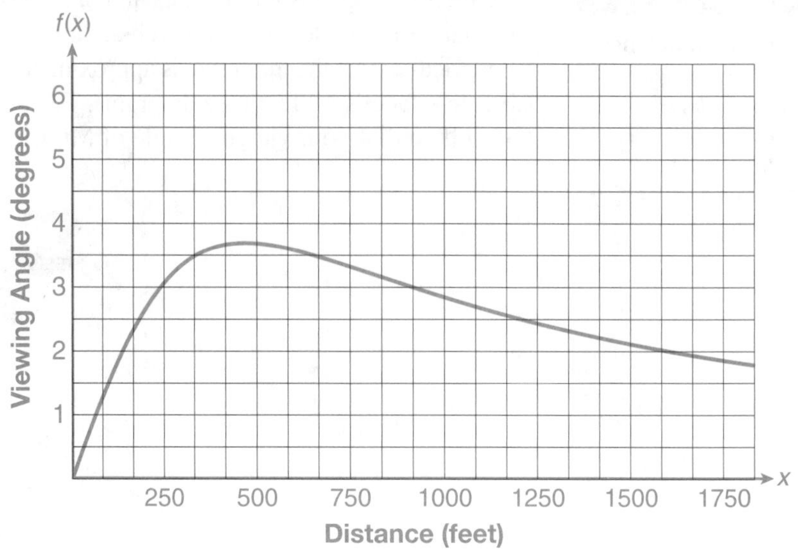

3. What is the largest value of the viewing angle? Justify your conclusion.

The largest viewing angle is approximately 3.7°. This is the output value of the highest point on the graph.

4. How far should you stand from the mountain to obtain this maximum value of the viewing angle? Explain.

I should stand approximately 470 feet from the mountain. This is the input value for the largest viewing angle as seen on the graph.

EXERCISES

1. Consider the function defined by $f(x) = \arctan \frac{20}{x} - \arctan \frac{10}{x}$ defined for $0.01 \leq x \leq 100$.

   a. Use your grapher to sketch a graph of this function.

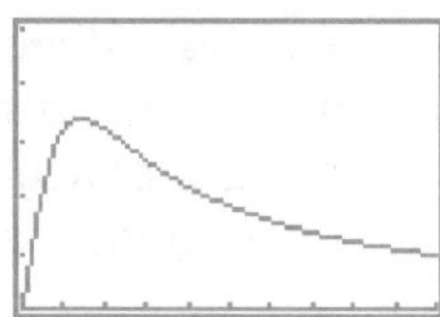

   b. Over the given domain, what is the maximum value of the function and where does it occur?

   Over the given domain, the maximum value of the function is approximately 19.5 and it occurs at $x = 14$.

   c. Over the given domain, what is the minimum value and where does it occur?

   The minimum value is difficult to see on the graph itself. I used the trace or the table feature on my grapher to determine that the minimum value in the given domain is 0.02865 and it occurs at $x = 0.01$.

Exercise numbers appearing in color are answered in the Selected Answers section of this book.

2. The Empire State Building rises 1414 feet above the ground, and you are standing across 34th Street, approximately 80 feet from the base of the building.

   a. If you look up to the top of the building, what is the angle of elevation you make with the ground?

Note: Not to scale

The angle of elevation is $\theta = \tan^{-1}(1414/80) = 86.8°$ or $87°$.

   b. How far from the building must you be to make your angle of elevation with the ground 85°?

Note: Not to scale

Let d represent the distance you stand from the Empire State Building.

$d = \frac{1414}{\tan 85} = 124$ ft

I must stand 124 feet from the base of the building so the angle of elevation is 85°.

What Have I Learned?

1. Classical right-triangle trigonometry was developed by the ancient Greeks to solve problems in surveying, astronomy, and navigation. For purposes of computation, the side opposite the angle θ, side O, is called the opposite, the side opposite the right angle, side H, is called the hypotenuse, and the third side, side A, is called the adjacent.

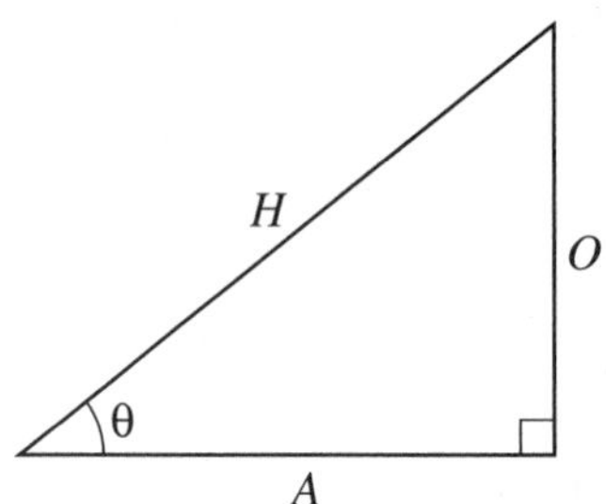

Define the three major trigonometric functions—sin θ, cos θ, and tan θ—in terms of H, A, and O.

$\sin \theta = \frac{O}{H}$ $\cos \theta = \frac{A}{H}$ $\tan \theta = \frac{O}{A}$

2. **a.** On any right triangle, which trigonometric function would you use to determine the opposite side if you know the angle measure and the length of the hypotenuse?

   I would use the sine function.

   b. Which trigonometric function would you use to determine the adjacent side if you know the angle measure and the length of the hypotenuse?

   I would use the cosine function.

   c. Which trigonometric function would you use to determine the adjacent side if you know the angle measure and the length of the opposite side?

   I would use the tangent function.

   d. Which trigonometric function would you use to determine the opposite side if you know the angle measure and the length of the adjacent side?

   The same as in part c, namely, the tangent function.

3. **a.** Suppose for a right triangle you know the length of the side opposite an angle and you know the length of the hypotenuse. How can you determine the angle?

   I would find the angle by using the arcsine function $(\sin^{-1})$.

   b. There is another way to solve part a. Describe this alternative technique.

   I could use the Pythagorean theorem to find the side adjacent and then find the angle by using the arccosine function.

c. If you know the lengths of any two sides of a right triangle, how can you determine all the angles in the triangle? Make up an example, and determine all the angles. Remember that all the interior angles of a triangle add up to 180°.

Example:

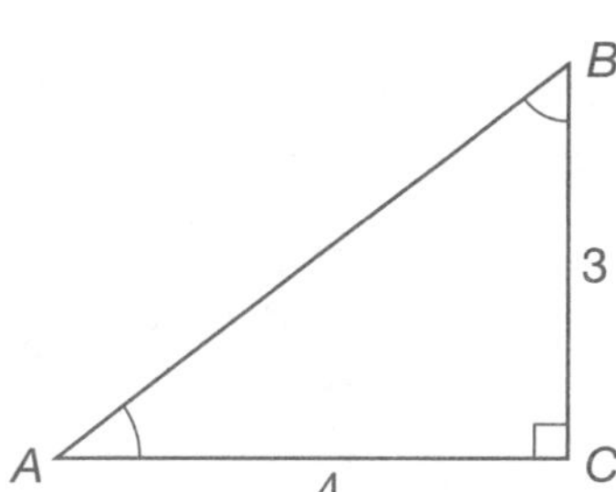

Angle C is 90° by definition of a right triangle.

Then $A = \tan^{-1}(3/4) = 36.9°$ and

$B = \tan^{-1}(4/3) = 53.1°$.

Alternatively, $B = 90° - 36.9° = 53.1°$

4. Consider the following right triangle.

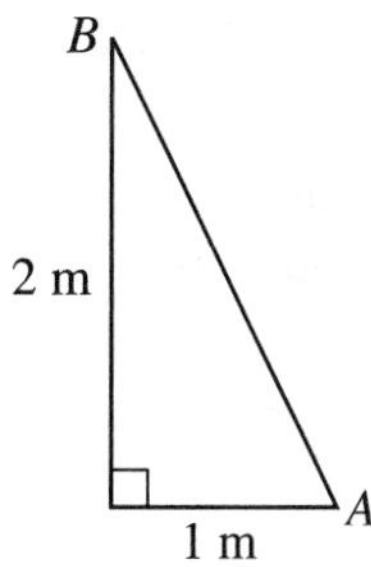

Calculate each of the following.

a. $\sin A$

$\sin A = \frac{2}{\sqrt{5}}$

b. $\cos A$

$\cos A = \frac{1}{\sqrt{5}}$

c. $\tan A$

$\tan A = \frac{2}{1}$

d. $\sin B$

$\sin B = \frac{1}{\sqrt{5}}$

e. $\cos B$

$\cos B = \frac{2}{\sqrt{5}}$

f. $\tan B$

$\tan B = \frac{1}{2}$

g. What trigonometric property is illustrated by parts a–f? Explain.

For complementary angles in a given right triangle, the cofunction values of those angles are equal. Specifically, if A and B are complementary angles, then $\sin A = \cos B$ and $\sin B = \cos A$.

5. Consider the following two calculator screens.

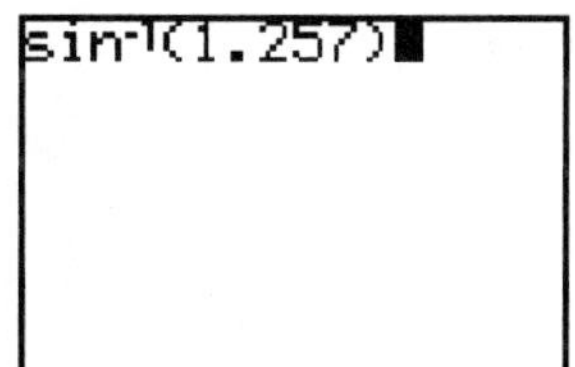

a. The second screen indicates that 1.257 is not in the domain of the inverse sine function. Do you agree? Explain.

Yes, I agree. The range of values for the sine function is from -1 to 1, that is, $y = \sin x$ cannot be greater than one in absolute value.

b. The following screen indicates that you do not have the same problem for the inverse tangent function. Why not? Explain.

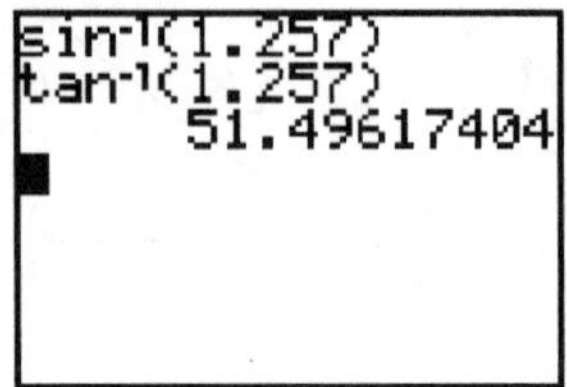

The range of values for the tangent function is from $-\infty$ to $+\infty$ and therefore $y = 1.257$ presents no problem.

6. Using diagrams, explain the difference between angle of depression and angle of elevation.

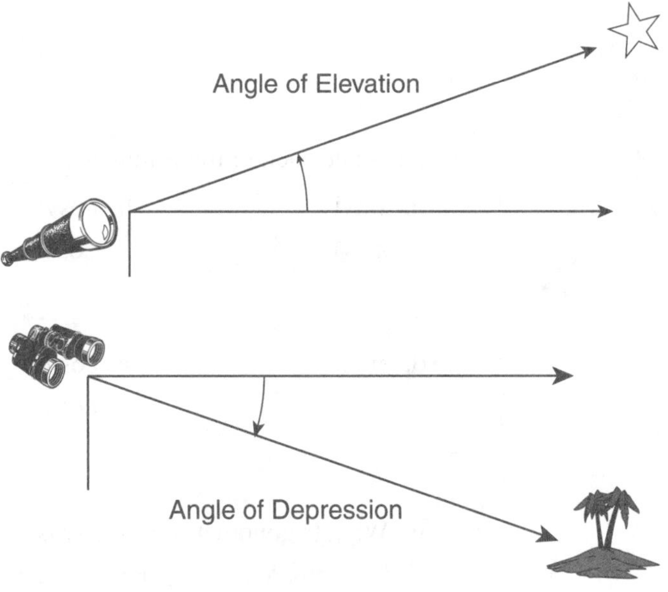

How Can I Practice?

1. Triangle *ABC* is a right triangle.

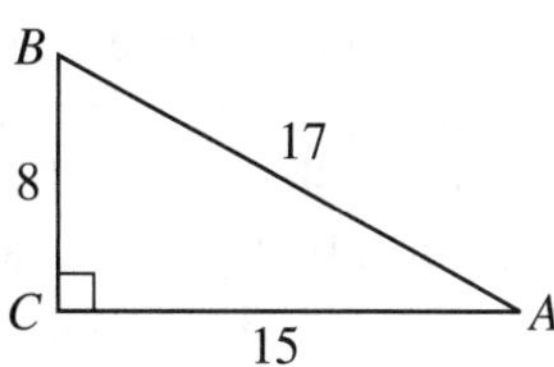

Calculate each of the following.

a. tan *A*

$\tan A = \frac{8}{15}$

b. tan *B*

$\tan B = \frac{15}{8}$

c. cos *A*

$\cos A = \frac{15}{17}$

d. cos *B*

$\cos B = \frac{8}{17}$

e. sin *A*

$\sin A = \frac{8}{17}$

f. sin *B*

$\sin B = \frac{15}{17}$

2. Given $\sin A = \frac{5}{13}$, determine cos *A* and tan *A* exactly.

$\cos A = \frac{12}{13}$ and $\tan A = \frac{5}{12}$

3. Given $\tan B = \frac{7}{4}$, determine sin *B* and cos *B* exactly.

$\sin B = \frac{7}{\sqrt{65}}$ and $\cos B = \frac{4}{\sqrt{65}}$

4. Using your calculator, evaluate the following for θ to the nearest 0.1°, where $0° \leq \theta \leq 90°$.

a. $\sin\theta = \frac{3}{4}$

$\theta = 48.6°$

b. $\cos\theta = 0.9172$

$\theta = 23.5°$

c. $\theta = \arctan\frac{7}{2}$

$\theta = 74.1°$

d. $\theta = \sin^{-1}\frac{2}{7}$

$\theta = 16.6°$

e. $\theta = \tan^{-1} 0.9714$

$\theta = 44.2°$

f. $\theta = \arccos 0.9714$

$\theta = 13.7°$

5. Solve the following right triangle. That is, determine all the missing sides and angles.

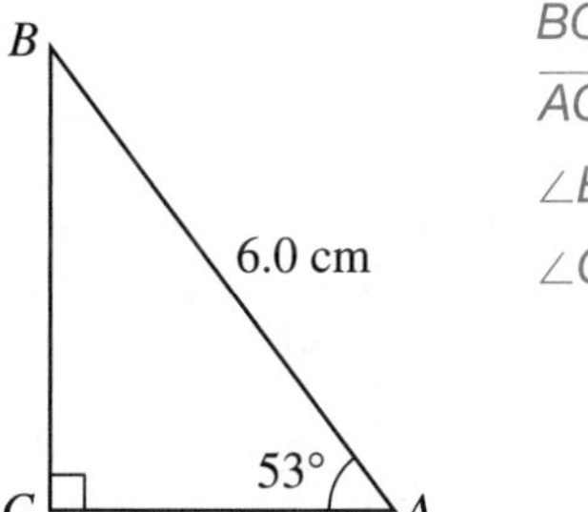

$\overline{BC} = 4.8$ cm

$\overline{AC} = 3.6$ cm

$\angle B = 37°$

$\angle C = 90°$

6. You are building a new garage to be attached to your home and investigate several 30-foot-wide trusses to support the roof. You narrow down your choices to three: One has an angle of 45° with the horizontal, and the others have angles of 35° and 25° with the horizontal. You determine that the walls of the garage must be 10 feet high. To match the height of the rest of the house, the peak of the garage should be approximately 20 feet high. Which truss should you buy?

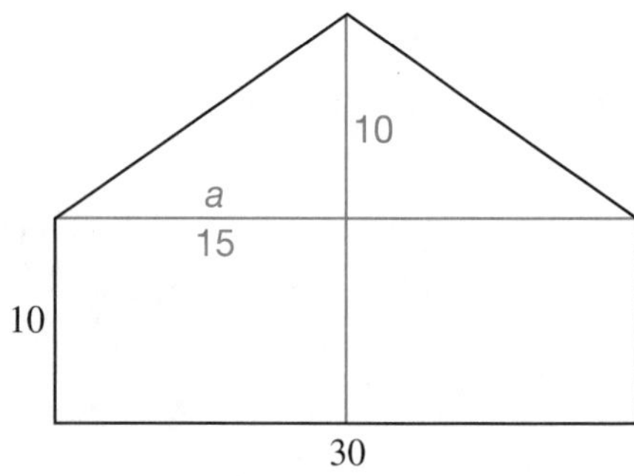

$A = \arctan\left(\frac{10}{15}\right) = 33.7°$ Therefore, I should buy the 35° trusses.

7. The side view of your swimming pool is shown here.

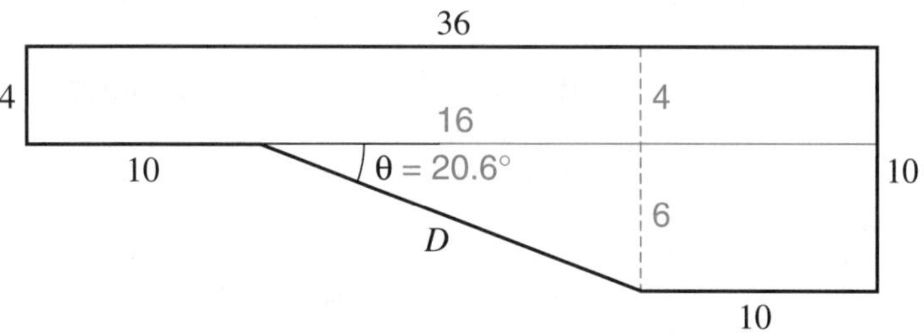

   a. What is the angle of depression, θ?

   The angle of depression, $\theta = 20.6°$

   b. What is the length of the inclined side, *D*?

   The length of the inclined side, $D = \sqrt{16^2 + 6^2} = 17.1$ ft.

8. **a.** As part of your summer vacation, you rent a cottage on a large lake. One day, you decide to visit a small island that is 6 miles east and 2.5 miles north of your cottage. Draw a diagram for this situation. How far from your cottage is the island?

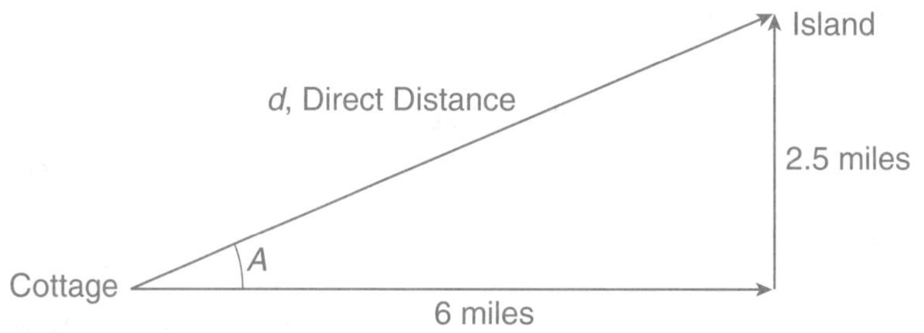

   The direct distance, *d*, from the cottage to the island is

   $d = \sqrt{2.5^2 + 6^2} = 6.5$ miles

   b. At what angle with respect to due east should you direct your boat to make the trip from your cottage to the island as short as possible?

   $A = \arctan\left(\frac{2.5}{6}\right) = 22.6°$

   I should direct my boat 22.6° north of east to get from the cottage to the island in the shortest distance.

CLUSTER 2

Why Are the Trigonometric Functions Called Circular?

ACTIVITY 6.8

Learn Trigonometry or Crash!

Topic: *Sine and Cosine as Circular Functions*

You are piloting a small plane and want to land at your local airport. Due to an emergency on the ground, the air traffic controller places you in a circular holding pattern at a constant altitude with a radius of 1 mile. Because your fuel is low, you are concerned with the distance traveled in the holding pattern. Of course, you communicate with air traffic control about your coordinates so that you do not collide with another airplane.

The given diagram shows your path in the air, with the airport located at the center (0, 0) of the circle on the ground. The radius of the circle is 1 mile. You begin your holding pattern at (1, 0).

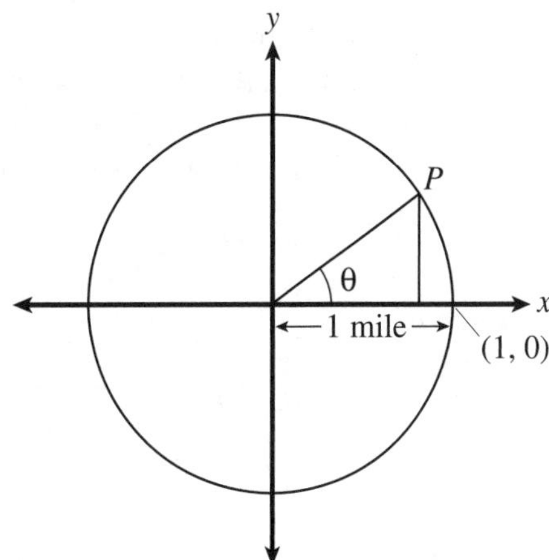

Let's examine the beginning of your first circular loop.

1. What distance (in miles) did you fly in one loop?

   One loop is the circumference of the circle $C = 2\pi \cdot 1$ mi $= 2\pi$ mi $= 6.28$ mi.

2. Let P represent your position after flying only $\frac{1}{10}$ of a loop. (See preceding diagram.)

   a. Compute the distance traveled from (1, 0) to P.

   $\frac{1}{10}2\pi$ mi $= \frac{\pi}{5}$ mi $= 0.628$ mi.

A **central angle** is an angle with its vertex at the center of a circle.

   b. Determine the number of degrees of the central angle, θ, when you fly $\frac{1}{10}$ of a loop (see diagram). Recall that there are 360° in a circle.

   $\frac{1}{10}360° = 36°$

3. Use the cosine and sine of angle θ from Problem 2 to determine the coordinates of point P. Place this information on the diagram in the form of an ordered pair.

$(x, y) = (\cos 36°, \sin 36°) = (0.81, 0.59)$

4. Repeat this procedure for the following fractions of a loop and record your results in the table and on the diagram.

LOOP	CENTRAL ANGLE θ	DISTANCE TRAVELED	(COS θ, SIN θ)
$\frac{1}{5}$	72°	$\frac{2\pi}{5}$ mi, or 1.26 mi	(0.31, 0.95)
$\frac{1}{8}$	45°	$\frac{2\pi}{8}$ mi or 0.79 mi	(0.71, 0.71)
$\frac{1}{20}$	18°	$\frac{2\pi}{20}$ mi or 0.314 mi	(0.95, 0.31)

RIGHT-TRIANGLE TRIGONOMETRY AND THE UNIT CIRCLE

Consider an object that is moving a distance d counterclockwise on the unit circle from the starting point (1, 0). Note that the unit circle has its center at the origin and a radius of 1. Let $P(x, y)$ be the position of the object on the unit circle after it has moved distance d, and let θ be the corresponding central angle.

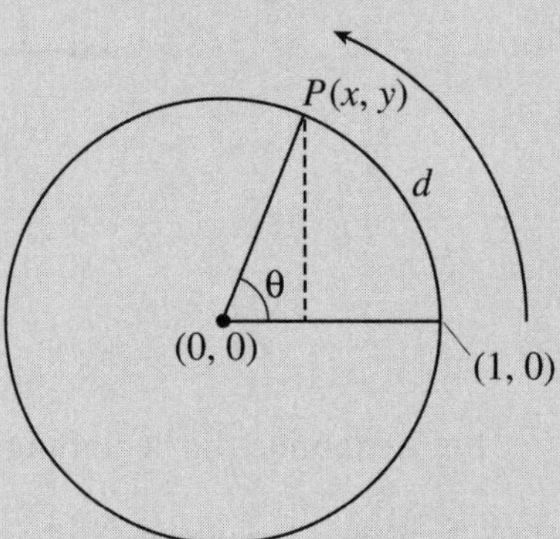

Then the coordinates of P are given by (cos θ, sin θ).

5. a. Your odometer tells you that you have traveled 2 miles in the holding pattern. What is the central angle θ? (*Hint:* What fraction of the loop have you traveled?)

2 mi means $\frac{2}{2\pi} = \frac{1}{\pi} = 0.32$ of a loop. The angle is $\frac{1}{\pi}360° = 0.32(360°) = 114.6°$

b. Use your calculator to determine the coordinates of point P from part a. Remember that $x = \cos\theta$ and $y = \sin\theta$.

$(\cos 114.6°, \sin 114.6°) = (-0.42, 0.91)$

For $\theta > 90°$, the coordinates of P are $(\cos\theta, \sin\theta)$ as before. Depending on where you are on the circle, these coordinates may be positive or negative.

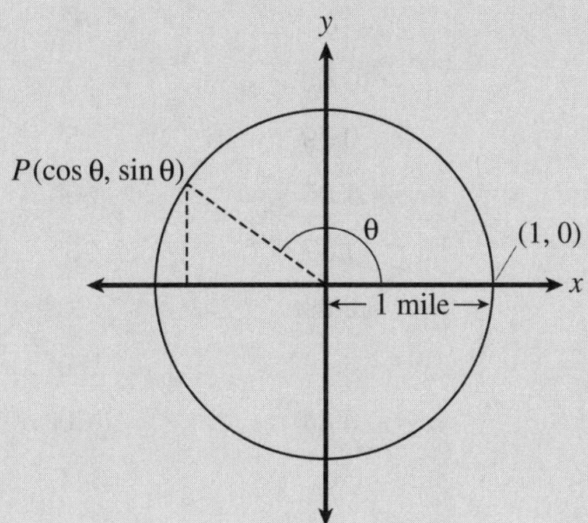

6. Give an example of where on the unit circle (circle of radius 1) both coordinates of P are negative. Place θ and the coordinates of P on the following diagram.

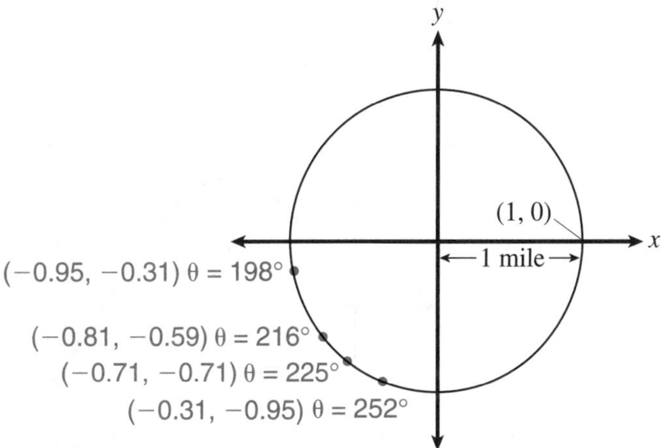

Answers will vary.

7. By the time you have traveled 5 miles in the holding pattern, what is the central angle θ, and what are the coordinates of point P?

5 miles means $\frac{5}{2\pi}$ of a loop, $\theta = \frac{5}{2\pi}360° = 286.5°$

$P(\cos 286.5°, \sin 286.5°) = (0.28, -0.96)$

8. Complete the following table.

Distance Traveled	Central Angle θ	cos θ	sin θ
0	0°	1	0
0.52	30°	0.866	0.5
0.79	45°	0.707	0.707
1.05	60°	0.5	0.866
1.57	90°	0	1
2.09	120°	−0.5	0.866
3.14	180°	−1	0
3.84	220°	−0.766	−0.643
6	344°	0.961	−0.276
6.28	360°	1	0

9. Plot the data pairs (θ, sin θ) on the following grid. Draw a smooth curve through these points. Verify the results with your grapher, by sketching a graph of $y = \sin x$. Use the window Xmin $= 0_1$ Xmax $= 360$, Ymin $= -1$, Ymax $= 1$, and degree mode.

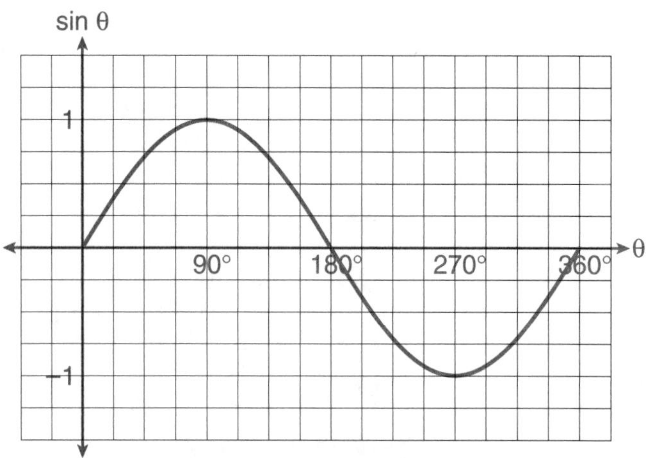

10. Repeat Problem 9 for data pairs (θ, cos θ).

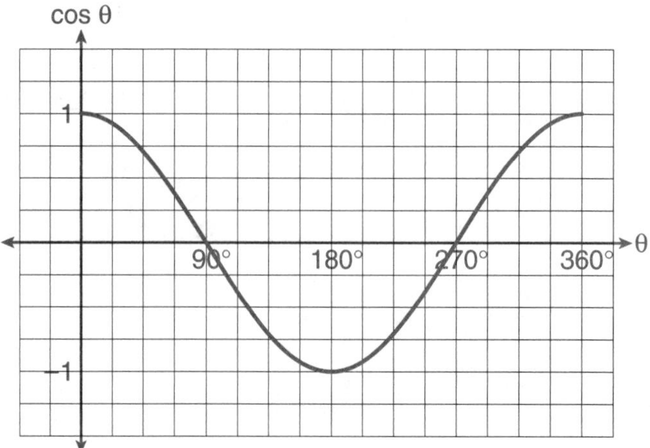

11. You notice that the odometer reads 11.28 miles from the start of the holding pattern. What is the central angle θ, and what are the coordinates of point *P*?

$\theta = \frac{11.28}{2\pi} \cdot 360° = 646.3°$

$P(\cos 646.3°, \sin 646.3°) = (0.28, -0.96)$.

12. Suppose you are at some particular point in the holding pattern. How many miles will you travel in the loop to return to the same coordinates?

2π or 6.28 miles.

13. Describe what the graphs of $y = \sin\theta$ and $y = \cos\theta$ each look like for values of θ greater than 360°.

The graphs will continue in the same patterns.

Note that these repeating graphs are the basis for the **periodic** or **cyclic** behavior of the trigonometric functions. Because many real-world phenomena involve this repeating behavior, the trigonometric functions are very useful in modeling these phenomena.

14. Choose three values of $\theta < 0°$ (i.e., θ measured clockwise). Plot the angles with their corresponding coordinates on the following diagram. Show how you arrived at the coordinates. (Answers will vary.)

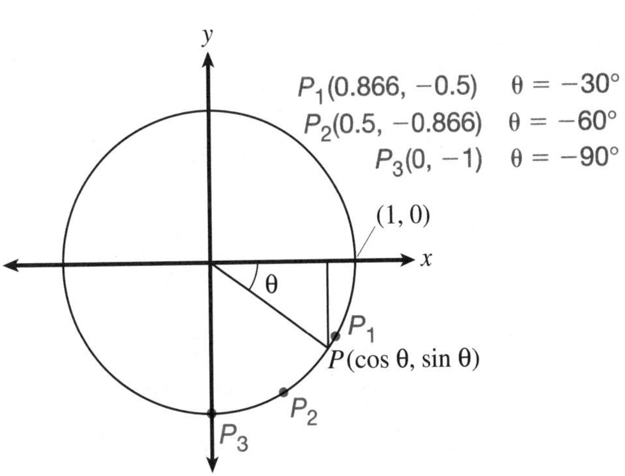

15. What is the domain (input values) of the sine and cosine functions?

All angles measured by degrees.

16. What is the range (output values) of the sine and cosine functions?

$-1 \le \sin\theta \le 1 \quad -1 \le \cos\theta \le 1$

SUMMARY

- A central angle is an angle whose vertex is the center of a circle.
- The position $P(x, y)$ of an object moving on the unit circle can be defined by $x = \cos\theta$ and $y = \sin\theta$, where θ is a central angle with its initial side as the positive x-axis and its terminal side OP. Because of this connection to the unit circle, the sine and cosine functions are often called circular functions.
- If the motion on the unit circle is counterclockwise, the angle measurement is positive. If the motion on the unit circle is clockwise, the angle measurement is negative.
- The domain of the sine and cosine functions is all angles, both positive and negative.
- The range of the sine and cosine functions is all values of N such that $-1 \leq N \leq 1$.

EXERCISES

1. Determine the coordinates of the point on the unit circle corresponding to the following central angles.

a. 72°

(0.31, 0.95)

b. 310°

(0.64. −0.77)

c. 270°

(0, −1)

d. 111°

(−0.36, 0.93)

e. 212°

(−0.85, −0.53)

f. 435°

(0.26. 0.97)

g. −70°

(0.34, −0.94)

2. For each of the points on the unit circle determined in Exercise 1, determine the distance traveled to the point.

a. $\frac{72}{360} \cdot 2\pi = 1.26$

b. $\frac{310}{360} \cdot 2\pi = 5.41$

c. $\frac{270}{360} \cdot 2\pi = 4.71$

d. $\frac{111}{360} \cdot 2\pi = 1.94$

e. $\frac{212}{360} \cdot 2\pi = 3.70$

f. $\frac{435}{360} \cdot 2\pi = 7.59$

g. $\frac{-70}{360} \cdot 2\pi = -1.22$ Distance is 1.22.

Exercise numbers appearing in color are answered in the Selected Answers section of this book.

3. Consider the graph of the following function.

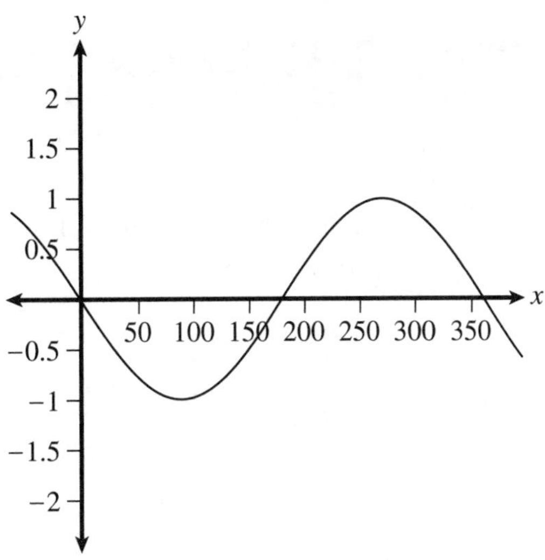

a. Does the graph represent a circular function (a function defined by points on the unit circle)? Explain.

Yes. The output values could be the x-coordinates of points starting at the point (0, 1) and moving counterclockwise. Other answers are possible.

b. If you answered yes to part a, what is the motion described by the graph?

Counterclockwise.

4. Consider the graph of the following function.

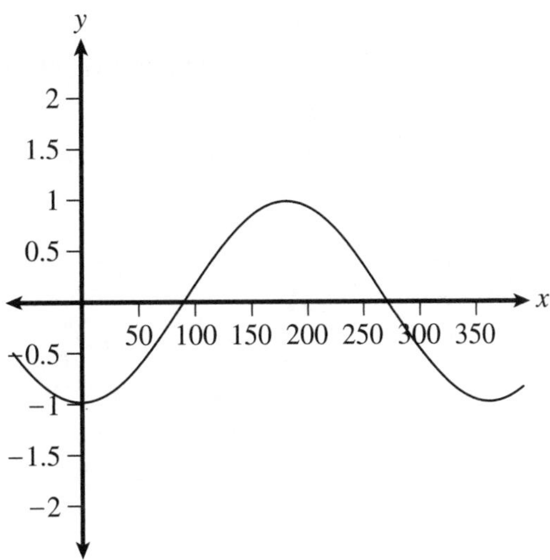

a. Does this graph represent a circular function? Explain.

Yes. The output values could be the y-coordinates of points starting at the point $(-1, 0)$ and moving counterclockwise. Other answers are possible.

b. If you answered yes to part a, what is the motion described by the graph?

Counterclockwise.

5. The following table represents the number of daylight hours for a certain city in the Western Hemisphere on the dates indicated.

MAR. 21	APR. 21	MAY 21	JUNE 21	JULY 21	AUG. 21	SEPT. 21	OCT. 21	NOV. 21	DEC. 21	JAN. 21	FEB. 21	MAR. 21
11.9	10.5	9.6	8.7	9.7	10.6	12.1	13.5	14.7	15.7	14.7	13.4	11.9

a. Plot the data on the following grid.

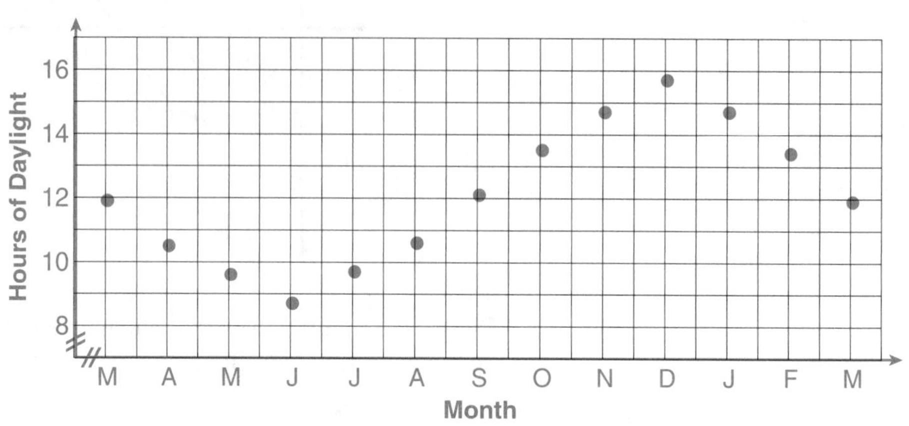

b. Do the data indicate a circular function? Explain.

Yes, the number of hours of daylight is cyclic.

c. How does this function compare with the others in this activity?

The graph has the same shape.

d. Is the city in question north or south of the equator? Explain.

South. The number of hours of daylight is greater from October to February, our winter.

ACTIVITY 6.9

It Won't Hertz
Topics: *Periodic Behavior, Radian Measure*

Household electric current is called alternating current, or AC, because it changes magnitude and direction with time. The household current through a 60-watt lightbulb is given by the equation

$$A = 2\sin(120\pi t),$$

where A is the current in amperes and t is the time in seconds.

Note that the input of the sine function in this activity is time measured by real numbers (seconds) and not angles measured in degrees. For this to make sense, an alternate real-number method for measuring angles must be introduced. This measurement is called **radian measure.**

The correspondence between degree and radian measure:

180° is the same as 1π, or about 3.14, in radians.

Therefore, $1° = \frac{\pi}{180°}$ radians and 1 radian $= \frac{180°}{\pi}$

Whenever you see an angle measure without a degree symbol, assume that the angle is measured in radians. For example, 90° is the same as $\frac{\pi}{2}$ radians. Here is how you can change degrees to radians:

$$90° = \left(\frac{90°}{1}\right)\left(\frac{1\pi \text{ radians}}{180°}\right) = \left(\frac{90°\,\pi \text{ radians}}{180°}\right) = \frac{\pi}{2} \text{ radians.}$$

1. Convert the following degree measures to radian measure.

DEGREE MEASURE	RADIAN MEASURE
10	$\pi/18 = 0.175$
20	$\pi/9 = 0.349$
30	$\pi/6 = 0.524$
60	$\pi/3 = 1.047$
120	$2\pi/3 = 2.094$
360	$2\pi = 6.283$

2. a. Describe a procedure to convert radians to degrees.

Multiply by $\frac{180 \text{ degree}}{\pi \text{ radians}} \approx \frac{180°}{1\pi \text{ radians}}$

b. How many degrees are in 1.5π radians?

$1.5\pi \cdot \frac{180}{\pi} = 270°$

c. How many degrees are in 2π radians?

$2\pi \cdot \frac{180}{\pi} = 360°$

d. How many degrees are in $\frac{\pi}{10}$ radians?

$\frac{\pi}{10} \cdot \frac{180}{\pi} = 18°$

B Appendix

For more practice converting degree measure to radian measure and vice versa, see Appendix B.

As stated, the function defined by $A = 2\sin(120\pi t)$, where A is the current in amperes and t is the time in seconds, gives the household current through a 60-watt lightbulb.

3. Graph this equation using the following window. Your calculator must be in radian mode, instead of degree mode.

$$\text{Xmin} = 0 \qquad \text{Ymin} = -3$$

$$\text{Xmax} = \tfrac{1}{20} \qquad \text{Ymax} = 3$$

$$\text{Xscl} = \tfrac{1}{240} \qquad \text{Yscl} = 1$$

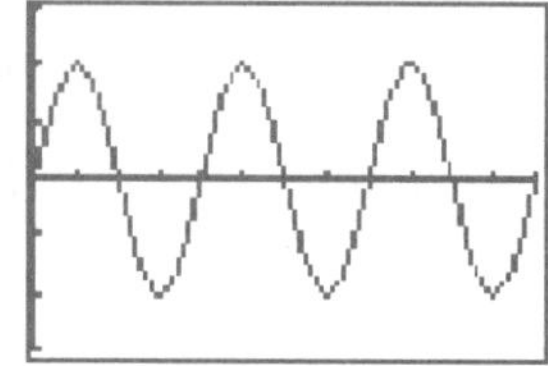

4. Using the graph, what is the maximum current? Explain.

2 amps, the highest and lowest points on the graph.

5. What do you think is happening to the current when the graph drops below the horizontal axis? (Reread the description of alternating current.)

It changes direction.

There is a pattern on the graph that repeats. This pattern is called a cycle. The shortest time it takes for one cycle is called the **period.**

6. What is the *period* of this function? (The tick marks on the horizontal axis are at $\frac{1}{240}$-second intervals.)

$\frac{1}{60}$th sec

7. Determine the period (shortest interval in which the graph repeats) of the following functions. Use the window Xmin $= 0$, Xmax $= 6\pi$, Xscl $= \frac{\pi}{4}$, Ymin $= -2$, Ymax $= 2$, and Yscl $= 1$.

a. $y = \sin x$ **b.** $y = \sin \frac{1}{2}x$ **c.** $y = \cos 2x$

2π 4π π

In general, the *frequency* of $y = a\sin(bx + c)$ or $y = a\cos(bx + c)$ is the number of cycles completed by 2π units.

8. Determine the frequency, the number of cycles completed in 2π radians, for each of the following functions.

a. $y = \sin x$

1

b. $y = \sin \frac{1}{2}x$

1/2

c. $y = \cos 2x$

2

9. For normal household current described by $A = 2 \sin(120\pi t)$, how many cycles occur in 1 second?

60 cycles per second.

SUMMARY

- Radian measure is used when the input of a repeating function is better defined by real numbers than by angles measured in degrees.
- To convert degree measure to radian measure, multiply the degree measure by $\frac{\pi \text{ radians}}{180°}$.
- To convert radian measure to degree measure, multiply the radian measure by $\frac{180°}{\pi \text{ radians}}$.
- The pattern of a graph that is repeated is called the cycle.
- The smallest interval of input necessary for the graph of a function to repeat is called the period.
- The frequency of the functions defined by $y = a \sin(bx + c)$ and $y = a \cos(bx + c)$ is b, where $b > 0$

EXERCISES

1. Convert the following degree measures to radian measures.

a. 45°

$45° \cdot \frac{\pi}{180°} = \frac{\pi}{4} = 0.785$

b. 140°

$140° \cdot \frac{\pi}{180°} = \frac{7\pi}{9} = 2.443$

c. 330°

$330° \cdot \frac{\pi}{180°} = \frac{11\pi}{6} = 5.760$

d. −36°

$-36° \cdot \frac{\pi}{180°} = \frac{-\pi}{5} = -0.628$

2. Convert the following radian measures to degree measures.

a. $\frac{3\pi}{4}$

$\frac{3\pi}{4} \cdot \frac{180°}{\pi} = 135°$

b. 2.5π

$\frac{2.5\pi}{1} \cdot \frac{180°}{\pi} = 450°$

c. 6π

$6\pi \cdot \frac{180°}{\pi} = 1080°$

d. 1.8π

$1.8\pi \cdot \frac{180°}{\pi} = 324°$

Exercise numbers appearing in color are answered in the Selected Answers section of this book.

For Exercises 3–10, be sure your calculator is in radian mode.

3. How do the graphs of each pair of functions compare? Use your grapher.

a. $y = 2\cos x, \quad y = \cos 2x$

$y = 2\cos x$ is $y = \cos x$ stretched vertically by a factor of 2. $y = \cos(2x)$ is $y = \cos x$ compressed horizontally by a factor of 2.

b. $y = \sin(x + \pi), \quad y = \pi + \sin x$

$y = \sin(x + \pi)$ is the graph of $y = \sin x$ shifted π units left. $y = \pi + \sin x$ is the graph of $y = \sin x$ shifted π units up.

c. $y = -3\sin x, \quad y = 3\sin x$

$y = -3\sin x$ is the graph of $y = 3\sin x$ reflected in the x-axis.

d. $y = \cos\frac{1}{3}x, \quad y = \cos 3x$

$y = \cos(\frac{1}{3}x)$ is $y = \cos x$ stretched horizontally by a factor of 3. $y = \cos(3x)$ is $y = \cos x$ compressed horizontally by a factor of 3.

For Exercises 4–10, graph each function and determine the following characteristics for each:

a. The largest (maximum) value of the function.

b. The smallest (minimum) value of the function.

c. The period (the shortest interval for which the graph repeats).

4. $y = 0.5\sin 2x$

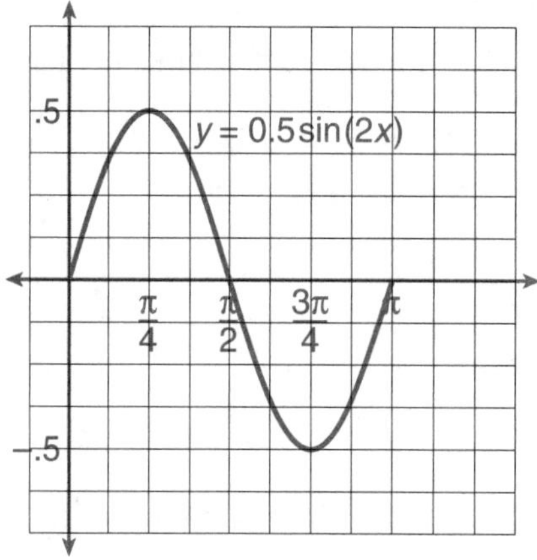

max: 0.5

min: -0.5

period: π

5. $g(x) = 14\cos(3x - 1)$

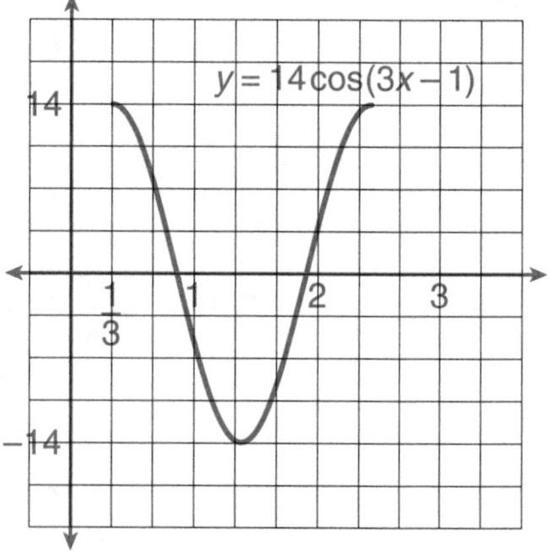

max: 14

min: -14

period: $2\pi/3$

6. $y = -3 \sin 3x$

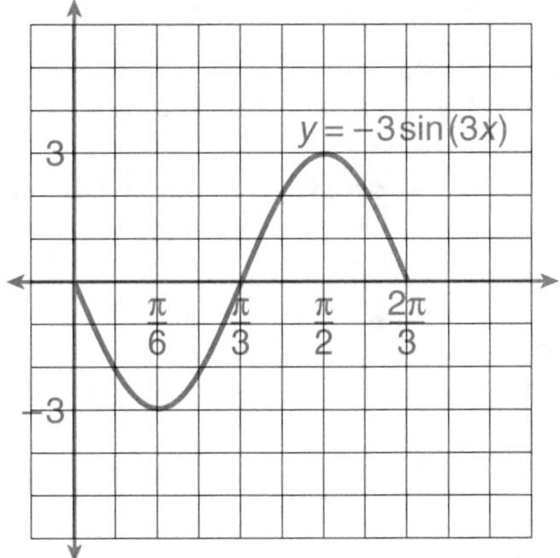

max: 3

min: −3

period: $2\pi/3$

7. $f(x) = 2.3 \cos(0.5x + 3)$

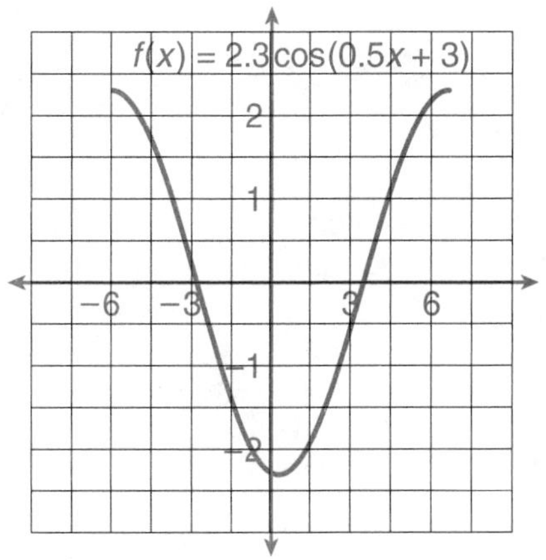

max: 2.3

min: −2.3

period: 4π

8. $y = 6 - 4 \sin(6 - x)$

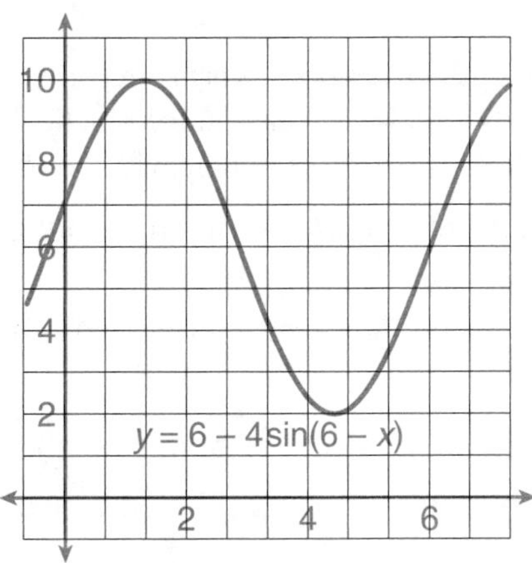

max: 10

min: 2

period: 2π

9. $y = 2 \sin x + 3 \cos x$

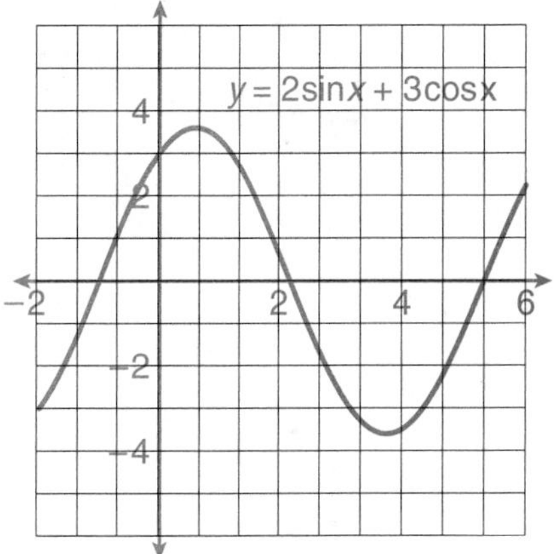

max: 3.606

min: −3.606

period: 2π

10. $y = 4 \cos 2x - 3 \sin 5x$

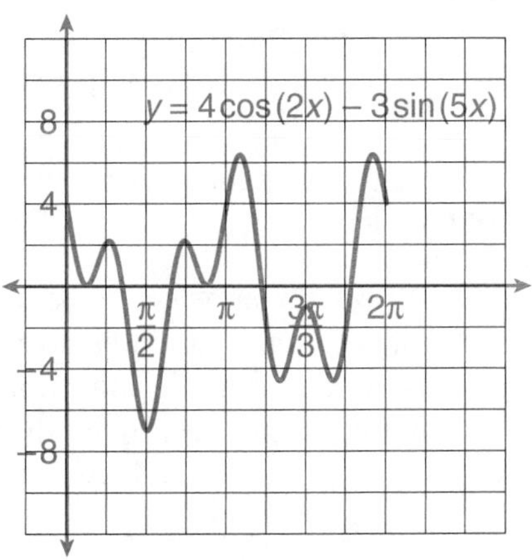

max: 6.362

min: −7

period: 2π

11. You are setting up a budget for the new year. Your utility bill for natural gas and electric usage is a large part of your budget. To help determine the amount you might need to spend on gas and electricity, you examine your previous three years' bills. Because you live in a rural area, you are billed every two months instead of every month. The data you obtain appear in the following graph.

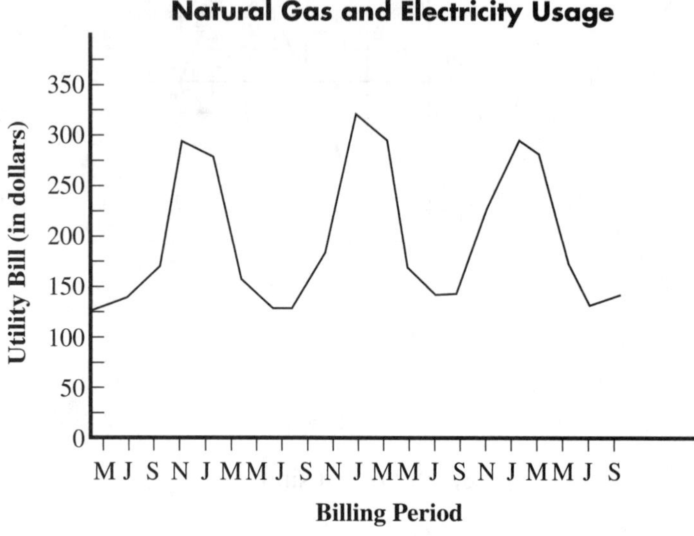

You notice that a pattern develops, which is repeated. This function, though not exactly periodic, models a periodic function for practical purposes. Label the horizontal axis with bimonthly periods, beginning with the June/July bill from three years ago.

a. What months of the year is the utility bill the highest? How much is this bill?

The bill is highest for December/January. The amount of the bill is approximately $300.

b. What months of the year is the utility bill the lowest? How much is this bill?

The bill is lowest for June/July. The amount of the bill is approximately $125.

c. What is the largest value for the function whose graph is given here?

The largest value is $325.

d. What is the period of the graph?

The period is 6 billing periods or 12 months.

e. Suppose that your power company has announced that its rates are going to increase by 5% beginning in April of the coming year. How will this change affect the graph of this function? Will it affect the periodic nature of the function?

The graph will be stretched vertically by a factor of 1.05. This will not affect the period of the function.

f. You heat your house and your water with natural gas and use electricity for all other purposes. You do not currently have air conditioning in your house. Suppose you install a central air conditioning unit next summer. What changes do you think might occur in the shape of the graph?

The amount of the bill for the summer months June/July August/September will increase. The graph would flatten out as the monthly charges become more equal.

ACTIVITY 6.10

Get in Shape

Topic: *The Amplitude of* $y = a \sin(bx + c)$ *and* $y = a \cos(bx + c)$

You decide to try jogging to shape up. You are fortunate to have a large neighborhood park nearby that has a circular track with a radius of 100 meters.

1. If you run one lap around the track, how many meters have you traveled? Explain.

   1 lap = the circumference of the circle. $C = 2\pi r = 2\pi(100 \text{ m}) \approx 628$ m.

2. You start off averaging a relatively slow rate of approximately 100 meters per minute. How long does it take you to complete one lap? Explain.

   $t = \frac{628 \text{ m}}{100 \text{ m/min}} = 6.28$ min

You want to improve your speed. Gathering data describing your position on the track as a function of time may be useful. You sketch the track on a coordinate system with the center at the origin. Assume that the starting line has coordinates (100, 0) and that you run counterclockwise.

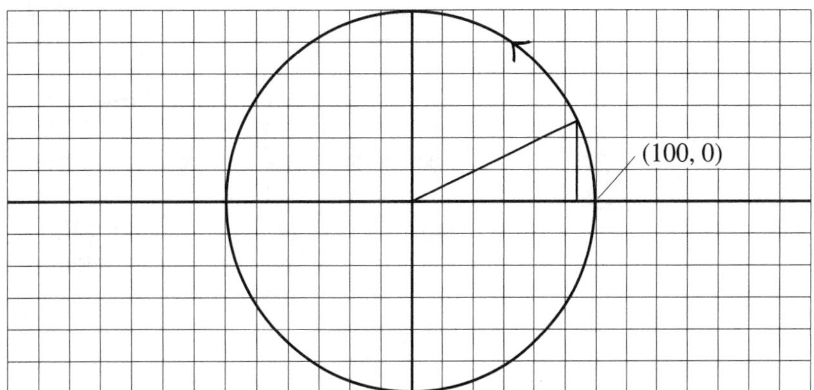

3. You begin to gather data about your position at various times. Using the preceding diagram and the results from Problem 2, complete the following table to locate your coordinates at selected times along your path.

t (min)	Your x-Coordinate	Your y-Coordinate
0	100	0
$\pi/2$	0	100
π	−100	0
$3\pi/2$	0	−100
2π	100	0
$5\pi/2$	0	100
3π	−100	0

4. What patterns do you notice about the numerical data in Problem 3? Predict your coordinates as your time increases.

The data are cyclic. $t = \frac{7\pi}{2}$ $(x, y) = (0, -100)$, $t = 4\pi$ $(x, y) = (100, 0)$

5. To better analyze your position at times other than those listed in the previous table, you decide to make some educated guesses. Consider $t = \frac{\pi}{4}$ minutes.

Use the graph to approximate the coordinates of your position P when $t = \frac{\pi}{4}$, and label these coordinates on the graph.

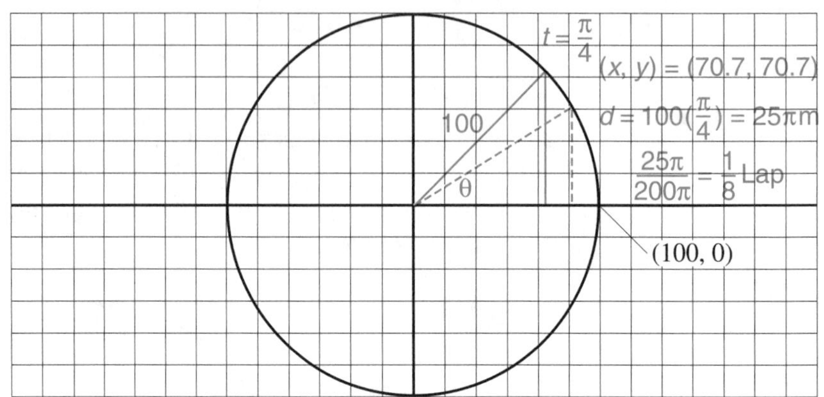

6. To check your guess, you recall that right-triangle trigonometry gives some useful information about special right triangles. If you are not familiar with special right triangles see Appendix B. First, however, you need to compute angle θ, given in the graph of Problem 5. Calculate θ and explain how you arrived at your answer.

$\theta = \frac{\pi}{4} = 45°$

$\frac{1}{8}(2\pi) = \frac{\pi}{4}$

$\frac{1}{8}(360°) = 45°$

7. You are now in a position to gather more data about your position. Complete the following table to give the coordinates of your position at the additional special points along your path.

t (min)	Your x-Coordinate	Your y-Coordinate
$\pi/4$	70.71	70.71
$3\pi/4$	−70.71	70.71
$5\pi/4$	−70.71	−70.71
$7\pi/4$	70.71	−70.71
$9\pi/4$	70.71	70.71

8. On the following grid, use the data from Problems 3 and 7 to plot (t, y), your y-coordinate as a function of t. Connect your data pairs to make a smooth graph, and predict what will happen to the graph for values of t before and after the values of t in the tables.

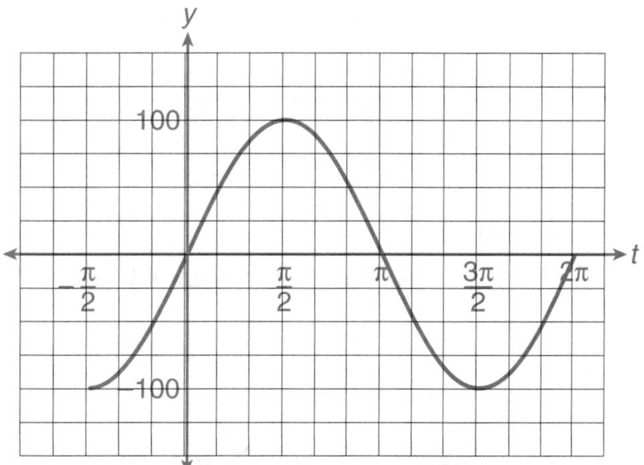

9. Use your grapher to plot $y = 100 \sin x$. Make sure your grapher is radian mode. Note that the name of the input t has been changed to conform with the calculator.

10. Compare your answers to Problems 8 and 9.

The graphs are the same.

11. a. What is the maximum value of the sine function in Problem 9? Explain.

100 is the maximum value.

b. What is the minimum value of the sine function in Problem 9? Explain.

−100 is the minimum value.

Another important feature of the graphs of function sine and cosine functions is called the **amplitude.** The amplitude of a periodic function is defined by

$$\text{amplitude} = \tfrac{1}{2}\left(M - m\right)$$

where M is the maximum output value of the function and m is the minimum output value of the function.

12. a. What is the amplitude of the sine function in the equation $y = 100 \sin x$?

Amplitude = 100.

b. Is there a relationship between the amplitude of $y = 100 \sin x$ and the coefficient 100? Explain.

Yes, the coefficient 100 is the amplitude.

13. Determine the amplitude of the following functions by inspection. Then verify using your grapher.

a. $y = 1.5 \sin x$ **b.** $f(x) = 15 \sin(x + \pi)$ **c.** $y = 3 \sin(2x)$

1.5 1.5 3

14. a. Is -2 the amplitude of $y = -2 \sin x$? Explain.

No. Amplitude is one half the maximum minus the minimum, so it can never be negative.

b. What is the amplitude of $y = -2 \sin x$?

2.

SUMMARY

The amplitude of trigonometric functions defined by $y = a \sin(bx + c)$ or $y = a \cos(bx + c)$ is defined by

$$\tfrac{1}{2}(M - m),$$

where M represents the maximum function value and m represents the minimum function value. The amplitude is equivalent to $|a|$, the absolute value of the coefficient of the function. Therefore,

$$|a| = \tfrac{1}{2}(M - m).$$

EXERCISES

1. On the following grid, repeat Problem 8 to plot the data pairs (t, x).

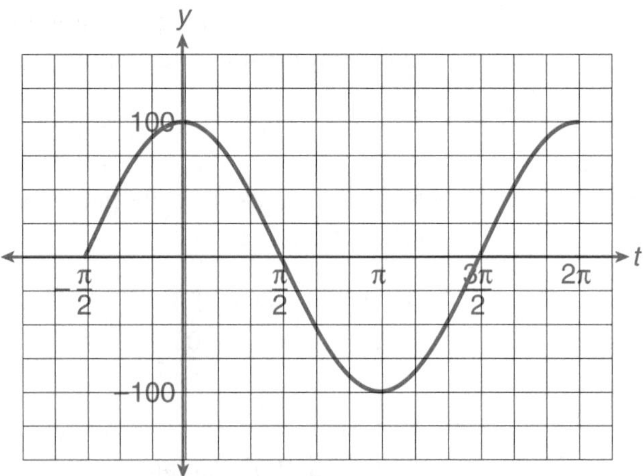

Exercise numbers appearing in color are answered in the Selected Answers section of this book.

2. Use your grapher to plot $y = 100 \cos x$. Make sure your grapher is in radian mode. Note that the names of both the input t and output (your x-coordinate) have been changed to conform with your calculator.

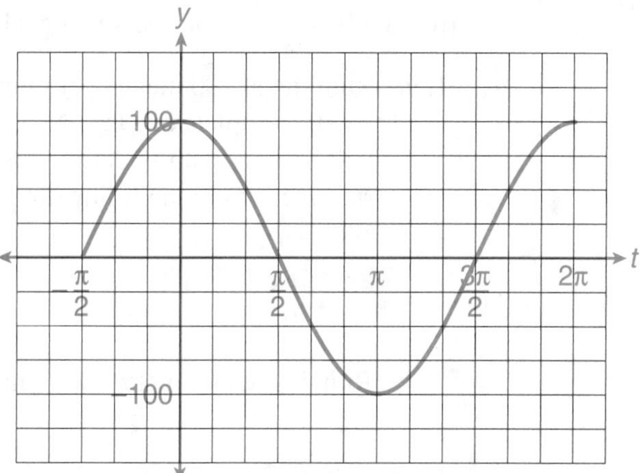

3. Explain why your answers to Exercises 1 and 2 are the same.

   $(x, y) = (100 \cos \theta, 100 \sin \theta)$

4. a. What is the maximum function value of this cosine function? Explain.

   The maximum value is 100.

   b. What is the minimum function value of this cosine function? Explain.

   The minimum value is -100.

5. What is the connection between the function values in Problem 4, the 100-meter radius of the circle, and the coefficient 100 of the function?

   100 is the amplitude of the function.

6. If you are forced to run on a larger circular track of radius 150 meters, and you increase your speed to 150 meters per minute, predict the equations of the functions describing the x- and y-coordinates of your position. Explain.

   $(x, y) = (150 \cos \theta, 150 \sin \theta)$

7. Determine the amplitude of the following functions by inspection. Then verify the results using your grapher. (Remember, amplitude cannot be negative.)

   a. $y = 3 \sin x$

   amp = 3

   b. $y = 0.4 \cos x$

   amp = 0.4

   c. $f(x) = -2 \cos x$

   amp = 2

   d. $g(x) = -2.3 \sin x$

   amp = 2.3

   e. $y = 2 \sin(3x - 1)$

   amp = 2

   f. $h(x) = -4 \cos(x + \pi)$

   amp = 4

ACTIVITY 6.11

Speeding Up

Topic: *The Period of* $y = a \sin(bx + c)$ *and* $y = a \cos(bx + c)$

After a lot of practice, you begin to speed up on your circular track of radius 100 meters.

You finally achieve your personal goal of 200 meters per minute.

1. **a.** Running at 200 meters per minute counterclockwise, how long does it take you to complete one lap? Note that this amount of time to complete one lap will be important in defining the key concept of period for the trigonometric functions in the following problems.

   One lap $= 2\pi(100 \text{ m}) = 200\pi \text{ m}$

   $t = \frac{200\pi \text{ m}}{200 \text{ m/min}} = \pi \text{ min} = 3.14 \text{ min}$

   b. Running at 200 meters per minute, how long does it take to complete $\frac{1}{2}$ of a lap?

   $\frac{1}{2}$ lap; $\frac{\pi}{2}$ min

   c. How long does it take to complete $\frac{1}{4}$ of a lap?

   $\frac{1}{4}$ lap; $\frac{\pi}{4}$ min

2. Use the results from Problem 1 to complete the following table that indicates coordinates at selected special points along your path.

t (min)	YOUR x-COORDINATE	YOUR y-COORDINATE
0	100	0
$\pi/4$	0	100
$\pi/2$	−100	0
$3\pi/4$	0	−100
π	100	0
$5\pi/4$	0	100
$3\pi/2$	−100	0
$7\pi/4$	0	−100
2π	100	0

3. On the following grid, use the data from Problem 2 to plot (t, y), your y-coordinate as a function of t. Connect your data pairs to make a smooth graph, as in the previous activity, and predict what will happen to the graph for values of t before and after the values of t in the table.

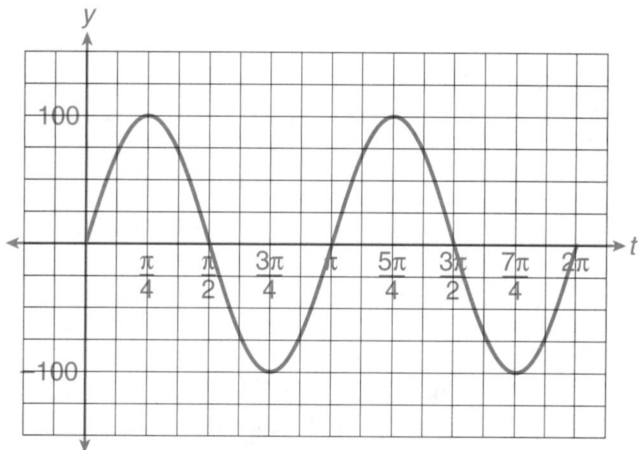

4. What is the amount of time it takes for the graph in Problem 3 to complete one full cycle (i.e., for you to complete one full lap)?

π minutes.

5. When you doubled your speed, what effect did that have on the amount of time to complete one cycle? Explain.

Doubling the speed cuts the time in half.

6. Use your grapher to plot $y = 100 \sin 2x$. Note that the name of the input has been changed to conform with your calculator.

7. Compare your results in Problems 3 and 6.

The graphs are the same.

8. Recall that the period of a trigonometric function is the shortest time (distance) to complete one full cycle. Determine the period of each of the following.

a. $y = 100 \sin x$

period $= 2\pi$ units.

b. $y = 100 \sin(2x)$

period $= \pi$ units.

9. On the following grid, repeat Problem 3 to plot the data pairs (t, x).

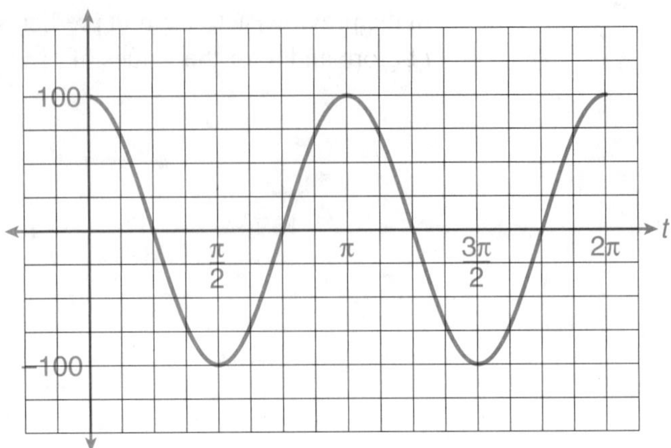

10. a. What equation should you enter into your calculator to produce the graph from Problem 8?

$y = 100 \cos(2x)$

b. Enter the equation from part a into your calculator and obtain a graph.

11. a. If you tripled your speed on the track from the original 100 meters per minute, what effect would this have on the amount of time to complete one lap?

The time would be reduced by a factor of 3 from 2π min (6.28 min) to $2\pi/3$ minutes (2.09 min).

b. What equations would describe the x- and y-coordinates of your position?

$x = 100 \cos(3t)$

$y = 100 \sin(3t)$

12. Determine the period of each of the following functions:

a. $y = 100 \cos x$

2π

b. $g(x) = 100 \cos(2x)$

π

c. $h(x) = 100 \cos(3x)$

$\frac{2\pi}{3}$

SUMMARY

- The smallest interval of input necessary for the graph of a function to repeat is called the period.
- For the trigonometric functions defined by $y = a \sin(bx + c)$ or $y = a \cos(bx + c)$, where $b > 0$ the period is $\frac{2\pi}{b}$.
- The frequency of these graphs over intervals of length 2π is b.

EXERCISES

1. For the following functions, identify both the amplitude and the period by inspection. Note that amplitude is always positive.

   a. $y = 3 \cos 1.5x$

   amp: 3, period: $\frac{2\pi}{1.5} = \frac{4\pi}{3}$

   b. $y = 0.5 \sin 2x$

   amp: 0.5, period: $\frac{2\pi}{2} = \pi$

   c. $f(x) = -2.3 \cos 0.4x$

   amp: 2.3, period: $\frac{2\pi}{0.4} = 5\pi$

   d. $g(x) = 36 \sin 2\pi x$

   amp: 36, period: $\frac{2\pi}{2\pi} = 1$

2. Is there any relationship between the amplitude and the period of the sine function? Explain.

   No, they are independent.

3. For each of the following tables, identify a function of the form $y = a \sin bx$ or $y = a \cos bx$ that approximately satisfies the table.

   a.

x	0	0.7854	1.5708	2.3562	3.1416
y	0	−15	0	15	0

   $y = -15 \sin (2x)$

   b.

x	0	2.244	4.488	6.732	8.976
y	1.3	0	−1.3	0	1.3

   $y = 1.3 \cos (0.7x)$

4. For each of the following graphs, identify a function of the form $y = a \sin bx$ or $y = a \cos bx$ that the graph approximates. Explain.

   a.

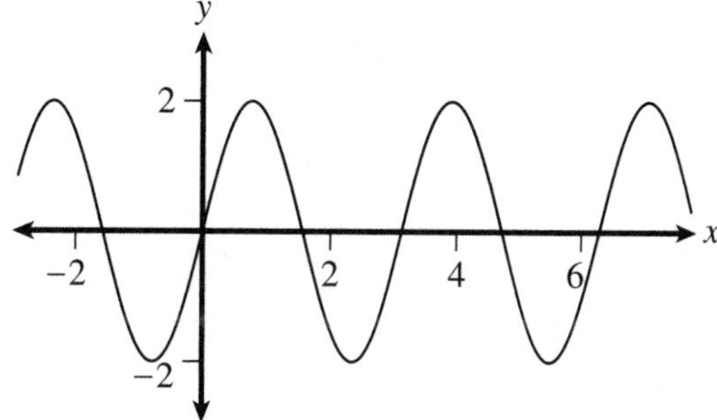

   amp: 2; period $= \pi = \frac{2\pi}{b}$ or $b = 2$

   $y = 2 \sin (2x)$

Exercise numbers appearing in color are answered in the Selected Answers section of this book.

b.

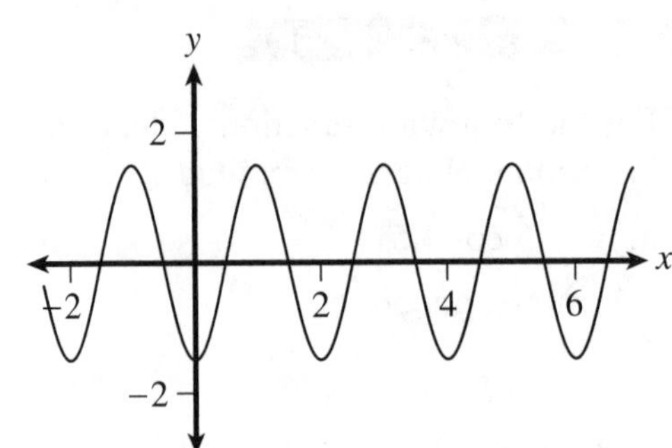

amp: 1.5; period $= 2 = \frac{2\pi}{b}$ or $b = \pi$

$y = -1.5 \cos(\pi x)$

5. Match the given equation to one of the graphs that follow. Assume Xscl = 1 and Yscl = 1.

a. $y = 2 \cos 0.5x$

Graph is i.

b. $y = -0.5 \sin 2x$

Graph is ii.

c. $y = 0.5 \cos 2x$

Graph is iii.

d. $y = 2 \sin 0.5x$

Graph is iv.

i.

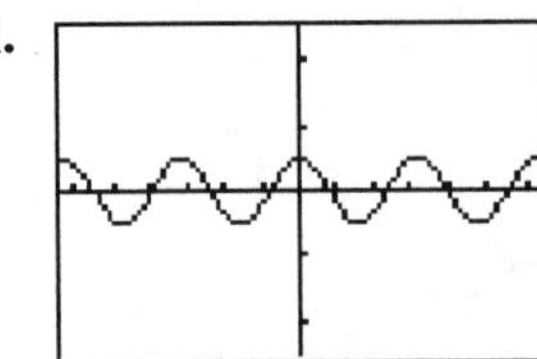

ii.

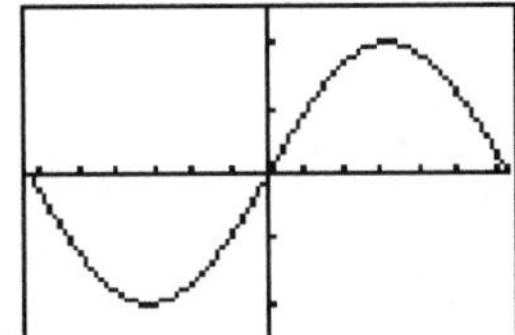

iii.

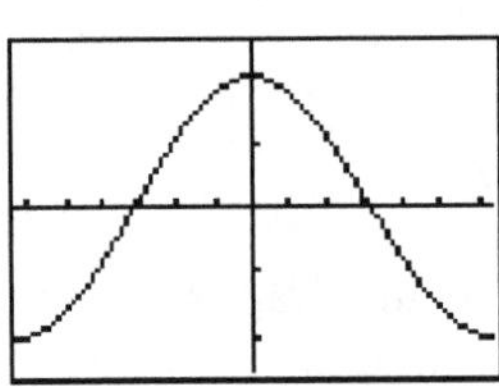

iv.

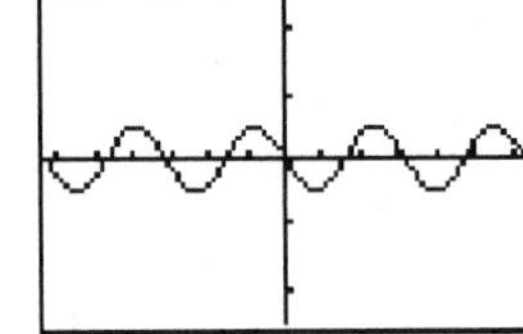

ACTIVITY 6.12

Running with a Friend

Topic: *Displacement of $y = a \sin(bx + c)$ and $y = a \cos(bx + c)$*

While jogging, you become good friends with another runner who started out, like you, with a speed of 100 meters per minute on the 100-meter track. You enjoy running together but prefer to keep a healthy distance between each other during the run. You start at (100, 0) and when you arrive at (0, 100), your friend starts at (100, 0).

1. Assume that you both maintain the same speed of 100 meters per minute.

a. How far ahead of your friend are you?

You are $\frac{1}{4}$ lap ahead.

$\frac{1}{4}(200\pi)$

$m = 50\pi$

$m = 157$ min

b. How long after you start does your friend wait before starting?

$t = \frac{50\pi \text{ m}}{100 \text{ m/min}} = \frac{\pi}{2} \text{ min} = 1.57 \text{ min}$

2. Complete the following table to give coordinates for both you and your friend at selected special points along the track.

t (min)	YOUR x-COORDINATE	YOUR y-COORDINATE	YOUR FRIEND'S x-COORDINATE	YOUR FRIEND'S y-COORDINATE
0	100	0	-----	-----
$\pi/2$	0	100	100	0
π	−100	0	0	100
$3\pi/2$	0	−100	−100	0
2π	100	0	0	−100
$5\pi/2$	0	100	100	0

3. On the following grid, use the data from Problem 2 to plot (t, y) for both you and your friend. Connect the points to smooth out your graphs.

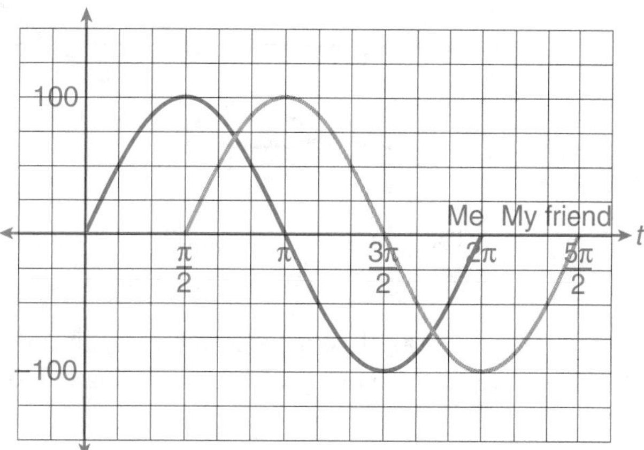

4. What is the relationship between the two graphs?

The graph for my friend is shifted $\frac{\pi}{2}$ units to the right.

The **displacement,** or **phase shift,** of the graph of $y = a\sin(bx + c)$ is the smallest movement (left or right) necessary for the graph of $y = a\sin(bx)$ to match the graph of $y = a\sin(bx + c)$ exactly. For example, consider the graphs of $y = \sin x$ and $y = \sin(x + 1)$.

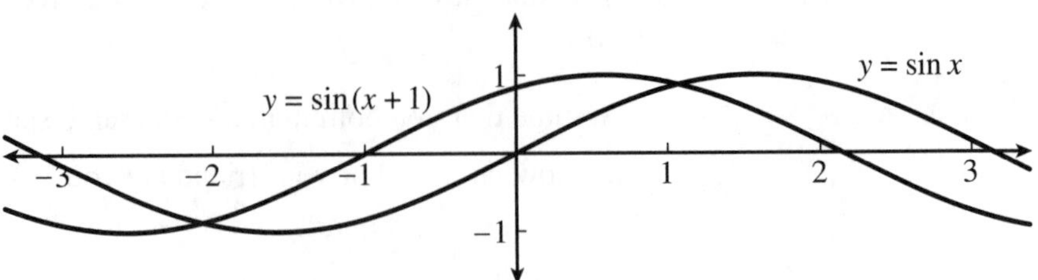

The graph of $y = \sin x$ must be moved 1 unit to the left to match the graph of $y = \sin(x + 1)$ exactly, so the displacement, or phase shift, is -1.

5. a. Which graph is displaced in Problem 3?

The graph for my friend.

b. What is the displacement?

$\pi/2$ minutes.

6. Would you expect the same type of relationship between the two graphs representing the x-coordinates? Explain.

Yes, you can see from the table that the x-coordinates are the same for values of t that differ by $\pi/2$ minutes.

Displacement, or phase shift, is defined for the cosine function in the same manner it is defined for sine. For example, consider the graphs of $y = 3\cos 2x$ and $y = 3\cos(2x - 1)$.

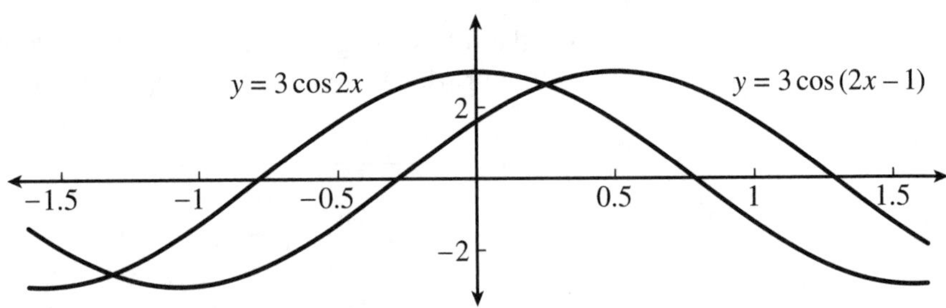

The graph of $y = 3\cos(2x - 1)$ appears to be about $\frac{1}{2}$ unit to the right of the graph of $y = 3\cos 2x$, so the displacement is approximately $\frac{1}{2}$.

7. a. If your x-coordinate is given by $100\cos t$, predict the defining equation of your friend's x-coordinate. Explain.

$x = 100\cos\left(t - \frac{\pi}{2}\right)$

b. Use your grapher to test your prediction.

In general, in the functions defined by $y = a\sin(bx + c)$ and $y = a\cos(bx + c)$, the values for b and c affect the displacement, or phase shift, of the function. The phase shift is given by $-\frac{c}{b}$. Note that if $-\frac{c}{b}$ is negative, the shift is to the left. If $-\frac{c}{b}$ is positive, the shift is to the right.

8. a. Using the expression $-\frac{c}{b}$, what is the displacement of $y = 3\cos(2x - 1)$?

$-\frac{c}{b} = -\frac{(-1)}{2} = \frac{1}{2}$

b. Is your result consistent with the graph preceding Problem 7?

Yes.

9. In this activity, your friend's y-coordinate is given by $y = a\sin(bx + c)$, where $a = 100$ and $b = 1$. Calculate c.

$-\frac{c}{b} = \frac{\pi}{2}$

$\frac{-c}{1} = \frac{\pi}{2}$

$c = -\frac{\pi}{2}$

SUMMARY

- The displacement, or phase shift, of the graph of $y = a\sin(bx + c)(b > 0)$ is the smallest movement (left or right) necessary for the graph of $y = a\sin bx$ to match the graph of $y = a\sin(bx + c)$ exactly.
- The displacement, or phase shift, of the graph of $y = a\cos(bx + c)(b > 0)$ is the smallest movement (left or right) necessary for the graph of $y = a\cos bx$ to match the graph of $y = a\cos(bx + c)$ exactly.
- For the functions $y = a\sin(bx + c)$ and $y = a\cos(bx + c)(b > 0)$, the phase shift is given by $-\frac{c}{b}$.
- If $-\frac{c}{b}$ is negative, the shift is to the left. If $-\frac{c}{b}$ is positive, the shift is to the right.

EXERCISES

1. For the following functions, identify the amplitude, period, and displacement.

a. $y = 0.7\cos\left(2x + \frac{\pi}{2}\right)$

amp: 0.7

per: π

disp: $\frac{-\frac{\pi}{2}}{2} = -\frac{\pi}{4}$

b. $y = 3\sin(x - 1)$

amp: 3

per: 2π

disp: $\frac{-(-1)}{1} = 1$

c. $f(x) = -2.5\sin\left(0.4x + \frac{\pi}{3}\right)$

amp: 2.5

per: 5π

disp: $\frac{-\frac{\pi}{3}}{0.4} = -\frac{5\pi}{6}$

d. $g(x) = 15\sin(2\pi x - 0.3)$

amp: 15

per: 1

disp: $\frac{-(-0.3)}{2\pi} = \frac{3}{20\pi} = 0.0477$

Exercise numbers appearing in color are answered in the Selected Answers section of this book.

2. For each of the following tables, identify a function of the form $y = a \sin(bx + c)$ or $y = a \cos(bx + c)$ that approximately satisfies the table.

a.

x	−0.7854	0.7854	2.3562	3.927	5.4978
y	0	3	0	−3	0

$y = 3 \sin\left(x + \frac{\pi}{4}\right)$

b.

x	1	2.5708	4.1416	5.7124	7.2832
y	−0.5	0	0.5	0	−0.5

$y = -0.5 \cos(x - 1)$

3. Sketch one cycle of the graph of the function defined by $f(x) = 2 \sin\left(x + \frac{\pi}{2}\right)$.

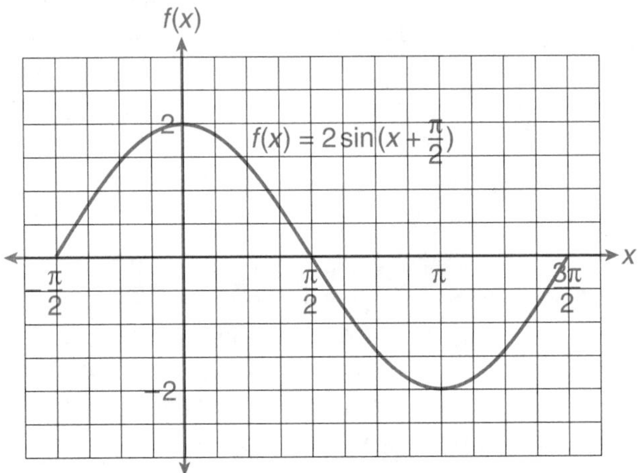

4. Determine an equation for the function defined by the following graph.

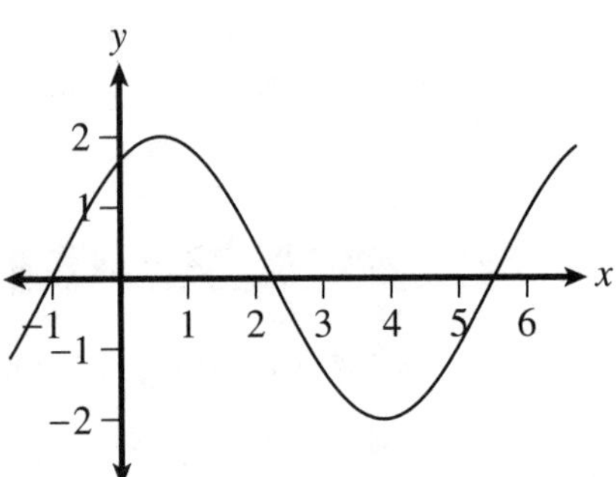

$y = 2 \sin(x + 1)$

5. Match the given equation to one of the graphs that follow. (Assume Xscl = 1 and Yscl = 1.)

a. $y = 2\cos(x - 1)$

Graph is iii

b. $y = 2\sin(x - 1)$

Graph is iv

c. $y = 2\cos(x + 2)$

Graph is i

d. $y = -2\sin(x + 2)$

Graph is iv

i.

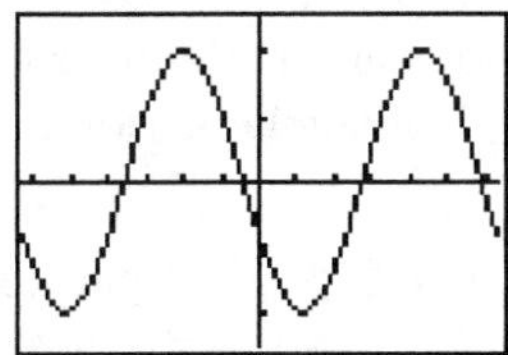

ii.

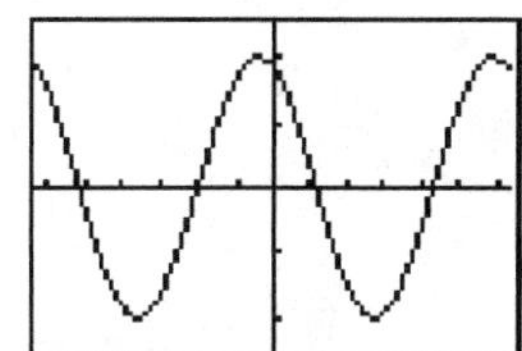

iii.

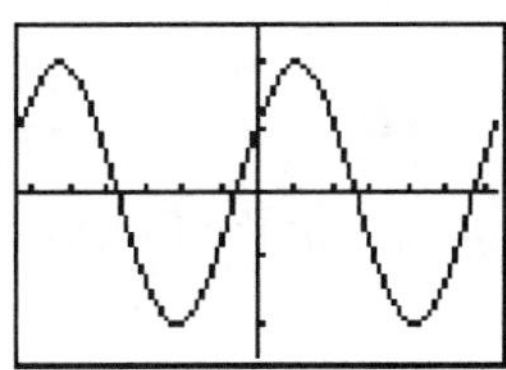

iv.

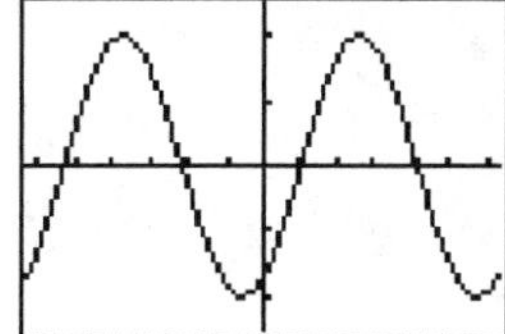

What Have I Learned?

1. Explain why the trigonometric functions could be called circular functions.

Their output values are coordinates of points on a circle.

2. Sometimes the difference between the trigonometric functions and the circular functions is explained by the difference in inputs. The input values for the trigonometric functions are angle measurements, and the input values for the circular functions are real numbers. How does your knowledge of radian measure relate to this?

An angle measured in radians is equivalent to the distance traveled along an arc of a circle of radius one intercepted by the angle. This distance is a real number.

3. a. Estimate the amplitude of the function defined by the following graph.

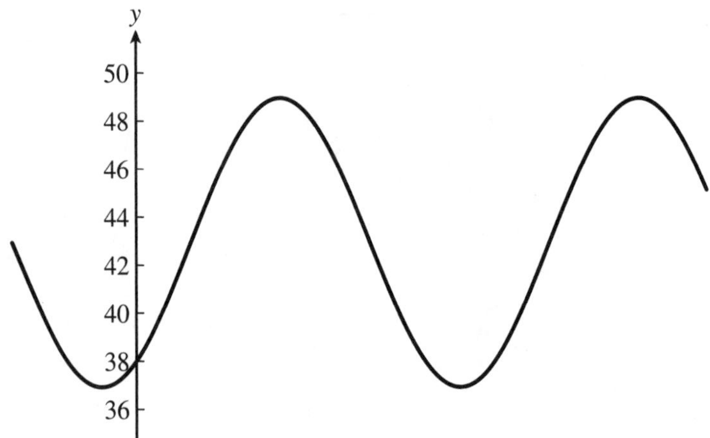

The amplitude is about 6.

b. Explain how you used the definition of amplitude to answer part a.

$\text{Amp} = \frac{1}{2}(M - m) = \frac{1}{2}(49 - 37) = \frac{1}{2}(12) = 6$

4. The period of $y = \sin x$ and $y = \cos x$ is 2π. Explain why this makes sense when sine and cosine are viewed as circular functions.

The circumference of a circle is $2\pi r$. If the radius is 1, then the length of the intercepted arc is 2π units.

5. Given a function defined by $y = a \sin(bx + c)$ and $b > 0$ and given the fact that b and c possess opposite signs, is the graph of the function displaced to the right or to the left? Explain.

If b and c have opposite signs, then $\frac{c}{b}$ is negative and $-\frac{c}{b}$ is positive. Therefore, the displacement is to the right.

How Can I Practice?

1. Determine the coordinates of the point on the unit circle corresponding to the following central angles. If necessary, round your results to the nearest hundredth.

a. 36°

(0.81, 0.59)

b. 210°

(−0.87, −0.5)

c. −90°

(0, −1)

d. 317°

(0.73, −0.68)

e. −144°

(−0.81, −0.59)

f. 450°

(0,1)

2. For each of the points on the unit circle determined in Exercise 1, determine the distance traveled along the circle to the point from (1, 0).

a. 0.63 units

b. 3.67 units

c. 1.57 units clockwise

d. 5.53 units

e. 2.51 units clockwise

f. 7.85 units

3. Convert the following degree measures to radian measures in terms of π.

a. 18°

$18° \cdot \frac{\pi}{180°} = \frac{\pi}{10}$

b. 150°

$150° \cdot \frac{\pi}{180°} = \frac{5\pi}{6}$

c. 390°

$390° \cdot \frac{\pi}{180°} = \frac{13\pi}{6}$

d. −72°

$-72° \cdot \frac{\pi}{180°} = \frac{-2\pi}{5}$

4. Convert the following radian measures to degree measures.

a. $\frac{5\pi}{6}$

$\frac{5\pi}{6} \cdot \frac{180°}{\pi} = 150°$

b. 1.7π

$1.7\pi \cdot \frac{180°}{\pi} = 306°$

c. -3π

$-3\pi \cdot \frac{180°}{\pi} = -540°$

d. 0.9π

$0.9\pi \cdot \frac{180°}{\pi} = 162°$

Exercise numbers appearing in color are answered in the Selected Answers section of this book.

Obtain the following information about each of the functions defined by the equations in Problems 5–9:

a. Use your grapher to sketch a graph.

b. From the defining equation, determine the amplitude. Then use your graph to explain why your amplitude is correct.

c. From the defining equation, determine the period. Then use your graph to explain why your period is correct.

d. From the defining equation, determine the displacement. Then use your graph to explain why your displacement is correct.

5. $y = 4 \cos 3x$

amp: 4

period: $\frac{2\pi}{3}$

displacement: 0

6. $y = -2 \sin (x - 1)$

amp $= 2$

period: $\frac{2\pi}{1} = 2\pi$

displacement: 1

7. $s = 3.2 \sin (-2x)$

amp: 3.2

period: $\frac{2\pi}{2} = \pi$

displacement: 0

8. $f(x) = -\cos \left(\frac{x}{2} + 1\right)$

amp $= 1$

period: $\frac{2\pi}{\frac{1}{2}} = 4\pi$

displacement: -2

9. $g(x) = 4 - 3 \cos (4x - 1)$

amp: 3

period: $\frac{2\pi}{4} = \frac{\pi}{2}$

displacement: $\frac{-(-1)}{4} = \frac{1}{4}$

10. You rent a cottage on the ocean for a week one summer and notice that the tide comes in twice a day with approximate regularity. Remembering that the trigonometric functions model repetitive behavior, you place a meter stick in the water to measure water height every hour from 6:00 A.M. to midnight. At low tide the height of the water is 0 centimeters, and at high tide the height is 80 centimeters.

a. Explain why a sine or a cosine function models this relationship between height of water in centimeters and time in hours.

Because of the repetitive nature of the height of the water as a function of time.

b. What is the amplitude of this function?

$$\text{Amplitude} = \frac{\text{range}}{2} = \frac{80 - 0}{2} = 40$$

c. Approximate the period of this function. Explain.

Period is approximately 12 hours, since high tide occurs twice a day.

d. Determine a reasonable defining equation for this function. Explain.

Let x represent the number of hours since midnight.

$y = a \sin(bx + c) + d$

$a = 40$, the amplitude

$$\text{Period} = \frac{2\pi}{b} = 12$$
$$b = \frac{\pi}{6}$$

$$\text{Displacement} = 3 = \frac{-c}{b} = \frac{-c}{\frac{\pi}{6}}$$
$$-c = 3 \cdot \left(\frac{\pi}{6}\right)$$
$$c = \frac{-\pi}{2}$$

Vertical shift $= d = 40$

$y = 40 \sin\left(\frac{\pi}{6}x - \frac{\pi}{2}\right) + 40$

Other equations are possible.

CHAPTER 6

Gateway Review

1. You walk 7 miles in a straight line 63° north of east.

a. Determine how far north you have traveled.

N = 7 sin(63°) = 6.24 miles

b. Determine how far east you have traveled.

E = 7 cos(63°) = 3.18 miles

2. Solve the following triangles.

a.

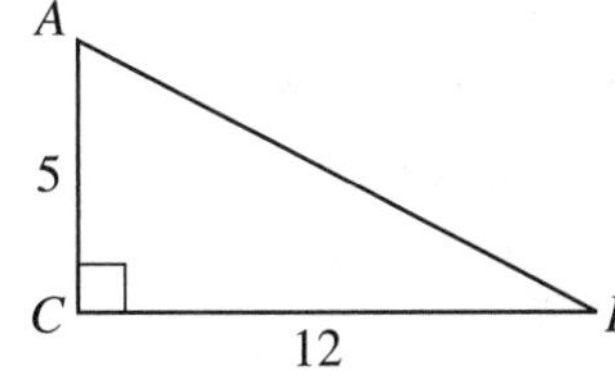

b.

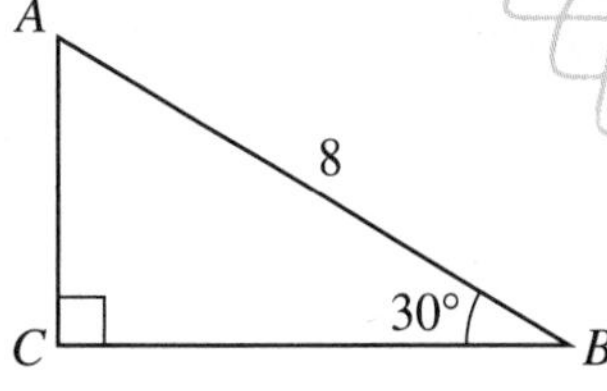

a. Side c = 13, angle A = 67.4°, angle B = 22.6°

b. Side a = 6.93, side b = 4, angle A = 60°

c.

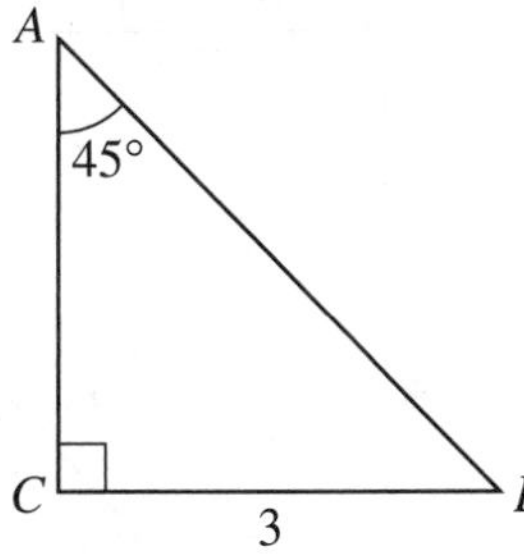

d.

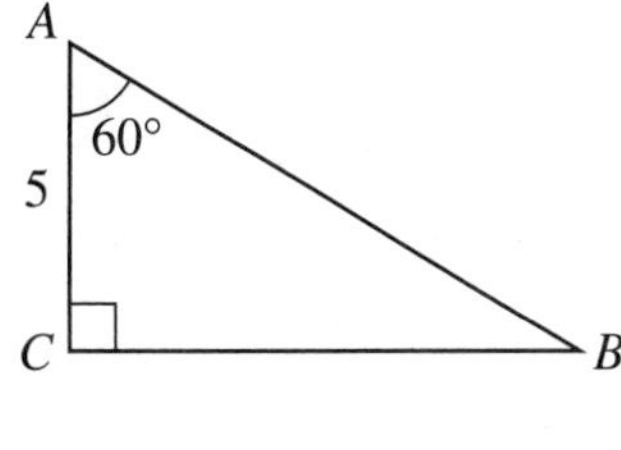

c. Side b = 3, side c = 4.24, angle B = 45°

d. Side a = 8.66, side c = 10, angle B = 30°

3. a. Given $\sin \theta = \frac{6}{10}$, determine $\cos \theta$ and $\tan \theta$ without using your calculator.

$\cos \theta = \frac{8}{10}$

$\tan \theta = \frac{6}{8}$

b. Given $\cos \theta = \frac{\sqrt{3}}{2}$, determine $\sin \theta$, $\tan \theta$, and θ without using your calculator.

$\sin \theta = \frac{1}{2}$

$\tan \theta = \frac{1}{\sqrt{3}}$

$\theta = 30°$

Exercise numbers appearing in color are answered in the Selected Answers section of this book.

c. Given $\tan\theta = \frac{8}{5}$, determine $\sin\theta$ and $\cos\theta$ without using your calculator.

$c^2 = 5^2 + 8^2 = 89$

$c = \sqrt{89}$

$\sin\theta = \dfrac{8}{\sqrt{89}}$

$\cos\theta = \dfrac{5}{\sqrt{89}}$

4. You are taking your nephew to see the Empire State Building. When you are 100 feet away from the building, you and your nephew look up to see the top. You are 6 feet tall, your nephew is 3 feet tall, and the height of the Empire State Building is 1414 feet. You notice that even though he is only half your height, your nephew does not have to tilt his head any more than you do. Is your observation correct? Is the angle always independent of people's heights? Explain.

No, there is a difference but it is so small that it is difficult to see.

For you: $\theta = \tan^{-1}\left(\frac{1408}{100}\right) = 85.9375°$.

For your nephew: $\theta = \tan^{-1}\left(\frac{1411}{100}\right) = 85.9461°$.

5. In the following diagram, determine the lengths of *a*, *c*, *b*, and *h*.

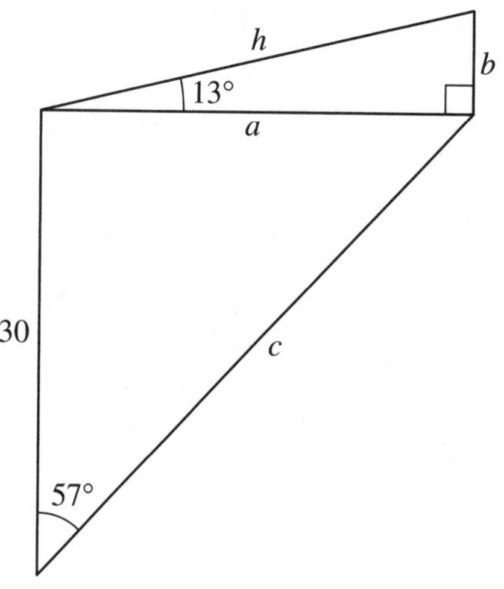

$\tan 57° = \frac{a}{30}$

$30 \tan 57° = a$

$a = 46.2$

$\tan 13° = \frac{b}{46.2}$

$b = 46.2 \tan 13°$

$b = 10.7$

$\cos 57° = \frac{30}{c}$

$c = \frac{30}{\cos 57°}$

$c = 55.1$

$\cos 13° = \frac{46.2}{h}$

$h = \frac{46.2}{\cos 13°}$

$h = 47.4$

6. In the following diagram, determine x and h without using your calculator. (*Hint:* See Exercises 2c and d.)

So, $(2x)^2 = x^2 + (200 + x)^2$

$4x^2 = x^2 + 40{,}000 + 400x + x^2$

$2x^2 - 400x - 40{,}000 = 0$

$$x = \frac{400 \pm \sqrt{400^2 + 4(2)(40{,}000)}}{2(2)}$$

$$x = \frac{400 \pm \sqrt{160{,}000 + 320{,}000}}{4}$$

$$x = \frac{400 \pm \sqrt{480{,}000}}{4}$$

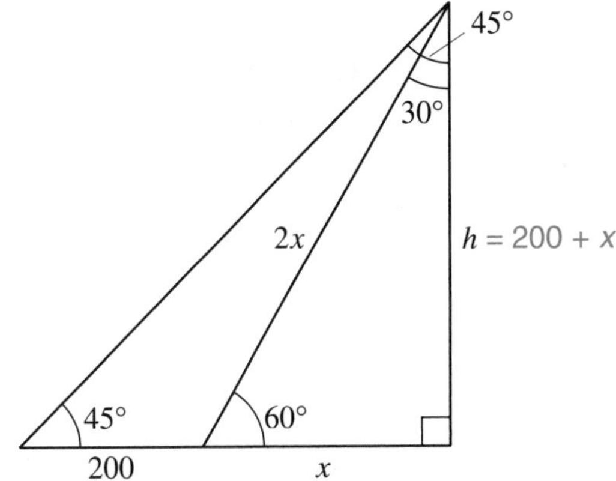

The negative does not make sense, thus $x = \dfrac{400 \pm 400\sqrt{3}}{4}$

$x = 100 + 100\sqrt{3}$; $h = 300 + 100\sqrt{3}$

7. Using the following triangles, complete the table without using your calculator.

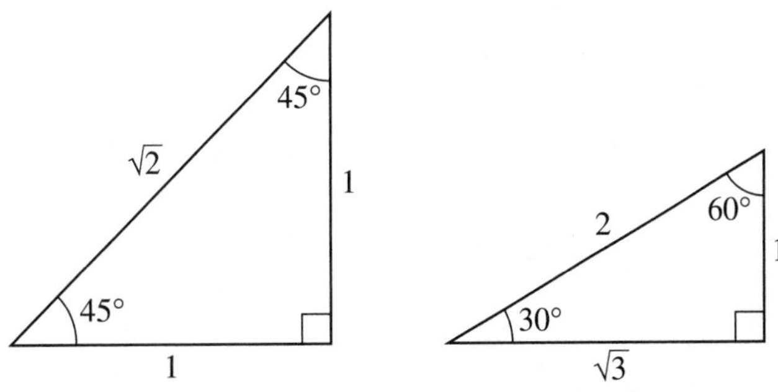

Angle θ	sin θ	cos θ	tan θ
120°	$\frac{\sqrt{3}}{2}$	$-1/2$	$-\sqrt{3}/1$
135°	$\frac{1}{\sqrt{2}}$	$-\frac{1}{\sqrt{2}}$	-1
150°	$\frac{1}{2}$	$-\frac{\sqrt{3}}{2}$	$-\frac{1}{\sqrt{3}}$
180°	0	-1	0
210°	$-1/2$	$-\frac{\sqrt{3}}{2}$	$\frac{1}{\sqrt{3}}$
225°	$-\frac{1}{\sqrt{2}}$	$-\frac{1}{\sqrt{2}}$	1
240°	$-\frac{\sqrt{3}}{2}$	$-1/2$	$\sqrt{3}$
270°	-1	0	undefined
300°	$-\frac{\sqrt{3}}{2}$	$\frac{1}{2}$	$-\sqrt{3}/1$
315°	$-\frac{1}{\sqrt{2}}$	$\frac{1}{\sqrt{2}}$	-1
330°	$-1/2$	$\frac{\sqrt{3}}{2}$	$-\frac{1}{\sqrt{3}}$
360°	0	1	0

8. Determine the amplitude and period of the given functions and then sketch their graphs. Use your grapher to verify your results.

a. $y = 2 \sin x$

amplitude = 2

period = 2π

b. $y = -2 \sin x$

amplitude = 2

period = 2π

c. $y = \cos 2x$

amplitude = 1

period = π

d. $y = \cos 2\pi x$

amplitude = 1

period = 1

e. $y = \sin \frac{x}{2}$

amplitude = 1

period = 4π

f. $y = \sin \frac{\pi x}{2}$

amplitude = 1

period = 4

g. $y = \cos x + 2$

amplitude = 1

period = 2π

h. $y = \cos x - 2$

amplitude = 1

period = 2π

i. $y = \sin(2\pi x - 3\pi)$

amplitude = 1

period = 1

j. $y = 3 \sin(2\pi x - 3\pi) - 1$

amplitude = 3

period = 1

9. Match the given equation to one of the accompanying graphs. (Assume Xscl = 1 and Yscl = 1.)

a. $y = -3 \sin x + 4$
is graph vi.

b. $y = 2 \sin\left(\frac{\pi x}{2} + \frac{\pi}{2}\right)$
is graph ii.

c. $y = 2 \sin\left(\frac{\pi x}{2} - \frac{\pi}{2}\right) + 4$
is graph iv.

d. $y = -3 \cos x + 4$
is graph v.

e. $y = 2 \cos\left(\frac{\pi x}{2} + \frac{\pi}{2}\right)$
is graph vii.

f. $y = -\cos\left(\pi x - \frac{\pi}{2}\right) + 3$
is graph viii

i.

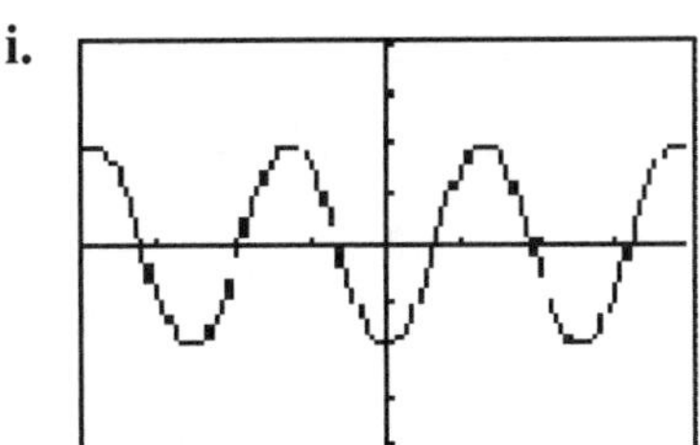

ii.

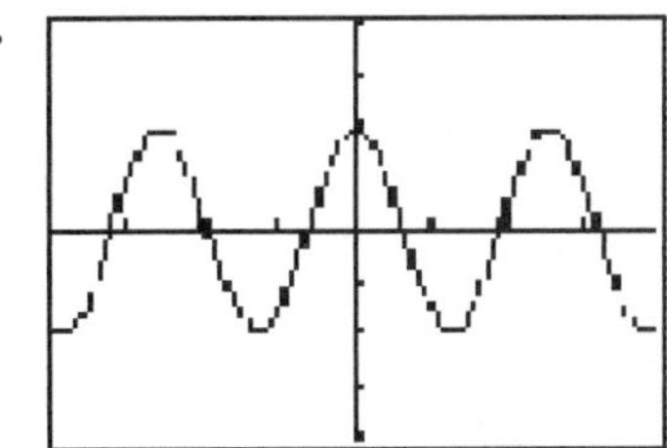

iii.

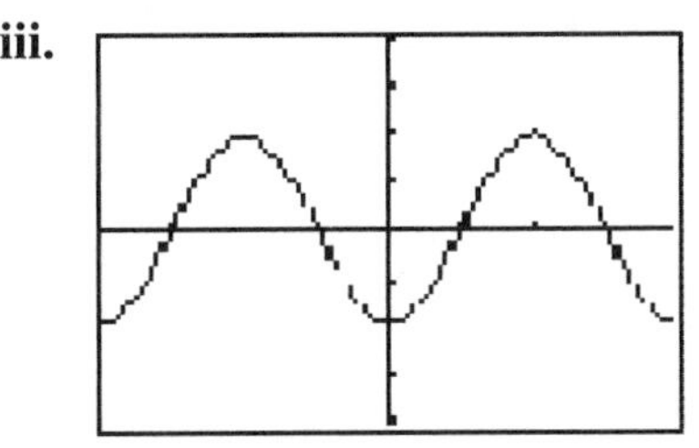

iv.

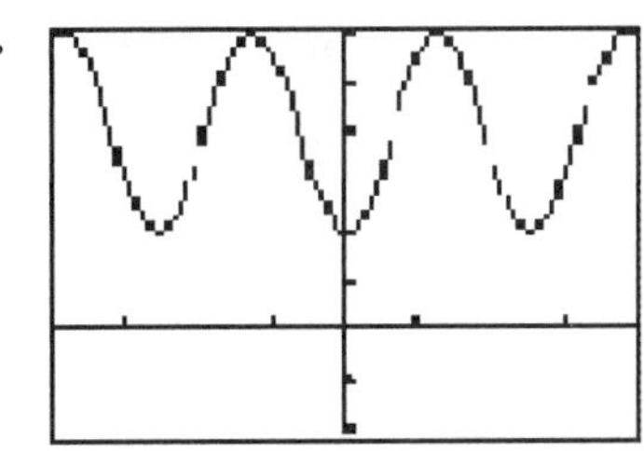

v.

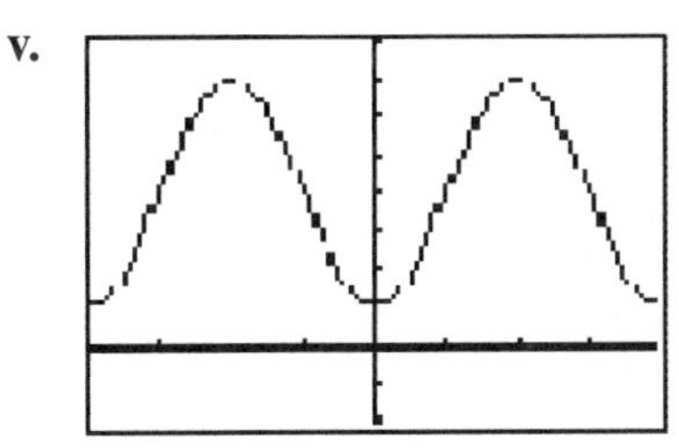

vi.

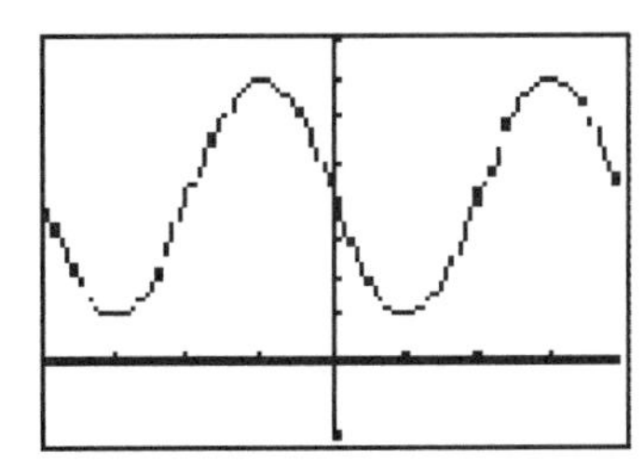

vii.

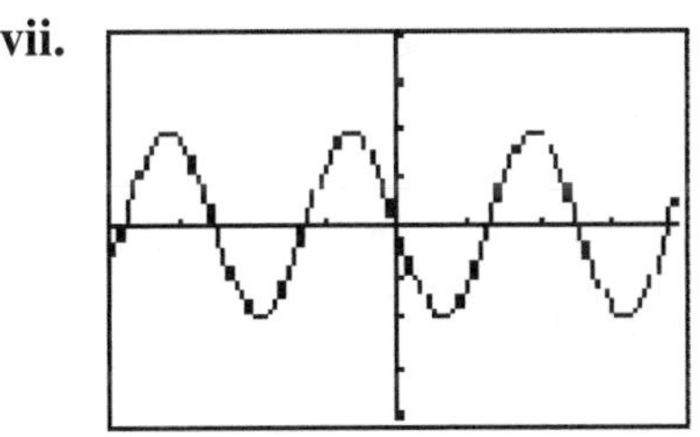

viii.

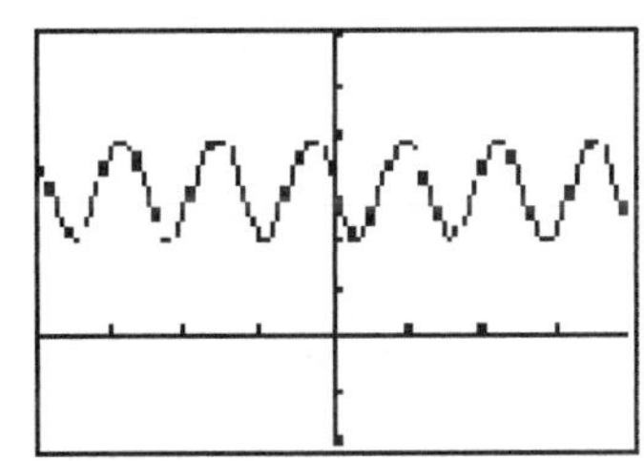

APPENDIX A

Concept Review

Note: Answers to all exercises in Appendix A can be found in the *Instructor's Resource Guide* supplement.

Properties of Exponents

The basic properties of exponents are summarized as follows:

If a is a real number greater than zero and n and m are rational numbers then,

1. $a^n a^m = a^{n+m}$ **2.** $\frac{a^n}{a^m} = a^{n-m}$ **3.** $(a^n)^m = a^{nm}$

4. $(ab)^n = a^n b^n$ **5.** $a^0 = 1$ **6.** $a^{-n} = \frac{1}{a^n}$

Property 1: $\mathbf{a^n a^m = a^{n+m}}$ If you are multiplying two powers of the same base, add the exponents.

Example 1: $x^4 \cdot x^7 = x^{4+7} = x^{11}$

Note that the exponents were added and the base did not change.

Property 2: $\frac{a^n}{a^m} = a^{n-m}$ If you are dividing two powers of the same base, subtract the exponents.

Example 2: $\frac{6^6}{6^4} = 6^{6-4} = 6^2 = 36$

Note that the exponents were subtracted and the base did not change.

Property 3: $(a^n)^m = a^{nm}$ If a power is raised to a power, multiply the exponents.

Example 3: $(y^3)^4 = y^{12}$

The exponents were multiplied. The base does not change. Can you justify this result in your own mind?

Property 4: $(ab)^n = a^n b^n$ If a product is raised to a power, each factor is raised to that power.

Example 4: $(2x^2y^3) = 2^3 \cdot (x^2)^3 \cdot (y^3)^3 = 8x^6y^9$

Note that since the base contained three factors each of those was raised to the third power. The common mistake in an expansion such as this is not to raise the coefficient to the power.

Property 5: $a^0 = 1, a \neq 0$ Often presented as a definition, property 5 states that any nonzero base raised to the zero power is one. This property or definition is a result of property 2 of exponents as follows:

Consider $\frac{x^5}{x^5}$. Using property 2, $x^{5-5} = x^0$. However, you know that any fraction in which the numerator and the denominator are equal is equivalent to 1. Therefore, $x^0 = 1$.

Example 5: $\left(\frac{2x^3}{3yz^5}\right)^0 = 1$

Given a nonzero base, if the exponent is zero, the value is one.

Property 6: $a^{-n} = \frac{1}{a^n}$ Sometimes presented as a definition, property 6 states that any base raised to a negative power is equivalent to the reciprocal of the base raised to the positive power. Note that the negative exponent does not have any effect on the sign of the base. This property could also be viewed as a result of the second property of exponents as follows:

Consider $\frac{x^3}{x^5}$. Using property 2, $x^{3-5} = x^{-2}$. If you view this expression algebraically, you have three factors of x in the numerator and five in the denominator. If you divide out the three common factors, you are left with $\frac{1}{x^2}$. Therefore, if property 2 is true, then .$x^{-2} = \frac{1}{x^2}$.

Example 6: Write each of the following without negative exponents.

a. 3^{-2} **b.** $\frac{2}{x^{-3}}$

Solution: a. $3^{-2} = \frac{1}{3^2} = \frac{1}{9}$ **b.** $\frac{2}{x^{-3}} = \frac{2}{\frac{1}{x^3}} = 2 \div \frac{1}{x^3} = 2 \cdot x^3 = 2x^3$

A **factor** can be moved from a numerator to denominator or from a denominator to a numerator by changing the *sign of the exponent.*

Example 7: Simplify and express your results with positive exponents only.

$$\left(\frac{x^3y^{-4}}{2x^{-3}y^{-2}z}\right) \cdot \left(\frac{4x^3y^2z}{x^5y^{-3}z^3}\right)$$

Solution: Simplify each factor by writing them with positive exponents only.

$\left(\frac{x^6}{2y^2z}\right) \cdot \left(\frac{4y^5}{x^2z^2}\right)$. Now multiply and simplify: $\frac{4x^6y^5}{2x^2y^2z^3} = \frac{2x^4y^3}{z^3}$.

EXERCISES

Simplify and express your results with positive exponents only.

1. 5^{-3}

2. $\dfrac{1}{x^{-5}}$

3. $\dfrac{3x}{y^{-2}}$

4. $\dfrac{10x^2y^5}{2x^{-3}}$

5. $\dfrac{5^{-1}z}{x^{-1}z^{-2}}$

6. $5x^0$

7. $(a + b)^0$

8. $-3(x^0 - 4y^0)$

9. $x^6 \cdot x^{-3}$

10. $\dfrac{4^{-2}}{4^{-3}}$

11. $(4x^2y^3) \cdot (3x^{-3}y^{-2})$

12. $\dfrac{24x^{-2}y^3}{6x^3y^{-1}}$

13. $\dfrac{(4x^2y^{-3}) \cdot (5x^3y^{-2})}{6x^2y^{-3}z^{-3}}$

14. $\left(\dfrac{2x^{-2}y^{-3}}{z^2}\right) \cdot \left(\dfrac{x^5y^3}{z^{-3}}\right)$

15. $\dfrac{(6x^4y^{-3}z^{-2})(3x^{-3}y^4)}{15x^{-3}y^{-2}z^2}$

Solving 2 × 2 Linear Systems by the Addition Method

The addition method is an algebraic alternative to the substitution method for solving a 2 × 2 linear system of the form

$$a_1x + b_1y = c_1$$
$$a_2x + b_2y = c_2,$$

where a_1, a_2, b_1, b_2, c_1, and c_2 are real numbers.

The basic strategy for the addition method is to reduce the 2 × 2 system to a single linear equation by eliminating a variable.

For example, consider the x-coefficients of the linear system

$$2x + 3y = 1$$
$$4x - y = 9.$$

The coefficients are 2 and 4. The LCD of 2 and 4 is 4. Use the multiplication principle to multiply each side of the first equation by –2. The resulting system is

$$\begin{aligned} -4x - 6y &= -2 \\ 4x - y &= 9 \quad . \end{aligned}$$

Note, multiplying by –2 produces x-coefficients that are additive inverses or opposites. Now add the two equations together to eliminate the variable x.

$$-7y = -7$$

Solving for y, $y = -1$ is the y value of our solution. To find the value of x, substitute –1 for y and solve for x in any equation that involves x and y. For an alternative to determining the value of y, consider the original system and the coefficients of y, 3, and –1 in the original system. The LCD is 3. Since the signs are already opposites, multiply the second equation by 3.

$$\begin{aligned} 2x + 3y &= 1 \\ 12x - 3y &= 27 \end{aligned}$$

Adding the two equations will eliminate the y-variable.

$$14x = 28$$

Solving for x, $x = 2$. Therefore, the potential solution is (2, –1). This should be checked to make certain that it satisfies both equations.

Depending on the coefficients of the system, you may need to change both equations when using the addition method. For example, the coefficients of x in the 2×2 linear system

$$\begin{aligned} 5x - 2y &= 11 \\ 3x + 5y &= -12 \end{aligned}$$

are 5 and 3. The LCD is 15. Multiply the first equation by 3 and the second by –5 as follows:

$$\begin{aligned} 15x - 6y &= 33 \\ -15x - 25y &= 60 \end{aligned}$$

Add the two equations to eliminate the x terms from the system.

$$-31y = 93$$

Solving for y, $y = -3$. Substituting this value for y in the first equation of the original system yields

$$\begin{aligned} 5x - 2(-3) &= 11 \\ 5x + 6 &= 11 \\ 5x &= 5 \\ x &= 1 \end{aligned}$$

Therefore, (1, –3) is the potential solution of the system.

EXERCISES

Solve the following systems using the addition method. If the system is dependent or inconsistent state this as your answer.

1. $x - y = 3$
$x + y = -7$

2. $x + 4y = 10$
$x + 2y = 4$

3. $-5x - y = 4$
$-5x + 2y = 7$

4. $4x + y = 7$
$2x + 3y = 6$

5. $3x - y = 1$
$6x - 2y = 5$

6. $4x - 2y = 0$
$3x + 3y = 5$

7. $x - y = 9$
$-4x - 4y = -36$

8. $-2x + y = 6$
$4x + y = 1$

9. $\frac{3}{2}x + \frac{2}{5}y = \frac{9}{10}$
$\frac{1}{2}x + \frac{6}{5}y = \frac{3}{10}$

10. $0.3x - 0.8y = 1.6$
$0.1x + 0.4y = 1.2$

Solving 3 × 3 Linear Systems Algebraically

Linear equations such as $3x + 2y - z = 4$ involve three variables, x, y, and z. A solution of such an equation is an ordered triple (x, y, z) such that if the values of x, y, and z in the ordered triple are substituted into the equation, the result is a true statement.

A system of three linear equations in three variables (a 3×3 system) such as

$$\begin{aligned} -x + y + z &= -3 \\ 3x + 9y + 5z &= 5 \\ x + 3y + 2z &= 4 \end{aligned}$$

has as its solution all ordered triples (x, y, z) that will make all three equations true.

SOLVING A 3 × 3 LINEAR SYSTEM ALGEBRAICALLY

1. Eliminate one variable using any two of the given three equations to obtain an equation in two variables (or less).
2. Eliminate the same variable using the third equation not used in step 1 and either of the other two equations to obtain a second equation in two variables (or less)

3. Solve the system consisting of the two equations found in steps 1 and 2.
4. Substitute the values obtained in step 3 into any equation involving all three variables to determine the value of the third variable.
5. Check your solution in all three equations.

Example 1: Determine all solutions of

$$\begin{aligned} -x + y + z &= -3 \\ 3x + 9y + 5z &= 5 \\ x + 3y + 2z &= 4. \end{aligned}$$

Solution: Since the coefficients of x are –1, 3, and 1, they have an LCD of 3. Thus, you may choose to eliminate x using the addition method.

Step 1 Multiply both sides of the first equation by 3 and add it to the second equation.

$$\begin{aligned} -3x + 3y + 3z &= -9 \\ 3x + 9y + 5z &= 5 \end{aligned}$$

The sum is $12y + 8z = -4$.

Step 2 Multiply the third equation by -3 and add to the second

$$\begin{aligned} 3x + 9y + 5z &= 5 \\ -3x - 9y - 6x &= -12 \end{aligned}$$

The sum is $-z = -7$.

Step 3 The 2×2 system resulting from steps 1 and 2 is

$$\begin{aligned} 12y + 8z &= -4 \\ -z &= -7. \end{aligned}$$

The second equation is equivalent to $z = 7$. Substituting this value into the first equation of the new system yields

$$\begin{aligned} 12y + 8(7) &= -4 \\ 12y + 56 &= -4 \\ 12y &= -60 \\ y &= -5. \end{aligned}$$

Step 4 Using the values of y and z in the third equation of the original system.

$$\begin{aligned} x + 3(-5) + 2(7) &= 4 \\ x - 15 + 14 &= 4 \\ x - 1 &= 4 \\ x &= 5 \end{aligned}$$

The potential solution is (5, –5, 7) and should be checked in all three of the original equations.

Not every 3×3 linear system has unique solutions; some have multiple solutions. These are called **dependent systems.** Some systems have no solution and are called **inconsistent systems.**

Example 2: Solve the following system.

$$x + 2y + 3z = 5$$
$$-x + y - z = -6$$
$$2x + y + 4z = 4$$

Solution: Since the coefficients of x are 1, –1, and 2, the LCD is 2. Again, you may eliminate x using the addition method.

Step 1 Sum the first two equations to eliminate x.

$$x + 2y + 3z = 5$$
$$-x + y - z = -6$$

The sum is $3y + 2z = -1$.

Step 2 Multiply the second equation by 2 and add it to the third.

$$-2x + 2y - 2z = -12$$
$$2x + y + 4z = 4$$

The sum is $3y + 2z = -8$. The new system is

$$3y + 2z = -1$$
$$3y + 2z = -8.$$

Step 3 To solve the new system, multiply the first equation by –1 and add it to the second.

$$-3y - 2z = 1$$
$$3y + 2z = -8$$

The sum is $0 = -7$.

Since $0 = -7$ is a false statement, the conclusion is there is no solution. The original system was an inconsistent system.

Had the sum of the equations in step three resulted in a true statement such as $0 = 0$, the conclusion would have been that there were an infinite number of solutions. That is, the system would have been dependent.

EXERCISES

Solve the following systems algebraically. If the system is dependent or inconsistent state this as the answer.

1. $x + y - z = 9$
$x + y + z = 5$
$x - y - z = 1$

2. $-2x + y - 4z = 3$
$x + y - 3z = 2$
$x - y + 2z = 1$

3. $x + 2y + 3z = 5$
$-x + y - z = -6$
$2x + y + 4z = 4$

4. $3x - 2y + 3z = 11$
$2x + 3y - 2z = -5$
$x + 4y - z = -5$

5. $x - 4y + z = -5$
$3x - 12y + 3z = -15$
$-2x + 8y - 2z = 10$

6. $2x + 3y + 4z = 3$
$6x - 6y + 8z = 3$
$4x + 3y - 4z = 2$

7. $x + 2y = 10$
$-x + 3z = -23$
$4y - z = 9$

Linear Inequalities

The properties of real numbers used to solve linear inequalities are similar to those for solving equations.

ADDITION PROPERTY

For any algebraic expressions A, B, and C, if $A < B$, then

$$A + C < B + C.$$

This implies that the same expression can be added to or subtracted from both sides of an inequality without changing the direction of the inequality.

MULTIPLICATION PROPERTY OF INEQUALITIES

For any algebraic expressions A, B, and C, if $A < B$

1. If $C > 0$, then $AC < BC$

2. If $C < 0$, then $AC > BC$

This implies if both sides of an inequality are multiplied or divided by the same positive quantity the direction of the inequality symbol is unchanged. However, if both sides of an inequality are multiplied or divided by a negative quantity, the direction of the inequality symbol is reversed.

Example 1: Solve the inequality $4(2 - x) + 7 > -3(x - 1)$.

Solution: The first step is to simplify each side of the inequality.

$$8 - 4x + 7 > -3x + 3$$
$$15 - 4x > -3x + 3$$

Add 3x to both sides and simplify.

$$15 - 4x + 4x > -3x + 3 + 4x$$
$$15 > x + 3$$

Subtract 13 from both sides.

$$15 - 3 > x + 3 - 3$$
$$\text{So, } 12 > x, \text{ or } x < 12$$

Example 2: Solve the inequality $-3x < 21$.

Solution: On the surface, this problem is not difficult. The solution is found by dividing both sides by -3. The important point is to remember to reverse the inequality.

$$\frac{-3x}{-3} > \frac{21}{-3} \quad \text{or} \quad x > -7$$

Compound Inequalities

When solving compound inequalities, the solution must be such that the variable will be isolated in the middle of the inequality. We still can use all of our properties, if we apply them to all three parts. We must reverse the direction of all inequalities if we multiply or divide by a negative number.

Example 3: Solve $-12 < 8 - 4x \leq 16$.

Solution: Subtract 8 from all parts and simplify.

$$-12 - 8 < 8 - 4x - 8 \leq 16 - 8$$
$$-20 < -4x \leq 8$$

Divide each part by -4 and reverse the inequalities.

$$\frac{-20}{-4} > x \geq \frac{8}{-4} \quad \text{or} \quad -2 \leq x < 5.$$

Inequalities Involving Absolute Value

The key to solving absolute value inequalities algebraically is to rewrite them using the following properties.

ABSOLUTE VALUE PROPERTIES

For any real number x and $a > 0$,

$$|x| < a \text{ is equivalent to } -a < x < a.$$

For any real number x and a > 0,

$$|x| > a \text{ is equivalent to } x > a \text{ or } x < -a$$

SOLVING ABSOLUTE VALUE INEQUALITIES

1. Rewrite the inequality with the absolute value isolated.
2. Rewrite the inequality as a compound inequality or pair of inequalities
3. Solve the resulting inequality(s)

Example 4: Solve $|2x - 3| + 3 \leq 8$.

Solution: Subtract 3 from both sides

$$|2x - 3| + 3 - 3 \leq 8 - 3 \text{ or } |2x - 3| \leq 5.$$

Using the properties.

$$-5 \leq 2x - 3 \leq 5$$

Add 3 to each part.

$$-5 + 3 \leq 2x - 3 + 3 \leq 5 + 3$$
$$-2 \leq 2x \leq 8$$

Divide each part by 2.

$$\frac{-2}{2} \leq \frac{2x}{x} \leq \frac{8}{2} \quad \text{or} \quad -1 \leq x \leq 4$$

Example 5: Solve $|4x + 3| - 4 > 7$.

Solution: Add 4 to both sides to isolate the absolute value.

$$|4x + 3| - 4 + 4 > 7 + 4$$
$$|4x + 3| > 11$$

Using the absolute value properties.

$$4x + 3 > 11 \quad \text{or} \quad 4x + 3 < -11$$

Solving these inequalities.

$$4x + 3 - 3 > 11 - 3 \qquad 4x + 3 - 3 < -11 - 3$$
$$4x > 8 \qquad x < -14$$
$$x > 2 \qquad x < -\tfrac{7}{2}$$

EXERCISES

Solve the following inequalities.

1. $2x + 4 < 3$

2. $4x + 3 \geq -2x + 5$

3. $4y + 6 < 3(y + 3) + 2y$

4. $-(x + 3) - 4 > -x + 5$

5. $-2 < x - 5 \leq 7$

6. $-12 \leq 1 - 3x \leq 7$

7. $6 < -3(2x - 4) \leq 12$

8. $0 < \frac{2x - 6}{5} < 12$

9. $|3x - 5| < 5$

10. $|x - 3| - 2 \leq 3$

11. $|4x - 1| > 3$

12. $|2x - 1| - 4 \geq 7$

Adding and Subtracting Polynomials

Adding polynomials is simply a process of collecting like terms.

ADDING TWO POLYNOMIALS

1. Write the polynomials vertically, aligning the like terms.
2. Add the coefficients of like terms.
3. Leave the variable factors unchanged.

Example 1: Determine the sum of $3x^3 - 3x^2 + x - 5$ and $4x^3 - 6x + 7$.

Solution:

Step 1 Since there is no x^2 term in the second polynomial, the alignment is as follows;

$$\begin{array}{llll} 3x^3 & - 3x^2 & + x & - 5 \\ 4x^3 & - & 6x & + 7 \end{array}$$

Step 2 The coefficients of the like terms are 3 and 4, 1 and −6, and −5 and 7. The sums are 7, −5, and 2 respectively.

Step 3 Since the second term of the first polynomial $-3x^2$ is not aligned with any term, it will remain unchanged and the sum is

$$7x^3 - 3x^2 - 5x + 2.$$

Subtraction is equivalent to adding the opposite (additive inverse). To find the opposite of any polynomial, simply change the signs of each term of the polynomial.

For example, the opposite of $x^3 - 4x^2 + 12$ is $-x^3 + 4x^2 - 12$.

SUBTRACTING TWO POLYNOMIALS

1. Determine the opposite of the polynomial to be subtracted.
2. Write the polynomials vertically aligning the like terms.
3. Add the coefficients of like terms.
4. Leave the variable factors unchanged.

Example 2: Determine the following difference.

$$2x^2 - 7x - 6 - (5x^2 - 3x + 9)$$

Step 1 The polynomial being subtracted is $5x^2 - 3x + 9$. Its opposite is $-5x^2 + 3x - 9$.

Step 2 Aligning this with the first polynomial.

$$\begin{array}{r} 2x^2 - 7x - 6 \\ -5x^2 + 3x - 9 \end{array}$$

Steps 3 and 4 The sums of the coefficients are $2 + (-5) = -3$, $-7 + 3 = -4$, and $-6 + (-9) = -15$. Therefore, the difference of the original two polynomials is given by

$$\begin{array}{r} 2x^2 - 7x - 6 \\ -5x^2 + 3x - 9 \\ \hline -3x^2 - 4x - 15 \end{array}$$

EXERCISES

Determine the following sums and differences.

1. $(5x + 6y - 3z) + (-2x + 3y + 2z)$

2. $(x^2 - 5y^2 - 9z^2) - (-5x^2 + 2y^2 - z^2)$

3. $(x^2 + 2x - 4xy + 5) + (-2x^2 + 5x - 3xy - 7)$

4. $(7xy - 3xz + 5yz) - (-3xy - 3xz + yz)$

5. $(2x^2 + 5x - 4) + (3x^2 - 4x + 1) + (4x^2 - 2x + 5)$

6. $(3x - 7) - (5x + 1) - 2x - 5)$

7. $(8x^2 - 3x - 4x^3) - (5x^2 + 5x - 7x^3)$

8. $(3y^3 - 4y^2 + 7) - (2y^2 + y - 4) + (-2y^3 - 6y + 9)$

Multiplying Binomials

FOIL (standing for First, Outer, Inner, Last) describes a process used to multiply two binomials. It may be helpful for organizing your work as you multiply each term in the first binomial by each term in the other binomial.

USING THE FOIL METHOD

1. Multiply the FIRST term in each binomial.
2. Multiply the OUTER terms.
3. Multiply the INNER terms.
4. Multiply the LAST terms.
5. Sum the products in steps 1-4.

Example 1: Determine the product $(x + 2)(x + 5)$.

Solution:

Step 1 Multiply the FIRST terms $x \cdot x = x^2$

Step 2 Multiply the OUTER terms $x \cdot 5 = 5x$.

Step 3 Multiply the INNER terms $2 \cdot x = 2x$.

Step 4 Multiply the LAST terms $2 \cdot 5 = 10$.

Step 5 Sum the products $x^2 + 2x + 5x + 10 = x^2 + 7x + 10$.

EXERCISES

Determine the following products.

1. $(x + 3)(x + 5)$

2. $(x - 2)(x + 6)$

3. $(3x - 4)(2x - 1)$

4. $(4x - 1)(x + 7)$

5. $(x + 3)(x - 3)$

6. $(3x + 1)(3x - 1)$

7. $(7x - 5)(3x + 4)$

8. $(5x - 7)(5x + 7)$

Factoring: Common Factors

A common factor is the first thing to check for whenever you wish to factor a polynomial.

REMOVING A COMMON FACTOR FROM A POLYNOMIAL

1. Identify the common factor.
2. Apply the distributive law.

Example 1: Given the binomial $3x + 6$, 3 is a common factor because 3 is a factor of $3x$, and 3 is also a factor of 6. Applying the distributive law, we could write $3x + 6$ as $3(x + 2)$.

You may always check this by multiplying: $3(x + 2) = 3(x) + 3(2) = 3x + 6$.

When you look for a common factor, you should find the largest, or greatest common factor. We can see that 3 is a common factor for $6x + 24$, because 3 is a factor of both 6 and 24. However, there is a larger common factor. What is it?

Example 2: Given $6x^2 + 14x - 30$, you can see that 2 is a common factor. Is 2 the greatest common factor? Yes, because no larger number is a factor of every term. If we divide each term by 2, we obtain. So, we may rewrite the trinomial in factored form as: $2(3x^2 + 7x - 15)$.

Check this now by multiplying.

If the common factor involves a variable, you may still use the same method of dividing by the common factor.

Example 3: Factor $4x^3 - 8x^2 + 28x$.

Solution: The common factor is $4x$. Dividing each term by $4x$ leads us to the factored form $4x(x^2 - 2x + 7)$.

EXERCISES

Factor the following and check by multiplying.

1. $9x - 27$

2. $18x - 6$

3. $8x^2 + 40x + 16$

4. $3x^4 + 12x^3 - 27x^2$

5. $6x^5 + 2x^4 + -24x^3$

Factoring: Trinomials

With patience, it is possible to factor any trinomial by trial and error, which is the reverse of FOIL.

FACTORING TRINOMIALS BY TRIAL AND ERROR

1. Remove the greatest common factor
2. Try combinations of factors for the first and last terms in two binomials
3. Check the outer and inner products to match middle term of the original trinomial.
4. If the check fails repeat steps 2 and 3.

Example 1: Factor $6x^2 - 7x - 3$.

Solution:

Step 1 There is no common factor, so go to step 2.

Step 2 You could factor the first term as $6x(x)$ or as $2x(3x)$. The last term has factors of 3 and 1, disregarding signs. Suppose we try $(2x + 1)(3x - 3)$.

Step 3 The outer product is $-6x$. The inner product is $3x$. The sum is $-3x$. The check fails.

Step 4 Suppose we try $(2x - 3)(3x + 1)$. The outer product is $2x$. The inner product is $-9x$. The sum is $-7x$. It checks.

EXERCISES

Factor completely.

1. $x^2 + 7x + 12$

2. $6x^2 - 13x + 6$

3. $3x^2 + 7x - 6$

4. $6x^2 + 21x + 18$

5. $9x^2 - 6x + 1$

6. $2x^2 + 6x - 20$

7. $15x^2 + 2x - 1$

8. $4x^3 + 10x^2 + 4x$

Solving Equations by Factoring

Many quadratic and higher-order polynomial equations can be solved by using factoring and the zero product rule.

The process is as follows.

SOLVING AN EQUATION BY FACTORING

1. Use the addition principle to remove all terms from one side of the equation. This results in the equation being set equal to zero.
2. Combine like terms and then factor.
3. Use the zero product rule to set each factor containing a variable equal to zero and then solve the equations.
4. Check your solutions in the original equation.

Example 1: Solve the equation $x(x + 5) = 0$.

Solution: This equation already satisfies the first two steps in our process, so we simply start at step 3.

$$x = 0 \qquad x + 5 = 0$$
$$x = -5$$

Thus we have two solutions $x = 0$ and $x = -5$. The check is left to the reader.

Example 2: Solve the equation $6x^2 = 16x$.

Solution: Setting the equation equal to zero, $6x^2 = 16x = 0$. Since there are no like terms, factor the binomial.

$$2x(3x - 8) = 0$$

Using the zero product rule

$$\begin{aligned} 2x &= 0 \quad \text{or} \quad 3x - 8 = 0 \\ x &= 0 \quad \text{or} \quad 3x = 8 \\ & \qquad\qquad x = \tfrac{8}{3} \end{aligned}$$

The two potential solutions are $x = 0$ and $x = 8/3$. The check is left to the reader.

Example 3: Solve $3x^2 - 2 = -x$.

Solution: Setting the equation equal to zero, $3x^2 + x - 2 = 0$. Since there are no like terms, factor the trinomial.

$$(3x - 2)(x + 1) = 0.$$

Using the zero product rule

$$\begin{aligned} 3x - 2 = 0 &\quad \text{or} \quad x + 1 = 0 \\ 3x = 2 &\quad \text{or} \quad x = -1 \\ x = \tfrac{2}{3} & \end{aligned}$$

The two potential solutions are $x = \frac{2}{3}$ and $x = -1$. The check is left to the reader.

Example 4: Solve $3x^3 - 8x^2 = 3x$.

Solution: Setting the equation equal to zero, $3x^3 - 8x^2 - 3x = 0$. Since there are no like terms, factor the trinomial.

$$x(3x^2 - 8x - 3) = 0$$
$$x(3x + 1)(x - 9) = 0$$

Using the zero product rule,

$$x = 0 \quad \text{or} \quad 3x + 1 = 0 \quad \text{or} \quad x - 9 = 0$$
$$3x = -1 \quad \text{or} \quad x = 9$$
$$x = -\tfrac{1}{3}$$

The three potential solutions are $x = 0$, $x = -\frac{1}{3}$, and $x = 9$. The check is left to the reader.

EXERCISES

Solve each of the following equations.

1. $x(x + 7) = 0$

2. $3(x - 5)(2x + 1) = 0$

3. $12x = x^2$

4. $x^2 + 5x = 0$

5. $x^2 - 2x - 63 = 0$

6. $3x^2 - 9x - 30 = 0$

7. $-7x + 6x^2 = 10$

8. $3y^2 = 2 - y$

9. $-28x^2 + 15x - 2 = 0$

10. $4x^2 - 25 = 0$

11. $(x + 4)^2 - 16 = 0$

12. $(x + 1)^2 - 3x = 7$

13. $2(x + 2)(x - 2) = (x - 2)(x + 3) - 2$

14. $18x^3 = 15x^2 + 12x$

Solving Quadratic Equations by Completing the Square

The square root property can be used to solve equations of the form $x^2 = a$.

> **SQUARE ROOT PROPERTY**
>
> If $x^2 = a$, where a is a real number then $x = \pm \sqrt{a}$.

Example 1: Solve the equation $(x + 3)^2 = 9$.

Solution: This equation fits the form of the hypothesis of the square root property, so

$$x + 3 = \pm 3.$$

You now have two equations to solve $x + 3 = 3$ and $x + 3 = -3$. The solutions are $x = 0, -6$. Both of these values make the original statement true. Hence, both are solutions.

This example illustrates the goal of an algebraic technique of solving quadratic equation known as *completing the square.* The strategy is to rewrite the quadratic equation $ax^2 + bx + c = 0, a \neq 0$ in the form $(x + h)^2 = k$ and solve as in Example 1. This requires an algebraic process know as completing the square.

Consider the binomial $x^2 + 6x$. What term must be added to the binomial to produce a binomial that is a perfect square. The answer is one half the coefficient of the linear term squared. In this case, one half of 6 is 3. $3^2 = 9$. And

$$x^2 + 6x + 9 = (x + 3)^2$$

This process can be helpful in solving quadratic equations as follows.

> **SOLVING A QUADRATIC EQUATION BY COMPLETING THE SQUARE**
>
> 1. Use the multiplication principle to make the coefficient of x^2 equal to 1.
> 2. Rewrite the equation with the constant term isolated on one side.
> 3. Use the addition principle to add one half the coefficient of the linear term to both sides of the equation.
> 4. Replace the trinomial with its factored form.
> 5. Apply the square root property.
> 6. Solve the resulting linear equations.
> 7. Check your solutions in the original equation.

Example 2: Solve $x^2 - 4x - 5 = 0$ by the completing the square method.

Since the coefficient of x^2 is one, step 1 is not necessary.

Step 2 Adding 5 from both sides to isolate the constant term yields

$$x^2 - 4x = 5$$

Step 3 The value need to complete the square is $\left(\frac{1}{2} \cdot (-4)\right)^2 = (-2^2 = 4$. Using the addition principle to add this to both sides produces

$$x^2 - 4x + 4 = 5 + 4$$
$$x^2 - 4x + 4 = 9.$$

Step 4 Replacing the trinomial with its perfect square form,

$$(x - 2)^2 = 9.$$

Steps 5 and 6 Applying the square root principle and solving,

$$x - 2 = \pm 3$$
$$x = 2 \pm 3$$
$$x = -1, 5.$$

The checking of the solutions is left to the reader.

Example 3: Solve $6x + 6 = -x^2$ by the completing the square method.

Step 1 Multiply each term by -1 to make the coefficient of x^2 equal to one.

$$-6x - 6 = x^2$$

Step 2 Using the addition principle to isolate the constant term.

$$-6 = x^2 + 6x$$

Step 3 The value necessary to complete the square is $\left(\frac{1}{2} \cdot 6\right)^2 = 9$. Completing the square yields

$$-6 + 9 = x^2 + 6x + 9.$$

Step 4 Factoring and simplifying.

$$3 = (x + 3)^2$$

Steps 5 and 6 Taking the square root of both sides and solving.

$$\pm\sqrt{3} = x + 3$$
$$x = -3 \pm \sqrt{3}$$

The check is left to the reader. Note the solutions in this case are real, but not rational.

EXERCISES

Solve the following quadratic equations using the completing the square method.

1. $x^2 - 6x + 8 = 0$

2. $x^2 - 9x + 14 = 0$

3. $-4x = -x^2 + 12$

4. $2x^2 + 2x - 24 = 0$

5. $3x^2 + 2x = 1$

6. $-\frac{1}{2}x^2 - x + \frac{3}{2} = 0$

7. $10x^2 + 6x = 5$

8. $15x^2 - 10x - 3 = 0$

Derivation of the Quadratic Formula

The quadratic formula results from applying the completing the square method to the general quadratic equation $ax^2 + bx + c = 0$, where $a > 0$.

Step 1: Make the coefficient of x^2 equal 1, by multiplying both sides of the equation by $\frac{1}{a}$.

$$x^2 + \frac{b}{a}x + \frac{c}{a} = 0$$

Step 2 Use the addition principle to isolate the constant term on one side of the equals sign.

$$x^2 + \frac{b}{a} = -\frac{c}{a}$$

Step 3 Complete the square of the binomial. The coefficient of the linear term is $\frac{b}{a}$. The term needed to complete the square is $\left(\frac{1}{2} \cdot \frac{b}{a}\right)^2 = \frac{b^2}{4a^2}$. Using the addition principle to add this term to both sides yields

$$x^2 + \frac{b}{a}x + \frac{b^2}{4a^2} = \frac{b^2}{4a^2} - \frac{c}{a}.$$

Rewriting the right-hand side as a single fraction

$$x^2 + \frac{b}{a}x + \frac{b^2}{4a^2} = \frac{b^2 - 4ac}{4a^2}.$$

Step 4 Express the left-hand side in factored form

$$\left(x + \frac{b}{2a}\right)^2 = \frac{b^2 - 4ac}{4a^2}.$$

Step 5 Apply the square root property to the resulting equation

$$x + \frac{b}{a} = \pm\frac{\sqrt{b^2 - 4ac}}{2a}.$$

Step 6 Solve for x.

$$x + -\frac{b}{2a} \pm \frac{\sqrt{b^2 - 4ac}}{2a}$$

or

$$x = \frac{-b \pm \sqrt{b^2 - 4ac}}{2a}$$

This equation can be used to solve any quadratic equation in standard form $ax^2 + bx + c = 0 \quad a \neq 0$, and is called the **quadratic formula.**

Complex Numbers

The study of mathematics involves the study of different sets of numbers. Three sets of numbers that arise in this course are *rational numbers*, *real numbers*, and *complex numbers*.

The **rational numbers** are all numbers that can be written in the form $\frac{a}{b}$, where a and b are integers and $b \neq 0$. This set of numbers includes 3, 5, -17, 0.45, and 76.9.

The **irrational numbers** are all numbers that are not rational. This set includes π, $\sqrt{2}$, $\sqrt[3]{5}$, and $\frac{-3\sqrt{5}}{7}$.

The **real numbers** consist of all rational and all irrational numbers.

An example of a number that is not real is $\sqrt{-3}$. The number $\sqrt{3}$ is not real because there is no real number that when squared will equal a negative number. This number does have some interest because it is a solution to the quadratic equation $x^2 + 3 = 0$. To continue the discussion of the square root of a negative number, a new number is defined.

> The number i is a number such that
>
> $$i = \sqrt{-1} \quad \text{and} \quad i^2 = -1$$
>
> This number i is often called the **imaginary unit.**

This number i is used to define the square root of any number.

> For any real number b, where $b > 0$
>
> $$\sqrt{-b} = i\sqrt{b}$$

Note: Whenever, you are working with the square root of a negative number, express the number as a product of i before proceeding any further.

Example 1: Express $\sqrt{-9}$ and $\sqrt{-7}$ in terms of i.

Solution: $\sqrt{-9} = i\sqrt{9} = 3i$

$\sqrt{-7} = i\sqrt{7}$

If we apply the properties of exponents to i, we find the following:

$$i = i \qquad i^5 = i^4 \cdot i = 1 \cdot i = i$$

$$i^2 = -1 \qquad i^6 = i^4 \cdot i^2 = 1 \cdot (-1) = -1$$

$$i^3 = i^2 \cdot i = -1 \cdot i = -1 \qquad i^7 = i^4 \cdot i^3 = 1 \cdot (-i) = -i$$

$$i^4 = i^2 \cdot i^2 = (-1)(-1) = 1 \qquad i^8 = i^4 \cdot i^4 = 1 \cdot 1 = 1$$

This shows that the powers of i go through a cycle i, -1, $-i$, and 1 every four consecutive powers of i.

Example 2: Simplify i^{87}.

Solution: Since $87 = 4 \cdot 21 + 3$,

$$i^{87} = i^{4 \cdot 21 + 3} = (i^4)^{21} \cdot i^3 = 1 \cdot (-i) = -i.$$

The complex numbers are all numbers that can be written in the form $a + bi$ where a and b are real numbers and $i^2 = -1$. For the complex number $a + bi$, a is called the real part and bi is called the imaginary part.

Two complex numbers $a + bi$ and $c + di$ are equal if and only if $a = c$ and $b = d$.

ADDING OR SUBTRACTING COMPLEX NUMBERS

1. Combine the real parts.
2. Combine the imaginary parts.
3. Express the results in the form $a + bi$

Example 3: Perform the indicated operations and simplify.

a. $(2 + 3i) + (-4 - 7i)$ **b.** $(-4 - 4i) - (3 - 6i)$

Solution: **a.** Add the real parts $2 + (-4) = -2$.

Add the imaginary parts $3i + (7i) = -4i$.

The sum is $-7 + 2i$.

b. Subtract the real parts $-4 - 3 = -7$.

Subtract the imaginary parts $-4i - (-6i) = -4i + 6i = 21$.

The difference is $-7 + 21$.

MULTIPLYING COMPLEX NUMBERS

1. Multiply as if the numbers were polynomials.
2. Simplify using the properties of i.
3. Combine like terms.

Example 4: Multiply $(3 - 5i)(-3 + i)$

Solution: $-9 + 3i + 15i - 5i^2$

$-9 + 28i - 5(-1) = -4 + 28i$

The conjugate of a complex number $a + bi$ is the complex number $a - bi$.

DIVIDING COMPLEX NUMBERS

1. Express the division as a fraction.
2. Multiply the fraction by 1 in the form of the conjugate of the denominator over itself.
3. Multiply and simplify the numerator and the denominator.
4. Write the quotient in the form $a + bi$.

Example 5: Perform the division indicated and simplify

$$(1 - \sqrt{-9}) \div (3 + \sqrt{-4}).$$

Solution: Write as a fraction and in $a + bi$ form.

$$\frac{1 - 3i}{3 + 2i} = \frac{(1 - 3i)}{(3 + 2i)} \cdot \frac{(3 - 2i)}{(3 - 2i)} = \frac{3 - 2i - 9i + 6i^2}{9 - 4i^2}$$

$$= \frac{3 - 11i - 6}{9 + 4} = \frac{-3 - 11i}{13} = -\frac{3}{13} - \frac{11}{13}i$$

EXERCISES

Express the following in the form a + bi.

1. $4 + \sqrt{-9}$

2. $3 + \sqrt{-72}$

Perform the indicated operations and simplify.

3. $12 + 6i + (4 - 3i)$

4. $\left(\frac{3}{5} + \sqrt{-4}\right) - \left(\frac{2}{3} - \sqrt{-9}\right)$

5. $(3 + 4i) \cdot (-2 - i)$

6. $\left(\frac{2}{3} - 2i\right) \cdot \left(-\frac{3}{4} + 3i\right)$

7. $\dfrac{3 - 4i}{3 + 4i}$

8. $(5 - 3i) \div (3 + 2i)$

Rational Expressions

You may need to practice skills relating to rational functions to enhance your understanding of these functions

SIMPLIFYING RATIONAL EXPRESSIONS

1. Factor the numerator and the denominator.
2. Divide the numerator and the denominator by the common factors.

Example 1: Simplify $\dfrac{x^2 - 10x + 24}{x^2 - 5x + 4}$.

Solution:

Step 1 Factor the numerator and the denominator.

$$\frac{x^2 - 10x + 24}{x^2 - 5x + 4} = \frac{(x - 4)(x - 6)}{(x - 1)(x - 4)}$$

Step 2 Divide the numerator and denominator by the common factor.

$$\frac{\dfrac{(x - 4)(x - 6)}{(x - 4)}}{\dfrac{(x - 1)(x - 4)}{(x - 4)}} = \frac{x - 6}{x - 1}.$$

MULTIPLYING OR DIVIDING RATIONAL EXPRESSIONS

1. Factor the numerator and denominator of each fraction completely.
2. Divide out the common factors (cancel).
3. Multiply remaining factors.
4. In division proceed as above after inverting the divisor (the fraction after the division sign).

Example 2: Divide and simplify $\dfrac{x^2 + 3x - 10}{2x} \div \dfrac{x^2 - 5x + 6}{x^2 - 3x}$.

Solution:

Step 1 Rewrite as multiplication.

$$\frac{x^2 + 3x - 10}{2x} \div \frac{x^2 - 5x + 6}{x^2 - 3x} = \frac{x^2 + 3x - 10}{2x} \cdot \frac{x^2 - 3x}{x^2 - 5x + 6}$$

Step 2 Factor each fraction completely.

$$\frac{x^2 + 3x - 10}{2x} \cdot \frac{x^2 - 3x}{x^2 - 5x + 6} = \frac{(x + 5)(x - 2)}{2 \cdot x} \cdot \frac{x \cdot (x - 3)}{(x - 2)(x - 3)}$$

Step 3 Cancel common factors.

$$\frac{(x + 5)(x - 2)}{2 \cdot x} \cdot \frac{x \cdot (x - 3)}{(x - 2)(x - 3)} = \frac{(x + 5)}{2} \cdot \frac{1}{(x - 2)}$$

Step 4 Multiply the remaining fractions.

$$\frac{(x+5)}{2} \cdot \frac{1}{(x-2)} = \frac{x+5}{2x-4}$$

ADDING OR SUBTRACTING RATIONAL EXPRESSIONS

1. Find the LCD (least common denominator.).
2. Build each fraction to have the LCD.
3. Add or subtract numerators.
4. Place the numerator over the LCD; and simplify if necessary.

Example 3: Add and simplify $\frac{x}{x+1} + \frac{3}{(x+1)^2}$.

Solution:

Step 1 Since the denominators are already factored, it is clear that the LCD is $(x+1)^2$.

Step 2 Build each fraction to have the LCD.

$$\frac{x}{x+1} + \frac{3}{(x+1)^2} = \frac{x(x+1)}{(x+1)(x+1)} + \frac{3}{(x+1)^2} = \frac{x^2+x}{(x+1)^2} = \frac{3}{(x+1)^2}$$

Step 3 Add or subtract the numerators.

$$\frac{x^2+x}{(x+1)^2} + \frac{3}{(x+1)^2} = \frac{x^2+x+3}{(x+1)^2}$$

Step 4 Since the numerator can't be factored we are done.

SOLVING RATIONAL EQUATIONS

1. Find the LCD of all fractions in the equation.
2. Multiply both sides of the equation by $\frac{\text{LCD}}{1}$ (clear all denominators).
3. Solve the resulting equation.
4. Check for extraneous roots.

Example 4: Solve $3 - \frac{4}{x} = \frac{5}{2}$

Solution:

Step 1 The LCD is $2x$.

Step 2 Multiply both sides of the equation by $\frac{2x}{1}$.

$\frac{2x}{1}\left(3 - \frac{4}{x}\right) = \frac{2x}{1}\left(\frac{5}{2}\right)$ this is equivalent to $6x - \frac{8x}{x} = \frac{10x}{2}$ or $6x - 8 = 5x$.

Step 3 Solving the resulting equation

$$6x - 6x - 8 = 5x - 6x \quad \text{or} \quad -8 = -x \quad \text{so} \quad x = 8.$$

Step 4 The check is left to the reader.

EXERCISES

Simplify the following.

1. $\dfrac{3x^2 - 6x}{x^2 + x - 6}$

2. $\dfrac{2x^3 + 4x^2 - 4x}{2x + 4}$

3. $\dfrac{x^2 + 2x - 15}{3 - x}$

Perform the indicated operations and simplify.

4. $\dfrac{4x^2y}{5xz} \cdot \dfrac{15x^6}{8xy^2}$

5. $\dfrac{x^2 + 2x - 15}{3x + 15} \cdot \dfrac{x - 3}{3}$

6. $\dfrac{3}{x^2} + \dfrac{5}{6x}$

7. $\dfrac{2}{x - 5} - \dfrac{3}{x + 3}$

8. $\dfrac{3}{x - 3} + \dfrac{x - 2}{x^2 - 9}$

9. $\dfrac{5}{x^2 - x - 2} - \dfrac{2}{x^2 + 4x + 3}$

10. $\dfrac{x - 3}{x^2 - 3x + 2} - \dfrac{x + 1}{x^2 - 4}$

Solve the following equations.

11. $\dfrac{x}{3} + \dfrac{2x}{7} = 10$

12. $\dfrac{-2}{x} + \dfrac{8}{3} = \dfrac{2}{x}$

13. $\dfrac{x - 2}{x - 4} = \dfrac{x}{x - 1}$

14. $\dfrac{1}{x - 4} + x = \dfrac{-3}{x - 4}$

15. Solve $\dfrac{1}{R_1} + \dfrac{1}{R_2} = \dfrac{1}{R}$ for R.

Complex Fractions

Complex fractions are fractions with a fractional expression in the numerator, the denominator, or both. Examples include

$$\frac{\frac{2}{5}+\frac{1}{3}}{7}, \quad \frac{x+3}{\frac{x}{x+1}-2}, \quad \frac{x+\frac{1}{x}-3}{x^3-x-\frac{2}{x^2}}$$

There are two methods commonly used to simplify complex fractions. The first is to express the numerator and denominator as single fractions then divide.

SIMPLIFYING A COMPLEX FRACTION BY SIMPLIFYING THE NUMERATOR AND DENOMINATOR

1. Express the numerator as a single fraction.
2. Express the denominator as a single fraction.
3. Divide the numerator by the denominator.
4. Simplify, if possible.

Example 1: Simplify $\dfrac{1-\frac{7}{16}}{3-\frac{2}{5}}$.

Solution:

Step 1 Simplify the numerator. $1-\dfrac{7}{16}=\dfrac{16}{16}-\dfrac{7}{16}=\dfrac{9}{16}$.

Step 2 Simplify the denominator. $3-\dfrac{2}{5}=\dfrac{3}{1}-\dfrac{2}{5}=\dfrac{15}{5}-\dfrac{2}{5}=\dfrac{13}{5}$.

Step 3 Divide the numerator by the denominator. $\dfrac{9}{16}\div\dfrac{13}{5}=\dfrac{9}{16}\cdot\dfrac{5}{13}=\dfrac{45}{208}$.

Step 4 Since the fraction cannot be simplified, simplified result is $\dfrac{45}{208}$.

Example 2: Simplify $\dfrac{\frac{1}{x}+\frac{2}{x^2}}{2+\frac{1}{x^2}}$.

Solution:

Step 1 Simplify the numerator. $\dfrac{1}{x}+\dfrac{2}{x^2}=\dfrac{x}{x^2}+\dfrac{2}{x^2}=\dfrac{x+2}{x^2}$

Step 2 Simplify the denominator. $2+\dfrac{1}{x^2}=\dfrac{2}{1}+\dfrac{1}{x^2}=\dfrac{2x^2}{x^2}+\dfrac{1}{x^2}=\dfrac{2x^2+1}{x^2}$

Step 3 Divide the numerator by the denominator.

$$\frac{x+2}{x^2} \div \frac{2x^2+1}{x^2} = \frac{x+2}{x^2} \cdot \frac{x^2}{2x^2+1} = \frac{x+2}{2x^2+1}$$

Step 4 The result in step 3 is simplified.

The second method of simplifying a complex fraction is to multiply the numerator and denominator by the LCD of the entire fraction.

SIMPLIFYING A COMPLEX FRACTION BY MULTIPLYING BY THE LCD

Step 1 Determine the LCD of the numerator fractions and denominator fractions.

Step 2 Multiply the numerator and denominator by 1 in the form $\frac{LCD}{LCD}$.

Step 3 Simplify, if possible.

Example 3: Simplify $\dfrac{1-\frac{7}{16}}{3-\frac{2}{5}}$.

Solution:

Step 1 The only denominators are 16 and 5. Since there are no common factors the LCD is 80.

Step 2 $$\frac{80\left(1-\frac{7}{16}\right)}{80\left(3-\frac{2}{5}\right)} = \frac{80-\frac{80\cdot 7}{16}}{240-\frac{80\cdot 2}{5}} = \frac{80-5\cdot 7}{240-16\cdot 2} = \frac{80-35}{240-32} = \frac{45}{208}.$$

Step 3 Since the fraction is simplified, $\frac{45}{208}$ is the desired result.

Example 4: Simplify $\dfrac{\frac{3}{n-5}-2}{1-\frac{4}{n-5}}$.

Step 1 The LCD is $n-5$.

Step 2

$$\frac{(n-5)\cdot\left(\frac{3}{n-5}-2\right)}{(n-5)\cdot\left(1-\frac{4}{n-5}\right)} = \frac{\frac{3(n-5)}{n-5}-2(n-5)}{(n-5)-\frac{4(n-5)}{n-5}} = \frac{3-2n+10}{n-5-4} = \frac{-2n+13}{n-9}$$

Step 3 Since the numerator and denominator have no common factors the simplified result is $\dfrac{-2n+13}{n-9}$.

EXERCISES

Simplify the following complex fractions.

1. $\dfrac{\frac{1}{2} - \frac{1}{4}}{\frac{5}{8} + \frac{3}{4}}$

2. $\dfrac{\frac{5}{6y}}{\frac{10}{3xy}}$

3. $\dfrac{\dfrac{8x^2y}{3z^3}}{\dfrac{4xy}{9z^5}}$

4. $\dfrac{3 - \frac{1}{x}}{1 - \frac{1}{x}}$

5. $\dfrac{\dfrac{x^2}{y} - y}{\dfrac{y^2}{x} - x}$

6. $\dfrac{4 + \dfrac{6}{n + 1}}{7 - \dfrac{4}{n + 1}}$

7. $\dfrac{\dfrac{1}{y - 2} + \dfrac{3}{x}}{\dfrac{5}{x} - \dfrac{4}{xy - 2x}}$

8. $\dfrac{\dfrac{x}{x + 1} - 1}{\dfrac{x + 1}{x - 1}}$

9. $\dfrac{1 + \dfrac{x}{x + 1}}{\dfrac{2x + 1}{x - 1}}$

10. $\dfrac{\dfrac{x + 1}{x - 1} + \dfrac{x - 1}{x + 1}}{\dfrac{x + 1}{x - 1} - \dfrac{x - 1}{x + 1}}$

Radicals and Fractional Exponents

You may need to practice skills relating to radical functions to enhance your understanding of these functions.

TRANSLATING RADICAL EXPRESSIONS TO EXPRESSIONS USING RATIONAL EXPONENTS

1. The power of the expression becomes the numerator of the exponent.
2. The index (root) becomes the denominator of the exponent.

For example, $\sqrt[3]{x^2} = x^{\frac{2}{3}}$. In reverse, $a^{\frac{5}{4}} = \sqrt[4]{a^5}$.

When a 7 is written without an index, the index is assumed to be 2.

Fractional Exponents also obey the laws of exponents as outlined on page A-1

1. $a^n a^m = a^{n+m}$
2. $\dfrac{a^n}{a^m} = a^{n-m}$
3. $(a^n)^m = a^{nm}$
4. $(ab)^n = a^n b^n$
5. $a^0 = 1$
6. $a^{-n} = \dfrac{1}{a^n}$

In Examples 1–6, the following steps are followed:

1. Write each expression using rational exponents.
2. Apply the appropriate property of exponents.
3. Write the expression using radical notation.

Example 1: $\sqrt[3]{x^2} \cdot \sqrt[4]{x} = x^{\frac{2}{3}} \cdot x^{\frac{1}{4}} = x^{\left(\frac{2}{3}+\frac{1}{4}\right)} = x^{\left(\frac{8}{12}+\frac{3}{12}\right)} = x^{\frac{11}{12}} = \sqrt[12]{x^{11}}$

Example 2: $\dfrac{\sqrt[5]{x^4}}{\sqrt[10]{x^7}} = \dfrac{x^{\frac{4}{5}}}{x^{\frac{7}{10}}} = x^{\frac{4}{5}-\frac{7}{10}} = x^{\frac{8}{10}-\frac{7}{10}} = x^{\frac{1}{10}} = \sqrt[10]{x}$

Example 3: $\left(\sqrt[3]{\sqrt{x^5}}\right) = \left(x^{\frac{5}{2}}\right)^{\frac{1}{3}} = x^{\frac{5}{2}\cdot\frac{1}{3}} = x^{\frac{5}{6}} = \sqrt[6]{x^5}$

Example 4: $\sqrt[3]{ab^2} = \left(ab^2\right)^{\frac{1}{3}} = a^{\frac{1}{3}} \cdot b^{\frac{2}{3}} = \sqrt[3]{a} \cdot \sqrt[3]{b^2}$

Example 5: $\left(\sqrt[4]{x}\right)^0 = \left(x^{\frac{1}{4}}\right)^0 = x^0 = 1$

Example 6: $x^{\frac{-2}{3}} = \dfrac{1}{x^{\frac{2}{3}}} = \dfrac{1}{\sqrt[3]{x^2}}$

EXERCISES

Rewrite the following using exponents.

1. a. $\sqrt[5]{x^4}$ **b.** $\sqrt[6]{x^3}$

c. $\sqrt[3]{(x+y)^2}$ **d.** $\sqrt[3]{(a-b)^3}$

Rewrite these expressions using a radical.

2. a. $9x^{\frac{3}{2}}$ **b.** $(9x)^{\frac{3}{2}}$

c. $(4x^2 - 9y^2)^{\frac{1}{2}}$ **d.** $(x-y)^{\frac{4}{5}}$

Simplify and express your results in radical form, if appropriate.

3. a. $\sqrt{x^{12}}$ **b.** $\sqrt[5]{6.87^5}$

c. $\sqrt{\sqrt{a^2b}}$ **d.** $\left(\sqrt[3]{a^4bc^3}\right)^{30}$

e. $x^{\frac{1}{4}} \cdot x^{\frac{3}{8}}$ **f.** $\dfrac{x^{\frac{1}{2}}}{x^{\frac{1}{3}}}$

g. $\left(x^{\frac{-2}{5}}\right)^{\frac{1}{4}}$ **h.** $\left(2x^{\frac{1}{3}}\right)^0$

Solving Equations Involving Radicals

Equations in which at least one side contains a radical with a variable in the radicand are called *radical equations.* A key to solving radical equations is a special case of the multiplication principle called the *property of nth powers.*

PROPERTY OF *N*TH POWERS

If the equation $a = b$ is true, and n is any positive integer, then $a^n = b^n$ is also true.

This implies that if x is a solution of $f(x) = g(x)$, then x is also a solution of $\left(f(x)\right)^n = \left(g(x)\right)^n$. The converse, however, is not necessarily true. If x is a solution of $\left(f(x)\right)^n = \left(g(x)\right)^n$, then x may or may not be a solution of $f(x) = g(x)$.

SOLVING RADICAL EQUATIONS

1. Isolate one radical term on one side of the equation.
2. Raise each side of the equation to the power that matches the index of the radical.
3. Solve the resulting equation. If a radical remains, repeat steps 1 and 2.
4. Check all solutions in the original equation.

Example 1: Solve $\sqrt{3x - 1} - 5 = 0$.

Solution:

Step 1 Use the addition principle to isolate the radical.

$$\sqrt{3x - 1} = 5$$

Step 2 Square both sides.

$$\left(\sqrt{3x - 1}\right)^2 = 5^2$$
$$3x - 1 = 25$$

Step 3 Solve the resulting equation.

$$3x = 26$$
$$x = \tfrac{26}{3}$$

Step 4 Check the solution.

$$\sqrt{3 \cdot \tfrac{26}{3} - 1} - 5 = \sqrt{26 - 1} - 5 = \sqrt{25} - 5 = 0$$

Example 2: Solve $\sqrt{x^2 - 8x} = 3$.

Solution:

Step 1 is not necessary since the radical is already necessary.

Step 2 Square both sides.

$$\left(\sqrt{x^2 - 8x}\right)^2 = 3^2$$
$$x^2 - 8x = 9$$

Step 3 Solve the resulting equation.

$$x^2 - 8x - 9 = 0$$
$$(x - 9)(x + 1) = 0$$
$$x - 9 = 0 \quad \text{or} \quad x + 1 = 0$$
$$x = 9 \quad \text{or} \quad x = -1$$

Step 4 Checking the solutions is left to the reader.

Example 3: Solve $\sqrt{x - 1} = x - 3$

Solution:

Step 1 can be skipped since the radical is isolated.

Step 2 Square both sides.

$$\left(\sqrt{x - 1}\right)^2 = (x - 3)^2$$
$$x - 1 = x^2 - 6x + 9$$

Step 3 Solve the resulting equation.

$$0 = x^2 - 7x + 10$$
$$0 = (x - 2)(x - 5)$$
$$x - 2 = 0 \quad \text{or} \quad x - 5 = 0$$
$$x = 2 \quad \text{or} \quad x = 5$$

Step 4 Note that $x = 2$ does not check. With $x = 1$, the left-hand side of the original equation simplifies to $\sqrt{2 - 1} = \sqrt{1} = 1$. With $x = 1$, the right-hand side of the original simplifies to $2 - 3 = -1$. Since $-1 \neq 1$, $x = 2$ is not a solution. $x = 2$ is known as an extraneous solution. The check of $x = 5$ is left to the student.

Example 4: Solve $\sqrt{5x + 1} - 1 = \sqrt{3x}$.

Solution: Since one of the two radicals is isolated, skip step 1.

Step 2 Square both sides.

$$\left(\sqrt{5x + 1} - 1\right)^2 = \left(\sqrt{3x}\right)^2$$
$$5x + 1 - 2\sqrt{5x + 1} + 1 = 3x$$
$$2x + 2 = 2\sqrt{5x + 1}$$

Since there is still a radical in the equation so repeat steps 1 and 2.

Isolate the radical.

$$x + 1 = \sqrt{5x + 1}$$

Square both sides.

$$(x + 1)^2 = \left(\sqrt{5x + 1}\right)^2$$
$$x^2 + 2x + 1 = 5x + 1$$

Step 3 Solve the resulting equation.

$$x^2 - 3x = 0$$
$$x(x - 3) = 0$$
$$x = 0 \quad \text{or} \quad x - 3 = 0$$
$$x = 3$$

Step 4 Check the solutions. This is left to the reader.

EXERCISES

Solve each of the following algebraically.

1. $\sqrt{5x + 1} - 10 = 0$

2. $2\sqrt{3y} = \sqrt{5y = 7}$

3. $\sqrt{2x^2 + 4x = 4}$

4. $\sqrt{x^2 + 3} - 2 = 0$

5. $x\sqrt{2} = \sqrt{6 - 4x}$

6. $\sqrt{3x + 10} - 3x = 4$

7. $1 + \sqrt{5x + 9} = x$

8. $3 - \sqrt{x + 4} = \sqrt{x + 7}$

APPENDIX B

Trigonemetry

Note: Answers to all exercises in Appendix B can be found in the *Instructor's Resource Guide* supplement.

Radian Measure of Angles

In *degrees*, a protractor measures angles from 0 to 180. In *radians*, the angles range in value from 0 to π:

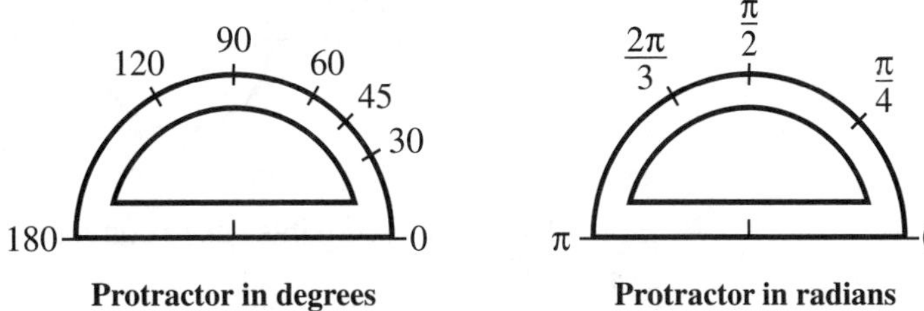

Protractor in degrees **Protractor in radians**

The fundamental idea given above is that the measure of a straight angle can be taken to be either 180 degrees or π radians.

$$180° \equiv \pi \text{ radians} \qquad \textbf{(1)}$$

All other angles are done proportionately. The following table gives some examples.

ANGLE (in degrees)	REASONING	CALCULATIONS	ANGLE (in radians)
90	90 is *one half* of 180	$\frac{1}{2} \cdot \pi$	$\frac{\pi}{2}$
60	60 is *one third* of 180	$\frac{1}{3} \cdot \pi$	$\frac{\pi}{3}$
45	45 is *one fourth* of 180	$\frac{1}{4} \cdot \pi$	$\frac{\pi}{4}$
30	30 is *one sixth* of 180	$\frac{1}{6} \cdot \pi$	$\frac{\pi}{6}$
120	120 is *two thirds* of 180	$\frac{2}{3} \cdot \pi$	$\frac{2\pi}{3}$
1	1 is *one one hundred eightieth* of 180	$\frac{1}{180} \cdot \pi$	$\frac{\pi}{180}$

The last line of the table is useful for converting *any* angle from degrees to radians:

$$1° \equiv \pi/180 \text{ radians} \qquad \textbf{(2)}$$

Examples of the use of formula (2).

ANGLE (in degrees)	REASONING	CALCULATIONS	ANGLE (in radians)
12	12 is *twelve* times 1	$12 \cdot \frac{\pi}{180}$	$\frac{\pi}{15}$
7	7 is *seven* times 1	$7 \cdot \frac{\pi}{180}$	$\frac{7\pi}{180}$
345	345 is *345* times 1	$345 \cdot \frac{\pi}{180}$	$\frac{85\pi}{34}$

The angle to wrap around a *full circle* is *twice* a straight angle of 180°, so it is 360° or 2π radians. You can also have angles that wrap around a circle more than once! (Think of a fishing reel or spool of wire, with the string or wire wrapped around many times.)

Twice around the circle
is 4π radians

π rad
or 180°

0 2π

4π

Equivalence (1) also enables us to convert angles from radians to degrees. Study these examples:

ANGLE (in radians)	REASONING	CALCULATIONS	ANGLE (in degrees)
$\frac{2\pi}{3}$	*Two thirds* of π	$\frac{2}{3} \cdot 180$	120
7π	*Seven* times π	$7 \cdot 180$	1260
1	From (1), $\pi \equiv 180°$ Divide both sides of this equivalence by π.	$345 \cdot \frac{\pi}{180}$	$\frac{85\pi}{34}$

The last line of the preceding table gives us an equivalence useful in converting from radians to degrees:

$$1 \text{ radian} \equiv \frac{180°}{\pi} \qquad \textbf{(3)}$$

Since $\pi \approx 3.14$, equivalence (3) shows that 1 radian $\approx 57.3°$. This is worth seeing on a protractor:

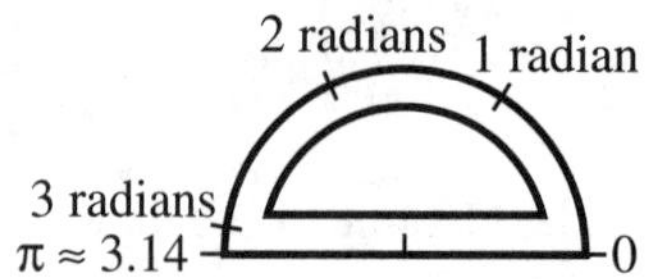

To convert 5 radians: $5 \cdot \dfrac{180}{\pi} = \dfrac{900}{\pi}$ degrees.

To convert 0.6 radians: $0.6 \cdot \dfrac{180}{\pi} = \dfrac{108}{\pi}$ degrees.

The answers just given can be written approximately: 5 radians ≈ 286.5° and 0.6 radians ≈ 34.4°.

EXERCISES

In Exercises 1–9, convert the given angle from degrees to radians or vice versa.

1. 30°

2. 135°

3. $\dfrac{2\pi}{5}$ radians

4. 150°

5. $\dfrac{5\pi}{3}$ radians

6. 1.5 radians

7. 27°

8. $\dfrac{2}{3}$ radian

9. 450°

10. How many times would you have to wrap a length of string around a circle to mark off an angle of 4π radians? 12π radians? 15π radians? 7 radians? 2000 radians?

11. Recall that the circumference of a circle, C, is given by the formula $C = 2\pi r$, where r is the radius of the circle. A **unit circle** is one whose radius is 1. Explain why the circumference of a unit circle equals the radian measure of the angle needed to wrap once around the circle.

12. **a.** Explain why a central angle of 1 radian in a unit circle subtends an arc whose length is 1 unit. (*Hint:* see Exercise 11.)

b. Explain why a central angle of t radians in a unit circle subtends an arc whose length is t units.

c. Explain why a central angle of t radians in a circle of radius r subtends an arc whose length is tr units.

13. Label the following radian measures on the circle: $\dfrac{\pi}{4}, \dfrac{\pi}{2}, \dfrac{5\pi}{4}, \dfrac{3\pi}{2}, 2\pi$.

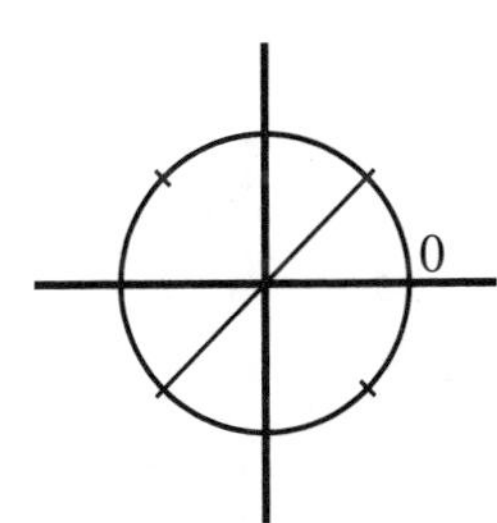

14. Label the following radian measures on the circle: $\frac{\pi}{3}, \frac{\pi}{2}, \frac{2\pi}{3}, \frac{4\pi}{3}, \pi$.

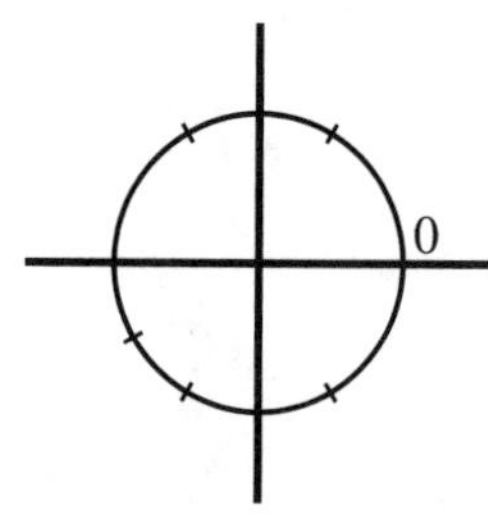

15. Label the following radian measures on the circle: $\frac{\pi}{6}, \frac{\pi}{2}, \frac{7\pi}{6}, \frac{4\pi}{3}, \frac{11\pi}{6}$.

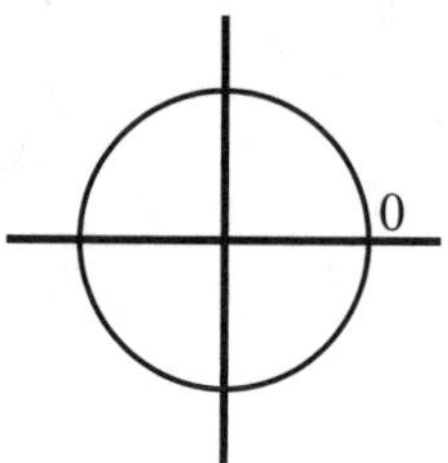

16. Locate approximately the following radian measures on the circle:

$1, \frac{\pi}{6}, 2, 0.6, 5, 3, \frac{3\pi}{4}, \frac{3\pi}{2,}, 1.4.$

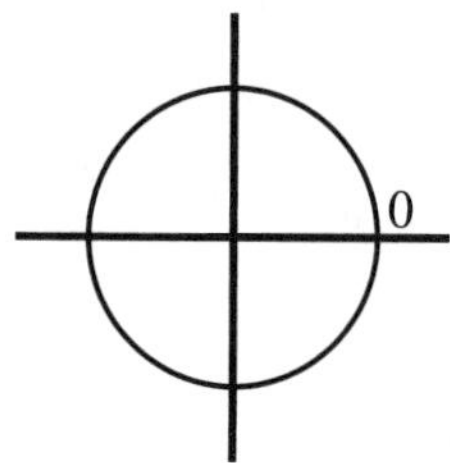

Trigonometric Functions in Right Triangles

For an angle θ in a right triangle (as pictured), the basic trigonometric functions (sine, cosine, tangent) are defined by

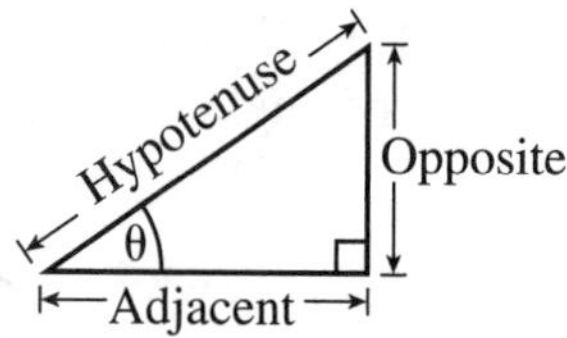

$$\sin\theta = \frac{\text{opposite}}{\text{hypotenuse}} \qquad \cos\theta = \frac{\text{adjacent}}{\text{hypotenuse}} \qquad \tan\theta = \frac{\text{opposite}}{\text{adjacent}}$$

The acronym **SOH CAH TOA** summarizes this; for example, **SOH** tells you that **s**ine equals **o**pposite over the **h**ypotenuse.

Using the accompanying triangle,

$$\sin\theta = \frac{\text{opp}}{\text{hyp}} = \frac{6}{10} = \frac{3}{5}$$

$$\cos\theta = \frac{\text{adj}}{\text{hyp}} = \frac{8}{10} = \frac{4}{5}$$

$$\tan\theta = \frac{\text{opp}}{\text{adj}} = \frac{6}{8} = \frac{3}{4}$$

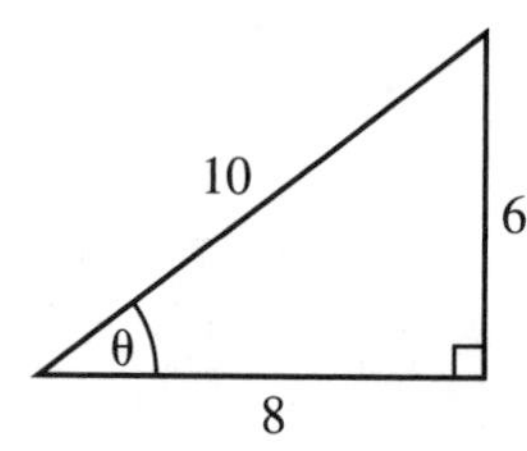

Frequently, you must use the **Pythagorean theorem** for right triangles. As you recall, the theorem says that in a right triangle, $c^2 = a^2 + b^2$. For example, to determine the values of trigonometric functions in the given triangle, you first use the Pythagorean theorem to determine the missing side:

$$2^2 = 1^2 + x^2 \quad \text{or} \quad 4 = 1 + x^2 \quad \text{or} \quad x^2 = 3$$

$$x = \sqrt{3}$$

Then, as before,

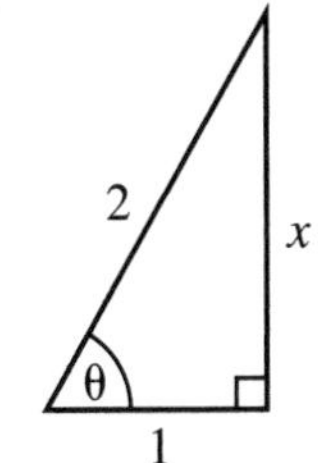

$$\sin\theta = \frac{\text{opp}}{\text{hyp}} = \frac{\sqrt{3}}{2}$$

$$\cos\theta = \frac{\text{adj}}{\text{hyp}} = \frac{1}{2}$$

$$\tan\theta = \frac{\text{opp}}{\text{adj}} = \frac{\sqrt{3}}{1} = \sqrt{3}$$

EXERCISES

In Exercises 1–6, find $\sin\theta$, $\cos\theta$, *and* $\tan\theta$.

1.

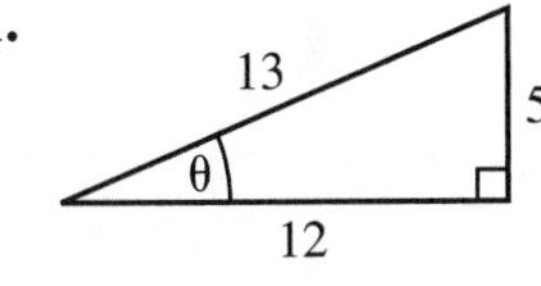

2.

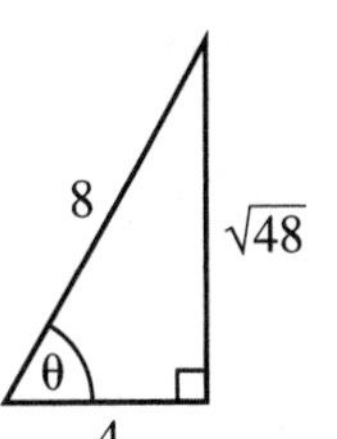

3.

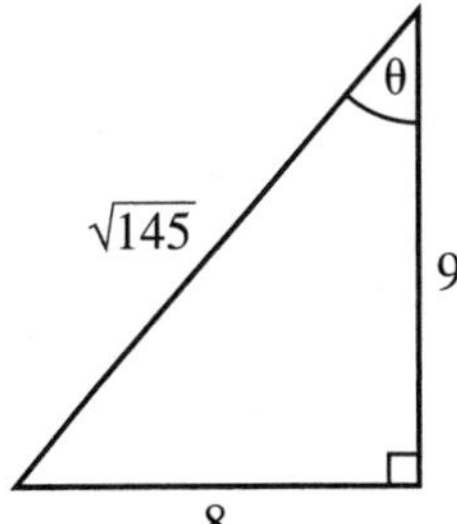

4.

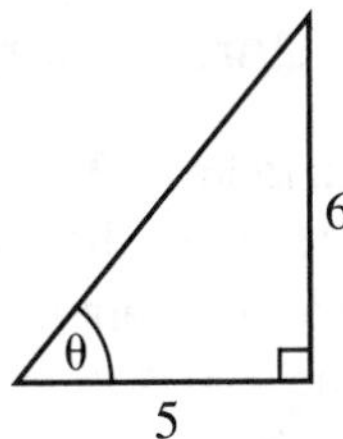

5.

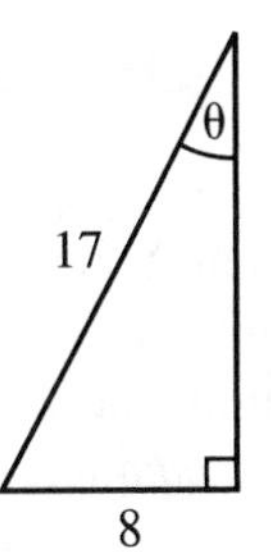

6.

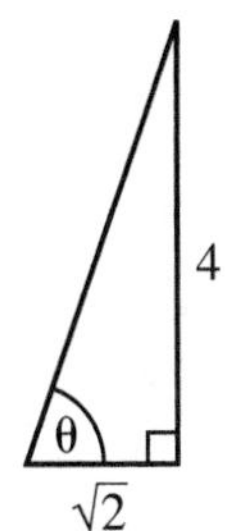

7. Using the Pythagorean theorem and SOH CAH TOA, show that $\sin^2\theta + \cos^2\theta = 1$ for any angle θ in a right triangle.

Special Triangles: 30–60–90 and 45–45–90

Certain angles arise frequently in nature and in engineering because of the symmetry involved. Look at bridges, and even honeycombs, and you will see 30-, 45-, 60-, and 90- degree angles. Because of this, 30-60-90 and 45-45-90 triangles are especially important. Here is what their basic proportions are:

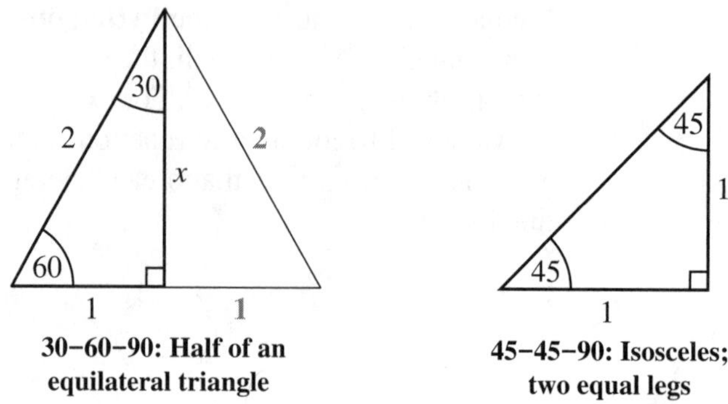

30–60–90: Half of an equilateral triangle

45–45–90: Isosceles; two equal legs

The third side in each triangle can be found using the Pythagorean theorem. The proportions are:

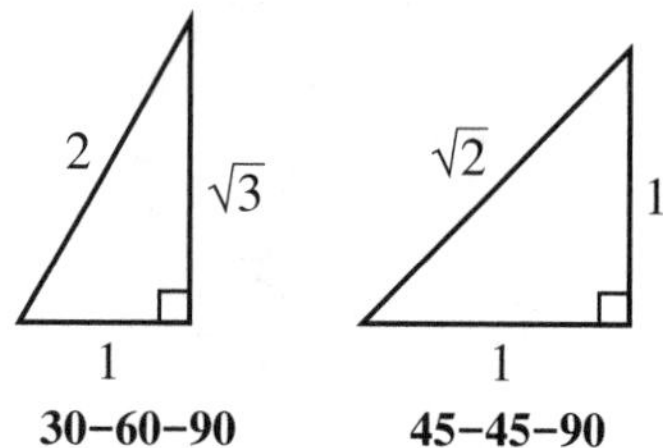

30–60–90

45–45–90

From the triangles, you obtain these important values for trigonometric functions:

ANGLE	SINE	COSINE	TANGENT
30	$\frac{1}{2}$	$\frac{\sqrt{3}}{2}$	$\frac{\sqrt{3}}{3}$
45	$\frac{\sqrt{2}}{2}$	$\frac{\sqrt{2}}{2}$	1
60	$\frac{\sqrt{3}}{2}$	$\frac{1}{2}$	$\sqrt{3}$

Trigonometric Functions for More General Angles

When an angle θ is larger than 90° (in radians, θ, $\frac{\pi}{2}$), you can still evaluate sine, cosine, and tangent. You work in an *xy* plane, make the positive x axis the initial side of the angle, and make a *reference triangle* by dropping a perpendicular from a point on the terminal side of the angle to the *x* axis. (See the figure.) For positive angles, you rotate *counterclockwise* to find the terminal side.

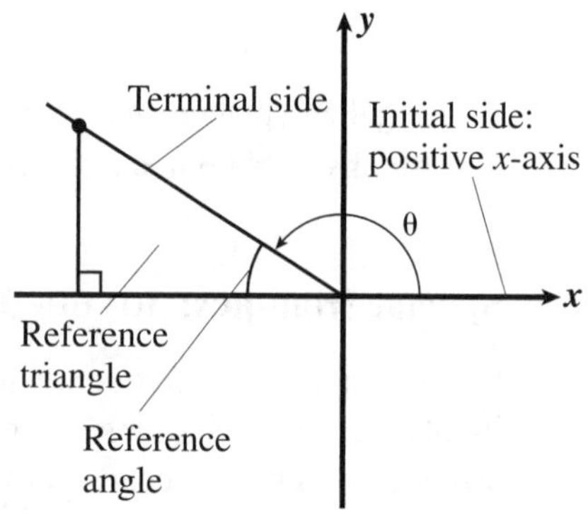

You then use SOH CAH TOA on the *reference triangle*. **Warning:** The adjacent and opposite sides may be *negative* in this situation, depending on the quadrant in which the terminal side of the angle lies.

For example, in the figure below, note the negative sign for the adjacent side. (It lies on the *negative* x axis.) You have

$$\sin\theta = \frac{\text{opp}}{\text{hyp}} = \frac{4}{5}$$

$$\cos\theta = \frac{\text{adj}}{\text{hyp}} = -\frac{3}{5}$$

$$\tan\theta = \frac{\text{opp}}{\text{adj}} = \frac{4}{(-3)} = -\frac{4}{3}$$

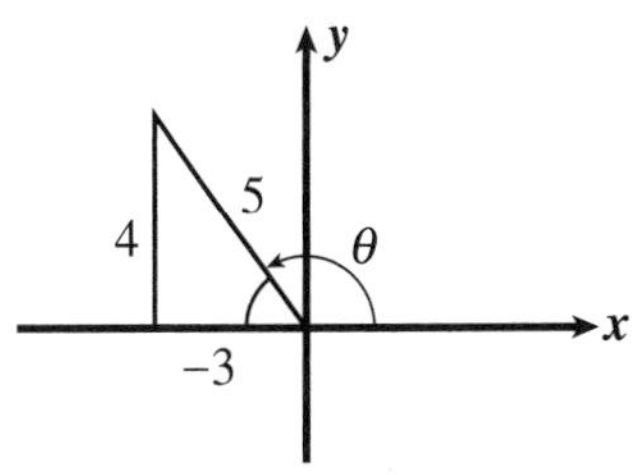

You also need to use the Pythagorean theorem at times. In the figure below, you have $6^2 = (-2) + y^2$ or $y^2 = 32$. Since y must be *negative* (do you see why?), $y = -\sqrt{32} = -4\sqrt{2}$. You now find

$$\sin\theta = \frac{\text{opp}}{\text{hyp}} = \frac{-4\sqrt{2}}{6} = \frac{-2\sqrt{2}}{3}$$

$$\cos\theta = \frac{\text{adj}}{\text{hyp}} = \frac{-2}{6} = \frac{-1}{3}$$

$$\tan\theta = \frac{\text{opp}}{\text{adj}} = \frac{-4\sqrt{2}}{(-2)} = 2\sqrt{2}$$

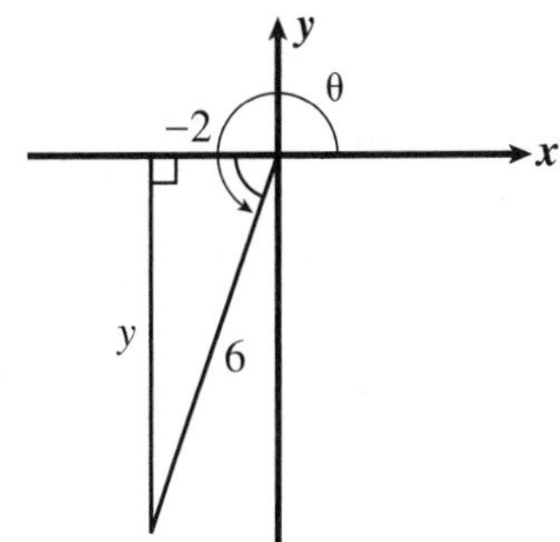

As noted previously, reference triangles with angles of 30°, 60°, or 45° show up frequently because of the symmetry involved. To find the values of the three trigonometric functions for $\theta = 5\pi/3$ radians, we convert to degrees and sketch the angle and the reference triangle:

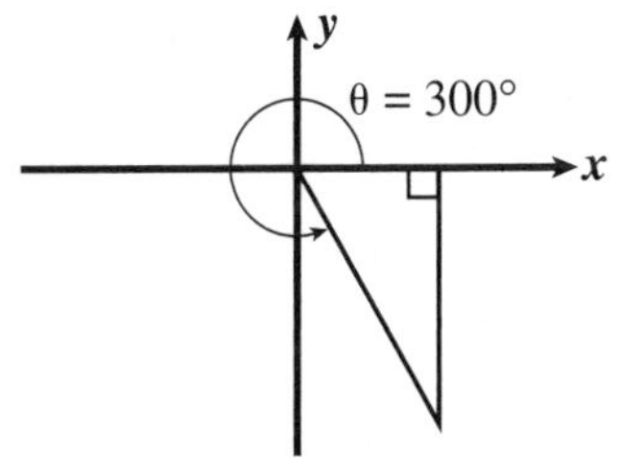

$$\frac{5\pi}{3} = \frac{5}{3}\cdot 180° = 300°$$

As noted previously, reference triangles with angles of 30°, 60°, or 45° show up frequently because of the symmetry involved. To find the values of the three trigonometric functions for $\theta = 5\pi/3$ radians, we convert to degrees and sketch the angle and the reference triangle:

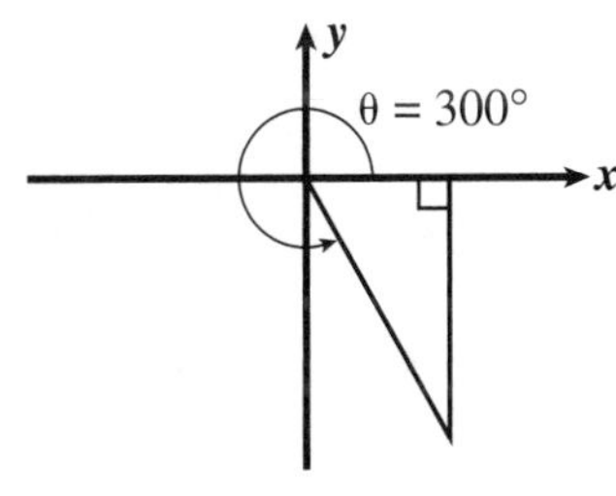

$$\frac{5\pi}{3} = \frac{5}{3}\cdot 180° = 300°$$

Then label the sides using our knowledge of 30-60-90 triangles:

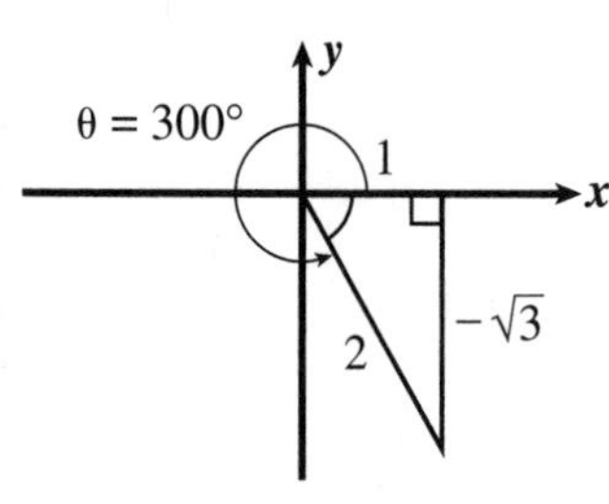

Finally,

$$\sin 300^\circ = \frac{\text{opp}}{\text{hyp}} = \frac{-\sqrt{3}}{2}$$

$$\cos 300^\circ = \frac{\text{adj}}{\text{hyp}} = \frac{1}{2}$$

$$\tan 300^\circ = \frac{\text{opp}}{\text{adj}} = \frac{-\sqrt{3}}{1} = -\sqrt{3}$$

To help remember the ± signs, the phrase *All Students Take Calculus* is useful. The four words go in the four quadrants of the *xy* plane:

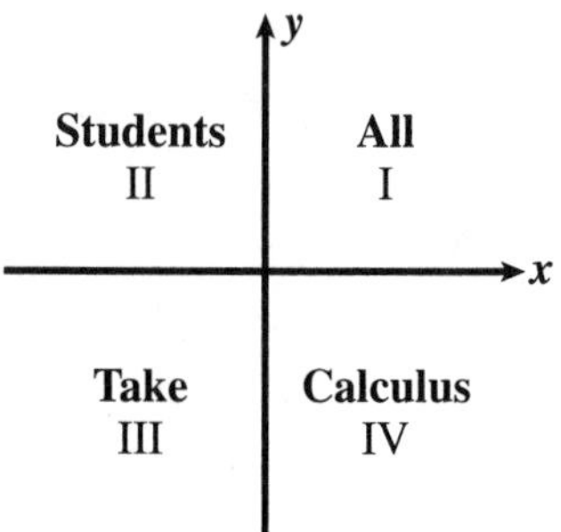

The ***All*** means *all* trigonometric functions are positive in the quadrant I; **S** for **S**tudents means ***S**ine* is positive in quadrant II; **T** for **T**ake means ***T**angent* is positive in quadrant III; **C** for **C**alculus means ***C**osine* is positive in quadrant IV.

Note that for *negative* angles we locate the terminal side by rotating *clockwise* from the positive *x* axis. The figure at the right shows that

$$\sin \frac{-3\pi}{4} = \frac{-1}{\sqrt{2}} = \frac{-\sqrt{2}}{2};$$

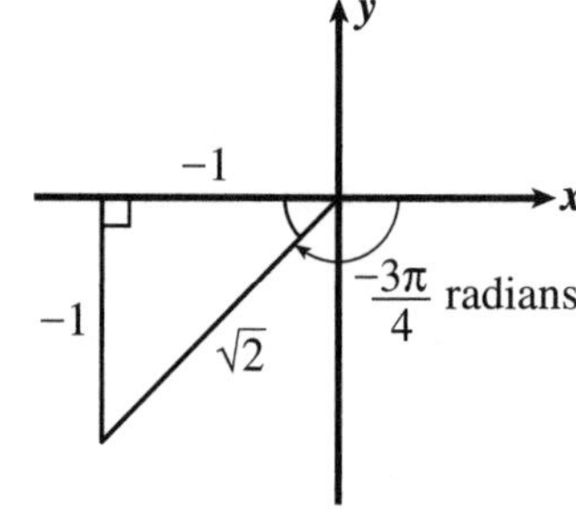

and by similar calculations,

$$\cos \frac{-3\pi}{4} = \frac{-\sqrt{2}}{2} \text{ and } \tan \frac{-3\pi}{4} = 1.$$

EXERCISES

In Exercises 1–4, find the remaining side of the reference triangle and evaluate sin θ, cos θ, and tan θ.

1.

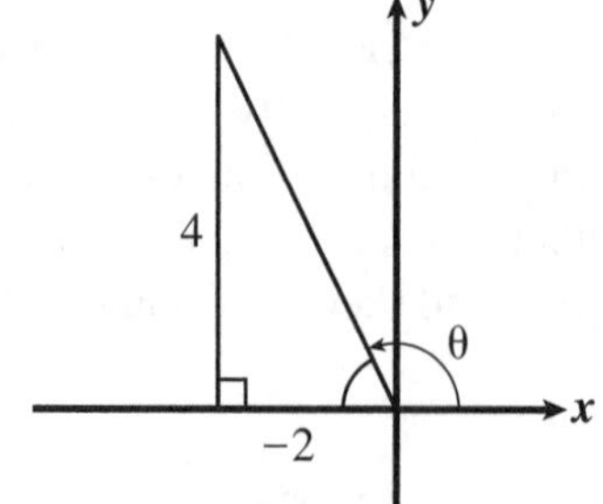

2.

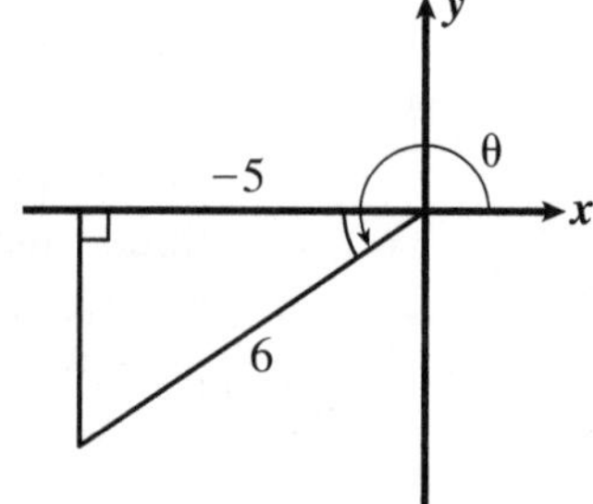

3.

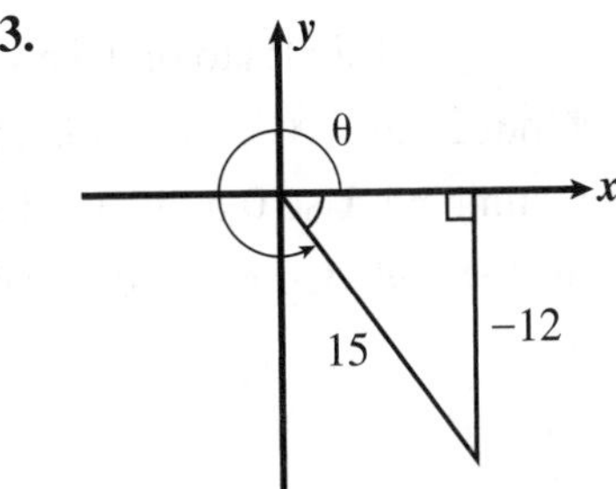

4.

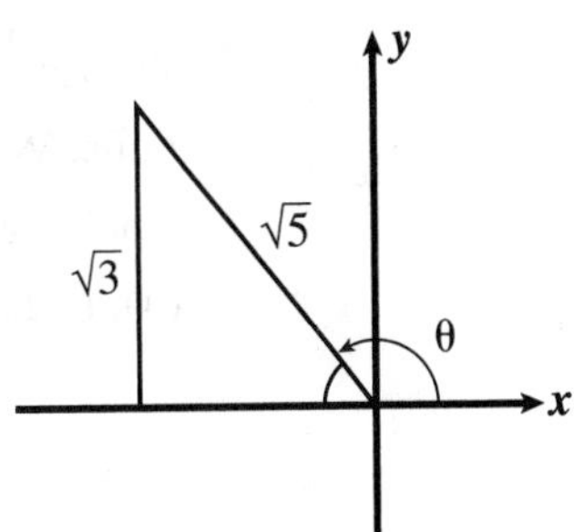

In Exercises 5–10, sketch the angle and reference triangle and then work out the values of the three trigonometric functions for that angle.

5. $\theta = \frac{\pi}{2}$radians

6. $\theta = 225°$

7. $\theta = -150°$

8. $\theta = 330°$

9. θ is fourth quadrant angle whose sine is $-\frac{6}{8}$.

10. θ is fourth quadrant tangent angle whose tangent is $-\frac{3}{5}$.

11. Show that for θ in *any* quadrant, the relationship $\sin^2\theta + \cos^2\theta = 1$ holds.

Dealing with Special Angles: 0°, ±90°, ±180°

For multiples of 90° (equivalently, multiples of $\frac{\pi}{2}$ radians), the reference triangle degenerates to a straight line. Either the adjacent or opposite side degenerates to 0:

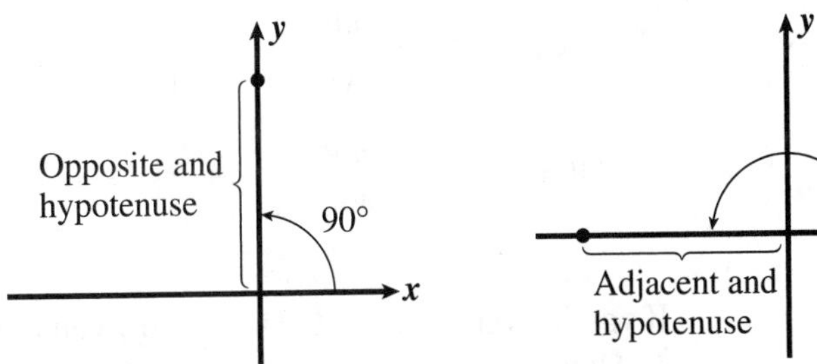

90 degrees: adjacent side is 0 **180 degrees: opposite side is 0**

For simplicity, notice that for ordinary angles, when we mark a point on the terminal side of an angle θ, the *x value* gives the value of the *adjacent* side, and the *y* value gives the *opposite*. Let us also use r for the length of the hypotenuse:

Therefore, we could have defined

$$\sin\theta = \frac{\text{opp}}{\text{hyp}} = \frac{y}{\text{hyp}} = \frac{y}{r}$$
$$\cos\theta = \frac{\text{adj}}{\text{hyp}} = \frac{x}{\text{hyp}} = \frac{x}{r} \qquad \textbf{(4)}$$
$$\tan\theta = \frac{\text{opp}}{\text{adj}} = \frac{y}{x}$$

We use $\frac{y}{r}$, $\frac{x}{r}$, and $\frac{y}{x}$ for the special angles to find the values of the trigonometric functions. When we have a multiple of 90°, we mark a point on the terminal side and label it with its x and y numbers. Use 0 and ± 1 for simplicity, then use formula (4). Here are the pictures for -90 degrees and 180 degrees.

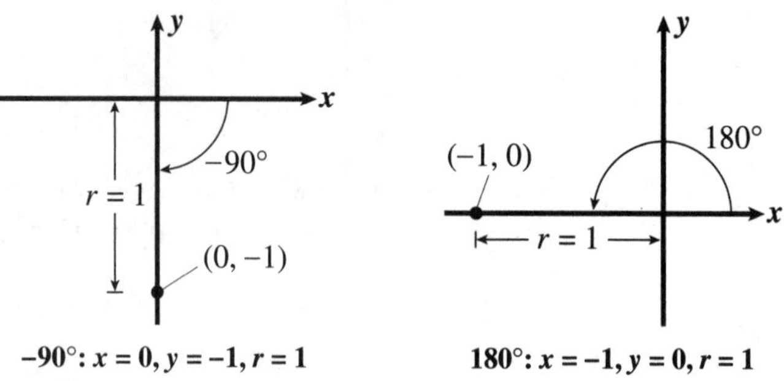

−90°: $x = 0, y = -1, r = 1$

180°: $x = -1, y = 0, r = 1$

Now the trigonometric values are:

$$\sin 180° = \frac{\text{opp}}{\text{hyp}} = \frac{y}{r} = \frac{0}{1} = 0$$

$$\cos 180° = \frac{\text{adj}}{\text{hyp}} = \frac{x}{r} = -\frac{1}{1} = -1$$

$$\tan 180° = \frac{\text{opp}}{\text{adj}} = \frac{y}{x} = \frac{0}{-1} = 0$$

$$\sin(-90°) = \frac{\text{opp}}{\text{hyp}} = \frac{y}{r} = \frac{-1}{1} = -1$$

$$\cos(-90°) = \frac{\text{adj}}{\text{hyp}} = \frac{x}{r} = \frac{0}{1} = 0$$

$$\tan(-90°) = \frac{\text{opp}}{\text{adj}} = \frac{y}{x} = \frac{-1}{0} = \textit{undefined}$$

If you use only 0 and ± 1 for x and y values of these special angles, r always equals 1. Also, whenever the x value is 0, the tangent is *undefined*, since the formula then involves division by 0.

EXERCISES

In Exercises 1–6, for each given value of θ draw the angle, label a point on the terminal side, and use formulas (4) to get the values of sin θ, cos θ, and tan θ.

1. $\theta = 90°$

2. $\theta = -\pi$ radians

3. $\theta = 720°$

4. $\theta = -630°$

5. $\theta = \frac{7\pi}{2}$ radians

6. $\theta = 23\pi$ radians

The TI–83 Graphing Calculator

Getting Started with the TI–83

ON-OFF

To turn on the TI-83 press the (ON) key. To turn off the TI-83, press (2nd) and then (ON).

In general, to access any of the white commands, press the black or gray key. To access the gold commands, press (2nd) and then the black or gray key below the desired command. Similarly, to access any of the green commands or symbols, press (ALPHA) followed by the appropriate black or gray key.

Contrast

To adjust the contrast on your screen, press and release the (2nd) key and hold (▲) to darken and (▼) to lighten.

Mode

The (MODE) key controls many calculator settings. The activated settings are highlighted. For most of your work in this course, the settings in the left-hand column should be highlighted.

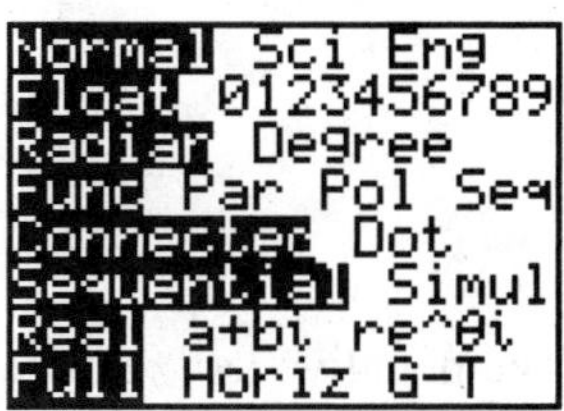

To change a setting, move the cursor to the desired setting and press (ENTER).

The Home Screen

The home screen is used for calculations.

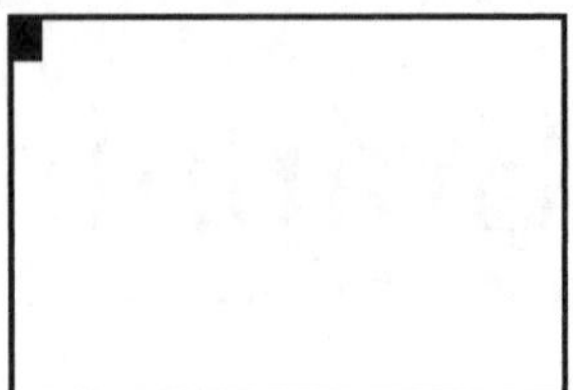

You may return to the home screen at any time by using the QUIT command. This command is accessed by pressing (2nd) (MODE). All calculations in the home screen are subject to the order of operations.

Enter all expressions as you would write them. Always observe the order of operations. Once you have typed the expression, press (ENTER) to obtain the simplified result. Before you hit (ENTER) you may edit your expression by using the arrow keys, the delete command (DEL), and the insert command (2nd) (DEL).

Three keys of special note are the reciprocal key (X^{-1}), the caret key (^), and the negative key ((–)).

The reciprocal command (X^{-1}) will invert the number in the home screen.

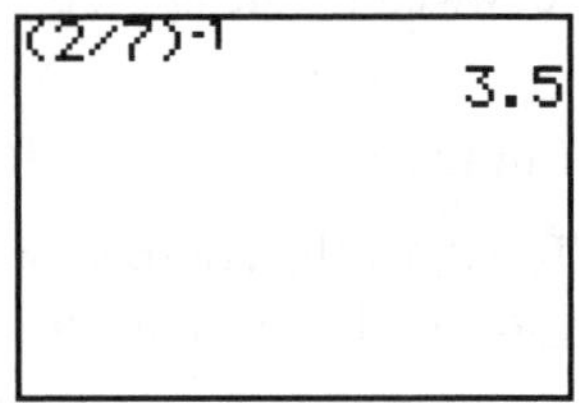

The caret key (^) is used to raise numbers to powers

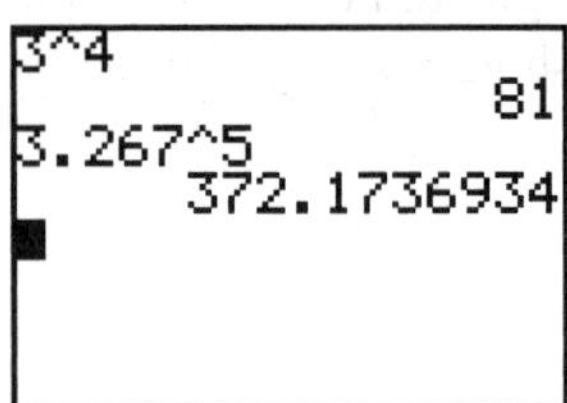

The negative key is different from the minus key. To enter a negative number use the gray key ((–)), not the blue (–) key.

```
15-6
                 9
15--6
                21
```

A table of keys and their functions follows.

Key	Function Description
ON	Turns calculator on or off.
CLEAR	Clears text screen.
ENTER	Executes a command.
(−)	Calculates the additive inverse.
MODE	Displays current operating settings.
DEL	Deletes the character at the cursor.
^	Symbol used for exponentiation.
ANS	Storage location of the last calculation.
ENTRY	Retrieves the previously executed expression.

ANS and ENTRY

The last two commands in the table can be real time savers. The result of your last calculation is always stored in a memory location known as ANS. It is accessed by pressing [2nd] [(−)] or it can be automatically accessed by pressing any operation button.

Suppose you want to evaluate $12.5\sqrt{1 + 0.5 \cdot (0.55)^2}$. It could be evaluated in one expression and checked with a series of calculations using ANS.

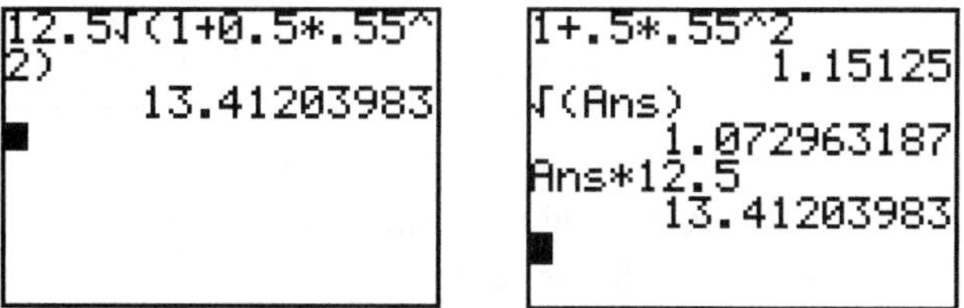

The ENTRY command recalls the last expression. Even if you have pressed [ENTER], you can edit the previous expression. The [2nd] [ENTER] sequence will recall the previous expression for editing.

Suppose you want to evaluate the compound interest expression $P\left(1 + \frac{r}{n}\right)^{nt}$, where P is the principal, r is the interest rate, n is the number of compounding periods annually, and t is the number of years, when $P = \$1000$, $r = 6.5\%$, $n = 1$, and $t = 2$, 5, and 15 years.

Using the ENTRY command, this expression would be entered once and edited twice.

```
1000(1+.065)^2
         1134.225
1000(1+.065)^5
      1370.086663
1000(1+.065)^15
      2571.841007
```

Note that there are many last expressions stored in the ENTRY memory location. You can repeat the ENTRY command as many times as you want to retrieve a previously entered expression.

Functions and Graphing with the TI-83

Y = Menu

Functions of the form $y = f(x)$ can be entered into the TI-83 using the Y = menu. To access the Y = menu press the [Y=] key. Type the expression $f(x)$ after Y1 using the [X,T,θ,n] key for the variable x and press [ENTER].

For example, enter the function $f(x) = 3x^5 - 4x + 1$.

```
Plot1 Plot2 Plot3
\Y1=3X^5-4X+1
\Y2=
\Y3=
\Y4=
\Y5=
\Y6=
\Y7=
```

Note the = sign after Y1 is highlighted. This shows Y1 is selected to be graphed. The highlighting may be turned on or off by using the arrow keys to move the cursor to the = sign and then pressing [ENTER].

```
Plot1 Plot2 Plot3
\Y1=3X^5-4X+1
\Y2=
\Y3=
\Y4=
\Y5=
\Y6=
\Y7=
```

Once the function is entered in the Y = menu, function values may be evaluated in the home screen.

For example, given $f(x) = 3x^5 - 4x + 1$, evaluate $f(4)$. In the home screen press [VARS].

```
VARS Y-VARS
1:Window...
2:Zoom...
3:GDB...
4:Picture...
5:Statistics...
6:Table...
7:String...
```

Move the cursor to Y-VARS and press [ENTER].

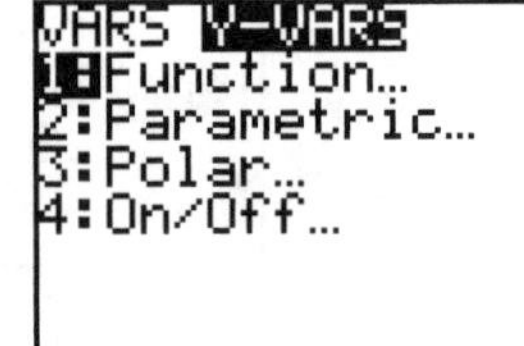

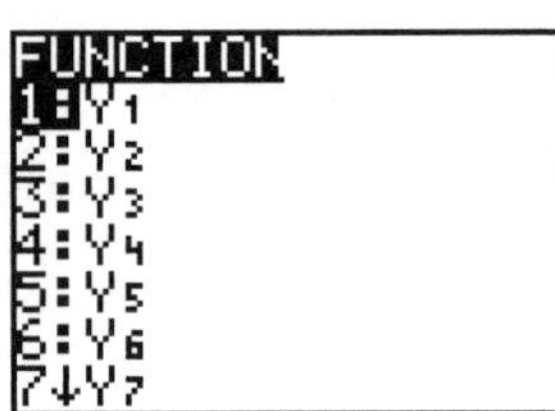

Press (ENTER) again to select Y1. Y1 now appears in the home screen.

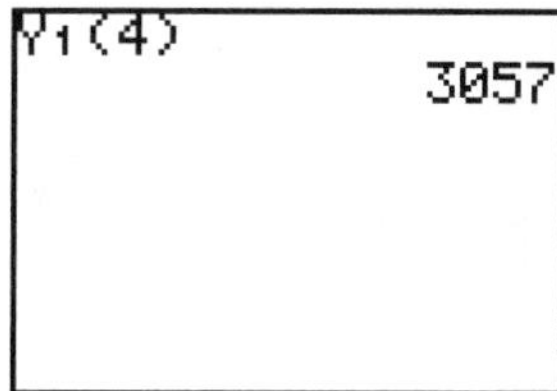

To evaluate $f(4)$, press (( ) (4) ( )) after Y1 and press (ENTER).

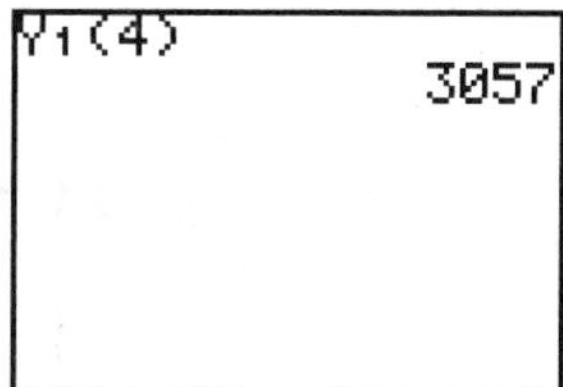

Tables of Values

If you are interested in viewing several function values for the same function, you may want to construct a table.

Before constructing the table, look at the settings in the Table Setup menu. To do this, press (2nd) (WINDOW).

TblStart tells you where the table of values will start. ΔTbl tells you the increment from one input value to the next. Set the TblStart at −2 and the ΔTbl at 0.5 then press (2nd) (GRAPH) to access the following table. (Make certain that the = sign following Y1 is highlighted.)

X	Y1
-2	-87
-1.5	-15.78
-1	2
-.5	2.9063
0	1
.5	-.9063
1	0

X= -2

Use the (▲) and (▼) keys to view other values in the table.

If the input values of interest are not evenly spaced, you may want to choose the ask mode for the independent variable from the Table Setup menu.

The resulting table is blank, but you can fill it by choosing any values you like for x and pressing (ENTER) after each.

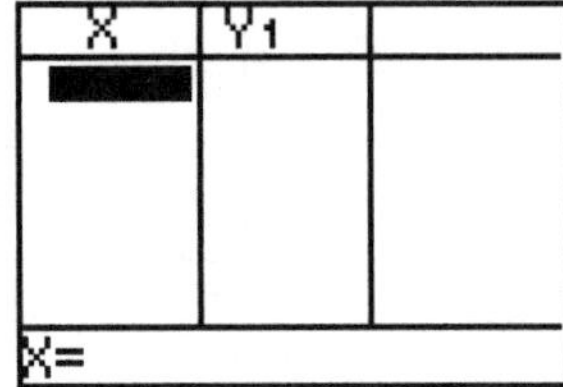

Note that the number of digits shown in the output is limited by the table width, but if you want more digits, move the cursor to the desired output and more digits appear at the bottom of the screen.

Graphing a Function

Once a function is entered in the Y = menu and activated, it can be displayed and analyzed. For this discussion, we will use the function $f(x) = -x^2 + 10x + 12$. Enter this as Y1.

The Viewing Window

The viewing window is the portion of the rectangular coordinate system that is displayed when you graph a function.

Xmin defines the left edge of the window.

Xmax defines the right edge of the window.

Xscl defines the distance between horizontal tick marks.

Ymin defines the bottom edge of the window.

Ymax defines the top edge of the window.

Yscl defines the distance between vertical tick marks.

In the standard viewing window, Xmin $= -10$, Xmax $= 10$, Xscl $= 1$, Ymin $= -10$, Ymax $= 10$, and Yscl $= 1$.

To select the standard viewing window, press ZOOM 6.

If you press the GRAPH key now, you will view the following:

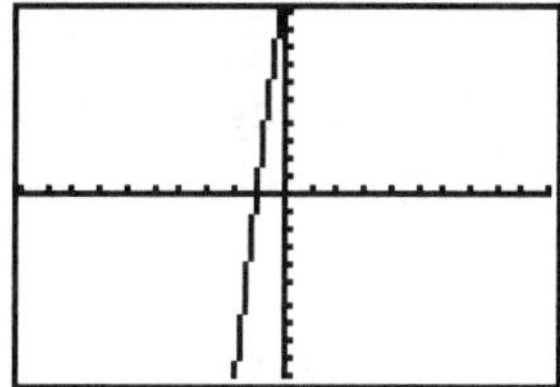

Is this an accurate and or complete picture of your function, or is the window giving you a misleading impression? You may want to use your table function to view the output values from -10 to 10.

X	Y1
4	36
5	37
6	36
7	33
8	28
9	21
10	12

X=10

X	Y1
-3	-27
-2	-12
-1	1
0	12
1	21
2	28
3	33

X=3

X	Y1
-10	-188
-9	-159
-8	-132
-7	-107
-6	-84
-5	-63
-4	-44

X=-10

The table indicates that the minimum output value is -188 and the maximum output value is 37. Press WINDOW and reset the settings to approximately the following;

Xmin $= -10$, Xmax $= 10$, Xscl $= 1$, Ymin $= -190$, Ymax $= 40$, Yscl $= 10$

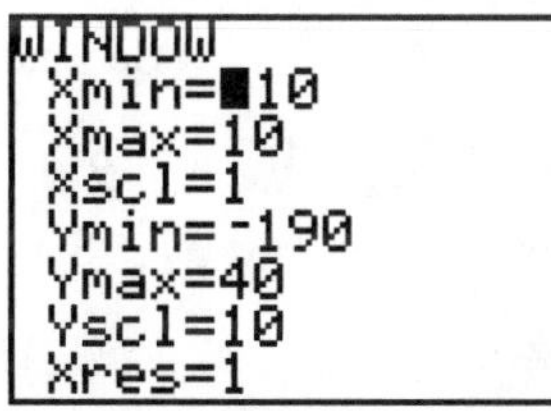

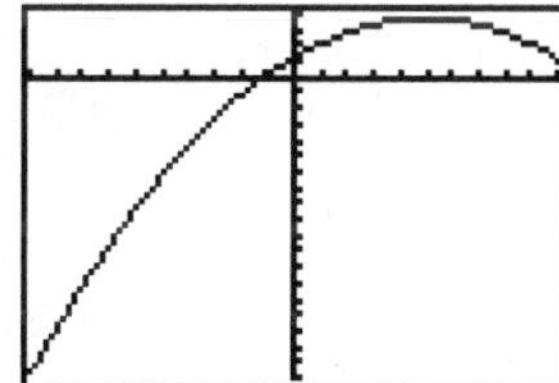

The new graph gives us a much more complete picture of the behavior of the function on the interval [–10, 10].

Specific points on the curve can be viewed by activating the trace feature. While in the graph window, press (TRACE). A flashing cursor will appear on the curve at approximately the midpoint of the screen.

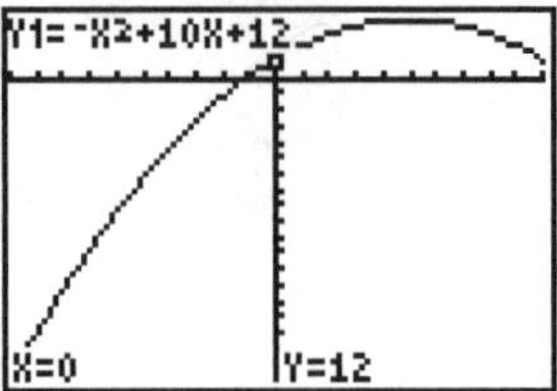

The left arrow key, (◀), will move the cursor toward smaller input values. The right arrow key, (▶), will move the cursor toward larger input values. If the cursor reaches the edge of the window and you continue to move the cursor, the window will adjust automatically.

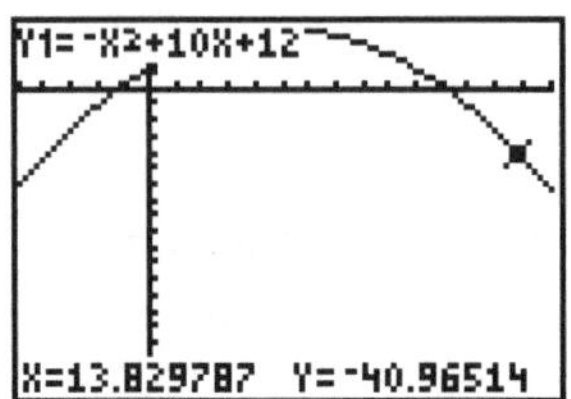

Zoom Menu

The Zoom menu offers several options for changing the window very quickly.

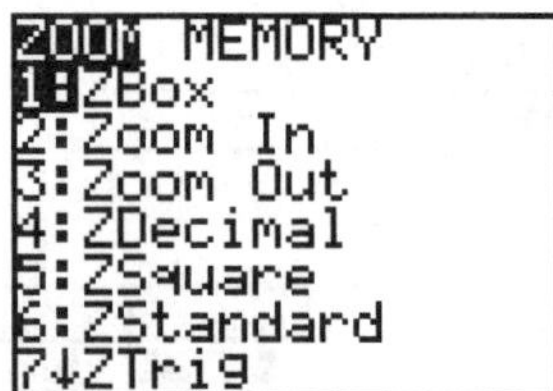

The features of each of the commands are summarized in the following table.

Zoom Command	Description
1:ZBox	Draws a box to define the viewing window.
2:Zoom In	Magnifies the graph near the cursor.
3:Zoom Out	Increases the viewing window around the cursor.
4:Zdecimal	Sets a window so that Xscl and Yscl are 0.1.
5:ZSquare	Sets equal size pixels on the x and y axes.
6:ZStandard	Sets the window to standard settings.
7:ZTrig	Sets built-in trig window variables.
8:ZInteger	Sets integer values on the x and y axes.
9:ZoomStat	Sets window based on the current values in the stat lists.
0:ZoomFit	Replots graph to include the max and min output values for the current Xmin and Xmax.

Solving Equations Graphically Using the TI-83

Two methods of an equation graphically with the TI-83 are:

A. the intercept method
B. the intersection method

The following will illustrate both methods for the equation

$$x^3 + 3 = 3x$$

A. The Intercepts Method

This method is based on the fact that the solutions of $f(x) = 0$ are the x-intercepts of the function $y = f(x)$.

Step 1 Write the equation in the form $f(x) = 0$.

$$x^3 - 3x + 3 = 0$$

Step 2 Enter $f(x)$ into the Y = editor.

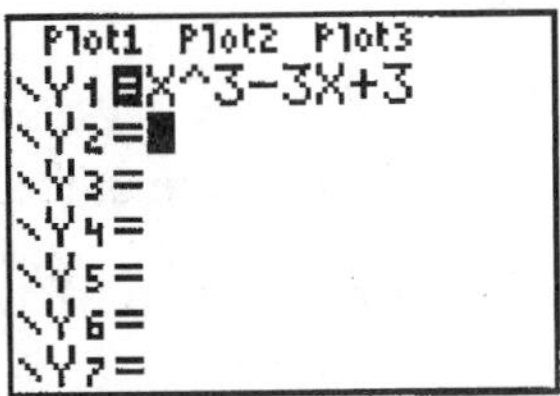

Step 3 Examine the graph to determine the number of x-intercepts.

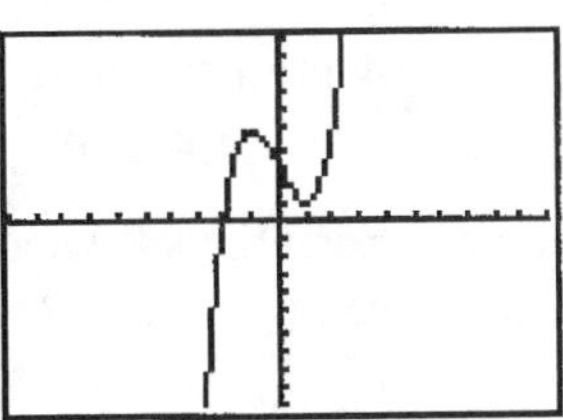

In this case, there appears to be only one x-intercept.

Step 4 Access the CALCULATE menu by pushing (2nd) (TRACE) and select option 2: zero. This will find zeros of functions.

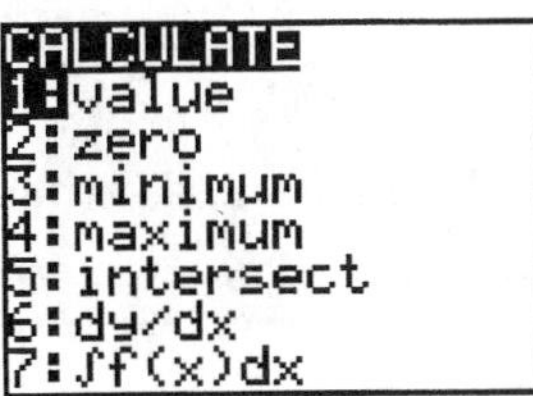

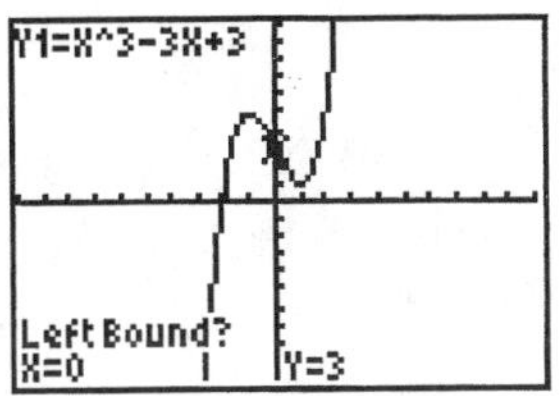

Step 5 Move the cursor to the left of the x-intercept and push (ENTER).

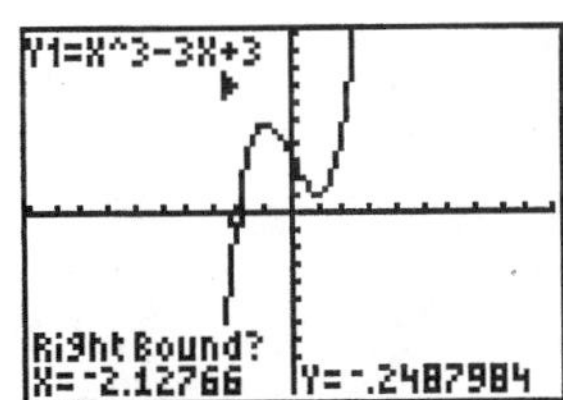

Step 6 Move the cursor a little to the right of the x-intercept and push (ENTER) again.

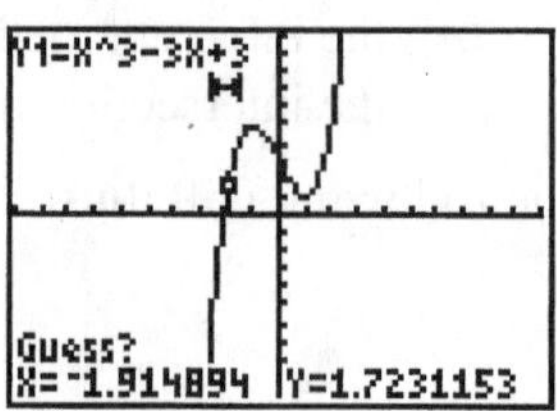

Step 7 The calculator asks you to guess. If you are reasonably close to the x-intercept just push (ENTER) again. The coordinates of the x-intercept appear under the word Zero. The x-intercept is a solution of the equation.

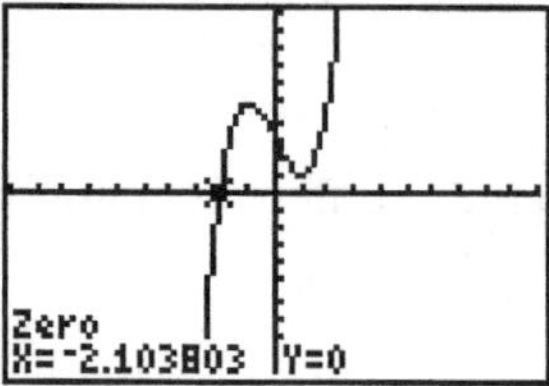

If there are other x-intercepts, repeat the process.

B. The Intersection Method

This method is based on the fact that solutions to the equation $f(x) = g(x)$ are input values of x that produce the same outputs for the functions f and g. Graphically these are the x-coordinates of the intersection points of $y = f(x)$ and $y = g(x)$.

The following procedure illustrates how to use the intersection method to solve $x^3 + 3 = 3x$ graphically.

Step 1 Enter the left-hand side of the equation as Y1 in the Y = editor and the right-hand side as Y2.

```
Plot1 Plot2 Plot3
\Y1=X^3+3
\Y2=3X
\Y3=
\Y4=
\Y5=
\Y6=
\Y7=
```

Step 2 Examine the graphs to determine the number of intersection points.

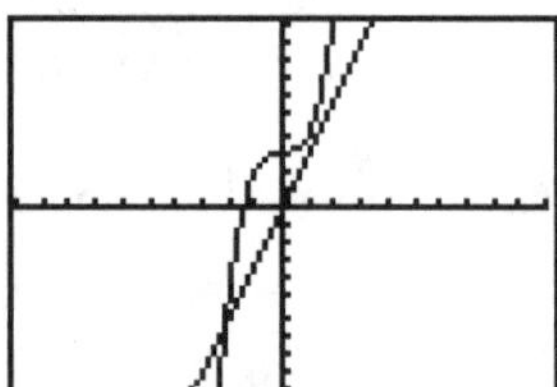

You may need a couple of windows to be certain of the number of intersection points.

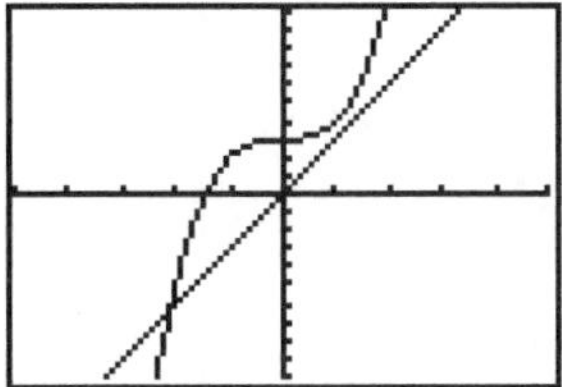

Step 3 Access the CALCULATE menu by pushing (2nd) (TRACE) then choose option 5: intersect.

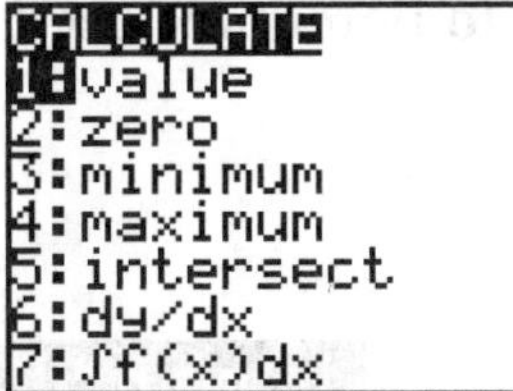

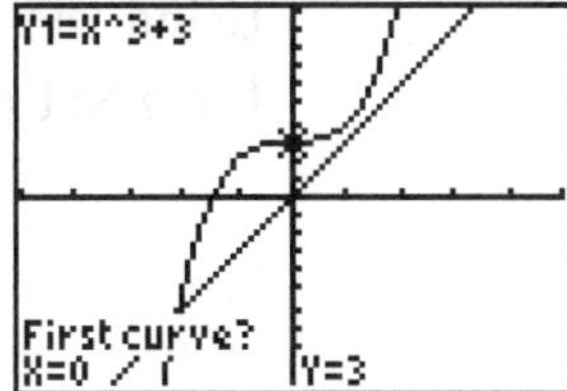

The cursor will appear on the first curve in the center of the window.

Step 4 Move the cursor close to the desired intersection point and press (ENTER).

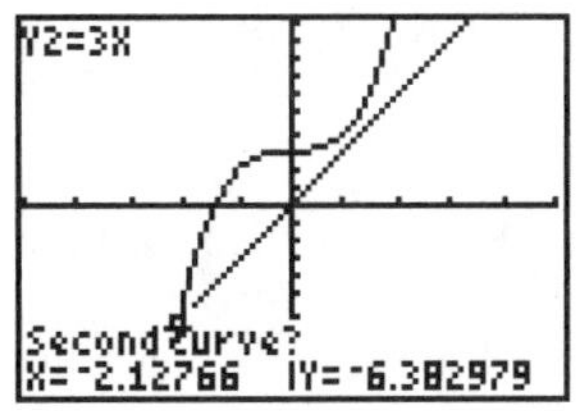

The cursor will now jump vertically to the other curve.

Step 5 Repeat step 4 for the second curve.

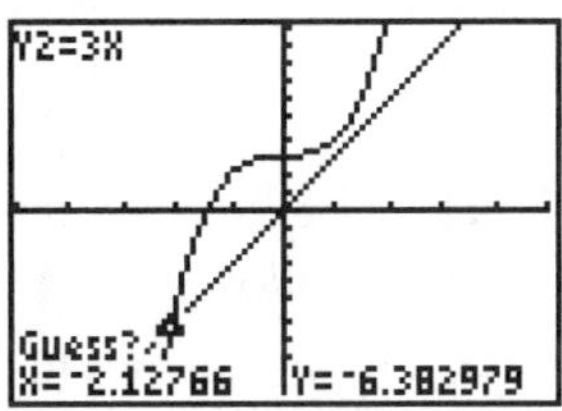

Step 6 To use the cursor's current location as your guess, press (ENTER) in response to the question on the screen that asks Guess? If you want to move to a better guess value, do so before you press (ENTER).

The coordinates of the intersection point appear below the word Intersection.

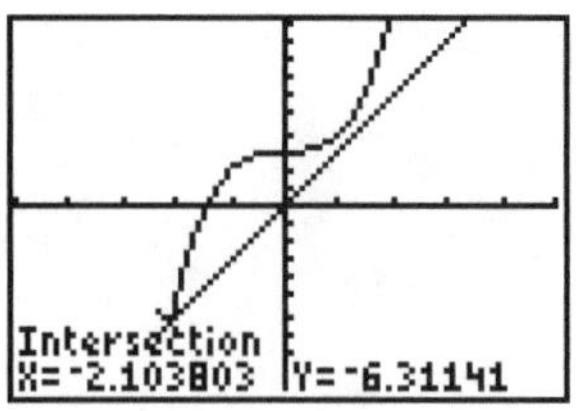

The x-coordinate is a solution to the equation.

If there are other intersection points, repeat the process as necessary.

Using the TI-83 to Determine the Linear Regression Equation for a Set of Data

Example:

INPUT	OUTPUT
2	2
3	5
4	3
5	7
6	9

A. Enter the data into the calculator as follows:

1. Press (STAT) and choose EDIT.

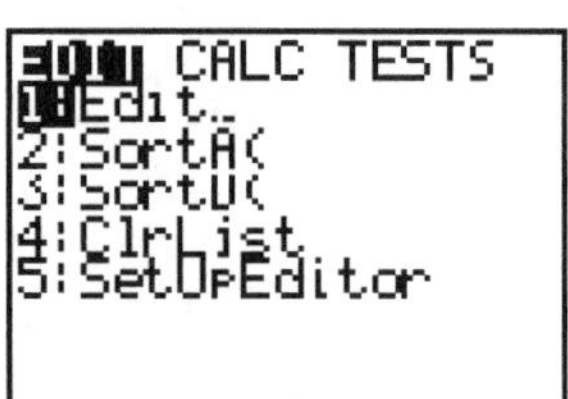

2. The TI-83 has six built-in lists, L1, L2, ..., L6. If there is data in L1, clear the list as follows:

a. Use the arrows to place the cursor on L1 at the top of the list. Press (CLEAR) followed by (ENTER).

b. Follow the same procedure to clear L2, if necessary.

L1 L2 L3 1

L1(1) =

c. Enter the input into L1 and the output into L2.

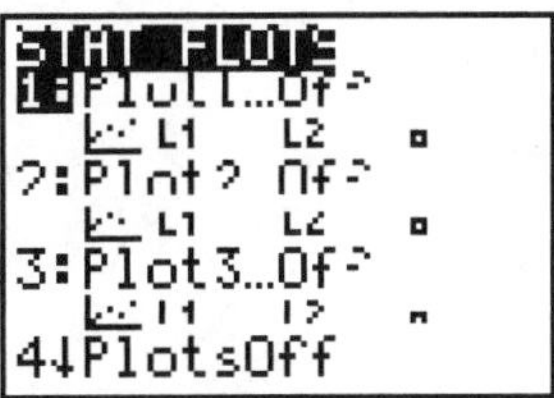

B. To see a scatterplot of the data proceed as follows.

1. STAT PLOT is the 2nd function of the (Y=) key. You must press (2nd) before pressing (Y=) to access the STAT PLOT menu.

2. Make sure plot 2 and plot 3 are off and choose plot 1. Highlight On, the scatter plot symbol and the square mark as indicated below. L1 is the Xlist and L2 is the Ylist. L1 is the 2nd function of the 1 button and L2 is the 2nd function of the 2 button, and so on.

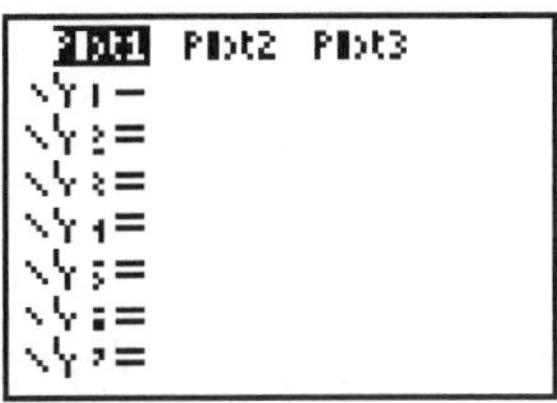

3. Press (Y=) and clear or deselect any functions currently stored.

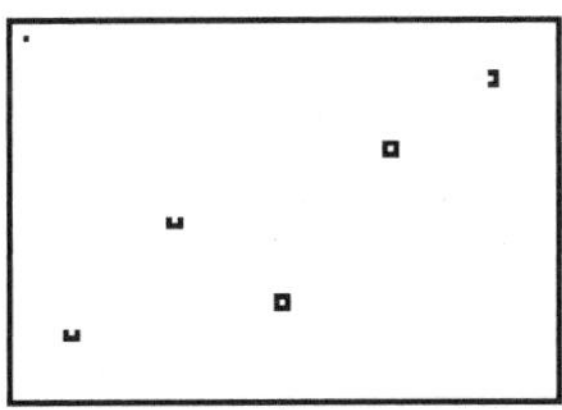

4. To display the scatterplot, have the calculator determine an appropriate window by pressing (ZOOM) and then (9) (ZoomStat).

C. Calculate the linear regression equation as follows.

1. Press STAT and right arrow to highlight CALC.

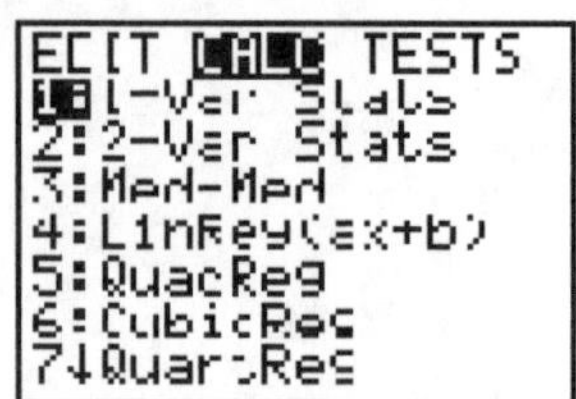

2. Choose 4: LinReg(ax + b). LinReg(ax + b) will be pasted to the home screen. To tell the calculator where the data is, press 2nd and 1 (for L1), then ,, then 2nd and 2 (for L2) so the display looks like this:

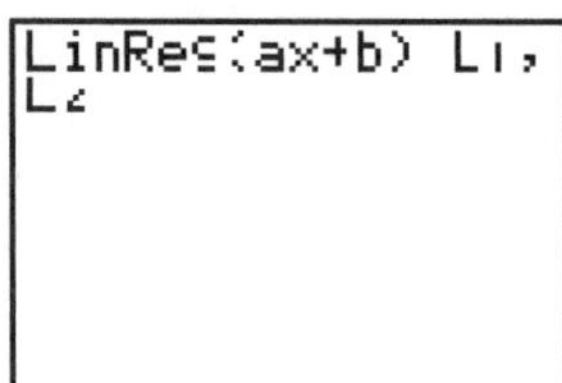

3. Press , and then press VARS.

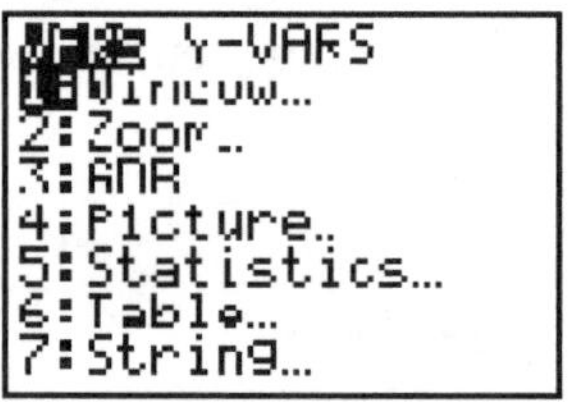

4. Right arrow to highlight Y-VARS.

5. Choose 1, FUNCTION.

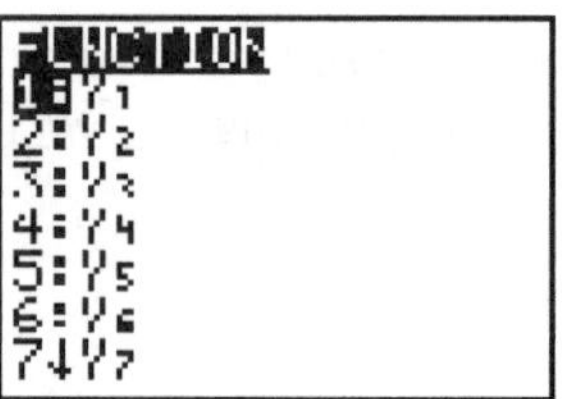

6. Choose 1 for Y1 (or 2 for Y2, etc.).

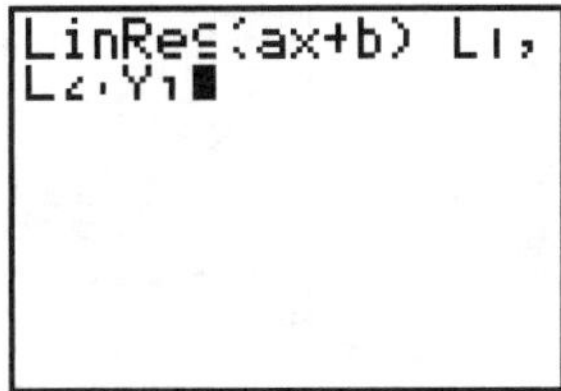

7. Press (ENTER).

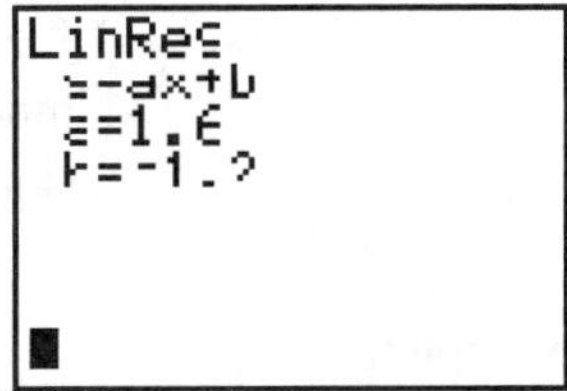

The linear regression equation for this data is $y = 1.6x - 1.2$.

8. To display the regression line, press (GRAPH).

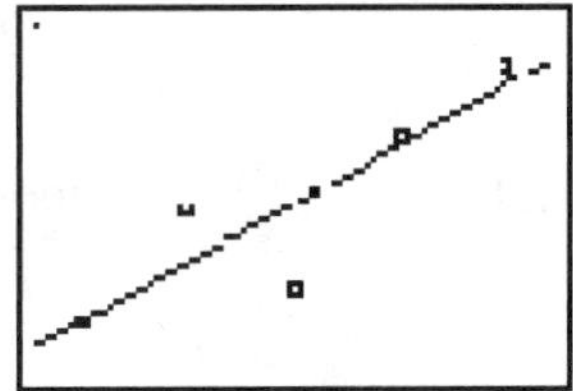

Histograms, Boxplots, and Statistics: Random Integers and Lists

Entering a Collection of Data

Press (STAT), then choose (EDIT). You will see a table with heading L1, L2, L3, (L is for List). If there is a list of numbers already stored under L1, move the cursor to the L1 heading, then press (CLEAR) and (ENTER). When the list is empty start entering the data one number at a time. If you wish to keep stored more than one set of data values, simply repeat the process for any of list L2 through L6.

Calculating One-Variable Statistics

Press (STAT), then choose (CALC). From the calculate menu, press (ENTER) to choose the one-variable statistics. When you see 1-Var Stats on your home screen, enter the name of the list where your data is stored (the second function of 1 through 6).

You will see the following display:

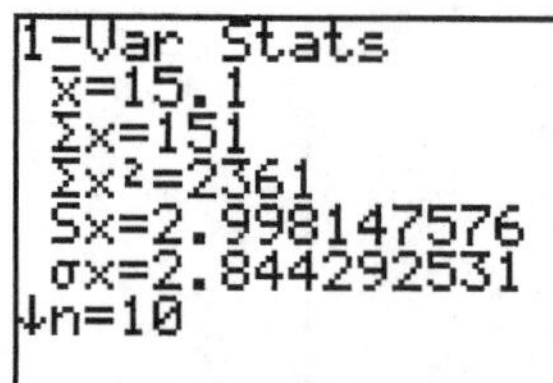

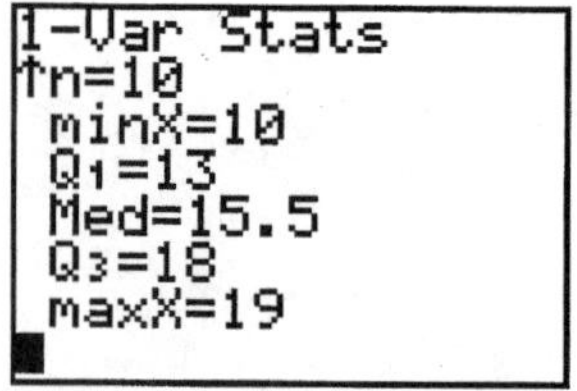

The statistics you will need to note are:

Mean, $x = 15.1$
Standard deviation, $\sigma_x = 2{,}844292531$
Number of data values, $n = 0$
Median, Med = 15.5

Example:

AGES OF STUDENTS IN YOUR CLASS				
18	20	19	23	20
19	25	21	18	27
20	35	23	19	21
28	18	21	28	33

1. Press (STAT) and choose (EDIT).

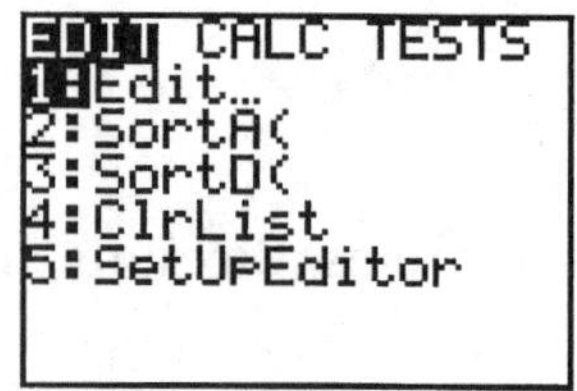

2. To enter one variable data, you will need only one list.
   a. If there is data in L1, clear the list (move the cursor to the top, highlighting L1, press (CLEAR) and then (ENTER).)
   b. Enter the data into L1.

3. To calculate the one variable statistics press STAT, highlight CALC, then choose option 1: 1-Var Stats.

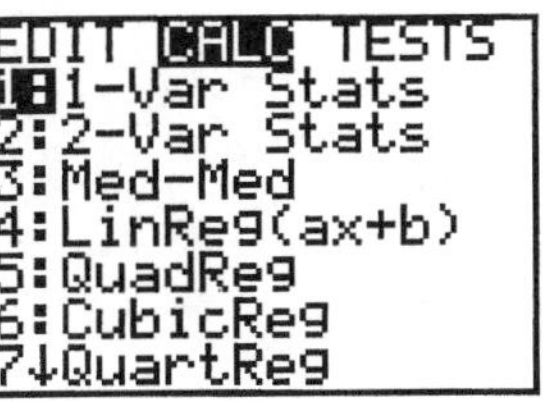

4. When 1-Var Stats appears on the home screen, enter 2nd 1 (for L1). The following basic statistics appear. Scroll down to see the second screen.

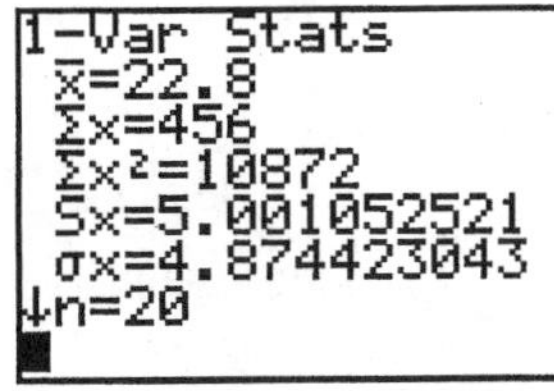

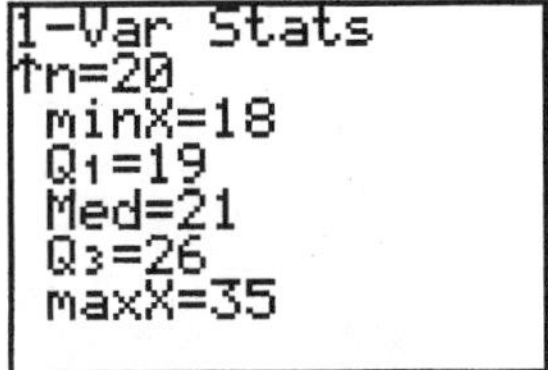

Creating a Histogram for One-Variable Data

1. Using the example data in L1, press 2nd Y= to get the STAT PLOT menu. Choose any of Plot1, Plot2, or Plot3, making sure the two you *don't* choose are Off.

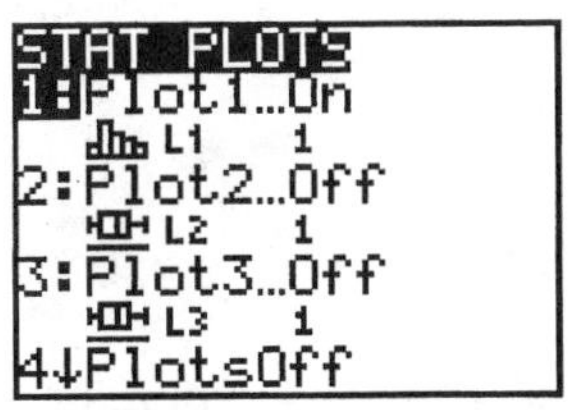

2. In the plot menu, highlight and select On, histogram type of plot, L1 for the Xlist, and 1 for the Freq, as shown

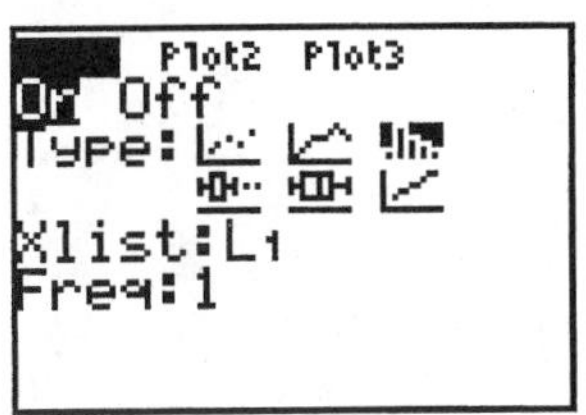

3. To see a histogram, press ZOOM and choose option 9: ZoomStat. The following histogram shows the domain of the distribution, grouping data values into classes.

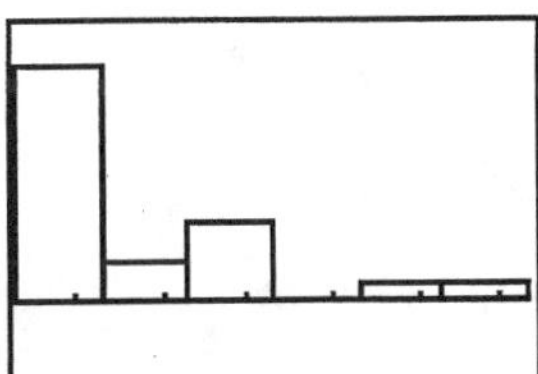

4. To show the histogram where each rectangle represents one data value, press WINDOW and set Xscl to 1, then press GRAPH.

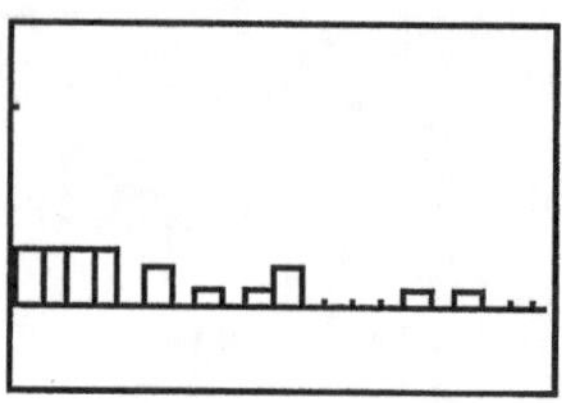

5. Pressing TRACE allows you to see the frequency for each data value.

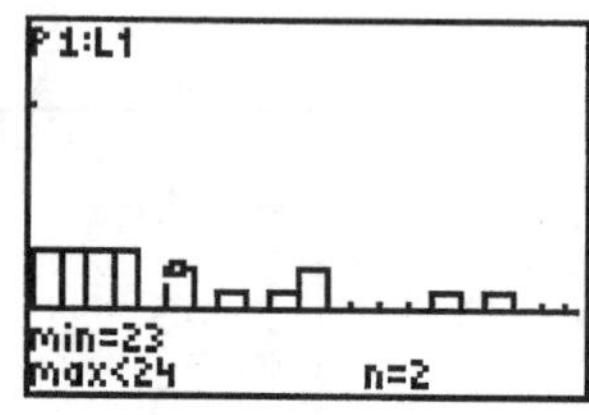

Creating a Boxplot for One-Variable Data

1. In the plot menu, highlight and select On, boxplot type of plot, L1 for the Xlist, and 1 for the Freq, as shown below

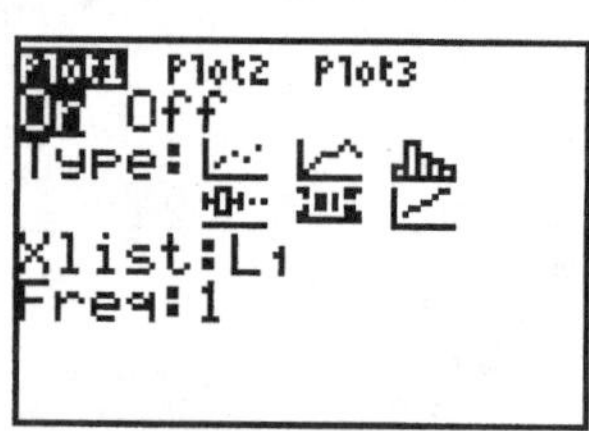

2. To see a boxplot, press ZOOM and choose option 9: ZoomStat.

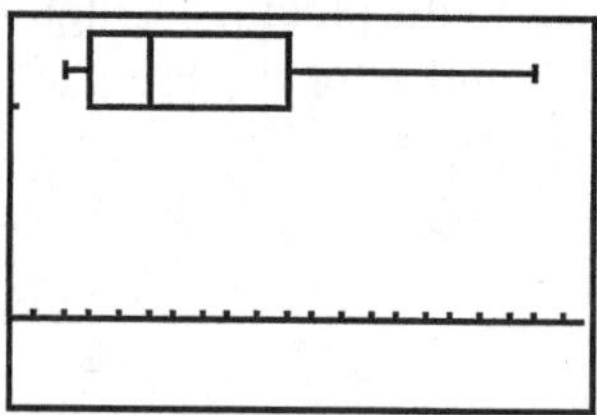

3. Pressing TRACE allows you to see the five-number summary for this distribution.

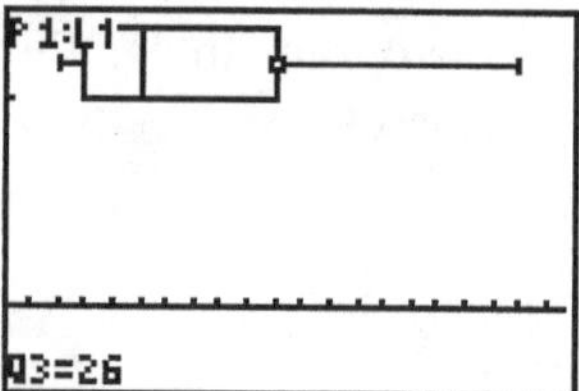

Generating a List of Random Numbers

1. Press (STAT) and choose (EDIT).

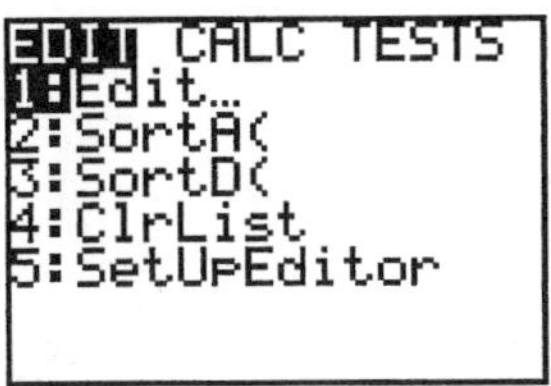

2. Clear list L1 and highlight the L1 heading. Press (MATH), choose the PRB menu, and select option 5: randlnt(.

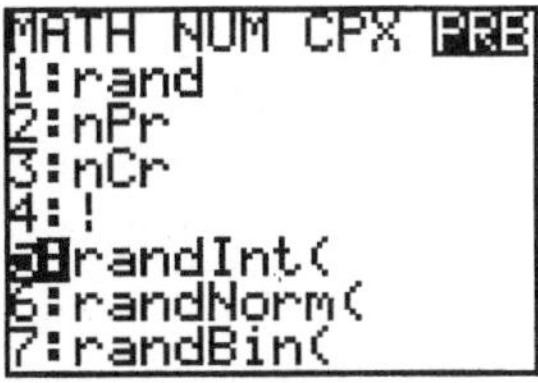

3. To randomly generate integers between 0 and 1, enter this domain, followed by the quantity of numbers desired, separated by commas. The following command generates a list of 50 zeros and ones. (Note that the command is too long to fit on the screen at once.)

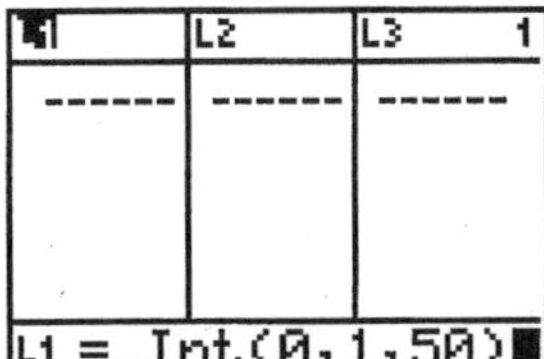

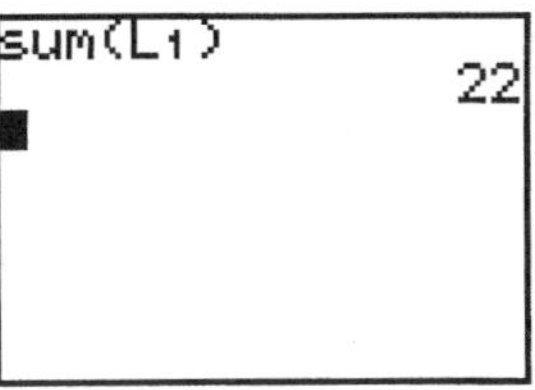

4. To quickly add the numbers in a list, from the home screen, press (2nd) (STAT) (for LIST), choose the MATH menu, and select option 5: sum(. Enter the name of the list, L1, and the sum will be displayed, as shown.

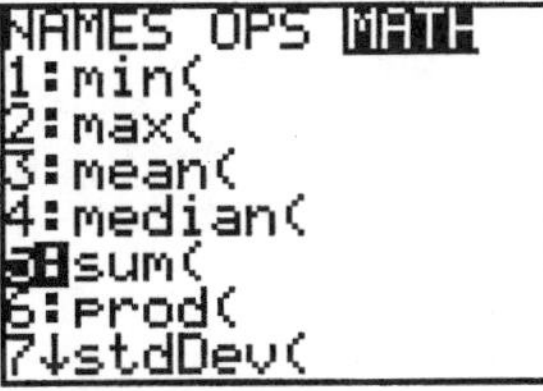

In this example, 22 of the 50 integers were ones.

Selected Answers

Chapter 1

Activity 1.1 Exercises: 2. a. Yes, it is a function. For each number of beers you drink, you will have a different blood-alcohol level; **b.** This is probably not a function, because if you drank three beers early, your blood-alcohol level may be different than if you spread them out over two hours; **3. a.** Yes, each numerical grade will correspond with one letter grade; **b.** No, the letter grades may correspond to several different numerical grades; **5. a.** Yes, each amount of snowfall is paired with one elevation; **b.** Yes, each elevation is paired with one quantity of snow; **7. a.** $f(4) = 2000$; **b.** At 4000 feet there is 9 inches of snow; **c.** (9, 4000); **d.** elevation.

Activity 1.2 Exercises: 1. $T(x) = 0.08x$; **3.** -1; -11.4; 1.2832; **5.** 4; 4; 4; **7.** Col. 1: 3, 5, 7, 9; Col. 2: 9, 25, 49, 81; **9.** Col. 1: 0, 5, 10, 15; Col. 2: 10, 9.75, 9.49, 9.22.

Activity 1.3 Exercises: 1. a. A function; **b.** No, not a function; **3.** Xmin = -2, Xmax = 3, Ymin = -6, Ymax = 36; **5. a.** Col. 1: 7238; Col. 2: 11,494; Col. 3: 17,157; Col. 4: 24,429; **b.** The dependent variable is the helium. The independent variable is the radius of the balloon; **c.** $V = f(\underline{\ r\ })$, $\underline{\ r\ }$; **d.** Domain $0 \leq r \leq 25$. The corresponding range is $0 \leq h \leq 65{,}450$; **e.** $100f(15) = 100(14{,}137) = 1{,}413{,}700 \text{ cm}^3$; **f.** $\frac{100{,}000}{14{,}137} \approx 7$ balloons; **g.** The helium is independent. The number of balloons is dependent; **h.** 6 in. is approximately 15.4 cm. $f(15.4) = 15{,}299 \text{ cm}^3\ \frac{100{,}000}{15{,}299} = 6$ balloons.

Activity 1.4 1. The balloon rises rather rapidly at first, but then rises more slowly as it reaches its maximum. Then it starts to come down very rapidly, but later slows its decent. Later it levels off before it finally reaches the ground; **2.** The profits increase with temperature. First it is a medium increase, then it is a fast increase. It levels off briefly, but then continues a rather steady rise as the temperature rises; **3.** Annual income is low and rather constant for a low number of years of education. It increases steadily as education increases for a while, then it takes a dip, but as the number of years of education gets large, the annual income increases sharply.

How Can I Practice? 1. a. Yes, because none of the total points values is repeated; **b.** Yes, for each numerical grade in the table, there is one value of total points; **c.** $f = \{(432, 86.4), (394, 78.8), (495, 99), (330, 66), (213, 42.6)\}$; **e.** $f(394) = 78.8$; **f.** The numerical grade that corresponds to 394 points is 78.8; **g.** $f(213) = 42.6$; **h.** The numerical grade that corresponds to 213 points is 42.6; **i.** If $f(n) = 66$, then $n = 330$; **2.** This is a function; **3.** This could be a function, depending on how activity level is measured; **4.** This is a function; **5.** This is not a function; **6.** This is a function; **7.** This is not a function; **8.** This is a function; **9.** This is a function; **10.** This is not a function; **11. a.** $c = 90h$; **b.** $f(h) = 90h$; **c.** Col. 1: 180; Col. 2: 360; Col. 3: 630; Col. 4: 720; Col. 5: 990; **d.** The output is cost; **e.** The independent variable is hours; **f.** For each value of input, h, there is only one value of output; **g.** The practical domain is 0 to 20 depending on the school; The practical range is 0 to 1800; **h.** The horizontal axis represents the input; **i.** $f(h)$ is a function because the graph passes the vertical line test; **k.** The cost of 9 credit hours is 810 dollars; **12. a.** $p(3) = 13$; **b.** $p(-4) = -1$; **c.** $p\left(\frac{1}{2}\right) = 8$; **d.** $p(0) = 7$; **13. a.** $t(2) = -3$; **b.** $t(-3) = 22$; **14. a.** The net profit increases during the first 2 quarters of 1993. The net profit then decreases for about 2.5 quarters, and then increases through the final quarter of 1994; **b.** The annual income rises rather steadily for 3 years. In the 4th year it rises sharply. It suffers a sharp decline during the next year. During the last year the income recovers to about the point it was originally.

Activity 1.5 Exercises: 1. a. $\frac{\Delta s}{\Delta t} = \frac{90 - 30}{86 - 81} = \frac{60}{5} = 12$ million/year; **b.** Sales were increasing at a rate of 12 million cards per year; **3.** $\frac{\Delta s}{\Delta t} = \frac{65 - 9.2}{96 - 78} = \frac{55.8}{18} = 3.1$ million/year; **5. a.** It means that sales decreased; **b.** Sales are decreasing. 86–88; 91–93; 94--96; **c.** The graph would go down;

7.

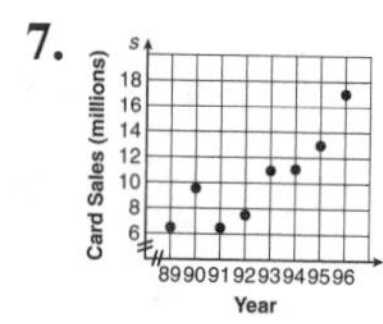

9. a. $\frac{\Delta\$}{\Delta t} = 56.9$ million dollars per year; **b.** $\frac{\Delta\$}{\Delta t} = -54.2$ million dollars per year; **c.** $\frac{\Delta\$}{\Delta t} = 1.35$ million dollars per year; **d.** $\frac{\Delta\$}{\Delta t} = 17.24$ million dollars per year.

Activity 1.6 Exercises:

1. a. The function is linear. The slope is 10; **b.** This function is not linear. The slope between the first and second points is $-\frac{3}{2}$. The slope between the second and third points is $-\frac{9}{2}$; **c.** This is a linear function. The constant slope is $\frac{9-18}{2-(-2)} = -\frac{9}{4}$; **3. a.** The data is linear because the input increases by 1 as the output decreases by 3; **b.** This data is not linear because as the input increases by 1, the output decreases by 5, then 4, then 3; **c.** This data is linear, because the output is constant. The slope is zero; **5. a.** $m = -6$; **b.** (0, 5); **c.** $f(x) = -6x + 5$; **d.** $\left(\frac{5}{6}, 0\right)$; **7. a.** Yes, the table demonstrates a constant change in t, 5 sec, and a constant change in h, -500, so the rate of change is constant; **b.** $m = -100$; **c.** The negative sign means the graph is decreasing and so is the jet's height above the ground; **d.** (0, 3500); **e.** $f(x) = -100x + 3500$; **f.** (35, 0) This means it takes the jet 35 seconds to reach the ground from a height of 3500 feet; **8. a.** $(-0.5, 0)$; **b.** (6, 0).

Activity 1.7 Exercises:

1. a. $f(x) = x - 2$; **b.** $f(x) = \frac{1}{2}x + 1$; **c.** $g(x) = -2x + 6$; **d.** $h(x) = 3x - 6$; **2. a.** 50 mph; **b.** $d = 50t + 25$; **3. a.** (0, 35) The vertical intercept occurs where $x = 0$; **b.** $m = \frac{1}{20}$ The cost is \$1 per 20 miles or \$0.05 per mile; **c.** $c = f(x) = \frac{1}{20}x + 35$; **5. a.** $y = \frac{1}{2}x - 1$; **b.** $y = -2x - 1$; **c.** $y = \frac{3}{2}x + 3$; **d.** $y = 3x - 11$; **7. a.** $(0, -8)$, $(1, -6)$, $(3, -2)$, $(4, 0)$, $(2, -4)$

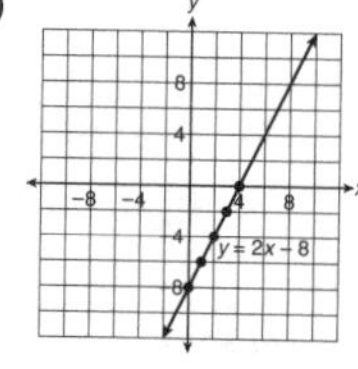

c. $\left(0, -\frac{1}{2}\right)$, $\left(1, \frac{3}{2}\right)$, $\left(\frac{1}{2}, \frac{1}{2}\right)$, $\left(\frac{1}{4}, 0\right)$, $\left(\frac{3}{2}, \frac{5}{2}\right)$

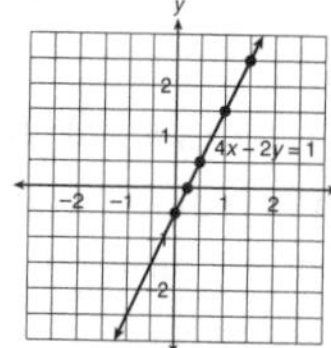

e. (0, 5), (1, 5), (2, 5), (3, 5), (4, 5)

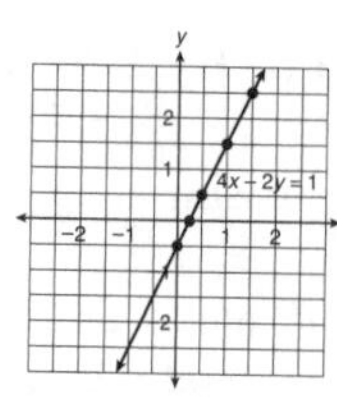

Activity 1.8 Exercises:

1. a. $y = 2x - 3$, $m = 2$, $(0, -3)$; **b.** $y = -x - 2$, $m = -1$, $(0, -2)$; **c.** $y = \frac{2}{3}x - \frac{7}{3}$, $m = \frac{2}{3}$, $\left(0, -\frac{7}{3}\right)$; **d.** $y = \frac{1}{2}x + 2$, $m = \frac{1}{2}$, (0, 2); **e.** $y = 4$, $m = 0$, (0, 4); **3. a.** $x = -2$; **b.** no slope (undefined); **c.** vertical; none; horizontal; $(-2, 0)$; **d.**

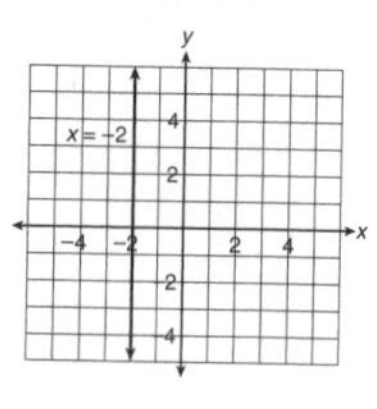

e. This is not a function. It does not pass the vertical line test; **f.** A line with 0 slope is a horizontal line. It does represent a function. A line with undefined slope is a vertical line. It does not represent a function; **5. a.** $250w$; **b.** $200d$; **c.** $250w + 200d = 10{,}000$; **d.** $d = \frac{10{,}000 - 250w}{200} = 50 - \frac{5}{4}w$; **e.** (40, 0) The maximum number of washers I can purchase is 40; **f.** (0, 50) The maximum number of dryers I can purchase is 50; **g.** The slope is $-\frac{5}{4}$. This means for every 5 dryers I purchase, that is 4 less washers I can purchase; **h.** The only relevant part is where both w and d are positive (quadrant I); **i.** Domain $0 \le w \le 40$; range $0 \le d \le 50$.

Activity 1.9 Exercises:

1. a.

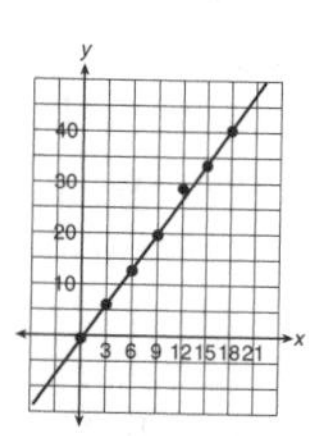

b. $y = 2x - 1$; **c.** $f(x) = 2.299x - 0.761$; **d.** My value of y would be 19; **e.** The value of y from the regression equation would be 22.229; **f.** For the x value of 25, my equation yields 51. The regression equation yields 56.714. I have more confidence in the regression equation; **3. a.** $d = 0.097t + 363.433$; **b.** When $t = 0$, $d = 363.433$. This is very close to 365.25; **c.** $d = 0.097(300) + 363.433 = 392.5$ days; **d.** $d = 0.097(700) + 363.433 = 431.3$ days This answer is not as likely to be as accurate as part c because you are outside the range of the data; **e.** The function probably is not linear, but over "short" time periods all functions are approximately linear. The length of the year may have been longer, but there are a lot of forces in the universe that we may not even have discovered yet.

How Can I Practice?

1. a. $g(x) = 2x - 3$; **b.** $h(x) = -2x - 3$; **c.** $x = 2$; **d.** none; **e.** $f(x) = -2x + 3$; **f.** $y = -2x$; **g.** $y = 2$; **h.** none; **i.** none; **2. a.** Col. 1: 28; Col. 2: 40; Col. 3: 52; Col. 4: 60; Col. 5: 68; **b.** Yes, it is linear. The slope is 4; **c.** $c = 4m + 20$; **d.**

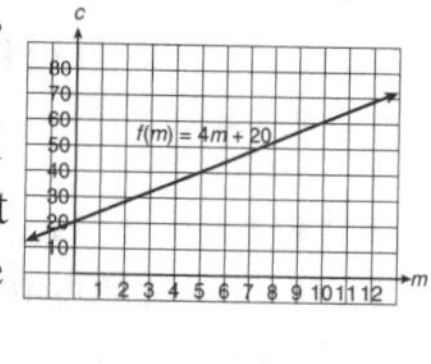

e. The slope is 4. This represents the monthly charge; **f.** The vertical intercept is (0, 20). It indicates that the initial rental cost is \$20; **g.** The horizontal intercept is $(-5, 0)$. It has no practical meaning in this case; **h.** $65 = 4m + 20$ or $45 = 4m$ or $m = 11.25$. I can keep the grapher for 11 months; **3. a.** 1.5; **b.** 1.5; **c.** $s(t)$ is a linear function because the rate of change is constant; **4.** $m = -\frac{1}{2}$; **5.** $m = -4$; **6.** $m = \frac{2}{5}$; **7.** $y = -7x + 4$; **8.** $y = 2x + 10$; **9.** $y = 5$; **10.** $x = -3$; **11.** $y = -\frac{1}{2}x - 2$; **12.** $y = \frac{1}{3}x - 3$;

13. 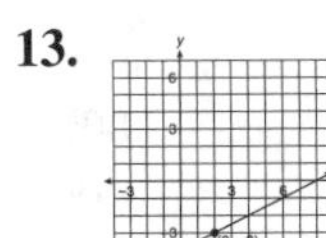

14. 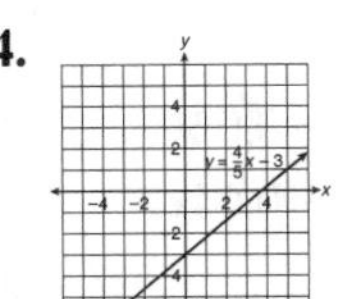
15. 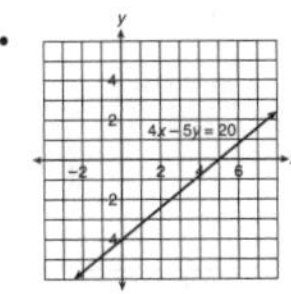

16. 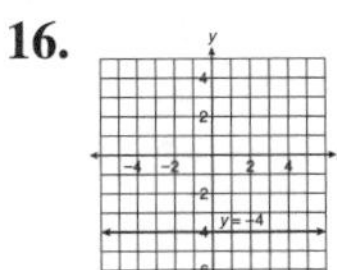

17. a. 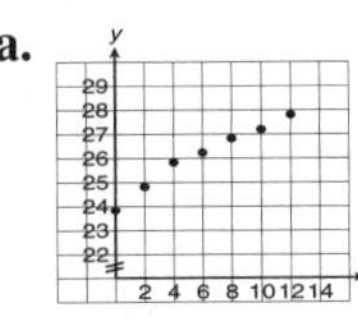

b. $f(x) = 0.322x + 24.156$; **c.** $y = 27.054$; **d.** $y = 30.596$; **18. a.** ; **b.** $f(x) = 0.657x + 4.533$; **c.** In 1986, $x = 17, f(17) = 15.7\%$ In 2010, $x = 41, f(41) = 31.5\%$; **d.** I have more confidence in 1986 because it was interpolated from the data. The 2010 percentage was a result of extrapolation, which is always less accurate.

Activity 1.11 **Exercises:** **1. a.** $d = 6t$; **b.** $d = 5t + 40$; **c.** $t = 40$ seconds; **d.** I am $6(40) = 240$ m from the starting point so I am $400 - 240 = 160$ m from the finish line; **3.**

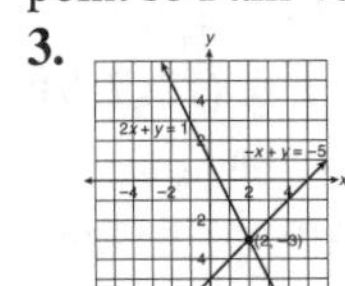

; **5.** The solution is (0.7368, 1.2105); **6.** Graphically, a dependent linear system consists of a single line; **7. a.** $(-3, -2)$; **b.** $(4, -1)$; **c.** $(3.5, -4)$; **d.** Inconsistent; No solution; **8. a.** $x = \frac{1}{2}, y = -1$; **b.** $x = -5, y = 8$; **9.** $(-4, -6)$.

Activity 1.12 **Exercises:** **1.** $(0, -3, 5)$; **3.** $(-5, 3, 1)$; **5. a.** dependent; **b.** inconsistent; **6.** Let x = number of first type of switch; y = number of second type of switch; z = number of third type of switch; **b.** $x = 1200$; $z = 3600$; $y = 7200$.

Activity 1.13 **Exercises:**

1. a. $P(x) = \begin{cases} 1.20 & 0 < x \le 1 \\ 0.90(x - 1) + 1.20 & x > 1 \end{cases}$

b. $P(15) = 0.90(15 - 1) + 1.2 = \$13.80$;

c.

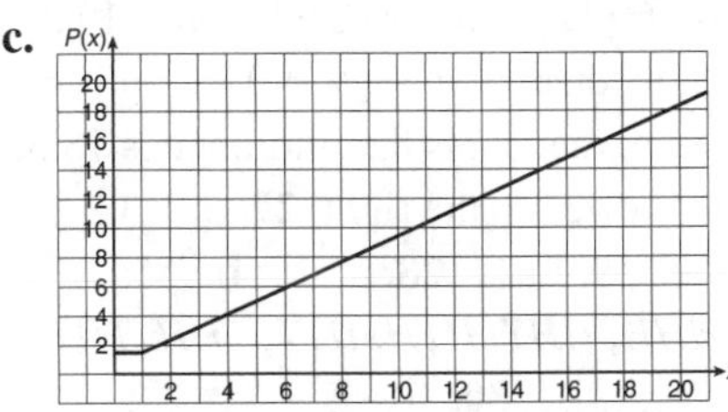

3. a. $f(x) = \begin{cases} 2.5x & x \le 15{,}000 \\ 3(x - 15{,}000) & 15{,}000 < x \le 21{,}000 \\ 4(x - 21{,}000) & x > 21{,}000 \end{cases}$

c. $f(18{,}000) = 46{,}500, f(25{,}000) = 71{,}500$; **d.** 23,375 books.

Activity 1.14 **Exercises:** **1. a.** 0.25 cm; **b.** $|x - 8| \le 0.25$; **c.** $7.75 \le x \le 8.25$; **3. a.** $|4 - (-3)| = 7$; **b.** $|x - (-3)| = 5$; **c.** $|x - 4| = 3$; **d.** $|x - 175| \le 5$; **e.** $|x - 10| \ge 3$; **f.** $|x - (-20)| < 5$; **g.** $|x - 83| = 12$; **h.** $|x - 123| > 5$; **4. a.** ; **b.** $x = -8$ or $x = 2$; **c.** $x = 1$ or $x = 7$; **d.** $170 \le x \le 180$; **e.** $x \le 7$ or $x \ge 13$; **f.** $-25 < x < -15$; **g.** $x = 71$ or $x = 95$; **h.** $x < 118$ or $x > 128$; **7. a.** ; **b.** ; **c.** ; **d.** ;

9. $y = |x - 6| = \begin{cases} x - 6 & x > 6 \\ -x + 6 & x > 6 \end{cases}$ **11.** .

How Can I Practice? **1.** $(1, -4)$; **2.** $(3, 2)$; **3.** $(-4, -5)$; **4.** Inconsistent, No solution; **6.** $(1, 5, -2)$; **7.**

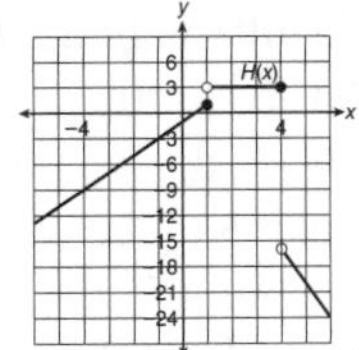

; **8. a.** 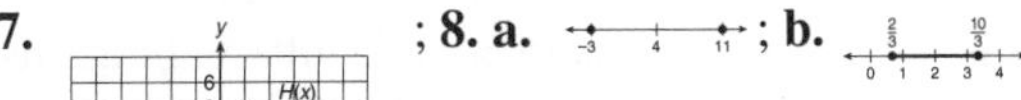 ; **b.**

Activity 1.15 **Exercises:** **1. b.** The distribution is somewhat skewed to the right; **c.** Mean = 38.28, median = 38; **d.** Since the distribution is fairly symmetrical, the mean and median are very close; **e.** The midrange is $(56 - 22)/2 = 39$; **f.** No, there is no mode, several values appear twice, but none more than that; **2.** Mean = 66, median = 66, midrange = 66; **3. c.** The domain is $\{0, 1, 2, 3, 4, 5, 6, 7, 8, 9, 10\}$; The range of the function is $\{0, 1, 2, 4, 5, 6, 7\}$; **d.** The distribution is skewed to the left; **e.** Mean = 8.2, median = 8, midrange = 7; **5.** Skewed to the left.

Activity 1.16 **Exercises:** **1. a.** Col. 1: 48; Col. 2: 52; Col. 3: 56, 44, 100; **b.** Col. 1: 0.24, 0.24, 0.48; Col. 2: 0.32, 0.20, 0.52; Col. 3: 0.56, 0.44, 1.00; **c.** 0.48; **d.** 0.20; **e.** 0.545; **f.** 0.429; **g.** There is a higher percentage of females that smoke; **3.** The probability of living to age 80 is 0.16. Or, there is a 16% chance of someone living to age 80; **5.** $P(\text{II}) = \frac{1}{4}$; **7. a.** Yes, could be a probability function; **b.** No, probabilities do not add up to one; **c.** No, every probability must be between zero and one, inclusive; **9. a.** 0.57; **b.** 0.32; **c.** 0.54.

Activity 1.17 **Exercises:** **1.** 1,280,000,000; **3.** $2^{10} = 1024$; **5.** 10,626 cones are possible, counting different orderings of the scoops. $10626/6 = 1771$ if the order doesn't matter; **6. b.** $P(2, B) = \frac{1}{18}$; **c.** $P(B) = \frac{1}{3}$; **d.** $P(2 \text{ or } B) = \frac{8}{18} = \frac{4}{9}$; **7. a.** 000, 001, 010, 011, 100, 101, 110, 111; **b.** $P(\text{one } 0) = \frac{3}{8}$; **c.** $(\text{at least one } 0) = \frac{7}{8}$; **9. a.** There are $20 \cdot 19 = 380$ different ways of choosing two socks. Of these, ten will be matched pairs. So, $P(\text{match}) = \frac{1}{38}$; **b.** 11.

Activity 1.18 **Exercises:** **1.** $\sigma = \sqrt{\frac{48}{6}} = 2.83$; **3.** 58, 70, 83.5, 90, 102; **5.** 120, 148, 162, 174, 202; **7.** DiMaggio: 12, 20.5, 30, 32, 46, Mantle: 13, 21, 28.5, 37, 54; **c.** Mantle's home run distribution is more variable and more evenly spread out.

How Can I Practice? **1.** Relative Frequencies; Col. 1: 0.079, 0.064, 0.019, 0.004, 0.165; Col. 2: 0.081, 0.120, 0.153, 0.098, 0.459; Col. 3: 0.025, 0.032, 0.113, 0.146, 0.316; Col. 4: 0.002, 0.006, 0.015, 0.036, 0.059; Col. 5: Total: 321; 365; 494; 468; 1648; Relative Frequency: 0.195, 0.221, 0.300, 0.284, 1; **a. i.** 0.002, **ii.** 0.064, **iii.** 0.182; **b.** 0.17; **c.** 0.532; **3.** $6^4 = 1296$; **5.** Col. 1: 1/16; Col. 2: 4/16; Col. 3: 6/16; Col. 4: 4/16; Col. 5: 1/16; **7.** 10! = 3,628,800; **8.** $\sigma = 1.53$; **9.** 58, 64.5, 69, 71, 85.

Gateway Review **1. a.** Yes, it is a function; **b.** No, it is not a function. There are two different outputs paired with 2; **c.** Yes, it is a function; **2.** Col. 1: 20; Col. 2: 36; Col. 3: 44; Col. 4: 60; Col. 5: 76; **a.** Yes, for each input there is one output; **b.** The input is x, the number of hours worked; **c.** The dependent variable is $f(x)$, the total cost; **d.** Negative values would not be realistic domain values. A negative number of hours worked does not make sense; **e.** The rate of change is 8; **f.** The rate of change is 8; **g.** The rate of change between any two points is 8; **h.** the relationship is linear; **i.** $f(x) = 8x + 20$; **j.** The slope is the hourly rate I charge; **k.** (0, 20) is the vertical intercept. This represents the fertilizer cost; **l.** $f(4) = 8(4) + 20 = 52$; **m.** $8x + 20 = 92$ or $8x = 72$ or $x = 9$; **3. a.** $f(-2) = 14$, $g(-2) = 10$; **b.** $-6 + (-5) = -11$; **c.** $24 - 16 = 8$; **d.** $36(-2) = -72$; **4. a.** linear; **b.** linear; **c.** not linear; **d.** linear; **5. a.** $m = -\frac{4}{3}$; **b.** $7y = 3x - 21$, $m = \frac{3}{7}$; **c.** $m = \frac{1}{2}$; **6. a.** $y = 4$; **b.** $y = 2x + 5$; **c.** $y = -3x + 4$; **d.** $y = 2x - 16$; **e.** $x = 2$; **f.** $y = -5x + 20$; **g.** $y = 4x + 8$; **h.** $y = -\frac{1}{2}x + 5$; **7.** $y = -\frac{2}{5}x + 2$; **8. a.** $f(x) = 300{,}000 - 10{,}000x$; **b.** $m = -10{,}000$. The building depreciates $10,000 per year; **c.** (0, 300,000) The original value is $300,000; **d.** (30, 0) It takes 30 years for the building to fully depreciate; **9. a.** $(0, -3)$; **b.** $(0, -3)$; **c.** $(0, -3)$; **d.** The graphs all intersect at the point $(0, -3)$; **e.** The results are the same; **10. a.** $m = -2$; (0, 1); **b.** $m = -2$; $(0, -1)$; **c.** $m = -2$; $(0, -3)$; **d.** The graphs are parallel lines; **11. a.** $m = -3$, (0, 2); **b.** $m = -3$, (0, 2); **c.** $m = -3$, (0, 2); **d.** The graphs are all the same; **e.** The slopes; **f.** The slopes and the y-intercepts; **g.** The results are the same; **12. a.** (0, 150) (75, 0); **c.** The domain and range are all reals; **d.** $w(t) = -2t + 150$; **e.** They are the same; **13. a.** $f(x) = 5$; **b.** Horizontal line through (0, 5); **c.** The slope is 0; **14.**

15. a. $f(x) = \begin{cases} 1500 & x \le 10{,}000 \\ 1500 + 0.02x & 10{,}000 < x \le 40{,}000 \\ 1500 + 0.04x & x > 40{,}000 \end{cases}$

b. 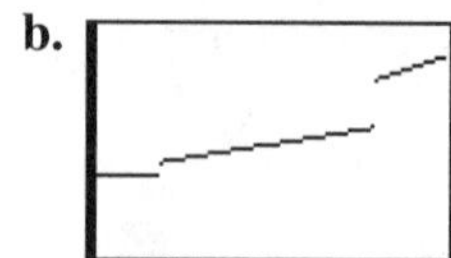 Xmin = 0, Xmax = 50,000, Ymin = 0, Ymax = 4000, Xscl = 100;

c. $f(25{,}000) = 1500 + 0.02(25{,}000) = 2000$; **d.** $1500 + 0.04x = 3150$, $0.04x = 1650$, $x = 41{,}250$; **16. a.** $y = 1040x + 7900$; **b.** 1040 The number of finishers increased at a rate of 1040 per year; **c.** (0, 7900) The model indicates there were 7900 finishers in the year 1994; **d.** Pretty good; **e.** 14,140; **f.** I used extrapolation, because I am predicting outside the original data; **g.** No, 2024 is farther from the data than 2000. The farther removed we are from the data, the more likely our prediction is in error; **17. a.** $(3, -1)$; **b.** $(-1, 6)$;

c. 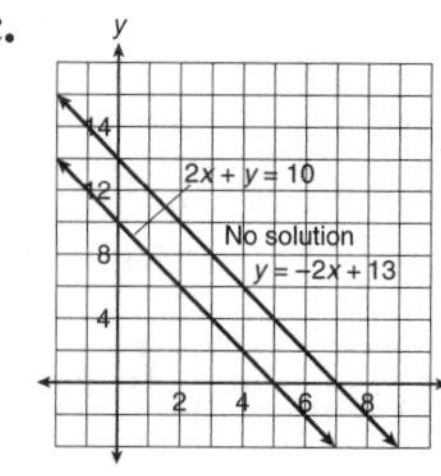

; **d.** dependent system, x = cost of one pizza = $4.40, y = cost of one cookie = $0.75; **19. a.** (0, 1, 2); **b.** $(-3, 1, 0)$; **c.** $(0.5, 0.25, -0.5)$; **d.** (12, 7, 9); **20. a.** x = cost of a small print = 0.50, y = cost of a medium print = 1, z = cost of a large print = 2, Yes, this is a good deal; **b.** Answers will vary. I would not take advantage of this. I don't give away many pictures;

21. a. 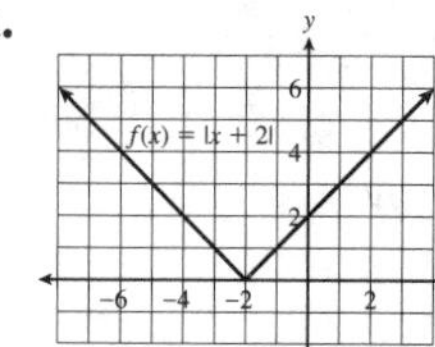

; **b.** Increasing $x > -2$, decreasing $x < -2$; **c.** Domain is all real numbers; **d.** Range is $y \ge 0$; **e.** g is the reflection through the x-axis; **f.** f shifts the graph of $y = |x|$ two units to the left. g shifts the graph of $y = |x|$ two units up; **22. a.** $x = 28$ or $x = 18$; **b.** $x = -5$ or $x = -19$; **c.** $x = \frac{11}{2}$ or $x = -\frac{1}{2}$; **d.** $x = \frac{1}{5}$ or $x = 1$; **23. a.** $2.3 \le x \le 2.7$; **b.** $x > -3$ or $x < -7$; **c.** $3 < x < 6$; **d.** $-\frac{20}{3} \le x \le -\frac{16}{3}$; **24. a.** $|x - 453| \le 8$; **b.** $445 \le x \le 461$; **25.** Mean is 160.12; Standard deviation is 19.8. min is 120, $Q_1 = 148$, median = 162, $Q_3 = 174$, max = 202; **26. a.** Mean is 82.4, median is 82, midrange is 78.5; **b.** The distribution is skewed to the right; **27. a.** .43; **b.** .50; **c.** .19; **d.** .05; **e.** .59; **f.** .11; **28. a.** .17; **b.** .55; **c.** .72; **d.** 0; **29. a.** {*HHH, HHT, HTH, HTT, THH, THT, TTH, TTT*}; **b.** Col. 2: $\frac{1}{8}, \frac{3}{8}, \frac{3}{8}, \frac{1}{8}$; **30.** $10 \cdot 9 \cdot 8 = 720$; **31.** $8 \cdot 10 \cdot 10 \cdot 10 \cdot 10 \cdot 10 \cdot 10 \cdot 10 = 8 \cdot 10^7 = 80{,}000{,}000$

Chapter 2

Activity 2.1 **Exercises 2.1:** **1. a.** Col. 2: 100, 100, 100; 100; Col. 3: 250, 500, 750, 1000, 1250; Col. 4: 350, 600, 850, 1100, 1350; **b.** $C(x) = f(x) = 12.50x + 100$; **c.** Col. 2: 6, 9, 12, 15; Col. 3: 4500, 6750, 9000, 11,250; Col. 4: 585, 877.50, 1170, 1462.50; **d.** $R(x) = 14.625x$; **e.** $P = 2.125x - 100$; **f.** $0 \le x \le$ number of people the banquet hall will accommodate; **g.** 48; **h.** 283; **3. a.** $(f - g)(x) = 6x - 3$; **b.** Col. 2: 1, 9, 17, 25; Col. 3: 4, 0, −4, −8; Col. 4: −3, 9, 21, 33; **c.** Answers will vary depending on the choices of x. Col. 1: 1, −1, 2.5, 3.2; Col. 2: 5, −3, 11, 13.8; Col. 3: 2, 6, −1, −2.4; Col. 4: 3, −9, 12, 16.2; **d.** Yes; **5. a.** $-x^2 + 5x - 8$; **b.** $x^2 + x - 2$; **c.** $-3x^2 + 12x - 19$; **d.** $2x^2 - x + 1$.

Activity 2.2 **Exercises:** **1. a.** $(f + g)(x) = -x + 1$; **b.** $(f - g)(x) = -x - 5$; **c.** $(g - f)(x) = x + 5$;

3.

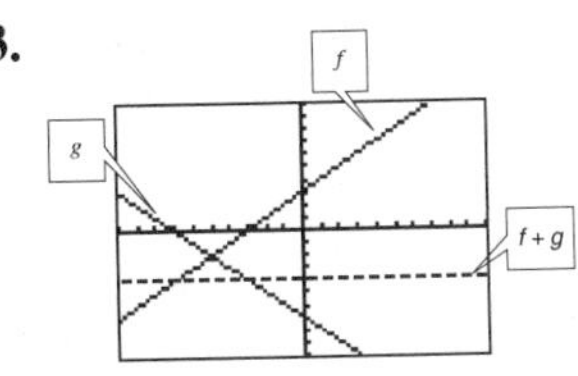

Activity 2.3 **Exercises:** **1. a.** $50 + x$; **b.** $7.50 - 0.05x$; **c.** $C(x) = (50 + x)(7.50 - 0.05x)$; **d.** Domain is $0 \le x \le 50$; **f.** $C(x) = -0.050x^2 + 5x + 375)$; **g.** The graphs are the same; **3.** Col. 1: $3x^2$; Col. 2: $9x$; Col. 3: $-5x$; $x^3 + 6x^2 + 4x - 15$; **5. a.** $x^2 + 5x + 6$; **b.** $x^2 - 5x + 6$; **c.** $x^2 - x - 6$; **d.** $x^2 + x - 6$; **7. a.** $x^3 + 6x^2 + 5x - 6$; **b.** $= 2x^4 - 5x^3 + 5x^2 + 4x$; **c.** $= 2x^3 - 11x^2 + 16x - 3$; **d.** $-x^3 + 4x^2 + 4x - 16$; **e.** $= 3x^4 - 14x^3 + 20x^2 - 11x + 2$; **f.** $-4x^3 + 2x^2 + 30x$; **8. a.** $(f \cdot g)(x) = 2x^2 - x - 3$; **b.** Col. 2: 1, 2, 3, 4, 5; Col. 3: −3, −1, 1, 3, 5; Col. 4: −3, −2, 3, 12, 25; **c.** Col. 1: 6, 7, 8, 9; Col. 2: 7, 8, 9, 10; Col. 3: 9, 11, 13, 15; Col. 4: 63, 88, 117, 150; Answers may vary depending on the choices of x; **d.** Yes, the output of the product function is the product of the outputs of f and g.

How Can I Practice? **1. a.** $x = 30$; **b.** $N = f(t) = 30 + t$, $C = g(t) = 20 - .5t$; **c.** Col. 1: 30, 20; Col. 2: 32, 19; Col. 3: 34, 18; Col. 4: 36, 17; Col. 5: 38, 16; Col. 6: 40, 15; **d.** Col. 1: 600; Col. 2: 608; Col. 3: 612; Col. 4: 612; Col. 5: 608; Col. 6: 600; **e.** $R(t) = -0.5t^2 + 5t + 600$; **g.** \$612.50 is the maximum revenue if 35 couples attend; **h.** 35 tickets must be sold to obtain the maximum revenue; **2. a.** $3x - 1$; **b.** $-x + 5$; **c.** $2x^2 + x - 6$; **d.** 2; **e.** 0; **f.** $3x + 6$; **3. a.** $-3x + 5$; **b.** $x^4 - x^3 - 5x^2 + 9x - 4$; **c.** 0; **d.** $-x^2 - 7x + 14$; **4. a.** $5x - 2$; **b.** $2x^2 - 2x - 8$; **c.** $-2x + 12$; **d.** $2x^2 - 13x - 8$; **e.** $5x^2 - x + 2$; **5. a.** x^4; **b.** x^9; **c.** $6x^8$; **d.** x^5y^6z; **e.** $10x^6y^5z^8$; **f.** $-30a^5b^3$; **6. a.** $x^2 - 7x + 10$; **b.** $4x^2 + 25x - 21$; **c.** $-x^2 + 2x + 3$; **d.** $x^3 + x^2 - 11x + 10$; **e.** $2x^3 - x^2 + 3x + 2$; **f.** $-2x^2 - 5x - 21$; **g.** $11x^2 - 2x$; **h.** $-x^5 - x^3 + 3x^2 + 2x - 1$.

Activity 2.4 **Exercises:** **1. a.** $g(2) = 200$. The radius of the slick is 200 ft 2 hours after the spill; **b.** $f(g(2)) \approx 125{,}663$ sq ft. The area of the oil slick is 125,663 sq ft; **c.** $f(g(10)) = 3{,}141{,}592$ sq ft. This is the area of the slick after 10 hours. **d.** $f(g(t)) = 10{,}000\pi t^2$; **e.** $f(g(10)) = 1{,}000{,}000\pi t^2$. The formulas are the same; **2.** $g(f(t)) = \frac{4}{3}\pi\left(t^2 + 2t + 1\right)$; **3. a.** $u(v(x)) = -18x^2 + 18x - 3$; **b.** $v(u(t)) = -6t^2 + 6t + 2$.

Activity 2.5 **Exercises:** **1. a.** 26,400 ft; **b.** 316,800 in.; **c.** 316,800 in.; **d.** $f(x) = 5280x$; **e.** $g(w) = 12w$; **f.** $g(f(5)) = 316{,}800$; **g.** $g(f(x)) = 63{,}360x$; **3. a.** $f(x) = x - 1500$; **b.** $g(x) = 0.9x$; **c.** $f(g(20{,}000)) = 16{,}500$ The sale price of a \$20,000 car after a 10% discount and a \$1500 rebate is \$16,500; **d.** $g(f(20{,}000) = \$16{,}650$ The sale price of a \$20,000 car after a \$1500 rebate and a 10% discount is \$16,650; **e.** Taking the discount first is better for the consumer. Taking the rebate is better for the dealership; **5. a.** 8; **b.** 4; **c.** 15; **d.** 2.

Activity 2.6 **Exercises:** **1. a.** $f(g(2)) = 6$; **b.** $g(12) = 9$; **c.** $f(x - 3) = 2x + 2$; **d.** $g(2x + 8) = 2x + 5$; **3.** $f(g(x)) = x^{18}$, $g(f(x)) = -x^{18}$; **5. a.** 10; **b.** 12; **c.** 4; **d.** 256; **e.** 1.90365; **f.** 4; **7. a.** 5; **b.** 0; **c.** Undefined.

Activity 2.7 **Exercises:** **1. a.** 7; **b.** 4; **c.** x; **d.** x; **3. a.** Col. 1: 2, 3, 4, 2; Col. 2: 0, 1, 2, 3; **b.** No, because the input value 2 is paired with two different output values, 0 and 3; **c.** The function does have an inverse, but the inverse is not a function.

Activity 2.8 **Exercises:** **1. a.** $P(x) = 0.05x + 250$; **b.** $P(6000) = 550$. The weekly salary for \$6000 worth of sales is \$550; **c.** $S(P) = \dfrac{P - 250}{0.05}$; **d.** $S(400) = 3000$. A weekly salary of \$400 means I sold \$3000 worth of merchandise; **e.** $S(P(8000)) = 8000$; **3. a.** $f^{-1}(x) = \dfrac{x + 4}{3}$; **b.** $g^{-1}(x) = 2z + 4$; **c.** $t = \frac{5}{s}$ or $s = \frac{5}{t}$; **5.** Yes, they are inverses because they are reflections in the line $y = x$;

7. a. $g^{-1}(x) = \dfrac{3x - 6}{4}$; **b.**

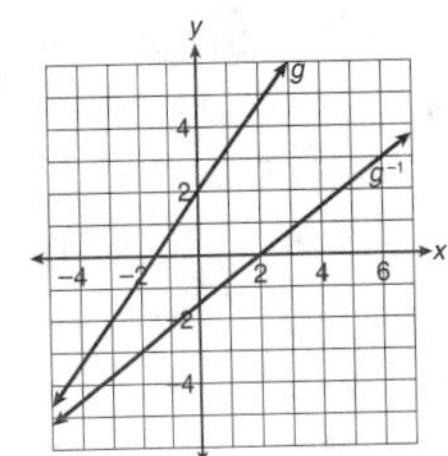

c. Yes, because the graphs are reflections in the line $y = x$; **d.** $g^{-1}\left(\frac{6 + 4x}{3}\right) = x$. Yes, because $g^{-1}(g(x)) = x$.

Activity 2.9 **1. a.** $f(1011) = 3$; **b.** $g(n) = 1$ when $n = 3$, $g(4) = 0$; **3.** Col. 2: 3, 4, 4, 5, 3, 4, 4, 5, 4; Col. 3: 1, 0, 0, 1, 1, 0, 0, 1, 0; **5.** No. Maybe the original string was 11101 and it was sent correctly or the original string was 111010 and the person forgot to add a 0 to the end of it.

How Can I Practice? **1. a.** -3; **b.** 7; **c.** $f(x + 2) = x^2 + 4x$; **d.** $g(x^2 - 4) = x^2 - 2$; **e.** $f(x^2 - 4) = x^4 - 8x^2 + 12$; **f.** $g^{-1}(x) = x - 2$; **2. a.** $f(-2) = -6$; **b.** $g(-1) = 22$; **c.** $g(-2) = -2$; **d.** $f(4 + x - x^2) = x - x^2$; **e.** $g(x - 4) = -x^2 + 9x - 16$; **f.** $f(x) = x + 4$; **3.** Col. 1: -1; Col. 2: 3; Col. 3: 2; Col. 4: 1; Col. 5: 0; **4. a.** x^8; **b.** x^3y^3; **c.** $32x^{20}y^5$; **d.** $(27x^6)(2xy^4) = 54x^7y^4$; **e.** 125; **f.** 16; **5. a.** $g(3x^2) = -54x^6$; **b.** $f(-2x^3) = 12x^6$; **c.** $g(48) = -221{,}184$; **6. a.** $s(4x - 1) = 16x^2 + 8x - 4$; **b.** $t(x^2 + 4x - 1) = 4x^2 + 16x - 5$; **c.** $t^{-1}(x) = \frac{x + 1}{4}$; **7. a.** $p(\sqrt{x + 2}) = \frac{1}{\sqrt{x + 2}}$; **b.** $c(\frac{1}{x}) = \sqrt{\frac{1}{x} + 2}$; **c.** $p^{-1}(x) = \frac{1}{x}$; **8.** $\{(6, 4),(-9, 7),(1, -2),(0, 0)\}$; **9.** Since $f(g(x)) = g(f(x)) = x$, f, and g are inverse functions; **10. a.** $f^{-1}(x) = \frac{x - 3}{4}$;

b.

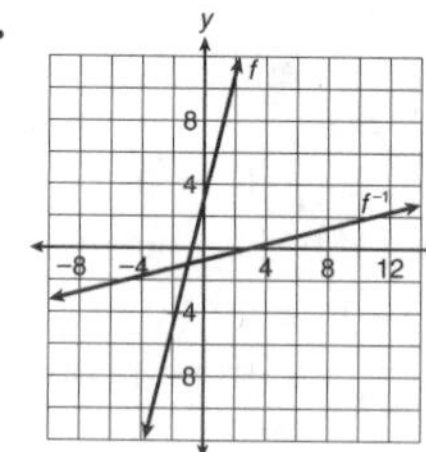

; **c.** The intercepts of f are (0, 3) and $(-3/4, 0)$. The intercepts of f^{-1} $(0, -3/4)$ and (3, 0); **d.** The slope of the graph of f is 4. The slope of the graph of the inverse is 1/4; **11. a.** $b = x^2$ $V = 10b$; **b.** $V = 10x^2$; **12.** $x = 3/4$.

Gateway Review **1. a.** $2x^2 - 2x - 1$; **b.** $-x^2 + 5x - 4$; **c.** $4x^2 - 13x + 3$; **d.** $x^3 - 7x^2 + 13x - 15$; **e.** $-11x + 11$; **2. a.** $6x^8$; **b.** $16x^6y^2$; **c.** $-2x^5y^3$; **d.** $-10x^5y^5z^4$; **3. a.** -20; **b.** $4x + 1$; **c.** 19; **d.** $-12x^2 + 22x - 6$; **e.** $-12x + 16$; **f.** $g(10) = -17$; **g.** $f^{-1}(x) = \frac{x + 2}{6}$; **4. a.** $x^2 - 4x + 5$; **b.** $3x^3 - 5x^2 + 11x - 6$; **c.** $f(3x - 2) = 9x^2 - 15x + 9$; **d.** $g(5) = 13$; **5. a.** 7; **b.** 4; **c.** 81; **d.** 3.214; **6. a.** $f(x) = 0.02x^2$; **b.** $g(x) = 0.048x^2$; **c.** $(f + g)(x) = 0.068x^2$; **d.** Col. 2: 0.08, 0.32, 0.72, 1.28, 2; Col. 3: 1.92, 7.68, 17.28, 30.72, 48; Col. 4: 2, 8, 18, 32, 50; **e.** $f(5) = 0.50$, $g(5) = 1.2$, $(f + g)(5) = 1.70$ For a box whose base is 5 in. by 5 in., the cost of the top and bottom of the box is \$.50, the cost of the 4 sides is \$1.70, and the total cost of the box is \$1.70; **7. a.** $f(x) = 12x + 300$; **b.** $g(x) = 25.95x$; **c.** $h(x) = 25.95x - (12x + 300) = 13.95x - 300$; **d.** 22 hats must be sold, since 21 hats is not quite enough. The solution was obtained graphically; **e.** $f(50) = 900$, the cost of producing 50 hats is \$900. $g(50) = 1297.50$, the revenue from 50 hats is \$1297.50. $h(50) = 397.50$, the profit from selling 50 hats is \$397.50; **f.** The profit is the difference between the revenue and cost functions; **8. a.** $f(x) = 60(110) + x(110 - 2x)$; **b.** $f(x) = 6600 + 110x - 2x^2$; **c.** Integers $0 \le x \le 30$; **d.** $f(15) = 7800$. At regular price the cost is \$8250, so the savings is \$450; **9. a.** -10; **b.** 41; **c.** 2; **d.** 5; **10. a.** Integers $0 \le x \le 30$; **b.** $f(22) = 2864.40$; **c.** $f(3.75t) = 150(3.75t) - 0.9(3.75t)^2 = 562.50t - 12.65625t^2$; **d.** The input variable is t; **e.** $C(g(4)) = \$2047.50$; **f.** $3500 = 562.50t - 12.65625t^2$, t is about 7.5 hours (determined graphically); **11. a.** $f^{-1}(x) = y = \frac{5x + 3}{2}$; **b.** The slope of f is 2/5. The slope of f^{-1} is 5/2. The slopes are reciprocals; **12. a.** Let $f(x) = -2x + 1$ and $g(x) = \frac{1 - x}{2}$.

$$f(g(x)) = f\left(\frac{1 - x}{2}\right) = -2\left(\frac{1 - x}{2}\right) + 1 = x$$

$$g(f(x)) = g(-2x + 1) = \frac{1 - (-2x + 1)}{2} = \frac{2x}{2} = x$$

Since $f(g(x)) = g(f(x)) = x$, f and g are inverses; **b.** ; **c.** f and g are symmetric with respect to the line $y = x$; **13. a.** Yes, the ratio (change in cost)/(change in number of tickets) is constant; **b.** $f(x) = 5.5x$; **c.** the cost of one ticket is \$5.50. This is represented by the slope; **d.** Col. 1; \$11.00, \$27.50, \$38.50, \$66.00; Col. 2: 2, 5, 7, 12; **e.** $g(x) = \frac{2}{11}x$; **f.** The slope is 2/11. The slopes are reciprocals; **g.** The functions are inverses since $f(g(x)) = g(f(x)) = x$.

Chapter 3

Activity 3.1 **Exercises:** **1. a.** Col. 1: 0.04; Col. 2: 0.2; Col. 3: 1; Col. 4: 5; Col. 5: 25; Col. 1: 25; Col. 2: 5; Col. 3: 1; Col. 4: 0.2; Col. 5: 0.04; **b.** ; **c.** The graphs are reflections in the y-axis; **3. a.** All three functions have the same shape, but different y-intercepts; **b.** The graphs intersect at (0, 1). They both have the x-axis as an asymptote. However, f is a decreasing function and g is an increasing function; **c.** The graphs are reflections over the x-axis; **d.** The graphs are reflections in the y-axis; **5. a.** Col. 2: 24.948; Col. 3: 26.944; Col. 4: 29.099; **b.** Col. 2: 7.5; Col. 3: 5.625; Col. 3: 4.219.

Activity 3.2 **1. a.** Yes, because the ratios of consecutive outputs are fairly close: 0.998, 0.997, and 0.995 respectively; **b.** $p = 148.3(0.997)^t$; **c.** $p = 143.9$ million; **2.** The graph of f is iii. The graph of g is i. The graph of h is ii; **3. a.** This is not exponential because the output ratio is not constant even though the input changes by 1 at each step; **b.** This is exponential. The growth factor is 4; **c.** This is not exponential because the output ratio is not constant even though the input changes by 2 at each step; **d.** This is exponential. The decay factor is 0.49; **5. a.** $f(-2) = \frac{3}{16}$; **b.** $f(\frac{1}{2}) = 6$; **c.** $f(2) = 48$; **d.** $f(1.3) = 18.189$; **7. a.** 2.5 parts per million; **b.**

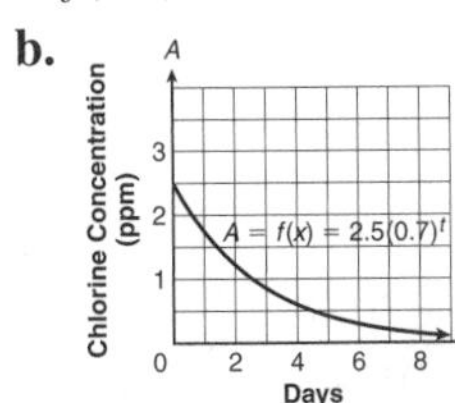

c. $f(3) = 2.5(0.7)^3 = 0.86$ parts per million; **d.** If the days are hot and sunny then chlorine should be added every 1.4 days.

Activity 3.3 **1. a.** If $r = 0.02$, the growth factor $1 + r = 1.02$; **b.** If $r = .23$, the decay factor $1 - r = 0.77$; **c.** If the growth factor $1 + r = 1.029$, then $r = 0.029$ or 2.9%; **d.** If the decay factor $1 - r = 0.32$, then $r = 0.68$ or 68%; **2. a.** Bozeman $P = 22{,}660(1.0046)^x$; Butte $P = 33{,}336(0.9891)^x$; **b.** Bozeman: $P(12) = 22{,}660(1.0046)^{12} = 23{,}943$; Butte $P(12) = 33{,}336(0.9891)^{12} = 29{,}228$; **c.** Bozeman's population will double in about 150 years; **d.** The populations will be about equal in 24.8 years or 2015; **4. a.**

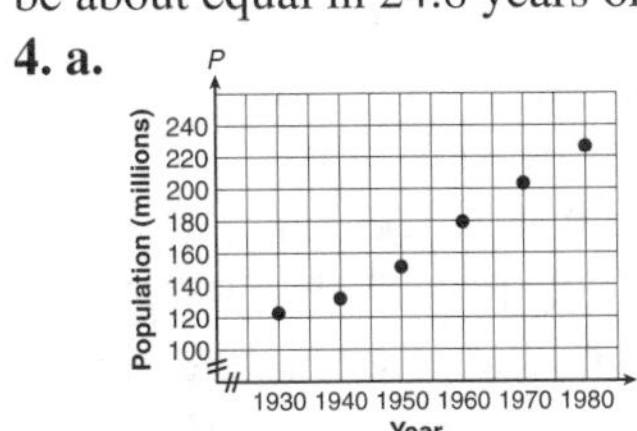

; **b.** Yes, the ratios are close; **c.** $P = 122.8(1.0125)^t$; **d.** $P(50) = 122.8(1.0125)^{50} = 228.5$ million; **5. a.** $V(t) = 20{,}000(0.85)^t$; **b.** 15%; **c.** 0.85; **d.** $V(5) = 20{,}000(0.85)^5 = 8874$; **e.** They agree; **f.** 4.3 years from purchase time.

Activity 3.5 **1. a.** $A = 2000\left(1 + \frac{.05}{12}\right)^{12(2)} = 2209.88$; **b.** About 14 years.; **c.** The growth rate is 0.0511619. The growth factor is 1.0511619; **3. a.** 12.277 grams; **b.** 20 to 10 about 28 years, 10 to 5 about 28 years, 5 to 2.5 about 28 years; **c.** The growth (decay) rate is 2.44%. The decay factor is 0.9759; **5. a.** 127.62 billion; **b.**

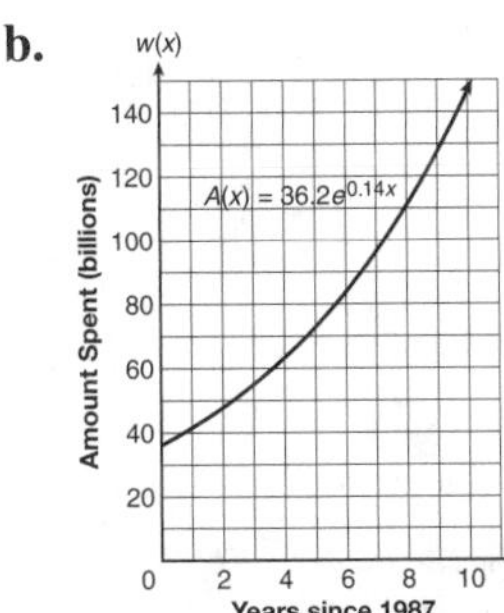

; **c.** (0, 36.2) This indicates the 36.2 billion spent in 1987; **d.** 1992; **e.** The doubling time is about 5 years. **7. a.** The number e is named for the Swiss mathematician Leonhard Euler; **b.** Additional irrational numbers are π, 2π, π, $\sqrt{3}$, $-2\sqrt[3]{7}$; **c.** Well over 100; **d.** When they were looking, they were not absolutely sure that a pattern did not exist.

Activity 3.6 **1. a.** The exponential model seems to be better since the rate of change appears to be increasing; **b.**

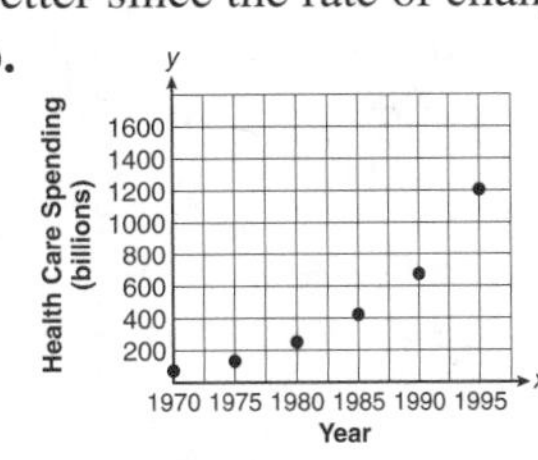

; **c.** The scatterplot reinforces part a because the points seem to be an increasing exponential curve; **d.** $C(t) = 77.41(1.1167)^t$ t = Number of years since 1970; **e.** 703.93 billion; **f.** Error = 28.93; Percent error 4.3%; **g.** 1.1167 billion dollars; **h.** $t = 23$ or 1993; **i.** doubling time is about 6.3 years; **3. a.** All reals; **b.** $y > 0$; **c.** Since $b > 0$, the function is always positive; **d.** if $a < 0$, the function is always negative; **e.** $(0, a)$.

How Can I Practice? **1. a.** $A = 17{,}000(1.04)^t$; **b.** The growth rate is 0.04, the growth factor is 1.04; **c.** $A = 17{,}000\left(1.04\right)^3 = 19{,}122.69$; **d.** 14.5 years; **2.** graph i is function b; graph ii is function c; graph iii is function a; **3.** i is function b because it is decreasing and the only growth factor between 0 and 1 is function b's 0.47; ii is function c because it is positive and increasing with the growth factor of 1.47; iii is function a because it is the only one that will yield negative output. ; **4. a.** Col. 3: 13.01; Col. 4: 33.18; Col. 5: 84.61; **b.** Col. 3: 1.26; Col. 4: 0.76; Col. 5: 0.46; **c.** Col. 1: 7.10; Col. 2: 12.78; Col. 5: 74.7; **5. a.** $y = 2(2.55)^x$; **b.** $y = 3.5(0.6)^x$; **c.** $y = 7.1(1.8)^x$; **6. a.** $f(0) = 1.3$; decreasing; **b.** $f(0) = 0.6$; increasing; **c.** $f(0) = 3$; decreasing; **7. a.** Yes; **b.** The constant ratio is 2.5 or $\frac{5}{2}$; **c.** $A = 2(2.5)^x$; **8.** The answer is, it depends. If I plan to be with the company 10 years or less, I would take Plan 1, because it takes Plan 2 about 9 years to catch up. If I expect to be with the company for a long time, say 20 years, I would choose Plan 2 because by then I am over $6000 per year better off; **9. a.** $N = f(t) = 2e^{0.075t}$; **b.** $N = 3.6442$; **c.**

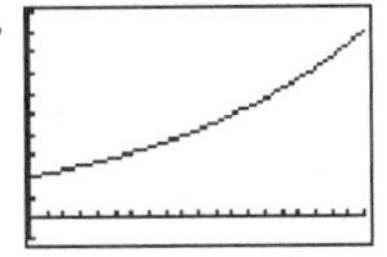

; **d.** 14.6482 or 15 weeks.

Activity 3.7 **1. a.** 5; **b.** 3; **c.** -1; **d.** -6; **e.** 0; **f.** 2; **g.** $\frac{1}{2}$; **h.** $\frac{1}{2}$; **3. a.** $\log_3 9 = 2$; **b.** $\log_{121} 11 = \frac{1}{2}$; **c.** $\log_4 27 = x$; **d.** $\log_y 19 = 3$; **5. a.** $0 < x < 1, x = \log 3.25$, $x = 0.5119$; **b.** $2 < x < 3, x = \log 590, x = 2.771$; **c.** $-6 < x < -5; x = \log 0.0000045; x = -5.347$; **7. a.** $x > 0$; **b.** All real numbers.; **c.** $x > 1$; **d.** $0 < x < 1$; **e.** $x = 1$; **f.** 10; **g.** Only f will change. $\log_b x = 1$ when $x = b$; **h.** c, d, and f will change. c and d will be interchanged; **9.** $y = \log_2 x$.

Activity 3.8 **1. a;**

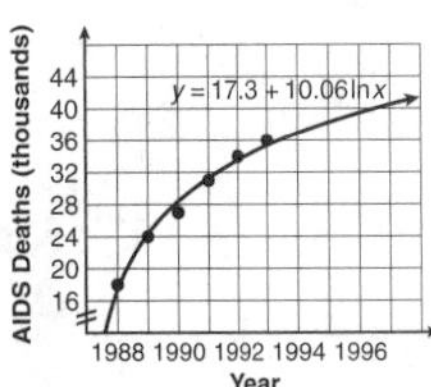

b. Yes, it is increasing, but more and more slowly; **d.** Yes, since all the points are close to the line and some are above, some are below; **e.** 36,900 deaths; **f.** Quite accurate. The error is 460 or 1.2%; **3. a.** $x > 0$; **b.** All real numbers.; **c.** When $x > 1$; **d.** $0 < x < 1$; **e.** $x = 1$; **f.** $x = e$; **5. a.** 0; **b.** 1; **c.** 2; **7. a.**

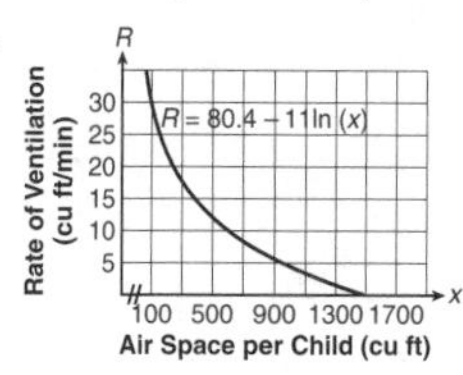

b. $f(300) = 17.66$.

Activity 3.9

1. a. $\log_b 3 + \log_b 7$; **b.** $1 + \log_3 13$; **c.** $\log_7 13 - \log_7 17$; **d.** $\log_3 x + \log_3 y - 1$; **3. b.** No, the graphs are the same because $\log(2x) = \log 2 + \log x$; **5. a.** $7.4 \log(15) = 8.7$ or 9 cars; **b.** Col. 2: 9, 13, 21; **c.** The sum of the sales from the smaller ads exceeds the sales from the larger ad by 1; **d.** Pretty close. 15 times 50 equals 750, so I would have expected the sum of the sales from the smaller ads to equal the sales from the largest. The error is due to rounding; **e.** Forget about the giant ad. It is a waste of money.

Activity 3.10

1. a. $5(\log_3 3) = 5 \cdot 1 = 5$; **b.** $x(\log_2 2) = x \cdot 1 = x$; **c.** $3\log_b x - 4\log_b y$; **d.** $\frac{1}{3}\ln x + \frac{1}{4}\ln y - 2\ln z$; **e.** $\log_3(2x + y)$; **3. a.** 12.5; **b.** 18; **c.** 15; **d.** $2\log_a x + \log_a y - \log_a a = 12 + 25 - 1 = 36$; **5. a.** **b.** 47.5%

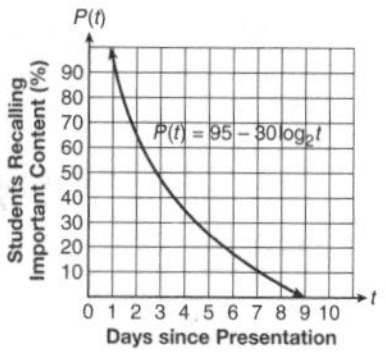

Activity 3.11

1. $x = 3.81$; **2.** $x = 0.946$; **3.** $t = 17.67$; **7.** $x = 1.36$; **9. a.** $t = 8$ days; **b.** $t = 19$ days.

Activity 3.12

1. $x = 2^5 = 32$; **3.** $x = 12.62$; **5.** $x = 9.57$; **7.** $x = 2.328$; **9.** $[H^+] = 10^{-2.4} = 0.00398$ moles/liter.

How Can I Practice?

1. a. $\log_b x + 2\log_b y - \log_b z$; **b.** $\frac{3}{2}\log_3 x + \frac{1}{2}\log_3 y - \log_3 z$; **c.** $\log_5 x + \frac{1}{2}\log_5(x^2 + 4)$; **d.** $\frac{1}{3}\log_4 x + \frac{2}{3}\log_4 y - \frac{2}{3}\log_4 z$; **2. a.** $\log \dfrac{x\sqrt[3]{y}}{\sqrt{z}}$; **b.** $\log_3[(x + 3)^3 z^2]$; **c.** $\log_3 \sqrt[3]{\dfrac{x}{y^2 z^4}}$; **3. a.** $\frac{\log 17}{\log 5} = 1.76$; **b.** $\frac{1}{3} \cdot \frac{\log 41}{\log 13} = 0.4826$; **4. a.** $x = 646.08$; **b.** $6(x - 1) = 7^{13}$,

$$x = \frac{7^{13}}{6} + 1 = 1.6148 \times 10^{10};$$

5. a. $x = \frac{\log 17}{\log 3} = 2.5789$; **b.** $\log 2 + x\log 3 = x\log 4$ or

$$x = \frac{\log 2}{\log 4 - \log 3} = 2.409;$$

c. $\log(1.5) + (2x + 1)\log 3 = \log 2 + (x - 1)\log(1.5)$
$\log(1.5) + 2x\log 3 + \log 3 =$
$\log 2 + x\log(1.5) - \log(1.5)$
$x[2\log 3 - \log(1.5)] = \log 2 - 2\log(1.5) - \log 3$
$x = -0.6789$;

6. a. **c.** $E = 3910.93$

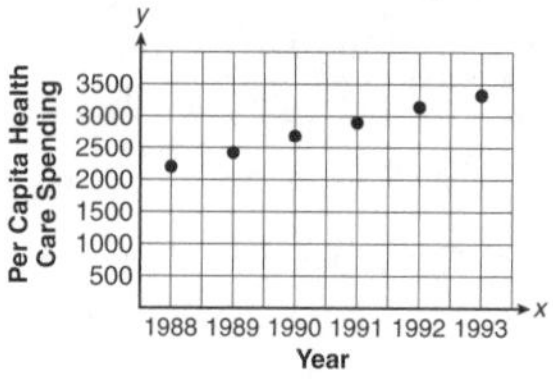

Gateway Review

1. a. Col. 1: $\frac{1}{8}$; Col. 2: $\frac{1}{2}$; Col. 3: 1; Col. 4: 8; Col. 5: 16; Col. 6: 64; Col. 7: 512; **b.** ; **c.** Increasing, since $b = 8 > 1$; **d.** The domain is all real numbers; **e.** The range is $y > 0$; **f.** There is no x-intercept. The y-intercept is (0, 1); **g.** There is one horizontal asymptote, the x-axis, $y = 0$; **h.** The domain and range are the same. The graphs are reflections in the y-axis. f is increasing, g is decreasing; **i.** h is moved upward 5 units; **j.** $x = 8^y$ or $y = \log_8 x$; **2. a.** The table is approximately exponential. The constant factor is about 1.55; **b.** $y = 10(1.55)^x$; **3. a.** Col. 1: 1999, 10,000; Col. 2: 2000, 10,150; Col. 3: 2001, 10,302; Col. 4: 2002, 10,457; Col. 5: 2003, 10,614; Col. 5: 2004, 10,773; **b.** $y = 10{,}000(1.015)^x$; **c.** $y = 10{,}000(1.015)^6 = 10{,}934.43$. This is reasonable if we assume that 10,000 is a reasonable starting salary; **d.** $2 = (1.015)^t$; **4. a.** $A = 8410.14$; **b.** $t = 13.5$ years; **5. a.** 125; **b.** 27; **c.** $\frac{1}{32}$; **d.** 25; **e.** -2; **f.** 4; **g.** -3; **6. a.** $\frac{\log 21}{\log 7} = 1.56$; **b.** $\frac{\log(8/9)}{\log 15} = -4.35 \times 10^{-2}$; **7. a.** $3\log_2^x + \log_2 y - 0.5\log_2 z$; **b.** $2\log x + \frac{3}{2}\log y - \frac{1}{2}\log z$; **8. a.** $\log \dfrac{x\sqrt[4]{y}}{z^3}$; **b.** $\log \sqrt[3]{\dfrac{x}{y^2 z^5}}$; **9. a.** $3 + x = \frac{\log 7}{\log 3}$; $x = -1.23$; **b.** $x = 7.50$; **c.** $x = -13.09$; **d.** $x = 1.75$; **e.** $x = 8$, or $x = -2$, -2 is extraneous; **10. a.**

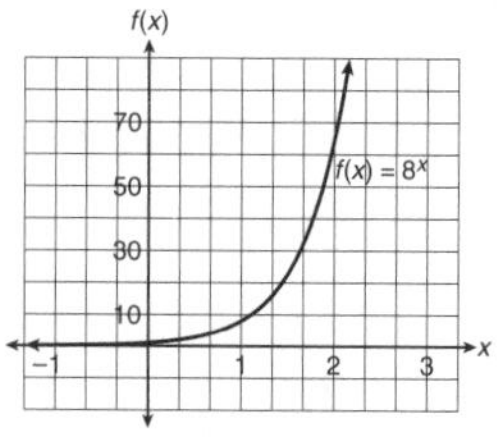

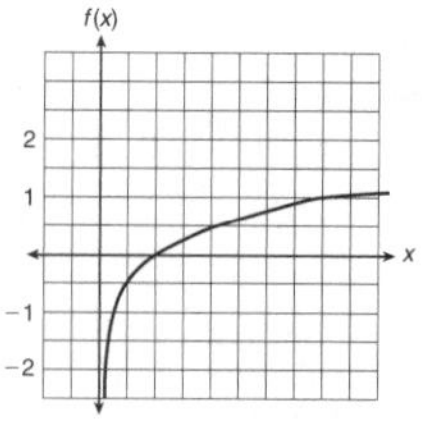

b. $f(x) = \log_2 \sqrt{x}$ or $f(x) = \frac{1}{2}\log_2 x$; **c.** 2.87744; **d.** $x = 24.9$ (by graphing); **e.** $g(x) = 2^{2x}$, $(2^2)^x = 4^x$; **11. a.** New York 18.2 million; Florida 14 million;

b. 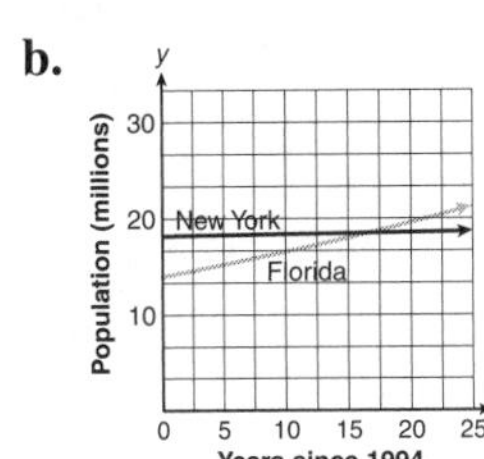

; **c.** $t = 17$; Florida's population will equal that of New York in the year 2011; **d.** $t = 35$; Florida's population will exceed 25 million in the year 2029; **e.** $t > 16.6$ At current rates, the population of Florida exceeds the population of NY sometime in the year 2010.

Chapter 4

Activity 4.1 Exercises: **1. a.** Col. 1: 4; Col. 2: 1; Col. 3: 0; Col. 4: 1; Col. 5: 9; Col. 6: 16; **b.** No, the rate of change between any two points is not constant; **c.** No, there is not a constant growth or decay factor; **e.** The coefficient is 1; **3. a.** ∪-shaped; vertical intercept (0, 5) symmetric with respect to the y-axis; **b.** ∩-shaped; vertical intercept (0, 1) symmetric with respect to the y-axis; **c.** ∪-shaped; vertical intercept (0, −3), symmetric with respect to the y-axis; **5. a.** $a = -2, b = 0, c = 0$; **b.** $a = \frac{2}{5}, b = 0, c = 3$; **c.** $a = -1, b = 5, c = 0$; **d.** $a = 5, b = 2, c = -1$.

Activity 4.2 Exercises: **1. a.** downward, **b.** (0, −4); **3. a.** upward, **b.** (0, 3); **5. a.** downward; **b.** (0, −7); **7. a.** The graph of $y = \frac{3}{5}x^2$ is wider than the graph of $y = x^2$; **b.** $y = x^2$ would have a greater output value; **9. a.** The functions are increasing when $x > 0$; **b.** $y = 8x^2$ is increasing more rapidly than $y = 0.5x^2$.

Activity 4.3 Exercises: **1. a.** upward; **b.** $x = 0$, **c.** (0, −3); **d.** (0, −3); **3. a.** upward; **b.** $x = -2$; **c.** (−2, −7); **d.** (0, −3); **5. a.** upward; **b.** $x = -1.5$; **c.** (−1.5, 1.75) **d.** (0, 4); **7. a.** upward; **b.** $x = 0.25$; **c.** (0.25, −3.125); **d.** (0, −3); **9. a.** (1, 0) (6, 0); **b.** D: all real numbers; R: $g(x) \le 6.25$; **c.** $x < 3.5$; **d.** $x > 3.5$; **11. a.** (3.46, 0) (−3.46, 0); **b.** D: all real numbers R: $y \ge -12$; **c.** $x > 0$; **d.** $x < 0$; **13. a.** (−1, 0) (3, 0); **b.** D: all real numbers R: $g(x) \le 4$; **c.** $x < 1$; **d.** $x > 1$; **15. a.** (0.2, 0) (1, 0); **b.** D: all real numbers R: $y \le 0.8$; **c.** $x < 0.6$; **d.** $x > 0.6$; **17. a.** 149 feet; **b.** 6.05 sec; **c.** It indicates when the arrow hits the ground.

How Can I Practice? **1.** Col. 1: 5, $\frac{1}{3}$, −2; Col. 2: 0, 3, 1; Col. 3: 0, −1, 0; **2. a.** downward; **b.** $x = 0$; **c.** (0, 4); **d.** (0, 4); **3. a.** upward; **b.** $x = 0$; **c.** (0, 0); **d.** (0, 0); **4. a.** downward; **b.** $x = 1$; **c.** (1, 10); **d.** (0, 7); **5. a.** upward; **b.** $x = 1/2$; **c.** (1/2, −1); **d.** (0, 0); **6. a.** upward; **b.** $x = -3$, **c.** (−3, 0), **d.** (0, 9), **7. a.** upward; **b.** $x = 1/2$; **c.** (1/2, 3/4); **d.** (0, 1); **8. a.** (−2, 0) (2, 0); **b.** D: all real numbers R: $y \le 4$; **c.** $x < 0$; **d.** $x > 0$; **10. a.** (0.91, 0) (−2.91, 0); **b.** D: all real numbers R: $y \le 11$; **c.** $x < -1$; **d.** $x > -1$; **12.**, (0.75, 26.125); **14. a.** $0 \le x \le 100$; **b.** $h(50) = 0.01(50)^2 - 50 + 35 = 10$ feet.

Activity 4.4 Exercises: **1.** $x = 6$ or $x = -2$; **3.** $x = 9$ or $x = -5$; **5.** $x = -11$ or $x = -1$; **7.** $x = \pm 5$; **9.** $x = -3$ or $x = 1$; **11.** $x = 7$ or $x = -4$; **13. a.** $-2 < x < 6$, **b.** $x < -2$ or $x > 6$; **15. a.** $d(55) = 181.5$ feet; **b.** $0.04v^2 + 1.1v = 200$, $v = 58$ mph.

Activity 4.5 Exercises **1.** $(3x - 1)(x + 4) = 0$, $x = \frac{1}{3}$ or $x = -4$; **3.** $x^2 - 7x - 18 = 0$, $(x - 9)(x + 2) = 0$, $x = 9, -2$; **5.** $a = 1, b = 6$, $c = -3$, $x = \dfrac{-6 \pm \sqrt{36 - 4(1)(-3)}}{2} = \dfrac{-6 \pm \sqrt{48}}{2}$ $x = 0.46$ or $x = -6.46$; **7.** $x^2 + 5x - 13 = 0$, $a = 1, b = 5$, $c = -13$, $x = \dfrac{5 \pm \sqrt{77}}{2} = 1.89$ or -6.89; **9.** $2x^2 - 3x - 5 = 0$, $a = 2, b = -3, c = -5$, $x = \dfrac{3 \pm \sqrt{49}}{4} = 2.5, -1$; **11.** $2x^2 + 4x - 40 = 0$; $x^2 + 2x - 20 = 0$, $x = \dfrac{-2 \pm \sqrt{84}}{2} = 3.58$ or -5.58; **13.** (3, 0) and (−2, 0); **15. b.** $t = 5.6$ Sometime in 1995; **c.** The answers are the same; **d.** We are only extrapolating a little, so I am fairly confident.

Activity 4.6 Exercises: **1.** $5i$; **3.** $6i$; **5.** $4i\sqrt{3}$; **7.** $\frac{3}{4}i$; **9.** $x = \dfrac{1}{3} \pm \dfrac{\sqrt{80}}{6}i$; **11.** $x = 1, -3.5$; **13.** $b^2 - 4ac = 49$, 2 distinct real solutions; **15.** $b^2 - 4ac = 0$, 1 repeated real solution; **17.** $12x^2 - 4x + 3 = 0$, $b^2 - 4ac = -128$, 2 distinct complex solutions.

Activity 4.7 Exercises: **1. a.** Col. 1: 225, 5625; Col. 2: 200, 10,000; Col. 3: 175, 13,125; Col. 4: 150, 15,000; Col. 5: 125, 15,625; Col. 6: 100, 15,000; Col. 7: 75, 13,125; Col. 8: 50, 10,000; Col. 9: 25, 5625; **b.** 125 feet by 125 feet; **c.** $l = 250 - w$, $A = f(w) = w \cdot (250 - w)$; **d.** $w = 125$, $f(125) = 15{,}625$; **e.** $w \cdot (250 - w) = 0$ $w = 0$, or $w = 250$. There can be no rectangle constructed with these dimensions; **f.** Domain: $0 < w < 250$, Range: $0 < A \le 15{,}625$; **3.** x = length of the base, $x(3x + 2) = 56$, Reject the negative, $3x + 2$ = height, $3x^2 + 2x - 56 = 0$, length = 4 inches, $x = 4$ or $x = -4.7$, height = 14 inches.

How Can I Practice? **1. a.** $x \approx 1.2$; Col. 1: 1, 5; Col. 2: 1.1, 6.05; Col. 3: 1.2, 7.2; Col. 4: 1.3, 8.45; Col. 5: 1.4, 9.8; Col. 6: 1.5, 11.25; **b.** $x \approx 0.8$; Col. 1: 0.5, 6.75; Col. 2: 0.6, 6.16; Col. 3: 0.7, 5.59; Col. 4: 0.8, 5.04; Col. 5: 0.9, 4.51; Col. 6: 1, 4; **c.** $x = 2$, Col. 1: 2, 2; **3. a.** $-8 < x < 2$, **b.** $x < -8$ or $x > 2$,

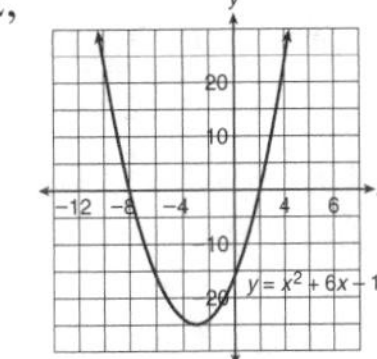

5. a. $a = 3, b = -1, c = -7$, $b^2 - 4ac = 85$, two real solutions, $x = 1.70, -1.37$; **b.** $a = 1$; $b = -4$; $c = 10$,

$b^2 - 4ac = -24$, two complex solutions, $x = 2 \pm \sqrt{6}i$, **c.** $a = 2, b = -5, c = -3, b^2 - 4ac = 49$, two real solutions, $x = 3, -0.5$, **d.** $a = 9, b = -6, c = 1$, $b^2 - 4ac = 0$, one real repeated solution, $x = 1/3$; **7. a.** $s(44) = 122.5$ feet away; **b.** $\frac{1}{32}v^2 + v + 18 = 50$ $v = -51.78$ or 19.78, Reject the negative $\frac{1}{32}v^2 + v - 32 = 0$ 19.78 ft/sec 13.5 mph.

Activity 4.9 Exercises:

1. a.

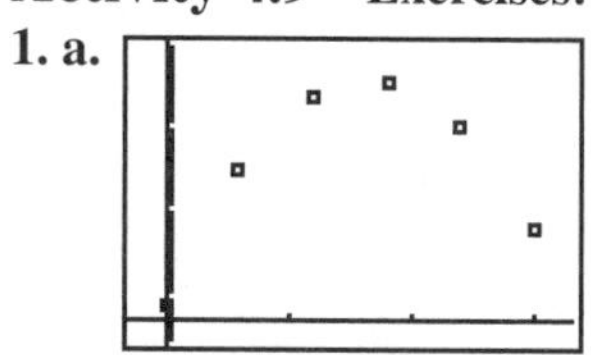

b. $y = -15.9752x^2 + 52.88875x + 2.5536$;

c.

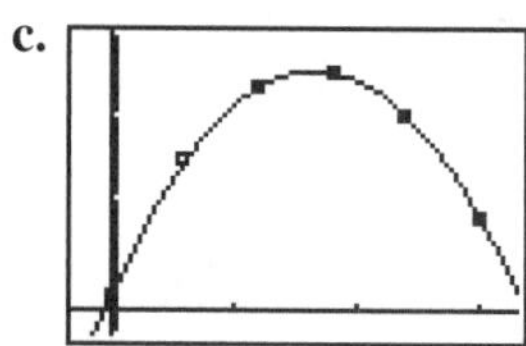

The curve is a great fit for the data, very close to all the points; **d.** Time could be between 0 and approximately 3.3 seconds (when the ball hits the ground); **e.** The height of the ball above the field is between 0 and approximately 47 feet; **f.** You can trace the regression curve to find that the ball is 35 feet above the ground at approximately 0.8 seconds, on the way up; **g.** The ball will also be at a height of 35 feet at about 2.5 seconds, on the way down (so, there are two solutions); **3. a.** $y = 0.086x^2 - 0.842x + 32.487$; **b.** Approximately 700 feet; **c.** $280 = 0.086x^2 - 0.842x + 32.487$ $0 = 0.086x^2 - 0.842x - 247.513$ Using the quadratic formula, a speed of 58.8 mph would require a stopping distance of 280 feet.

Activity 4.10 Exercises:

1. a. $y = 8x$, $8 = k1$, so $k = 8$, Col. 1: 2; Col. 3: 32; Col. 4: 64; **b.** $y = x^3$, $1 = k1^3$, so $k = 1$, or $y = x^3$, Col. 1: $\frac{1}{8}$; Col. 3: 27; Col. 4: 216; **3.** $12 = k2^2$, so $k = 3$, So $y = 3x^2$. When $x = 8$, $y = 3(8)^2 = 192$; **5.** $d = kt^2$, $20 = k(2)^2$, so $k = 5$. Now $d = 5t^2$, so in 2.5 seconds you travel $d = 5(2.5)^2 = 31.25$ meters; **9.** $f(x) = x^6$

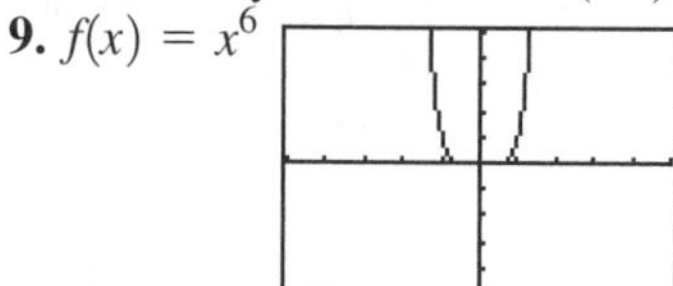

11. $f(x)$ is increasing for $x > 0$; **13.** $y = x^2$ is rising more slowly than $y = x^3$ for $x > 1$; **15.** $y = -2x^3$ is decreasing and goes through (0, 0), while $y = 2x^3 + 1$ is increasing and does not pass through the origin. Both have a similar "S" like shape.

Activity 4.11 Exercises:

1. $x = 0, -1, -2$; **3.** $x = \pm 2, \pm 3$;

5.

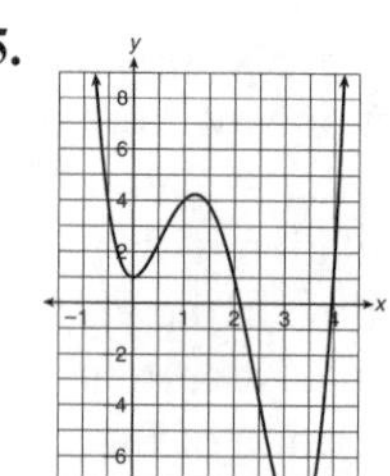

No maximum point, a minimum point at (3.28, −8.91); **7.** No, as x increases without bound, y increases without bound; **9. a.** Increase; **b.** Decreasing; **c.** One.

Activity 4.12 Exercises:

1. a.

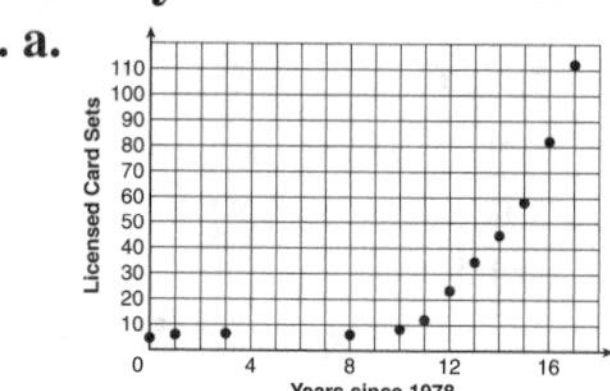

No, the data points do not form a straight line;

3. a.

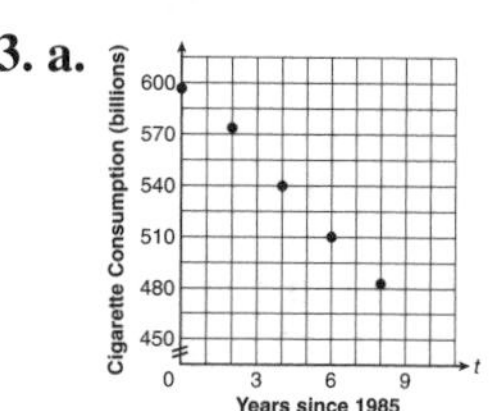

b. $y = -14.15x + 597.4$; **c.** $y = -0.125x^2 - 13.15x + 596.4$; **d.** There appears to be no difference between the two models. Both fit closely to the data; **e.** The linear model predicts 314.4 and the quadratic predicts 283.4; **f.** We are predicting quite far outside our practical domain, so I am not very confident in either model's prediction.

How Can I Practice?

1. $y = kx^2$, $45 = k3^2$, so $k = 5$, $k = 5(6)^2 = 180$; **3.** $v = kt$, $60 = k3$, $k = 20$ $v = 20(4) = 80$ ft/sec;

4. a. These are the same shape and size, however, $y = 3x^2 + 5$ is shifted up by five units;

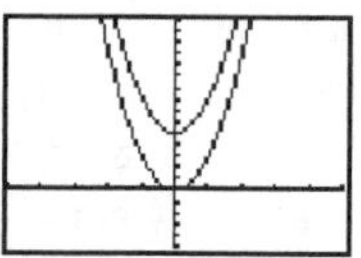

b. These are the same shape but are reflections of each other in the x-axis;

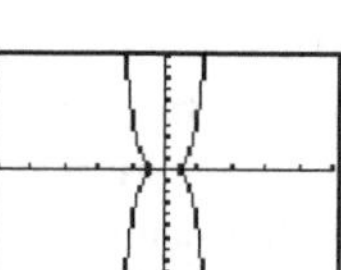

c. These are the same shape and size but are shifted vertically by five units;

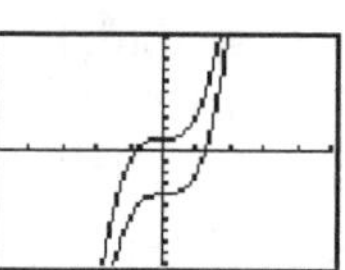

d. These are the same shape and size but are shifted horizontally one unit to the right;

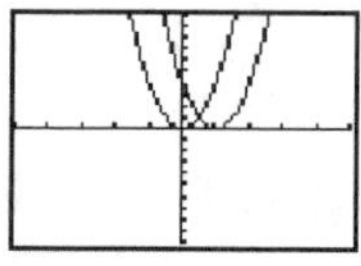

5. a. i. (0, 0); **ii.** (0, 0), (−4, 0), (2, 0); **iii.** (−2.4, 16.9), (1, −5); **b. i.** (0, 3); **ii.** (−1, 0), (1.57, 0); **iii.** (0.77, 4.2); **7. a.** (−5, 6); **b.** (0, 0), (−5, 6), (−10, 0); **c.** $y = -0.24x^2 - 2.4x$; **9. a.**

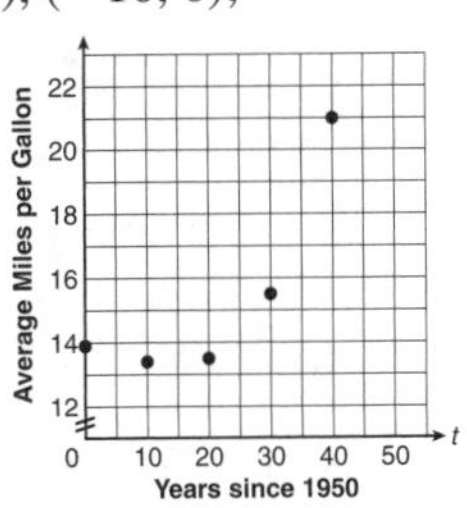

b. $y = 0.0099285714x^2 - 0.2341428571x$; $+ 14.18571429$; **c.** 27.3 mpg; **d.** 2003.

Gateway Review **1. a.** up; **b.** $x = 0$; **c.** (0, 2); **d.** (0, 2); **2. a.** down; **b.** $x = 0$; **c.** (0, 0); **d.** (0, 0); **3. a.** down; **b.** $x = 0$, **c.** (0, 4); **d.** (0, 4); **4. a.** up, **b.** $x = \frac{1}{4}$; **c.** $\left(\frac{1}{4}, -\frac{1}{8}\right)$; **d.** (0, 0); **5. a.** up; **b.** $x = -\frac{5}{2}$; **c.** (−2.5, −0.25); **d.** (0, 6); **6. a.** up; **b.** $x = \frac{3}{2}$; **c.** (1.5, 1.75); **d.** (0, 4); **7. a.** up; **b.** $x = 1$; **c.** (1, 0); **d.** (0, 1); **8. a.** down; **b.** $x = 2.5$; **c.** (2.5, 0.25); **d.** (0, −6);

9. a. (−3, 0), (−1, 0);
b. D: all real numbers R: $g(x) \geq -1$;
c. $x > -2$; **d.** $x < -2$;

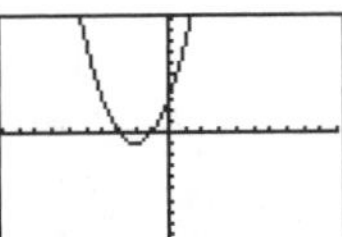

10. a. (−3, 0), (1, 0);
b. D: all real numbers, R: $f(x) \geq 4$;
c. $x > -1$; **d.** $x < -1$;

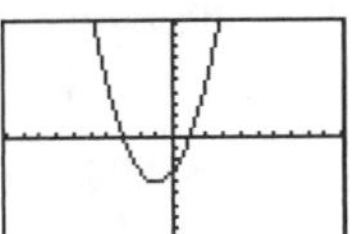

11. a. (0.382, 0), (2.62, 0);
b. D: all real numbers, R: $y \geq -1.25$;
c. $x > 1.5$; **d.** $x < 1.5$;

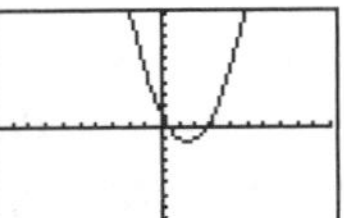

12. a. (−3.22, 0), (−0.775, 0);
b. D: all real numbers, R: $h(x) \geq -3$;
c. $x > -2$;
d. $x < -2$;

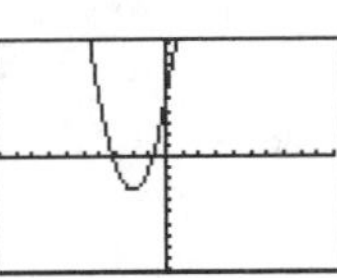

13. a. (−2, 0), (2, 0);
b. D: all real numbers R: $y(x) \leq 8$;
c. $x < 0$, **d.** $x > 0$;

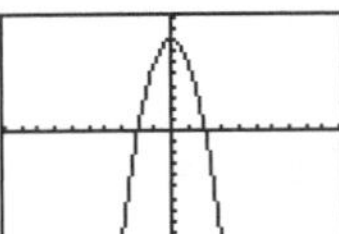

14. a. $(\frac{1}{3}, 0)$, (1, 0);
b. D: all real numbers R: $f(x) \leq \frac{1}{3}$;
c. $x < 2/3$;
d. $x > 2/3$;

15. a. none;
b. D: all real numbers R: $g(x) \geq 5$;
c. $x > 0$;
d. $x < 0$;

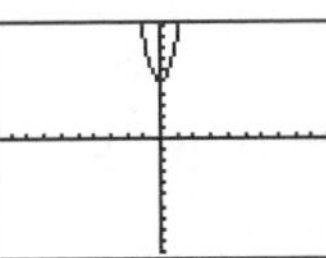

16. $x = -2$; **17.** $x = 2, 3$; **18.** $x = -0.51, 6.5$; **19.** $x = -5, 2$; **20.** $x = \pm 1.1$; **21.** $x = -0.21, -4.79$; **22.** $x = \pm 3$; **23.** $x = \pm 6$; **24.** $x = 3, 4$; **25.** $x = -3, 9$; **26.** $x = 0, -1$; **27.** $x = -0.7, -4.3$; **28.** $x = 0.25 \pm 1.2i$; **29.** $x = \pm 2.83$; **30.** $x = -3, \frac{4}{3}$; **31.** $x = -1, 2.5$; **32.** From the grapher: (0.419, 0), (3.581, 0),

$$x = \frac{-(-8) \pm \sqrt{(-8)^2 - 4(2)(3)}}{2(2)} = \frac{8 \pm \sqrt{40}}{4}$$

$= 3.581, 0.419$; **33. a.** $7i$; **b.** $= 4\sqrt{3}i$; **c.** $3i$; **d.** $\sqrt{23}i$; **e.** $\frac{\sqrt{5}}{3}i$; **f.** $\frac{\sqrt{17}}{4}i$; **34.** Two real solutions.; **35.** Two real solutions.; **36.** Two real solutions.; **37.** Two complex solutions; **38.** $x = \frac{-2 \pm \sqrt{2^2 - 4(3)(2)}}{2(3)} = \frac{-2 \pm \sqrt{-20}}{6}$

$= \frac{-2 \pm 2\sqrt{5}i}{2(3)} = \frac{-1 \pm \sqrt{5}i}{3}$; **39. a.** $-2 < x < 3$; **b.** $x < -2$ or $x > 3$; **40. a.** $y = 20$; **b.** $y = 32$; **c.** $y = 40$; **41. a.** (2, 0); **b.** D: all real numbers R: all real numbers; **c.** inc: all real numbers; **42. a.** (−1, 0); **b.** D: all real numbers R: all real numbers **c.** decreasing all real numbers; **43. a.** (−1.68, 0), (1.68, 0); **b.** D: all real numbers R: $y \geq -8$; **c.** Inc: $x > 0$, dec: $x < 0$; **44. a.** (0, 0), (−1.26, 0); **b.** D: all real numbers R: $y \geq -1.19$; **c.** Inc: $x > -0.8$ dec: $x < -0.8$; **45. a.** none; **b.** D: all real numbers R: $y \geq 5$; **c.** inc: $x > 0$ dec: $y < 0$;

Chapter 5

Activity 5.1 **Exercises:** **1. a.** average speed = 16 km per hr; **b.** Col. 1: 20; Col. 2: 16; Col. 3: 13.33; Col. 4: 11.43; Col. 5: 10; Col. 6: 8.89; Col. 7: 8; **c.** $s = f(t) = \frac{20}{t}$; **d. i.** The domain is the set of all nonzero real numbers; **ii.** $1 \leq t \leq 5$; **e.** The average speed decreases, approaching zero; **f.** The average speed increases without bound; **3. a.** $D = \frac{1200}{N}$; **b.**

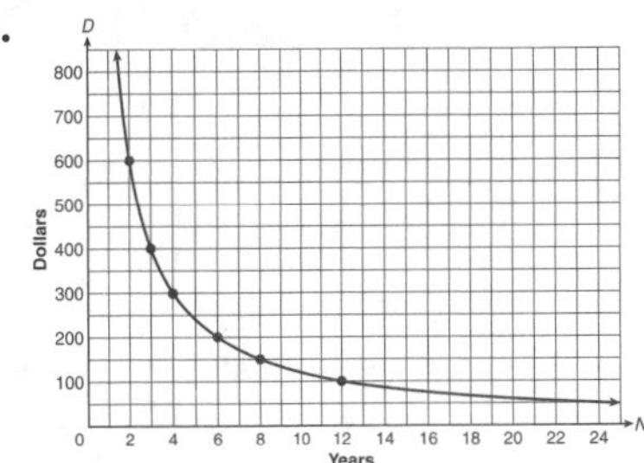

c. Decrease. As N gets larger, D gets smaller.

Activity 5.2 **Exercises:**

1. g is the reflection of f about the x-axis; **3.** The graphs have the same asymptotes and the same domain. Neither has a max or a min. $\frac{1}{x^2}$ is symmetric with respect to the y-axis. $\frac{1}{x^3}$ is symmetric with respect to the origin; **5.** The output corresponding to a given input will be the opposite in sign. The graphs will be reflected in the x-axis; **6. a.** $y = 2/x$, Col. 2: 4, 1, 1/3; **7.** $k = 128$; **9.** $I = 0.11$ unit.

Activity 5.3 Exercises **1. a.** $= \frac{80{,}000}{P - 2.5}$; **b.** Col. 2: 160,000; Col. 3: 32,000; Col. 4: 10,667; Col. 5: 3555.55; **c.** It decreases; **d.** $V(2) = -160{,}000$ A price of \$2 per cubic meter is not practical; **e.** $P > 2.5$;
f.

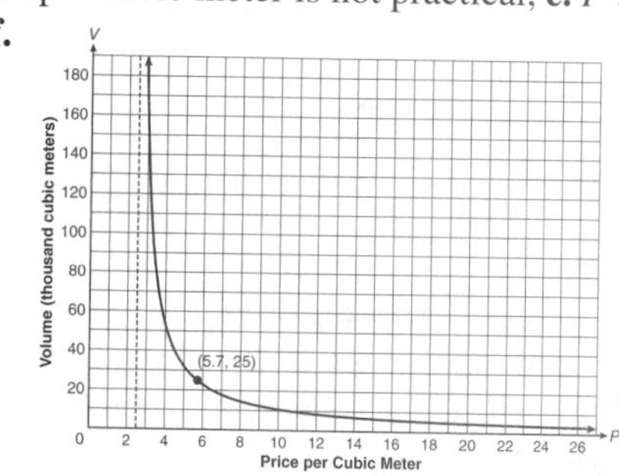

3. a. D: all real numbers, except $x = 7$, Vert. asy: $x = 7$; **b.** D: all real numbers, except $x = 25$,Vert. asy: $x = 25$; **c.** D: all real numbers, except $x = 5$, Vert. asy: $x = 5$; **d.** D: all real numbers, except $x = 14$, Vert. asy: $x = 14$; **e.** D: all real numbers, except $x = -2.5$, Vert. asy: $x = -2.5$; **5. a.** $x = 5$; **b.** $f(x)$ gets large, approaching infinity; $g(x)$ gets small, approaching negative infinity; **c.** $f(x)$ gets small, approaching negative infinity; $g(x)$ gets large, approaching infinity.

Activity 5.4 Exercises
1. a. H: $y = 4$, V: $x = -2$; **b.** H: $y = -1$, V: $x = -1$; **c.** H: $y = 0$, V: $x = \pm 2$; **d.** H: $y = 15$, V: $x = \frac{1}{2}$;

a.

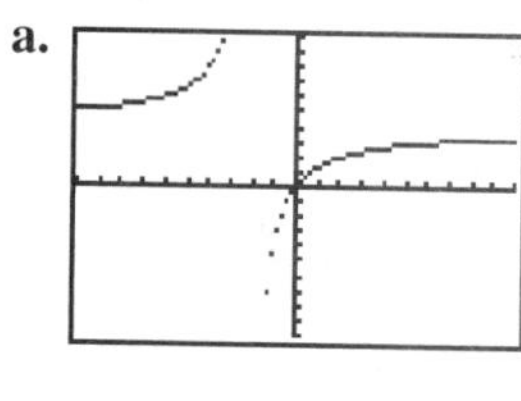

b.

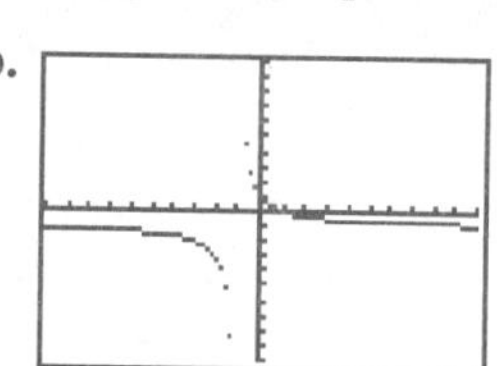

c.

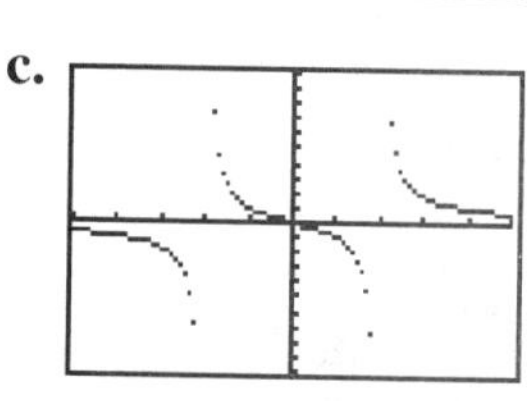

d.

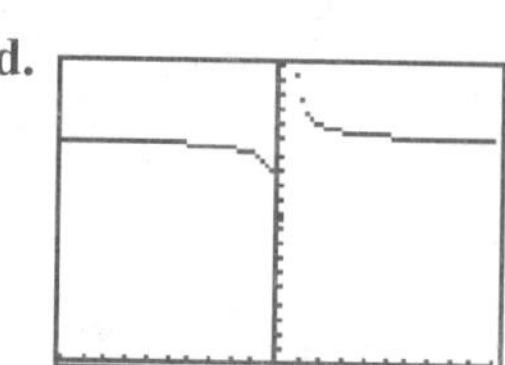

3. a. $x < 0.5$, x 0.778; **b.** $x < -0.2$, $x > 0.66$; **c.** $x < 0.0345$, $5.766 \le x < 6$;

a.

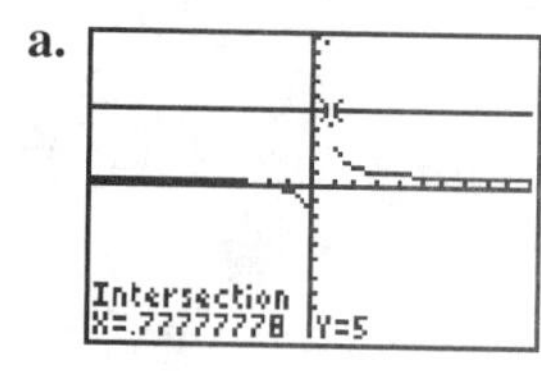

b.

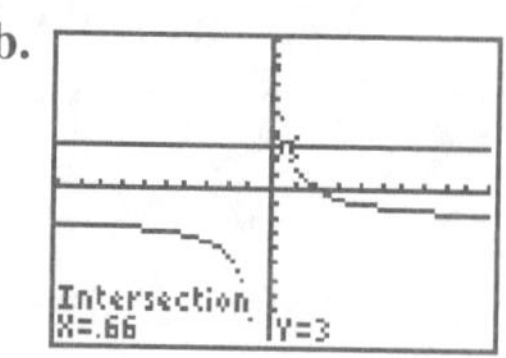

c.

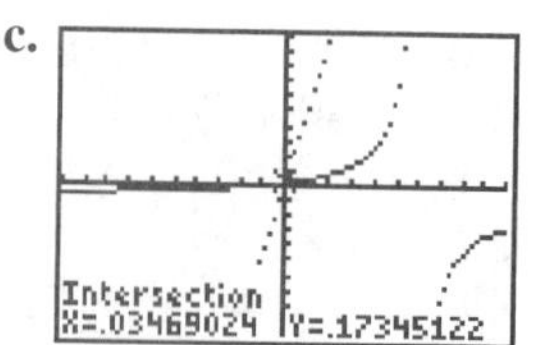

5. a. $d = \pm 10$ ft, but only 10 makes sense; **b.** $d = 0.433$ ft; **7. a.** 7.85 prey per week; **b.** n is approximately 62 prey per square mile; **c.** $18 < n < 62$.

How Can I Practice? **1.** f and g are reflections of each other about the x-axis (and the y-axis!). **2.** The graph of g is the same as f, but shifted 5 units to the right; **3.** They are similar, but the graph of g is closer to the x-axis, and the graph of f is closer to the y-axis; **4. a.** T = time in hours, s = speed in mph $T = \frac{145}{s}$; **b.** $0 < s < 80$; **c.** domain all real numbers except 0; **5. a.** D: all real numbers, except $x = -5$, Vert. asy: $x = -5$; **b.** D: all real numbers, except $x = 13/2$, Vert. asy: $x = 13/2$; **c.** D: all real numbers, except $x = 8/5$, Vert. asy: $x = 8/5$; **d.** D: all real numbers, except $x = 0.5614$, Vert. asy: $x = 0.5614$; **6.** Answers will vary: three different linear factors in the denominator, not repeated in the numerator; **7.** $w \approx 79.01$ lb; **8. a.** Practical domain: all positive integers, with some realistic upper limit, depending on the specific situation; **b.** $x = 1123$ mowers; **c.** between 2787 and 5788 lawn mowers must be sold; **9. a.** 93.32 is practical; **b.** The drug will be at its highest concentration 0.913 min after injection; **10. a.** $x = -0.25$; **b.** $x \approx 2.94$; **c.** $x \approx -2.9$; **d.** $x \approx 8.788$; **11. a.** (answers will vary) 200-lb man ≈ 90.9 kg, $W = 90.475$ kg; **b.** $W(h) = \frac{70}{(1 + \frac{h}{6400})^2}$; **c.** Col. 1: 70; Col. 2: 69.78; Col. 3: 67.86; Col. 4: 52.36; Col. 5: 45.94; Col. 6: 40.64; Col. 7: 10.66; Col. 8: 4.11; **d.** The weight decreases; **e.** 1.3317 kg; **f.** (Answers will vary some at the upper end), Domain is $0 \le h \le 40{,}000$;
g.

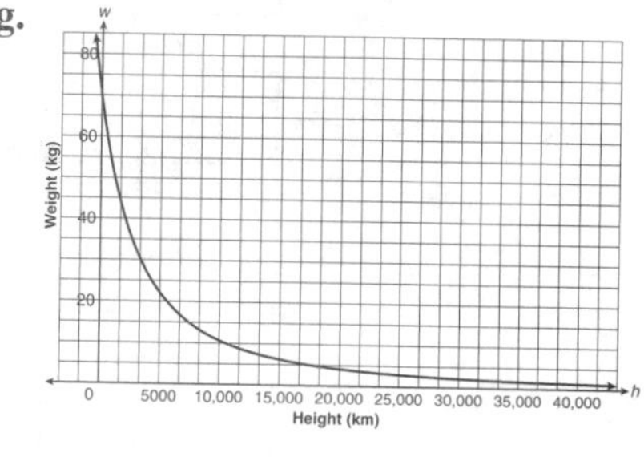

; **h.** $h = 2650.9668$

Activity 5.5 Exercises: **1. a.** 5.48; **b.** 2.45; **c.** 169; **d.** 27; **3. a.** $f(14) = 32{,}180$ The approximate income of an individual with 14 years of education is \$32,180; **b.** 21 years of education; **5. a.** No, the graph of f is below the graph of g for $0 < x < 1$; **b.** Yes, the graph of f is above the graph of g for $x > 1$.

Activity 5.6 Exercises: **1. a.** Has a solution. $x = 4$; **b.** No solution. The equation would be true only if the radical were negative; **c.** Has a solution. $x = -2$;

3. a. $x = \frac{26}{3}$; **b.** $x = 12.75$; **c.** $x = 1$; **d.** $x = -1.17$; **5.** $x = 1.75$; **7. a.** approximately 27,798; **b.** $0 \leq x \leq 100$; **c.** $x = 97$ years; **d.** $x = 75$ years.

Activity 5.7 Exercises:

1. a. 4; **b.** 2; **c.** -3; **d.** 5; **e.** $\frac{1}{6}$; **f.** Not a real number; **g.** 10; **h.** Not a real number; **3.** $l_1 = \sqrt[3]{1450}$, $l_2 = \sqrt[3]{1280}$, $l_1 - l_2 = 0.46$ inches; **5. a.** All real numbers; **b.** $x \geq 3$; **c.** All real numbers; **d.** $x \leq 2$; **7.** a. $x = 64$; **b.** $x = 81$.

How Can I Practice?

1. a. $x = 98$; **b.** $x = 41$; **c.** $x = 12$; **d.** $x = \pm\sqrt{61}$; **e.** No solution; **f.** $x = 10$; **g.** $x = 10.5$; **h.** $x \approx 0.95$; **2. a.** $x > 7$; **b.** $x \geq 1.2141$; **c.** $x \leq -0.686$ or $x \geq 0.686$; **3. a.** $x \leq 6$; **b.** All real numbers; **c.** $x \geq 2$ or $x \leq -2$; **4.** Length is approximately 7.71 inches; **5.** $r = \sqrt[3]{\frac{3V}{4\pi}}$, $V = 620$, $r = 5.29$ cm; **6.** $d = 156.25$; **7.** $x = 6.5$ inches; **8. a.** $x = 115$; $s = \sqrt{24 \cdot 115} \approx 53$ mph; **b.** $s = 80$: $80 = \sqrt{24x}$; $x \approx 267$ feet; **c.** Probably something like $0 \leq x < 600$; **9.** The graphs are reflections about the line $x = 2$.

Gateway Review

1. a. $d = \frac{1200}{w}$; **b.** Col. 1: 30, 40; Col. 2: 35, 34.286; Col. 3: 40, 30; Col. 4: 50, 24; Col. 5: 60, 20; **c.** As width increases, the depth decreases; **d.** The depth is 12 feet, not enough room for any theater set; **e.** (Answers may vary.) $40 \leq w \leq 60$; **f.** No. Division by zero is undefined; **g.** Rational function; **h.** All real numbers except 0; **i.** $w = 0$; **j.** $d = 0$, as w increases, d approaches 0; **2. a.**

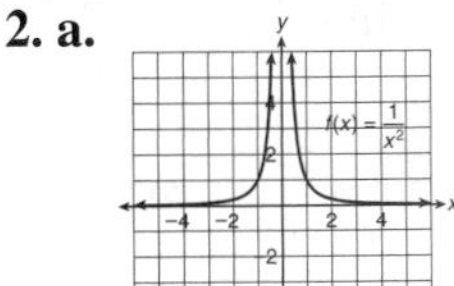

b.

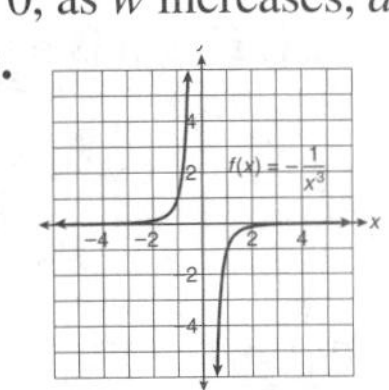

c. The graphs have the same horizontal and vertical asymptotes. $f(x) = \frac{1}{x^2}$ is symmetric with respect the y-axis. $f(x) = -\frac{1}{x^3}$ is symmetric with respect to (0, 0) in quadrants II and IV; **3. a.** $y = 4$; **b.** 5.12 decibels; **c.** 1.28 inches; **4. a.** H: $y = 0$, V: $x = 3$, $(0, \frac{4}{3})$, No x-intercept; **b.** H: $y = 2$, V: $x = -2$, (0, 0), (0, 0); **c.** H: $y = \frac{1}{3}$, V: $x = \frac{2}{3}$, $(0, -\frac{1}{2})$, $(-1, 0)$; **5. a.** $x = \frac{8}{3}$; **b.** The solution is the x-coordinate of the x-intercept;

6. a.

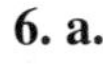

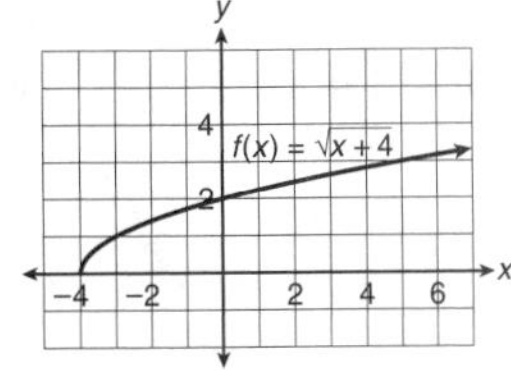

b. The output is increasing; **c.** $x \geq -4$; **d.** $x \geq 0$; **e.** The x-intercept is $(-4, 0)$. The y-intercept is (0, 2); **f.** g has the same shape, but is shifted 8 units to the right; **g.** The graphs are reflected through the x-axis; **7. a.**

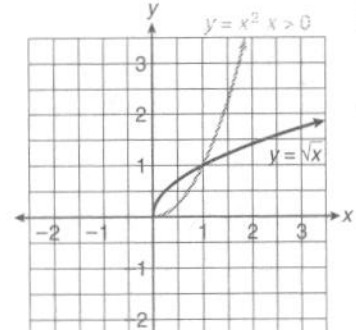

; **b.** $f^{-1}(x) = x^2$ $x \geq 0$; **d.** The graphs are reflections in $y = x$; **e.** $f(f^{-1}(x)) = x$, $f^{-1}(f(x)) = x$; **8. a.** $x = 6$; **b.** $x = 6$; **c.** $x = 4.6$; **d.** No solution; **e.** $x = -1.4$; **f.** $x = 1$; **g.** $x = 27$; **h.** $x = \pm\sqrt{2}$

Chapter 6

Activity 6.1 Exercises:

1. a. $\sin A = 0.6000$; **b.** $\sin B = 0.8000$; **c.** $\cos A = 0.8000$; **d.** $\cos B = 0.6000$; **e.** $\tan A = 0.7500$; **f.** $\tan B = 1.3333$; **3. a.** Given $\tan B = \frac{7}{4}$, the side opposite angle B is 7; the side adjacent to angle B is 4. Use Pythagorean theorem to determine that the hypotenuse is $\sqrt{65}$.; **b.** $\sin B = 7/\sqrt{65} = 0.8682$; **c.** $\cos B = 4/\sqrt{65} = 0.4961$; **5. a.** The sine function relates angle B and sides c and y; **b.** $\sin B = \frac{y}{c}$; **7. a.** $x = 7.9$; **b.** $x = 85.6$; **c.** $x = 61.4$.

Activity 6.2 Exercises:

1. a. I would travel 0.68 miles going back directly south and then directly west; **b.** $s = 0.5 \cos 30° = 0.43$ miles; $w = 0.5 \sin 30° = 0.25$ miles, These calculations confirm the result in part a; **3. a.** Col. 2: 83, 73, 66, 57, 42, 23, 13; Col. 3: 0.9925, 0.9563, 0.9135, 0.8387, 0.6691, 0.3907, 0.2250; Col. 4: 0.9925, 0.9563, 0.9135, 0.8387, 0.6691, 0.3907, 0.2250; **b.** the table in part a illustrates the property that cofunctions of complementary angles are equal.

Activity 6.3 Exercises:

a. $\theta = 30°$; **b.** $\theta = 64.62°$; **c.** $\theta = 67.04°$; **d.** $\theta = 63.82°$; **e.** $\theta = 66.81°$; **f.** $\theta = 64.62°$; **g.** $\theta = 22.28°$; **h.** $\theta = 20.76°$; **3.** I must turn the rowboat 110° to head directly south; **5. b.** The ramp makes an angle of 5.7° with the horizontal; **c.** The elevation changes 1.5 feet from one end of the ramp to the other.

Activity 6.4 Exercises:

1. a. The side adjacent to the 57° angle = 4.2 ft. The hypotenuse is 7.8 ft. The other acute angle is 33°; **b.** The hypotenuse is 19.0.The angle adjacent to side 18 = 18.4°. The other acute angle is 71.6°; **c.** The other leg = 7.9 in. The angle adjacent to side 9 in. is 41.4°. The other angle is 48.6°.

Activity 6.5 Exercises:

1. a. The slope is 5/100 or 1/20, or 0.05; **b.** $A = \tan^{-1}(0.05) = 2.86°$. The highway makes angle of 2.86° with the horizontal. This angle is called the angle of elevation; **c.** I would be 264 feet above sea level after 1 mile. 1 mile is equivalent to 5280 ft. If x

represents the number of feet above sea level after climbing 1 mile, then $x = 5280 \cdot \sin(2.9) =$ approximately 264 ft.

Activity 6.6 **Exercises:** **1. b.** The height of the tower is 556 feet since $h = 92 \tan 80.6° = 555.7$ feet; **2.** The runway is approximately 2 miles long; **3. a.** $A = \frac{1}{2}h(10 + 2x)$ or simplifying, $A = h(5 + x)$ or $A = 5h + hx$; **b.** $A = 5(\sin t)(5 + 5 \cos t)$ or $A = 25 \sin t(1 + \cos t)$ or $A = 25 \sin t + 25 \sin t (\cos t)$; **d.** The graph in part c indicates that the area of the trapezoidal cross section (output) is the greatest when the angle t is 60° ; **e.** The area is approximately 32.5 sq. ft. as read from the graph in part c; **f.** $V = 1250 \sin t(1 + \cos t)$; **h.** The graph indicates the greatest value for the volume between 0° and 90° is 1625 cubic feet when the angle t is 60°; **i.** The angle is the same, namely 60° for this scenario.

Activity 6.7 **Exercises:** **1. b.** Over the given domain, the maximum value of the function is approximately 19.5 and it occurs at $x = 14$; **c.** The minimum value is difficult to see on the graph itself. I used the trace or the table feature on my grapher to determine that the minimum value in the given domain is 0.02865 and it occurs at $x = 0.01$.

How Can I Practice? **1. a.** $\tan A = \frac{8}{15}$; **b.** $\tan B = \frac{15}{8}$; **c.** $\cos A = \frac{15}{17}$; **d.** $\cos B = \frac{8}{17}$; **e.** $\sin A = \frac{8}{17}$; **f.** $\sin B = \frac{15}{17}$; **2.** $\cos A = \frac{12}{13}$ and $\tan A = \frac{5}{12}$; **3.** $\sin B = \frac{7}{\sqrt{65}}$ and $\cos B = \frac{4}{\sqrt{65}}$; **4. a.** $\theta = 48.6°$; **b.** $\theta = 23.5°$; **c.** $\theta = 74.1°$; **d.** $\theta = 16.6°$; **e.** $\theta = 44.2°$; **f.** $\theta = 13.7°$; **5.** $\overline{BC} = 4.8$ cm, $\overline{AC} = 3.6$ cm, $\angle B = 37°$, $\angle C = 90°$; **6.** Therefore, I should buy the 35° trusses; **7. a.** The angle of depression, $\theta = 20.6°$; **b.** 17.1 ft; **8. a.** $d = \sqrt{2.5^2 + 6^2} = 6.5$ miles; **b.** $A = \arctan\left(\frac{2.5}{6}\right) = 22.6°$.

Activity 6.8 **Exercises:** **1. a.** (0.31, 0.95); **b.** (0.64, −0.77); **c.** (0, −1); **d.** (−0.36, 0.93); **e.** (−0.85, −0.53); **f.** (0.26, 0.97); **g.** (0.34, −0.94); **3. a.** Yes. The output values could be the x-coordinates of points starting at the point (0, 1) and moving counterclockwise; **b.** counterclockwise; **5. b.** Yes, the number of hours of daylight is cyclic; **c.** The graph has the same shape; **d.** South. The number of hours of daylight is greater from October to February, our winter.

Activity 6.9 **Exercises:** **1. a.** 0.785; **b.** 2.443; **c.** 5.760; **d.** −0.628; **3. a.** $y = 2 \cos x$ is $y = \cos x$ stretched vertically by a factor of 2. $y = \cos(2x)$ is $y = \cos x$ compressed horizontally by a factor of 2; **b.** $y = \sin(x + \pi)$ is the graph of $y = \sin x$ shifted π units left. $y = \pi + \sin x$ is the graph of $y = \sin x$ shifted π units up; **c.** $y = -3 \sin x$ is the graph of $y = 3 \sin x$ reflected in the x-axis; **d.** $y = \cos\left(\frac{1}{3}x\right)$ is $y = \cos x$ stretched horizontally by a factor of 3. $y = \cos(3x)$ is $y = \cos x$ compressed horizontally by a factor of 3; **5.** max: 14; min: −14; period: $2\pi/3$; **7.** max: 2.3; min: −2.3; period: 4π; **9.** max: 3.606; min: −3.606; period: 2π; **11. a.** The bill is highest for December/January. The amount of the bill is approximately \$300; **b.** The bill is lowest for June/July. The amount of the bill is approximately \$125; **c.** The largest value is \$325; **d.** the period is 6 billing periods or 12 months; **e.** The graph will be stretched vertically by a factor of 1.05. This will not affect the period of the function; **f.** The amount of the bill for the summer months June/July August/September will increase. If the increase is large enough the graph will have a period of 3 billing periods (6 months).

Activity 6.10 **Exercises:**

1.

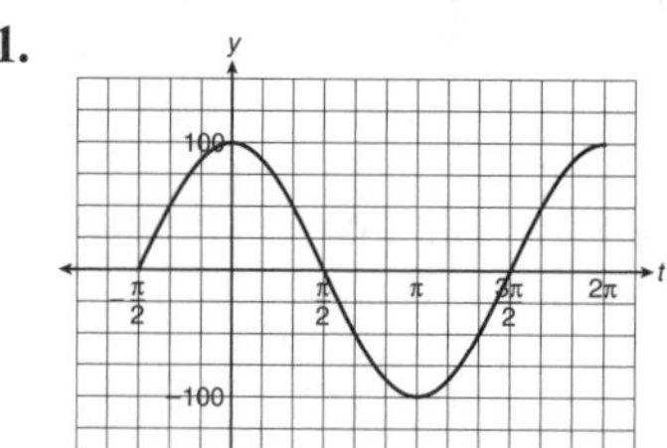

3. $(x, y) = (100 \cos \theta, 100 \sin \theta)$; **5.** 100 is the amplitude of the function; **7. a.** amp = 3; **b.** amp = 0.4; **c.** amp = 2; **d.** amp = 2.3; **e.** amp = 2; **f.** amp = 4.

Activity 6.11 **Exercises:** **1. a.** amp: 3, period: $\frac{2\pi}{1.5} = \frac{4\pi}{3}$; **b.** amp: 0.5, period: $\frac{2\pi}{2} = \pi$; **c.** amp: 2.3, period: $\frac{2\pi}{0.4} = 5\pi$; **d.** amp: 36, period: $\frac{2\pi}{2\pi} = 1$; **3. a.** $y = -15 \sin(2x)$; **b.** $y = 1.3 \cos(0.7x)$; **5. a.** Graph is i; **b.** Graph is ii; **c.** Graph is iii; **d.** Graph is iv.

Activity 6.12 **Exercises:** **1. a.** amp: 0.7, per: π, disp: $\frac{-\frac{\pi}{2}}{2} = -\frac{\pi}{4}$; **b.** amp: 3, per: 2π, disp: $\frac{-(-1)}{1} = 1$; **c.** amp: 2.5, per: 5π, disp: $\frac{-\frac{\pi}{3}}{0.4} = -\frac{5\pi}{6}$; **d.** amp: 15 per: 1, disp: $\frac{-(-0.3)}{2\pi} = \frac{3}{20\pi} = 0.0477$;

3.

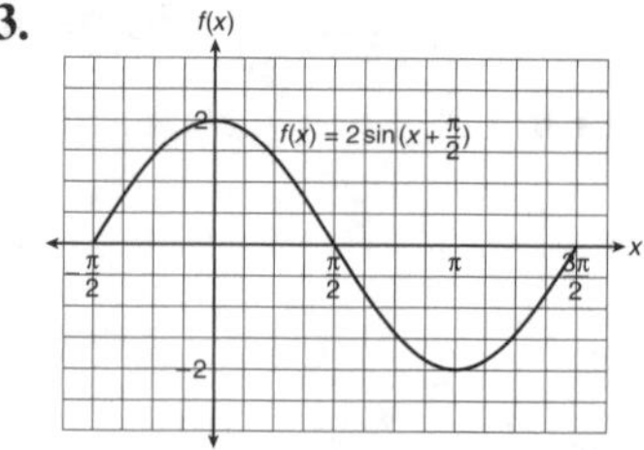

4. $y = 2 \sin(x + 1)$; **5. a.** Graph iii; **b.** graph iv; **c.** Graph i; **d.** Graph iv.

How Can I Practice? **1. a.** (0.81, 0.59); **b.** (−0.87, −0.5); **c.** (0, −1); **d.** (0.73, −0.68); **e.** (−0.81, −0.59); **f.** (0, 1); **2. a.** 0.63 units; **b.** 3.67 units;

c. 1.57 units clockwise; **d.** 5.53 units; **e.** 2.51 units clockwise; **f.** 7.85 units; **3. a.** $18° \cdot \frac{\pi}{180°} = \frac{\pi}{10}$; **b.** $150° \cdot \frac{\pi}{180°} = \frac{5\pi}{6}$; **c.** $390° \cdot \frac{\pi}{180°} = \frac{13\pi}{6}$; **d.** $-72° \cdot \frac{\pi}{180°} = \frac{-2\pi}{5}$; **4. a.** 150°; **b.** 306°; **c.** −540°; **d.** 162°; **5.** amp: 4, period: $\frac{2\pi}{3}$, displacement: 0; **6.** amp = 2, period: $\frac{2\pi}{1} = 2\pi$, displacement: 1; **7.** amp: 3.2, period: $\frac{2\pi}{2} = \pi$, displacement: 0; **8.** amp = 1, period: $\frac{2\pi}{\frac{1}{2}} = 4\pi$, displacement: −2; **9.** amp: 3, period: $\frac{2\pi}{4} = \frac{\pi}{2}$, displacement: $\frac{-(-1)}{4} = \frac{1}{4}$; **10. a.** Because of the repetitive nature of the height of the water as a function of time; **b.** Amplitude = 40; **c.** Period is approximately 12 hours, since high tide occurs twice a day; **d.** Other equations are possible.

Gateway Review **1. a.** $N = 6.24$ miles; **b.** $E = 3.18$ miles; **2. a.** Side $c = 13$, angle $A = 22.6°$, angle $B = 22.6°$; **b.** Side $a = 6.93$, side $b = 4$, angle $A = 60°$; **c.** Side $b = 3$, side $c = 4.24$, angle $B = 45°$; **d.** Side $a = 8.66$, side $c = 10$, angle $B = 30°$; **3. a.** $\cos\theta = \frac{8}{10}$, $\tan\theta = \frac{6}{8}$; **b.** $\sin\theta = \frac{1}{2}$, $\tan\theta = \frac{1}{\sqrt{3}}$, $\theta = 30°$; **c.** $c^2 = 5^2 + 8^2 = 89$, $c = \sqrt{89}$, $\sin\theta = \frac{8}{\sqrt{89}}$, $\cos\theta = \frac{5}{\sqrt{89}}$; **4.** No, there is a difference, but it is so small that it is difficult to see. For you: $\theta = \tan^{-1}\left(\frac{1408}{100}\right) = 85.9375°$. For your nephew: $\theta = \tan^{-1}\left(\frac{1411}{100}\right) = 85.9461°$; **5.** $\cos 57° = \frac{30}{c}$, $c = \frac{30}{\cos 57°}$, $c = 55.1$; **6.** $x = 100 + 100\sqrt{3}$; $h = 300 + 100\sqrt{3}$; **7.** Col. 2: $\frac{1}{\sqrt{2}}, \frac{1}{2}, 0, -1/2, -\frac{1}{\sqrt{2}}, -\frac{\sqrt{3}}{2}, -1, -\frac{\sqrt{3}}{2}, -\frac{1}{\sqrt{2}}, -1/2, 0$; Col. 3: $-1/2, -\frac{1}{\sqrt{2}}, -\frac{\sqrt{3}}{2}, -1, -\frac{\sqrt{3}}{2}, -\frac{1}{\sqrt{2}}, -1/2, 0, \frac{1}{2}, \frac{1}{\sqrt{2}}, \frac{\sqrt{3}}{2}, 1$; Col. 4: $-\sqrt{3}/1, -1, -\frac{1}{\sqrt{3}}, 0, \frac{1}{\sqrt{3}}, 1, \frac{\sqrt{3}}{}$, undefined, $-\sqrt{3}/1, -1, -\frac{1}{\sqrt{3}}, 0$; **8. a.** amplitude = 2, period = 2π; **b.** amplitude 2, period = 2π; **c.** amplitude = 1, period = π; **d.** amplitude = 1, period = 1; **e.** amplitude = 1, period = 4π, ; **f.** amplitude = 1, period = 4; **g.** amplitude = 1, period = 2π; **h.** amplitude = 1, period = 2π; **i.** amplitude = 1, period = 1; **j.** amplitude = 3, period = 1; **9. a.** is graph vi ; **b.** is graph ii; **c.** is graph iv; **d.** is graph v; **e.** is graph vii; **f.** is graph viii.

Glossary

addition of functions *see* sum function.

argument Another name for the input, or independent variable, of a function.

average rate of change, or simply, the **rate of change** The ratio $\frac{\Delta t}{\Delta w}$, where Δt represents the change in output and Δw represents the change in input.

axis of symmetry A vertical line that separates the graph of a parabola into two mirror images.

change of base formula $\log_b x = \frac{\log_a x}{\log_a b}$, where $b > 0$, $b \neq 1$, is the formula used to change logarithms of one base to logarithms of another base.

coefficient The numerical multiplier of a variable.

common logarithms Base 10 logarithms.

complex numbers Numbers of the form $a + bi$ such that a and b are real numbers and $i = \sqrt{-1}$.

composition function, $f \circ g$ The function that is created when the output of the function, g, becomes the input for a second function, f. the rule is given symbolically by $f \circ g(x) = f(g(x))$.

consistent system of linear equations A system with exactly one solution.

constant function A function in which there is no change in the output. The graph of a constant function is a horizontal line.

constant of proportionality A constant, k, that gives the rate of variation in the direct proportional relationship $y = kx^n$.

constant term A term that does not change in value.

continuous compounding of an investment Occurs when the period is so short it is essentially an instant in time. The formula for continuous compounding is $A = Pe^{rt}$.

cubic A third-degree polynomial function having the general equation $y = ax^3 + bx^2 + cx + d$, where a, b, c, and d are real numbers and $a \neq 0$.

decay factor of an exponential function The number, b, in the equation $y = a \cdot b^x$, where $0 < b < 1$, where a is the amount when $x = 0$.

decreasing function A function in which the output decreases in value as the input increases. The graph goes down to the right.

degree of a polynomial function The exponent of the term with the largest exponent.

dependent variable of a function The output variable.

DERIVE The name of a computer algebra system.

difference function, $f - g$ The function that is created from two functions, f and g, by the rule $(f - g)(x) = f(x) - g(x)$.

direct variation between two variables A relationship in which as the independent variable (input) increases in value, the dependent variable (output) increases. Also the independent variable decreases as the dependent variable decreases.

discriminant The expression $b^2 - 4ac$ under the radical of the quadratic formula. The value of the discriminant determines the type of solutions of the equation $ax^2 + bx + c = 0$.

domain of a function The set of all possible input values of a function.

exponential function A function of the form $y = a \cdot b^x$ where the independent variable, x, is the exponent.

extraneous solution A potential solution that is not really a solution to the original equation or problem.

function A relationship between the input and the output such that for each input value there is exactly one output value.

general form of a linear equation $Ax + By = C$, where A, B, and C are real numbers.

growth factor of the exponential function $y = a \cdot b^x$ The number b, where $b > 1$ and a is the amount when $x = 0$.

horizontal intercepts All points of the graph of the function whose y-coordinate is 0. (*see* x-intercept)

identity function The function in which the output value is always identical to the input value.

imaginary unit $i = \sqrt{-1}$.

inconsistent system of linear equations A linear system with no solution. Graphically, two parallel lines represent the system.

increasing function A function in which the output increases in value as the input increases. The graph goes up to the right.

input variable The independent variable.

inverse functions Two functions f and g related such that $f(g(x)) = x = g(f(x))$. Graphically, these functions are mirror images in the line $y = x$.

inverse variation between two variables A relationship in which as the independent variable (input) increases in value, the dependent variable (output) decreases. Also, the independent variable decreases as the dependent variable increases.

irrational number Any real number that cannot be written as a rational number.

linear function Any function in which the rate of change, or slope, is constant.

linear term The term of a polynomial function of the form bx, where b is a real number.

logarithm function A function of the form $\log_b x = y$, where the base $b > 0$, $b \neq 1$.

magnitude The relative size of a number or quantity, expressed as a distance or absolute value (and therefore not negative).

mathematical model A function that best fits the actual data and can be used to predict output values for input values not in the table.

natural logarithm A logarithm to the base e. The logarithm is written as $\log_e x = \ln x$.

ordered pair A pair of values, separated by a comma and enclosed in a set of parentheses. The input value is written to the left of the output value.

output variable The dependent variable.

parabola The graph of a quadratic function (second-degree polynomial function). The graph is U-shaped, opening either upward or downward.

piecewise function A function in which the function rule for determining the output is given separately, or in pieces, for different values of the input.

polynomial function Any function defined by a finite number of terms of the form ax^n, where a is a real number and n is a non-negative integer.

practical domain The set of all input values that make sense in a problem situation.

practical range The set of all output values that make sense in a problem situation.

product function, $f \cdot g$ The function that is created from two functions f and g, by the rule $(f \cdot g)(x) = f(x) \cdot g(x)$

profit function A function that is common in the business world and is defined by Profit = Revenue – Cost.

quadratic formula The formula $x = \frac{-b \pm \sqrt{b^2 - 4ac}}{2a}$ that represents the solutions to the quadratic equation $ax^2 + bx + c = 0$.

quadratic function A second-degree polynomial function defined by an equation of the form $f(x) = ax^2 + bx + c$, where a, b, and c are real numbers and $a \neq 0$.

quartic function A fourth-degree polynomial function defined by an equation of the form $f(x) = ax^4 + bx^3 + cx^2 + dx + e$, where a, b, c, d, and e are real numbers and $a \neq 0$.

radical function Any function involving a radical (square root, cube root, etc.)

radicand The expression under the radical.

range The collection of all values of the dependent variable.

ratio The growth or decay factor, b, of the exponential function $y = a \cdot b^x$ where $b > 0$ and $b \neq 1$.

rational equation An equation composed of fractions where the numerators and denominators are polynomials, with the variable appearing somewhere in a denominator.

rational function Any function that can be defined as the ratio of two polynomial functions.

real numbers All numbers that are either rational or irrational.

slope of a line The constant rate of change of output to input.

slope-intercept form of the equation of a line The equation $y = mx + b$, where m represents the slope of the line and $(0, b)$ is the vertical intercept.

solution of a system of equations in two variables The ordered pair of numbers (x, y) that make both equations true.

sum function, $f + g$ The function that is created from two functions f and g by the rule $(f + g)(x) = f(x) + g(x)$.

system of linear equations in two variables A pair of equations that can be written in the form , and where a, b, c, and d are real numbers.

variation How the dependent variable changes when the independent variable changes. (*see* direct variation or inverse variation.)

vertex The turning point of the graph of a parabola having coordinates $\left(\frac{-b}{2a}, f\left(\frac{-b}{2a}\right)\right)$, where a and b are determined from the equation $f(x) = ax^2 + bx + c$. The vertex is the highest or lowest point of a parabola.

vertical asymptote A vertical line that a curve approaches, getting progressively closer, without ever touching that vertical line.

vertical intercept The point of the graph of the function whose x-coordinate is 0. (*see* y-intercept)

x-intercepts All points of the graph of the function whose y-coordinate is 0. (*see* horizontal intercept.)

Xmax The largest value of input visible in the window of a graphing calculator.

Xmin The smallest value of input visible in the window of a graphing calculator.

y-intercept All points of the graph of the function whose x-coordinate is 0. (*see* vertical intercept.)

Ymax The largest value of output visible in the window of a graphing calculator.

Ymin The smallest value of output visible in the window of a graphing calculator.

zero product rule The algebraic rule that says if a and b are real numbers such that $a \cdot b = 0$, then either a or b, or both, must be equal to zero.

Index